No Right to Be Idle

The first two pupils admitted to the New York State Asylum for Idiots. The first spent nine years at the asylum, then lived with his parents, and later his siblings. The second died at the asylum fifty-two years later, in 1902. Courtesy of the New York State Archive.

SARAH F. ROSE

No Right to Be Idle
The Invention of Disability, 1840s–1930s

The University of North Carolina Press *Chapel Hill*

© 2017 The University of North Carolina Press
All rights reserved
Set in Arno Pro by Westchester Publishing Services
Manufactured in the United States of America
The University of North Carolina Press has been a member of the
Green Press Initiative since 2003.
Library of Congress Cataloging-in-Publication Data

Names: Rose, Sarah F., author.
Title: No right to be idle : the invention of disability, 1840s–1930s / Sarah F. Rose.
Description: Chapel Hill : University of North Carolina Press, [2017] |
   Includes bibliographical references and index.
Identifiers: LCCN 2016021462 | ISBN 9781469630083 (cloth : alk. paper) | ISBN
   9781469624891 (pbk : alk. paper) | ISBN 9781469624907 (ebook)
Subjects: LCSH: People with disabilities—Government policy—United
   States—History. | People with disabilities—United States—Public
   opinion—History. | People with disabilities—Rehabilitation—United
   States—History. | People with disabilities—Employment—United
   States—History. | People with disabilities—Civil rights—United
   States—History. | People with disabilities—Legal status, laws,
   etc.—United States—History—19th century. | People with
   disabilities—Legal status, laws, etc.—United States—History—20th
   century. | Marginality, Social—United States—History—19th century. |
   Marginality, Social—United States—History—20th century.
Classification: LCC HV1553 .R66 2017 | DDC 331.5/9097309034—dc23 LC record available at
https://lccn.loc.gov/2016021462

Cover illustration: Female residents of Rome (N.Y.) Custodial Asylum at dinner in dining hall,
ca. 1890–1915 (NYSA_A1994-77_B2_F1_P10, courtesy of the New York State Archives).

*In loving memory of Grandma Jennie Scott Rose
and in honor of Frank Scott*

Contents

Acknowledgments xi

INTRODUCTION 1

CHAPTER ONE
Her Mother Did Not Like to Have Her Learn to Work: Disability, Family, and the Spectrum of Productivity, 1840s–1870s 14

CHAPTER TWO
He Had No Home but the County Poor House: Family Incapacity, Charity Policy, Wage Labor, and the Shift to Custodial Care, 1870s–1900s 49

CHAPTER THREE
I Wish to Thank You for My Freedom: Paroling Feeble-Minded People into Farm and Domestic Work, 1900s–1930s 91

CHAPTER FOUR
We Do Not Prefer Cripples, but They Can Earn Full Wages: Mechanization, Efficiency, and the Quest for Interchangeable Workers, 1880s–1920s 111

CHAPTER FIVE
The Greatest Handicap Suffered by Crippled Workers: The Perverse Impact of Workmen's Compensation, 1900s–1930s 137

CHAPTER SIX
Saving the Human Wreckage Cast on the Industrial Scrap Heap: Goodwill Industries and the Imperative of Efficiency, 1890s–1920s 172

CHAPTER SEVEN
The Duty to Make Himself a Useful, Self-Supporting Citizen: Disabled Veterans and the Limits of Vocational Rehabilitation, 1910s–1920s 190

Conclusion 223

Appendix. A Note on Sources 229

Notes 233

Bibliography 339

Index 369

Charts and Illustrations

CHARTS

1-1 How sex shaped discharge at the New York State Asylum for Idiots, 1851–1893 38

1-2 Disability, ability, and the possibility of life at home after the New York State Asylum for Idiots, 1851–1893 45

1-3 Parents' occupations and the possibility of life at home after the New York State Asylum for Idiots, 1851–1893 46

1-4 Parents' occupations and length of stay at the New York State Asylum for Idiots, 1851–1893 47

2-1 Origins of admittees to the New York State Asylum for Idiots, 1851–1890 55

2-2 Origins of admittees to the New York State Asylum for Idiots and prospects for life outside institutions, 1851–1893 56

2-3 Family disruption prior to arrival at the New York State Asylum for Idiots, 1851–1890 58

2-4 Family disruption and the prospects for life at home after the New York State Asylum for Idiots, 1851–1893 64

2-5 Shifting origins and levels of family disruption at the New York State Asylum for Idiots, 1851–1890 66

2-6 Admittees' origins, family disruption, and lives lived in institutions at the New York State Asylum for Idiots, 1851–1893 66

2-7 Ability and death rates at the New York State Asylum for Idiots, 1851–1890 83

ILLUSTRATIONS

Frontispiece. The first two pupils admitted to the New York State Asylum for Idiots. The first spent nine years at the asylum, then lived with his parents, and later his siblings. The second died at the asylum fifty-two years later, in 1902. ii

Founding superintendent of the New York State Asylum for Idiots, Hervey B. Wilbur 21

Early pupils at New York State Asylum for Idiots 26

Female inmates working in the canning plant, Syracuse State Institution for Feeble-Minded Children, ca. 1910–1930 79

Boys painting buildings, Syracuse State Institution for Feeble-Minded Children, ca. 1910–1930 79

Group of female inmates with tuberculosis on veranda of the New York State Custodial Asylum for Feeble-Minded Women at Newark, ca. 1910–1914 84

Superintendent of the Rome State Custodial Asylum, Charles Bernstein 94

Colony "girls" in front of their house, Syracuse State School for Mental Defectives, ca. 1920s–1930s 106

Interior view of ward for "low-grade" and "crippled" children, Rome State Custodial Asylum, ca. 1910–1914 109

"The Crippled Watchman, A Type" from *Work-Accidents and the Law* by Crystal Eastman, 1910 119

Man with amputation working in the upholstery department at Ford Motor Company, 1917 129

Blind men sorting bolts and nuts at Ford Motor Company's River Rouge plant, 1934 135

Social investigator and workmen's compensation advocate Crystal Eastman 140

Statistician, social insurance advocate, and workmen's compensation analyst Isaac Max Rubinow 154

Methodist minister and founder of Goodwill Industries, Edgar James Helms 175

Cartoon from "They Don't Want Your Charity—They Demand Their Chance," by H. T. Webster, *Carry On*, August 1918 200

Poster from rehabilitation exhibit put together by the Red Cross Institute for Crippled and Disabled Men and the Red Cross Institute for the Blind, 1919 203

Acknowledgments

Shortly after I finished graduate school, my aunt sent me a letter to the editor written in 1944 by her grandfather Frank Scott, in which he explained why he saw "the Workmen's Compensation law here in New York [as] a direct slap in the face for anyone who has a permanent physical disability." To my surprise, I had unknowingly chosen to research the very beliefs and policies that prevented him, along with many other people with disabilities, from finding permanent work and "enjoy[ing] 'Freedom from want.'" In the years since, Frank Scott's daughter—my grandmother Jennie Scott Rose—and I spent many wonderful hours talking about history, disability policy, and virtually everything else under the sun. She did not live to see this book's publication, but it is dedicated in loving memory of her and in honor of her father, Frank Scott.

Many others played crucial roles in helping me bring this book to fruition. I would especially like to thank my dissertation advisor Susan Levine for her willingness to explore a brand-new historical field that was not her specialty, her fine sense of how to put together research projects, her impeccable editing skills, her patience and generosity, and her gift for saying exactly what I needed to hear when I needed to hear it. Leon Fink's incisive grasp of historical arguments, his ability to see where a project needs to go (often well before its author does), and his challenging questions have been invaluable. I will also always be grateful to him for founding the Work, Race, and Gender in the Urban World (WRGUW) program in the University of Illinois at Chicago's Department of History, which provided an incredibly lively and creative academic environment for my colleagues and me during graduate school. Richard John not only shared his encyclopedic knowledge of historical literature and research strategies, but also made this project stronger by always asking the difficult questions and challenging me to reflect on its theoretical foundations. Arwen Mohun, in turn, provided one of the key intellectual springboards and encouraged me to pursue the topic of working-class experiences and notions of disability.

I could not have finished this book without the help of research assistants—and now friends—Kallie Kosc and especially Trevor Engel. Both gamely undertook the painstaking task of helping me build a database of nearly 2,000 pupils and inmates of the New York State Asylum for Idiots and research their family histories. Kallie helped me recognize that much of my story lay not simply in idiot asylums but rather in the families of people who passed through or who remained in those institutions, while Trevor assisted with virtually every aspect of the manuscript over the course of more than two years. Not a single chapter was left untouched by his insightful questions, careful edits, and dedicated research. His good humor and staunch commitment made the revision process far easier.

I am deeply grateful to UNC editor Brandon Proia for all he has done to make this book possible, especially his patient yet persistent cheerleading, his enthusiastic advocacy, and his readiness to advise on virtually any aspect of the project. I am also thankful to former UNC acquisitions editors Sian Hunter and David Perry for taking on this project in the first place, while the final manuscript benefited considerably from Barbara Goodhouse's fine copyediting. I am especially appreciative of the thought-provoking and meticulous reviews provided by Paul K. Longmore, Eileen Boris, and an anonymous reader, which challenged me in the best way possible to further hone my arguments, think more broadly, and highlight the people whose lives were shaped by this history and who, in turn, shaped it.

I could not have found a better—or more fun—way to refine my thinking about narratives and themes in disability history or sharpen my storytelling than to teach multiple parts of the manuscript to undergraduate and graduate students in historical methods, disability history, and disability studies at the University of Texas at Arlington. I am also deeply grateful to the many colleagues in Texas, Chicago, and elsewhere who read the entire manuscript or significant segments or who provided other invaluable advice: the members of the University of Illinois at Chicago History Department Dissertation Workshop; the Newberry Library Seminar on Technology, Politics, and Culture; and the Dallas Area Society of Historians (DASH); as well as Douglas Baynton, Edward Berkowitz, Laurie Block, Jeff Brune, Susan Burch, Guy Chet, Stephanie Cole, Trevor Engel, Anne Finger, Leon Fink, Mary Furner, Jeff Helgeson, Nate Holdren, Kathryn Irving, Richard John, Nate Kogan, Catherine Kudlick, Susan Levine, Allison O'Mahen Malcom, Alexis McCrossen, Sonya Michel, Andrew Milson, David Mitchell, Arwen Mohun, Christopher Morris, Kim Nielsen, Alice O'Connor, Anne Parsons, Michael Perman, John Reda, Joshua Salzmann, Walt Schalick, Richard Scotch, Graham Warder, and John Williams-Searle. Thanks, too, to anyone whose name I have inadvertently omitted.

Over the fifteen some-odd years that I worked on and off this project, I received crucial financial support from the University of Texas Arlington's

College of Liberal Arts/Festival of Ideas Global Research Institute, the National Academy of Education, the Spencer Foundation (twice), the New York State Archives, the American Association of University Women, the University of Illinois at Chicago, the Harvard Business School, the Schlesinger Library, the Social Welfare History Archives, the Illinois State Historical Society, and the Henry Ford Museum. I was also fortunate enough to be able to stay with family and friends for much of my research, including Janelle Snider, Lesli Stinger, Jessica Sebeok, Sonya Michel and Jeffrey Herf, Christopher and Kelly Cantwell, Katie Beilfuss, and Betsy and Eric Mendelsohn. In particular, Susan and Jack Penney's house and Jennie Rose's apartment became homes away from home, as well as the sites of a very long-running pinochle game.

The J. Gilligan's Irish traditional music session and the TIMES Session Players—an Irish music community in North Texas, of all places—provided invaluable humor, much-needed breaks, and wonderful tunes while I was revising the manuscript. The disability studies community at the University of Texas at Arlington and the local disability rights community provided both moral support and cheerleading. Friends Stephanie Cole and Gregg Cantrell, Carol Thompson and Bob Young, Rick Roberts, Trevor Engel, Gypsy Youngraven, Carla and Ron Murawski, Lisa Vanderlinden and Rob Garnett, Kenyon Zimmer, John and Phyllis Reda, Mary Caraway and Erik Carlson, Joshua Salzmann, and Sue Levine and Leon Fink, as well as family members Don and Sue Rose, Sue and Jack Penney, Jennie Rose, and Janelle Snider did so much to keep me going through the long haul.

Our beloved South Side Chicago cat Aviva kept me company through much of the research, writing, and revision process, although sadly she did not live to see the book published. She did, however, spend a glorious summer lounging on my desk while I did nothing else but revise the manuscript! Aoife and Fionn have brought much laughter and purrs during the final stages.

Finally, my husband Dave Aftandilian cooked meals and ran the house—for months—while also learning far more about disability, labor, and policy history than he probably ever wanted to know. He read large portions of the manuscript multiple times and provided an invaluable sounding board. I could not ask for a more supportive or wonderful partner.

No Right to Be Idle

Introduction

In the 1870s, Lily Westbrooke was an unassuming, ordinary resident of the New York State Asylum for Idiots. An "industrious and faithful worker," she spent her days laboring in the institution's laundry, where she had "assume[d] the responsibility of looking after a great deal of the children's clothing." An affectionate woman who loved taking charge of younger pupils, Westbrooke had come far since arriving at the asylum from a "pauper" family in 1858 as a bashful nine-year-old who understood only simple language and was unaware that "printed words stood for objects of any kinds." Now a "great talker" and an avid reader, she showed no signs of the obstinacy, violent temper, and reputed "moral deficiency" that Madison County Poorhouse officials claimed had led them to send her to the Asylum for Idiots in the first place.

But Westbrooke's ability as a worker counted for little when the superintendent, James C. Carson, discharged her in 1888 to her mother. Within less than a year, she once again entered the Madison County Poorhouse, this time for good. Presumably, her mother had died, remarried, or become unwilling or unable to house her. Without relatives who were willing and able to either help her find a paid position as a laundress or make use of her skills themselves, Westbrooke had no options other than following in her parents' footsteps by becoming a county pauper. Labeled by poor-law officials as a "cripple & idiotic" with "no hope" for recovery, she remained at the poorhouse until her death sometime in the 1920s. Since the poorhouse keeper noted that she could do simple housework, she may have performed unpaid care work at the almshouse, as she had at the Asylum for Idiots.[1]

At roughly the same time as Westbrooke died in the Madison County Poorhouse, Philadelphia resident Walter Pratt, who had lost an eye to a flying piece of steel, was likewise struggling to find a way to subsist off his labors. Despite wearing a natural-looking glass eye, he could not convince an employer to hire him for even the most menial job. In 1928, he complained to an investigator from the Consumers' League of Eastern Pennsylvania: "You know nowadays you have to pass a physical examination and I would get along fine until they would test my eyes, one at a time, and then it was all off." After being rejected for yet another janitorial position, he exclaimed, "Well the fact that I have only one eye doesn't affect my hands and feet, I can do this work just as well as a man with both his eyes." But the employer told him, "Why should we bother with a one-eyed man when we can find plenty with two good eyes?" Pratt reflected, "Here I am, an able bodied man and willing to do any kind of work, dependent upon my two youngsters for support."[2]

At first glance, Westbrooke and Pratt might seem to have had little in common. After all, she had a cognitive impairment that reportedly dated back to birth and spent virtually all of her life inside institutions, performing uncompensated care work. He, in contrast, toiled for pay on the mainstream labor market until an industrial accident cost him an eye. Pratt had children on whom he could rely, while Westbrooke ended her days in the poorhouse because no relatives were willing or able to house her. But a closer look reveals striking similarities between their stories—similarities that highlight the changing meanings and lived experiences of disability at the turn of the twentieth century.

Both Westbrooke and Pratt could and wanted to work. But like a growing number of people in the late nineteenth and early twentieth centuries who had what we might today term "disabilities," Westbrooke and Pratt found themselves deemed incapable of contributing to either a household economy or the wage labor market. In effect, they had been made unproductive and left dependent on others' aid by three interlocking factors, as well as the complexity and mutability of disability itself. First, the transition to industrial capitalism and an urban wage labor economy reduced families' capacity to care for and make use of partly productive relatives such as Westbrooke. Second, as mechanized factory labor became increasingly central to the economy, employers in nearly all sectors began to demand workers who, unlike Pratt, had intact, interchangeable bodies. Third, public policies intended to prevent public dependency, such as workmen's compensation laws and programs that classified and redirected diverse poorhouse residents into suitable institutions, had unexpected and sometimes even perverse results for people with diverse bodies and capabilities. As policy makers grappled, often unknowingly, with the multifaceted, ever-shifting nature of disability, some of their well-intentioned programs in fact served to exclude people with disabilities from both the wage labor market and economic citizenship.

By the end of World War I, these four factors had combined to render people with disabilities unproductive citizens in the cultural imagination: a concept central to disability policy in the United States during the rest of the twentieth century.[3] Disability, in turn, became synonymous with reliance on public dependency, poor citizenship, and the inability to care for oneself or work productively. In other words, disability was believed to pose risks both to individuals' own morals and to those of the nation as a whole. Speaking at the first national conference on vocational rehabilitation in 1922, the social worker George B. Mangold highlighted the ways in which definitions of disability, work, and citizenship had intertwined, arguing, "Every man ought to be self-supporting and also able to support a family, and no man has a social right to refuse to contribute in some way to the wealth and to the progress of society.... Nor has any man who is crippled a right to be idle and enjoy the gratuitous support of relatives or of a philanthropic agency or of the public." He called on the nation to provide the training necessary to return such *men* to work.[4]

Although Mangold focused only on "crippled" men, reflecting the power of male breadwinner ideology, the new concept—and, in many ways, the experiences—of disability in fact brought together populations that policy makers, employers, and the public had long viewed as distinct. People who toiled on the wage labor market, those who labored in rehabilitative institutions for no pay, and those who could not work and relied on public relief all fell under the umbrella of "disability." So too did people with all sorts of impairments—blindness, idiocy, amputations, withered limbs, shell shock, even tuberculosis—that occurred at various ages and stemmed from very different origins, both acquired and congenital. But despite this vast bodily diversity, people with disabilities had much in common. As Westbrooke's and Pratt's cases demonstrate, the "problem" of disability lay not in their actual impairments or the work they did but rather in the meanings attributed to those impairments by policy makers and employers, as well as in how those meanings intersected with a rapidly shifting workplace, changing family capacities, policies aimed at preventing dependency, and the complexity of disability itself.

As Mangold's proclamation suggests, the separation of people with disabilities from the status of "workers" and the paid labor market hardly went unchallenged. Both disabled people and a diverse array of vocational rehabilitators recognized the long-standing importance of work to social standing and economic citizenship, as well as the ways in which dependency has historically been equated with poor citizenship in the United States.[5] People with disabilities fought to maintain—or regain—their places in the paid labor market. Crippled widows started their own newsstands when they could not find employment, leg amputees learned to mount ladders so that they could paint signs, rheumatic men pulled stuffing from couches in sheltered workshops, and feeble-minded girls competed to be paroled from custodial institutions as domestic servants, among many other examples. But with the notable exception of Ford Motor Company, which hired thousands of disabled workers at full pay, their labors were rarely not recognized or compensated as real work.

Vocational rehabilitation initiatives such as Goodwill Industries' sheltered workshops and the Veterans' Bureau program for disabled World War I veterans found decidedly mixed success with helping disabled workers enter—or re-enter—the paid labor market. Saturated with the Protestant work ethic, these programs frequently focused more on trying to avert the civic and individual moral risks traditionally associated with dependency than on providing training suitable for an increasingly industrial economy. Rehabilitators likewise struggled to cope with the complexity of disability, especially when mixed with shifting family structures, a rapidly industrializing economy, and the unexpected effects of public policies. Nevertheless, rehabilitation initiatives did provide some disabled people and their families with modest, albeit often poverty-level, incomes.

But as the hundreds of African American migrant laborers who fell ill from silicosis while digging a dam tunnel in West Virginia in the late 1920s and early 1930s could testify, these shifts did not uniformly affect all who might be said to have "disabilities."[6] Existing hierarchies of race, gender, and class mattered. Within working-class communities, disabling injuries were often so common that they served at least as a marker of poverty, if not class itself. In addition, employers' beliefs that certain races or genders were more productive and better suited to particular jobs—that women could more easily paint radioactive radium on watch dials, for instance—ensured that occupational hazards, as well as the resulting disabilities, were not equally distributed.[7] At the same time, policy makers' racialized and gendered assumptions about health, "fitness," accidents, and the nature of "breadwinners" and family often barred nonwhites and women from gaining equal access to compensation and rehabilitation programs and, in some cases, life outside institutions for the feeble-minded.[8]

Ultimately, despite the efforts of a wide range of policy makers, reformers, and disabled people themselves, by the 1920s many people with disabilities and their families were relegated to poverty and second-class economic and social citizenship. Although the causes of this shift lay in forces far beyond the control of individuals with disabilities, disability was becoming inextricably linked with personal immorality and economic dependency. Throughout the remainder of the twentieth century and into the twenty-first, moreover, legislators and disability rights activists would struggle to integrate the roughly 20 percent of Americans with disabilities into the mainstream labor market.

Vocational rehabilitation programs, National Employ the Handicapped Week, and even the Americans with Disabilities Act would prove unable to undo the shifts that took place between the 1850s and 1920s. Even in 2017, nearly thirty years after the passage of the Americans with Disabilities Act in 1990, 70 percent of working-age adults with disabilities are not employed—in contrast to just 25 percent of nondisabled individuals—and nearly 30 percent of disabled people live in poverty.[9]

Disability in the Antebellum United States

Today, disability is a familiar category. But prior to the early twentieth century, people with what now might be termed "disabilities" or "impairments" fell under a multiplicity of terms, from lame, simple, deaf-mute, and invalid to worn out, cripple, feeble, and lunatic, among others. These terms did not imply an inability to work and care for oneself, as would be the case with later definitions of disability. Only in one sector—laws aimed at disabled veterans and seamen (sailors)—did "disability" appear with its more contemporary meaning: a bodily variation or incapacity that made one "incapable afterwards of getting a livelihood."[10]

During the nation's early decades, the lives of people with disabilities were as diverse as the terms used to describe them. While some fell under the category of dependents on public aid, living in poorhouses, receiving cash aid, or being boarded out with community members, most were integrated into their families and communities. In a society in which few lived into adulthood without acquiring scars from smallpox, poverty, or occupational hazards, variations in bodily function and appearance were common and rarely prevented people from continuing to work. Few sailors finished their careers without having an extremity broken, mashed, or amputated outright; slaves lost digits to frostbite and developed "bandy-legged" walks due to nutritional deficiencies; and laborers suffered from rheumatism, to give just a few examples.[11] Even those who required some assistance, such as Revolutionary War veteran Seth Delano, likely helped care for others in their household. Delano's head wound had earned him an invalid pension, which he used to support himself as well as his wife, who was "so feeble as to be confined to her bed" much of the time, and their sole child, Rebecca, who was "blind and able to do nothing towards her support."[12]

Early American communities also tended to tolerate unusual behavior, as long as a person did not become violent or commit arson. Samuel Coolidge, who completed his degree at Harvard in 1738 and preached for a few years in

Massachusetts, served as Watertown's schoolmaster between 1749 and 1763. During his periodic episodes of insanity, "he wandered the streets... half-naked, yelling profanities, and disrupting classes at his alma mater." In exchange for Coolidge's teaching when sane, the community housed and fed him. But to guarantee that their children would have an instructor in the morning, town residents locked him in the schoolhouse most nights. Only when his behavior became uncontrollable did residents discharge him from his teaching responsibilities and restrain him in a room—the same room in which he died one year later, in 1764.[13]

As in the case of Coolidge, communities stepped in only when relatives proved unwilling or unable to provide care; family, not the community, was the default locus of care in the early United States. Enfeebled Revolutionary War veterans such as James Trowbridge, who reported in 1820 that his wounds had caused him to be "laid up" for much of the preceding decades, relied on their wives and adult daughters. He claimed, in fact, that his wife had "ruined her health in taking care of me."[14] Likewise, the family of Revolutionary leader James Otis Jr. struggled to manage his violent behavior for years themselves before eventually deciding to have him boarded elsewhere.[15] Yet, the privacy of family care also left people with disabilities vulnerable to abuse. Patrick Henry's wife, Sarah, spent the last several years of her life "confined to a cellar room, bound in a straitjacket, and attended by a servant [slave]" in the family estate.[16]

If absolutely necessary, communities would provide care, but such care could be harsh. Early Americans typically classified people deemed to be lame, blind, consumptive, idiotic, or otherwise impaired and who could not care for or support themselves as members of the deserving poor: those who became poor through no fault of their own, as opposed to dissolutes and drunks. Consequently, towns boarded out some impoverished people with disabilities, especially women, and offered others tax reductions. But for some, the almshouse loomed—an institution whose poor conditions and stringent labor requirements were specifically intended to discourage impoverished people from entering.[17] Poorhouse officials often broke up families by age and gender, restricted rations of meat and tea, and required able-bodied inmates to work at breaking stones, weaving, or caring for ill residents.[18]

Early American communities strictly enforced residency requirements for assistance, deporting those who had not attained the status of inhabitant and requiring ship captains to post bonds for passengers who might not be able to support themselves.[19] After goldsmith John Treby became ill in the 1780s, for instance, the town of Providence "warned him out" to his hometown of

Newport and deposited him with the overseers of the poor. Treby was far from the only impoverished person with a disability (or without one) to be deported from Providence.[20]

Not only were people with disabilities ubiquitous in the early United States; so too were concepts of disability. Indeed, language about disability played a central role in antebellum debates over slavery. Proslavery advocates justified bondage of African Americans on the grounds that slaves suffered from "Drapetomania" and "Dysaesthesia Aethiopis"—diseases that purportedly provided slaves with intense urges to run away and evade labor, respectively.[21] Abolitionists and ex-slaves, in response, contended that abusive masters caused slaves to develop epilepsy and insanity.[22]

Far from being a marginal aspect of human life or a phenomenon of certain eras in American history, disability is both a central, "normal" element of human experience and one of the ways in which societies have justified power hierarchies—two of the key contributions of the new field of disability history. Instead of seeing disabilities as aberrant conditions or as medical impairments in need of a cure, disability historians argue that disability is socially constructed. That is, the experience of a disability, and even what counts as a disability, varies by historical era and by culture. The ways in which race, class, gender, age, and kind of impairment—whether sensory, psychosocial, physical, cognitive, or chronic illness, and at what level—intersect with disability also matter, of course.[23] Early twentieth-century Pittsburgh steel mills were so dangerous, for example, that missing a finger was considered normal and did not prevent laborers from finding employment. Nor did such an impairment cause stigma within working-class communities; rather, such injuries were often seen as indicating manly mastery of a dangerous workplace. As workmen's compensation laws took effect in the 1910s, however, companies began to screen out workers with even such minor impairments as amputated fingers or, as Walter Pratt discovered, missing eyes. What had been a "normal" working body instead became read as a sign of carelessness or inefficiency, and ultimately a reason to keep people out of the workplace. Managers and safety inspectors castigated the largely white immigrant workforce for being too "simple" and "backwards" to follow basic safety protocols. By the 1920s, workers with minimal impairments had thus become too *disabled* to find work in many industries. Both the meaning and the lived experience of disability shifted dramatically within just a few decades.

But this study also suggests that it is not sufficient simply to look at the lives of people with disabilities. As the stories of both Lily Westbrooke and Walter Pratt reveal, individuals' family and community contexts matter. If

Westbrooke had an intact family to whom she could return and who could make use of her hard-won skills, she might not have died in a county poorhouse. Likewise, if Pratt's children had not been able to support him, he might have shared Westbrooke's fate. In other words, the relatives and neighbors of people with disabilities play a crucial role in determining how, and perhaps even whether, a person's impairment shapes their life.[24]

Although many, if not most, people with disabilities have historically worked (even though their labors have not always been defined or rewarded as such), the history of disability has also been shaped by centuries-old debates over who is worthy of public charity. Since the Elizabethan Poor Law of 1601, charity officials and lawmakers have sought to distinguish the "deserving poor"—those whose poverty resulted from factors beyond their control, such as old age, illness, youth, or widowhood—from the "undeserving poor," who were perceived as able but unwilling to work. The desire to aid the deserving poor while simultaneously discouraging the undeserving poor drove early American lawmakers to follow their English forebears in instituting residency requirements for aid, such as those encountered by ill goldsmith John Treby, and to experiment with various methods of limiting relief only to those deemed worthy of assistance.[25]

Disabled people, however, have long fallen between the categories of deserving and undeserving. First, disability's complexity and sheer variety posed considerable hurdles to charity officials who sought to enact clear rules about who was worthy of aid. Second, some impairments—idiocy, insanity, crippled limbs, perhaps blindness or deafness—could potentially be faked for gain.[26] Third, widely held beliefs about certain impairments raised questions about who actually bore responsibility for disabled people who required public aid: should it be society, families, or individuals, or some combination thereof? Antebellum Americans, for instance, debated whether people labeled as "idiots" were the products of family sin, evidence of poor heredity, not even human, or indicative of the vast diversity of nature; each interpretation, of course, led to different solutions. Likewise, employers, workers, and legislators battled over whether disabling work accidents originated out of unsafe workplaces or laborers' own negligence.[27] Consequently, as legislators and reformers struggled to make sense of why people with disabilities had such trouble finding paid work in the early twentieth century, their proposed remedies reflected their fears that disabled people might in fact be lazy rather than truly worthy of aid.

Policy makers' unsuccessful efforts to reintegrate people with disabilities into the rapidly shifting mainstream labor market underscore the importance of investigating how public policies functioned in the real world, as well as the assumptions that guided the policy-making process. As scholars have pointed out in recent decades, the implementation and outcomes of policies are just as important as the policy makers' ideologies. Unintended consequences matter.[28] For example, by no means did legislators and labor law reformers intend to provide employers with convincing and publicly acceptable rationales for screening out people with disabilities from their workforce—that is, by raising the potential cost of compensating such workers for accidents—but workmen's compensation laws unexpectedly reinforced employers' growing skepticism about disabled workers. Perversely, while attempting to solve the social problems caused by industrial accidents, policy makers rendered disabled people dependent.

But policy makers and reformers faced enormous hurdles. By its very nature, policy generalizes specific conditions; for instance, legislators struggled to distinguish between the occupational impact of a crushed joint and that caused by an outright amputation.[29] Indeed, disability's innate complexity and mutability—the vast diversity of types, the way impairments evolve over time in individuals, the fact that new technologies create new kinds of impairments, and the ways which they intersect with race, class, gender, and age—posed serious challenges. Complicating matters for lawmakers, family structures and the labor market were shifting dramatically at the same time. As a result, what constituted disability in one family context or economic situation might not have done so at another time. Policy makers, moreover, rarely realized that they were making disability policy per se. Rather, legislators and reformers believed they were simply trying to address diverse issues such as households that struggled to care for idiotic children, families left impoverished by industrial accidents, feeble-minded women who had no choice but to live in poorhouses, and disabled veterans who could not return to their former jobs. Yet policy makers' fears about encouraging dependency, their concerns about state funding capacity, and desires to preserve the distinctions between the deserving and undeserving poor fundamentally shaped how they approached these issues. And in so doing, their policies unintentionally helped to define disability as a policy category and edge disabled people out of one of the basic standards for "good citizenship": paid work. Undoing the pernicious, if unintended, effects of these policies proved a difficult—if not impossible—task.

Finally, this book aims to expand the notion of who counts a worker, while also highlighting the importance of more consciously incorporating bodies into labor history. Scholars of women's history, among others, have long emphasized that unpaid work, whether caring for children or managing a household, is still work, even if it is not recognized with wages. Labor historians have also begun to explore less formal economic sectors, such as the "gray" (or informal) labor market, as well as the ways in which workers move in and out of formal workplaces. However, the boundaries of what constitutes "work" have been demarcated not only by the actual labor performed but also by the bodies doing that work.[30] Because of the function and appearance of their bodies, disabled people's labors, for instance—whether in institutions for the feeble-minded, sheltered workshops, rehabilitation programs, or the gray market—have rarely been recognized as work. At the Rome State Custodial Asylum in New York State, for instance, the "feeble-minded" inmates virtually ran the asylum, producing most of the food, doing the cooking, helping care for fellow inmates, and printing the inmate newsletter, receiving only room, board, clothing, and perhaps a small amount of pocket money in exchange. Such permanent "training," however, seldom offered a path to the paid labor market. Given that access to paid work has long served as the foundation of social and economic citizenship in the United States, this dynamic had profound consequences for the social standing of people with disabilities. Incorporating disabled people's labors into the history of work thus raises important questions about the reasons certain people's bodies and their toils have been defined, respectively, as nonproductive, noncompensable, and as something other than real work.

No Right to Be Idle opens by tracing the ways in which the postbellum shift to an urban, wage-based, and often unsteady industrial economy undermined families' abilities to accommodate relatives with disabilities. Chapter 1 uses the nationwide spread of idiot asylums in the mid-nineteenth century as a lens into how families understood productivity and issues of care prior to the emergence of large-scale wage labor and intense urbanization. Although superintendents of asylums depicted "idiots" as unproductive, immoral drains on society, in part to obtain funding from lawmakers, families resisted these pejorative depictions. Relatives viewed productivity as a spectrum that varied by age, gender, and ability, reflecting the fact that people with a wide range of bodily capabilities had long participated in household economies and the wage labor market.

In an economy and a society of farms and small communities, superintendents could easily return most of their pupils home—often at parents' request—but by the late 1870s this was no longer true. Chapter 2 explores how the shift to an unpredictable, urban wage economy left many families unable to care for or make use of "idiotic" relatives who might be only partly productive.

Complicating matters, charity policies intended to prevent public dependency—scientific charity programs and efforts to separate diverse poorhouse residents into specialized institutions—increasingly selected pupils who had no home to which they could return. In response to this rapidly increasing and permanent population, asylum directors allied with proto-eugenicists such as Josephine Shaw Lowell to convince lawmakers to fund dedicated custodial asylums for "feeble-minded" people. In these institutions, inmates' labors no longer led to discharge. Instead, perceived abilities determined every facet of life, from institutional conditions to inmates' likelihood of dying shortly after arrival, and often in perverse ways. Despite being depicted by superintendents as unemployable in mainstream society, "feeble-minded" women who were institutionally productive were much less likely to be discharged and remained for decades, performing vast amounts of unpaid care work that defrayed much of the costs of these custodial asylums. Nonetheless, for some inmates, their toils offered some meaning and a small measure of control over their lives.

But as Charles Bernstein demonstrated at New York's Rome State Custodial Asylum, even the early twentieth century job market still allowed for a spectrum of ability, if carefully analyzed. Individual employers, in turn, and transition services could substitute for absent relatives. Chapter 3 explores how, during the 1910s and 1920s, Bernstein moved hundreds of people labeled "feeble-minded"—most of whom lacked families—into paid positions as farm laborers, domestic servants, laundresses, and seamstresses. The superintendents of dozens of other institutions for the feeble-minded across the nation copied his program, in part because it offered a means for addressing relentless pressure for new admissions and perpetual funding challenges. By providing what were, in effect, early group homes and astutely fitting people to appropriate positions, Bernstein managed to turn many, albeit not most, asylum inmates into wage workers living in mainstream society.

The middle chapters turn to the reasons why people with a wide array of disabilities, mostly acquired ones, lost access to the paid labor market between the 1890s and the 1920s. Chapter 4 opens by investigating the ways in which working-class communities and workers had traditionally understood disability: as an anticipated, if feared, outcome of working life, but not as a cause for stigma. While bodily modifications such as missing fingers, crushed limbs, blinded eyes, or weakened lungs often brought a loss of skill and income, injured workers continued to work, often in the informal labor market. Mechanization and the drive for efficiency, however, provided employers with new notions of what made a good worker. With the striking exception of the Ford Motor Company, almost all major industrial employers began to believe that a modern, mechanized, and efficient workplace required employees with intact, interchangeable bodies. Henry Ford, however, demonstrated that, if carefully handled, mechanization could actually expand the range of employable bodies.

As Chapter 5 shows, another public policy intended to prevent dependency—workmen's compensation—greatly exacerbated disabled workers' difficulties on the mainstream labor market. Originally intended to aid families who had lost a breadwinner to death or disability, compensation laws could not encompass the immense diversity of disabilities and their mutability over time. The statutes also did nothing to address the long-term financial challenges faced by workers who became permanently disabled. Due to the segregated nature of the labor force, furthermore, rarely did women and African Americans receive compensation for their work-induced illnesses and disabilities. Making matters worse, the structure of compensation tables created financial incentives for employers to exclude workers with disabilities, regardless of their origin. By the 1920s, nearly all major employers made it a practice to require physical examinations before hiring workers. Even Ford Motor Company substantially reduced its hiring of new workers with disabilities, although it retained many existing ones.

As workers with a wide array of both acquired and congenital disabilities lost access to the paid labor market, legislators and reformers began to search for a way to return people with disabilities to productivity and self-support. Influenced by the Protestant work ethic and the long-standing association of dependency with poor citizenship, rehabilitators tended to focus more on restoring their clients' putatively damaged morality than on determining how to integrate disabled people into the wage labor market. Nevertheless, vocational rehabilitation programs did offer some disabled people and their families modest incomes during times of considerable stress. Chapter 6 traces the emergence of Goodwill Industries and the ways in which its sheltered workshops replicated mainstream employers' use of piecework and concerns with efficiency—dynamics that led managers to exclude many disabled workers as too inefficient. Due to the complexity of disability and the ways that it intersected with age, gender, and family status, few clients moved into the outside labor force.

In contrast, while most disabled World War I veterans eventually returned to the wage labor market, little credit could be given to the vast rehabilitation program created to restore them to the status of breadwinners and self-sufficient citizens. As Chapter 7 shows, veterans and rehabilitators clashed over how to define disability and rehabilitation, in part because new tools of war caused so many injuries that led to chronic pain. Often, veterans found that their disabilities did not qualify them for training even when they could not find work, that rehabilitation did not meet their family's economic needs, and that even after training they could not locate jobs in their fields. In effect, the ways in which policy makers had attempted to generalize disability failed to encompass its diversity, its mutability within and across individuals, how it was reshaped by the shifting economic context, and the ways that technological shifts produced unexpected new impairments. The program's storied administrative dysfunction did not help. In the end, many disabled veterans, especially white ones, ultimately found employment—some equivalent to their prewar earnings. But much of their success was due to the fact that most employers were more willing to hire veterans with disabilities than disabled civilians. Significant numbers, moreover, struggled to manage chronic pain and other impairments and remained on the margins of the economy.

By the 1920s, people with many different types and origins of disabilities had been pushed out of household economies and the paid labor market, like Lily Westbrooke and Walter Pratt (whom we met at the beginning of this chapter). Their bodies were now deemed unproductive, or insufficiently productive, by employers and lawmakers—a shift compounded by changes in family capacity, the rapidly evolving labor market, public policies that sought to deter dependency, and the mutability and complexity of disability itself. Like Westbrooke and Pratt, disabled people continued to seek paid work and to labor, albeit often for minimal or no pay, while often being told that they had "no right to be idle." As we will see, the common twentieth-century notion of equating "disability" with unproductivity, poor citizenship, and dependency on public or charitable assistance was, truly, an invention.

CHAPTER ONE

Her Mother Did Not Like to Have Her Learn to Work

Disability, Family, and the Spectrum of Productivity, 1840s–1870s

In 1869, Paul and Amelia Tucker removed their eighteen-year-old daughter, Emily, from the New York State Asylum for Idiots. As its superintendent, Hervey B. Wilbur, reported, during her two yearlong stints at the asylum Emily had "learned to read a little and write a little"; she had also "learned to work." On the face of it, the Tuckers' decision to bring their daughter home was not particularly unusual. During the asylum's first two decades, parents routinely withdrew their children from the institution or kept them home at the end of summer vacation. In this case, however, the superintendent recorded an unusual rationale: "She was kept at home . . . because she was useful and perhaps because her mother did not like to have her learn to work."[1]

Tucker's mother's comment flew in the face of contemporary rhetoric about "idiots." This term encompassed people with a wide range of impairments, including cerebral palsy, epilepsy, deafness, and what would later be described as autism, as well as cognitive disabilities that could arise from thyroid disorders, head injuries, and high fevers. But in general, "idiot" referred to a person who was not able to care for himself or herself, do useful labor, or understand the legal consequences of his or her actions.[2] In part to obtain funding for asylums from legislators skeptical that idiots could be educated, advocates such as Samuel Gridley Howe variously represented untrained "idiots" as specimens of humanity in need of uplift, as entirely unproductive burdens on overwhelmed families, and, often, as morally dangerous parasites on society.[3]

Educators' and charity reformers' elastic rhetoric proved successful politically. By the 1870s, a network of public idiot asylums, along with a few private ones, had emerged across the northeastern and midwestern states, thanks in no small part to the proselytizing and organizational efforts of Hervey B. Wilbur of the New York State Asylum for Idiots.[4] The founders of these institutions sought to teach their pupils basic self-care and, if possible, the rudiments of reading and writing. Depending on their gender, pupils also learned either farm labor or household skills. Eventually, superintendents aimed to return their charges to their presumably rural families as "useful laborers" or, at least, as needing less daily personal care. Such an approach also proved popular with lawmakers perennially concerned with cost-cutting; consequently, Wilbur and his counterparts often relied on mixed public-private schemes to fund asylums. By and large, however, his training program—as well as those modeled upon it—worked remarkably well during the 1850s and 1860s.

But as suggested by Wilbur's cryptic notation in Tucker's file quoted above, families did not simply adopt superintendents' oft-pejorative depictions of "idiotic" relatives. If we look beyond the asylum walls to examine the lived experiences of "idiots" in their families and communities—where, after all, the vast majority resided—a rather different perspective emerges.[5] To be sure, relatives appreciated when pupils returned home more able to care for themselves and, in some cases, capable of contributing to the household economy—especially under the supervision of relatives. But families often fought hard to ensure that their "idiotic" relatives could live at home, even those who needed considerable care. Families did not view productivity in the simple black-and-white terms suggested by asylum superintendents, nor did the ability or inability to do useful labor determine an individual's value in their eyes. Rather, relatives understood their "idiotic" children in light of the fact that people with diverse bodies and capacities had long performed domestic and manual labor in an economy and society of farms and small communities; such an economy also helped to sustain relatives' capacity for caring. Indeed, such individuals were seen as simply part of a broad spectrum of productivity that varied according to age, gender, and ability.[6]

The Problem of Idiocy

The problem of "idiocy" first emerged as a social issue ripe for intervention in the mid-1840s, when several European and American educators and doctors challenged the long-standing presumption that idiots were incurable. Inspired by the common school movement and immersed in a transatlantic network of asylum builders, three men—Edouard Séguin, Samuel Gridley Howe, and Hervey Wilbur—set out to prove that idiots could in fact benefit from training. Howe, in particular, would make a crucial rhetorical contribution, one that would shape discourse on people labeled as "idiots" and, later on, "feeble-minded," for decades to come.

In the mid-nineteenth century, idiots were hardly an unfamiliar sight to most Americans. Yet, idiocy itself was somewhat ill-defined medically and would remain so well into the twentieth century. For one thing, idiocy did not refer simply to people with cognitive or developmental impairments, such as those stemming from iodine deficiency, Down's syndrome, or brain injuries induced by accidents or high fevers. Rather, the category included those who appeared "idiotic" because of mobility impairments, poor hearing or eyesight, or abuse and neglect, as well as what would become known as autism by the 1940s. English and early American legal theorists and social commentators, meanwhile, had defined idiocy as a permanent, "natural" lack of understanding (or mental deficiency) that typically dated from birth and which prevented self-support and moral judgment. In theory, lawmakers, judges, and doctors distinguished between the temporary nature of "distractedness," which was roughly equivalent to insanity, and the permanent nature of idiocy, but such distinctions were challenging in practice.[7] Charity officials, as well as many members of the public, had a clear, nonmedical definition of idiocy: the inability to care for oneself or do "useful labor." Equally critically, idiots supposedly could not improve, even with training.[8]

Idiocy had yet more meanings: the result of sin, an appropriate object of study for those seeking to understand the natural world, and an innate characteristic of certain races. Both Puritan ministers and nineteenth-century charities officials, for instance, considered idiots to be evidence of parental sins such as intemperance and unchaste behavior. Yet, Cotton Mather and his fellow clerics also saw idiots as innocent beings and manifestations of "God's diverse creations"—"curiosities" to be studied, in effect. In fact, Mather included the tale of two "uncommon Idiots" among his regular reports to London's Royal Society.[9] Antebellum proslavery advocates, meanwhile, sought to define African Americans as inherently feeble-minded. After the 1840 federal census purportedly tallied far higher rates of insanity and idiocy among free blacks than among slaves, southern writers proclaimed that freedom would bring only misery and disability to their human property. Samuel Cartwright, for instance, contended in 1851 that "it is this defective hematosis, or atmospherization of the blood . . . that is the true cause of that debasement of the mind, which has rendered the people of Africa unable to take care of themselves."[10]

In antebellum America, people labeled as idiots encountered both extreme vulnerability and relative integration—often based on their family context. Because families served as the primary locus of care, disinterested or cruel relatives could confine individuals with cognitive or psychosocial impairments without any interference from authorities, such as Patrick Henry's aforementioned "mad" wife, Sarah Shelton Henry, who died after spending several years in a basement in a straitjacket and accompanied only by a slave.[11] Idiots' presumed incurability, as well as their perceived inability to care for themselves or do useful work, also contributed to their neglect by charity officials. Following Elizabethan poor-law precedents, charity officials categorized idiots, simpletons, and imbeciles, among others, as part of the "deserving" poor; this status, however, did not necessarily lead to kind, or even good, care of those whose families could or would not look after them.[12] While Dorothea Dix is best known for her advocacy on behalf of people deemed insane, her famed 1843 *Memorial to the Legislature of Massachusetts* raised awareness about the abuse and neglect suffered by "idiots" and "imbeciles" in poorhouses and jails. She came across "one idiotic subject chained" in a poorhouse, while another had lived "in a close stall for 17 years."[13] As Dix investigated the conditions of those labeled insane or idiotic in almshouses and jails across Massachusetts and New York, she discovered that the type of impairment mattered little. Rather, poorhouse keepers routinely relegated "incurables," whether labeled insane or idiotic, to "close, unventilated rooms; narrow, dark cells, cheerless dungeons, cold and damp," and, often, death.[14]

At the same time, as suggested by the numerous literary accounts of "town idiots" and "simpletons," many idiots were relatively integrated into their communities. In part, this was due to the fact that antebellum Americans demonstrated considerable tolerance for nonviolent neighbors with cognitive and psychosocial impairments. The residents of Brampton, Massachusetts, for instance, lived with Jack Downs, who "regularly enjoyed plucking wigs off the heads of church worshippers with a string and fishhook, and was well known for throwing rotten apples at the minister during the sermon."[15]

As might be expected, families' financial resources also eased integration. Thomas Cameron, the oldest son of the wealthiest plantation family in South Carolina, attended several boarding schools in northern states during the 1820s, including a military academy. His parents hoped that he would thereby gain physical and intellectual strength. As an adult, he returned to his family's plantation in South Carolina, where he served as a messenger between plantations, attended social functions such as weddings, voted and attended Whig political rallies, and developed close ties with his nieces and nephews. Later on, Cameron even became the local postmaster.[16]

Nevertheless, legislators and professional charity reformers viewed idiots through a different lens: as utterly resistant to education and, therefore, as inappropriate subjects for state intervention. Consequently, the asylum building movement of the 1820s and 1830s initially bypassed idiots.[17] During these decades, legislators and professional charity reformers such as Samuel Gridley Howe established a wide variety of state institutions aimed at rehabilitating groups such as the poor, criminals, and blind and deaf children into moral, self-supporting inhabitants. These institutions reflected a millennialist faith in human perfectibility and societal progress, as well as a fervent belief in work as both a form of rehabilitation and a means of defraying expenses. In theory, segregating criminals, orphaned children, the insane, the poor, and children with disabilities in a bucolic yet disciplined setting would improve their morality, teach the value of steady labor, and perhaps even cure them.[18] Prisoners at the Auburn and Ossining (now Sing Sing) state prisons in New York, for instance, labored six days a week in a communal workshop, from 5 A.M. until 6 P.M. Superintendents and legislators alike argued that inmates' labors would inculcate industry and prevent criminal interaction among them.[19] But since few thought idiots capable of improving, lawmakers saw no need to waste state money on a group whose morality could not be improved and who could not be made self-sufficient. Dorothea Dix's exposés of the mistreatment endured by idiots in county poorhouses in Massachusetts and New York in 1842 and 1843, respectively, finally piqued lawmakers' interest, as did the 1845 New York State census, which tallied sixteen hundred idiots in the state.[20]

Edouard Séguin's work with idiots in Paris also played a central role in challenging the assumptions of legislators and professional charity reformers and legislators that idiots could not be educated. While completing his medical training, Séguin spent several years in the late 1830s working under famed physician Jean-Marc Itard, who had earlier tried and failed to educate Victor, the "wild boy of Aveyron." Along with the rest of the French medical establishment, Itard believed idiots to be incapable of improvement, but Séguin found some success with his individualized "physiological" method. After stimulating his charges' senses and muscles, he taught them to speak; finally, he trained his students in morals and occupational skills. Séguin viewed his approach as helping idiots to develop their own will, the lack of which he saw as a crucial element of idiocy. He also relied heavily on Phillipe Pinel's notion of "moral treatment," a doctrine that became popular among lunacy reformers starting in the 1790s and which gained considerable sway during the first half of the nineteenth century. Rather than chain or confine mad or idiotic individuals, advocates of moral treatment sought to recognize an individual's humanity and model kind behavior and personal composure, and they often provided work therapy as well.[21] In 1839, Séguin opened the world's first school for idiots in Paris. By the mid-1840s, reports of his work had begun to appear in English; they soon caused a minor sensation among American insane asylum superintendents, who had long been frustrated by the steady accumulation of seemingly incurable "idiots" in their institutions.[22]

The Boston-based educator and reformer Samuel Gridley Howe, who had long taken an interest in improving insane asylums, took on the cause and soon proved to be a powerful advocate for state-funded idiot asylums in Massachusetts and beyond. In so doing, he also played a key role in defining the "problem of idiocy" as a dire economic and moral issue. By the time Séguin's work reached the shores of the United States in the mid-1840s, Howe had acquired a sterling reputation in the Bay State as a professional reformer, in part due to his adept self-promotion. A Unitarian physician who fervently believed in humanity's essential goodness and perfectibility but who could at times be arrogant, he had already served in the Greek War of Independence, cofounded and directed the Perkins Institution and the Massachusetts Asylum for the Blind in Boston, and helped Dorothea Dix expose the mistreatment of insane inmates at the East Cambridge jail, among other achievements. After reading about Séguin's work, Howe published a series of letters in the Boston *Daily Advertiser* on the benefits of establishing a state idiot asylum. This reflected his passionate, lifelong belief in the public's responsibility to provide all children with an equivalent education appropriately modified to their capabilities—a passion shared with his close friend Horace Mann, leader of the common school movement.[23] Working in conjunction with State Representative Horatio Boyington and Samuel Woodward, the superintendent of the Worcester State Lunatic Hospital, Howe helped establish an investigative committee in 1846 to survey the care of idiots in Massachusetts. Drawing on his successful experiences with training a few idiots at the Perkins Institution, he arranged for himself to be appointed chairman.[24] The committee offered a brief preliminary report in March 1847 that featured a letter from Senator Charles Sumner's brother George endorsing Séguin's work and stressing the "imperative duty" of republics to educate "the deaf, the blind, the infirm in intellect."[25]

Howe's final report, released in mid-1848, stressed both idiots' possible educability and the dire financial and moral risks they posed to society. After discussing the 361 "idiots" examined by the committee, he estimated that as many as 1,500 such people resided in Massachusetts, living in "dreadful degradation" and "always a burden upon the public."[26] As this characterization suggests, Howe's report positioned idiots as both potentially deserving of assistance and fitting many of the criteria of those typically deemed undeserving of state or community assistance. He emphasized two themes that would shape discourse on idiocy and idiots throughout the rest of the nineteenth century: the parasitic dependence of idiots on their families and the state, and the immorality they spread within their communities and, by extension, American society as a whole. Howe's report became a seminal work in the study of the feeble-minded and, later, in the American eugenics movement—a work from which advocates in those overlapping fields would borrow liberally in the following decades. He contended:

> There are at least a thousand persons of this class who not only contribute nothing to the common stock, but who are ravenous consumers; who are idle and often mischievous, and who are dead weights upon the material prosperity of the State. But this is not all; they are even worse than useless; they generally require a good deal of watching to prevent their doing mischief, and they occupy a considerable part of the time of more industrious and valuable persons.... Every such person is like an Upas tree, that poisons the whole moral atmosphere around him."[27]

Howe's intertwined condemnations of idleness, attacks on those who required "excessive care," and celebrations of self-sufficiency reflected the fact that, like many other mid-nineteenth-century elites and reformers, he saw public dependency and overgenerous charity as morally corrosive to both individuals and the republic. He put such views into practice both at the Perkins Institute, where he made vocational training a centerpiece of blind children's schooling, and, later in life, as chairman of the Massachusetts Board of Charities, when he won passage of a vagrancy law in 1866 that "enforced labor for the paupers who can work, but will not."[28] Undoubtedly, Howe was also motivated by his growing belief that people labeled as idiots, as well as blind and deaf people, constituted hereditary evidence of their parents' sins. In large part, this proto-eugenic turn arose from his "failed" effort to educate deaf-blind student Laura Bridgman so as to validate phrenology, Unitarianism, and his views of human development. When she proved to have a free will of her own and found evangelical Christianity more attractive than Howe's Unitarianism, Howe blamed her "deranged constitution"—a critique he soon extended to other blind students and their families.[29]

Simultaneously, Howe argued that idiots deserved equal education and treatment. With training, he predicted that idiots could "attain a respectable mediocrity, and surpass, in mental power, the common peasant of many European states."[30] His persistent faith in human goodness, moreover, led him to reject the idea of permanently institutionalizing idiots in a custodial asylum. Further reflecting his millennialist hopes in progress, as well as his belief that

Founding superintendent of the New York State Asylum for Idiots, Hervey B. Wilbur from *Proceedings of the Association of Medical Officers of American Institutions for Idiotic and Feeble-Minded Persons*, 1884.

idiots warranted aid, Howe maintained that after finishing their schooling, idiots should be encouraged to return to their home communities to deter others against poor choices in marriage or behavior.[31] Howe's report proved convincing. In May 1848, the Massachusetts legislature appropriated funds for the first educational program for idiots in the United States: an experimental wing for idiot training in the Perkins Institute for the Blind, which soon became the Massachusetts School for Idiotic and Feeble-Minded Youth.[32]

While Howe played a crucial role in outlining the problem of idiocy and its potential solutions, another man, Hervey Backus Wilbur, undertook the practical labor of spreading idiot asylums across the country. A young physician with a reputation for imprudence and a zealous devotion to his causes, Wilbur found his curiosity piqued after he read a review of Séguin's first book and a report on the idiot training program at Paris's Bicêtre hospital in British journals. In 1847, he sent an order abroad seeking any and all books that might explain how to treat idiocy. In return, he received only Séguin's newly released *Traitement moral, hygiene, et education des idiots*. Although Wilbur had previously been rather restless—he had yet to establish a medical practice, had previously worked as a civil engineer, and had moved seven times since graduating from Berkshire Medical College in 1843—he found himself fascinated by Séguin's methodology.[33]

Soon afterwards, in July 1848, a prominent local lawyer asked Wilbur to try educating his seven-year-old idiot son. Wilbur promptly welcomed the boy into his house in Barre, Massachusetts, much to the dismay of friends who feared that teaching idiots would prove both impossible and unprofitable. Later that year, he formally founded the privately funded Institute for Idiots in Barre. While at the institute, pupils resided in Wilbur's house, along with his infant daughter and his wife, Harriet Holden. By early 1851, Wilbur had recruited enough pupils—approximately a dozen—that he, his family, and his students moved to a larger residence. Much like those he later admitted to the New York State Asylum for Idiots, his pupils at Barre had a wide range of impairments. Several could not speak or understand language, one did not have control of his bowels, a few had regular seizures, whereas others already spoke some words and could walk. Wilbur soon began to gain regional renown as an expert on the training of idiots, even referring pupils to Howe's asylum.[34]

Meanwhile, in New York, State Senator Frederick F. Backus had also become intrigued by the possibility of educating idiots but had little success convincing his state legislature to establish a school. Wary of new budgetary commitments after the enormous expense of constructing the Utica State Lunatic Asylum, which had exceeded its initial budget by eight times, the state legislature rejected Backus's proposals in 1846 and 1847.[35] Not until Howe (who had already learned that public demonstrations by his blind students provided an invaluable means of fund-raising and public relations) visited Albany in 1850 with several of his idiotic students in tow did the New York legislature finally act. Several trustees, bemused by their appointments and convinced that "none but fools would think of teaching fools," traveled to Massachusetts to consult with Wilbur and Howe. Their two-day visit at the Institute for Idiots in Barre so impressed the trustees that they immediately hired Wilbur, who had in fact been angling for the position for over a year.[36] The following year, the New York State Asylum for Idiots opened in the former Bull's Head Tavern near the shore of the Hudson River just a few miles north of Albany, on land donated by Stephen van Rensselaer IV with the aim of encouraging legislators to fund the asylum. The trustees and Wilbur hoped that locating the asylum in a "retired yet accessible" spot near a major city would aid legislative oversight and help to educate the populace about the social and economic benefits of training idiots.[37]

A Method for Educating Idiots

Despite many inducements, Wilbur never left the New York State Asylum for Idiots. He died in 1883 at the asylum, which had moved to Syracuse in 1855. Nevertheless, Wilbur played a far more central role in spreading idiot asylums across the country than did Howe, who spent much of the 1850s and 1860s advocating on behalf of the abolition of slavery, charity reform, and oral education for deaf children.[38] Not only did Wilbur train many, if not most, of the individuals who founded and staffed over a dozen idiot schools from Michigan to California, but he also personally advised on the establishment of several others in the United States and Canada between the 1850s and the 1880s.[39] As a result, other asylums adopted Wilbur's methods for educating idiots, which relied on the assumption that, once as fully trained as possible in self-care and vocational skills, pupils would return to their families—presumably in rural areas—as at least less burdensome and, preferably, at least somewhat capable of working. His approach also reflected widespread mid-nineteenth-century notions that linked being a producer—or, at the very least, not being dependent—with good morality and citizenship, as well with Protestant notions of work as being key to salvation. As Wilbur and his counterparts in other states were aware, such a focus played well with legislators perennially concerned with asylums' costs and reluctant to fully support institutions as well as the private funders on whom his institution and others also relied.

Wilbur was in many ways an exemplar rather than a precursor, perhaps nowhere more than in his use of Enlightenment rhetoric about people perceived as "idiots." Enlightenment thinkers such as Denis Diderot, Jean-Jacques Rousseau, and John Locke all employed people with impairments such as deafness, blindness, and idiocy in thought-pieces that considered the nature of humanity and human capacity. People with physical disabilities, in turn, played key roles in evolutionary scientists' attempts to classify the natural world and in statisticians' attempts to define normality during the first half of the nineteenth century. In his annual reports to the New York legislature, however, Wilbur argued fervently on behalf of idiots' humanity—a decidedly minority viewpoint at this time.[40] He often stressed the "human origin" of idiots, noting that pupils suffered from homesickness, and stated that "they [we]re not responsible for their unfortunate condition, whether inherited or as the result of disease."[41] Wilbur's younger brother Charles Toppan Wilbur studied with him and promulgated those views as he established state idiot asylums in Illinois, Indiana, Nebraska, and Minnesota, as well as private asylums in Connecticut and Michigan. In his first annual report to Illinois legislators, Charles argued that "however they may differ in physical, mental or moral organization, they are yet human beings."[42] The younger Wilbur also reproduced his brother's argument verbatim from the first annual report for the New York State Asylum for Idiots, contending that idiots' "degradation in the scale of humanity ... constitute[d] no absolute release or outlawry from the duties or rights ... of human beings." The following year, he went even further, characterizing his pupils as "fellow-citizens."[43]

Undoubtedly, the brothers hoped that such claims might convince skeptical legislators of the virtues of supporting their asylums, thereby assuring a steadier stream of funding. But the Wilbur brothers' passionate advocacy on behalf of idiots' "human soul" and "human destiny" contrasts with the rhetoric of their contemporaries as well as with later superintendents' efforts to permanently confine, sterilize, or entirely eradicate people deemed "feeble-minded." To help win over state legislators to support an idiot asylum, Howe, of course, had strategically defined idiots as "dead weights on the material prosperity of the state" and as "like an Upas tree, that poisons the whole moral atmosphere about him."[44] The eventual head of the Massachusetts School for Idiotic and Feeble-Minded Youth, James B. Richards, likewise emphasized idiots' "low [place] in the scale," as well as their deformities and infirmities.[45] Both Wilburs also rejected the hereditarian and proto-eugenic understandings of idiocy that became so popular starting in the 1870s.[46]

Despite some scholars' claims that Hervey Wilbur carefully selected the most promising and least disabled pupils to more easily fulfill legislators' expectations, the initial students at the asylum reflected the trustees' mandate that they "exhibit a fair average of the great varieties of idiocy."[47] Such attacks are based on similar critiques made by the second generation of asylum superintendents, who were trying to distinguish themselves from their forebears and gain more funding. Half of the New York State Asylum for Idiot's first cohort of twenty-six students could not speak at all, and a quarter did not understand language. Harry Goodnow, for instance, arrived at age ten, without knowing his own name. He liked being out in the sun bareheaded, but spent his time twisting his fingers and, if left alone, eating out of the swill pail.[48] Others could not walk or feed themselves. In fact, Wilbur reported that one "would have starved to death with food within her reach and before her eyes."[49] Like Goodnow, many had "destructive habits" that their families found challenging to handle. Alexander Mitchell, a "low-grade idiot" who entered as the asylum's tenth pupil at age eight, could not control his bowels or bladder or speak and was "always covered with saliva to the waist." Describing Mitchell as "exceedingly bad-tempered and ugly," Wilbur noted that he spent his first three months at the asylum "in a rage ... from being forced [to] wear shoes on his feet." A few, meanwhile, had already attended common school or received instruction at home but had struggled to learn.[50]

While some of the Wilbur brothers' counterparts, such as Howe, initially sought out the most "malleable" students to ensure steady funding for their experimental asylums, they too accepted students with a wide array of abilities. More than half of Howe's first class of twenty-eight students at the Massachusetts Experimental School for Teaching and Training Idiotic Children were "dumb, many of them absolutely so, the others only making two or three sounds resembling words indeed," and only seven could feed themselves. Fewer than one-third were "cleanly."[51] In Illinois, meanwhile, all of Charles Toppan Wilbur's first ten students could walk, but almost none could dress themselves. He noted that one girl "was so habituated to tearing her clothes, in her fits of passion, that it was found very difficult to keep her decently clad." Only a select few had any training in "useful labor" such as basic sewing or "household occupations."[52]

In the case of state-funded pupils, a county judge had to first certify that the child was an appropriate candidate for admission. The application form requested information about the family's finances and the relationship between the "idiot" and the person requesting that they be admitted, as well as the candidate's nativity, residence, and age. Circulars sent to family physicians, meanwhile, asked about "history of the case: whether resulting from any know[n] predisposing causes in the condition or habits of ancestors, or produced by disease or accident in infancy." These answers gave particulars as to "bodily health, mental characteristics and capacities, disposition, peculiar habits." Pupils typically began with a one-month trial and were to be apportioned equally among judicial districts or senatorial districts, depending on the state.[53]

Even early on, idiot asylums served a diverse population not limited to people with cognitive disabilities—a pattern that would remain in effect in succeeding decades and which regularly posed challenges for superintendents. Officially, all idiot asylums followed Hervey Wilbur's, Charles Toppan Wilbur's, and Howe's practice of barring "cripples," students with epilepsy, insanity, or "incurable diseases." In reality, however, the Wilburs and their counterparts regularly accepted students with mild epilepsy, deafness, and various physical impairments, generally excluding only those with insanity or dementia, or whose "serious ill-health seemed likely to terminate in a speedy death."[54] In 1853, for instance, Hervey Wilbur reported admitting two boys, Natty and Willie, directly from Manhattan's poorhouse on Randall's Island. The boys were "partially paralyzed, both entirely dumb," and one had a chronic eye infection, but both eventually learned to fingerspell and, later, to speak. Natty became well known in the city of Syracuse and remained at the asylum until his death in 1902.[55] Other early pupils had facial paralysis, curved spines, paralyzed limbs, palsy, chorea, club feet, significant hearing loss or deafness,

Early pupils at New York State Asylum for Idiots. Courtesy of the New York State Archive.

or partial blindness, or were labeled as "cripples," in the parlance of the time.[56] In fact, Wilbur often observed that many of his pupils had some sort of physical impairment or general ill health, and he even seemed to have relished the challenge of educating children with severe and multiple impairments, perhaps seeing such cases as making for good publicity.[57]

Aside from the nearly 20 percent of students identified as having a congenital impairment (one dating from birth), the causes of pupils' idiocy were just as diverse as their abilities. Superintendents struggled to make sense of the range of causes.[58] As was the case with Margaret McDonogh, about 7 percent of students' impairments originated from the high fevers caused by scarlet fever and, to a lesser extent, measles and what doctors termed "meningitis." Although she was "like other children" before a bout of "what her mother called 'the black measles,'" it left her "quite idiotic" and incapable of walking or speaking for five years. Once at the asylum, however, McDonogh eventually learned to use the sewing machine and became "very useful in all domestic matters" but never learned to read or write.[59] A smaller fraction (3 percent) had suffered head injuries. After a "log of wood" fell on Walter McNeil's head, for instance, he had lost the ability to speak; the person who recommended him to the New York State Asylum for Idiots noted that his "intelect [sic] seems paralized [sic]" and that he was "like a log so inactive."[60] Yet others' impairments arose from uncontrolled seizures or, far more rarely, from thyroid deficiencies, Down's syndrome, or physical abuse.[61] More than a few were deaf or hard of hearing or had physical impairments often assumed to be associated with idiocy at the time, such as cerebral palsy, physical deformities, or chorea. An illness at six weeks of age left John Foster, for instance, with "want of use of [his] left leg." After he failed to retain what he learned in school, he arrived at the New York State Asylum for Idiots in 1860 labeled as a "cripple." But during his four years in the asylum, he "learned rapidly"; in fact, Wilbur commented, "before he left he was regarded by visitors as possessed of normal intelligence."[62]

From the first, Wilbur's assumption that his pupils would return home shaped his approach; he focused initially on teaching his charges the self-care skills that would make them less burdensome both at the asylum and at home. He sought to render them "decent in their habits, more obedient, furnished with more extended means of happiness, educated in some simple occupations and industry, capable of self support under judicious management in their own families."[63] As at Barre, he modeled the institution's program on Séguin's method of beginning with "exciting the will" of the pupils by providing "appropriate stimuli, and then by its continued exercise giving it the capability to control the other attributes of the individual."⁶⁴ Fanny Paterson, for instance, arrived at the asylum in 1859 after a bout of measles, which had "left her weak in body and mind." No longer could she walk or talk; instead, she "l[ay] on the floor and beat her head with a constant moaning noise."⁶⁵

Once pupils began to gain control over their movements, often via mimicking each others' behaviors in groups, they began learning to "take care of themselves as far as possible in all personal matters" so as to ease their reintegration into their families.⁶⁶ In particular, Wilbur emphasized training students to control their bladder and bowels, feed themselves, dress themselves, and communicate insofar as possible—all skills that would greatly reduce their need for care once at home. Nine-year-old Albert Page, for instance, arrived in 1856, described as "filthy" and unable to walk or feed himself fully. Wilbur described him as "very mischievous, restless, throws everything out of the window or hides articles." But after an eleven-year stay, Page departed "improved greatly in his habits—[he had] learned to care for himself." Not only had he "made some progress in school studies" but his father "report[ed] him as being of some service on his farm."⁶⁷

As in Paterson's case, Wilbur placed great weight on eliminating or at least reducing "destructive habits" with which relatives struggled to cope that might discourage them from retaining idiotic children at home. Frances Alden, for example, "rock[ed] almost constantly & scream[ed] a good deal of the time," while Diana Heller "str[uck] other children or anyone else with whom she c[ame] into contact," and Christopher Collins "br[oke] windows when in a passion." All three eventually returned home, although only Alden's conduct improved; after six years, Wilbur noted that although she was "not entirely over her obstinacy ... she now walks a few steps along when she chooses. Cannot dress herself."⁶⁸

Reflecting Wilbur's aim of articulating a place for his institution—and his pupils—within the broader movement for common schools, those pupils who mastered basic self-care moved on to introductory academic classes and occupational training. As did his counterparts in other states, he envisioned educating the most capable so that they could enter ordinary schools with "the same ends and objects as the other pupils; to be qualified ... for civil usefulness and social happiness."⁶⁹ Stressing the fact that the state had long provided education to deaf and blind children, he argued that legislators had established "the principle that any physical infirmity ... constituted no bar to [children's] enjoyment of the public provision for education whenever the education was practicable."⁷⁰ Pupils began as in common schools, learning words and, later on, letters and numbers; if able, they progressed to simple reading and writing. In many ways, Floyd Nelson's experiences with schooling proved typical. When he arrived in 1867, he could speak, albeit "very slowly leaving out all connecting words," and had no grasp of numbers or letters. After three years' time, Nelson had learned the alphabet and many printed words, enabling him to work slowly through the first reader.[71]

Wilbur further hoped to prove that a very few "exceptional" students had been falsely labeled as idiots and might eventually cross "beyond the line of social disability, the line between idiocy and ordinary human intelligence." He recognized that some children labeled as "idiots" had suffered severe neglect or had some sort of sensory deprivation, such as deafness, that prevented typical cognitive development.[72] A select few of his students did advance to the third or fourth readers, or even to geography and division. Some, such as Carrie Munson, later attended ordinary schools. After a five-year stay at Syracuse prompted by her inability to learn at a regular school, Munson's parents retained her at home "with the expectation of sending her to a common school." By then, she had also become "quite capable in household work."[73] Wilbur celebrated these accomplishments, crowing over Charles Buckner's mastery of "the four rules of arithmetic, written and mental," as well as the fact that he "enjoy[ed] any storybook, paper, or magazine, reading them with pleasure and profit."[74]

Nevertheless, occupational training remained crucial, especially for the majority of pupils, such as Lillian Gaffer, who would never improve enough to attend common schools but who could be productive within the context of a family—or an asylum. After she had resided at the asylum for fourteen years, Wilbur reflected, "she had some school exercises but it was thought better to give her some useful occupation, as it was almost impossible to teach her anything pertaining to school." Instead, Gaffer did a full day's labor in the bakery.[75] Indeed, Wilbur commented in 1856 that although relatives might fixate on "mere school acquirements ... the capability for useful occupation" is the "true end and aim of his education."[76]

Like other members of the Protestant, property-owning, middle class—the source of nearly all asylum builders, charity reformers, and, crucially, legislators—Wilbur and his counterparts adhered to the widespread antebellum belief that doing useful labor was a crucial element of good morality. At a time when idleness remained associated with sin, and when politicians, workers, and public media alike celebrated "producers," he argued that "the capability for useful occupation and the willingness to be thus occupied, satisfies the greatest need of the idiot and will insure his future comfort and happiness."[77] Other superintendents made similar arguments, knowing full well that many if not all of the legislators reading his annual reports shared their belief that work was the "core of moral life."[78] Howe promised, for instance, "All are to be kept busy and rendered industrious; and if possible taught some simple and useful work, if it be but doing *chores* about a house and farm."[79] Joseph Parrish, founding superintendent of the Pennsylvania School, argued in turn that "labor is the first duty, as it is the noblest privilege of man; it is the rudimental life from which emanates the entire physical, and moral structure."[80] More than one reiterated Wilbur's argument that their asylums had no higher aim than "impart[ing] a capacity for usefulness."[81]

Relatively speaking, idiot asylums lagged behind the other rehabilitative institutions that arose out of the Second Great Awakening: the state penitentiaries, insane asylums, state schools for the deaf and blind, and revamped local poorhouses that were established by legislators and charity officials in northern and midwestern states in the 1820s and 1830s. Nevertheless, the founders of idiot asylums shared their predecessors' belief in the moral benefits of work, while also recognizing the political utility of using occupational training programs to convince skeptical legislators that state funds were being used efficiently. At Utica State Lunatic Asylum, for instance, most inmates worked in the wards, in industrial shops, or on the asylum farm. Officials believed that inmates would thereby learn the regularity and self-discipline thought necessary to restoring sanity.[82] Wilbur stressed similar themes, arguing that not only did digging vegetables or making beds physically tire out his students but, as he explained in 1859, such work also "substitute[d] a normal direction, and a spontaneous exercise of the various human faculties, with which they are endowed, for a blind subserviency to mere habit, or the misdirection of those same powers, by appetite and passion." Such language, moreover, bore marked similarities to arguments that missionaries made about the moral benefits of manual labor training for "heathens" in Hawai'i and Indian Territory and at American Indian boarding schools.[83]

In practice, idiot asylums' occupational training programs largely but not entirely imitated their institutional antecedents. While schools for deaf and blind children trained their students in trades such as printing, music, broom making, and, sometimes, in basic skills such as sewing, idiot asylum superintendents tended to view skilled trades as unlikely to ensure self-support in the countryside and, even more problematic, as likely to lead their charges into the dangerous environment of towns and cities.[84] Accordingly, in keeping with nineteenth-century gender mores, female students studied domestic skills, whereas boys learned primarily agricultural labor. Wilbur observed in his second annual report, "Some of the little girls can do little more than hold a needle in their hands or even a piece of cloth, but they will gradually acquire a curiosity to notice what the others are doing, and will in the same gradual manner make the first attempts towards sewing."[85] Male students began occupational training with simple tasks such as gathering stones or filling in a swampy area, eventually moving on to more advanced duties such as gathering fruit, watering, and hoeing—at first working under constant supervision, but eventually learning to do farm labor by themselves.[86] After the asylum's 1855 move to a more spacious site in Syracuse, Wilbur expanded occupational programs even further, using female students to complete nearly all duties in the bedrooms, dining rooms, and laundry and having male pupils undertake most of the farm work during the summers.[87]

The asylum's relocation to Syracuse illustrated the deeply political nature of asylum building as well as the crucial role played by mixed public-private funding schemes. Wilbur and the asylum's trustees had initially hoped to expand the still-experimental institution at its original site in Troy, in order to keep the asylum near the state capital. The state bought a nearby farm, but State Senator Clarkson Crosby became incensed that the state did not select his land instead and had a provision passed that required the state to select another site. In an example of the sort of civic speculation common in the nineteenth century, General E. W. Leavenworth, a prominent Syracuse banker and ex officio member of the asylum board of trustees (courtesy of his position as acting secretary of state), simultaneously organized a group of twenty speculators willing to pay the trustees $7,500 to bring the asylum to Syracuse. The *Syracuse Daily Standard* editorialized that the asylum would provide a "novelty that will draw many to the city ... with a probable expense of $50,000 annually falling into the hands of the city and the vicinity." The state eventually purchased an even larger parcel of Leavenworth's land than he had initially offered (at the price of $10,300); Leavenworth also profited from later sales of land to the asylum. In order to prevent the appearance of a conflict of interest, the board of trustees suggested in its annual report that Leavenworth was unwilling to sell his land. Wilbur's prior experience as a civil engineer allowed him to quickly modify the plans for the Troy site and build the new asylum in Syracuse before any local opposition developed.[88]

Wilbur's influence, moreover, extended well beyond the state of New York; he had a profound and even international influence on the structure and staff of idiot asylums during the second half of the nineteenth century. As the founder of the first private asylum for idiots in the United States and the superintendent of the first state asylum dedicated specifically to training idiots, he was the acknowledged expert on idiot education during the 1850s and 1860s. In fact, Wilbur was one of the leading men in the field until his death in 1883. Although Howe founded what would later become the Massachusetts School for Idiotic and Feeble-Minded Youth and served as general superintendent for many years, he had many other interests than idiots and, in fact, did not teach at the experimental school for idiots within his Perkins Institute for the Blind. Wilbur and Séguin, who became increasingly close starting in the late 1850s, were the key leaders of the first generation of superintendents. Séguin, however, while renowned as the pioneer of idiot training, was hampered by his weak grasp of English, his tendency to take offense at small slights, and his desire for full control, which led to his short tenures as superintendent at the experimental Massachusetts school and the Pennsylvania Training School for Idiotic and Feeble-Minded Children.[89]

Despite the ill health of his first wife, Harriet Holden, throughout the 1860s and his daughter's death in 1871, Wilbur remained committed to what he had early on described to Howe as *"missionary labor."* The governors of Ohio and Kentucky asked him to demonstrate his students' achievements to their state legislatures, while legislative committees from Connecticut and Ohio traveled to Syracuse to consult with him before establishing institutions in their own states. Wilbur trained not only his younger brother Charles Toppan Wilbur, who established institutions in six different states, but also the founders of the Kansas State Asylum for Idiotic and Imbecile Youth and the California Home for the Care and Training of the Feeble-Minded.[90] Reflecting the transatlantic nature of both the asylum movement and early educational programs for children with disabilities, Hervey Wilbur maintained a lively correspondence with superintendents of European schools located in France, Saxony, Prussia, Switzerland, and Wurtemburg and consulted at idiot asylums in England and Ontario during the 1870s.[91] That same decade, in 1876, Wilbur helped Isaac N. Kerlin of the Pennsylvania Training School establish the first professional association for superintendents of idiot asylums, the Association of Medical Officers of American Institutions for Idiotic and Feeble-Minded Persons, and then served as the association's second president.[92] At the association's meetings, members repeatedly recognized Wilbur's leading role in occupational training. In fact, Séguin termed the New York State Asylum for Idiots a "mecca."[93]

Consequently, many asylums adopted Wilbur's approach wholesale. Echoing both Séguin and Wilbur, the Illinois Institution for Feeble-Minded Children, for instance, began by teaching students "the more practical matters of every day life, the cultivation of habits of decency, propriety, self-management and self-reliance."[94] And reflecting the weight that superintendents placed on teaching their charges to require less care at both home and the asylum, the Massachusetts School for Idiotic and Feeble-Minded Youth sought to instill the virtue of "decency" as well as "regularity and cleanliness."[95] As in New York, every asylum provided some academic training; Illinois's Charles Toppan Wilbur proudly reported, for instance, that some pupils had advanced to the third and fourth readers and had begun learning multiplication and forms of measure.[96]

But illustrating Hervey Wilbur's influence, occupational training programs took center stage. His stature here was such that at least one superintendent, Iowa's O. W. Archibald, drew on Wilbur's expertise while negotiating with state legislators. To strengthen the case he made in his biennial report as to why the legislature should fund the asylum's purchase of a large farm, Archibald directly reproduced his correspondence with Wilbur: "The experience of all similar and older institutions is that farming is the most beneficial, profitable and satisfactory. Dr. H. B. Wilbur, who has been superintendent of the New York Asylum for Idiots for over twenty-five (25) years, says, in answer to inquiries regarding this matter: 'I still believe that farming and gardening occupations are the best forms of employment for persons of deficient intelligence.'"[97]

Overall, superintendents continued to assume that students would eventually return to their families in small, often rural, communities and trained their charges accordingly. Massachusetts's general superintendent Samuel Gridley Howe contended, for instance, "It is quite clear, that domestic service, or what is called housework, is the best occupation for girls."[98] In the Bay State's asylum, as well as in those in Iowa, Pennsylvania, and other states, girls made beds, did the dishes, set tables, scrubbed floors, did laundry, swept, and sewed.[99] With the exception of the Massachusetts School, which was located in a densely populated part of Boston, idiot asylums focused on teaching boys to do farm work. Charles Toppan Wilbur, for instance, argued that "experience has shown that agricultural labor is the best employment." Echoing his older brother, he observed that "coming ... as so many of the pupils will, from the rural districts, when they enter the Institution, and returning to the same on leaving it, education in agricultural employments would seem the best adapted. ... It can certainly be made to contribute more towards reducing the current expenses of an establishment than any other."[100]

As the younger Wilbur's comment suggested, superintendents' discussions of occupational programs were hardly apolitical, given the funding challenges inherent in establishing asylums and legislators' reluctance to devote additional dollars. Prior generations of asylum builders had promised legislators that the new insane asylums, penitentiaries, schools for deaf and blind children, and poorhouses would prove to be wise economic investments. As Howe had done in his 1848 report on the status of idiots in Massachusetts, these advocates blended lofty humanitarian rhetoric with economic arguments. They relied on the new science of statistics, pride in the state-financed building of progressive institutions, and sympathy for pitiful or powerless beings to argue that proper training and treatment would save taxpayers money by turning dependents into self-supporting inhabitants.[101] In his first report to the New York legislature after opening the New York State Asylum for Idiots, for instance, Hervey Wilbur contended that the asylum would replace "capacities for incapacities." He continued, "A class of human beings, now a burden to community, destitute of intelligence, degraded and miserable, to their friends and to society ... [would be rendered] more capable of self-assistance, of self-support, of self-respect, and of obtaining the greatest degree of comfort and happiness with their small means."[102] The trustees of the New York State Asylum for Idiots eagerly endorsed Wilbur's blend of humanitarianism and economic frugality, suggesting that the new asylum would replace "encumbrances and annoyances" with independent, self-sufficient individuals.[103]

Complicating matters for the older Wilbur brother, New York lawmakers remained skeptical about funding new institutional projects in the wake of the cost overruns involved in the construction of Utica State Lunatic Asylum. He knew that his experimental asylum had to demonstrate a "wise political economy" and find additional sources of revenue in order to continue receiving state funds.[104] Indeed, Wilbur had already displayed his financial acumen in an 1850 letter to Howe, in which he argued that Howe had set the fees of his experimental state idiot asylum too low to offset cost-cutting attempts by the Massachusetts legislature.[105] The younger man contended that, given the experimental nature of idiot asylums, such institutions needed to become economically stable if legislators were to continue funding them.[106] Wilbur, as well as his counterparts, assiduously courted paying pupils as a means of helping support the asylum. Fees from paying pupils helped balance the ledgers, covering as much as 13.5 percent of regular expenditures in 1870.[107]

Wilbur knew full well that asylums' annual reports were, in effect, "begging letters" directed toward state legislators who held the purse strings. Accordingly, he carefully highlighted the institutional costs defrayed via pupils' labors.[108] In his 1852 annual report, he observed, "During the summer past, the elder members of the class have made twenty-four sheets; twenty-four towels;

forty pillow-cases, besides hemming a large number of pocket handkerchiefs. Their success already gives promise that they will in time be able to do much of the sewing required in such an institution. Nor need this, or will this be the only industrial occupation to be profitably carried on in the asylum."[109] Using language that would have resonated strongly in legislators' ears, in 1858 Wilbur lauded his older male charges as "actual producers," proclaiming the next year that their labor—if properly directed—equaled the cost of their support.[110] By that point, male students were producing all of the asylum's vegetables, as well as at least thirty tons of hay, eighty bushels of oats, and five hundred bushels of potatoes per year, defraying the costs of provisions and supplies by more than 15 percent.[111] The asylums' trustees, meanwhile, were so pleased that they announced that they "would dispense with the school-room rather than with the farm, so far as the boys are concerned."[112]

Other superintendents followed Wilbur's rhetorical cues and political strategies. Superintendent Parrish of the Pennsylvania Training School boasted in 1860 that "little children . . . from seven to twelve years old" had "gathered tons of surface-stone . . . by which fields have been greatly improved"; he suggested that not only had their work saved money but that the "fact of their being useful" served as a "stimulus to their moral development." His older male students had planted and harvested the potato crop and assisted in haying, while a male teenager served as "butler of the house . . . assist[ing] in the housekeeping department, and occupies a place that would be entrusted to a *hired* person."[113] The head of the Iowa asylum likewise promised legislators that with a proper farm the "large number of boys in the Asylum who are able and willing to work . . . [could] furnish the Asylum with all the necessary vegetables for its use."[114]

Often superintendents combined such proclamations with language more reminiscent of Howe's harsh economic definition of idiots as nonproducers who drained a family of its vitality—language that spoke directly to legislators' cost-cutting concerns. Wilbur's younger brother Charles, for instance, argued in the late 1860s: "As a matter of political economy, the moneys appropriated for their education will most assuredly result in the relief from the burden of their support at the public expense in a greater degree than in the case of any other subjects of education in the State. . . . With appropriate education will develop a capacity for productive industry, where, without it, an utter inability for useful occupation would exist."[115] Hervey Wilbur himself suggested in 1871 that caring for even one idiotic child imposed an impossible burden on families. Contending that state provisions were "very inadequate" at this time, he argued, "The extra care and attention these demanded so fettered the industry of other members as to turn the scale and land the whole family in the poor-house."[116]

Families and the Spectrum of Productivity

In the late 1850s, Robert Jeffries returned home to his parents' farm near Syracuse "improved only in habits." A "long fever" at age two had left him nonverbal, and he did not know his own name. Jeffries continued to require substantial daily care upon his departure from the asylum, yet he lived with his parents for the next fifty-one years. Only upon their death did he enter the Onondaga County Almshouse.[117] After being discharged in 1860, Sally Goode, in turn, "acted as a nurse for years for her foster-mother." While in the asylum, she had learned to read and write and had also become "capable of any simple household occupation." Later on, once she gained experience, she maintained herself for more than two decades by working as a servant.[118] And, of course, Emily Tucker's parents retained her at home after two years at the New York State Asylum for Idiots because she was "useful" and her mother had qualms about her learning to work.[119]

Despite superintendents' nakedly political attempts to paint idiots as unproductive burdens, their dire rhetoric appears to have had little effect upon pupils' families. In fact, superintendents in New York, Massachusetts, Illinois, and elsewhere achieved their goal of reintegrating many, if not most, of their charges into their largely rural families in the 1850s and 1860s. Like Jeffries, Goode, and Tucker, most pupils—especially those who were less "able"— remained at asylums for only a few years and then returned home permanently.[120] To be sure, relatives appreciated when their children became more able to care for themselves, and many proved capable of significant work, at least in rural and small communities where they could rely on support from relatives. But unlike most superintendents, families adhered to older and more flexible understandings of productivity that did not label individuals as either fully productive or entirely unproductive. Rather, as Hervey Wilbur recognized, families eagerly sought to make use of "idiotic" relatives even when they were only partly productive. Bonds of loyalty and affection mattered too, as did the way in which mid-nineteenth-century occupational structures extended families' capacity for caring.

For most students, their families had far more influence on their lives than the asylum. At the New York State Asylum for Idiots, the overall discharge rate averaged 52.4 percent during the asylum's first four decades. In other words, just over half of those admitted did not remain in the asylum and, in many cases, returned home within a year or two, sometimes within a few months.[121] New York was far from alone in this trend; in fact, short stays were common throughout idiot asylums' early years. Only half of the students at Howe's experimental asylum in Massachusetts remained more than a year, while students' stays at the Illinois Institution for Feeble-Minded Children averaged just over two years during the first fifteen years.[122]

Discharge, however, did not necessarily mean that pupils had successfully completed their training. Upon discharge, some pupils had mastered self-care, gender-appropriate work, and basic academic skills. But often, superintendents used "discharge" to refer to those students whom they deemed incapable of improving, either because of age or a lack of ability. Additionally, "discharged" encompassed the considerable number of pupils removed by their parents, as well as those who removed themselves by eloping from the campus. In other words, those discharged constituted an extremely diverse population, not simply the most capable.[123]

Admittedly, asylums were more central to others' lives, especially for female pupils. Rebecca Stahl, for instance, arrived at the New York State Asylum for Idiots in 1857 and never left, dying there in 1875. In a photo attached to her admission record, her hair is tied back and she is wearing a dress with a lace collar. Next to her picture is a handwritten notation, "scrofulous," indicating that she may have had tuberculosis-induced swellings in her neck. Like Stahl, 16 percent of pupils admitted died at the asylum, sometimes after being institutionalized for more than half a century.[124] Another 24 percent were eventually transferred to other institutions—a phenomenon discussed in chapter 2.

Discharge patterns, moreover, were deeply gendered. While girls and young women comprised about 40 percent of the asylum's population, like Stahl they were disproportionately likely to remain permanently at the asylum until death or to be transferred directly to another state or county institution (see Chart 1-1 as well as "Appendix: A Note on Sources").[125] In Stahl's case, she passed away after an eighteen-year stay during which she had learned to dress herself and younger children, speak English rather than German, eat "in a proper way," and count and read a little. Wilbur noted, "She listens with pleasure whenever anyone reads aloud" and can "sew on any plain work and knit some."[126] But during the asylum's first two decades, Stahl's tale of a life lived largely inside an institution represented the exception, not the rule.

A select few students fulfilled superintendents' optimistic projections early on that most "idiots" could be trained to be self-supporting. Wilbur, for instance, confidently estimated in 1857 that, if admitted early enough,

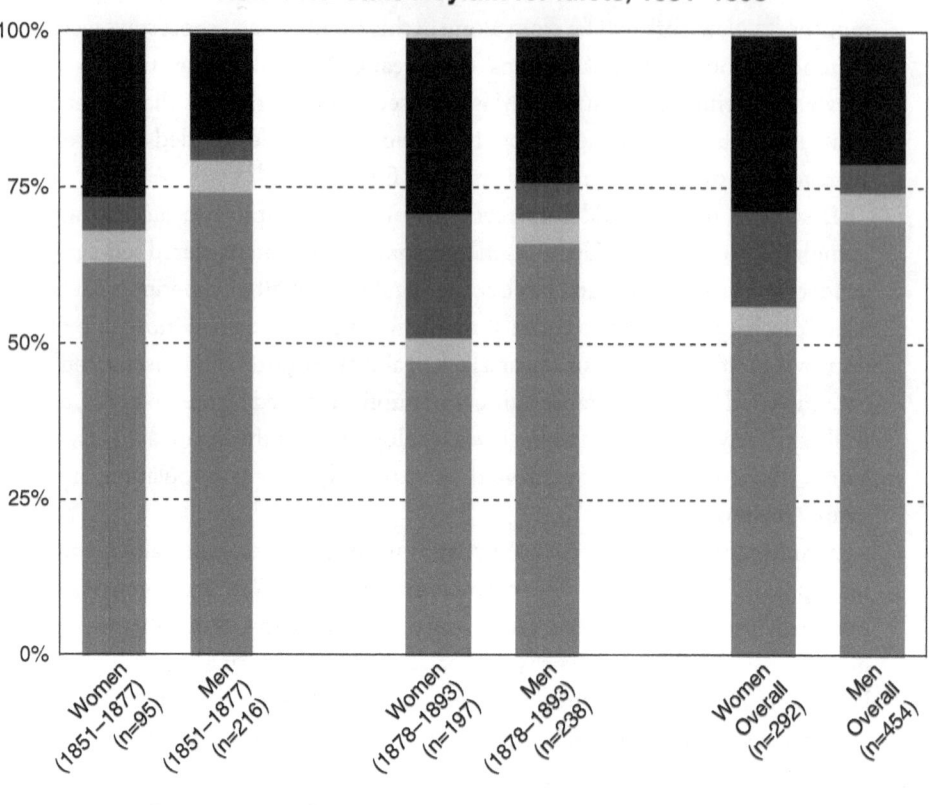

Chart 1-1: How sex shaped discharge at the New York State Asylum for Idiots, 1851–1893

■ Discharged   ■ Reinstitutionalized   ■ Transferred   ■ Died   ▫ Unclear

70 percent of idiots could achieve such a state; of course, such claims must be read in light of the fact that asylums' annual reports were, in effect, pleas for continued state funding.[127] Several boys did acquire trades after departing the New York asylum. Joseph Calvert, who was deaf, worked as a bookbinder in New York City, not only supporting himself but also helping maintain his mother. Nathaniel Bucher, in turn, a "feeble child" who arrived at the asylum speaking both English and his native German, left able to do very simple math and read in the third reader; more importantly, he had learned to sew well enough to join his family's business as a tailor. Later on, he earned enough from working in a clothing factory to single-handedly support his sister and elderly mother.[128] By the end of the Civil War several former pupils had served in the Union Army, while others had helped widen the Erie

Canal.[129] Still others, such as Alexander Tilton, whom Wilbur described as a "first-rate painter," remained at the asylum as paid staff, earning full wages.[130]

Some former female pupils also managed to support themselves despite the fact that the labor market offered single women little other than ill-paid positions as seamstresses, domestics, or, in some areas, mill workers.[131] Melina Cogswell, for instance, who arrived at the asylum in 1860 with only a limited ability to speak and having received no prior instruction, became so competent at "all ordinary household occupation" that her newly widowed mother presumably requested her discharge around 1870. For the next decade and a half, the two women jointly ran their family farm in northern New York, with help from her deaf and "idiotic" sister Emily, who had "bec[ome] capable of ordinary household occupations" while at the asylum. Melina, whom Wilbur had found an apt pupil "much pleased to learn anything," also maintained a regular correspondence with the asylum's officers; presumably, she reported her marriage to a railroad fireman in 1884 and the birth of her three children. Decades later, after their marriage failed, she once again drew on her asylum training to support herself as a housekeeper.[132]

Discharged pupils such as Cogswell often relied on backing from relatives and, at times, neighbors, as they transitioned into self-supporting work, reflecting the crucial importance of family capacity for early idiot asylums. Paddy Sullivan, for instance, arrived in Syracuse in 1859 unable to speak due to scarlet fever, which had "destroyed his vocal organs [and] impaired his intellect." He did not learn to read or write during his tenure at the asylum. But after two years of training, he obtained a trackman's position on the railroad alongside his brother, earning "ordinary wages." In the 1870s, after his brother married and started his own family, Sullivan worked as a laborer, supporting his elderly mother.[133] Jane Carlisle, in turn, had learned to sew "very neatly" and became "very capable as an assistant in house-work" after seven years at the asylum. After leaving the asylum, she lived on a farm as a boarder with her father's neighbors, where, from all reports, she "ma[de] herself quite useful." Over the next forty years, she would live with and work for several different farm families who resided near her relatives.[134] Others, such as Alice Fahey, lived on and off with family members. Initially, Fahey resided with her siblings and her widowed mother, laboring first as a "day servant" and then attaching facings (hems) in a knitting mill. By age forty, she had moved out and was earning enough to pay for a room in a boardinghouse. But later in life, perhaps too old to work as a servant, she once again returned to live with her widowed brother, who supported both of them as a laborer in a woolen mill.[135]

Superintendents in other states reported similar success in training pupils to be self-sufficient, at least during the first few decades. In the late 1870s, the superintendents of both the Ohio Institution for Feeble-Minded Youth and the Connecticut School for Imbeciles estimated that a quarter of the pupils discharged since their institutions opened in 1857 and 1858, respectively, were self-sufficient.[136] The numbers were even more impressive in Kentucky, which focused on serving a "higher-grade" of "imbecilic" pupils and rejected idiots outright: 3 percent of the total residents of the Institute for the Feeble-Minded in Frankfort were placed in community employment during 1884 alone, and roughly 19 percent of newly admitted students, not just those discharged, eventually became self-supporting.[137] Characteristically, Howe framed the issue in blunt economic terms when he reported in 1858 on a pupil whom "any stranger would set . . . down as a low case of idiocy." Much to Howe's surprise, the boy was "willing to work if urged to do so" and was now earning six dollars a month. He reflected that this "will suffice to show that some of our pupils can be made self-supporting, instead of being a tax on their friends during the whole of their lives."[138]

Few students, however, became as independent as Melina Cogswell or Paddy Sullivan, let alone those male pupils who learned a skilled trade. More often, those discharged from the asylum contributed in some way to the household's economy, reflecting the fact that at this time only the wealthiest families could afford to adopt superintendents' rhetoric about productivity being an all-or-nothing proposition. In keeping with an era in which children were viewed as little adults and expected to work and the aged labored until their bodies gave out, relatives seem to have understood productivity as falling on a spectrum that varied according to age, ability, and gender.[139]

As a matter of fact, parents explicitly requested their children be discharged to care for younger siblings or disabled relatives or assist with the family farm or business, although Wilbur rarely deemed such pupils fully productive. Eleanor Wills's mother kept her at home following vacation after three years "on account . . . of needing her services in the care of children," while Hannah Baxter departed in the early 1870s to aid her ill mother and blind stepfather. William Gilbert, in turn, returned home to Tennessee to labor on his widowed mother's farm and help with her basket-making business, and James Barnes left the asylum to assist in his father's bakery.[140]

Few, if any, of these former pupils could complete the equivalent of an able-bodied adult's full day of work, but Wilbur recognized that they could still be of considerable value to their family. Gilbert, for instance, had periodic seizures and only limited use of his right arm and leg, and had learned to read just "a little" and to count to twenty. Although Barnes had learned to read and write and spoke more freely, his speech remained "indistinct."[141] Wilbur also advised the parents of sixteen-year-old Irene Little, for instance, to retain her at home after just one year of training, although she was "an improvable case" who would be expected to gain more skills with time. He cited both her age and "the fact that she was capable of work at home."[142]

At times, families' eagerness to make use of even less than fully productive children frustrated superintendents keen to see promising students advance further. Illinois's superintendent, Charles Toppan Wilbur, complained in 1868 that "some of our best pupils have not returned, because their parents have found them so much improved and so useful at home that they seem unwilling to spare them to return." He grumbled, "Unfortunately these could be spared the least."[143]

Often, as with Eleanor Wills, parents learned about their children's newfound abilities for self-care and labor during annual summer vacations—visits that Hervey Wilbur and other early superintendents explicitly intended both to preserve family ties and publicize the work of their institutions. In 1858, for instance, he confidently predicted that "a knowledge of what has been accomplished in particular cases has been communicated to neighborhoods in all sections of the State, by the return of our pupils to their homes, at the annual vacations."[144] Illinois's Charles Toppan Wilbur illustrated how this process worked when he sent a survey home during the summer of 1868 asking parents to scrutinize their child's behavior and compare it with their capacities prior to admission. Given the highly political nature of annual reports, he may well have redacted less positive remarks, yet the comments are telling. Parents praised their children's new abilities to dress and undress themselves with less help or even do so with a "great deal of ease," rarely "soil" their beds and clothing, and "understand all that is said . . . about the ordinary affairs of the house or family." Some directly addressed superintendents' core aim of making their charges less burdensome on families' capacity for caring. One responder noted that their daughter no longer "displace[d] articles of furniture" and did not "make so much confusion." Another stated outright that "he requires less care and oversight."[145] Parents also highlighted some children's newfound capacities for labor, with one praising the fact that their daughter was "more careful in taking care of the younger children." In fact, one father proclaimed that, although he previously "could not teach him at home to work," his son was now so familiar with garden tools that he "would now rather pay him ten dollars a month for his labor than [hire] average laboring men." The father added, "He was worth nothing when he went to the Institution."[146]

Families' eagerness to make use of even partly productive children also reflected the long-standing integration of many but not all people with what we might today term "disabilities" in both the mainstream labor market and household economies. Historically, even those literally deemed "disabled"—such as Revolutionary War veterans who drew the nation's first pensions, farmers deemed incompetent to manage their business affairs, or slaves whose epilepsy or blindness made them unsalable—had typically continued to work as best they could, often on the margins of the labor market. Under the Invalid Pension Act of 1793, for instance, Revolutionary War veterans could receive assistance only if two doctors certified the "nature of the said disability, and in what degree, it prevents the claimant from obtaining his livelihood, by labor."[147] Although such "invalid pensioners" could not perform the strenuous physical labor required in an agricultural economy prior to mechanization, by no means were they idle. Day laborer William Leech reported being "able to perform about one quarter of the labor of a man," while others cared for disabled relatives or helped to run a family farm.[148] Likewise, during antebellum times, men deemed to be "altogether unfit and unable to govern" themselves by a *writ de lunatico inquirendo* (local commission in lunacy) typically continued to work as hired hands on their farms under the direction of their guardians. In fact, such labor often served as the pathway by which they proved that they had regained their sanity.[149] "Useless" slaves, in turn—slaves whose bodily differences or infirmities had reduced their monetary value to that of infants or even one cent—did a wide variety of work. Blind people looked after chickens or even drove carts, "feeble" women cooked, and a one-armed man served as a carpenter; others cared for children, carried water, or tended garden plots, among other forms of care work.[150]

Like disabled Revolutionary War veterans, mad farmers, and disabled slaves, those "idiotic" children and teenagers who could not transition fully to the mainstream labor market did menial tasks or care work at home; some also scraped by as occasional day laborers.[151] As in asylums themselves, this mix reflected both contemporary gender norms and the gendered nature of the labor force, and, as such, may partly explain why female pupils were overall less likely to be discharged (see Chart 1-1). Befitting superintendents' assumption that most students would return home to rural communities and require guidance from family members, male pupils who could not master a trade typically helped on their family's farm or were placed as farm laborers on nearby farms. Hervey Wilbur noted about one: "Can go to post-office and store to trade things by himself, feeds animals by himself, catches and harnesses horses and attaches them to buggy. Not trusted to manage team."

Another earned board and clothing in exchange for his labor.¹⁵² Others, such as James Barnes or William Gilbert, assisted with their families' businesses of baking or basket making, respectively or, like Conrad Ulrich and Simon Thomas, lived with a relative and found irregular work as day laborers.¹⁵³

With few exceptions, former female pupils performed care work. Wilbur noted in 1862 that four girls had "left the Asylum not only able to read and write a little, but what was of far more importance they had acquired considerable dexterity in common feminine employments, and were quite capable and willing in the performance of simple household occupations."¹⁵⁴ Like Eleanor Wills, more than one female pupil departed the asylum to care for younger siblings. After helping to raise five sisters and brothers, she reprised the same role later on with her brother's family in Virginia. In fact, Wilbur complained when Melissa Campbell's mother withdrew her to "take a place in care of children" in Chicago, contending that she should have remained at the asylum for another year or two.¹⁵⁵

The predominance of care work among female pupils, furthermore, hints at one reason girls may have been so much less likely to be discharged from the New York State Asylum for Idiots even prior to the emergence of hereditarian policies in the 1870s. Not only did the gendered nature of the labor market offer women only a limited number of poorly paid positions, but there was also no female equivalent to the day laborer and farmhand positions taken by some less able male pupils. As a result, households that did not require much care work—or care workers—may have been reluctant to have their daughters return home.¹⁵⁶

Clearly, these former pupils helped to contribute toward their household's livelihood, but their marginal economic position left them vulnerable as their family's capacity for caring shifted. As parents aged and died, pupils who had scraped by as day laborers or farm workers struggled to maintain themselves. Simon Thomas, for instance, lived with his mother, a seamstress, for decades after being discharged from the New York State Asylum for Idiots. As she grew older, he helped to support her by working as a day laborer. But after her death in the early 1890s, he found himself in the Tompkins County Almshouse in the Finger Lakes region; he remained there through at least 1910.¹⁵⁷ James Barnes, meanwhile, who had been brought home to assist with his father's bakery, managed to survive for more than a decade as a farmhand and laborer after the business failed. But when the economy contracted sharply in the 1890s, he had little recourse but to turn to the Oswego County Poorhouse.¹⁵⁸ Siblings, too, sometimes proved less than willing to take on the burden of caring for an "idiotic" relative when a parent died. After Jason Cage's mother died, for instance, his three brothers—all of whom were skilled tradesmen—placed him in the Monroe County Almshouse.[159] And as children grew up and departed the household, or when ill relatives passed away, families had less use for members who might be able to perform care work but were only partly productive otherwise. Hannah Baxter, for instance, who had been retained at home to tend to her sick mother and assist her blind stepfather, was sent to the Newark State Custodial Asylum for Feeble-Minded Women after both parents died.[160]

Yet the absence of productivity did not necessarily sunder familial bonds. Even when children could not contribute any labor at all and instead imposed a "tax" of substantial daily personal care, relatives rarely abandoned them to the asylum or the poorhouse. In fact, more-able individuals were significantly less likely to be discharged and were much more likely to eventually be transferred to another institution. Strikingly, when those deemed more capable were discharged home, they were also *more likely* to later be "reinstitutionalized" by their families in a county almshouse, the New York State Asylum for Idiots, or one of the state custodial asylums for "feeble-minded" people that emerged starting in the late 1870s, or another type of institution. Although superintendents had good economic reason to retain the more-able people, especially women, as will be explored in chapter 2, parents may have been more comfortable with "idiotic" children who needed care than with those who were more independent. Alternatively, parents may have become frustrated when their "able" children did not live up to expectations. In contrast, as shown in Chart 1-2, pupils who were "filthy," could not walk fully or partly, or required assistance in feeding or dressing were slightly more likely than their more-able counterparts to return home in the first place, as well as remain home, often for decades (see "Appendix: A Note on Sources" for more on the language used in this chart).[161] Winston Grant, for instance, arrived at the asylum in 1852 at age seven, identified as a "low-grade idiot." Convulsions in infancy and early childhood had left him unable to speak or comprehend language, feed himself, or control his bladder or bowels. After six years at the New York State Asylum for Idiots, Wilbur dismissed Grant as "unimprovable." His abrupt return home to northern New York almost certainly tested his family's capacity for care. While at the asylum, Grant had learned few, if any, self-care skills. His parents, moreover, had limited familial and financial resources: just one other surviving child, an able-bodied boy still too young to earn a wage, plus his father's modest income from working as a furniture clerk. But, by reaching outside the immediate family for assistance, relying first on a young servant, then taking in a wealthy widowed neighbor as a

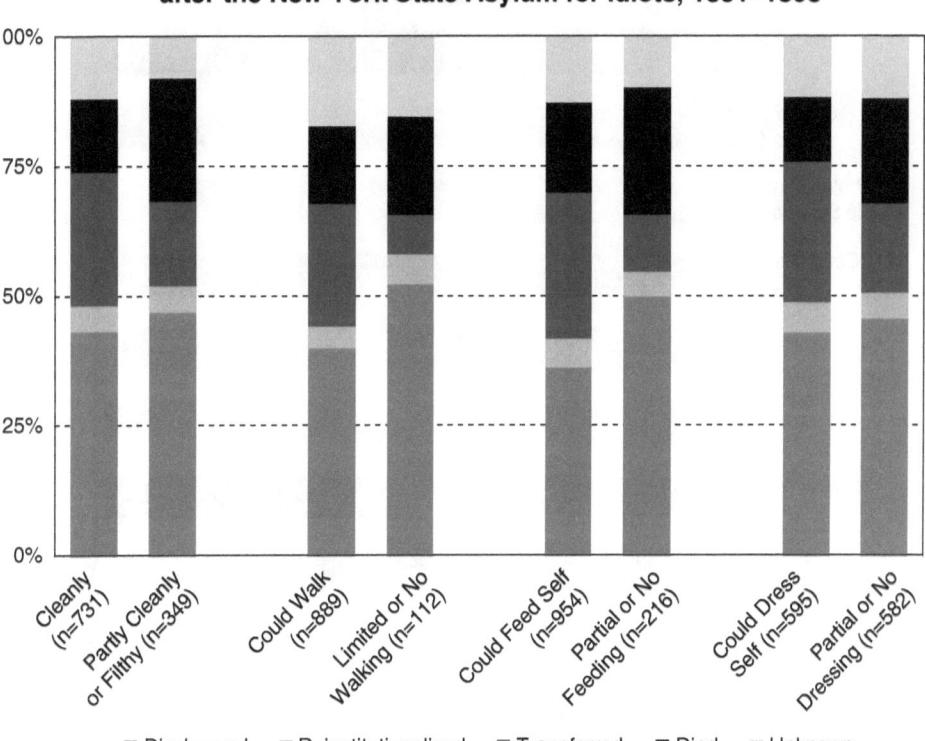

Chart 1-2: Disability, ability, and the possibility of life at home after the New York State Asylum for Idiots, 1851–1893

boarder, and finally drawing on the aid of an aunt, Grant's parents maintained their son at home for at least two decades.[162]

Even relatives who could muster far fewer resources fought hard to keep their children at home. Robert Jeffries's widowed mother cared for him, apparently single-handedly, for more than thirty years after her husband died, while Fanny Paterson's aging parents kept her at home on their farm with little outside aid for at least two decades.[163] Parents' reluctance to turn to the county poorhouse—or perhaps their inability to do so—likely also reflected the fact that poor-law officials tried hard to maintain the family as the locus of care. County facilities only reluctantly accepted people labeled as "idiots" and "insane" when relatives could no longer care for them.

Even as poor and middling families went to great lengths to maintain their children at home, pupils from exceptionally wealthy and prominent families found themselves abandoned to the asylum, suggesting that class status may have shaped attitudes toward "idiots." Robert Sherbourne, for instance, arrived in 1851 as the asylum's second pupil. Hopeful that their "quite good looking"

Chart 1-3: Parents' occupations and the possibility of life at home after the New York State Asylum for Idiots, 1851–1893

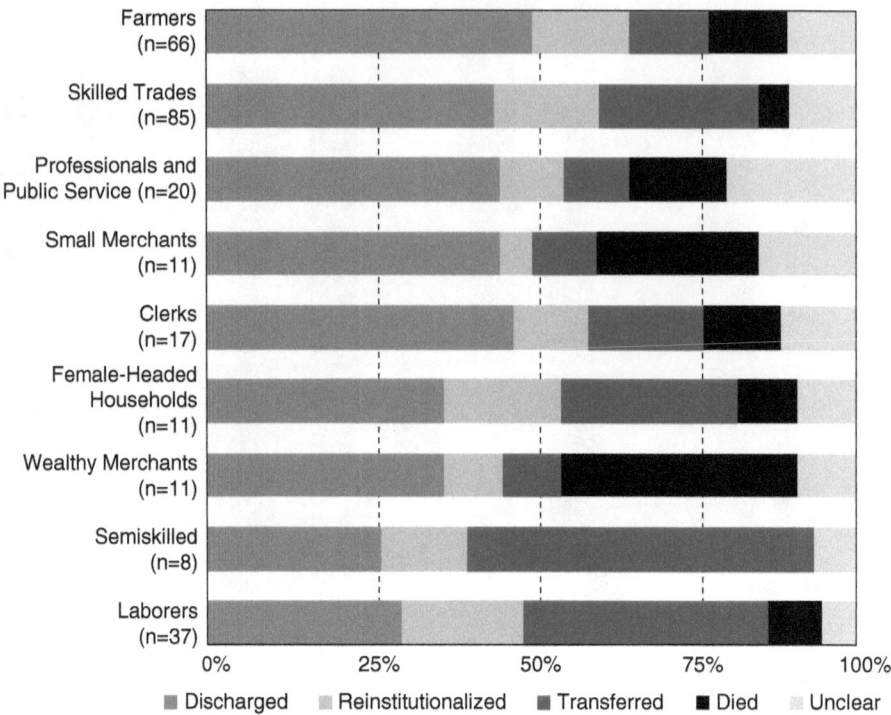

and well-spoken yet "awkward" son would improve under Wilbur's tutelage, his parents sent hundreds of books along with him although he "did not know six letters" and could count only to two. Compared with most pupils admitted to the asylum, Robert came from extraordinary wealth; he was the great-great-nephew of one of the most successful industrialists of the mid-nineteenth century, and his father and uncle were leading military officials. "Owing to instruction at home," he could use a knife and fork and speak far more fluently than most other pupils, but he could not identify colors or tie his shoes or cravat. Despite his parents' initial hopes, they seem to have abandoned him to the asylum. Unlike the vast majority of pupils from poor and middling families, Robert was never again listed as part of his family in the census, nor did he appear in any books on his family; he died at the asylum in 1902 at age sixty-two after living there for fifty-one years.[164] Likewise, Orson Cobb's parents resorted to a measure typically used by poor-law officials rather than well-heeled lawyers and congressmen: boarding one son out with another family as a farm laborer after his discharge from the asylum. Orson's

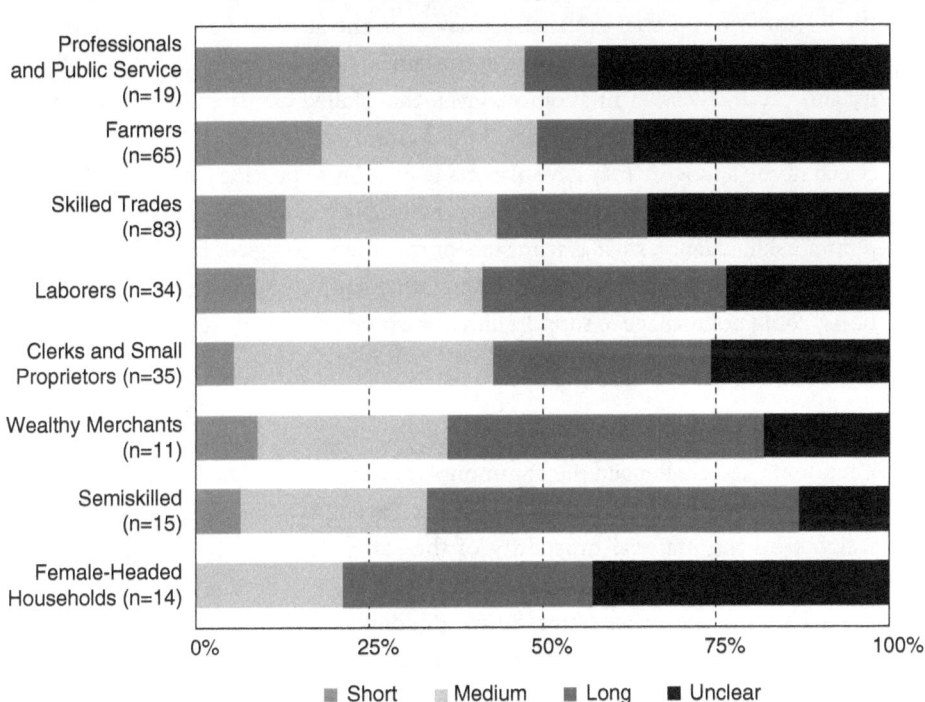

Chart 1-4: Parents' occupations and length of stay at the New York State Asylum for Idiots, 1851–1893

brother, who also spent time at the New York State Asylum for Idiots, was sent to the Willard Asylum for the Insane, where he died.[165] Of course, these wealthy parents could also afford to pay for decades of asylum-based care and had no need for their children's labor, but the exclusion of these children from census forms suggests more: perhaps the notion that "idiots" were unseemly in such a refined setting.

Finally, in a trend that boded ill for the future, given New York's rapid industrialization, parents' immigration statuses and their occupations played a significant role in determining whether children went home from the asylum or remained there. Although discharge rates did not vary according to whether parents were native-born or immigrants, pupils from immigrant families were 50 percent more likely to be reinstitutionalized by their families after discharge or transferred outright from the New York State Asylum for Idiots to another institution, such as an insane asylum, a custodial asylum for the feeble-minded, or a county almshouse. And as shown in Charts 1-3 and 1-4, farm families proved by far the most capable of accommodating "idiotic" relatives. Their children were more likely to be discharged home in the first place, less likely to be transferred to another institution, tended to remain for shorter periods at the asylum overall, and, intriguingly, were also generally less able upon arrival at the institution. A partial explanation may lie in the fact that farmers had little choice but to make use of everyone in the family, despite varying levels of ability and productivity.[166] In addition, given that skilled craftspeople and small proprietors also commonly retained their children at home, the overlap between home and work may have also made it easier to provide care as needed. In contrast, the families of wage workers, especially female ones and those who did semiskilled labor, such as teamsters or milkmen, struggled. Henry Parkes's mother, a widowed washerwoman whose other son worked as an unskilled laborer, could not manage to support him upon his discharge. Instead, he entered the Chenango County Poorhouse.[167]

BY 1870, HERVEY WILBUR, Samuel Gridley Howe, and other asylum superintendents had challenged the commonplace notion that "idiots" were uneducable. Howe's characterization of idiots as "ravenous consumers" and "dead weights on the material prosperity of the state," furthermore, had proven strikingly effective in convincing skeptical legislators to fund asylums in both Massachusetts and other states. Superintendents, moreover, achieved some measure of success returning pupils to their families as at least less burdensome if not actually useful.

Yet superintendents' dire depictions of their potential pupils appear to have had little impact on how pupils' families viewed their "idiotic" relatives. Unlike Howe, families had long understood productivity as falling on a spectrum that evolved throughout the life course rather than as the black-and-white dyad of able-bodied and disabled put forth by eugenicists and asylum advocates in the early twentieth century. Nor did relatives see productivity as the sole aim of education or as an essential requirement for maintaining family ties. In so doing, families simply reflected the long-standing integration of many people with what we might today call disabilities into both the mainstream labor force and household economies. Of course, relatives' willingness, even eagerness, to have their children return home also reflected familial loyalty and affection, as well as the ways in which the mid-nineteenth-century economy of farms and small communities sustained families' capacity for caring.

But in the coming decades, the industrializing economy would sorely test families' ability to care for idiotic relatives. Shifting charity policies, in turn, would alter institutions' populations in ways that made it increasingly challenging to return students home. For the "feeble-minded" inmates of these asylums, lives lived in institutions would increasingly become the norm.

CHAPTER TWO

He Had No Home but the County Poor House
Family Incapacity, Charity Policy, Wage Labor, and the Shift to Custodial Care, 1870s–1900s

CUSTODIAL PROTECTION [is] the most economical system of caring for this class of the State's wards [the feeble-minded, who] are—must be—a public burden and expense, either in the charitable or penal institutions of the State. This system assures economy by limiting its beneficiaries to the minimum, and at the same time answers the highest demands of philanthropy.[1]

Fourteen-year-old Amelia Harlow arrived at the New York State Asylum for Idiots in 1886 already familiar with institutional life. Described by the Broome County superintendent of the poor, M. B. Payne, as "good-hearted [and] quick to learn in school," Amelia's parents had nevertheless abandoned her to an orphanage years earlier. While she could already read, write, and do housework, Payne complained about her thick speech and characterized her to asylum staff as "entirely irresponsible."[2]

Although she could care for herself and perform useful labor even before arriving at the asylum, Harlow never left the confines of an institution. Unlike previous generations of pupils, her ability to be at least partly productive did not garner her discharge. After spending twenty-one years at the New York State Asylum for Idiots, where she almost certainly performed unpaid labor in the wards, dining room, sewing room, or laundry, she was transferred to the State Custodial Asylum for Feeble-Minded Women in the Finger Lakes town of Newark—an institution notorious for abuse and poor conditions. She remained there through at least 1910, at which point her trail goes cold. Most likely she died there or was transferred to her home county's poorhouse after reaching menopause.[3]

By the 1880s and 1890s, Harlow's tale of a life lived almost entirely in institutional confines would become increasingly typical, not only at the New York State Asylum for Idiots but also at similar institutions across the country. Only rarely did pupils—or, as they were referred to more commonly, "inmates"— return to live with their families at home. Instead, asylum directors presided over perpetually expanding institutions that focused on supplying permanent custodial care for "the feeble-minded": a mutable category that encompassed "idiots" and "imbeciles" but which could at times also refer to people with nearly any physical impairment that dated to birth or early childhood.

Charity officials, asylum officials, and members of the burgeoning eugenics movement, moreover, argued that feeble-mindedness lay at the root of a vast array of social ills, from criminality and prostitution to dependency on public aid and alcoholism.[4]

By the start of the twentieth century, growing numbers of inmates lived in vast custodial institutions for the feeble-minded that soon housed as many as 2,000 or 3,000 people. At the 1902 meeting of the American Association for the Study of the Feeble-Minded, superintendent Martin Barr of the Pennsylvania Training School explained the rationale for this new policy of containment, proclaiming, "There is a consensus that abandons the hope long cherished of a return of the imbecile to the world.... We need ... to convince the world that by permanent segregation only is the imbecile to be safe-guarded from certain deterioration and society from depredation, contamination, and increase of a pernicious element."[5]

How can we account for this dramatic shift in outcomes: from reintegration into families and sometimes communities, to lifetime custodial care? Scholars have explained this move toward permanent incarceration in a number of ways: as the inevitable outcome of superintendents' institution-building ambitions, as the consequence of the burgeoning eugenics movement, or as the result of growing numbers of individuals admitted with severe impairments. Certainly, some asylum directors may have cared more for their careers than for their charges, and, clearly, the rapidly growing popularity of eugenic thought and policies did much to stigmatize people labeled as feeble-minded, especially females and those from immigrant families. There is less evidence that individuals' levels of ability shifted over time, however, and yet less that these inmates lost the ability to work and became burdens on the public purse.[6]

But if we once again look beyond the asylum walls to focus on disability in the family and community, a different explanation emerges for the collapse of integration programs and the shift to custodial care—one that highlights the ways in which a rapidly changing economy and society weakened families' capacity to care for and make use of relatives with what we might call disabilities, as well as how charity policies aimed at preventing public dependency inadvertently produced a class of inmates without families. In sum, the phenomenon of the "idiot who couldn't go home" was hardly just the result of eugenic stigma, nativist hostility, or superintendents' greed. Rather, Harlow's tale of a life lived in institutions was, in many ways, the result of aggressive postbellum charity campaigns that brought in more admittees from vulnerable or nonexistent families, the ways in which the shift from an economy and society of farms and small communities toward an unstable urban wage labor economy undermined families' capacities to care, and the mismatch between the rural focus of asylum training programs and an increasingly urbanizing, industrializing society. In effect, many families no longer lived in a context in which they could tend to idiotic relatives and potentially draw on their labor.

Since most superintendents, lawmakers, and charity officials did not fully grasp why it became so difficult to return those formerly termed "pupils" to their families, asylum directors such as New York's Hervey B. Wilbur saw few alternatives other than expanding their institutions to serve—and in many cases, employ—a permanent custodial population of *inmates*. Aided by the furor over pauperism and the reproduction of public dependency that arose out of the depression of the 1870s, as well as by the slippage between the deserving and undeserving poor, superintendents cast "feeble-minded" people as unproductive burdens on their families and society and soon convinced lawmakers to fund custodial programs that could rely on inmates' commodified labors. Once again, Wilbur led the way, this time with the State Custodial Asylum for Feeble-Minded Women in Newark.

In these new custodial programs, as well as in older educationally focused institutions such as the New York State Asylum for Idiots, ability shaped every aspect of inmates' lives, from clothing to survival rates. As superintendents were fond of proclaiming, the vast quantities of unpaid work—especially care work—done by inmates served to defray the cost of their dependency on the state, yet their labor did not lead to discharge, especially for women. Despite being cast as unproductive in mainstream society, female inmates were simply too productive within institutional settings. Regardless, inmates sometimes still found meaning in their work, albeit not necessarily in ways intended by superintendents.

Charity Reform and Homeless Idiots

During the 1850s and 1860s, it was so unusual for pupils to arrive directly from poorhouses or orphan asylums that New York asylum superintendent Hervey Wilbur noted that Alan Cooper "was retained longer than usual because he had no home but the Co. Poor House."[7] But starting just after the Civil War, charity reformers began seeking to rationalize aid programs and thereby discourage what they perceived as hereditary dependency on private and especially public assistance. Within just a decade, these new policies would significantly alter the background of those admitted to the State Asylum for Idiots, posing a serious challenge to Wilbur's system of eventually discharging students to live and, in many cases, work with their families. As these reforms spread across the country, superintendents in other states discovered that many of their incoming pupils, too, lacked homes to which they could return.

Officially, legislators in New York, Illinois, Massachusetts, and other states had always encouraged and, at times, required superintendents to give preference to children from impoverished families, reflecting the economic logic behind idiot asylums. Lawmakers in New York, for instance, required in 1851 that "idiots shall be selected from those whose parents or guardians are unable to provide for their support." In Massachusetts, legislators mandated that no fewer than ten of the first batch of pupils should come from "indigent families"; by 1856, the school was obligated to educate at least thirty of its approximately forty pupils for free.[8]

Despite such rules, during the 1850s and 1860s, pupils at state idiot asylums came from a wide array of economic backgrounds. The children of farmers, bakers, and shoemakers rubbed shoulders with the offspring of unskilled laborers and seamstresses and, occasionally, those of lawyers or wealthy merchants.[9] Notably, every public asylum admitted significant numbers of paying pupils to cover costs, often with the encouragement of legislators who were skeptical about the experimental nature of educating idiots and wary of providing funding. Illinois superintendent Charles Toppan Wilbur, for instance, explained in his first annual report that although many applications had arrived from parents unable to pay board, "unfortunately the selection [of pupils] was influenced by the necessity of requiring the parents of those seeking admission to pay a certain sum, because of the inadequacy of the appropriation."[10] In Massachusetts and New York, where legislators mandated that superintendents accept and train a large proportion of children from indigent families gratis, paying pupils comprised a smaller but still financially significant portion of the asylums' populations.[11] Fees from privately funded students such as Rachel Gannon, the daughter of a wealthy merchant in New York City, or James Stranger, the son of a prosperous lawyer and farmer in upstate New York, contributed approximately 15 percent to the total income of the New York asylum through the mid-1870s. The fact that paying pupils often remained at the institution for decades, not infrequently dying there, made their fees all the more valuable.[12]

Early on, even "state-funded" pupils typically did not come from the most impoverished backgrounds or from poorhouses, but rather from intact families in modest circumstances. During the 1850s in New York, for instance, less than 1 percent of pupils arrived directly from almshouses or orphan asylums. Rather, the fathers of state-funded pupils typically worked in skilled trades such as carpentry and wagon making, owned small farms or, less commonly, ran small shops—all places that could easily make use of trained "idiotic" children after discharge. Only a few families scraped by via unskilled labor or, in the small number of female-headed households, ill-paid seamstress work.[13] Virtually all parents of children in asylums in both New York and Illinois, moreover, could afford their children's rail fare home for summer vacation, and many could also afford to contribute toward the cost of their children's clothing.[14]

But during the first two decades after the Civil War, state idiot asylums' populations would change significantly as a result of charity reformers' attempts to streamline charity programs and extend state supervision to poorhouses, county jails, and other institutions. Fearful that overly generous aid would produce a hereditary plague of paupers, and desirous of eliminating what they saw as rampant abuse and waste, a largely female corps of activists convinced Massachusetts legislators to establish a Board of State Charities in 1863. More than a dozen other states, including New York, Illinois, Ohio, and Connecticut, soon followed suit.[15]

During the 1870s and 1880s, state charity boards attempted to intervene in a wide range of public welfare issues, including sanitation and compulsory schooling laws. Board officials focused most intensely, however, on inspecting public and private institutions to standardize practices, investigate conditions, and help them operate economically, as well as investigating the causes of dependency and deviancy and ensuring that aid was provided only to those who truly needed it. Often working in conjunction with voluntary organizations such as Louisa Lee Schuyler's State Charities Aid Association, a New York–based entity, these charity reformers fanned out across their states, providing reams of detailed annual reports on the conditions in county almshouses and jails, insane asylums, schools for the deaf and idiotic, houses of refuge, and private orphan asylums, among others.[16]

Reformers sought to prevent "indiscriminate mixing" in poorhouses, believing that allowing children to mingle with the elderly, people labeled as insane or idiotic, single mothers, the ill, and out of work but able-bodied men encouraged the spread of public dependency. After inspecting several New York county poorhouses, State Charities Aid Association's Schuyler, for instance, charged in her organization's first annual report that "an absence of classification" led to "gross immorality, a want of enlightened treatment of the insane, no nursing for the sick; the children badly fed, badly clothed, badly taken care of, and exposed to the degrading influence of those in immediate charge of them."[17] In theory, separating able-bodied children from the "vicious idle poor," the insane from single mothers, and the deaf from the elderly, among others, then placing each group in an appropriate rehabilitative institution, would ensure better care and prevent future dependency on public aid.[18]

Reflecting the influence of Charles Loring Brace's child-saving movement, charity reformers fought hard to enact laws banning all able-bodied children over the age of two or three years from poorhouses. By the late 1870s, they had succeeded in several states, including Massachusetts and New York. Although no laws barred children labeled as deaf, idiotic, blind, or crippled from residing in poorhouses, inspectors nonetheless tended to note their presence and, if they seemed teachable, often contacted the superintendent of the relevant asylum.[19]

While charity reformers never managed fully to implement their classification schemes, their efforts nevertheless began to alter the population of state idiot asylums in profound ways. At the New York State Asylum for Idiots in Syracuse, for instance, only fourteen out of the first six hundred pupils came directly from almshouses during the institution's first twenty years; another fourteen came from orphan asylums. But starting in 1874, as the State Charities Aid Association and other charity reformers began conducting regular inspections, batches of homeless, idiotic children began arriving at the asylum from county poorhouses. In December 1877, while the country was still in a severe depression, three new pupils came from a Brooklyn orphan asylum and six arrived from New York City's almshouse department on Randall's Island. Just two months later, three girls arrived from Erie County's poorhouse in Buffalo.

Unlike their earlier counterparts, students from poorhouses rarely left the asylum. Of these twelve pupils—or inmates—ten died at the asylum or were transferred to the Rome State Custodial Asylum or a county poorhouse; most remained at the asylum in Syracuse for more than twenty years.[20] Only two ever returned to mainstream society, in both cases after spending nine years at the asylum: John Weiman, who learned to "work out of doors" after arriving barely able to speak, and Mary Butters, who became "competent to do any kind of sewing" and could "make a dress for herself without assistance."[21] Crucially, both could support and care for themselves without assistance from family members—unlike many of their fellow homeless pupils at the asylum.

By the 1880s, such homeless children made up an ever-increasing percentage of those admitted to idiot asylums. In fact, superintendents now rarely accepted new paying pupils, although most superintendents allowed older

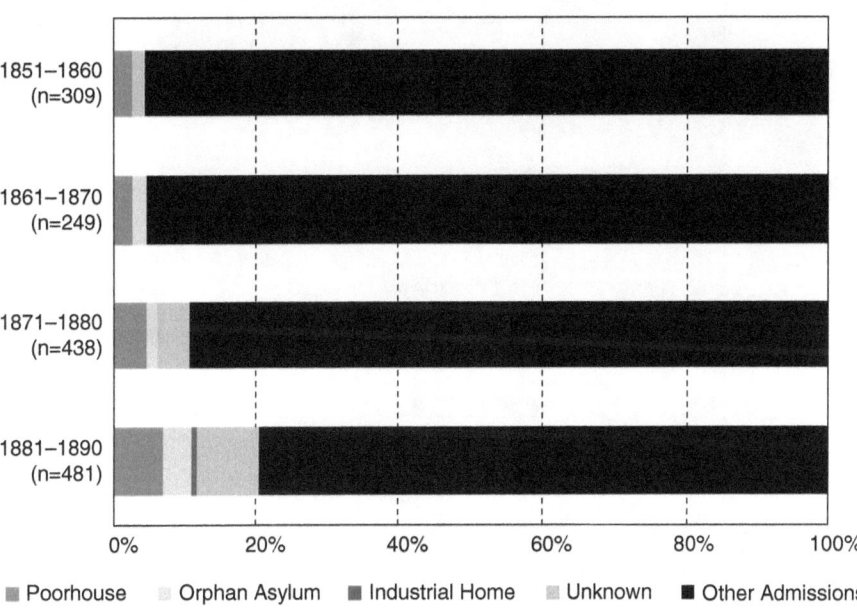

Chart 2-1: Origins of admittees to the New York State Asylum for Idiots, 1851–1890

■ Poorhouse　　■ Orphan Asylum　　■ Industrial Home　　■ Unknown　　■ Other Admissions

private inmates to remain. In New York, upward of 20 percent of new admissions came directly from poorhouses, orphan asylums, or industrial homes, or via recommendation from poor-law officials (see Chart 2-1; for more on the data used in these charts, see "Appendix: A Note on Sources"). Fred Calhoun typified this new population. He arrived at the New York State Asylum for Idiots in 1885 courtesy of Charles S. Hoyt, the secretary of the State Board of Charities (SBC). While on a routine annual inspection of the Essex County Poorhouse, Hoyt had examined "three or four young idiotic persons." He declared that while the seven-year-old Calhoun was clearly idiotic, there was "no doubt about his being teachable."[22] Illinois superintendent William B. Fish reported much the same story in 1888, complaining that he had to turn away "children who ought to be admitted" because of seventy-five or so "deformed, crippled, idiotic, and comparatively helpless" custodial cases and a large number of "simple-minded girls," most of whom were "paupers .... [or] abandoned waifs" with "no other home than this asylum." He pleaded for the legislature to appropriate enough funds to build a custodial wing.[23]

As Fish's plea suggests, the growing percentage of homeless children posed a serious challenge to superintendents accustomed to being able to discharge students to relatives. Indeed, the dramatic shift in admittees' origins threatened

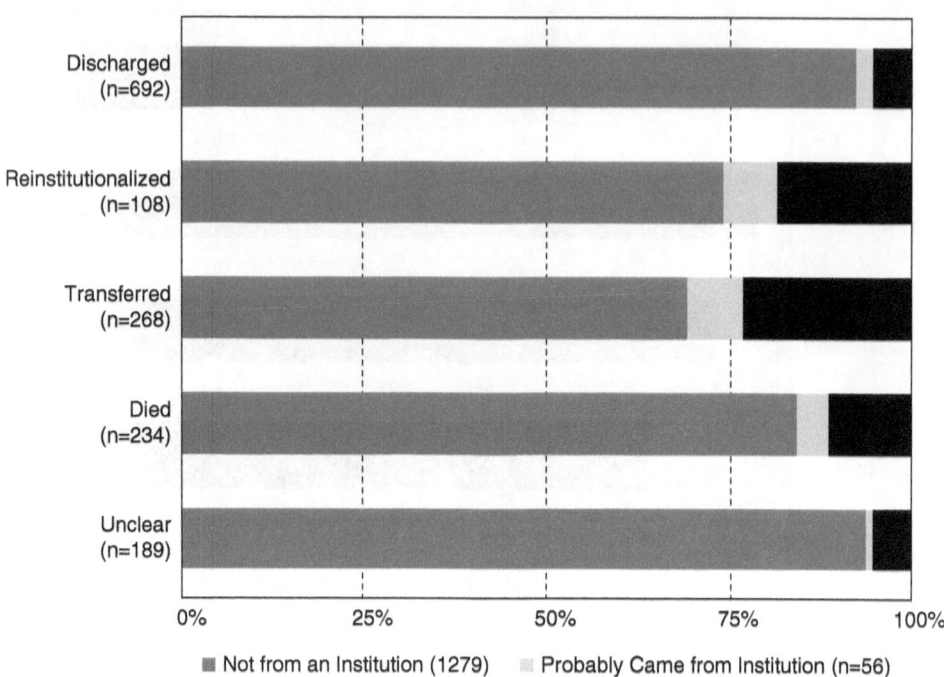

Chart 2-2: Origins of admittees to the New York State Asylum for Idiots and prospects for life outside institutions, 1851–1893

to upend the entire system. Asylums could accommodate a few homeless individuals like Alan Cooper, who was "capable of simple farm work" but whom Wilbur hesitated to discharge, since he had no home but the county poorhouse. But a system that relied on relatives' willingness to care for and, when possible, employ discharged students had no solutions for the dozens of homeless children who now arrived each year (see Chart 2-2). Consequently, such admittees were far less likely to be discharged in the first place; instead, they generally died after spending decades in the asylum or were transferred to another institution, most commonly either a county poorhouse or one of the custodial asylums established in the late nineteenth century, as will be discussed in the next section. In effect, charity reformers' efforts to rationalize charity provisions and thereby discourage dependency on public aid had inadvertently created a population of inmates who had no home to which they could go. By 1869, Wilbur could not ignore the steady drumbeat of requests for new admissions, and he reluctantly released Cooper to the Genesee County poorhouse, where he remained for at least a decade. In succeeding decades,

Cooper's narrative of a life lived in institutions would become increasingly common.[24]

Wage Labor, Urbanization, and the Challenge to Family Capacity

Compounding these issues of family *in*capacity, in the decades after the Civil War growing numbers of asylum admittees also came from urban, poor, and wage-dependent families in transition or in outright crisis. Walter Goodrich, for instance, arrived at the New York State Asylum for Idiots from Albany in 1882, just months after his mother had died of consumption. His admission record noted, "Father is poor & hard-working, had not the means or chance to take care or notice of the boy properly." Millie Landon entered the asylum in 1886 following her mother's admission to a state insane asylum; her father/grandfather was already incarcerated in Sing Sing Prison due to the incestuous relations that had produced her. Elderly laborer John Kovacevich, in turn, foresaw trouble looming ahead; in 1888, he petitioned the Illinois Asylum for Feeble-Minded Children to take his two sons, both "helpless as infants" and incapable of walking or caring for themselves. Although he and his wife had cared for them and a third "afflicted" child at home for more than ten years, his aging body had begun to reduce his earnings, threatening his family's stability.[25]

Unlike Alan Cooper, who "had no home but the Co. Poor House," these individuals theoretically had relatives to whom they could return. But the death, disablement, illness, divorce, or remarriage of a parent or other caretaker had pushed families beyond their capacity—or willingness—to provide care and supervision. The economic turmoil of the postbellum decades, combined with the large-scale shift away from farms and artisanal work and toward wage labor, left many families living on the edge. Complicating matters, asylums' training programs continued to emphasize skills most suitable for rural households even though more and more children came from wage-dependent families living in urban areas. In addition, the rapidly growing charity infrastructure served to connect struggling families with idiot asylums and other institutions with the express aim of preventing entire households from slipping into dependency on public aid, ensuring that a disproportionate percentage of new admissions came from families that rarely regained the capacity to make use of or tend to their "idiotic" relatives.[26]

Prior to the Civil War, only rarely did pupils at idiot asylums arrive from households in crisis. At the New York State Asylum for Idiots in Syracuse, less than 10 percent of students admitted during the 1850s had experienced

Chart 2-3: Family disruption prior to arrival at the New York State Asylum for Idiots, 1851–1890

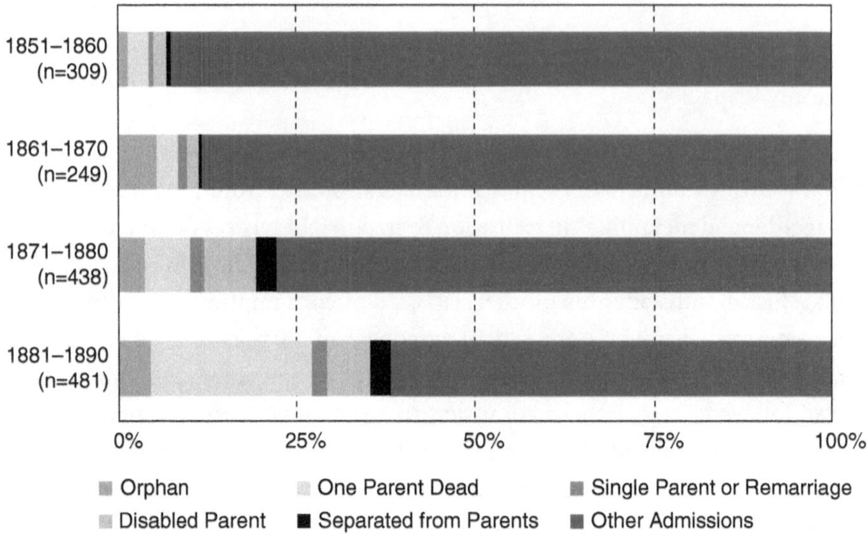

- Orphan
- One Parent Dead
- Single Parent or Remarriage
- Disabled Parent
- Separated from Parents
- Other Admissions

some form of family disruption, primarily the death of one parent. An even smaller percentage had a parent perceived as having what today might be called a "disability," most commonly ill health of some form. But by the 1870s—a decade that included one of the United States' worst depressions—nearly 25 percent of children admitted to the asylum came from families who identified themselves or were labeled as being in some sort of distress. By the 1880s, almost 40 percent did (see Chart 2-3). In other words, even those children who *had* families, unlike Cooper, became ever less likely to leave the asylum.

Most commonly, these children arrived sometime after the death of one or both parents. Three years after his wife died of consumption, James Dassler, for instance, sent his lively eight-year-old daughter Irma to the asylum, explaining that he was "not able to give the child the proper attention, it takes his time & keeps him from making enough to live on."[27] Often, however, individuals arrived in the months immediately following a parent's death while a family fought to reconstitute itself and regain its economic footing. Harvey Straw came to Syracuse in 1883 at age twelve just after his father died of malaria-induced heart trouble, whereas fourteen-year-old Anna Wiebe arrived following her mother's death in childbirth. Both were in fact partly productive; Straw could "spade, split wood, pump water, [and] drive cows," while Wiebe could help with washing dishes and "caring for baby" despite the fact her arms were slightly paralyzed. But at a time when Straw's mother and Wiebe's father were each struggling to support seven other children, sending a child to the New York State Asylum for Idiots likely seemed an attractive means of extending their family's weakened capacity for care.[28]

Others' parents had been institutionalized or had acquired disabilities or chronic illnesses, sometimes both. Martha Rudd's alcoholic father had entered an inebriate asylum just prior to her admission to the asylum at Syracuse, whereas Calvin Teesdale's father "became insane at intervals [but] recovered after a few months' confinement" in the Willard Asylum for the Chronic Insane. The generosity of benefits for disabled Union veterans, in turn, may explain why only one parent is known to have entered a soldiers' home.[29]

Lest these examples suggest that fathers were the only ones to enter institutions or acquire disabilities, mothers did too; the way their travails were characterized on children's admission forms, however, reflected the racialized and gendered constructions of ability, health, and poverty at this time. Adaline O'Donnell's Irish immigrant mother, for instance, was described as a "partly weak-minded" woman who had "lived for years at the Poor House in Otsego Co" and had "several nominal husbands," while Polish-born Bartholomew Rabinowitz's mother was labeled as "nervous" and "scrofulous" (having a tuberculous infection of the neck).[30] At a time when many lawmakers and charity officials alike assumed that Irish, German, and especially southern and eastern European immigrants were inherently less vigorous and more prone to particular diseases such as trachoma or tuberculosis, such descriptions were hardly neutral.[31]

But admission forms characterized even native-born mothers in terms that suggested the growing power of hereditarian (proto-eugenic) and biological explanations for poverty, as well as gendered understandings of disability and, in particular, cognitive impairments. Mother after mother was characterized as "simple-minded," "feeble-minded," "weak-minded," "idiotic," "imbecilic," "slightly deranged," or "scrofulous." In contrast, only a few fathers were labeled as such.[32]

Remarriage, too, contributed new and often permanent pupils or, more accurately, inmates. The wealthy parents discussed in chapter 1 were not the only ones to question whether "idiotic" children belonged at home; so too did some stepparents. After Margaret Lambeth's mother died and her father remarried, for instance, she was first abandoned to a truant home and then to the Monroe County Poorhouse in Rochester, whence she was sent to the New York State Asylum for Idiots. Lambeth could do "cleaning & washing under supervision" and was overall "quite capable in household matters," but her "ordinary looking" parents complained that scarlet fever had left her "dull... dumb & idiotic." Unlike many partly productive individuals admitted to the New York State Asylum for Idiots early on, Lambeth never returned home, despite becoming "useful in many ways" and mastering "quite difficult" sewing projects. After she had spent thirty-four years there, the superintendent, O. H. Cobb, returned Lambeth to the Monroe County Poorhouse in 1912. Unlike most "idiotic" children of the lower and middling sort, she never appeared again in her family's census record. Other stepparents abused their stepchildren so viciously that they caused impairments, as did some birth parents.[33]

The reasons so many more admittees came from families in crisis after the Civil War are complex. Clearly, the economic turmoil of the late nineteenth century, combined with the large-scale shift to wage labor, left families living on a financial knife's edge. The sharp depression of the 1870s put approximately three million people out of work, many for several years. Veritable armies of tramps and vagrants roamed the countryside even after the economy began to rebound in 1879. Workers protested drastic pay cuts and unemployment by the tens of thousands, most notably during the massive general strikes of the Great Upheaval in 1877. Further depressions followed in the 1880s and, in particular, the 1890s. The simultaneous move toward hourly, wage-based labor, moreover, made working-class households' finances even more unstable. Even skilled workers could hardly expect more than eight or nine months of reliable work per year, meaning that they, too, often had to turn to charity or even beg.[34]

While some children continued to come from farm families and those in artisanal trades, more and more came from urban areas and had fathers who toiled at either skilled work or unskilled labor, brothers who labored as clerks, sisters who worked as factory operatives, and mothers who sweated as seamstresses—wage-based positions that typically required labor outside the home and which made it hard to care for and potentially draw on the labor of a discharged "idiotic" relative.[35] When New York's asylum opened in 1851, for instance, the state was predominantly rural, under a third of the population living in urban areas and a small fraction working in manufacturing. By 1890, however, two-thirds lived in urban areas, and nearly 20 percent labored in the manufacturing sector.[36] Hervey Wilbur recognized the challenges that poverty and urbanization posed to families' capacity to care, noting in 1882, not long before his death, that "almost all the cases of idiocy occurring in indigent families become, sooner or later, a public charge." He added, "This is especially true of city populations."[37]

Yet, New York's Asylum for Idiots, as well as the many others modeled after it, continued to teach housekeeping, farming, and other skills suitable for rural economies. Of course, such skills also served to defray institutional costs, compensate for limited state funding, and, in theory, illustrate that superintendents practiced a "wise political economy."[38] As a result, it became progressively harder to integrate children into families that were increasingly likely to live in urban areas. Polish-born Moishe Abrams, for instance, proved "very studious" despite arriving with "very dirty habits." Wilbur noted that he "would soon be able to work on a farm." But Abrams came from a Jewish family that worked in New York City's garment industry. Unsurprisingly, his family never took him back. Instead, prominent members of the Jewish community housed him for a few years as a boarder.[39] While Abrams found his way home to his community, if not his family, for others the disjunction between their skills and their family's economic context meant that they lived the remainder of their lives in asylums. Beatrix Wetzel could "do plain sewing quite readily by hand" and was capable in "all the household occupations," but her Brooklyn-based parents could find little use for her. After spending twenty-five years at the New York State Asylum for Idiots, she was transferred to the Rome State Custodial Asylum to live out her days.[40]

Given the economic context, few households in distress—especially the growing numbers that relied on wage labor outside the home—could make use of a partly productive child or tend one who required substantial daily care. The German-born Beckers, for example, had maintained their "idiotic" sons Johann and Wilfred at home for years, relying on the considerable income their father earned from helping to build pianos, as well as their sister's labor at a confectionery shop. Like other pupils who arrived from disrupted families, both boys were relatively able when compared with the asylum's average pupils. Although Johann and Wilfred could speak, walk, and feed themselves, they nonetheless required regular care from their mother and other relatives. Neither could dress himself entirely, and, perhaps more importantly, neither was fully "cleanly." Their father's death, left their mother unable to support her sons, and within months the two boys entered the asylum in Syracuse. As in Johann and Wilfred's case, children who arrived at the asylum from families in distress were slightly more able than the average, meaning that they were more likely to be able to feed themselves, dress themselves, walk, and/or control their bladder and bowels, suggesting that family disruption, not ability, proved the tipping point in relatives' decisions to institutionalize their children.[41]

The Beckers were far from the only family that depended on wages to face the dilemma of how to care for and utilize "idiotic" relatives. In fact, during the

1870s nearly half of those newly admitted to the New York asylum from wage-dependent families had experienced some form of family disruption, as opposed to just over a quarter of students overall. Immigrant families were also slightly more likely to experience family disruption: 34.6 percent versus 25.2 percent of children from native-born families. In part, this distinction reflected the fact that immigrants comprised a disproportionate share of urban residents and wage workers: one-third of industrial workers in 1870, for instance. On the whole, individuals from immigrant families were also very slightly (3–13 percent) more able to care for themselves, suggesting that such families were less able to accommodate "feeble-minded" children, even those who were partly productive.[42] Illinois superintendent William B. Fish reported much the same story, noting in his annual report for 1888—perhaps with an eye to politics—that nearly all of the 300 applicants he had turned away for "want of room" came from "families in straitened circumstances to whom the care of an imbecile child is a most serious burden."[43]

Superintendents could hardly help but recognize families' increasing fragility. Fewer and fewer parents could afford to outfit their children before sending them to asylums, let alone cover the cost of their travel there. New York superintendent Hervey Wilbur reported that in 1868, for example, the parents of over 60 percent of those newly admitted "were so indigent that they could not afford to supply them with necessary clothing." In a growing number of states, local charities or counties now had to pick up the bill.[44] Poignantly, superintendents in Pennsylvania and Ohio, as well as in New York and Illinois, observed that only a few families could still afford to fund their children's summer vacations at home—the same trips originally intended to preserve family ties and demonstrate students' progress to their home communities. Illinois asylum director Charles Toppan Wilbur commented in 1876, "A large proportion of the pupils must be inmates of the asylum for the entire twelve months of the year ... remain[ing even] during the summer months, when all the pupils of the deaf and dumb and blind asylum go to their homes to spend a three or four months' vacation."[45]

The dramatic postbellum expansion of state and voluntary charity infrastructures also helped to identify households in crisis and inform them about the possibility of placing their "idiotic" children in asylums. The organized charity societies that emerged in New York and many other states in the late 1870s sent out hundreds of "friendly visitors" across cities and towns to investigate those who requested assistance. Adhering to the middle-class values of "rationality, efficiency, foresight, and planning," fearful of encouraging dependency on public or private assistance, and convinced that the causes of poverty lay in individual morality (or lack thereof), these visitors did not directly grant aid, monetary or otherwise. Instead, they interviewed struggling families to determine their moral worthiness and referred those deemed "deserving" to an appropriate charitable agency or, as in the case of the DeNiro family of Chicago, to a state institution.[46] After learning that Mrs. DeNiro was in "delicate health" and had been "abandoned by her husband and left without any means of support," the Charity Organization Society of Chicago arranged for her "attractive ... but very helpless" six-year-old daughter, Francesca, to be admitted to the Illinois Institution for Feeble-Minded Children. Although Mrs. DeNiro desired to keep her daughter at home, Francesca's care took so much time that she could hardly tend to her three other children. Because orphan asylums typically barred children deemed feeble-minded, crippled, blind, or in other ways not able, few if any options existed other than sending her to either the Cook County (Chicago) poorhouse or a state institution.[47]

This burgeoning charity infrastructure had an especially striking impact in the rapidly expanding city of Buffalo, where an English-born reverend, Stephen Humphreys Gurteen, established the first Charity Organization Society (COS) in the United States in 1877. Although Buffalo residents typically sent only a minuscule number of children to the New York State Asylum for Idiots—one or two per year during the 1850s and 1860s—admissions spiked sharply at two points in the 1870s, both directly in connection with charity reform initiatives. After State Charities Board (SCB) officials spent months investigating the city's poorhouses, orphan asylums, dispensaries, and the like in late 1873, nine children from Buffalo arrived at the idiot asylum in just two months. Most came directly from the Erie County almshouse, where charity board officials had presumably encountered them and deemed them "trainable." Six either died at the New York State Asylum for Idiots or were eventually transferred to county poorhouses or custodial asylums for "the feebleminded." And as friendly visitors for the new COS fanned out across the city in the late 1870s, admissions from Buffalo once again soared. Eighteen new admittees came between 1878 and 1880, primarily from households in which a parent had just died or become disabled and which, in all likelihood, had requested charitable relief.[48] Wallace Wheeler, for instance, arrived at the asylum in Syracuse after his father became "nearly blind." Reflecting the rising vogue of eugenic thinking, his mother, in turn, was described as "feeble-minded."[49]

Upon occasion, households in distress—especially those headed by single mothers who could draw on assistance from other children—managed to reconstitute their capacity for caring and find a way to make use of relatives discharged from the asylum. Harvey Straw, for instance, who could already

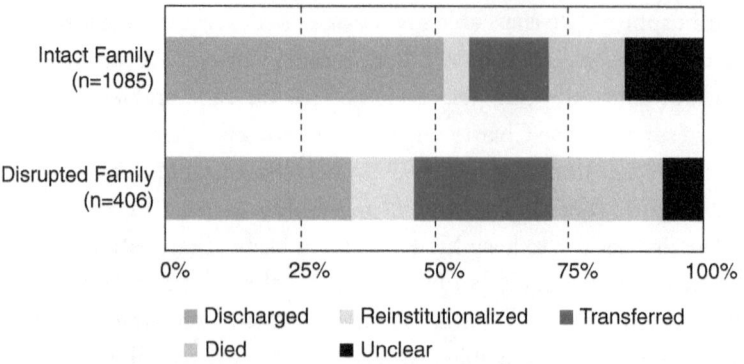

Chart 2-4: Family disruption and the prospects for life at home after the New York State Asylum for Idiots, 1851–1893

do basic farm work prior to his arrival in Syracuse at age twelve, remained only three years in New York's asylum. By 1886, his four younger siblings required less care; the youngest had grown out of toddlerhood, and several had entered adolescence. His mother took him home to help her jointly run their farm.[50] Likewise, after a decade in the New York State Asylum for Idiots, the Becker boys, for instance, went home to Buffalo to live with their mother and sister and, later on, their sister and niece; the two younger women supported the family by working as servants. Johann may have worked at odd jobs to help support the household, given that, when he entered the Erie County Poorhouse nearly three decades later in 1918 at age sixty, he was identified as able to perform labor. His brother's fate after 1900 remains less clear.[51]

More commonly, disrupted households struggled to reclaim their children, even though relatives have historically been reluctant to place or leave family members in institutions. As shown in Chart 2-4, children from households in distress were far less likely to return home from the New York State Asylum for Idiots and remain with their families. Walter Goodrich, whose widowed father could no longer care for him, as mentioned earlier, was one of the many pupils from families in crisis who were eventually transferred to other institutions. After Goodrich spent twenty years in the asylum at Syracuse, Wilbur's successor, James C. Carson, sent Goodrich to the Albany County Almshouse, whence he was eventually transferred to the Rome State Custodial Asylum. Others, such as Eileen Bagshaw, who came after her mother developed "a cancer," remained at the asylum in Syracuse until their deaths.[52]

Even when families managed to reconstitute themselves and their capacities for caring and making use of partly productive relatives, such stability sometimes proved only temporary. Just over a quarter of those taken home by their families from the New York State Asylum for Idiots eventually found themselves living in another institution. Randolph Sutton's father, for instance, had originally sent him to the asylum after his mother became ill. After hiring a live-in housekeeper whom he later married, the father took Randolph home to Brooklyn, dying soon afterward. Sutton's stepmother housed him for a few years while he did odd jobs, but then she placed him in the New York Farm Colony on Staten Island, where he remained for several decades.[53]

The gravity of the challenge facing asylum superintendents in the 1870s becomes even clearer when the growing numbers of children from disrupted families are combined with those of homeless individuals. At the New York State Asylum for Idiots, nearly 35 percent of those admitted during the 1870s could not readily be returned home, while 65 percent of children who arrived during the 1880s fell into that category (Chart 2-5). In comparison with individuals from intact families, students who came from institutions or families in distress, especially both, or who had no family history at all, were disproportionately likely to live the rest of their lives in institutions (Chart 2-6). No longer could superintendents count on discharging a large proportion of pupils to families who could tend and make use of idiotic relatives in an economy and society of rural and small communities. Combined with charity reform campaigns, the rise of the inherently unstable urban wage labor economy had decimated the necessary family and community supports. Asylum *inmates* could perform useful labor, but their families—if they even still existed—could no longer make use of those hard-won skills or look after them.

The Solution: Custodial Care

With individuals such as the homeless and friendless Walter Goodrich filling their asylums, superintendents could hardly ignore the growing evidence that many, if not most, families now lacked the capacity to care for their "idiotic" relatives and make use of their acquired skills. But the way in which Wilbur and his counterparts responded to both their inability to return individuals to their families and legislators' continuing pressure to hold down costs would have fateful consequences for the lives of those now deemed "feeble-minded." With few viable alternatives other than relegating their charges to county poorhouses, asylum directors, led by Wilbur, chose to push lawmakers to establish custodial care facilities that could rely on the commodified labor of trained *inmates* who lacked homes, especially female ones. Harkening back to Samuel Gridley Howe's 1848 report on the status of idiots,

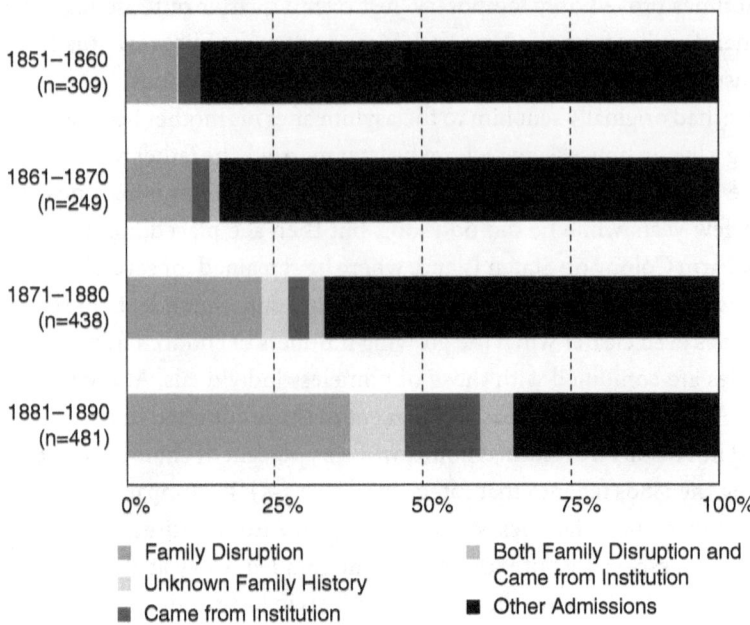

Chart 2-5: Shifting origins and levels of family disruption at the New York State Asylum for Idiots, 1851–1890

- Family Disruption
- Unknown Family History
- Came from Institution
- Both Family Disruption and Came from Institution
- Other Admissions

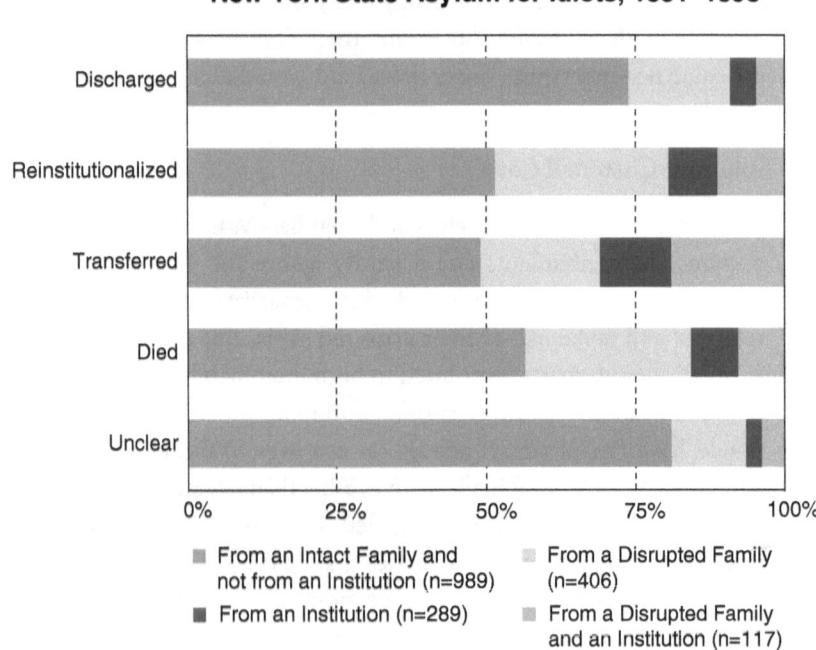

Chart 2-6: Admittees' origins, family disruption, and lives lived in institutions at the New York State Asylum for Idiots, 1851–1893

- From an Intact Family and not from an Institution (n=989)
- From an Institution (n=289)
- From a Disrupted Family (n=406)
- From a Disrupted Family and an Institution (n=117)

superintendents cast "feeble-minded" people as unproductive burdens on wage-dependent families, yet promised that institutional settings would make such individuals productive. At first, legislators hesitated to fund such proposals.

But the depression of the 1870s and, in particular, the resulting furor over pauperism and hereditary public dependency provided superintendents with a far more welcoming rhetorical and policy environment in which to argue that establishing custodial asylums for people identified as feeble-minded would save state funds twice over. In theory, such institutions would both make use of inmates' otherwise seemingly wasted capacities for labor and prevent impoverished yet respectable wage-earning families from slipping into the poorhouse. Such tales played on the contemporary slippage between the deserving and undeserving poor and, as such, proved compelling. In 1878, New York legislators established the first such dedicated asylum: the Custodial Asylum for Feeble-Minded Women in Newark. In the years to come, state after state would follow New York's lead, and Goodrich's narrative of a life lived almost entirely in the confines of institutions would become increasingly common.

While asylum superintendents did not fully grasp why families became less able to care for "idiotic" relatives in the 1870s and 1880s, they used annual reports to highlight the financial and practical challenges posed by the rapid accumulation of homeless, friendless inmates in institutions. Wilbur, for instance, reported that by 1875, only 56 of 196 present at New York's asylum—almost 30 percent—still had both parents living. Another 56 had lost both parents.[54] A few years later, he baldly stated, "Each year there are an increasing number of our pupils admitted from orphan asylum[s] and county poorhouses, who have and will have no home to go to when dismissed from the institution. Need custodial branch for males."[55] Illinois superintendent William B. Fish shared Wilbur's concerns, noting in 1880 that over 60 percent of the 338 "inmates" were "county charges whose clothing and transportation were furnished by the different counties of the State." Soon afterward, Fish called on the legislature to expand the institution, explaining that 300 "urgent" applications had accumulated "for want of room," nearly all of them "from families in straitened circumstances."[56] Pennsylvania Training School superintendent Isaac N. Kerlin, in turn, contended that 60 percent of the "feeble-minded" came from "the middle and poorer classes." Acknowledging the growing impact of the urban wage labor market on family capacity, he asserted that "the sadness and burden are found to be especially severe in the families of mechanics and artisans, who are bravely striving to keep themselves above pauperism."[57]

More so than other superintendents, Wilbur fretted over what to do with individuals from families that lacked the ability to care for them and utilize their skills, knowing full well the abysmal conditions in county poorhouses. In his annual reports, he stressed the "wanton neglect" faced by homeless idiots discharged to almshouses, especially those deemed "unteachable." Of course, such comments were hardly apolitical given the context in which they appeared, yet like antebellum lunacy reformer Dorothea Dix, who famously reported on her visits to poorhouses and insane asylums, Wilbur had gained firsthand knowledge of the potentially dire circumstances. In 1860, he reported that one boy had been "found naked in a county poor-house, and had been in that condition for two years. He had not only been without clothing by day, but he had slept in the straw, like a dog, at night."[58] Hinting at the likelihood of wasting hard-won skills and thereby effectively squandering state funds, he warned that others would "relapse into [their] former habits of stupidity and idleness" due to the lack of stimulation or training in poorhouses.[59]

But without community-based services that could extend the capacity of struggling families, Wilbur and his counterparts had few choices other than reluctantly releasing people to poorhouses or retaining them in asylums. Only Kentucky offered an alternative. Prior to the establishment of the Kentucky Institution for Feeble-Minded Children in 1860, the legislature had devoted $25,000 each year to helping indigent parents of "idiots" maintain them at home. After 1860, the legislature supported only those deemed "unteachable or too old for instruction." Wilbur was familiar with the program—he had advised Kentucky lawmakers prior to the opening of their institution—but saw little hope that the New York legislature would adopt Kentucky's program. Wilbur ruefully reflected that had lawmakers known better when they established the State Asylum for Idiots, they might have provided better from the beginning for those whose families could not easily take them home.[60]

Instead, Wilbur chose to press for custodial facilities that could permanently house and take advantage of the commodified labors of people whose families lacked the capacity to care for them. As the leading figure in idiot education and care in the country, his approach would also carry great weight in other states.[61] Prior to the depression of the 1870s, Wilbur had no luck enticing legislators to fund a custodial facility, but the question of what to do with homeless pupils or those from disrupted families was not entirely unfamiliar to him. As early as 1860, he had inklings that a custodial program might eventually become necessary—especially for those deemed "unteachable" and therefore the most subject to abuse in poorhouses—due to what was at that time a slow accumulation of students from institutions and disrupted families.⁶² After New York lawmakers established the State Board of Commissioners of Public Charities in 1867 (renamed the State Board of Charities in 1873), Wilbur curried favor with the board's members with the express aim of winning their support for a custodial program on the grounds of the Willard State Lunatic Asylum in Ovid. He proposed that after undergoing the standard period of training at the New York State Asylum for Idiots in Syracuse, capable homeless individuals could care for their "unteachable" counterparts, while also undertaking "simple industrial occupations, that would help to diminish the cost of support in such an asylum." By providing low-cost care for unteachable "non-producers," contended Wilbur, such a system would also prove "a positive gain to the productive power of the State."⁶³ Board members proved supportive, as did the trustees of the custodially oriented Willard Asylum, but legislators blanched at the prospect of spending yet more tax dollars on Willard.⁶⁴ Nevertheless, when the depression of the 1870s made pauperism and public dependency newly visible to lawmakers, charity officials, and professional charity reformers, Wilbur's plans finally gained traction.

The depression that wracked the United States between 1873 and 1878 left charity officials convinced that there were few truly deserving dependents. Professional charity reformers and state charity officials rejected workers' contention that no jobs existed, as well as the notion that massive industrialization had created structural unemployment. According to classical economic theory, unemployment was "a transitory and essentially insignificant phenomenon." Consequently, charity officials argued that workers were simply prone to idleness and were too lazy and irresponsible to look for work.⁶⁵ As a result, local and state charity officials offered aid erratically and, following tradition, poorhouse keepers required able-bodied men to complete a work test by chopping wood or breaking stones before receiving relief. State after state passed or strengthened vagrancy laws that criminalized public dependency and tramping in search of employment.⁶⁶ Members of the newly formed state charity boards and professional charity reformers, especially those involved with the "scientific charity" movement, redefined beggars as "swindlers" who refused to engage in the wage-based contract economy or to do their proper share of work in exchange for alms.⁶⁷ Charity officials and professional charity reformers would maintain their skeptical view of the poor and public dependents well past 1900.

The growing influence of hereditarian thought—especially degeneracy theory—intensified the fears of charity officials and professional charity reformers about public dependents. Professional charity reformers such as Josephine Shaw Lowell believed that socially undesirable behaviors like intemperance or prostitution were inherited, perhaps even racial, in nature. A tendency toward public dependency, therefore, could be passed down to children, while a poor environment contributed to an individual's degenerate state and would be reflected in future generations. On the other hand, a moral environment could potentially improve a family's germ plasm. This mixture of environmentalist, racialist, and Lamarckian hereditarian thinking reached its peak in Richard L. Dugdale's 1877 tract, *"The Jukes": A Study in Crime, Pauperism, Disease, and Heredity*, which traced a 1,200-member clan of drunkards, thieves, bastards, beggars, prostitutes, syphilitics, and murderers. In a manner reminiscent of Howe's 1848 report on idiots, Dugdale stressed "human cost accounting" and argued that the 1,200 members of the Jukes clan had cost New York more than $1.3 million over the past seventy-five years.[68]

During the mid- to late 1870s, state charity officials in New York and other states even adopted a pejorative, hereditarian view of those typically deemed to be part of the "deserving poor": children, widows, some people with "disabilities," and others who could not attain self-sufficiency and therefore deserved public aid. This transformation is perhaps best illustrated by Charles S. Hoyt's exhaustive 1876 survey of county poorhouse inmates, "Report on the Causes of Pauperism." Nearly all such inmates were originally domestic servants or unskilled laborers. Hoyt, the secretary of the SBC and a leading figure in charity reform nationally, nonetheless argued that "the number of persons in our poor-houses who have been reduced to poverty by causes outside of their own acts is, contrary to the general impression, surprisingly small."[69] Accordingly, the SBC began experimenting with requiring county poorhouses to extend work programs to public dependents—even the traditionally deserving and disabled poor. SBC member Martin B. Anderson, for instance, contended, "We believe that work should be provided for weak-minded and partially infirm paupers, even if it shall return no profit to the counties. The inmates of our poor-houses will always be healthier and happier when employed than when idle."[70]

Leading charity reformer—and advocate of scientific charity—Josephine Shaw Lowell played a key role in popularizing charity officials' harsher vision of public dependency and the deserving poor. In 1876, at only thirty-three years of age, Lowell became the first woman to be appointed to the New York State Board of Charities following her precedent-setting report on able-bodied paupers for the New York State Charities Aid Association, which many professional charity reformers saw as "a model of the new social-scientific approach." Her report blended statistics and anecdotes in order to discover "the 'truth' about public dependency" and present it in a seemingly neutral manner.⁷¹ One of the most prominent charity reformers of the postbellum decades, Lowell came from a Boston Brahmin family deeply involved with radical politics; among other causes, her Unitarian family supported abolitionism, women's rights, and the utopian Brook Farm community. Later in life, she would support mothers' pensions, the living wage, wage-earning women, binding arbitration, and the Homestead Strike and would also found the New York Consumers' League. But in the 1870s, Lowell shared with other leaders of the scientific charity movement a devout belief in the moral value of work and an environmentalist faith that properly structured institutions could prevent degeneracy.⁷² Her report lambasted charity officials' current approach to public dependency, suggesting that charity policy effectively told "the vicious and idle: 'We will board you free of cost, if you will only come and stay among us.' The money wasted in this way is the least of the evils of the present system; the corrupting influence of these worthless men and women, as they pass from town to town, lodging among the people, must be incalculable."⁷³ And along with her fellow charity reformers, furthermore, she had recently become fascinated with hereditarian (or proto-eugenic) explanations for social problems. By preventing people who might rely on public aid from reproducing, Lowell hoped to solve the problem of public dependency.

Lowell's advocacy, the rise of an urban wage economy, and the intellectual and political fallout of the 1870s depression created new openings for Wilbur and, eventually, his counterparts in other states to frame custodial facilities for people labeled "feeble-minded" as a wise use of state funds. By telling stories of impoverished yet respectable wage-dependent families, especially those headed by widows, who struggled to care for idiotic children, superintendents played on the murky boundaries between the deserving and undeserving poor at this time, as well as the moral dangers reputed to lurk in poorhouses.⁷⁴ Wilbur, for instance, argued in 1877 that those pupils admitted from "orphan asylums and county poor-houses are often sent to prevent breaking up families or relieve [the] burden of poor families."⁷⁵ Two years later, he explained why he had declined to discharge a girl with epilepsy, commenting, "To have returned her to her mother, struggling to support the other helpless [albino] members of her family, by teaching school, would possibly have consigned the whole family to the county poor-house."⁷⁶

Wilbur was far from the only superintendent to suggest that the urban wage-based economy posed serious challenges to families with idiotic relatives and might produce troubling social consequences as well. Notably, asylum directors did not acknowledge that, in the right context, such individuals could and did contribute to household economies; rather, superintendents cast "feeble-minded" people as entirely unproductive outside of institutional settings. Iowa's O. W. Archibald, for example, contended in 1879 that idiots always became "burdens" either to their parents or as "pauper charges" to the county.[77] William B. Fish of the Illinois Institution, in turn, told a heart-wrenching story of a widowed washerwoman in 1888. Despite a long-standing illness, she had undertaken a "brave struggle" to "keep her family together." But according to Fish, her nineteen-year-old idiotic daughter, Nadine Weiman, "required so much of the personal care of the mother that she [wa]s unable to earn enough" to support herself and her other three children. He warned that "unless she is relieved of the care of this child there remains nothing in store for the whole family but the county house."[78] Such stories were not entirely new to asylums' annual reports; in many ways, they illustrated the lasting impact of Samuel Gridley Howe's 1848 *Report to the Legislature of Massachusetts upon Idiocy*.[79]

But these tales of respectable impoverished widows struggling to earn enough to support their families and care for an idiotic child acquired a new power when counterposed against the unstable urban wage economy and a second class of single mothers grappling with cognitive impairments: feeble-minded women, especially those residing in poorhouses. After Lowell claimed her seat on the SBC in 1876, such women became her bête noire. In fact, she redefined the question of custodial care for the feeble-minded in such fearful terms that neither the board nor the legislature could dismiss the issue. Her first presentation on the topic, in January 1878, proved so convincing that board secretary Charles S. Hoyt immediately arranged for her to meet with Wilbur and the Syracuse trustees and ordered 1,000 copies of Lowell's report printed.[80] Although the text of her report has not survived, Lowell's message can be pieced together from the Syracuse asylum's annual report for 1878 and speeches in which she used a similar methodology.[81] As the institution's trustees recounted, she documented that in county poorhouses, "carelessness in the administration ... in the matter of a proper and rigid separation of the sexes" contributed to high rates of illegitimate births among "imbecile and idiotic females." Such women, Lowell argued, were easily seduced. Their children invariably "became a permanent burden upon the counties." Feeble-minded women were even more vulnerable outside local poorhouses, although the story ended the same way: with mother and child "abandoned to the charge of the county authorities."[82] Lowell thus suggested that by failing to control feeble-minded women, local poorhouses were *reproducing public dependency*, a notion anathema to charity officials. Her gendered understanding of public dependency and feeble-mindedness, moreover, proved influential in the formal eugenics movement that began to emerge in the 1880s.[83]

Unlike Lowell, Wilbur held that idiots rarely reproduced and saw little need to incarcerate feeble-minded women purely to prevent them from becoming pregnant, but he reluctantly joined forces with her in order to establish a custodial asylum.[84] Lowell's help—along with Wilbur's carefully cultivated relationship with the SBC and, in particular, his strong public support for the board in its battle to gain more oversight over state insane asylums in the mid-1870s—proved decisive.[85] In June 1878, the legislature approved an $18,000 appropriation for the new institution. Later that year, the New York State Custodial Asylum for Feeble-Minded Women opened its doors in the Finger Lakes town of Newark under the supervision of Wilbur and the Syracuse-based trustees of the New York State Asylum for Idiots. Reflecting Lowell's defining influence on the new asylum, lawmakers and the SBC declared that the Newark asylum would serve only women of childbearing age, and only those capable of useful work. Even if inmates—no longer termed pupils—became capable of supporting themselves, they could not leave the asylum, nor could relatives easily extract them from the institution.

All about Ability

Just as Wilbur had played a leading role in driving the establishment of idiot asylums across the country during the 1850s and 1860s, so too did his turn toward custodial care reshape the asylum landscape in the 1870s and beyond. As a dedicated custodial facility, the State Custodial Asylum for Feeble-Minded Women at Newark eventually proved to be an outlier; nearly every other state established "congregate" asylums that mixed inmates deemed in need of custodial care with those thought capable of benefiting from education and, crucially, of learning to do work useful in institutional settings. Nevertheless, by demonstrating the cost-effectiveness of relying extensively on inmates' unpaid labor—commodifying their work, in effect—the Newark asylum served as an invaluable model for superintendents seeking to create custodial wings and colonies within their own institutions. For inmates, especially female ones, the vast amounts of care work they performed no longer provided a pathway to release and integration into their families and mainstream society; rather, their toils merely served to defray the cost of their dependency on the state. Despite being cast as unproductive burdens by Lowell and asylum superintendents—at least if allowed to live outside institutions—such inmates were too productive to discharge. In these custodial asylums, moreover, inmates' ability—or inability—to perform useful labor and care for themselves shaped nearly every aspect of their lives, from clothing and living conditions to the prospects for survival and, perversely, discharge.

To a fair degree, Wilbur's 1873 outline for a custodial program shaped life at Newark: namely, that the more capable inmates would help to care for the less able.[86] Accordingly, Wilbur sent the Newark asylum a mixture of "higher-grade" and "lower-grade" inmates from the New York State Asylum for Idiots at Syracuse. The first group ranged from Lillian Mallard, who, despite her "defective eyesight" and poor hearing, had learned to sew and "made herself useful in a variety of ways at scrubbing, dining-room work, and in the Laundry," to Lucy Halloran, who could not control her bowels or bladder and had learned little other than how to recognize colors and shapes while at the asylum.[87] Most inmates, however, came from county poorhouses, sometimes without even a change of clothing.[88] Officially, "young and healthy" women received priority for admission; Wilbur also rejected women whom poorhouse officials classified as "unteachable."[89] In practice, women with epilepsy, cerebral palsy, partial blindness, various types of paralysis, and chronic diseases soon made up a considerable proportion of Newark's population—one-third in 1881. Superintendents and the board repeatedly complained that the county superintendents of the poor sent insane, delinquent, aged, or otherwise troublesome women as potential inmates, not idiotic, imbecilic, or feeble-minded ones. And despite Lowell's interest in hereditarianism and her decisive influence on the asylum, the majority of women admitted to Newark, likely upwards of 75–80 percent, had neither given birth to children nor were pregnant. Regardless, the asylum's trustees described the institution in 1889 as serving "imbecile women in our State, born in alms-houses and never having had any other home" who "have been mothers from once to four times."[90]

The asylum's superintendents lauded the caretaking abilities of inmates, who at times watched over as many as seventeen women—work that not only reduced costs but also addressed superintendents' continual problems with retaining employees. The superintendents of idiot asylums in New York and other states—and state institutions in general—could rarely match the going wage rates.[91] In fact, although most inmates arrived not knowing how to do any domestic work, superintendents found that "higher-grade" inmates did a better job caring for "unteachable" inmates than did paid employees; they "not only tolerated the monotony and unpleasantries but, indeed, seemed to thrive on them."[92] Ironically, professional charity reformers deplored such practices in the county almshouses and state insane asylums on the grounds that relying on inmates' labor encouraged poor care. Nevertheless, having inmates care for each other would become increasingly common in state idiot asylums and institutions for the feeble-minded across the nation during the late nineteenth century.[93]

But whereas first-generation superintendents such as Wilbur had used occupational training programs not only to defray institutional costs but also to ease pupils' reintegration into their families, by the late 1870s and the 1880s charity officials and asylum directors used inmates' labor at Newark to provide care on the cheap. In its 1879 report to the legislature, for instance, the SBC promised that "the various household occupations necessary in so large a family [will] be done, as far as possible, by the inmates, for economy's sake."[94] The first superintendent of Newark, C. C. Warner—the former superintendent of the poor for the well-regarded Onondaga County Almshouse—required all inmates capable of any type of work to labor; usually roughly half could.[95] By 1886, inmates were making all of the clothing for the 134 residents, and in 1893 they produced 713 dresses, 519 chemises, and 43 straitjackets, among other items.[96] Other inmates worked in the kitchen, laundry, canning room, bakery, and garden; in 1909, for instance, they also made $600.21 worth of canned goods ranging from strawberries and plums to floor wax and lard, raised $2,483.57 in farm produce, and saved $2,116.07 in provisions and $1,189.06 in household stores.[97] Thanks to inmates' toils, between 1880 and 1920 Newark's cost of maintenance (excluding clothing) averaged just 68 percent of that at the Syracuse asylum—about the same cost of care as at county poorhouses.[98] Since institutional expenses remained a potent political issue well past the turn of the century, superintendents' frugality undoubtedly pleased the state charity officials and legislators.[99]

Despite inmates' considerable productivity, their unpaid labors only rarely provided a pathway to discharge; instead, superintendents' hereditarian beliefs and the value of inmates' labors led them to retain nearly all inmates at the Newark asylum. The four "higher-grade" inmates whom asylum director W. L. Willett discharged in 1892 represented a rare exception. He later reported that all four had obtained "good places to work through the efforts of the superintendents of the poor of the counties from which they were committed." Nine inmates were released to their relatives in 1894 after improving considerably; most became self-sustaining, while a few others were dismissed in 1912 because they were no longer seen as "menace[s] to society." But between 1879 and 1920, the Newark asylum had an average annual discharge rate of only 3.92 percent.[100] The Syracuse asylum, in contrast, discharged nearly 10 percent of its pupils outright each year. Nearly a third of those released from Newark, moreover, were discharged solely because they had reached menopause.[101]

Most released inmates returned to the poorhouses whence they had originally come, in part because even when inmates had families, the Newark superintendents paid little attention to whether their relatives could receive them. In 1894, Mrs. Elizabeth Goodings, for instance, wrote to the SBC begging that superintendent Winspear not discharge her daughter: "I am totally without income (77 years of age) and dependent on my soninlaw [sic].... He will not be wiling to receive Emily into his home.... It would break my heart if my oldest child should be obliged to go to a county house or an insane asylum.... Does it not seem cruel to throw these children back into the condition from which you have taken them ... [?] With the exception that they cannot propogate [sic] their kind, will not there [sic] last condition be as sad as their first[?]"[102]

In the decades to come, state after state would open dedicated custodial facilities or, more commonly, expand educationally oriented asylums to include separate custodial wings or colonies. In either case, superintendents and lawmakers cited the Newark asylum's pioneering frugality and extensive use of commodified inmate labor as a model.[103] Willett noted in 1890 that other states "are agitating the question of custodial care for the feeble-minded, and are looking to this State with considerable interest to see if our method is the best. There are a variety of opinions in regard to it."[104] In Illinois in 1882, Charles Toppan Wilbur won legislators' approval to purchase a farm explicitly intended to employ adult male inmates, as did Isaac Kerlin of the Pennsylvania Training School. Whereas Samuel Gridley Howe had barred custodial inmates from the Massachusetts School for Feeble-Minded Children and had warned late in life against the establishment of custodial programs, his death in 1876 allowed his successors to add both a dedicated custodial annex for those deemed "unimprovable" and a farm for adult men in 1883. Newer institutions with more available land close by, such as those in Iowa, Indiana, Minnesota, and Kansas, integrated custodial care into their programs from the start.[105]

Just as at Newark, these other institutions relied on immense quantities of inmates' unpaid labor—especially that performed by female inmates—to reduce costs to the public purse. Speaking at the 1885 National Conference of Charities and Correction, Pennsylvania Training School superintendent Isaac N. Kerlin, for instance, reported that "our children's work" saved the institution "four thousand dollars in wage labor annually." He proudly noted that savings "permit[ed] the institution to retain about thirty inmates on the non-paying list; that is, thirty *free* patients are actually supported by the saving in the service."[106] Much as officials at Newark had argued, Kerlin asserted that feeble-minded girls provided far better care for "lower-grade" cases than did paid, able-bodied employees. After taking an extended tour of the Pennsylvania Training School, *Christian Register* editor, prison reformer, and eventual Congressman Samuel J. Barrows advocated on behalf of this approach at the National Conference of Charities and Correction, contending that "higher-grade" custodial inmates "sympathize with [lower-grade cases] and gain their affection as no other class can do." He added, "through this combined labor the expenses of the institution were reduced, while its efficiency was increased."[107] Per capita costs at the Pennsylvania Training School, in fact, dropped from $183 in 1890 to $152 in 1893, justifying Kerlin's hope that adding a formal custodial care program would help stabilize the asylum's finances. The Illinois Asylum for Feeble-Minded Children at Lincoln demonstrated an even more dramatic decrease in costs, going from $280 per year in 1875 with 81 inmates to an annual cost of $184 in 1885 with 312 inmates and, finally, to $135 per year in 1894 with 546 inmates.[108]

Even with a dedicated custodial asylum located in the state, the theoretically educationally oriented New York State Asylum for Idiots at Syracuse followed these trends. After Hervey Wilbur's death in 1883, his successors virtually abandoned academic training in favor of developing pupils' vocational skills, as did similarly focused institutions in other states. Pennsylvania Training School superintendent Kerlin argued, for instance, that it was "hard to convince the parents that old forms of letters and numbers do not constitute an education for an imbecile child, even when they may be acquired." Instead, he contended that students should learn "conformity to the habits and actions of normal people" in case they might be one of the few to be discharged. Far more critically, they needed to acquire vocational skills to ensure that their "cost and care shall be as moderate as possible."[109]

Prior to his death, Wilbur had already begun to enlarge the asylum's occupational training programs and workshops to provide occupation for the growing population of older male students for whom lawmakers declined to dedicate an asylum until 1894, when the state opened the Oneida State Custodial Asylum for Unteachable Idiots at Rome (soon renamed the Rome State Custodial Asylum).[110] Illustrating the growing commodification of inmates' labors, under Wilbur's successor, James C. Carson (1885–1912), young girls alternated lessons in ironing with their academic studies "with the view of fitting them in time for useful work in the laundry. A number of boys work[ed] in the tailor shop in the same way."[111] By 1888, moreover, Carson had expanded Syracuse's sewing workshops so significantly that he was able to reduce by a third the annual fees charged to counties for clothing their pupils; other asylums did the same. And in Massachusetts, "a large part of [their] girls" went to the sewing-room each day, completing all of the sewing required by the institution.[112] He also enlarged the asylum's farm colony, which, combined with the garden at the main campus, defrayed the cost of provisions for the entire asylum by an average of 28 percent between 1884 and 1920.[113]

Carson also redoubled efforts to train multiply disabled and "unteachable" students—those long deemed incapable of working—to be somewhat productive or at least less burdensome. In so doing, he helped lay the groundwork for the approach that superintendent Charles Bernstein would adopt at the Rome State Custodial Asylum for Unteachable Idiots at the turn of the twentieth century. Dismissing received wisdom that children with impairments in addition to idiocy—blindness, cerebral palsy, and other forms of paralysis— could not learn to care for themselves, Carson arranged for them to join sewing workshops and learn to braid mats. He explained his reasoning in 1885: "These mats are not made neatly enough for the market but answer their purpose very well, and are used about the asylum to good advantage when needed. Their making gives occupation to these boys who could not otherwise be employed, which is the chief object sought."[114] In addition, Carson assigned "low-grade boys" to help grade (level) the grounds, moving thousands of cubic feet of earth.[115] Teachers kept those pupils deemed completely "unteachable" busy with games, music, singing, marching, and practicing with apparatus such as dumbbells, and learning self-care skills.[116] Echoing Howe's rhetoric about "ravenous consumers" and reflecting the low value placed on care work, Carson stressed the larger social benefits of teaching pupils to care for themselves, even if those were the only skills they learned: "If a child who cannot feed or dress itself, button its shoes, comb its own hair, or perform many other of the simple and necessary acts in every-day life, can be taught to do any one of them unaided, something has been gained; the labor of another person more valuable for other purposes has been saved to that extent, and the efforts at training have not been expended in vain."[117]

Here, too, superintendents' increasingly hereditarian bent, concerns about reproduction of public dependence, and the value placed on inmates' work meant that the ability to care for oneself or perform useful labor no longer provided a pathway to discharge, especially for women. After his arrival at the New York State Asylum for Idiots in 1885, Carson, for instance, began to track the parentage of all applicants, looking for "hereditary taints" such as idiocy, imbecilism, insanity, epilepsy, intemperance, consanguinity, convulsions,

Female inmates working in the canning plant, Syracuse State Institution for Feeble-Minded Children, ca. 1910–1930. Courtesy of the New York State Museum.

Boys painting buildings, Syracuse State Institution for Feeble-Minded Children, ca. 1910–1930. Courtesy of the New York State Museum.

general sickliness, physical deformities, delinquency, criminality, and pauperism. After nearly thirty years of study, he reported that of 3,000 applications, only just over a third "came to us from a parentage recorded as free from degeneracy or some hereditary family stain."[118] He advised against discharging any female inmates, contending in 1886 that "in fact it is a wise policy to retain all females, if possible, unless they can be provided for in places other than the county poor-houses." In 1898, he added, "With reference to the widespread army of degenerates scattered here and there throughout the land, and who are annually adding to the general plethora of feeble-mindedness, we believe that humanity, economy, the protection of society and the prevention of degeneracy demand the permanent sequestration of the entire body of the feeble-minded within our borders in institutions."[119] Carson's successor, O. H. Cobb, shared his hereditarian views and, like most of his fellow superintendents in the 1910s, saw feeble-mindedness—and especially feeble-minded women—as the source of most social problems, especially public dependency.[120] Accordingly, Carson and Cobb discharged female students at considerably lower rates than male students between 1886 and 1920, although female students made up slightly more of the asylum's population: male students comprised 59.46 percent of discharges, while female students made up only 41.17 percent of discharges.[121]

Perversely, the gendered division of labor within the asylum likely also prevented female inmates from winning their release; in other words, women's unpaid care work proved especially valuable in the context of custodial programs. It is challenging to sort out the various factors that could prevent discharge, since superintendents' hereditarian bents, family incapacity or unwillingness to take a relative home, and perhaps even personal preference all could play a role. Yet, it is telling that, after the mid-1870s, Wilbur and Carson discharged virtually no women who were able to perform ward work, clean, sew, or do laundry—all skills that, as scholars have pointed out, were in increasingly high demand as custodial programs expanded. Instead, female pupils such as Maud Halford, who "understood . . . nearly all kinds of work" and could manage a room with six beds, and Irma Ramsey, who could sew "very well" on a machine, spent the remainder of their lives in asylums. After fifteen years at the Syracuse State Institution, Halford was transferred to the Newark asylum in 1884; by 1900, she was living in an old-age home in Buffalo. Ramsey, meanwhile, remained at the Syracuse State Institution for Feeble-Minded Children for thirty-eight years before being discharged to the Suffolk County Poorhouse in 1917 at age forty-three. Since her trail goes cold then, she may well have died soon after entering the almshouse.[122] Halford and

Ramsey, furthermore, were far from the only such accomplished women to live their lives in institutions. Sybil Keene, for instance, worked in the dining room and could make her own dresses but was eventually transferred to the Rome State Custodial Asylum and then Orange County's poorhouse. Lisa Lancaster, in turn, was "very good at taking care of younger children" and worked in the dining room during every meal; she, too, was sent to the Rome Asylum after a long stay at Syracuse.[123] Other superintendents, especially those at older asylums that lacked space for a farm colony, likewise preferentially retained adult female inmates because their ability to do care work was so valuable.[124]

In contrast, Carson and his counterparts followed Wilbur's example by occasionally discharging male pupils as either entirely self-supporting or partly productive in the context of their families. One young man trained for several years with the asylum's carpenter; after being discharged in 1892, he began working as a carpenter in New York City, where he earned $12 to $14 a week. Another moved to California, where he supported himself by working in a raisin vineyard. Others discharged themselves by "eloping" (or escaping), as in the case of Adolphus Whitman, who left the asylum in 1889 to work as a farm laborer and railroad gripman (and strikebreaker) for several years, among other jobs.[125] Yet other male students departed the asylum to live with their families after having been deemed "very useful on farm," able to do errands, or able to "do many useful things very nicely both in and out of doors."[126]

Male students, moreover, could at times still access the community outside the asylum. Willie, for instance, who had arrived at the New York State Asylum for Idiots in 1851 along with his brother Natty, lived there until his death in 1898 at age fifty-five. Superintendent Carson noted that Willie "became a constant reader of the Bible, a member of the Fourth Presbyterian Church in this city and a regular, interested and devoted attendant at all of the services in that church. His conscientious Christian life was a most worthy example to those better endowed and won many friends to him in the church, at the Y.M.C.A. and throughout the city. During his last illness these friendships were well attested by the many inquiries about him and the almost daily calls he received."[127] Willie's long tenure at the asylum and cheerful demeanor gave him special privileges, but Carson permitted a few other male pupils to wander nearby streets.[128]

Meanwhile, superintendents readily discharged inmates deemed to have "no occupational capacity"—even some women—provided that they had relatives who could take them. A few months after Carson's arrival at Syracuse in 1884, for instance, he released Clara Heinrich to her German immigrant parents in Brooklyn. While at the asylum, she had learned to speak much more fluently; in fact, she often sang and "talk[ed] too much." No longer did she "tear her clothing and pinch and strike the children about her," but it remains less clear if she learned to control her bowels and bladder. Despite remaining for eight years at the asylum, she never advanced to vocational classes. Nor was Heinrich the only female inmate discharged by Carson; a few years later, he released Eileen Kavanaugh to her family's care. She was unable to speak, feed herself, dress herself, or "walk well owing to physical weakness" after twelve years in the asylum, and Carson likewise had little hope that she would become able to work.[129]

Commodified inmate labor became so central to these institutions that inmates' perceived abilities and occupational capacities shaped every aspect of their lives, from the clothes they wore to the length of time they were likely to survive in institutionalized life. Upon becoming superintendent at New York's Rome State Custodial Asylum for Unteachable Idiots in 1903, superintendent Charles Bernstein, for instance, discarded his predecessor's method of classifying newly admitted inmates by medical categories such as "idiot," "idio-imbecile," "imbecile," and so on—the standard method used by asylum directors.[130] Instead, he recategorized individuals by their ability to care for themselves and do work considered valuable within the asylum or at least undertake vocational training. Bernstein's new scheme ranged from no ability to work in class one, to "self-care" in class two, "assist others" in class three, "usefulness in industrial departments" in class four, and "good workers" in class five. Inmates' clothing indicated their level of productivity according to this scheme. Those who misbehaved had to wear the clothing of the least capable group and eat with those inmates who could not feed themselves.[131] The following year, Bernstein established a credit system whereby inmates could obtain new clothing only by working or attending vocational training or self-care classes—to which the school was nearly entirely devoted—and showing good deportment.[132]

Ability also played a crucial role in determining whether an inmate would live or die. Even at comparatively well-funded educational asylums such as the New York State Asylum for Idiots, those pupils less capable of caring for themselves died at roughly double the rate of those classified as "cleanly" or able to walk, feed themselves, and dress themselves between 1851 and 1890.[133] Often, such students died within mere months, as in the case of Janette Farmer, who arrived at Syracuse in 1873 labeled as "filthy," hardly able to walk, and unable to talk. Despite having arms that were partly paralyzed, she could feed and dress herself. She "underst[ood] no language, except to recognize

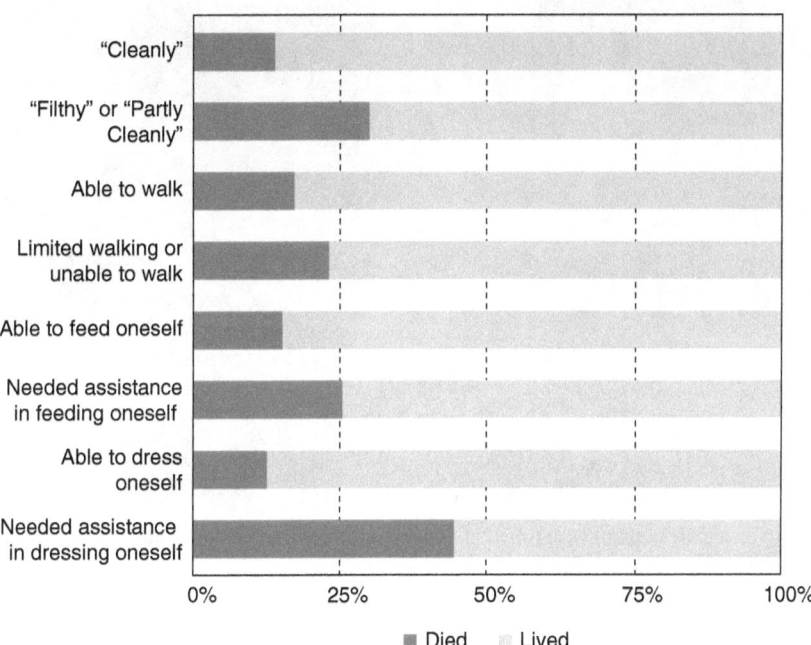

Chart 2-7: Ability and death rates at the New York State Asylum for Idiots, 1851–1890

her own name when called." Within five months, Farmer was dead from spinal meningitis, having "suffered greatly" because "she could not tell the seat of pain."[134] And during the Rome State Custodial Asylum for Unteachable Idiots' first decade, nearly two-thirds of those deemed least able—"idiots"—died shortly after admission, often within just a year or two. With the exception of inmates who had epileptic fits, death rates for more able classes of inmates never reached above 23 percent and sometimes ranged as low as 1.5 percent per year. As in many state institutions, not simply idiot asylums, tuberculosis took much of the toll.[135]

Undoubtedly, the abysmal living conditions common in custodial wings and facilities increased death rates. At Newark, inmates suffered the consequences of Wilbur's rush to find quarters for the asylum. Eager to lure an asylum and the resulting jobs to their town, Newark's leaders had offered him their "uninhabited religious academy, rent-free, if the state would refurbish the building." The building had previously served as the Wayne and Ontario Collegiate Institute (a Baptist school) and as a Lutheran academy, but it was still incomplete when the asylum opened in 1878. The water supply and sewage provisions remained inadequate at the Newark asylum until the early

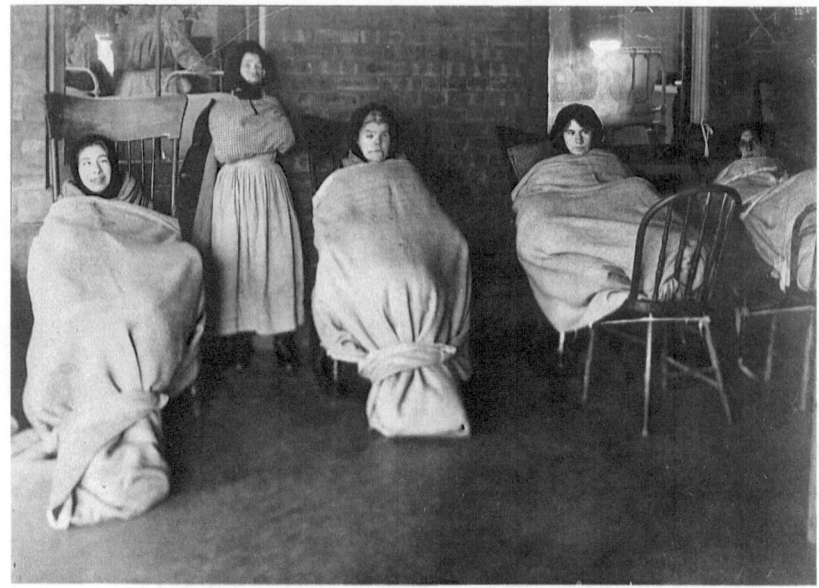

Group of female inmates with tuberculosis on veranda of the New York State Custodial Asylum for Feeble-Minded Women at Newark, ca. 1910–1914. Courtesy of the New York State Archive.

1910s, when the state finally built a sewage disposal plant. The poor sanitary conditions likely contributed to high rates of disease; in 1889, the asylum reported sixty-nine cases of cholera morbus.[136]

Conditions were hardly better at the Rome State Custodial Asylum for Unteachable Idiots when Bernstein became superintendent in 1902, reflecting the fact that superintendents' tendency of using frugality to obtain state funding was at best a tenuous strategy. He inherited a decaying asylum that the *New York Tribune* argued had long been known as "one of the most discreditable asylums for the care of the insane and aged poor in the State." The *Tribune* continued, "The plumbing might well inspire the thought that it had been put in while Washington was President and never repaired."[137] Bernstein's predecessor, John Fitzgerald, had already improved conditions somewhat during his tenure. With the board's help, Fitzgerald had persuaded lawmakers to replace the old basement dining halls, whose stone and dirt floors were "saturated with refuse water and grease" and where inmates ate their meals with pipes and a first-floor water closet dripping on them.[138] Yet by 1900, most wards still remained bare, lacking even enough furniture for all of the inmates to sit down at once. The piggery, cow yard, and slaughterhouse were all upwind of residential buildings, and during the summer, mosquitoes proliferated in marshy holes near the wards.¹³⁹ Inmates did not receive any dental care—a practice that, upon becoming superintendent in 1903, Bernstein forthrightly challenged as inhumane and counterproductive.¹⁴⁰ Some, meanwhile, continued to reside in wards locked at all times or in old insane asylum cells. With the board's support, he finally succeeded in ending both practices.¹⁴¹ Nevertheless, funding remained so scant that the board of managers reported in 1909 that most beds lacked sheets or pillowcases and that curtains were in such scant supply that inmates had to undress in full view of the public traveling a nearby road.¹⁴²

Abuse was also often rife in custodial institutions or on custodial wings. In 1893, the SBC discovered that Newark's superintendent Willett, matron Kate Rose Willett, and the assistant matrons had all beaten inmates. The most notable cases were two ill women, one of whom was physically abused in bed when she refused to take her medication; the other, "being an invalid, was brought to the matron, with the medical advice that the patient was sick, to which advice the matron replied in substance that she knew better and that the patient was only ugly; whereupon the matron punished the patient with the ferule. A few days later, the patient developed meningitis; within ten days, she had died." In addition, Willett punished patients "by tripping them from behind and letting them fall on their backs," without "any means used to graduate the fall or force of contact with the ground . . . except such species of garroting or pressure on the throat or neck." Superintendent Willett, matron Willett, and the first assistant matron resigned.¹⁴³

Multiple Meanings of Work

Although inmates' toils in custodial institutions led to discharge only in extremely rare cases, some still experienced their unpaid work as more than unpaid drudgery. Within oft-bleak and sometimes abusive institutions such as New York's Custodial Asylum for Feeble-Minded Women at Newark, work provided a source of entertainment, or at least a means of passing free time. Vocational training classes helped fill the hours when "higher-grade" inmates were not laboring in the kitchen, laundry, or sewing rooms, or helping on the wards. Sometimes inmates' labors enabled them to earn pocket money and, thereby, limited choice over their clothing. The ability to work could also bring much-desired status within the institution itself.

At the Newark asylum, work offered an escape from the boredom of an institution that, for its first fifteen years, had no pictures on the walls, no outdoor exercise, and no regular parties or other forms of amusements. Superintendents periodically closed the school—which taught primarily vocational subjects—because of a lack of space and teachers.[144] Inmates had considerable free time, even after the staff established weekly public entertainments in 1892, in which inmates demonstrated to visitors their talents at music, dancing, dumbbell exercises, and marching, along with evening amusements twice a month and winter sleigh rides (two each annually for all inmates).[145]

Upon his arrival as superintendent in 1893, Charles W. Winspear revitalized the asylum's school and encouraged inmates to plan their own masquerade balls and arranged for concerts, cinematograph showings, picnics, and performances by showmen, along with seasonal parties.[146] But after his departure in 1909, the school closed once again, and entertainments declined dramatically until the SBC ordered Winspear's replacement, superintendent Dr. Ethan A. Nevin, to provide the inmates with activities other than work. He hired a physical director who taught games and folk dancing, among other activities, to 240 of the nearly 800 inmates at the asylum. The managers also began reading to a large group of inmates on a weekly basis, and cottage residents (who generally had multiple disabilities and were classed as fully or somewhat helpless) began having regular picnics outside, among other innovations—likely their only source of outside excursions or exercise. And after encouragement from administrators, fifty inmates formed a Mutual Improvement Society.[147] Despite the growing number of activities within the institution, inmates remained isolated from the outside world. The Newark asylum's "Circular of Information" for 1911 revealed that inmates were allowed to write home only once a month; friends and relatives of inmates were urged to not share any news that might make inmates "discontented."[148]

Inmates demonstrated their boredom in the early 1910s, when they eagerly responded to Nevin's efforts to expand industrial training beyond the usual duties of doing laundry, sewing, cooking, and caring for less capable inmates. After consulting with industrial teachers at other state institutions, he organized voluntary classes in basketry, art, and a wide range of fancy work (embroidery, crocheting, and lace making, among other skills), as well as daily gardening parties. The classes filled immediately, and many inmates added their names to waiting lists. Nevin also arranged for an attendant to teach a kindergarten class to forty inmates as "an experiment intended to help overcome their destructive tendencies."[149] In at least one case, Nevin's efforts to engage his inmates succeeded admirably: the board reported in 1912 that "a deaf and dumb girl" had been "very discontented and unhappy but since being employed in basket making and other industrial enterprises of the Institution has seemed entirely satisfied."[150] By September 1913, he had placed 782 out of the 800 total inmates in work or vocational training. Nevins proudly reported: "The girls are more efficient in their work, happier and prouder about it than they used to be, partly, we think, because we try to give each girl the work she would rather do, partly because we change the girls from one congenial activity to the other, and partly because we are careful not to give them too much to do at once."[151]

Inmates' labors could also offer a means of earning money, and in particular, gaining some choice over the standard issue (and inadequate) clothing, as revealed in the 1907 investigation that eventually ended Winspear's reign as superintendent. Early that year, the inspector of state charitable institutions, Henry M. Lechtrecker, discovered courtesy of the resident physician, Dr. Anna Warnecke, that board members and the asylums' matron were paying inmates a pittance to do "fine linen" and "open linen work," and then selling inmates' work in town for a considerable price or keeping the fancy work for personal use. Warnecke had repeatedly raised her concerns to the board, but with little success. Lechtrecker reported to the SBC, in turn, that the inmates appeared to be working constantly on "dining room sets and pieces for dresser decoration [that] were of the most intricate and difficult kind of drawn linen work," even in the "uncertain light of the early evening, much to the injury of eyesight."[152] By early 1908, the resulting scandal had brought down the matron and seven of the nine members of the board, including Edwin K. Burnham, a leading local businessman and former state representative who had played the central role in the town's fight to retain the asylum in Newark in the 1880s.[153] Superintendent Charles Winspear's reputation was irrevocably tarnished, and he resigned in 1909.

While Inspector Lechtrecker and the SBC focused primarily on the "doubtful propriety" of the board members and matron profiting from inmates' labors, inmates clearly understood the fancy work as a means for improving their perennially poor living conditions.[154] Without fail, they used their minuscule earnings to buy stockings better than those available at the institution, which Lechtrecker described as made from "inferior grade yarn... unseasonable, poorly made and without any attempt at sizes." As Lechtrecker reported, shoes, sheets, and pillowcases were perennially in short supply; combs were so rarely supplied that inmates went "about the grounds with their individual hair brushes tied to waist band of skirts." And until 1912, the inmates seem to have had only winter wraps and shawls instead of coats.[155]

The question of who should benefit from inmates' labors remained a subject of fervent debate on the asylum's board for several years. Initially, the board arranged for a local merchant to value inmates' fancy work and pay them individually, with inmates allowed to dispose of their income as they wished. In 1909, the two remaining members of the old board (who had both been involved in the 1907 scandal) successfully regained control of the pricing and selling process. By 1911, those board members had resigned, and the matron began depositing the proceeds from selling inmates' fancy work in a general entertainment fund (the same policy as in the early 1890s). The new board also went on record as officially "encourag[ing] all sorts of handiwork within the capacity of the inmates."[156]

Finally, as suggested by the way in which inmates' clothing at the Rome asylum visually indicated whether Bernstein deemed them to be "good workers," labor could also offer a source of status within institutions—a much-desired one at that, especially for those deemed incapable of working. More than one-quarter of pupils admitted to the New York State Asylum for Idiots, for instance, could already do some "useful labor" upon their arrival, typically housework such as setting the table or helping to wash dishes in the case of girls and, for boys, bringing in wood or water. Like other children, moreover, many students in the asylum had imitated their parents' tasks at home. Terrence Flaherty "like[d] to make believe to do carpenter's work"—work that he could not easily master due to his "slightly emaciated" limbs and the fact that he could move only a few steps by himself even with crutches. Frances Hertzfeld, in turn, "amuse[d]" herself by scrubbing and doing other work.[157] Consequently, it should be no surprise that some of those whom superintendents considered too impaired to work desperately wanted to do so. Arnold Painter's epilepsy and limited sight meant that he could not undertake the standard vocational classes at the New York State Asylum for Idiots, but he managed to "make himself useful in many ways." Indeed, Wilbur noted, he was "very fond of doing errands." And even though Wilbur barred Myra Percy from occupational training classes, he ruefully observed that had she not been partly blind, she "would be very capable [of occupation]." Regardless, Percy was "very desirous of learning to work."[158]

BY THE LATE 1870S and the 1880s, admission to custodial facilities such as the New York State Asylum for Idiots at Syracuse typically served as the prelude to (or, in many cases, the continuation of) a life spent entirely in institutions. No longer did individuals return home to live with their relatives, as they had in the 1850s and 1860s. Instead, the rapidly shifting economy and society and, in particular, the emergence of urban wage labor undermined families' capacity to care for "feeble-minded" children. Charity reforms intended to prevent dependency on public aid, moreover, had inadvertently led asylums to preferentially admit people who could not easily be returned home.

Superintendents struggled to manage this sudden accumulation of individuals who, like Amelia Harlow, had no home. While asylum directors recognized families' growing incapacity to some degree, their institutions nevertheless continued to operate based on the assumption that they could eventually reintegrate pupils into their families. Seeing few viable alternatives, superintendents soon joined with charity reformers such as Josephine Shaw Lowell to advocate for custodial wings and dedicated custodial institutions that could house adult "feeble-minded" inmates—especially women—and make use of their commodified labors. While legislators initially hesitated to provide funding, the depression of the 1870s heightened charity officials' and legislators' concerns about pauperism, feeble-minded women, and the reproduction of public dependency and made them far more willing to finance custodial facilities.

In these new custodial institutions and wings, ability shaped every aspect of inmates' lives, including the clothing they wore, their chances of discharge, and their chances of survival within the asylums. From superintendents' point of view, the immense quantities of unpaid labor done by inmates defrayed the cost of their dependency on the public purse. Perversely, asylum directors had cast "feeble-minded" individuals, especially women, as unproductive burdens on their families in order to persuade lawmakers to fund custodial institutions, but female inmates' care work proved so valuable to the functioning of asylums that they rarely won discharge. Yet, some inmates nonetheless found meaning in their toils and used them to gain some small measure of control over their lives.

But because the creation of custodial programs did not address the root causes of why families increasingly struggled to provide for and make use of "feeble-minded" relatives, or why charity policies disproportionately selected pupils who were homeless and friendless, the pressure for admissions continued unabated. States' new custodial facilities filled almost immediately, leaving legislatures scrambling to establish additional institutions. By 1947, New York State alone had twelve "state schools for the mentally retarded." Nationally, over 128,000 people lived in such facilities by 1955.

The unraveling of Wilbur's approach for reintegrating "idiotic" children into their families also highlights the importance of family in shaping the lived experiences of people with diverse bodies and abilities. Along with increasing eugenic stigma and well-intentioned charity policies that had unexpected outcomes on asylums' populations, relatives' growing incapacity for care effectively led superintendents to cast people labeled as idiots or feeble-minded as socially dangerous, unproductive in mainstream society, and suited only for unpaid labor within institutions. As charity officials, social workers, managers of sheltered workshops, and vocational rehabilitators worked to reintegrate people with acquired disabilities into the mainstream labor market in the early twentieth century, they too would discover that a person's family context played a crucial role in determining his or her experience of "disability."

Despite superintendents' dire—and self-serving—rhetoric about the inevitable dependency of "feeble-minded" people outside institutions, as superintendent Charles Bernstein of the Rome State Custodial Asylum would show, even such people who lacked families could in fact be reintegrated into the wage labor market. The solution lay in recognizing that the job market itself allowed for a spectrum of ability and that individuals could be "fitted" to suitable positions. Even while working with a population that had few relatives who could ease their entry into the labor force, Bernstein nevertheless transitioned hundreds of "feeble-minded" people into paid positions in the manual and domestic labor.

CHAPTER THREE

I Wish to Thank You for My Freedom
Paroling Feeble-Minded People into Farm and Domestic Work, 1900s–1930s

Julia Cuyper crowed over her new position as a domestic servant in Gloversville, New York. Since the family had invited her along on an auto ride and a visit to the circus, she only had time that day to write a few chatty lines updating her beloved former teacher, Miss Sullivan. Cuyper reported that she "like[d] it very much" at her new place and inquired about the girls in the sewing room, asking Sullivan to give them her love. She reported that she did "quite a good deal of sewing out here" and was planning to make a dress that week; she added, "I am mighty glad I know how to sew."

Clearly close to her former teacher, Cuyper ended with "Wish I were with you in the sewing room, but I don't want to come back." "Back" in this case meant the Rome State Custodial Asylum for the Feeble-Minded, an institution established by state legislators in 1894 as the Oneida State Custodial Asylum for Unteachable Idiots and intended to permanently contain adults labeled as idiots, imbeciles, or feeble-minded at minimal cost, thereby protecting society from the "burden" and "menace" of feeble-mindedness.[1] Like hundreds of inmates at Rome, Cuyper had been paroled to live with her employer while earning full wages, room, and board as a domestic servant. After four years of labor, the superintendent, Charles Bernstein, discharged her in 1921. Just a few months later, she wrote once again, explaining that she was married and now had a one-year-old son. She asked two of her friends who remained in the asylum's colony system—a frequent precursor to the parole process—to write.[2]

The 1910s and 1920s marked one of the high points of the American eugenics movement: decades that witnessed the expansion of federal attempts to bar immigrants with a wide array of disabilities, growing state efforts to restrict marriages involving people labeled as "idiots, imbeciles, or feeble-minded," and the Supreme Court's upholding of state-sponsored compulsory sterilization in *Buck v. Bell*. Yet Julia Cuyper was far from the only inmate of the Rome asylum to be reintegrated into the wage workforce and mainstream society.[3]

In effect, Bernstein found a solution to the family capacity challenges that had so bedeviled Hervey Wilbur and that had helped lead to the emergence of large custodial asylums such as Rome. As had started to become the case at the New York State Asylum for Idiots in the 1870s—and as was always true at the New York State Custodial Asylum for Feeble-Minded Women at Newark—most inmates at the Rome asylum came from a combination of disrupted families, impoverished and wage-dependent urban households, or poorhouses or orphan asylums. Bernstein's colony system and his practice of placing people such as Julia Cuyper with individual employers, however, created a method of easing their transitions into the wage labor force even when they lacked relatives to aid that transition. Indeed, the colonies provided social services that, in some ways, resembled the group homes and community living programs that began to emerge in the 1970s.

Given that, by this time, "feeble-minded" had become synonymous with the inability to function in mainstream society, let alone support oneself, Bernstein's colony and parole system constituted a striking, if temporary, achievement. His system rested on an astute analysis of the labor market and a shrewd assessment of the limited funding available from state lawmakers, as well as what could only be described as an obsession with the moral and practical benefits of productivity. He recognized that the job market itself allowed for a spectrum of ability and that individual employers could, to a degree, substitute for absent relatives. And in effect, he returned to the types of work long embedded in family economies and taught to pupils at idiot asylums and inmates of institutions for the feeble-minded: domestic service and non-mechanized farm labor.

While Bernstein's fellow superintendents initially expressed horror at the thought of releasing feeble-minded girls into mainstream society, they soon realized that a colony and parole system could help to alleviate perennial funding challenges and the relentless pressure for new admissions. By the late 1920s, almost every institution for the feeble-minded would adopt elements of Bernstein's system.

An Evolution

When Charles Bernstein first arrived at the Rome State Custodial Asylum for Unteachable Idiots at age twenty-three in 1895, he hardly seemed likely to challenge the very rationale behind custodial care for "the feeble-minded." Although the young medical intern and assistant superintendent never adhered to the harshest eugenic views expressed by some of his colleagues, early on he was deeply skeptical of the idea of releasing any inmates. The reasons Bernstein's views evolved remain less than fully clear, but in part, he simply became more familiar with his charges and their capabilities. Ever the astute politician, Bernstein also recognized that an asylum for "unteachable" inmates would receive minimal funding and offer little in the way of professional stature. His own personal experiences with disability may have also played a role.

Orphaned at nine, Bernstein was raised in rural New York by his maternal uncle, Madison Young—an experience that shaped his outlook and which undoubtedly contributed to his passionate belief in the power of environments to shape individuals' destinies. A local schoolmaster, Young proved to be a "severe disciplinarian" to the boy and his two older siblings. Bernstein said little to colleagues about his childhood, but one noted at his memorial that his uncle's abuse "developed a feeling of injustice in the nephew."[4] Later in life, Bernstein reflected, "If ever I have the care of children I shall be fair to them and let kindness rule my acts."[5] Perhaps paradoxically, given that he later ran a custodial asylum, Bernstein's own disability of severe eczema eventually provided a means for escaping his uncle's abuse. The family's physician, Dr. Alfredo Guffin, had long been fond of the boy and eventually took him to Albany City Hospital, fifty-five miles away, in an attempt to find a viable treatment. Bernstein never returned to his uncle's house. Instead, he lived with the physician, helping around the house and accompanying him on house calls. Inspired by Guffin's example, Bernstein entered medical school and also spent one year studying law prior to arriving at the Rome State Custodial Asylum for Unteachable Idiots. Despite Guffin's efforts, however, Bernstein's eczema never disappeared; he lived with it his entire life.[6]

Once at Rome, the young assistant superintendent demonstrated his fervent belief in the moral benefits of work. Soon after starting his duties at the asylum in 1895, he began to press the founding superintendent, John Fitzgerald, to expand the institution's vocational programs. Bernstein argued that not only would such training help defray the perpetually ill-funded asylum's costs, but it would also help occupy inmates living in a bleak and run-down facility. Fitzgerald proved amenable. By 1900, the 43 percent of inmates who were working defrayed nearly one-fifth of the total cost of maintenance by raising produce on the asylum's farm. Inmates also graded roads and paths at one-third the cost of contract labor, harvested most of the ice supply, made nearly 6,000 articles of clothing, and repaired over 18,000 items of clothing.[7] That same year, Fitzgerald explicitly defined inmates' labor in shrewdly political terms as "compensation for [the state's] generous contributions for their support."[8]

After Bernstein replaced Fitzgerald as superintendent in 1903, he expanded inmate labor programs even further, requiring that all "able-bodied inmates"

Superintendent of the Rome State Custodial Asylum Charles Bernstein from *Hello Doctor: A Brief Biography of Charles Bernstein* by James G. Riggs, 1936.

and most "cripples" at Rome work. By 1904, female inmates at the asylum provided much of the labor force in the dining rooms and kitchens and on the wards. They also manufactured all of the clothing except "heavy knit underwear and 'dress-up suits' for men, and this without employing any additional citizen labor in connection, with occasional assistance from attendants": more than 8,000 items of clothing all told. Although the asylum's population had increased by 10 percent in just one year, Bernstein managed to reduce clothing costs by 15 percent by using inmate labor.[9] Male inmates laboring on farms defrayed nearly 20 percent of the asylum's total costs, while others built an artificial lake to produce ice, painted the buildings and roofs, excavated cellars and foundations for new buildings, and repaired shoes, among other "remunerative labor ... directly profitable to the State." Those not yet capable of work attended daily classes aimed at making them more able to care for themselves, and thereby less burdensome.[10] And, as mentioned in chapter 2, Bernstein mandated that inmates wear clothes indicating their level of productivity and allowed them to obtain new clothing only by working or attending vocational training or self-care classes.[11]

Bernstein, moreover, recognized the political challenges inherent in asking legislators to fund an asylum for "unteachable" inmates. Accordingly, he adopted two distinct strategies to portray his charges as more capable, less dependent, and therefore worthy of additional investment. Like many of his counterparts, he sought to curry favor with lawmakers by reducing the asylum's cost to the state. Charities officials closely monitored the yearly costs of each state institution, and Bernstein delivered. As Rome's population rose to his goal of 1,100 by 1907, the asylum's per capita maintenance dropped to $139.49 per inmate, lower than nearly any other state institution.[12]

In addition, Bernstein fought to shift legislators' perceptions of his inmates from idle subjects of chronic care to capable workers. Immediately after replacing Fitzgerald as superintendent, he began trying to remove "unteachable idiots" from the asylum's name as an "unwarranted stigma." Reflecting his environmentalist beliefs, Bernstein argued in the 1903 annual report that less than 1 percent of inmates were "truly unteachable." He noted that many could read and write, and "over 50 per cent of them have been taught to be useful." Complaining that "the interests of the asylum are jeopardized by the idea existing among many people that only unteachables are cared for here," he lamented, "In the matter of supplies, the idea prevail[s] that the smallest variety possible in diet and clothing is sufficient for unteachables, who must necessarily live like animals."[13]

Bernstein argued that even the least capable inmates needed and deserved more than food, clothing, and housing. Indeed, that same year he lambasted a trustee of the Syracuse State Institution for Feeble-Minded Children (the former New York State Asylum for Idiots, renamed in 1891) after the man grumbled at a professional conference about the large number of custodial cases at the educationally oriented Syracuse institution, claiming that such children could never benefit from its programs. An infuriated Bernstein replied: "Anyone who has spent any time with the custodial class of feeble-minded and observed them closely would soon be impressed with the fact that housing, clothing, and feeding them, and that alone, was surely a shortsighted policy, as, under such treatment, they are bound to grow more dull, stupid, destructive, filthy or violent (this depending on treatment) and require a constantly increasing amount of personal attention from the attendants."[14]

Yet early on in his career, Bernstein held strikingly harsh views of his charges—views characteristic of eugenicist counterparts who headed other state institutions for the feeble-minded. At the national conference of the American Association of Institutions for the Feeble-Minded in 1905, he stated, "I firmly believe that no feeble-minded person should be taught to read and write, because I know some of the results of that teaching." He continued, "They find what they are losing in the world and are constantly hankering after it, and it makes them miserable ... and they oftentimes run away."[15] Warning that educated inmates would also make their parents unhappy if they came to visit, he particularly emphasized the dangers inherent in teaching "custodial cases" to read.

Bernstein likewise had little regard for inmates' families. At the 1909 superintendents' conference, for instance, Bernstein related the story of "a rather peculiar accident ... an especially funny one." The prior year, he explained, the asylum had received a shipment of boys from New York City, only half of whom could say their own names; the attendant who traveled with them, moreover, knew none of the boys. His staff nevertheless eventually identified all of the new inmates. But soon thereafter, "a fellow who had red hair and blue eyes died." When they notified the mother to come claim his body, she said, "That is never my boy, my boy had black hair and black eyes." She looked all through the institution but could not find her son. The asylum sent the boy's remains to New York City, where charity officials convinced her that "living up here in the country his hair and eyes had bleached out—and she buried him."[16]

And like many of his colleagues, Bernstein refused to discharge inmates except by court order, arguing that releasing the "feeble-minded" was tantamount to courting disaster. In 1907, he justified this policy as ensuring "the protection of society in general and for the economic interest of the State, as well as for the protection of the individual." Suggesting that, freed from custodial care, female inmates, in particular, were "sure to drift into immorality and crime," he claimed that within a short time families invariably asked to return the inmate to the institution.[17]

But over time, Bernstein's harsh views began to soften; he even began to experiment in 1909 with paroling a few inmates to family members and trusted colleagues, as well as expanding his roster of so-called farm colonies. The asylum's board proved willing, but within a few months the state's attorney general had shut down the experimental program on the grounds that the asylum "had no right to parole inmates." In part, state officials cited concerns over the costs of paroling inmates whose "friends" could not cover their travel expenses. Bernstein played hardball, arguing that a parole system would likely save the state money. He noted, "We very frequently have requests for both boys and girls to act as helpers in families, especially for boys on farms.... It would seem that a legal system of parole or placing out of such cases might well be tried under proper supervision, and thus to a like extent relieve the overcrowded condition of the asylum, or make room for additional needy cases."[18] He estimated that as much as 10 percent of the populations of male and female inmates could benefit. After two years of agitating, Bernstein won permission from the attorney general and the state legislature to parole and discharge inmates, with the caveat that the asylum could no longer retain inmates whose families were not indigent.[19]

Bernstein never explained why his views of his charges mellowed over time, but three factors seem crucial. First, he had never been a strong advocate of eugenics. In fact, in his annual report for 1913—reprinted in the State Board of Charities report and likely sent to other superintendents—he openly attacked the eugenics movement, arguing that the sociologists and psychologists who led the movement had "little or no insight into the pathological conditions underlying many of these defects." Bernstein continued, "On reflection, the thought occurs, does any one more inherit mental and nervous peculiarities and state of mind or physical attitudes than they do their various physical malformation[s] and religious or political beliefs? Those who care for small children well know what apt students or rather mimics they are."[20] In effect, he was arguing that one's environment had far more impact than one's heredity. Second, Bernstein's increasing familiarity with his charges—namely, his pragmatic knowledge of his inmates—worked in tandem with his environmentalist tendencies. He began to argue that some inmates had temporarily become feeble-minded through poor nutrition, disease, neglect, or masturbation. If placed in the proper environment, he contended, they could be reeducated and "saved to society as producers."[21] Finally, like other superintendents of institutions for feeble-minded people, he faced relentless pressure for more admissions from parents and county officials, as well as for cost-cutting from state officials.[22]

In addition, Bernstein was a canny political operator who had already discovered a means for not only opening beds but also making himself popular with legislators: farm colonies. Superintendents of idiot asylums, including Hervey Wilbur and the heads of the Illinois and Massachusetts asylums, had first begun to establish such programs in the 1880s. Generally, a small group of inmates lived near the asylum on a farm and grew produce or raised dairy cattle and chickens; whatever they produced fed inmates and employees at the asylum. The Illinois Institution for Feeble-Minded Children, for instance, established a 400-acre colony in 1887 that housed a farmer, milkman, maid-of-all-work, and twenty male inmates. Institutional farms such as these were also common in insane asylums, prisons, and, at times, poorhouses from the mid-nineteenth century on. Bernstein began pressing for a farm colony system starting in 1904, when he asked for a legislative appropriation of $45,000 to purchase seven to nine farms with 1,000 acres of land to house one hundred males.[23]

As usual for a superintendent later known for regularly "working over" the legislature, Bernstein made a hard sell.[24] He promised that farm colonies could produce all of the asylum's vegetables and butter and all of the feed for pigs, cattle, and horses, and also supply extra vegetables that could be canned and sold to cover provisions that could not be self-produced, such as sugar and condiments. In sum, Bernstein predicted that the colonies could cover 68 percent of the cost of all provisions for the entire asylum. He added that the program would also enable the institution to "give profitable employment to a much larger number of inmates than we are able to at the present time. In this way we are very sure we will be able to reduce to a considerable extent our present direct per capita cost of maintenance to the State. The farm life will also be decidedly beneficial to the brighter class of boys."[25] By 1905, Bernstein had received $10,000 to buy 150 acres of land and employ sixteen boys under the supervision of a farmer and his wife.[26] This initial appropriation did not satisfy him—by 1906, he was contending that 10 percent of male inmates could work on farm colonies and that they could be made "almost, if not wholly self-supporting in such colonies."[27] As it turned out, the colonies provided significant savings for the asylum as a whole. Not only did lawmakers have to fund fewer new wards, but in 1910, for example, every dollar spent on maintaining and renting property for colonies returned two dollars in produce, meat, and dairy products.[28]

Releasing Feeble-Minded Girls

Bernstein's colonies for female inmates, proved even more visionary but also provoked far more hostility from his colleagues. In 1914, at the height of the eugenics movement and its hysteria over the so-called burden and menace of the feeble-minded, he took the stunning step of establishing a "working girls' colony" in downtown Rome. Within three years, Bernstein had founded four more colonies for female inmates. In so doing, Bernstein effectively launched a frontal attack on one of the cornerstones of eugenics: the link between feeble-minded women and hereditary public dependency. Leading eugenicist and superintendent of the Massachusetts School for the Feeble-Minded Walter E. Fernald, for instance, proclaimed in 1912: "The high-grade female imbecile group is the most dangerous class . . . . They are never able to support themselves." He continued, "Their numerous progeny usually become public charges as diseased or neglected children, imbeciles, epileptics, Juvenile delinquents or later on as adult paupers or criminals."[29] Yet after a suitable period of observation, Bernstein planned to parole and then discharge colony residents. And in fact, by using the colonies to create early proxies for group homes, he created a solution for the lack of family capacity that had so frustrated Hervey Wilbur at the New York State Asylum for Idiots and that had led to the emergence of vast custodial asylums such as Rome.

Bernstein never explained the origins of his "working girls' colonies," and in many ways his program was so innovative that it is hard to identify a clear model. Some distant precursors existed, nonetheless. Perhaps the closest antecedent was the centuries-old colony in Geel, Belgium, in which those deemed "insane" lived with families in the town and interacted with community members. This system arose in the thirteenth century and was well known in the Atlantic world during the nineteenth and early twentieth centuries. In fact, Vincent van Gogh's family considered sending him there to recover.[30] In addition, Bernstein was likely inspired by the prison parole systems that New York State pioneered in the 1870s and which had become widely accepted by the 1910s. Around the same time, state mental asylums in both New York and Massachusetts began experimenting with parole programs. Finally, Bernstein undoubtedly knew of the efforts made by British teachers of "special" or "ungraded classes"—what was later termed "special education"—to integrate their pupils into the mainstream workforce. Such classes had originated in the 1890s, and by 1903 a vigorous transatlantic debate had emerged over whether graduates could become self-supporting.[31] Regardless of the sources of Bernstein's inspiration, through his colony and parole program he created a distinctive model of how people with cognitive—and sometimes physical—impairments could be integrated into the mainstream wage labor force.

Bernstein established his first working girls' colony in the city of Rome proper. Under the supervision of a house mother—his sister-in-law, social worker Inez F. Stebbins—approximately twenty girls lived in the house while doing sewing and domestic work except for "special cooking" by the day, week, or month "at the rate of fifty cents per day and thirty cents per half day."[32] Bernstein soon permitted those deemed most trustworthy—about half of the colony's residents—to board at the house where they worked, but pressed them to return to the colony for social events planned by the residents themselves, night school, and supervised excursions to movies and other public events. Other girls worked only a few days a week away from the colony or, in the case of those deemed in need of more supervision, sewed and did hand laundry at the house itself.[33] Within a year, the girls' colony housed sixty-seven women, and by 1916, Bernstein had added a site in Rome; these were soon followed by a domestic servant colony on Staten Island and two knitting mill colonies in Oriskany Falls, not far from the asylum itself. By 1919, Rome had eleven farm colonies for 220 male residents and seven urban colonies with 172 female residents.[34] The colonies housed nearly 20 percent of the asylum's population. But Bernstein did not stop there; he added forestry colonies in the Adirondack Mountains, more colonies for women, and one urban labor colony for men.[35] In addition, he began sending the "most promising women," as well as men trained as farm laborers, to communities all across the state.

Bernstein and Stebbins established a gradual progression from asylum to colony to parole—or sometimes from the asylum to parole directly—a process that allowed inmates to gain the vocational, social, and practical skills necessary to live independently. Reflecting their shared belief in the influence of a good environment, Bernstein "decided that colony officials should know nothing definitely of the girl's past history, giving each girl the best chance possible to bury her past if she were so disposed."[36] Often, inmates spent years honing their skills and proving their reliability in the asylum or colonies before winning a chance to try parole. Typically, Bernstein first had inmates complete short trials in colonies; some progressed to regular colony life, then began living at their workplaces and returning to the colony for social events, and finally were discharged.

Bettina McMann's experiences exemplified inmates' often halting progress through the colony, parole, and discharge system, as well as the fact that some "high-grade" inmates experienced real community at the asylum. She began by working for board member James Douglass in the nearby town of Oriskany Falls in early 1914. After a monthlong trial, she returned to the asylum, as did many inmates who entered the colony and parole system—a few for "social offenses" such as flirting, others for medical treatment, and some "because their services were worth more to the institution than they were getting outside,—namely $3.50 a week."[37] McMann remained at the institution throughout 1915 and most of 1916. Once back at the asylum, she labored in the sewing room, which she disliked; nevertheless, the editors of the *Custodial Herald* said that "'actions speak louder than words' in this case. She makes great headway."[38] In fall 1916, she finally gained parole as a domestic worker in Fort Plain and later in Gloversville. Even after being discharged and marrying, McMann maintained contact with friends on the staff and among the inmates. In 1927, she reported that her son was almost seven and said, "My greatest pleasure is writing to you all at the School as I don't think I could ever forget the place and the friends who dwell within. How often I wish I could come back for a couple of days just to pay a little tribute to you all."[39]

On the whole, the colonies fulfilled Bernstein's grandiose financial promises to legislators, at least until the start of the Great Depression. During the

Rome colony's first year, for instance, the seventy-seven "girls" who had worked at the colony earned nearly $3,300, more than double the amount necessary to cover the costs of rent, furniture, provisions, salary of matron, material for clothing, utilities, transportation, and entertainments. Each resident received twenty-five cents of spending money per week, as well as fifty cents to deposit in their savings account.[40] A typical 1913 contract for a paroled farm laborer, in turn, paid $10 per month for ten months, plus room and board.[41]

Bernstein predicted, furthermore, that up to 40 percent of the Rome asylum's inmates could eventually join the colony and parole program. His numbers were not far off. By 1921, Rome's nearly two dozen colonies housed over 700 inmates, or a third of the entire institution's population; 180 of the 339 girls in the colonies "were entirely self-supporting, with savings to the amount of $4,672 ... to the credit of 122 girls." Bernstein proudly reported that the "state is saved the annual maintenance cost of $250 to $300 per inmate for over 700 patients, totaling more than $200,000 annual saving," as well as the roughly $500,000 it would cost to house inmates at the home institution.[42] He crowed about his parolees' successes, contending, "The very marked improvement occurring in these parole cases [in colonies] is most favorably commented on by all who come in contact with such cases and there is no doubt but that it is just these normal experiences in life which these cases lacked in their earlier environment and the absence in their lives during their earlier habit forming period of these normal home and social experiences was the real cause of their previous misfit or failure."[43] And if inmates did well, as Prudence Tedesco did, they might eventually earn discharge. Several years after being discharged in 1921, the now-married woman wrote to Bernstein, opening with "I wish to thank you for my freedom."[44]

Fitting Workers to the Job

Why was the colony—and the dozen other girls' colonies that followed—so successful economically? After all, for many people in the 1910s, the inability to "get along in the regular world" was the very definition of feeble-mindedness. Bernstein's genius lay in his analysis of the labor market. He realized that the job market itself called for a spectrum of ability, much like that of his charges. In addition, Bernstein targeted two economic sectors that suffered from chronic labor shortages: domestic work and nonmechanized farm labor.

Indeed, Bernstein seems to have been inspired to establish the colony and parole program partly because of the dozens of requests he received each year from farmers and wealthy or middle-class families in need of help all across the state, even prior to the labor shortage wrought by the United States' entrance into the Great War in 1917. He explained in 1915, "We are able to assist the community by supplying the two kinds of labor, for which there is a great demand and a most scanty supply—namely, farm help and domestic service."[45] Crucially, both sectors were also nonunionized, which enabled him to largely but not entirely avoid critiques from other workers.[46]

Moreover, the shift from "common hand labor" to mechanized work, he suggested, had left few viable work options for "morons" and "borderline" cases: those whom eugenicists deemed the most able of the "feeble-minded." No longer could they sustain themselves by their own labors without guidance. Yet if placed in the proper work situation, not only would such people no longer appear to be "social failures or misfits" but they could also be "save[d] to something better than lives of institutional servitude."[47]

Employers eagerly sought to hire colony workers, suggesting that employers, too, recognized that not every job required the same level of ability. Indeed, the colony workers were so popular that Bernstein received far more requests than he could fill—from a request for a servants' colony in Clayville, New York, to a query for millworkers in Gloversville. A trial servant colony on Staten Island was so successful that the Women's City Club sought to make it a permanent institution based out of New York City's poorhouse on Randall's Island. The *New York Times* reported, "Everyone is pleased with the idea of its [the colony] being taken over by the city at Randall's Island except the Staten Island women, who see themselves again without household helpers."[48] The knitting mill colony in Gloversville—one of two established in the town—encountered more hostility. Bernstein's assistant Ward Millias recalled, "Organized labor was not entirely happy over the arrangement, but accepted it because local labor supply was insufficient to keep the mill operating to capacity. On a production basis our girls were found to be 75 per cent efficient as compared to the usual run of labor."[49]

Bernstein was not only an economic pioneer but also a social pioneer. His colonies provided social services not unlike the group homes and community living programs that haltingly began to emerge in the 1970s: advice on how to handle relations with employers and tutoring in money management, letter-writing, even reading, and other skills crucial to life outside institutions.[50] He explained in 1916: "These girls are not markedly defective, but are girls who have been orphans or have never known a normal home, and when later in life they have gone out into the world they have been unable to get along because of lack of proper home training and normal worldly experience."[51]

Equally critically, the colonies also provided their residents—as well as those living with an employer nearby—with a community, complete with holiday celebrations and game nights. Bernstein and parole director Inez Stebbins sought to replace at least some of the "fun" of the institution through the colonies.

This community-building aspect served as one of Bernstein's prime motivations for creating the colony system in the first place. When he first began paroling inmates in the early 1910s, he had placed them individually. Many got homesick; some "begged to be allowed to return to the institution, or actually did return of their own accord."[52] Simply put, parolees missed the institution—their friends, the band and orchestra, social dances, and so on. Matilda Connor, one of the few African Americans at the institution, may have been one of those who preferred the community of the asylum. She worked as a servant for the Douglasses in Oriskany Falls during 1913; in fact, she was one of the first female inmates to be paroled to an individual employer. Despite receiving praise for her work ethic and musical talents in nearly every issue of the *Rome Custodial Herald*, Connor remained at the asylum throughout the 1910s—perhaps by choice. Instead, she ran the "girls' sewing room," learned to play the viola for the institution's orchestra, and became well known as the ever-reliable "telephone girl" for the asylum.[53]

As Connor's story suggests, some inmates built communities within the asylum—connections they maintained with "good old RSCA" even long after departing. Former inmates regularly visited the asylum for dances and other social events and to visit friends among the staff and inmates alike. In turn, staff members frequently called on discharged individuals while traveling on vacation or asylum business. But perhaps most compellingly, scores of former inmates wrote asylum staff and current inmates to report their successes outside the asylum and, sometimes, their travails, as well as to convey their genuine fondness for the asylum's staff. Amanda Cahn, for instance, opened her March 1917 letter to former teacher Miss Samson with "Was glad to hear from you and to know that you are alive still and breathing. I am getting along O.K. and like my place very much." Cahn continued, "When you come to Utica just let me know and we will have some time. Who went with you to the movies [sic] I wish I had been there to have gone with you." In closing, she wrote, "I am always glad to hear from you, so write when you can . . . from your little girl, Amanda Cahn."[54]

The timing of Bernstein's colony and parole program—it came at a peak in the American eugenics movement—made it all the more striking. His fellow superintendents were, by and large, fervent eugenicists who advocated sterilizing inmates and adamantly opposed discharging any of their charges. Dr. Albert E. Carroll, the head of the School for Feeble-Minded Youth in Fort Wayne, Indiana, declared at the national superintendents' meeting in 1906, for instance: "I have half a dozen cases now that I would like to dispose of, but I am just as sure that if they leave our institution they will enter some other, as I am of anything.... We thought of turning those girls out to become servants in private families [but] there was not one of those girls that did not have a bad family history." Ultimately, Carroll canceled the entire "domestic class," declaring that he had no right to experiment by releasing those students.[55]

Other superintendents believed that people labeled as feeble-minded could not compete on the mainstream labor market. George Knight of the Connecticut Training School for the Feeble-Minded predicted that, as a class, inmates' labor "would command absolutely nothing if brought into competition with even the most unskilled labor of persons of normal mind."[56] Dr. A. C. Rogers of the Minnesota School for the Feeble-Minded, in turn, focused more on his fears about inmates' abilities to manage life outside the institution. He reported that even the "boys" had "made absolute failures in trying to work outside." He warned, "They get into bad society, form bad habits, get in drinking, and lose their positions that they may have had for a while, especially when the hard times come." Others, such as Boston-based special class teacher Ada Fitts, complained that their former students bounced from job to job. She reported that one had held eighteen positions over two years, none for longer than three months and one for a single day.[57]

During the first few years of Bernstein's colony and parole program, the reactions of his fellow superintendents and charity reformers ranged from nonresponse to outright hostility. He first outlined his plans to provide a comprehensive system of state care for "the feeble-minded" in 1914 at the annual meeting of the American Association for the Study of the Feeble-Minded. Arguing that farm colonies on "abandoned or undeveloped farms" in central New York could house 500 to 1,000 inmates and produce farm commodities for charitable institutions at a "great savings to the state," Bernstein further proposed employing residents as farm laborers in the community. He noted that not only would the colonies have an "excess of labor above that required" but also that "the surrounding farmers ... are unable to secure labor to assist them in their farm work." Attendants, proposed Bernstein, could accompany the inmates to each farm. The minutes recorded dead silence after his talk; the members then proceeded to discuss every other paper presented during that particular session, ignoring Bernstein's.[58]

Charity officials responded rather more directly. Between 1911 and 1915, the New York State Charities Aid Association and the State Board of Charities' Standing Committee on Idiots and the Feeble-Minded issued three different reports aimed at demonstrating the foolhardiness of Bernstein's colony and parole program; the Children's Aid Society published a fourth report specifically about inmates discharged from Rome to Erie County a few years later. Hundreds of pages long, these reports suggested that Bernstein lacked the ability to accurately classify inmates as idiots, imbeciles, morons, or borderlines; traced their "poor heredity"; and argued that most inmates discharged were idle, immoral, and violent.[59]

Bernstein's astute political skills and attention to the dynamics of state funding, however, eventually enabled him to sell his plans to lawmakers. According to disability rights activist Gunner Dybwad, Bernstein once got "the attention of New York state legislators by placing women from colonies . . . in the lobby of a prominent Albany hotel where legislators lived during legislative sessions. After legislators noticed these *normal* women for several days, he announced to the legislators that the women were inmates at Rome." Bernstein also recognized that while the State Board of Charities might be filled with advocates of eugenics, legislators had more interest in dollars and cents. His colony and parole program provided a means for opening beds and reducing costs at a time of constant pressure for admissions and spiraling expenses. He stressed that the colonies quickly became self-supporting and emphasized that they "provided comparatively cheap custody and supervision."[60]

He also had fortuitous timing. By 1917, Just a few years after Bernstein had established his colony and parole program, eugenicists had labeled so many people as feeble-minded—including 47 percent of army recruits, infamously—that lawmakers and charity officials began questioning whether it was even possible to institutionalize everyone labeled as "feeble-minded." Joseph P. Byers of the Pennsylvania Committee on Provision for the Feeble-Minded observed, for instance, "We know that in the state having the greatest number of feeble-minded under public care in proportion to the general population, Massachusetts, the ratio is but one to 1,245 on the basis of the 1910 census."[61]

Consequently, Bernstein's colony and parole program therefore promised to address a pressing concern of superintendents and social welfare officials alike. When he once again presented a report about his colony program at the annual meeting of the American Association for the Study of the Feeble-Minded in mid-1917, his "experiments" were greeted with "wonderment" and acclaim.[62] Dr. C. S. Little of Letchworth Village in New York—a custodial state institution established near New York City in 1911—called the colony

Colony "girls" in front of their house, Syracuse State School for Mental Defectives, ca. 1920s–1930s. Courtesy of the New York State Museum.

and parole program "a bully good thing" and, acknowledging the massive amount of work required, claimed that nobody else "could do it but Bernstein, he has more energy than any six men I have ever known."[63] E. J. Emerick, the superintendent of the Ohio School for the Feeble-Minded, praised in turn the ways that Bernstein's program drew on the fact that the job market allowed for a spectrum of ability: "The facts are, we need different degrees of mental level in order to carry on successfully the business of the world." He continued, "A man who has not the mental capacity for a bricklayer may make a very good hodcarrier and be perfectly happy and contented with his work, and it is just as essential to have hodcarriers as it is to have bricklayers, and the latter probably would not have been contented to have done the work of the former."[64] Perhaps even more valuable was the support offered by Massachusetts superintendent Walter Fernald, a nationally prominent eugenicist who had fervently opposed discharging inmates. In 1919, Fernald concluded a study of 646 former inmates, finding that less than half discharged had turned to public relief or run into legal difficulties. He then declared that "the survey shows that there are bad defectives and good defectives."[65]

The so-called Rome plan soon spread nationwide. Virginia's, Michigan's, and Pennsylvania's commissions on the feeble-minded announced plans to establish similar systems, and observers from all over the country—and even abroad—visited Rome to inspect the colonies and study the parole program. By the mid-1920s, most other state institutions for the feeble-minded had adopted versions of Bernstein's system, with superintendents viewing it as a way to open more beds. Massachusetts's Waverly School for the Feeble-Minded even began paroling a few men to Morgan Memorial Goodwill Industries in Boston for that very reason.[66]

The Impact of the Colony System

While Bernstein's program was clearly successful politically and economically, how should one evaluate its impact on the thousands of inmates who traveled through the colonies and parole programs? For some, the system amounted to a true second chance, or even a first chance, to transition to life outside an institution and, in some cases, connect with relatives whom they barely knew. Others managed to live for a few years in mainstream society before returning to Rome. But the majority of inmates at the asylum never left; many died of disease endemic to crowded institutions within a few years or even within a few months.[67]

By any measure, Luke Tangemann's early life took a dramatic series of turns; nevertheless, his story of parole likely constitutes one of the most dramatic of all inmates'. He arrived at Rome in 1911 or 1912, having lost both feet to frostbite. As he told a reporter from the *Washington Post* in 1906, "It was last February, and a cold day too, when [my stepmother] tied me outdoors to a tree. I hadn't done nothin' to get such punishment for." His father and stepmother then abandoned him at a hospital in northern New York; he never heard from them again. After he spent several years in the county orphanage, officials sent Tangemann to Rome.[68] Once he arrived, Bernstein purchased two prosthetic feet for the boy, and Tangemann began learning how to farm and to cane chairs, among other tasks. He then became a celebrated head of the chair-caning, mattress, and mat-making workshops. After running the workshops for several years, Bernstein paroled Tangemann in October 1914 to the latter's maternal uncle as a farm laborer; he worked on his uncle's farm and other farms nearby and caned chairs in the off-season. By 1930, he had married, had a son and a young daughter, and had become a galvanizer in the steels mills in Cortland County. By the time he died in the late 1960s, Tangemann had several grandchildren and at least one great-grandson, who was named for him.[69]

Some individuals attended and graduated from high school while living in the colonies, while others, such as Tina Hutmacher, attended the asylum's nurse preparation program and began working independently. After spending several years working at the Syracuse girls' colony, where—as a fellow resident reported, she "ha[d] charge of the dining room and [house mother] Mrs. D. likes her work very much"—Hutmacher went through a yearlong training course in nursing at the asylum, then started serving as both a dental and a private nurse. She cared for children with diphtheria and measles, as well as for a woman with quinsy (abscesses in the throat), among others, earning as much as $25 a week during the 1920s.[70]

Other inmates gained their freedom but never managed to become fully self-supporting, relying on family members who reestablished the capacity to support and make use of them. After several years in various colonies, Lola Wegener, for example, was paroled home to her parents in northern New York in 1921 at age twenty-six. She soon sent a photo so that the asylum staff could "see what a nice home I have."[71] Several years later, she wrote again with an update: "I am always doing something to keep busy. . . . I did the raking with a little pony and [my father] gave me $12.00 for doing that. I do my mother's washing and ironing and she gives me $1.50 for the work. I am starting a bank account with the money I am earning and besides I buy all my clothing. . . . I try to live a good life and go to church with my people every Sunday." She proudly reported that she had a "white silk poodle that weighs five pounds." Wegener never lived independently, but she was thrilled to have the opportunity to reside at home.[72]

Finally, many inmates managed to live in colonies for a few years outside the asylum, but eventually returned and spent the rest of their lives in the institution. Herschel Obermeyer, for instance, was one of three deaf sons born to Russian and Romanian Jewish immigrants during the 1890s. After briefly attending Syracuse State Institution for Feeble-Minded Children as well as schools for deaf children in Rochester and New York City, he arrived at the Rome asylum in the 1910s, as did his older brother Barny; a third brother worked as an officer at the Rochester School for the Deaf. After mastering sewing, Obermeyer was given the opportunity to learn how to farm at the Stook Farm colony. He remained there for two years, but for unknown reasons, he was sent back to the main institution in 1918, where he began serving as a press-feeder in the printing shop. A few years letter, he sent Charles Bernstein a letter from the Institute for Male Defective Delinquents at Napanoch, pleading, "Would you please send me a nice book to read. I like to read." He remained at that institution for two years but was then returned to the Rome

Interior view of ward for "low-grade" and "crippled" children, Rome State Custodial Asylum, ca. 1910–1914. Courtesy of the New York State Archives.

asylum, where he rejoined the printers' corps. Both brothers resided at the Rome asylum in 1930 and presumably remained for the rest of their lives; Barny died at the renamed Rome Developmental Center in the 1980s.[73]

The Great Depression and, to a lesser degree, World War II brought an end to Bernstein's colonies. By the mid-1930s, few of the colonies had enough demand from employers to do more than provide housing outside the asylum. Discharged inmates wrote to the *Herald*, reporting that they were struggling to find work. And, paradoxically, workers' successful campaign for the eight-hour day during the New Deal left Bernstein short-handed at the asylum. Consequently, he turned for assistance to the most capable inmates—the ones who previously would have been sent to colonies or paroled outright. By the time of Bernstein's death in 1942, the Rome State School had become one of the largest institutions in the country, housing 3,950 inmates.[74]

Nevertheless, Bernstein's program offered a striking model for how to integrate people labeled as "feeble-minded" and who lacked families into the wage workforce and the broader society. Facing constant pressure for new admissions, perennially short on funding, and opposed to eugenic "solutions" such as sterilization, he came to realize that the job market itself allowed for a spectrum of ability. Equally important, he recognized that individual employers and "colonies" could substitute somewhat for absent relatives. And by targeting economic sectors with frequent labor shortages—domestic work and farm labor—he integrated hundreds of feeble-minded inmates into mainstream society, many permanently. In effect, Bernstein created forms of employment out of the same types of labor that had been embedded in family economies in the nineteenth century and that had long been taught to pupils in idiot asylums and inmates of institutions for the feeble-minded.

Bernstein's preferred forms of labor, however, reflected the jobs of the old economy, not those of the increasingly mechanized economy of the early twentieth century. As Henry Ford would show at Ford Motor Company, the same approach of *fitting* people to particular positions could be used in heavily mechanized factories to employ people with a wide array of disabilities—predominantly but not entirely acquired physical and sensory impairments, as well as chronic illnesses—and most of whom had long lived and worked regardless of their bodily status. But, like Bernstein, Ford would prove a conspicuous exception.

CHAPTER FOUR

We Do Not Prefer Cripples, but They Can Earn Full Wages

Mechanization, Efficiency, and the Quest for Interchangeable Workers, 1880s–1920s

During the first two decades of the twentieth century, Ford Motor Company hired thousands of workers with impairments that ranged from dual-arm amputations and total blindness to epilepsy and tuberculosis.¹ These workers received full pay and could not be fired except with the explicit approval of the head of the Employment Office. By 1919, over 9,000 of the 33,000 total Ford employees—nearly a third—were "actual cripples or men suffering with some ailment or disease or otherwise physically below par, including many men between 70 and 80 years old."² But as the *New York Times* reported in 1927, few other firms at this time willingly hired people with physical or sensory disabilities or chronic illnesses. Summarizing a report from the Sage Foundation, the article contended that "employers' prejudice against the engagement of handicapped persons is the chief contributing factor" preventing "handicapped men and women from being self-supporting." To quote the article's subhead, "Henry Ford [was] an exception."³

Much as Charles Bernstein had for "feeble-minded" people in farm labor and domestic service, Ford argued that if supervisors made proper use of mechanization and placed "handicapped" people in the correct jobs, workers with a wide array of disabilities could be as efficient and productive as their able-bodied counterparts, perhaps even more so. Few firms agreed. Starting in the late nineteenth century, employers had begun to assume that "disabled" people could not be efficient, productive workers. While companies sometimes kept on workers injured in their employ, albeit often in ill-paid positions, they increasingly refused to hire new applicants whose disabilities could be identified with medical examinations. In fact, as American workplaces became ever more mechanized, and as businesses introduced mass production techniques and welfare capitalist programs, employers began to demand workers with intact, fully functional bodies: namely, standardized workers who could themselves serve as interchangeable parts.

Employers' rejection of adults with permanent injuries—even minor impairments such as a missing finger—as too *disabled* to work represented a dramatic shift in traditional understandings of the impact of injuries and old age on productivity. During the nineteenth and early twentieth centuries, workers expected to be injured at some point, perhaps several times, in their working lives, although the dangers were not distributed equally across race and gender. Others simply "wore out." Over time, workers' toils left their bodies irretrievably altered, sometimes even consuming them. Consequently, workers moved up and down a spectrum of productivity during the course of their lives.

Within working-class communities and families, moreover, such injuries did not indicate unproductivity. Rather, what we often now term physical or sensory "impairments" or "disabilities," as well as "chronic illnesses," served as markers of poverty, if not class itself. Indeed, workers typically fought hard to retain their place in the labor force after receiving permanent injuries, although few managed to maintain the same occupational status or income as before acquiring a disability. They also remained integrated into their families and communities.

Nevertheless, the sharp division that employers and, to a lesser extent, labor unions began to draw between "productive" workers and people with a wide variety of disabilities at the turn of the twentieth century limited disabled people's access to paid work and, thereby, their ability to sustain themselves and their families. Traditionally the key to social standing in American public life, the ability to be self-supporting—and to be a male breadwinner—gradually slipped away from men and, to a lesser extent, women who suffered industrial accidents and diseases, as well as many people with congenital or childhood impairments. By excluding "disabled" workers from the wage labor market, employers helped to cast people with disabilities as unproductive citizens—even as disabled people continued working in other economic sectors, albeit not always for pay. Henry Ford, however, challenged the simple equation of disabled people with inefficiency, demonstrating that workers with a broad array of disabilities could in fact be productive in the increasingly mechanized economy of the twentieth century.

The Normal Costs of Working Life

Through at least the early 1920s—and longer in dangerous industries—disabling injuries were an expected, if feared, aspect of working-class life and, in particular, of poverty. During the mid- to late nineteenth century, for instance, railroaders' missing and crushed fingers signified experience, along with the good judgment and competence necessary to survive a train wreck. In fact, knowledgeable observers could spot brakemen by their missing fingers; few survived a career in railroading's most dangerous job without losing at least one digit.[4] This acceptance of high physical costs of work continued into the twentieth century, even as workplaces became ever larger and more mechanized. In 1922, the punch-press operator crew at Ford Motor Company's plant in Highland Park "lost . . . an average of sixteen fingers a month." Nearly thirty years later, a safety worker at Ford proudly recollected, "We kept reducing that figure until now, well, if we lose a finger, it's a calamity. In those days it was just a common occurrence; they expected it. It was considered part of the job."[5]

In fact, industrial injuries were so common during the late nineteenth and early twentieth centuries that some workers barely took note of their injuries, even serious ones.[6] The social reformer and investigator Crystal Eastman, for instance, found while serving during 1907 and 1908 as a researcher and author for the notable social investigation known as the Pittsburgh Survey that many workers saw their injuries and disabilities as just one of many expected misfortunes of life: "An old steel worker whom I questioned about his injuries answered, 'I never got hurt any to speak of.' After persistent inquiry, however, he recalled that he had once fractured his skull, that a few years later he had lost half a finger, and that only three years ago he was laid up for nine weeks with a crushed foot."[7] Eastman's colleague on the Pittsburgh Survey, John Fitch, encountered much the same phenomenon while researching his contribution to the study: *The Steel Workers*. Fitch interviewed a ladle man at a steel mill whose shoes had filled with molten steel after the stopper malfunctioned. Although "he could not turn over in bed without help for six weeks," the man had termed this a "minor" accident that "he seemed to think barely worth mentioning."[8]

Becoming disabled was often not traceable to a single accident, but rather to the ordinary process of "wearing out." This process clearly overlapped with aging, but also reflected the physical costs of heavy labor. Steelworkers, for instance, repeatedly told Fitch that they would not be able to work in the mills past the age of forty or fifty because of the strenuous work required of them. A furnace man reported that his eyes were "failing on account of the bright light of the furnace into which he has to look." Fitch noted, "He is 40 years old and his strength is failing; was at his best at 30."[9] In the late nineteenth century, many anthracite miners, in turn, "tried to retrace their steps on the job ladder" as their strength faded; once they could not sustain the workload of a skilled miner, they would become miner's helpers or laborers, and later breakers or slate pickers, at a considerable loss in income, of course.[10] Because adult miners could not earn enough to support their large families, their sons went to work at an early age as slate pickers or breaker boys. Consequently, adult miners' early exposure to coal dust made them much more likely to develop miner's asthma, increasing their family's dependence on children's wages and starting the cycle all over again.

Although the threat of work-induced accidents spared neither men nor women, the segregation of the labor force on the basis of gender exposed women and men to different rates and types of disabling injuries and illnesses.[11] Men's concentration in heavy industry ensured that they faced far higher rates of industrial accidents. In 1890, for instance, wage-earning men died from accidents at five times the rate of women; men also disproportionately suffered physical injuries such as lost or crushed limbs or the loss of sight in an eye.[12] During 1899 alone, one out of every twenty-seven railroad workers suffered an injury.[13]

Women, in contrast, encountered general debility in service work and occupational illnesses in light industrial work. Domestic servants reported that decades of service left them with "lower back problems, varicose veins, and, most common, ankle or foot problems," while laundry workers faced "swollen or ulcerated legs from the persistent damp" and pelvic problems from using foot-powered irons.[14] Gendered beliefs about women's suitability for certain types of work often left them disproportionately vulnerable to occupational diseases as well. Women made up the majority of victims of benzene and radium poisoning as well as "phossy-jaw"—a form of phosphorus poisoning that rotted the bones in victims' jaws—because employers viewed them as particularly well matched to light but chemical-laden jobs in dry cleaning, rubber manufacturing, cloth dyeing, and pottery manufacturing.[15]

Nor were occupational dangers distributed equally across races. Rather, those deemed nonwhite—or not fully white—faced different kinds of occupational risks and perhaps more dangerous workplaces overall. Indeed, no less an authority than the late immigration historian Oscar Handlin attributed what he interpreted as immigrants' apparent lack of patriotism to the fact that "from day to day [the prototypical immigrant] ran the risk of total calamity from illness or disabling injury."[16] Most immigrants, African Americans, Latinos, and Asians had little choice but to accept the most backbreaking, dangerous jobs. Irish immigrant miners in the Pennsylvania coalfields, for instance, had to work much longer hours in more dangerous conditions than their German supervisors, who had arrived earlier in the United States, while Latin cigar makers in Florida had such high rates of tuberculosis that they had to "take a collection every week for some consumptive comrade."[17]

Employers' racialized assumptions about health and fitness further endangered certain groups. Farmers in California, for instance, preferred to hire Mexicans and Asians for the grueling work of tending ground crops, arguing that their supposed shortness made them better suited to the work.[18] Ford Motor Company, in turn, reserved positions in blast furnaces and foundries for African Americans based on the notion that they could more easily withstand searing temperatures that routinely exceeded 130 degrees.[19] Reformers, moreover, repeated these racialized notions. The economist Jesse Pope, for instance, argued that eastern European Jews had a "singular dexterity" that made them excel at garment work, despite the fact that he also saw them as "the most helpless and inefficient immigrants that ever entered this county."[20]

People with imperfect bodies, however, continued to work after acquiring disabilities. In fact, the staff of the 1915 Survey of Cleveland Cripples, which had expected to find "dependents" in desperate need of charity and vocational training, expressed surprise that so many "cripples" in the city were self-supporting. Survey codirector Amy Hamburger later acknowledged, "Cripples unaided have contributed to their own successful economic independence. . . . The lives of unknown cripples are much more normal than had been supposed."[21] This self-sufficiency was far from unusual. Railroaders with minor impairments such as missing or crushed fingers generally returned to work prior to the 1890s.[22]

People with more serious impairments also remained in the workforce. The Pennsylvania house painter and decorator David Chapman, for example, lost the use of a hand in a work accident early in his career. Since many coworkers had lost their eyesight from the chemicals used in most paint removers, and one of his eyes had suffered the same kind of damage, he developed a safer paint remover and successfully marketed it to Wanamaker's and other stores. Unmarried, "with no family to care for," Chapman could afford to take risks. By the time a representative of the Consumers' League of Eastern Pennsylvania interviewed him in 1928, Chapman could report that his business had "prospered very well."[23] Robert Winthrop likewise found regular employment after losing a leg halfway between his hip and his knee at age sixteen. At the time of his accident, he had not yet learned a trade. But he had always wanted to be a painter, and "the inability to mount ladders that has proved the Waterloo of so many crippled men has seemed to be no obstacle to Winthrop." He developed his own method for climbing ladders and stabilizing himself without the artificial leg for which he had used his workmen's compensation.[24] Unsurprisingly, the Survey of Cleveland Cripples did find, however, that people with multiple impaired limbs had far higher rates of unemployment than those with more "simple" disabilities such as an amputated hand or leg.²⁵

Some disabled workers managed not only to remain in their old jobs, but also to maintain their old wage levels. The Consumers' League of Eastern Pennsylvania reported in 1928 on the case of Frank Kelly, an unmarried longshoreman who had lost three fingers in a work accident. After unsuccessfully trying to operate a cigar shop, he returned to work at the port, this time as a hatch tender, earning the same wages as before his accident.²⁶ Likewise, Philip Sampson continued to work as a painter and earned full wages after losing an eye to a dislodged barrel hoop. The interviewer noted that Sampson "trie[d] to fix it so he will not have the 'high up' jobs as he is a bit fearful of climbing but otherwise seems to [have] adjusted himself very well indeed."²⁷

The case of Richard Mayberry illustrates how ambition and luck might enable a disabled person actually to improve on his pre-injury social standing. In 1888, Mayberry lost his right arm above the wrist in a machine while working as an engineer at a paper factory. An earlier accident some years before had left his other hand "almost entirely useless." Although his employer, Cleveland Paper, blamed Mayberry for his accident, the company still paid most of his salary during his two-year-long recovery. Afterward, likely to discourage Mayberry from filing suit, Cleveland Paper offered to hire him back at his full salary with an assistant to tend the machines. Mayberry sued anyway, attempting to negotiate a life job as a chief engineer. By the time the lawsuit was over, Mayberry had used his political connections to become the examiner of engineers for the city of Cleveland, earning a lofty $1,500 a year.²⁸

More often, permanent injury precluded a return to one's prior job and resulted in a significantly lower standard of living. Crystal Eastman noted this tendency in her treatise, *Work-Accidents and the Law*, declaring that "every work-accident leaves a problem of poverty behind."²⁹ George Geiger, for instance, was fired from his position at "a catering and ice cream business he had held since he was a boy in short pants" after he lost "his right arm and several toes on each foot." Beforehand, Geiger had taken home $25 per week, but "afterward, he could hardly earn what he used to take home in tips alone. No one was much interested in hiring a black man who had only one arm."³⁰ Geiger's dramatic drop in wages was far from unusual. After losing his right arm above the elbow a salesman and demonstrator at a vacuum cleaner factory who had made $60 per week before his accident, drifted from job to job. Finally, he began working as a telegraph messenger for $60 a month.³¹ A sawyer at a lumber mill suffered an equally drastic collapse in income after also losing his right arm above the elbow; although he had previously earned $4 per day, he could only find work in the street trade selling paring knives.³² Of course, familial support, when available, eased the transition, but medical costs compounded the "dual economic burden" caused by workplace injuries.³³

As the cases of the salesman and sawyer suggest, acquired disabilities effectively deskilled workers, forcing them into unskilled positions with lower salaries. New York City hat maker John Schnapper, whose leg was crushed in a streetcar accident, found himself unable to return to work because the only sitting job available was classified as a "girl's job." A witness in his lawsuit against the streetcar company explained to the defense lawyer: "A man has not got the skill of girls sewing and felting, and a man would not earn half as much as a girl does, and the girl earns little enough."³⁴ Even minor disabling injuries, such as the partial loss of two fingers on a left hand, could effectively bar a worker from his skilled trade, as in the case of William Babcock, who earned $50 per week as a skilled carpenter before his accident and only $25 with a newspaper company afterward.³⁵

The process of "wearing out" had similar effects on workers' living standards and access to skilled work. As skilled laborers' toils consumed their bodies, they sank back down the ranks, eventually turning to unskilled work.³⁶ Pittsburgh steel puddler Andrew Gallagher had to leave the mills because of rheumatism brought on by the "extremes of heat and cold to which the men are subjected." Fitch reported that although Gallagher had been able to save money while in the mills and purchase his house—unlike most of his friends—he was now working "at common laborer's wages" in a foundry.³⁷ Like Gallagher, many workers "wore out" at an age past when they could easily learn a new trade. Recognizing these challenges, the *Official Journal* of the Amalgamated Meat Cutters and Butcher Workmen of America advised that, like a manufacturer who budgets "every year a certain amount, often ten per cent., to cover wear and tear of his machinery, a wage worker should set aside the same proportion of his wages for old age, recognizing the fact that he is wearing out and losing his vim and energy year by year."³⁸

To a certain extent, newly disabled workers could expect that their former employer would rehire them—a practice that, of course, encouraged injured workers to refrain from filing lawsuits. Firms tended to extend such offers only to workers whose own negligence had not caused their accidents, however.³⁹ The Illinois Central Railroad, among others, often rehired newly disabled employees, such as a brakeman assigned work as a flagman after injuring his wrist. The Atchison, Topeka, and Santa Fe line, meanwhile, staffed its employee reading rooms with workers with disabilities.⁴⁰ Such practices were so common that Henry N. Peters filed an amendment to his 1894 damages lawsuit against Standard Oil, claiming that he had been discharged "contrary to the established custom" of the company, which "retained in its employment men crippled therein."[41] Companies retained such policies through the turn of the century; in New York City, 20 percent of establishments offered positions to permanently injured workers in 1899 and 1907.[42]

While companies proved willing to reemploy their own newly disabled workers, rarely did firms spend much time exploring what workers *could* do with their reshaped bodies to earn full wages, as Ford Motor Company did. Seaman Michael Finnie's experience after he was injured in a streetcar accident proved a rare exception, although his story did not end well. Despite the fact that his accident had not occurred at work, the steamship line "tried to make work for Finnie sewing life preservers, but Finnie could not do even that."[43] More commonly, companies assumed that workers with physical or sensory disabilities or chronic illnesses could do little. Charles W. Holmes of the Massachusetts Commission for the Blind recounted a typical conversation with a potential employer in the 1910s, explaining, "The employer usually says, 'Yes, I admit that a blind man might do some things, but there is nothing here that he can do.' "[44] Instead, firms offered charity or a pension. To convince companies, Holmes and his fellow employment agents often carefully had to inspect a factory, pointing out the operations that could be completed by a blind worker.[45] The Pennsylvania Institution for the Instruction of the Blind, meanwhile, reported spending two years searching for a position for one of their graduates. The staff of the institution wrote more than 120 letters on his behalf and personally visited more than twenty factories and stores before finding him a place in a "distant city."[46]

Often companies provided ill-paid "life jobs"—such as the prototypical watchman's job—that reflected little other than their sympathy and desire to avoid lawsuits. A barrel company in Cleveland, for instance, offered a teenage boy a lifetime position at $5 per week in the 1870s, albeit with no compensation, after he lost his right arm while leaning over to look at an unguarded stave-cutting machine. He rejected the offer as insufficient and, after working as an elevator operator and a tinner, eventually became a well-respected locksmith.[47] The *Railroad Trainmen's Journal*, in turn, highlighted the financial challenges posed by employers' unwillingness to hire disabled workers at full wages, sardonically remarking in 1900, "The P. & R. motto is 'Be our slave, Join our relief and if you are killed your wife and family can starve; if you are disabled you can have a crossing to flag, at wages from 98¼[¢] to $1.00 day, that is enough for any cripple.' "[48]

"The Crippled Watchman, A Type" from *Work-Accidents and the Law* by Crystal Eastman, 1910.

Few firms other than Ford Motor Company—and for a brief time, Automatic Electric—willingly hired large numbers of new workers with disabilities, especially without intercession from charitable organizations. The Dayton Association for the Blind, for instance, persuaded the National Cash Register Company to hire three blind women in 1908. The women performed well, earning "as much as any woman has earned" at piecework jobs. Two more followed at the association's request in 1910 and 1911, one of whom became the main breadwinner for her family when her father lost his job during a downturn, but the company did not seek out additional blind workers.[49] A few other employers also discovered that disabled workers could be efficient employees during the 1910s and actively sought to hire them, albeit only in small numbers: the P. Goldsmith's Sons' baseball factory in Des Moines, Iowa, the A. & M. Haydon carriage bolt factory in Philadelphia, and, most notably, the Dennison Manufacturing Company. The last firm began making small but regular hires of blind workers after being contacted by the Massachusetts Association for Promoting the Interests of the Blind in 1904. In fact, owner Charles S. Dennison became a lauded "friend of the blind" until his death in the early 1910s.[50]

Although their numbers remained minuscule, such employees challenged employers' preconceptions about their abilities. A paper box factory that hired a young blind woman, for instance, told the Dayton Association that she "did more work than any seeing girl they ever had there."[51] More dramatically, in 1902 the Automatic Electric Company of Chicago recruited roughly 150 deaf workers after discovering that "two deaf employees... hired on a trial basis proved to be even more productive than their hearing counterparts." This opportunity did not last long, however. After machinists at the plant struck for shorter hours, deaf workers joined them on the picket line; although the company conceded within a week, they promptly fired their deaf employees for not being loyal enough to management.[52]

In response to the challenges posed by the mainstream mechanized labor market, some disabled people turned to self-employment. A former cabinetmaker and foreman in a planing mill who had lost his right arm above the elbow at age twenty-three in the early 1880s and also suffered from inflammation of the kidneys "had [a] saloon for years after [his] accident though he disliked [the] type of business." Although he perhaps played to the expectations of the Cleveland survey workers, he explained that such "work seemed [the] only opening."[53] The Consumers' League likewise lauded a number of people with disabilities who, recognizing that they could not easily return to their prior jobs, used their workmen's compensation payments to start small businesses. The league cited the cases of a "badly incapacitated Italian" who had successfully invested his commutation in an ice cream parlor and confectionery run by his mother, as well as that of "an elderly Irish" widow whose hand was left "a mutilated stump and utterly useless" by a laundry mangle. She opened a "neighborhood shop" and earned a small but regular income by opening at 5 A.M. and closing late at night, long past when other stores closed.[54] More dramatically, Elias Jones, a young African American carpenter for a Philadelphia shipbuilding company whose knee was fractured by a crane when it slipped, "soon found it was impossible for him to work at it with his leg stiff and partially useless." While he recovered in a hospital for fourteen months at the company's expense, his wife took in laundry work to keep the family going. Once released, Jones nevertheless established a good-sized contracting business within the African American community and invested in the Florida land boom.[55]

As suggested by Jones's tale and that of the Italian immigrant, adjusting to a work-induced disability often required reworking the entire household's economy. Family capacity played a crucial role in helping newly disabled workers remain in the workforce.[56] William Babcock's wife, for instance, took in boarders after her newly one-handed husband struggled to persuade employers to hire him; with his wages cut in half, however, the household soon fell into debt.[57] In contrast, the Irish widow's excruciatingly long hours at her newsstand—from 5 A.M. to 11 P.M.—reflected the loss of wages that often accompanied a disabling accident as well as the fact that she had no relatives willing or able to help her.

Other workers found success and relative acceptance in professional circles. Lacy Simms, for instance, had lost both forearms below the elbow at age five while visiting a cotton oil mill, but he nevertheless worked as both a teacher and a school superintendent in New Mexico prior to attending Oberlin College. Pushed hard by his father to become fully independent, Simms lived on his own as a young adult, relying on his neighbors only for help with his top collar button and tie.[58] While at Oberlin, a college official who was taken aback by Simms's appearance contacted Henry Ford to see if he would loan Simms $450 to purchase artificial arms to make him "less conspicuous." The official thought prosthetic limbs would help Simms to look "more like the normal person," thereby allowing him to "meet strangers to better advantage."[59] Reflecting his interest in disabled people, Ford loaned Simms the money. Simms, however, found the artificial arms utterly awkward and difficult to use, and promptly buried them in his backyard, where they stayed. Despite "making his friends uncomfortable" with his uncovered stumps, Simms became a Presbyterian minister in New Mexico, well known for his penmanship (he held his pen with his stumps).[60] The Survey of Cleveland Cripples documented the case of a similarly successful dual-arm amputee, David Moylan, who had lost both arms to railroad accidents but learned to hold a pen in his teeth. After working as a real estate agent and insurance salesman, Moylan attended law school, graduating seventh in a class of 200, and at the time of the survey was considering several offers from prominent Cleveland law firms.[61]

The variety of cases presented here suggests that disability was an expected aspect of working-class life—and of the life cycle of many workers—in the late nineteenth and early twentieth centuries. Disabled people continued to work, although often in unskilled positions and at lower wages. But they stayed integrated into their families and communities. And in some particularly dangerous industries, such as manufacturing and agriculture, acquiring physical or sensory "disabilities" or chronic illnesses remained a "normal" part of the work process well into the twentieth century. Memoirist Anne Finger, for instance, characterizes the "missing digits" caused by jewelry work as Rhode Island's "state symbol." In the 1970s, she rejected a relatively well-paid position in a jewelry factory because "few foot-press operators retired from their jobs with all their fingers intact—getting at least one lopped off in a machine was almost inevitable." Instead, she chose to work as a carder: a position that paid only minimum wage but which was far safer.[62] In his 1978 autobiography, American novelist Harry Crews, in turn, described his childhood fascination with the people in the Sears catalogue: "All the people in its pages were perfect. Nearly everybody I knew [in rural Georgia] had something missing, a finger cut off, a toe split, an ear half-chewed away, an eye clouded with blindness from a glancing fence staple."[63]

The Exclusion of Disabled Workers

Like Harry Crews, Henry Ford recognized that many workers lived and worked productively with what we now call disabilities—even at highly mechanized workplaces such as Ford Motor Company. By the turn of the twentieth century, most employers, however, began to feel otherwise. As the American economy became ever more mechanized and dependent on piecework and as the idea of efficiency became ever more popular, large corporations and small proprietors alike began to reject job applicants with a wide array of disabilities, fearing they would be inefficient workers. Increasingly, employers sought laborers with intact, fully functional bodies: workers who, like the items they produced, could be used as interchangeable parts.

The rise of workmen's compensation laws in the 1910s—and the incentives they offered to reject disabled job applicants—undoubtedly discouraged employers from hiring people with disabilities. So too did the Safety First movement, which emerged simultaneously and which tended to blame newly disabled workers for their injuries.[64] Yet, notions of pace and efficiency had a distinct impact on employers' choice of workers, especially in mechanized sectors, but also in less-mechanized, smaller-scale workplaces such as farms. Trade unions too—if unintentionally—participated in this process, which redefined who could be a worker, altered the meaning of work, largely barred disabled people from the paid labor market, and helped to cast people with sensory and physical impairments as well as chronic illnesses as "unproductive citizens." This new linkage of productivity and intact bodies developed at different rates in different industries, but spread even to welfare capitalist firms such as Eastman Kodak, H. J. Heinz Company, Proctor & Gamble, and Pullman. Over time, employers' narrowed vision of workers as intact, vigorous, and interchangeable largely replaced older conceptions of workers' bodies as "resource[s] to be used up over time."[65]

Employers in mechanized sectors—in particular, railroads—were the first to associate disabled people with inefficiency and unproductivity. During the early years of the American railroad industry, for instance, railroad workers and employers alike had seen minor disabilities such as the loss of a finger as a sign of experience and perhaps even courage on the job. In effect, a limited amount of bodily damage indicated an adept, efficient worker. Railroad companies therefore welcomed newly disabled workers when they wanted to return to work.[66] But by the 1880s, all of the major railroad corporations began to reject employees with even minor physical or sensory disabilities, particularly if they worked with the public. Managers questioned whether disabled workers could handle their duties and increasingly barred "cripples" from working on trains, in part because companies feared that a conductor's or engineer's missing finger might make passengers uncomfortable or lead the public to question the line's safety record.[67]

Ironically, efforts to redress the social costs of accidents further helped to define disabled railroaders as inefficient and therefore undesirable employees. Spurred on by the virtual certainty that railroad workers would experience at least one temporarily disabling accident during their career, if not be killed outright, railroad unions (also known as brotherhoods) began creating mutual insurance plans during the late 1860s and 1870s. Since most private insurance companies refused to cover railroaders, workers had little alternative but to create their own benefit associations. After several years of massive strikes in the late 1870s, railroad corporations followed suit and began establishing corporate accident relief funds in the hope that they would help to mollify workers.[68]

Both developments would eventually serve to stigmatize workers with even slight disabilities. Although both railroad managers and the brotherhoods had long seen crushed fingers and other impairments as indications of expertise, they now began to identify such injuries with intemperance, reckless behavior, and poor judgment.[69] Fearful that workers with disabilities might make fraudulent claims, moreover, companies instituted physical examinations for all employees, both veterans and new applicants. Such examinations built off of the limited inspections of railroaders' vision and hearing mandated by many states starting in the 1870s as well as the medical departments and hospital systems that railroad lines created to treat injured and ill workers in the 1880s.[70] By the early 1890s, virtually every company required all operating employees to undergo physical exams. Applicants for positions at the Chicago & North Western Railroad, for instance, could expect company physicians to scrutinize them for missing fingers, heart problems, lung issues, hernias, poor vision, and hearing loss; the line rejected nearly 15 percent of applicants.[71]

Veteran railroaders were, of course, particularly hard hit. As a result, "the slight disability of a missing finger" was transformed "from a badge of honor and a sign of experience" into "a bar to continued employment."[72] In effect, railroad companies now considered it more efficient to avoid potential payouts to workers with disabilities and prevent such workers from causing accidents. No longer did they seek to preserve an experienced staff of railroaders, especially one with a culture that celebrated heroic self-sacrifice.[73]

To a large degree, railroad workers were complicit in the move to exclude their disabled comrades. The brotherhoods generally supported the barring of workers with acquired disabilities and, like the railroad owners, began to blame them for causing their own injuries. Reflecting the power of the late nineteenth-century temperance movement—and an attempt to curry favor with the railroad companies by accepting the tenets of efficiency and workplace rationalization—brotherhood leaders increasingly associated disabling injuries with drunkenness and unnecessary risk taking. Although disabled unionists tried to remain active in the organizations, able-bodied members gradually pushed them out, aiming to shunt them into an ill-supported union home where they could be held up as evidence of the brotherhoods' generosity and the need for union organization.[74]

Employers in other mechanized workplaces also began to question whether people with physical, sensory, and other impairments could be efficient workers. In the mid-1910s, the foreman of the sanding department in a Cleveland furniture factory experienced employers' growing skepticism about disabled workers' abilities. When he lost his right arm above the elbow at age forty-seven, his company offered him a lifetime position at his current status. After losing all of his savings in a bank failure, however, he became depressed and asked to step down as foreman. He invented a special artificial limb to allow him to operate machines and lift heavy loads. After he "demonstrat[ed] its usefulness," his employer allowed him to once again become a sander. A few years later, the factory came under new ownership, and he once again had to prove that he could keep pace. He advised the staff of the Survey of Cleveland Cripples, "I appreciate that you must convince your employer not only that you can do the work, but that you can do it with as much rapidity and efficiency as your competitors. This I was able to do, and if you wish to assist cripples, always keep this in mind."[75]

Other recently disabled workers had less success proving their efficiency. William Babcock, for instance, had earned $50 per week as a skilled carpenter and woodworking finisher. After he lost his left hand to an unguarded saw, his employers offered him a job, but only temporarily. An investigator reported that "the bosses fe[lt] that his incapacity prevent[ed] him from working as fast as he should, although he himself contends that he can do the work as well, even if not quite so quickly as before."[76] Like Babcock, Ralph Fletcher struggled to meet his former employer's expectation of efficiency, even though they too agreed to rehire him. He had held a well-paid job as an upholsterer at a motor company, but during the late 1910s he had to have his right hand amputated "a few inches above the wrist." Another employee had turned on the picker machine while Fletcher was cleaning out the refuse. After his injury healed, he obtained a hook for his arm and, on the suggestion of a fellow workman at the motor company, returned to his company to ask for work. After persisting for two weeks, "they gave him sorting bolts and screws," but the manager "complained that he was too slow." Fletcher asked to work as a watchman instead, which he did for a short time before being laid off. An investigator from the Consumer's League of Eastern Pennsylvania reported in 1928, "Then followed another period of several months' attempts to find a job, with the old story repeated of 'no work for a cripple.' At last he answered a blind ad for a night watchman job and was given an interview." He received the job, but eventually returned to the motor company at their request as a night watchman. His family, however, struggled to make ends meet. Fletcher complained, "If only I had my hand I could be making my $1.25 an hour now at my trade."[77]

Employers in less mechanized environments, such as farming, also began to reject job applicants with many types of disabilities on the presumption that disabled workers would be inefficient. In September 1916, the rehabilitation magazine *American Journal of Care for Cripples* reprinted a telling story from *World's Work* about the U.S. Employment Service's efforts to place disabled workers. In this case, a "cripple" had applied through the New York branch to work at a dairy farm. But "when the cripple arrived at the dairy farm, the farmer, greatly incensed at the man's infirmity, refused to let him go to work, and immediately communicated to the agent his indignation at being supplied with a 'poor excuse for a man.'" The story ended happily for one party, however, since the employment agent convinced the farmer to give the man a fair try for a month and pay him $1 for each cow that he could handle. Although the farmer had originally offered only $25 per month, the man successfully cared for thirty cows, thus earning $30.[78] The U.S. Civil Service, in turn, barred civilians with impairments such as tuberculosis, complete deafness, epilepsy, loss of two limbs, heart disease, kidney disease, insanity, or badly crippled hands from even taking the qualifying examinations.[79]

"Worn-out" men likewise were deemed inefficient and increasingly had trouble retaining their jobs. A steelworker, for example, told John Fitch: "There are few old men working in the mills now, because the Steel Trust doesn't want old men. Their policy is to work out the old men and fill their places with younger men. This is so that they may keep up the highest standard of efficiency. If an old man can get as much work done as a young man he will hold his position, but the moment a man begins to fail an excuse will soon be found for letting him go."[80] The Carnegie Steel Company enforced an age limit of forty years for new hires, while the American Steel and Wire Company hired men over thirty-five years of age only if they were experienced.[81] Efficiency became an even more explicit criterion for employment at U.S. Steel when, in 1912, a committee of U.S. Steel stockholders commissioned by Judge Elbert H. Gary had decided that "the corporation was justified in making 'efficiency' the one standard by which continuance of employment in its plants is determined."[82]

U.S. Steel was only one of many welfare capitalist firms to begin screening out disabled workers during the 1910s. This shift cannot be disentangled from the ways in which workmen's compensation laws encouraged employers to discriminate against disabled workers, a topic that is the focus of chapter 5. Nevertheless, it remains striking that the two benefits offered by virtually every welfare capitalist program—company doctors and onsite hospital facilities—served to exclude some employees. Overall, these companies aimed to limit unionization efforts and reduce turnover by offering employees extensive medical care, as well as benefits like showers, baseball teams, English classes, disability and life insurance, pensions, and company housing. Montgomery Ward, for instance, instituted annual physicals in 1912 and began firing workers of "questionable" fitness, while starting in the mid-1910s, General Electric used its Medical Department to identify and reject disabled job applicants.[83] Given that employers had long believed that workers' own carelessness caused most accidents, these firms' pioneering safety programs may have also served to exclude disabled workers. Even after safety engineers proved that poor design made many if not most accidents virtually inevitable—a development that helped lay the groundwork for the Safety First movement of the 1920s—disabled employees continued to be blamed for ignoring safety rules.[84]

Only during labor shortages did companies change their exclusionary policies. Goodyear Tire and, to a lesser extent, Firestone hired hundreds of deaf workers during World War I, even creating Deaf sports teams and bringing on a dedicated recruiter to conduct national outreach within the Deaf community. But during the postwar recession, those last hired were the first employees laid off; once business picked up again, the companies favored the permanent—and able-bodied—residents of Akron. By 1921, the city's "Silent Colony" had faded away.[85]

By the 1920s, workers with a wide variety of disabilities found themselves unwelcome in nearly all heavily industrialized and mechanized workplaces—and in a growing number of less-mechanized workplaces as well. Employers increasingly demanded interchangeable workers with intact, fully functional bodies. In fact, in 1928 a survey of 600 of the nation's major companies found that more than half were unwilling to hire any disabled workers at all, partly on account of the belief that they were unsuited to the type of work available in their factories.[86]

Efficient Producers at Ford Motor Company

Henry Ford and key managers at Ford Motor Company held a distinctly different view of disability than most other early twentieth-century industrial employers. Ford rejected the increasingly commonsense notion that people with disabilities were simply too inefficient and unproductive even to consider hiring for mechanized work.[87] He often recounted the story of a blind man, for instance, who "was assigned to the stock department to count bolts and nuts for shipment to branch establishments. Two other able-bodied men were already employed on this work. In two days the foreman sent a note to the transfer department releasing the able-bodied men because the blind man was able to do not only his work but also the work that had formerly been done by the sound men."[88] This true story, which Ford retold from the 1920s through the 1940s, illustrated his belief that disabled people could be productive workers and underscored his efforts to convince his fellow industrialists to hire people with disabilities.[89] He argued that if supervisors made creative use of mechanization and physical examinations to place disabled people in the proper positions, workers with disabilities could be as productive and efficient as their able-bodied counterparts. No longer would they struggle to find employment.

Under the direction of Henry Ford and key supervisors, particularly John R. Lee (who founded the company's Sociological Department in 1914), the Reverend Samuel Marquis (who headed the Sociological Department between 1915 and 1921), and Dr. James E. Mead (the chief surgeon of the Medical Department), Ford Motor Company hired substantial numbers of new employees with disabilities.[90] By 1911, the company had 957 disabled workers out of approximately 3,700 total employees.[91] When the five-dollar day went into effect at Ford Motor Company in 1914, Henry Ford mandated that applicants should never be turned away because of their physical condition except when they had a contagious disease, and that no disabled workers should be fired because of their disabilities.[92]

While other employers used company doctors, medical departments, and physical examinations to filter out ill and disabled applicants and even current employees, Ford Motor Company used its screenings to place new hires with disabilities in jobs appropriate for their physical capabilities.[93] During two days late in 1918, for instance, just 43 out of 348 applicants qualified as "physically perfect." The others had a host of impairments: poor eyesight, flat feet, heart trouble, poor teeth, varicose veins, hernias, kidney trouble, club feet, deafness, tuberculosis, missing eyes, "deformed legs," hemorrhoids, mental deficiency, poor hearing, and crippled legs, among others. Company physicians determined the type of labor that each applicant was "physically able to do," sending those who required more specific adjustments to the Medical Transfer Department.[94] As at other large corporations that instituted scientific management techniques and human resources departments during the early twentieth century, Ford managers sharply restricted foremen's duties. The authority to fire employees rested not with foremen, but rather with the Employment Department, which preferred to transfer employees rather than fire them. Instead, "once hired, a man [wa]s assured of permanent employment," as Medical Department head James E. Mead explained. He continued, "One rule of this company which is hard and fast and which to my knowledge has never been broken, is that no person shall be discharged or laid off because he is physically unable to do his work." Ill employees, in turn, could obtain sick leave if necessary and had their jobs guaranteed. Such policies, of course, also helped to reduce worker turnover, which had hit 370 percent annually by 1913.[95] By 1918, more than 18 percent of the company's nearly 30,000-person workforce were "cripples or men physically sub standard." Another 207 men were blind in one eye, 60 had epilepsy, 234 were missing one foot or leg, and 900 had tuberculosis, among other disabled workers. The following year, Mead reported, "Ford employees are minus 1,031 of their allotted number of fingers or thumbs."[96]

Man with amputation working in the upholstery department at Ford Motor Company, 1917. From the collections of The Henry Ford, gift of Robert Gearhart.

Unlike other firms that offered disabled workers little other than ill-paid "life jobs," at Ford workers with disabilities received the same wages as their able-bodied counterparts (including the profit-sharing portion, if deemed eligible). They were, however, expected to be efficient at their jobs. Medical Department director Mead reported that as of fall 1918, foremen identified 85 percent of disabled and elderly employees as "fully efficient." Those who were "unable to keep up with their able bodied fellow workmen" were only slightly less efficient.[97] Employees with disabilities worked in a variety of positions, including on the production lines. Until 1916, most "defectives were confined" to the Magneto and Commutator Departments, when production supervisor Peter E. Martin ordered that "each department be given their percentage of defectives." The Magneto Department, which held the company's first production line and later fed into the main chassis line, manufactured the wire coils necessary to ignite the engine, while the Commutator Department produced the electrical switches used to generate torque in motors.[98] "Cripples" and other people unable to remain standing for long periods typically worked in those two departments, while other disabled people helped manufacture ammeters or worked on stamping machines or presses.[99] Deaf people likewise worked at a variety of machine and bench positions, albeit ones where they did not have to move around much.[100]

Rather than use Safety First campaigns to justify excluding disabled workers en masse, Ford Motor Company sought to place such workers in positions where they were unlikely to incur another injury; such practices, of course, also benefited the company by reducing accidents and payouts of workmen's compensation. For safety reasons, certain groups, such as blind people and people with epilepsy or tuberculosis, almost always worked off the line. Totally blind men sorted and assembled bolts, nuts, small gaskets, and washers, safely away from the assembly lines.[101] Men with one functional eye worked as inspectors, stock checkers, doormen, watchmen, or cleaners, or in the Salvage Department, in order to prevent them from losing that eye to a flying particle; some amputees also filled these positions.[102] Epileptics, in turn, were kept "away from all moving machinery, and off high places" to prevent injuries during a seizure.[103] And in line with contemporary standards for treating people with tuberculosis, the company generally placed "tuberculars" in non-dusty jobs, primarily in the Material Salvage Department. Others served as chassis drivers or worked as watchmen or doormen, and a few labored in the Magneto Department.[104] Ford Motor Company even ran a "Lungers Camp," a specially designed shed where men with advanced tuberculosis could sit while they "sort[ed] scrap, reclaim[ed] twine, nails, bolts . . . that formerly were a total loss to the Company, but now a valuable asset." Those with less serious cases worked in Lumber Salvage, where "broken and discarded boxes [we]re sawed into proper lengths and again made into boxes for export work, again saving the company many thousands of dollars." Combined, the two salvage programs produced profits of over $3,200 per week.[105] Finally, severely disabled workers did light assembly at home, as did workers recovering from leg or foot injuries in the firm's hospital. In the latter case, laborers received their full wages, but the company also avoided having to pay them workmen's compensation.[106]

Henry Ford's belief that disabled workers could continue to be productive derived in large part from his understanding of mechanization. While other industrial employers assumed that mechanization required workers with intact bodies, Ford understood that machinery could actually expand the potential of human labor by making work easier and more specialized. Just as other employers divided their product lines (a practice termed "flexible specialization"), he divided the workforce.[107] Reflecting back on the rise of mechanization, Ford observed: "There is no doubt that the machine not only makes it possible for more people to earn more money, but it also makes work more humane. . . . The notion that machinery was invented as a labor-saving device is a mistaken one. *Machinery was invented by labor for labor-serving purposes!*"[108] In particular, he cited the potential of mechanized, subdivided labor—if taken to its logical extreme—to increase employment among disabled people: "I am quite sure that if work is sufficiently subdivided—subdivided to the point of highest economy—there will be no dearth of places in which the physically incapacitated can do a man's job and get a man's wage."[109] Notably, experts in the efficiency movement such as Frank Gilbreth, who helped pioneer time-motion study and was later memorialized as the main character in the book *Cheaper by the Dozen*, agreed with Ford's belief that breaking down each work process and "adjusting" men to the proper positions could make disabled workers just as efficient and productive as their able-bodied counterparts.[110]

Consequently, in the 1910s, Ford's Sociological and Medical Departments classified each job in the vast plant according to whether it was "dry or wet . . . whether one or both hands [were] used; whether the employee [sat or stood] at his work; whether the room [was] noisy or quiet; . . . the weight of the material or piece handled; and a description of any strain the workman [was] under."[111] Because of this job classification system, the staff knew that "670 operations could be performed by legless men; about 2,600 by one-legged men; 2 by armless men; 715 by one-armed men; and 10 by blind men," and the staff could easily place disabled workers in appropriate positions.[112]

Furthermore, the Sociological and Medical Departments' staff routinely reassigned disabled employees to new positions if the current one was deemed unsafe. Workers diagnosed with tuberculosis, for example, would be moved to the Lungers Camp or Lumber Salvage, depending on their stage.[113] A World War I veteran with shell shock found Ford Motor Company to be exceptionally understanding. Since he had "nervous spells" in which he "just fell to pieces," the Employment Department initially assigned him a safe job weighing pistons away from all machinery.[114] One day, however, the veteran had a spell and threw one of the pistons at a fellow worker. When queried, the veteran said, "I don't know. It just got out of my hand and I threw it away." Rather than fire this veteran, however, the Ford staff assigned him to a position hanging fenders on the paint conveyer, where there was nothing to throw. The veteran did a fine job for three months, but then dove into the 500-gallon tank of paint enamel.[115] The assistant superintendent of the plant, William Klann, tried to take him off that position, but the veteran protested, saying that he liked that job. The veteran never caused any further problems; Klann later stated, "We cured that fellow by one job."[116]

Henry Ford's policy of hiring disabled workers was not a matter of charity. Indeed, he also hired African Americans, women, and felons.[117] His attitude toward disabled job applicants stemmed from his belief in social efficiency, his faith in the moral value of work, and his dislike of waste, dependence, and almsgiving. Ford argued that because "the maimed and halt are always with us," they needed to be part of the cross-section of society hired by his company.[118] Of course, such groups tended to make for loyal employees—an important consideration for a company that had massive turnover prior to the five-dollar-day program and which had expanded its manufacturing capacity extremely rapidly.

Ford's belief in the power of work to encourage individual uplift and regeneration also echoed reformers' and legislators' growing interest in vocational rehabilitation. In fact, the company broke its long-standing silence about hiring disabled workers in 1918, just as Congress began considering bills that would create a rehabilitation program for disabled civilians; earlier in the year, legislators had chosen to dedicate the first such federal program solely to serving injured soldiers. Writing in the trade journal *Iron Age*, Medical Department director James E. Mead argued that the "employment and care" of disabled veterans "is receiving universal attention," but demanded to know "why have the thousands and tens of thousands of cripples resulting from civil and industrial accidents received so scant attention . . . ?"[119] Other publications, such as the trade journals *Economic World* and *Modern Hospital*, the U.S. Bureau of Labor Statistics' *Monthly Labor Review*, and even Canada's *Labour Gazette* soon picked up the story.[120] Invariably, authors noted that Ford Motor Company stood alone among large industrial concerns in willingly hiring disabled job applicants and finding a means of making them profitable employees. An unsigned editorial in *Modern Hospital*, for instance, contended, "A human rubbish heap is a very expensive institution to maintain, and, when there are really potentialities of usefulness in much or most of the rubbish, the question of the efficiency of a system that maintains such a scrapheap becomes embarrassing."[121]

Unlike many rehabilitators, Ford rejected the idea of sheltered workshops. "It is economically most wasteful to accept crippled men as charges," he commented, "and then to teach them trivial tasks like the weaving of baskets or some other form of unremunerative hand labour in the hope, not of aiding them to make a living, but of preventing despondency."[122] Reflecting back in 1947, Ford explained further: "Life has taught me that adults, like children, want to be doing something. Men wear out when idle, just as machines do. . . . I believe in the kind of charity that helps a man to help himself. Give him a decent job with a living wage and he won't need charity."[123]

During the 1910s, the Sociological Department put Ford's faith in the moral value of work into practice, offering work over compensation or charity whenever possible. Marquis explained, "In the sociological department one rule was that no problem should be solved by the use of money when the solution could be reached through work." In addition, the department mandated that "no case should be undertaken that could not be placed ultimately on a self-supporting basis."[124] Like other firms, Ford Motor Company rehired workers who had been permanently disabled in workplace accidents. In part, Ford and his supervisors felt that it was cheaper to "fit" a man to a job that he could do than to fire him.[125] "It helped the employee and the Company," explained William Baxter, who worked in the Medical and Employment Departments in the 1910s and 1920s. "The Company didn't have to pay Workmen's Compensation because the man was employed, and it helped the employee too, to retain his self-respect by working. If other companies had done the same, a large number of physically handicapped would never have become public charges."[126] Only workers who were too badly injured to work again were deemed appropriate subjects for public charity: in other words, suitable members of the deserving poor.[127]

Ford Motor Company even rehired employees who sued for additional compensation when their disabilities worsened or the job market tightened.[128] Lithuanian immigrant Peter Banionis, for instance, lost the second and third fingers on his right hand in 1916 while cleaning a die press after another worker removed the blocks holding up the press. After recovering, he returned to work at Ford in 1917 but was laid off in 1933 during the depths of the Depression. Claiming that he could not find another job, he sued unsuccessfully for additional compensation; nonetheless, Banionis eventually returned to work at Ford, remaining there through at least World War II. Workers whose injuries had less clear-cut origins continued on too. In 1928, Frank McCracken claimed that the infection that eventually cost him the sight in both eyes arose after he "struck [his left] eye with edge of cloth he was shaking." Twice denied compensation, he soon settled for $4,500 and coverage of his hospital bills. The company kept him on as a laborer, while his son-in-law worked at the firm as a toolmaker.[129]

Ford Motor Company's hiring of disabled workers arose in part out of Henry Ford's passion for efficiency and his hatred of charity, but also out of his sincere interest in disabled people themselves, as well as in the challenges they faced in finding employment. William P. Baxter, who worked in the Employment Office and the Medical Department and eventually became employment manager, commented, "Mr. Ford was very much interested in these handicapped people. He seemed to show genuine interest in people of that type."[130] In at least one case, Ford personally ordered that a disabled worker be kept on at the company. In April 1913, L. B. Robertson, the head of the Legal Department, recommended terminating Warren Stevenson's employment, due to his increasingly frequent seizures and the "danger of serious injury from such cause with resulting compensation to be paid." The next day, plant superintendent P. E. Martin noted, "Man kept in our employ per order of Mr. Ford."[131]

Ford's attention to disabled people reached well beyond the issue of employment. Despite Ford's dislike of sheltered workshops, he and his wife arranged for the Detroit League for the Handicapped and the Needle and Loom Guild to sell workshop and homemade products at the Highland Park factory (or perhaps to supply them to the factory).[132] In addition, Ford maintained a correspondence with Helen Keller for nearly three decades and stayed abreast of developments in the crippled children's movement. Marquis, in turn, used Sociological Department investigators to find crippled children in Detroit and Dearborn so that they could receive medical treatment at the Henry Ford Hospital (often free of charge).[133] And perhaps most tellingly, Ford and his wife regularly frequented the Bay Cliff Health Camp in the Upper Peninsula during the 1930s and 1940s in order to visit the disabled children staying at the camp. Director Elba Morse recollected that Ford did not donate any money directly to the camp, but instead gave his time to the children "in direct service. He said that he would do anything for any child at any time." He conveyed children down to Dearborn for free surgery and employed their fathers at Ford Motor Company when necessary. Morse recalled Ford saying that coming to Bay Cliff made him feel better: "I think he probably sat still longer up here than he did any place else, because he seemed much more relaxed."[134]

Starting in the early 1920s, disabled job applicants found Ford Motor Company less welcoming, as discussed in the next chapter. Nonetheless, Ford's and Marquis's beliefs that people with disabilities were fully capable of being efficient workers and self-supporting citizens, even in a highly mechanized economy, lived on. Although fewer disabled workers overall found a welcome mat at Ford in the 1920s and 1930s, the company continued to re-employ workers who acquired disabilities on the job.[135] During and after World War II, Ford's older policies resurfaced as the company hired massive numbers of disabled workers—more than 100 "completely deaf-mutes," 687 sightless in some form, 66 who were deaf and dumb, 112 "who suffer from epilepsy"—and even provided a special grade-level entrance at the River

Blind men sorting bolts and nuts at Ford Motor Company's River Rouge plant, 1934. From the collections of The Henry Ford.

Rouge plant, complete with traffic officers and warning signs.[136] Ford also established Camp Legion, which provided disabled veterans with vocational rehabilitation, room, and board free of charge from 1944 to 1946. More importantly, Henry Ford's notion that people with disabilities could be productive in mechanized workplaces entered the mainstream of the rehabilitation movement through the company's own publicity and demonstration work during and after World War I, and then by the employment of so many disabled workers at full pay during World War II. By the 1940s, all of the most prominent rehabilitationists espoused the idea that, to be productive, workers with disabilities merely needed to be fitted to the appropriate job.[137]

FORD WAS A complex figure who could at once espouse anti-Semitism and a haughty paternalism, while at the same time evincing empathy and even respect for disabled people. His policy toward workers with disabilities stemmed from a hard-edged quest for efficiency and productivity but also derived from an understanding of mechanization and the industrial process that set him apart from his contemporaries. Ford demonstrated that disabled workers could make highly productive and efficient employees if properly placed. His policies further suggested that increasingly mechanized workplaces of the late nineteenth- and early twentieth centuries did in fact not require the standardized workers with intact, fully functional bodies so desired by most employers: workers who were, in effect, interchangeable parts. In fact, Ford's approach to disabled workers anticipated post–World War II developments in vocational rehabilitation, even though his efforts to convince his fellow employers to hire workers with disabilities came to naught at the time.

For most workers with disabling injuries, the ability to obtain work on the wage labor market slipped out of their grasp during the late nineteenth and early twentieth centuries. Few stopped working entirely; rather, they created jobs for themselves in the informal labor market. Nonetheless, many employers' shifting understandings of what made "a good worker" helped to redefine productivity on the wage labor market not as a spectrum but rather as a stark dyad of desirable able-bodied employees and inefficient and even dangerous disabled workers.

Ironically, workmen's compensation laws would only add to the challenges disabled workers faced in obtaining paid work. While labor reformers and legislators intended compensation programs to alleviate the social burden of industrial accidents and prevent public dependency, the laws further encouraged employers to discriminate against workers with all types of disabilities. By the 1920s, even Ford Motor Company had reduced its hiring of new workers with disabilities.

CHAPTER FIVE

The Greatest Handicap Suffered by Crippled Workers
The Perverse Impact of Workmen's Compensation, 1900s–1930s

In the early 1920s, disabled workers discovered that Ford Motor Company had, to some degree, rolled up its welcome mat. No longer did the firm embrace job applicants with a wide variety of disabilities, although disabled workers remained in the company's employ. The firm also adopted a confrontational approach toward injured workers who tried to claim compensation for their newly acquired disabilities.

Outside Ford Motor Company, however, disabled workers faced a far more hostile environment. After working for three months as a mechanic at an electrical company in the 1910s, Joseph Bartosz, for instance, found himself labeled a "liability ... concern" and fired. During one of the firm's periodic physical examinations, a company physician had realized that the mechanic was blind in his left eye. Although "this did not interfere in his work ... an injury to his good eye" would result in the company paying as much as $3,000 in compensation for what legislators termed "a total permanent disability."[1] Bartosz was just one of tens of thousands of one-eyed, one-armed, epileptic, tubercular, crippled, worn-out, hard-of-hearing, blind, four-fingered, herniated, hypertensive, and otherwise disabled workers who lost their jobs to compensation statutes during the 1910s and 1920s—even in nonindustrial sectors. At least on the wage labor market, the laws truly were "the greatest handicap suffered by crippled workers."[2]

But why would the workmen's compensation laws passed in forty-three states between 1910 and 1920 have such a dire effect on the job prospects of people with "disabilities"?[3] After all, lawmakers had intended for compensation statutes to alleviate the economic hardships wrought by industrial accidents. The answer lay in how labor reformers and legislators understood the social problem of workplace mishaps: namely, as causing workers to lose wages, leaving households without breadwinners, and potentially leading respectable working-class families to depend on public aid. Like labor reformers, lawmakers feared that overly generous compensation—or compensation for too long a period—would sap the households' work ethic and morality, perhaps even allowing them to slip into the undeserving poor. In effect, they saw the problem of industrial accidents as one of dependency, not disability. Indeed, legislators had hardly recognized that they were making disability policy.

Admittedly, compensation statutes provided modest yet invaluable aid to newly disabled workers during the first few years after their accidents. But unwittingly, lawmakers had also included financial incentives for insurers and already skeptical employers to screen out workers with a wide range of congenital and acquired physical, sensory, and cognitive disabilities as well as chronic illnesses: workers such as Bartosz. The effect on disabled workers was devastating. By the end of World War I, virtually every industrial employer required job applicants to undergo a medical examination. And by 1928, most major employers cited workmen's compensation laws as making it too financially risky to hire any disabled workers.[4] Making matters worse, the statutes did little to address the long-term financial challenges of living with a disability. Nor were the laws really equipped to handle disability's complex and shifting nature. Racialized and gendered notions of "fitness" and who qualified as a worker further limited the reach of compensation programs.

A few labor reformers tried to alter the statutes to aid workers with disabilities, but within just a few years the nature of the compensation system had already been set. Disabled workers, sometimes accompanied by their able-bodied counterparts, fought to retain access to wage work, but with little success. Perversely, workmen's compensation laws impoverished people with disabilities and made them more likely to have to depend on aid from charities, government, or family members.

Looking at the history of workmen's compensation through the lens of disability suggests the critical importance of looking at the unforeseen and often ironic implementation and outcomes of public policies. More than conservative initiatives intended to appease labor unions and address a significant rise in industrial accidents and lawsuits during the first decade of the twentieth century—and also more than simple reflections of the antilabor bent of protective legislation at that time—compensation laws reshaped the meaning and lived experiences of "disability" on the wage labor market.[5] Regardless of policy makers' intentions in enacting compensation statutes, the laws proved remarkably powerful in creating disability as a new policy problem synonymous with poverty and dependency.

The Social Problem of Industrial Accidents

After spending a year haunting the coroner's office, workingmen's homes, railroad yards, and blast furnaces of Pittsburgh's Steel District, in 1910 the young socialist lawyer Crystal Eastman released her sensational and painstakingly documented accounting of the toll taken on families by industrial accidents, *Work-Accidents and the Law*. Tracing the impact of 526 fatal accidents and 294 nonfatal injuries, she argued, "The continuing recurrence of preventable work-accidents is not only an injustice to the victims but also clearly a tremendous social waste."[6] Among the most pernicious effects she noted were children forced to leave school, widows required to work outside the home, and families having to stretch scarce meals.[7] Focusing much of her attention on the "industrial accident widow" and her children, Eastman defined the social problem of work accidents as an issue of families left destitute after the death or disabling of a breadwinner.[8] Unlike many of her colleagues, she did not suggest that such families automatically fell into the trap of public dependency. She charged the current method for compensating accident victims—the court-based employers' liability system—with being woefully inefficient and ineffective at preventing the workplace accidents that seemed inherent to an industrial economy. With the support of the American Association for Labor Legislation (AALL) and the reform magazine *Survey*, Eastman would set the agenda for the workmen's compensation movement of the 1910s.

Eastman was raised in western New York by two progressive Protestant ministers. Her work reflected her lifelong radicalism, her interest in a vast area of reform topics, and her commitment to careful social investigation—a trait shared by other authors involved with the Pittsburgh Survey. The daughter of one of the first women ordained in a Protestant church, as an adult Eastman advocated for women's suffrage, helping to draft the Equal Rights Amendment, and also served as investigating attorney for the U.S. Commission on Industrial Relations under Woodrow Wilson.

Part of what made Eastman's work (and that of other volumes in the Pittsburgh Survey) so pioneering was her commitment to a sociological approach. When Eastman's mother, Annie, fretted that her daughter would become depressed by her research, Crystal replied, "Strange to say my spirits thrive on all this atmosphere of death and destruction. I make a point of being gay and frivolous at work—and anyhow statistics—records of tragedies, don't depress you nearly as much as one would suppose. They are so interesting to me sociologically."[9]

Reflecting her socialist beliefs, Eastman rejected her fellow reformers' assumption that accident victims' families nearly invariably became dependent on public aid; rather, she emphasized how accidents produced poverty. In fact, she advised readers not to be "too quick to conclude that a great share of [the accident] burden must eventually be borne by the community through some form

Social investigator and workmen's compensation advocate Crystal Eastman. Photo by Bain News Service, courtesy of the Library of Congress.

of charity, public or private, organized or individual." Reporting that the city of Pittsburgh had needed to fund the burials of only 6 of 526 workmen killed during the year, she continued, "Apart from this, there were, out of 825 cases studied ... only seven in which any demand had been made upon organized or institutional charity." She noted that these demands were "very small," explaining, "For instance, two orphan children are being cared for in an asylum, and one blind old man whose son was killed received one dollar and fifty cents a month from the county for part of a year." She attributed this seemingly unexpected self-reliance on families' fortitude, noting, "That poor people are used to trouble is a commonplace."[10] Eastman also highlighted the fact that 149 of the men killed had dependents living abroad, "leav[ing] a poverty problem not in America, but in Europe." In effect, she suggested, the United States escaped its rightful share of the social burden wrought by unsafe workplaces and industrial accidents.[11]

Most other Progressive reformers assumed that industrial accidents invariably led to public dependency—a dynamic that exposed impoverished yet respectable families to the moral ills of poorhouses. Chicago settlement house worker Florence Lattimore, for instance, argued that because few families received compensation from employers in the early years of the twentieth century, local charities had to struggle to fill the gap. She contended that orphanages in Chicago spent hundreds of dollars for every family that as a result of an accident was unable to care for its children.[12] The head of the charity service of Illinois's Cook County likewise complained: "Hundreds of able bodied men in the prime of life are annually receiving injuries which result in the loss of life, limbs or health, and make many of them and their families county charges."[13] As the first decade of the twentieth century came to a close, many Progressives came to the same conclusion as Edward T. Devine, the head of the New York Charity Organization Society and coeditor of reform magazine *Survey*. He identified industrial accidents as one of the "fundamental causes" of poverty and "dependence on charitable relief."[14] At a time when reformers already feared that social problems ranging from immigration to prostitution were overwhelming the nation's resources, industrial accidents seemed to threaten families' morality and social stability.

As in the late nineteenth century, dependency constituted both a moral and a political threat for most Progressive reformers. Social worker Belle Lindner Israels noted in a 1908 *Survey* article, for instance, "In individual cases it is often difficult to determine if poverty is the result of idleness, or idleness the result of poverty."[15] Whether in the form of charity or governmental support, any assistance needed to be monitored carefully and, if possible, avoided entirely. Overly generous aid, in turn, would encourage immorality and laziness and, in the eyes of many reformers, could lead to the sort of patronage politics that they held largely responsible for the dramatic expansion of the Civil War pension system in the decades following the war.[16] Charity workers further fretted that aid would demoralize upstanding, independent workers and "degrade them to the rank of dependents."[17]

Men's dependence on charity posed more than simply a moral threat, however. As in the nineteenth century, reformers fretted about whether poor, ill, or disabled men retained the independence assumed necessary for good citizenship. But not only did industrial accidents jeopardize men's citizenship; by allowing workplaces to disrupt homes and potentially force women to enter the wage labor market, accidents threatened to undermine a gender system premised on separate spheres. In reality, of course, working-class women had long had little choice but to engage in paid work, whether taking in boarders, doing home production, or working for wages.[18]

Eastman also paid far closer attention than did her fellow reformers to the different ways in which disability and death affected workers' families. She contended that the families of men who suffered disabling injuries faced especially difficult and long-lasting hurdles. "When a working man is disabled ... it may involve a more exhausting struggle with poverty than is caused by the death of a wage-earner," she explained. "When a man dies as a result of injury there is at least one less consumer in the family." By contrast, the families of disabled workers not only lost the breadwinner's wages but also had to cover medical expenses and provide care, food, and lodging.[19]

Even as Eastman attempted to raise awareness among lawmakers about the social costs of industrial accidents, her fellow Progressive reformers feared that workers were part of the problem. Many of the Progressive Era's most forward-looking thinkers clung to unflattering assumptions about the nation's rapidly increasing unskilled and semiskilled labor force.[20] Echoing views widely held by employers, economist and AALL member Henry Seager, for instance, blamed a peculiar "recklessness of American workers" that made them prone to negligence that he believed stemmed from the large immigrant population, or even the youth of the workforce.[21]

Some skilled laborers agreed that workers bore partial blame for industrial accidents—a line of argument that often reflected union leaders' ethnic blinders. In 1908, *Charities and the Commons* (a predecessor of *Survey*) printed a commentary by a railroad signalman who claimed, "Unchecked negligence can be shown to be the root and direct cause of nearly all preventable accidents, and loss of life there from, on American railroads."[22] The unionized machinists, who also had high rates of accidents and disability, likewise argued that workers were often careless. The *Machinists Monthly Journal*, however, laid equal blame for accidents on employers, asserting, "Carelessness of employer and of employee is inevitable. Both these things, both imperfection of machinery and carelessness of human beings, may be diminished by wise laws, but they cannot be eradicated."[23] Yet, as the signalman and other writers in *Survey* and *Machinists Monthly Journal* noted, it was the duty of employers to prevent the negligence that would naturally occur in a monotonous industrial workplace.[24]

Of course, workers' attitudes toward safety were always clouded by economic need and low wages. Miners, for instance, denied for decades that coal dust could explode despite ample evidence to the contrary; they could not afford to upgrade open flame lamps to portable electrical ones, nor did they have the wherewithal to convince employers to sprinkle water on coal dust or provide proper ventilation.[25] Writers in *Survey* rued the fact that it took several years, thousands of deaths, and several thousand dollars of federal expenditures on testing galleries in order to convince mine workers of the fact that coal dust could spontaneously combust: "But these men who pushed at the ropes, and saw the smoke belch up, understand what the roar was saying. They knew that 30,000 miners were killed in the United States in the last ten years; that 75,000 were injured, many maimed for life."[26]

Simultaneously, engineers and statisticians were becoming convinced that accidents were an unavoidable and even routine aspect of industrial labor—an interpretation that fit well with reformers' assumptions that workers bore some responsibility too. Starting in the 1880s, engineers gradually recognized that it might be possible to design safer workplaces that would protect even the most careless workers; moreover, companies, not workers, seemed best positioned to undertake this work.[27] Eastman's research helped support this new approach. In *Work-Accidents and the Law*, she documented that in Pittsburgh, roughly one-third of accidents occurred not because of any negligence on the part of employers or workers, but because "danger to life and limb is inherent in modern manufacture, construction and transportation. Accidents happen *in the course of industry*."[28] A few years later, Alice Hamilton likewise proved that only rarely did workers' carelessness cause occupational illnesses. Starting with the lead industry, Hamilton documented how workers' ignorance—or "greenness"—and lack of power created tragic results. A newly arrived immigrant from Russia, for instance, "was set to working with the red lead paste and used to moisten his fingers in his mouth as he worked, because he had never been told that the stuff was dangerous. He was seriously leaded at the end of ten days." She added, "House and sign painters often have the choice between a lunch eaten with paint-smeared hands and no lunch at all."[29] Building off such research, statisticians such as Isaac Max Rubinow—whom we will meet again later—argued that "an industrial accident is not an accident at all."[30] Since no one was at fault for many accidents or diseases, a no-fault, automatic compensation system made increasing sense to reformers such as Eastman as well as to her regular partner in labor law advocacy: the AALL.

Founded in 1906 by Progressive economists John R. Commons and Richard T. Ely, the AALL started life as a research think tank that promoted uniform labor legislation and investigated labor conditions. But when Wisconsin-trained economist John B. Andrews became secretary in 1909, he took the AALL in a new direction. Soon it became one of the most active policy advocacy organizations in the fields of social insurance and protective labor legislation, pressing lawmakers to address workplace hazards, provide compensation for unemployed and injured workers, and enact health insurance. Often writing in the pages of the reform magazine *Survey*—edited jointly by Edward T. Devine, the founder of the New York Charity Organization Society, and Paul U. Kellogg, the director of the Pittsburgh Survey—the AALL's members contended that the power of the state could remedy some of the economic insecurities endemic to working-class life in the early twentieth century. By reducing the vulnerabilities brought on by accidents, illnesses, unemployment, and old age, protective labor legislation would lessen class conflict, prevent socialism, and improve national efficiency.[31]

As Eastman and AALL leaders considered how to address the social problems caused by industrial accidents, they turned an increasingly critical eye on the employers' liability system, the contemporary legal means for dealing with work accidents. Instead of aiding the struggling households that resulted from industrial accidents, the employers' liability system seemed to be fueling what reformers perceived as an explosion of public dependence.[32] When workers or their families tried to sue an employer for compensation, they were often stymied by one of the three dominant employers' liability doctrines which courts had constructed largely to protect employers. The "fellow-servant" doctrine entirely exempted employers from liability for accidents caused by other workers; "contributory negligence" enabled an employer to disregard a lawsuit if an employee had been at all negligent; and "assumption of risk" allowed an employer to argue that an employee had voluntarily accepted the risks inherent in a particular line of employment by taking the job. Of course, the anger of the AALL and other reformers at the employers' liability system also stemmed from the fact that it was a court-based rather than an administrative system; many Progressives, particularly those working on labor legislation, detested the judiciary for its conservatism.[33]

Companies regularly used the employers' liability doctrines to deny accident victims any compensation. The managers of Pacific Mills in Lawrence, Massachusetts, for instance, determined that all but 69 of 1,000 work accidents between 1900 and 1905 were due to carelessness or inattention on the part of a worker or fellow employee.[34] Judges, in turn, interpreted these doctrines strictly. For instance, under the assumption of risk doctrine, employers could argue that workers had accepted the risks if they had reported a hazard to a superior but remained at work under threat of losing their job. One seventeen-year-old girl lost her hands to a laundry mangle after she told her supervisor that she was frightened of one that was running at an unusually high speed. Her supervisor ordered her to either work on the mangle or lose her job. The judge ruled that by remaining at work, the girl had assumed the risk of using the equipment and forfeited any right to compensation.[35]

While researching *Work-Accidents and the Law*, furthermore, Eastman had discovered that, like the laundry worker, the vast majority of those injured or killed in industrial accidents received no compensation at all. Eastman recounted, for instance, the fate of six men "who were totally disabled for life: four of these men will walk on two crutches for the rest of their lives, one lost an arm and a leg, and one is paralyzed. Of these six men three received no compensation whatever; one $365, one $125, and one $30. The total loss of income for these men up to the end of their lives, according to their earnings at the time of the injury and the mortality tables, will amount to $12,365. The total compensation for the six cases amounted to $520—in other words four per cent of the loss."[36] Such uneven, minimal compensation was far from unusual under the American liability system. Legislative commissions and Progressive labor law reformers repeatedly confirmed that, depending on the year and location, only 10 to 50 percent of victims' families received compensation, even as legislatures began to weaken the reach of employers' liability doctrines and juries began granting larger awards in the 1890s.[37] Nevertheless, in most cases lawyers claimed the small amount of money that plaintiffs received after their long legal fights. A man in Duluth, Minnesota, for instance, received a $1,357 award, including interest, after a two-year legal struggle. The lawyer took $635, expert witnesses and additional lawyers charged $313.14, and court fees came to $73.20. After $147.20 in medical fees and $25 for an interpreter, the man had "less than $100 and [was] still in debt to the institutions that had taken care of him until his leg healed."[38]

Eastman and her allies—as well as workers themselves—directly connected paltry and sporadic liability awards with family impoverishment and social waste. She argued: "Instead of making the least of the industrial accident loss, we are making the most of it. We are allowing the bulk of it to be borne by those least able to bear it. We are distributing it so that it means the greatest possible amount of hardship to individuals."[39] Although Eastman downplayed families' reliance on public aid, *Survey* editor Devine noted that 80 percent of families suffering work accidents in New York City had to apply for aid from charity.[40] Likewise, the International Association of Machinists (IAM) queried: "Why shouldn't the workman who goes into his daily fight with modern machinery be assured that his injury will be regarded as an honorable wound, entitling him to decent consideration? Why should not the industrial soldier, meeting his death in forms as terrible as those of any battlefield, die knowing that he will leave, if not glory, at least a few years' food for his family?"[41]

Employers, too, complained that the liability system was ineffective. Only a fraction of the premiums that employers paid to insurance companies actually reached their workers. In 1904, Wisconsin's Special Committee on Industrial Insurance found that if an employer owed "$18 to an injured employee . . . on account of injury," another $82 went to the insurance companies. New

York State's Wainwright Commission—which put together the state's first workmen's compensation bill with help from the AALL—discovered that New York firms fared only a little better. Just 36.34 percent of the money that employers paid for liability insurance reached workers (exclusive of lawyers' fees).[42] Even when employers genuinely wanted to pay compensation for accidents, liability companies fought virtually every claim, leaving generous companies no choice but to pay workers themselves. And as legislators and juries weakened the common-law defenses, employers' insurance premiums rose from $203,137 in 1887 to $35 million in 1911.[43]

Eastman's reform colleagues—in particular, leaders of the AALL—argued that the common-law defenses exempted employers from responsibility, leaving workers and society bearing nearly the entire burden of industrial accidents. To some, such as Pittsburgh Survey director Paul U. Kellogg, it seemed as if companies derived part of their profits from the destruction of families. He thundered, "The fact that at Monongah [where 367 men died in an explosion in 1907] the very homes of the miners were part of the producing plant, does no more than emphasize the break where an industry turns back to society the families it has used and crippled."[44]

Instead, Eastman and AALL leaders hoped to force employers to "internalize" the costs of industrial accidents; in effect, compensation would become just another routine business expense.[45] William F. Willoughby, an economist and fourth president of the AALL, contended in 1913, for instance, "In regard to insurance against old age and invalidity, a strong case can also be made out for throwing a large part of, if not the entire burden upon the industry." He continued, "The workers are literally worn out in the industry as are other pieces of machinery, and it may well be maintained that the industry should provide for this human depreciation as it does for that of inanimate machinery."[46] Eastman, in turn, asserted that an employer should be "'liable' for compensation to all his workmen injured just as he is 'liable' for wages."[47] But in the view of AALL leaders, making employers internalize the costs of accidents offered benefits far beyond simply ensuring more compensation for accident victims' families and, thereby, reducing public dependency.

In fact, *Survey*, the AALL, and labor unionists all contended that the employers' liability system implicitly discouraged factory owners from trying to prevent accidents. Because "compensation for accidents is still on such a primitive, unreal, and fantastic basis," *Survey* editor Devine argued, employers had little incentive to make the workplace safer.[48] If employers were forced to pay their fair share by contributing to a compensation fund, he suggested, market forces would compel manufacturers to install safer equipment and properly train their employees.[49] The AALL thought that this approach might even be cheaper.[50] Although the machinists' union agreed that the employers' liability system encouraged factory owners to disregard safety provisions, like many unions, the IAM's leaders remained skeptical of a government-mandated compensation program. Rather, the IAM's socialist leadership argued that nothing less than nationalization of the railroads and mines would prevent accidents. In a commentary on mine disasters in West Virginia, the *Machinists Monthly Journal* contended: "This terrible carnage will be kept up as long as dividends are the principal things considered in the running of railroads. When the element of profit is eliminated and they are run for the people's benefit by the people ... then and not till then will there be a dearth of one-legged trainmen and one-armed switchmen throughout the land."[51]

Making employers cover the costs of industrial accidents would also improve national efficiency—a popular topic among Progressive reformers, industrial employers, and government officials in the 1910s. Given the AALL's estimates that 30,000 wage earners were killed each year and a minimum of 500,000 severely injured, industrial accidents and the employers' liability system seemed to directly undermine the goals of the efficiency movement. In 1910, the organization reported that industrial accidents cost the United States $1.5 billion a year, or 5 percent of the nation's economy.[52] AALL secretary John B. Andrews, in turn, fretted that the United States could not afford the social costs of industrial accidents or the resulting waste in manpower. Devine backed him up, remarking in *Survey*, "Our failure to conserve labor power is even more conspicuous than our wasteful exploitation of natural resources."[53] The machinists took a similar view, arguing that a third to half of all accidents could be prevented, and that "with the resulting physical impairment," this wastage was of "considerable economic value to the nation as a whole."[54] An automatic, equitable compensation system that could prevent dependency was not only an attractive financial proposition but also promised to relieve a court system straining under the burden of liability suits. In 1910 alone, Washington's state courts spent half their time on liability cases, of which only one out of every ten cases resulted in compensation for the plaintiff.[55]

Last but not least, AALL leaders believed that using the power of the state to force employers to internalize accident costs could potentially reduce class conflict. In 1909, philanthropist and AALL president Henry W. Farnam argued that reforming the liability system would help "steer the Ship of State ... to avoid both the Scylla of conservatism and the Charybdis of radicalism."[56]

Reformers of all stripes agreed with Farnam, among them John Mitchell of the United Mine Workers, Social Gospel leader John Graham Brooks and other religious leaders, and the National Civic Federation.[57] After 1911, the National Association of Manufacturers signed on as well, reflecting many employers' frustration with the uncertainty, expense, and constant conflict inherent in the liability system.[58]

As the fight for workmen's compensation laws picked up steam, the AALL played a critical propaganda role. In 1909, its leaders launched a two-pronged plan for addressing the social and economic problems caused by industrial accidents. The platform called on legislators to remove the common-law defenses that protected employers, require companies to absorb accident costs, and establish an automatic state-based system of workmen's compensation that would help injured workers regardless of negligence.[59] Like most Progressive organizations, the AALL advocated administrative—rather than judicial—supervision of labor legislation, preferably through an omnibus industrial commission of experts like themselves.[60] In so doing, the organization's leaders hoped to use workmen's compensation as a means to expand paternalist social welfare legislation and as a model for an expanded administrative state.[61] In the coming years, the AALL would organize four major conferences on workmen's compensation as well as several on occupational diseases, publish a wide array of press releases and educational pamphlets, and begin producing its own journal, the *American Labor Legislation Review* (in 1911). But one of the organization's proudest moments likely came in 1909 when it managed to place two members on the Wainwright Commission charged by the New York State legislature with developing a workmen's compensation law: economist Henry R. Seager and Crystal Eastman.

The Limits of an Administrative Solution

Reflecting the intense frustration of virtually every party involved with the employers' liability system, other states quickly followed New York's example after the Empire State passed its first compensation law in 1910—a law that was soon overturned. Within just one year, nine legislatures passed compensation laws and, by 1920, forty-three states had statutes on their books.[62] In many ways, compensation statutes proved at least a temporary boon to the families of workers who suffered industrial accidents. But at the same time, the programs reflected lawmakers' and labor reformers' fears of encouraging dependency on public aid, as well as their racialized and gendered assumptions about "fitness" and who counted as a worker.

Although most states began with elective programs, legislators provided both workers and employers with inducements to join. Workers would gain prompt, automatic compensation for their injuries: usually half of weekly wages, plus medical expenses.[63] Employers, in turn, would obtain protection from lawsuits by injured employees; universally, compensation statutes reduced or eliminated the employer-friendly legal doctrines of fellow-servant, assumption of risk, and contributory negligence. And in nearly every state, lawmakers removed the compensation process from the courts. Reflecting the consensus among employers, workers, lawmakers, and reformers that a court-based system of compensation would be unfair and unpredictable, legislators arranged for administrative commissions to oversee the process. In so doing, compensation statutes were part and parcel of a larger shift: the rise of the administrative state.[64]

Compensation advocates and legislators alike argued that overly generous benefits, or excessively long payments, would discourage workers and their families from returning to work and self-sufficiency. Theodore Roosevelt stated in 1908, for instance, "True you have lost an arm, and for a considerable period of time it will be difficult for you to engage in the labor to which you have been accustomed, or to acquire this ability to do other work." At the same time, he contended, "one armed men are not necessarily drones, and it is your duty to try again to become a self-supporting member of society as soon as you can do so." Like other Progressive reformers, Roosevelt cautioned lawmakers against encouraging public dependency. He advised, "Any law which, by its provisions for indefinite payments, would invite the injured man to remain in a perpetual state of idleness would be thoroughly unwise."[65]

American workmen's compensation acts drew on precedents from Germany, France, and other European countries, but offered considerably more-limited benefits. Low compensation levels reflected a distinctively American reluctance to encourage public dependency. While nearly every European country provided lifetime pensions for permanent total and partial disability, every state except Washington set time limits of four to eight years; Washington's law only covered workers in industries designated as particularly hazardous.[66] The federal law of 1908, which covered only 25 percent of federal employees, provided just a year of compensation for death or disability—support more akin to the lump sum settlements awarded by juries under the employers' liability system.[67] Under the dismemberment schedules popularized by New Jersey's pioneering statute, workers with certain disabilities received a predetermined number of weeks of compensation. In New York, for example, workers were awarded sixty weeks for the loss of a thumb, 240 weeks for the loss of an arm, and 128 weeks for the loss of an eye. In addition, most states capped the total payment at approximately $3,000.[68] At the end of the designated period, compensation ended.[69] Moreover, in order to discourage "malingering," American states before 1921 routinely mandated a two-week waiting period for compensation. European nations, in contrast, required only a three-day waiting period, while both Italy and Spain began compensation payments the same day as the accident.[70]

Several different factors contributed to the stinginess of compensation programs in the United States, including court rulings on the legality of early compensation programs, lawmakers' assumptions that workers shared responsibility for accidents, and the federal system. Unlike the more generous Continental programs, states provided only 50 percent of wages, with a proportional reduction for partial temporary and permanent disability.[71] Although most legislatures mandated a minimum payment of $4 or $5 per week for total temporary or permanent disability, U.S. compensation acts routinely capped payments at $10 or $12 per week, far below the wages of skilled workers, in part because legislators assumed workers bore much of the responsibility for accidents.[72] As compensation expert Isaac Max Rubinow later explained, "it was to be a quid pro quo—in accepting it the wageworker was asked to relinquish not only the chance of a liberal verdict, but even a part of the loss sustained."[73]

In part, this quid pro quo aspect of American workmen's compensation acts arose out of the 1911 *Ives v. South Buffalo Railway* decision, which overturned the first New York compensation statute. By prohibiting the compulsory taking of employers' property, the *Ives* decision led lawmakers in other states to establish voluntary programs with low compensation rates.[74] In such states, legislators encouraged employers to join by eliminating the common-law defenses—the fellow-servant, contributory negligence, and assumption of risk doctrines—for companies that refused to enter the state compensation programs.

Finally, the federal system of the United States exerted downward pressure on compensation rates. The Ohio compensation committee, for instance, complained, "It is absolutely impossible for Ohio—a lone State—to pay to the widow and children of the injured employe [sic] any approach to compensation commensurate with their loss." The commission suggested that if states had been able to work together, they could have tripled the amount offered to industrial accident victims and their families.[75]

Not only did U.S. compensation statutes provide far stingier benefits than their European counterparts, but the programs also reflected both the gender and racial segmentation of the labor market and lawmakers' and employers' assumptions about who qualified as a "worker" and who was "fit." Unlike their European counterparts, the bills excluded large categories of workers, most notably farm and domestic workers. Because the majority of African Americans and women labored in the agriculture and service sectors, these exclusions meant that compensation statutes served white men, largely immigrants, laboring in the industrial sectors.[76] Rubinow hinted at the gendered assumptions behind the exclusion of domestic servants, noting that "the whole subject of domestic service [was] one which didn't seem... to deserve serious consideration. The servant girl was a standard joke like the mother-in-law." He added that legislators feared the wrath of millions of farm families and households with servants.[77] Edwin S. Lott, the president of the United States Casualty Company, pointed to the illogical nature of such blanket exclusions, noting that compensation acts covered stable boys in livery stables but not cowboys on farms. Despite being less than liberal on some aspects of compensation—for instance, he wanted workers to cover their own medical costs—Lott argued that compensation acts should cover all employees. He observed, "I do not think it right to pay the house or hotel mechanic while he is laid up from an accident, and force the house or hotel maid to rely on the common law [of employers' liability] when she is blown up by a gas stove in the kitchen. Do you? I do not see any difference between the needs of the man working in the shop and the woman working in the kitchen—except votes."[78]

Due to gendered notions of dependency and assumptions about who qualified as a worker, the families of female industrial accident victims collected but little. Compensation advocates such as Eastman and the leaders of the AALL believed in encouraging men to provide for their households—to be male "breadwinners."[79] Lawmakers agreed. Accordingly, they modeled compensation laws on the wrongful death statutes of the 1840s and 1850s, which had barred widowers from suing for the deaths of their wives. The New York State compensation act designed by the Wainwright Commission in 1910, for instance, provided far more aid to dependent widows than to widowers; in effect, commissioners had assumed that only men were breadwinners.[80]

Racialized and gendered concepts of "fitness" meant that some groups of workers and their families sacrificed far more. During the Hawk's Nest Tunnel disaster in the early 1930s, for instance, thousands of African American migrant laborers developed the lung disease silicosis after drilling a dam tunnel through deadly silica without any protective equipment or safety precautions. Firm in their view that such a disfranchised and oppressed workforce would hardly complain, Union Carbide and Carbon never even informed workers of the dangers.[81] As many as 1,500 workers died in the "Village of the Living Dead"; the company arranged for a local mortician to bury them in unmarked graves in a cornfield. Aided by the popular belief that "Negroes didn't know how to care for themselves," the company successfully defended itself against most compensation claims, paying the parents of single black workers just $30. White families garnered up to $1,600.[82]

Nevertheless, the AALL, *Survey*, and unions such as the IAM hailed early versions of workmen's compensation as solving many of the social problems that stemmed from the employers' liability system. Foremost, compensation programs, they believed, would make employers responsible for preventing both accidents and families' dependence on charity or public aid, rather than placing the entire burden on workers.[83] As Jane Addams stated: "We must insist that the livelihood of the laborer shall not be beaten down below the level of efficient citizenship. From the human standpoint there is an obligation upon charity to discover how much of its material comes as the result of social neglect, remediable incapacity, and the lack of industrial safeguards. Is it because our modern industrialism is so new that we have been slow to connect it with the poverty all about us?"[84] The machinists desired foremost to establish "a compensation principle," which Arthur Holder argued was "one of the growths of civilization, one of the advanced movements to protect humanity."[85]

Although the machinists wanted a predictable, fair system of compensation, they were not sure if the government was the best administrator. Burned by years of judge-made rule by injunction, they preferred union control and, if not that, a nationally administered system of compensation to ensure fairness.[86] A 1909 story from the *Machinists Monthly Journal* illustrated the depths of union members' anger at the judiciary: "A little girl in Trenton[,] N.J., was run down by a street car and had one of her legs cut off.... The jury in the case returned a verdict awarding the little girl $8,500 for her accident." The writer wryly remarked, "The great and wise judge who presided set aside the verdict of the jury on the grounds that artificial legs were now perfected to such an extent that it was a positive pleasure to possess one, inferring thereby that the little girl, instead of being awarded damages, ought to piously return thanks to the good and kind corporation who had made such pleasure possible for her by butchering her beneath their wheels"[87]

The new workmen's compensation system, AALL leaders contended, was fair to employers and employees alike.[88] The commission-based organization of all state plans except New Jersey undoubtedly played a role in *Survey* and AALL's enthusiasm—it allowed experts like themselves to properly and actively enforce regulations.[89] The AALL and *Survey* also hoped that employers would find it in their financial interest to prevent accidents now that employers had lost the common-law defenses that let them avoid financial penalties in most cases.[90] Germany's experiences made them hopeful, since German employers had quite unexpectedly "invested in safety devices at a rate matched by employers nowhere else in the North Atlantic economy."[91] Finally, workmen's compensation would help repair the tattered relationship of employers and employees, potentially preventing socialism.[92] In December 1911, *Survey* printed (and officially endorsed) a petition calling for a federal commission on industrial relations. The petition argued that lawmakers had done little to address employers' failure to safeguard workers against occupational diseases and accidents, while quickly acting to crush strikes. "[The workingman] believes that the hand of the law, strong in the protection of property, often drops listless whenever measures are proposed to lighten labor's heavy burden."[93]

Did Workmen's Compensation Prevent Dependency?

Just as the AALL and its allies began to celebrate the compensation statutes spreading across the nation, some reformers began to express doubts about whether the new system had addressed the scope of social problems caused by industrial accidents. In late 1912, AALL member Isaac Max Rubinow launched a broadside on the new compensation statutes and the organization's entire approach to compensation law. A socialist like Eastman and one of the leading statisticians in the country, he approached the field of social insurance out of a deep concern about the hardships caused by poverty rather than a fear of public dependency. In 1913, AALL president William F. Willoughby had defined social insurance as "a device for accomplishing two exceedingly important welfare objects: providence, that is provision against a contingency certain or likely to occur, and distribution of the burden of loss entailed by the contingency when it does occur so that it can be more easily borne.... Under a purely savings system, the burden of loss falls with crushing force upon the individual." Willoughby continued, "Social insurance competes directly with charitable relief."[94]

Drawing on his expertise in the statistical analysis of work accidents and accident insurance, Rubinow argued that reformers' single-minded concern about temporary dependency was fundamentally misguided. Instead, he argued that the AALL and its counterparts should have focused their attention on "disability"—a term he used often. He suggested, in fact, that the compensation laws for which AALL members had fought so hard would fail to prevent public dependency among workers with newly acquired sensory and

Statistician, social insurance advocate, and workmen's compensation analyst Isaac Max Rubinow. Photo by Savony, courtesy of the Kheel Center for Labor-Management Documentation and Archives, Cornell University.

physical disabilities, as well as chronic illnesses. Cognizant that most would continue to work in some fashion, albeit likely not at the same wages or status as before, Rubinow contended that compensation laws would leave these workers mired in poverty. His critiques of the AALL approach to compensation law ultimately persuaded the organization to alter its approach. But by the time the AALL began proposing model legislation that reflected his advice, the nature of the compensation system had been set. Policy makers could not easily reshape the statutes for which they had advocated—and helped draft—just a few years before.

Rubinow's unusual insights into the challenges that workmen's compensation laws would pose to workers with acquired disabilities arose out of both his early work as a doctor and his pioneering role in the development of actuarial statistics. Born in Russia in 1875 to a wealthy Jewish family and trained as a physician, he first recognized the links between poverty and ill health while seeing patients in New York's Lower East Side. Distraught at their sufferings, Rubinow often gave them money instead of charging them, much to his wife's dismay.[95] After studying economics, sociology, political philosophy, and statistics at Columbia University, he moved to Washington, D.C., to work for the Civil Service Commission.[96] Following brief stints in the Department of Agriculture and the Department of Commerce and Labor, Rubinow secured a position in the Bureau of Labor Statistics. While in the nation's capital, he published on a vast array of topics ranging from domestic service and discrimination against African Americans to Russian agriculture, as well as much of the Bureau of Labor Statistics' eleven-volume *Workmen's Insurance and Compensation Systems in Europe*.[97] Desirous of leading the state-based workmen's compensation movement but frustrated by his spot on the sidelines in Washington, Rubinow returned to New York City in 1911 to take a position as chief statistician for the Ocean Accident & Guarantee Company. He hoped that his time at the firm would eventually qualify him to direct a state workmen's compensation fund.

Rubinow's return to New York put him in close contact with the interlocking communities of reformers around *Survey* and the AALL. Elected to the organization's General Administrative Council in 1912, he soon became a member of the new Social Insurance Committee as well, where he played a central role in developing the AALL's model compensation and sickness insurance bills.[98] He also served as a contributing editor and frequent writer for *Survey* from 1911 to 1916 and drafted the social insurance plank for Theodore Roosevelt's presidential campaign in 1912. The following year, he published his first magnum opus, *Social Insurance*, which long stood as the major text in the field.

Rubinow quickly emerged as a leading expert on compensation within the statistical and insurance communities—experience that would give him unique insights into the structure of compensation law and its impact on newly disabled workers' lives. Illustrating his children's recollections that he was "always working...he didn't know what it meant to play," Rubinow founded the Casualty Actuarial and Statistical Society of America in 1914 and served as the society's first president; he also led the rate committee for the Workmen's Compensation Service Bureau for much of the 1910s.[99] Later on, he summed up his work for the Service Bureau with his characteristic lack of humility: "I was...the committee."[100] In addition to these endeavors, Rubinow developed a "standard accident table" that would allow states to estimate the frequency and type of accidents. At a time when state and federal officials had only a scant grasp of accident rates, the table constituted a crucial accomplishment.[101] Soon, state officials from around the country began calling on Rubinow to advise on compensation rates and calculate the "pure premium": the rate that companies should pay for compensation insurance.[102] Despite his groundbreaking work and rising fame, what coworkers termed his "unfortunate personality" prevented him from ever fulfilling his dream of heading a state compensation fund.[103]

Nevertheless, within just four years, Rubinow would articulate a prescient critique of the ways the statutes would impoverish workers with disabling injuries—a critique that would lead the AALL to adopt an entirely new approach to workmen's compensation laws. Soon after returning to New York and joining the AALL's Committee on Social Insurance, he began using the organization's annual conference as well as pieces in *Survey* and *American Labor Legislation Review* to share his opinion that compensation laws failed people with partial permanent disabilities.[104] Shortly after New York passed a revised compensation act in 1913, he faulted the law in *Survey* for the "highly unsatisfactory" way it treated workers with such disabilities. He noted that "barring fatal accidents, the class of 'permanent partial disability' is economically the most important one," those affected being "from twenty-five to forty times more numerous" than those with total permanent disability, adding that many accidents causing partial disabilities "lead to a very serious impairment of 'standards,' not a few to actual destitution."[105]

While it is not entirely clear why Rubinow became fascinated by the issue of disability, his interest probably dated from his work at the Bureau of Labor Statistics and perhaps also his time as a physician on the Lower East Side. Reflecting on the process of constructing his standard accident table, he termed the "measurement of degree of permanent or partial incapacity" to be "both theoretically and practically one of the most difficult of the technical problems in the entire field of social insurance."[106] Disability raised critical questions about subjectivity and who could and should define disability.

Although only a small fraction of workplace accidents led to permanent disabilities—4,742 of every 100,000 accidents—Rubinow argued that such permanently disabled people constituted a crucial class for labor reformers. "Here we are dealing with cripples, cripples both surgically and economically, cripples made year in and year out, surviving for many years, and swelling the army of defective and therefore partly dependent wage workers," he noted. "While their economic condition may not be always as desperate as that of the victims of total permanent disability, their greater importance collectively is due to the fact that they are 40 to 50 times as numerous."[107] Rubinow suggested that no one involved in the compensation movement—from legislators and insurance companies to engineers and physicians—was equipped to deal with the issue of workers disabled by industrial accidents. He explained, "So long as industrial injuries were adjudicated in courts under liability laws through verdicts and always in a lump sum ... there was no apparent necessity to develop the body of experience as to the economic effects of physical injuries which, after all, is the crux of the problem."[108]

Unlike fellow AALL members, Rubinow recognized that most people with acquired disabilities would continue to work, but he feared that they would struggle to survive on their compensation and what little they could earn. "Instead of incapacity or disability, we really have to think in terms of reduced capacity or ability to work except . . . where absolute inability to continue a specific occupation may of course be combined with only partial disability for other occupations," he argued.[109] Recognizing that disabling injuries often caused workers to lose both status and income, he observed that only rarely could such workers find jobs that would cover the gap between their previous wages and compensation payments, let alone once their compensation stopped. He therefore contended that a partial disability—of 40 percent, for instance—was in practice much more than that, although such a worker received well under 40 percent of wages as compensation. But low compensation rates were far from the only flaw that Rubinow saw with the design of compensation statutes.

Disabilities, Rubinow suggested, had to be evaluated in the context of individual lives, rather than according to states' rigid "dismemberment schedules." The schedules varied from state to state but in general attached a set number of weeks to each major type of injury. In Iowa, for example, workers were entitled to 50 percent wages for 300 weeks for the loss of an eye, 200 weeks for the loss of an arm, 40 weeks for the loss of a thumb, 15 weeks for the loss of a little finger, and so on.[110] Workers who lost the function of a digit or limb—but not did not suffer an actual amputation—received proportionally less. To treat disabled workers fairly, compensation acts, in his view, had to incorporate factors such as age, occupation, economic context, and adaptability to new occupations, as well as the rate at which an individual healed, the ways in which a disability evolved over time, and the worker's overall physical condition.[111] Rubinow lamented the presence of a dismemberment schedule in the revised New York Compensation Act enacted in 1913, complaining: "An iron-clad rigid scale. So much for an arm, so little for a finger." He continued, "The obvious fact is disregarded that the same organs often have a very different economic value in different trades; a leg means everything to a stevedore, but economically much less to a watchmaker; the loss of two fingers may seriously disable the latter but not the former."[112]

While Rubinow considered occupation to be the critical issue in making a fair determination of compensation, he also stressed the importance of age, as well as the ways that disabilities might evolve over time and the ways in which various demographic factors intersected. On this basis, he found fault with the much-lauded California act, for which he had served as an adviser, and which provided detailed schedules determining the effect of 306 different injuries on 1,150 different occupations and ages from fifteen to seventy-five.

"It is furthermore obviously untrue that if the degree of disability has been determined at the time of the accident at 70 percent, that the remaining 30 percent will be retained during life," complained Rubinow. "A seriously disabled workman is grossly handicapped in the competitive labor market." He continued, "The combined handicap of advancing age and serious physical disability is almost unsurmountable."[113]

Rubinow urged states to replace their dismemberment schedules with more flexible, expert determinations that could better suit disabled workers' evolving needs. Reflecting his characteristically Progressive faith in administrative solutions, he advocated personalized evaluations that could reflect such intersecting factors as age, occupation, economic context, and individuals' evolving degree of disability. While he acknowledged that failing to provide a set time and amount of compensation eligibility might encourage malingering, Rubinow argued that lawmakers could not possibly hope to accurately determine the degree of disability for the rest of a worker's life. "No decision should be considered as absolutely final and irrevocable because circumstances may change," he advised.[114] In a letter to fellow statistician and compensation expert E. H. Downey, Rubinow added: "It takes time to develop [total permanent disabilities]. It may take two or three years. Some cases will get better and others will gradually grow worse. I think that will especially hold true of permanent partial disability."[115] In addition, more flexible determinations would better enable compensation committees to deal with the many disabilities that were not simple dismemberments, as well as dismemberments that did not precisely fit the schedules. He noted that such disabilities as frozen joints could be more troublesome than the actual loss of an arm.[116]

The key issue, Rubinow believed, was the gradual impoverishment of workers with acquired disabilities—a problem that compensation statutes failed to remedy. After an AALL meeting that focused on determining the best method of insurance for compensation acts, he remarked:

> If I were a wage worker, I would go away from this meeting with very mixed feelings. Let us assume a fairly light accident, one that disables a workingman for six weeks without leading to permanent disability. If he was earning $12 a week, his compensation in most states will be $6 a week. For the first two weeks he will receive nothing. Thus his entire compensation will amount to $24, out of which he will be forced to pay the entire cost of medical aid after the first two weeks, because in most states the payment of medical benefits is limited to two weeks. Do you call that compensation? Will these $24 really prevent want?[117]

Indeed, Rubinow noted that in many states, a totally temporarily disabled worker who earned minimal wages would receive only $4 or $5 per week to support his family. But he found the plight of people with permanent disabilities even more unsettling. While attacking the revised New York Compensation Act, Rubinow queried: "A loss of the right arm creates the right of compensation for 312 weeks or six years, but what of the many years to follow?"[118] The low rates paid by most states also failed to cover the extra expenses encountered by families when they had to care for a disabled member. Like Eastman had, he noted that a dead breadwinner was cheaper than a disabled one.[119]

In addition, Rubinow recognized that employers were increasingly rejecting elderly workers and those with many different types of disabilities in favor of those with intact, interchangeable bodies. "Everyone knows of the handicap of gray hair in applying for employment," he reflected. "How much greater the handicap of the wooden leg, or the sleeveless arm, even the ugly stumps of amputated fingers." Like railroad corporations who refused to hire conductors with a missing finger, employers in sales, clerical, and white-collar sectors enforced particularly high standards of bodily perfection. He noted, "From this point such economically inconsequential injuries, as loss of ear, nose, or scalp, or even ugly scars, may prove to be serious handicaps in the struggle to retain a foothold upon the road to opportunity."[120]

Although Rubinow expressed considerable interest in the burgeoning vocational rehabilitation movement—which aimed to train workers with all sorts of physical, sensory, and even cognitive and psychosocial disabilities, as well as chronic illnesses, to reenter the labor market and teach them the moral value of work—he cautioned labor reformers and legislators against assuming that rehabilitation would fully restore disabled workers' earning capacity or convince employers to drop their prejudice against disabled workers. "The phenomenal success of the individual who rides a bicycle with the aid of two artificial legs and threads a needle with two artificial hands must not be taken as typical," he wryly observed. "Besides actual disability, the question of employability is an important one. From this point of view the industrial cripple is in a very much less favorable position than the military cripple who will be favored both by law (civil service preferences, etc.) and public opinion."[121]

At the same time, Rubinow was not unconcerned about the moral issues raised by workmen's compensation payments. He acknowledged that malingering existed but dismissed it as far less important than the destitution brought on by disability and insufficient compensation.[122] To a limited degree, he shared his fellow labor reformers' fears that too much aid could prove morally corrupting. Dismemberment tables could, Rubinow feared, create an "aristocracy of cripples" accustomed to an "artificial[ly] high standard." For instance, Bruno Lasker, a member of *Survey*'s staff, contended that the best way to make sure that injured workers went back to work was to do periodic medical examinations and revise compensation down if "functional adaptation had progressed."[123] For Rubinow, compensation always had to be directly connected to the actual economic damage done to a worker—if a disability did not interfere with a worker's ability to earn a living, then there was no need to pay compensation for a permanent partial disability.[124]

By the mid-1910s, Rubinow's forceful critiques of workmen's compensation bills succeeding in reshaping the AALL's approach to the compensation issue and forcing the organization's leaders to grapple with the issue of disability. During the organization's initial push for workmen's compensation acts (1909–1912), the members and their editorial allies at *Survey* had uncritically accepted states' compensation rates and time limits.[125] Accordingly, they focused on providing statistics and discussing the social benefits of shifting from employers' liability to compensation.[126] In fact, the AALL and *Survey* had never set a baseline for compensation rates, nor did they discuss the issue of permanent disability prior to late 1912, when Rubinow joined the AALL's new Social Insurance Committee. After his arrival, the organization's leaders promptly began criticizing workmen's compensation statutes in their articles in *Survey*, focusing in particular on the ways in which low compensation rates, waiting periods, and time limits helped create public dependency—and on the issue of disability.[127]

The statistician's influence on the AALL's view of compensation laws became even more apparent in early 1914, when an unsigned editorial proclaimed in the *American Labor Legislation Review* that "the federal government and twenty-four states enacted compensation laws all more or less inadequate."[128] In effect, the piece announced that the AALL would no longer play just a supporting role in the compensation movement. Rather, the organization promised to release its own model compensation standards—standards that would better prevent public dependency among industrial accident victims, especially disabled ones. The AALL's "Standards for Workmen's Compensation" followed Rubinow's recommendations nearly word for word, advising extended coverage of medical expenses, waiting periods of only three to seven days, 67 percent compensation, coverage for disabilities as long as they lasted, permanent coverage for dependents (including widows and widowers) until remarriage, and inclusion of occupational diseases.[129] From the mid-1910s on, the AALL made improving compensation standards a prominent part of its "Immediate Legislative Program."[130]

The AALL had a few notable triumphs. Members such as John B. Andrews successfully advocated for more generous compensation scales in New Jersey and helped establish a workmen's compensation service bureau in the same state to advise workers on the compensation process.[131] Rubinow, Henry Seager, and Andrews also drafted the Kern-McGillicuddy Federal Employees Compensation Act of 1916, which provided compensation nearly up to Rubinow's standards.[132]

Overall, however, Andrews and his fellow AALL members discovered that altering the existing compensation laws was a difficult endeavor. The multiple interest groups involved in compensation programs—lawyers, insurance companies, trade unions, and state industrial commissions—made reform nearly impossible.[133] Only a few states revised their scales upward to account for permanent and temporary total disability; by the mid-1930s, even the most generous states paid injured or disabled workers only two-thirds of their former wages. Lawmakers also retained time limits and monetary caps on compensation payments, and only a third of states added coverage for occupational diseases.[134] Nor did workmen's compensation laws provide disabled workers with an effective alternative to litigation. Due to the difficulty of objectively defining and assessing disability and occupational diseases, disabled workers continued to sue employers for compensation.[135] The AALL regularly pressed for higher rates, shorter waiting periods, and uniform, nationwide compensation legislation but could make no headway against the hodgepodge of state programs.[136] Rubinow's calls to action had come too late. Within just a few years, the fundamental structure of the compensation system had already been fixed. The negative impact of compensation statutes on workers with disabilities would be even more devastating than he had predicted.

And despite his enormous contributions to the field of workmen's compensation, after 1916 Rubinow's difficult personality and his socialist affiliations would exile him from his beloved field of social insurance.[137] His second book, *The Quest for Security*, published in 1934, reportedly helped to inspire Franklin Roosevelt to organize the Committee on Economic Security (out of which would come Social Security), but Rubinow had antagonized so many of his fellow reformers and policy makers that he found himself excluded from the policy-making process.[138]

The Impact of Workmen's Compensation on Disabled Workers

Despite the efforts of Rubinow, the AALL, and *Survey* to improve the original workmen's compensation statutes, the laws had a devastating impact on workers with both congenital and acquired disabilities. Simply put, workmen's compensation provided employers who were already skeptical of disabled workers with a perverse financial incentive to use physical examinations, company doctors, and medical departments to exclude them. Rubinow proved prescient about the ways in which compensation statutes would fail to meet the needs of newly disabled workers. In fact, lawmakers' and reformers' fears about encouraging public dependency had shaped the statutes in ways that made such workers all the more likely to fall into poverty or have to rely on public aid. Like other public policies, compensation laws sought to generalize specific conditions, but disability's immense complexity posed great hurdles. So too did the fact that workers' injuries—and the impact on their earning capacity—often shifted over time. Thus, while many people with acquired disabilities continued to labor, just as people with congenital impairments did, workmen's compensation acts helped to exclude both groups from the wage labor force—and often from paid work as well. Ironically, compensation laws helped to create disability as a social problem of poverty and public dependency.

Much to labor reformers' surprise, workmen's compensation laws almost immediately began limiting the wage work prospects of workers with virtually all types of disabilities, but especially people with physical or sensory impairments and chronic illnesses. In its first annual report, the Industrial Accident Board of Massachusetts commented, "One of the logical but most unexpected developments of the Workmen's Compensation Act [of 1912] was shown almost immediately in the throwing of aged and infirm employees out of industry." The report explained that as soon as the compensation statute went into effect, one firm, for instance, conducted physical examinations of its workers and discharged twenty-two employees as "aged or under par physically."[139] Some companies, such as the Republic Iron & Steel Company in Youngstown and the Avery Company of Illinois, took action even before compensation statutes took effect. Both examined all employees in the month before their respective states' compensation acts went into effect in 1911. For Avery, this practice proved highly profitable. Not only did the firm's relief association have so many fewer requests for aid that it reduced fees by half, but insurance rates plummeted from $3.35 to 85 cents [per worker]. The owner, G. L. Avery, explained that "in dealing with the men, they are given to understand that they are treated as *profitable or unprofitable investments* rather than *desirables or undesirables*."[140]

Given employers' long history of retaining—and, to a lesser degree, hiring—employees with imperfect bodies, why did compensation statutes suddenly turn employers against disabled workers? In large part, the structure of the laws was to blame. Legislators had recognized the catastrophic economic damage often caused by severe impairments, such as total loss of eyesight, amputation of both legs, or loss of both hands. In the hope of preventing severely disabled workers from slipping into public dependency, the "dismemberment schedules" used to set compensation rates provided disproportionately more money for the most serious injuries. Pennsylvania, for instance, mandated 125 weeks of compensation at 50 percent of wages for the loss of one eye and 150 weeks for the loss of one foot, but 500 weeks for total disabilities such as the loss of two eyes or two feet.[141] State industrial accident commissions eventually granted equivalent compensation to workers with partial impairments who became totally disabled in a second accident.[142]

In effect, these provisions meant that a second injury to a worker with an existing physical or sensory disability might well cost employers far more in compensation than a first injury to an able-bodied worker. As firms began to realize the potential financial risks, they began to use physical examinations to exclude disabled job applicants and, to a lesser extent, current employees with disabilities, along with aged workers. Some companies shied away from married men as well, fearful of the cost of supporting dependents should a married worker be injured or killed.[143] Large industrial employers with company physicians and full-fledged medical departments were the first to bar such workers, but as time went on, even department stores and smaller manufacturers rejected current and potential employees with a wide variety of disabilities. Typically, workers with visible disabilities such as the loss of an eye, a hand, or a leg were fired first. But employers also sought to use the growing ranks of industrial physicians to screen out workers with less visible disabilities such as reduced vision or hearing, tuberculosis, hernias, varicose veins, and "hardened arteries," fearing that these impairments might be exacerbated by future injuries and therefore require compensation.[144] The Knights of Labor *Journal* argued, in turn, that compensation acts had imposed a "new status for the workman ... the duty of maintaining a condition of health, alertness and strength not before demanded of him from the employer."[145]

Perversely, physical examinations even became a venue for competition between firms. In effect, having a workforce largely free of "defective" workers now constituted a means for improving efficiency, at least in theory. When Republic Iron & Steel Company began requiring employees to undergo regular exams in 1914, Youngstown Sheet & Tube Company, the Carnegie Steel Company, and other firms followed suit. The inspections covered all workers, "whether in the mills or in the offices."[146] The head physician of "one of the largest industries in the country," for instance, remarked that his firm had no examination policy prior to the compensation act. He commented to fellow industrial surgeon Harry E. Mock: "It was thought best to let every man apply for a job, try himself out, if he could stand up under the work and wished the job, it was his." But when "everybody [wa]s doing it," the firm had little choice. Otherwise, they received only "the refuse of the railroads and steel mills, men who could not qualify in competitive physical examinations." Managers disliked discriminating against "defective men," such as those with one eye, but "the compensation liability [wa]s too great."[147]

Twice-disabled workers pressed industrial accident commissions to grant them compensation for second injuries that led to total disablement, but their success in winning compensation only made employers even more fearful of hiring workers with impairments. After 1914—when a "one-eyed" man in Michigan, Charles Weaver, temporarily won full compensation for the loss of vision in his second eye in a case that received widespread publicity—many more employers instituted physical examinations. The plaintiff's lawyers had acknowledged that the "social effects of an award favorable to Weaver were not unforeseen" and had advised states to amend their compensation laws to address the problem of second injuries. Otherwise, the attorneys predicted that "employers will not hire men with one eye, one leg, or one arm."[148] And within just a month of a 1930 Oklahoma court ruling favorable to a worker with a second injury, employers had fired 7,000 to 8,000 disabled men.[149]

Insurance companies, in particular, helped make disabled workers "undesirable" in the eyes of employers. Once states passed compensation statutes, insurers dropped their practice of rating companies by the "physical condition of the plant and the types of processes carried on." Instead, insurers began to charge companies based on the number of accidents at that plant and granted rate reductions for lower accident rates—giving employers even more incentive to screen out workers with a broad range of different disabilities.[150] Although little direct evidence exists of insurers actively encouraging companies to discriminate against disabled workers, the insurance journal *The Problem* "made no secret of the fact that examination of workmen should be used as a means of eliminating the unfit." The editors advised employers to institute physical examinations for all job applicants, in order to push the costs of taking care of "defectives" back onto society.[151] Companies who self-insured, covering their own compensation expenses without help from an insurer—a practice allowed in some states and adopted by major companies such as International Harvester and Standard Oil—likely had even more reason to bar workers with disabilities. The case of Ford Motor Company, which also self-insured, challenged such logic, of course. Nevertheless, recognizing this temptation, the New York State Industrial Commission required employers who sought to insure themselves to "sign a pledge that [they] will not discriminate against the partially disabled applicants for work."[152]

Complicating matters, most early twentieth-century industrial employers and safety advocates continued to believe that workers—especially those with physical or sensory disabilities—were careless and were responsible for most workplace accidents. Safety advocates, in particular, became increasingly cynical about whether workers actually wanted to protect themselves from accidents. Although overall accident rates began to drop in 1907, safety educators argued that workers' carelessness made the goal of preventing all accidents unreachable. Workers routinely removed safety guards, ignored signs, and disobeyed orders.[153] Don Leschohier of the Minnesota Bureau of Labor, for instance, explained the death of a man at a flour mill as follows: "He had been repeatedly warned against crawling through the belts and unquestionably lost his life through a willful taking of unnecessary risks."[154] In fact, safety managers at steel companies became so frustrated that they shifted their educational focus to the children of workers. Safety workers argued that it would be easier to ingrain "safety first" in children's minds than to change the work habits of their parents.[155] In workers' defense, the spread of piecework, low wages, and speedups made ignoring certain safety rules or equipment financially attractive—or at least worth the risk.[156]

Employers assumed that disabled workers, in particular, were inherently more careless and, therefore, more likely to be involved in industrial accidents. After all, such workers had presumably already had one accident, and their impairments might well contribute to another accident.[157] John Weller of the Packard Motor Car Company explained in 1914 that "all employers of labor today feel that they don't want to take any extra chances.... They think that a man by reason of some physical defects is more liable to accident than others."[158] Policy makers shared—and often affirmed—employers' skepticism about disabled workers. In a 1918 article in the *Monthly Labor Review*, Carl Hookstadt of the U.S. Bureau of Labor Statistics, for instance, advised employers to avoid hiring any disabled workers at all, arguing that a disabled worker was "more liable to injury ... and a greater source of danger to his fellow workman than a normal man."[159]

Workers fought industrial employers' efforts to institute physical examinations but had only limited success. Before the New York Compensation Act came into effect in 1913, several New York City printing firms posted notices that physical examinations would be required of all employees. The Allied

Printing Trades Council of New York informed the firms that the union would allow such exams to be made only by union doctors and suggested that the workers might go on strike; as a result, the printing firms reconsidered.[160] The printers were not the only workers to fight employers' attempts to institute physical examinations. In 1914, 16,000 General Electric workers threatened to strike over the company's use of medical examinations as a means of rejecting disabled job applicants with disabilities.[161] The same year, the Executive Council of the American Federation of Labor (AFL) warned that compensation laws were "creating an unemployable class."[162] Nevertheless, physical examinations became an increasingly popular means of limiting compensation payouts even outside the industrial sector. Indeed, the Kern-McGillicuddy federal compensation act of 1916 required medical examinations of all federal employees. AALL member Edwin W. De Leon praised this provision, arguing that "the best possible man can be assured only by a physical examination ... [and] it will reasonably follow that he will do the best possible work, and with the best possible effect."[163]

Ironically, the "second-injury problem" was not as unexpected as the Industrial Accident Board of Massachusetts had claimed. In fact, it was widely known in Great Britain and other European countries that had already established compensation programs.[164] The British Home Office, for instance, found that the institution of workmen's compensation in 1897 resulted in the exclusion of all one-eyed workers from the boilermaking and shipbuilding industries. Elderly and even middle-aged workers, too, found themselves unwelcome in many sectors.[165] Given the transatlantic nature of Progressive reform movements such as workmen's compensation, American compensation advocates and possibly even lawmakers may have known about the second-injury issue.[166] Railroads, furthermore, provided an earlier example closer to home—an example whose relevance apparently went unrecognized by legislators. During the 1880s and 1890s, the American railroad brotherhoods and companies established relief departments and insurance plans, as well as mandatory physical examinations. Workers with even the "slight disability of a missing finger" soon began to lose their jobs. Instead of celebrating such workers' courage and experience, the railroad companies and brotherhoods portrayed workers with disabilities, especially visible physical ones, as intemperate and reckless, and as posing an unnecessary financial risk.[167]

As a result of compensation statutes and, in particular, the second-injury problem, workers with many different types of disabilities had an ever more difficult time finding employment during the late 1910s and the 1920s, especially in the industrial sector. As early as 1916, a study of manufacturers in

Cincinnati "revealed that 50 per cent of the group did not wish to employ handicapped men because of the added liability in case of second accident."[168] Based on research conducted in the early 1920s, the Consumers' League of Eastern Pennsylvania reported that the "loss of the sight of one eye may not appear to be a very serious disability" in itself. They noted, however, that "whether the fear of losing the other eye and permanent disability resulting therefrom is the determining factor or not, employers seem most unwilling to hire a man who has lost the sight of one eye."[169] And by the late 1920s, various divisions at the Pullman Company reported rejecting between 10 and 21.5 percent of applicants based on physical examinations.[170] Even nonindustrial firms such as Montgomery Ward began to screen out workers whom examiners found to be of "questionable" fitness.[171]

But as policy makers discovered when they tried to rework compensation laws, there was no easy way to solve the second-injury problem. By 1915, sixteen of thirty-five states had altered their compensation statutes to attempt to eliminate the financial hazards of hiring disabled workers. Led by New York, states tried various ways of limiting payouts to disabled workers who had a second accident, such as restricting twice-disabled workers to compensation for only one injury at a time, apportioning compensation based on the degree of new disability or the combination of disabilities, or creating public second-injury funds to fully compensate such workers. States also stopped using dismemberment schedules for minor injuries (e.g., the loss of two fingers) and placed greater weight on the difference in earnings before and after injuries. In 1919, Minnesota even banned insurers from discriminating against "the handicapped."[172] Nonetheless, employers—industrial and nonindustrial alike—continued to discriminate against workers with many different types of disabilities. The second-injury problem reemerged after World War II, when employers cited it as a reason for barring disabled veterans from employment. One disabled World War II veteran reported: "I get the same story everywhere I go. Either they don't have a job I can do, or if I do, they can't hire me because of insurance rules."[173]

Workmen's compensation laws even affected disabled workers at Ford Motor Company. Starting in the early 1920s, job applicants with a wide array of disabilities encountered increasing hostility, as did some current employees with newly acquired disabilities. Workmen's compensation helped to drive this dramatic shift in employment policy. To make matters worse, workers newly disabled at Ford Motor Company found that the laws failed to meet their financial needs, just as Rubinow had predicted.

In 1921, the chief advocate for disabled workers at Ford Motor Company—Reverend Samuel Marquis, the head of the Sociological Department—left the company. After an intense dispute with infamously harsh production manager and plant superintendent Charles Sorenson over how best to treat and motivate workers, Marquis decided that their goals were incompatible. Sorenson cared about little else than increasing production, while Marquis desired to improve workers' lot.[174] In addition, after the labor turmoil of World War I, the postwar recession, and the Ford Motor Company's consequent near-failure, Ford had lost interest in paternalistic programs aimed at ensuring "loyalty and good-will."[175] Sorenson's elevation and Marquis's departure left disabled workers vulnerable because they were now considered to be too hard to fit into the production line. Workers with disabilities were occasionally fired outright. Robert A. Shaw, the head of the Safety Department in the late 1910s and early 1920s, explained that after Marquis left, "there was a little drop-off on ... [setting up special jobs for disabled people] except where a foreman or superintendent firmly believed in the principle ... [and] the principle I think lost its real force."[176]

Several different factors accounted for the Ford Motor Company's new hostility toward disabled workers. One of the most important factors was workmen's compensation. Michigan had passed a compensation act in 1912, but thanks to Marquis and Henry Ford himself, the act did not have a negative impact on disabled workers at Ford until the early 1920s. Evidence is scant, but it seems that Sorenson's rise to power allowed the head of the Legal Department, L. B. Robertson, to implement a strategy designed to limit the company's potential liability to disabled workers. In fact, Robertson had long been concerned about the second-injury problem, but his concerns had gained little traction with Henry Ford until the 1920s.[177] One worker who had become "crippled" while loading trucks with heavy materials highlighted the dramatic nature of the shift in 1927, remarking "When employees are injured, usually they are thrown out and new ones employed."[178]

At the same time, the Ford Legal Department suddenly adopted an aggressive stance in compensation cases, fighting tooth and nail to avoid paying compensation. Prior to Sorenson's takeover, the Legal Department had tried to be "very liberal" in paying compensation, often providing more than the law required, and generally trying to pay enough to ensure that injured employees would not fall into debt. Such practices also helped to keep compensation cases outside the courts and away from the Michigan Industrial Commission.[179] While discussing a difficult case in 1915, for example, L. B. Robertson reminded James Couzens, Ford's business manager, that the company preferred "to pay compensation in cases where there might be some technical question involved rather than take advantage of the law to defeat same."[180] Starting in the early 1920s, however, company lawyers began to take advantage of legal loopholes such as an expired statute of limitations, the absence of an actual accident, and the lack of clear negligence by the employer.[181] David McKenzie, for instance, lost one finger in a machine after having a dizzy spell and falling. Because his accident could not be attributed to negligence on the part of the Ford Motor Company, both the firm and the state compensation board refused to grant any award.[182] Ford's Legal Department also began to appeal cases to Michigan's Supreme Court to avoid paying compensation.[183]

Nevertheless, in striking contrast to other firms, Ford Motor Company retained many of its workers with disabilities. An investigator with the Sage Foundation found more than 13,000 "'physically sub-standard' men and women" laboring at Ford in 1927.[184] The company even kept on workers who had acquired disabilities while in its employ and later sued for additional compensation. Machine repairman Frank Alampi, for instance, had a steel fragment enter his eye in 1926; within two years, he had lost all use of the eye and demanded compensation. Ford Motor Company paid up, and by 1940 Alampi had advanced to the position of arc welder. The company likewise kept on Fred Albers despite the fact that his disability claim was dubious at best. In 1927, he had received a concussion after being struck on the side of the head by an iron bar. After four days, he developed "traumatic psychosis," for which the firm paid three weeks of compensation. Albers continued to work at Ford as a machinist but in 1933 suddenly filed for further compensation, "alleging still disabled as result of injury." The company successfully fought off the claim but retained him; in 1940, he was supporting his wife and two youngest sons as a laborer at Ford.[185]

Injured workers also suffered from what seems to have been a profound disconnect between the ways that workers and the Sorenson-era Legal Department experienced and understood injuries and disabilities. As Rubinow had argued, reporting an injury often meant that the injured worker incurred a substantial economic loss. In 1919, Michigan raised compensation for total disability from 50 percent to 60 percent of wages, with a minimum of $7 per week and a maximum of $14—rates far below what most Ford workers made with the implementation of the five-dollar day (and later the six-dollar day). Throughout the entire period, Michigan enforced a two-week waiting period for compensation.[186] Ford Motor Company also calculated compensation based on the minimum wage—not the profit-sharing portion.[187] Therefore, reporting an accident and taking time off to heal generally meant that workers lost at least half of their wages for several weeks, more if they did not win compensation. The fact that workers expected to be injured at some point in their working lives—often several times—likely also led many workers to underreport minor accidents.[188] Ford Motor Company's Legal Department, in turn, assumed that any delay on the part of a worker in reporting an accident meant that the employee was lying.

The impact of old disabilities and injuries on workers' earning capacity also changed over time, as Rubinow had suggested—a dynamic that the Ford Motor Company's lawyers, compensation statutes, and dismemberment schedules take into account. Often, what seemed at first to be a minor injury eventually became a serious impairment. In these cases, workers generally won compensation from Ford Motor Company, but only after long legal fights. Vahan Harootian, for instance, lost the sight in his right eye a year and a half after part of a saw blade broke off and hit him in the eye. After a two-year-long legal battle, Harootian won $1,800 in compensation and an additional $400 intended to allow him to buy a truck and enter the vegetable business.[189]

Workers with injuries such as hernias that were not the result of a clearly defined accident had markedly less success claiming compensation when their disabilities became more severe. As Rubinow had predicted, compensation statutes and dismemberment schedules functioned best in the cases of workers who suffered a simple accident. A former Ford employee, for instance, complained in 1927 that he had not received compensation for his two hernia operations or for his time off work. He exclaimed, "This speaks well for Henry Ford and the Workingmen's Compensation Law!"[190]

Economic downturns also made workers newly aware of their disabilities, since, as Rubinow had predicted, disabled workers were the last hired and first fired. During the Great Depression, but especially between 1933 and 1935, Ford Motor Company was deluged with delayed compensation claims from workers with a broad range of disabilities who could no longer find a job. Alex Marshall, for instance, whose left eye had been struck by a chip from a drill rod in 1926, had lost enough vision by 1933 that he no longer possessed the "industrial vision" required to gain a job. Marshall eventually won $1,400 in compensation, but most workers did not have his success.[191] Hundreds of workers reported developing hernias and bad backs from their time at Ford Motor Company. The company denied nearly all of these claims—even when the worker had a verifiable disability—and if necessary, appealed cases to Michigan's Supreme Court. Because workers had not reported their initial minor injury, the current disability could not be tied to a specific accident.[192]

Amidst the depths of the Depression, few disabled workers had the resources to fight a long legal battle.[193]

THE EXPERIENCES OF disabled workers at the Ford Motor Company and other industrial employers illustrate the simultaneous power and weakness of public policies and policy makers. Progressive Era reformers and reform organizations such as Crystal Eastman and the AALL had intended for workmen's compensation to prevent the families of industrial accident victims from slipping into public dependency. State legislatures, in turn, passed compensation laws that provided families with temporary, limited aid. But as Rubinow pointed out, workmen's compensation did not address the needs of permanently disabled workers. In fact, by unintentionally encouraging companies to bar workers with a wide array of congenital and acquired disabilities from employment, compensation statutes impoverished both people with disabilities and their families.

In large part, policy makers helped to create disability as a public policy problem of poverty and public dependency, albeit entirely unintentionally. Industrial employers had laid the groundwork for this shift by deeming workers with many types of disabilities inefficient and increasingly refusing to hire them during the late nineteenth and early twentieth centuries. The workmen's compensation acts of the 1910s, however, provided all employers with an even more convincing rationale for screening out all people with disabilities from their workforce, especially those with physical or sensory impairments and chronic illnesses. Perversely, workmen's compensation laws effectively barred disabled people from the wage labor market and often from paid work itself, although many found ways to continue to labor. Undoing the pernicious and impoverishing, if inadvertent, effects of these policies proved a difficult—if not impossible—task.

Reformers established sheltered workshops such as Goodwill Industries in which disabled workers would theoretically learn marketable skills that they could use on the paid labor market. But such programs struggled with the complexity of disability and their clients' family contexts. And ironically, sheltered workshops exhibited much the same concern for efficiency that had led employers on the mainstream labor market to exclude disabled workers in the first place.

CHAPTER SIX

Saving the Human Wreckage Cast on the Industrial Scrap Heap

Goodwill Industries and the Imperative of Efficiency, 1890s–1920s

In 1926, Edgar James Helms, the founder of Goodwill Industries, described his work as "the essential saving of the human wreckage that has been cast upon the industrial scrap heap."[1] At that time, Goodwill Industries' nationwide network of sheltered workshops employed thousands of disabled, elderly, and temporarily unemployed—but able-bodied—people in salvaging everything from rubber and rags to dolls and paper. Helms believed that his organization did far more than merely provide employment to "crippled, disabled, and needy people" left destitute by "improved machinery, mass production and competition."[2] Harkening back to the rhetoric used by early advocates of scientific charity, such as Josephine Shaw Lowell, he proclaimed that Goodwill Industries was "building up a great fence of prevention at the top of the precipice for through their work they are giving disadvantaged people a self-respecting chance to help themselves in their time of distress and before they have fallen into the abyss of alms and pauperism."[3]

Goodwill Industries was just one of hundreds of sheltered workshops to emerge during the tail end of the nineteenth and the early twentieth century. It exemplified the how the Protestant work ethic and fears about encouraging dependency shaped how workshop managers approached the problem of "disabled" people—those whose bodies had been deemed largely unfit for wage labor by a changing economy and public policies.[4] Like the superintendents of custodial asylums for people deemed feeble-minded, reformatories, manual labor boarding schools, vocational training programs for immigrant children, and other work-based reform programs, Helms and his counterparts placed great weight on instilling the moral virtues of work in their clients. In their minds, labor, especially craft labor, was a moral panacea for nearly any ill. And also like Helms, the founders of other sheltered workshops hoped to address the ways in which mechanization, employers' growing desire for workers with fully intact and interchangeable bodies, and workmen's compensation laws had begun to exclude disabled workers from the mainstream labor market and self-support. Indeed, Helms began his work in the mid-1890s by focusing on those whom he termed the "economically, physically, morally, and socially disabled."[5]

But in an increasingly mechanized economy in which public policies encouraged employers to discriminate against workers perceived as having disabilities, craft labor could not provide disabled workers with a path to the mainstream labor market. Nor did most sheltered workshops have the resources necessary to persuade skeptical employers to hire trainees with disabilities. The complexity of clients' situations, especially old age and widowhood, posed further challenges.

Making matters worse, Helms and other sheltered workshop managers discovered that even their institutions could not escape the logic of efficiency that had so pervaded the mainstream economy. To ensure Goodwill Industries' survival, he had little choice but to adopt piecework methods, rate workers by efficiency, conduct time-motion studies, and limit the number of disabled workers hired.

Even as the largest network of sheltered workshops in the country, and likely the best funded, Goodwill Industries consequently managed to employ only a small number of disabled people. Ultimately, sheltered workshops returned just a handful of their disabled clients to the mainstream wage labor market. Instead, most workers with disabilities remained permanently in the workshops, earning low wages and learning few marketable skills.[6] But ironically, disabled and elderly workers proved extremely useful for Goodwill Industries in one aspect: advertising.

The Birth of Goodwill Industries

"Not Charity but a Chance" and "Saving the Waste in Men and Things": these two slogans, which emerged at Boston's Morgan Memorial Goodwill Industries during the 1910s, summed up the hopes of Edgar James Helms for his rapidly growing network of industrial programs.[7] A Methodist Episcopal minister, Helms saw Goodwill Industries as inculcating self-respect and productive citizenship by providing temporary work and vocational training to disabled, elderly, and, in particular, unemployed able-bodied people who, in theory, would eventually return to the mainstream wage labor market. In so doing, he hoped to blunt the economic impact of mechanization and industrial downturns. Just one of many work-based rehabilitative endeavors that arose in the late nineteenth century, Goodwill Industries epitomized the ways in which these projects blended concerns about the moral ills of dependency and scientific charity practices with the Protestant work ethic and, often, the Social Gospel.[8]

Goodwill Industries arose out the devastating depression of the 1890s as part of the relief program of Morgan Chapel in Boston's South End neighborhood. The chapel—an odd amalgamation that was owned by the Unitarian Church but run by the Methodist Episcopal Church—had lost nearly all of its members by the time Edgar James Helms became the pastor in 1895.[9] A young Methodist Episcopal minister from Iowa, Helms promised to revitalize the church's membership and improve its vice-ridden vicinity. When Helms took charge of Morgan Memorial, the immediate neighborhood had a reputation as "a notorious red-light district ... [with] sixteen saloons, eleven pawnshops, two theaters, and innumerable pool rooms and gambling dens operating within two square blocks of the church." Gamblers attended church services "to distribute policy slips," and a beat cop used the vestry room as a place to meet prostitutes.[10] Helms planned to reinvent the chapel as an "institutional church": a chapel that combined welfare and religious work in an immigrant working-class neighborhood to reach young migrants, in particular, and build "the Kingdom of God on earth."[11]

Such rhetoric reflected the influence of the Social Gospel movement, which arose in the late nineteenth century and aimed to redress the ills of poverty, poor living conditions, economic inequality, and poor environments, especially in so-called industrial cities. In so doing, figures such as Richard T. Ely, Walter Rauschenbusch, and Josiah Strong sought to put the Lord's Prayer into action: "Thy Kingdom come, Thy will be done on earth as it is in heaven." Much like antebellum reformers in the wake of the Second Great Awakening, advocates of the Social Gospel viewed repairing the earthly world as a necessary precursor for bringing about the Millennium. And although Social Gospel activists sought to remedy economic injustices and thereby reduce societal conflict, they too placed great weight on the moral value of work. While the movement emerged first in mainline denominations such as the Episcopalians, Unitarians, and Congregationalists in the mid-1880s, Baptists and Methodists such as Helms soon joined.[12]

Helms arrived at Morgan Chapel already experienced in organizing urban missions and doing settlement house work, having helped found the Boston University Settlement in the North End. While working there during the early 1890s, he had begun with a classical evangelistic approach: preaching in Hebrew from a "Gospel Wagon" on the streets of the Jewish area.[13] Helms soon took the settlement in a new direction after discovering Toynbee Hall,

Edgar James Helms, Methodist minister and the founder of Goodwill Industries. Courtesy of Goodwill Industries International.

the British cooperative movement, and the new field of sociology; he also began research how other city churches connected with and served their "unchurched" working-class neighbors.[14] Discarding his efforts to aggressively evangelize his Jewish, Italian, and Portuguese neighbors, Helms instead focused on providing the community with much-needed practical services: boys' and girls' clubs, a mothers' group, reading rooms, meals and clothes for those in need, and classes in sewing, music, and basic academic skills.[15]

At the same time, Helms began to volunteer at Morgan Chapel in Boston's impoverished South End, where he helped Reverend E. P. King establish an industrial school for children and "a relief department where women could earn money from sewing."[16] In a failed attempt to increase membership, the ministers at Morgan Chapel had begun to serve free Sunday breakfasts to homeless men—who were then locked into services. Although the men increased attendance, their presence drove away nearly all of the older members. Helms thus took over the church's pastorate in 1895 at a difficult time. He arrived, however, with a promise of supplementary aid from the Unitarian Benevolent Fraternity of Churches for industrial education and relief programs and support for terminating the breakfasts, which both he and the Unitarian fraternity viewed as entrapment.[17]

Fresh off his success in using institutional church programs to win over skeptical residents of the North End, Helms immediately established industrial relief programs aimed at helping Morgan Chapel's immigrant neighbors cope with the devastating economic depression of the mid-1890s. Soliciting donations from the wealthy Boston neighborhoods of Back Bay and Beacon Hill, Helms used a wheelbarrow to transport items to a streetcar and then back to the South End, at least until the conductors banned him and his wheelbarrow for causing a public disruption. Since most of the donated clothing required repair, Helms hired a few local women to mend the items. According to the story he often retold later on while attempting to raise money, he invited neighborhood residents to help themselves to the clothing, which he had laid out on the church pews. Rushing the sanctuary, they fought over items. Horrified, he decided to stop giving out clothes. But later that day, an elderly woman refused to accept an overcoat for free, "convinc[ing] him that the poor could retain their self-respect only if they were required to pay something, even a token amount, for whatever was offered to them." This tale is likely apocryphal, since Helms had experimented with similar industrial programs during his earlier postings. The story nonetheless illustrates his firm belief in the moral threat posed by charity—a belief shared by many contemporary lawmakers, reformers, and advocates of the Social Gospel. Following John Wesley's precepts, Methodists had also long placed great value on hard work and frugality.[18]

Initially, Helms and his colleagues focused primarily on assisting able-bodied men, as well as some women, through temporary periods of unemployment or underemployment. Given the depth of the depression, the program met real needs and consequently took off quickly. During the winter of 1896–1897, more than 1,000 people labored in Morgan Chapel's industrial programs, which ranged from skilled work such as printing, mending garments, and repairing shoes to more menial tasks such as sawing wood and sorting scrap paper. While some workers remained for up to three weeks, others stayed as little as one hour—just long enough to earn a little fuel or a garment for a child.[19] Such extensive industrial programs constituted an unusual innovation within the institutional church movement, which generally provided only limited piecework relief programs for women, plus wood chopping for a few men.[20] By 1902, Helms had established a formal "Salvage Plant" along with a host of other programs reminiscent of secular settlement houses: a day nursery, an employment and placement bureau, a temperance saloon, a cafeteria with free or low-cost food, children's classes in immigrant languages and industrial skills, an industrial night school, a music school, summer camps for convalescents and poor children, residences for single intemperate men and elderly working women, and, for a brief time, a cooperative grocery store.[21]

Helms recognized that dramatic changes had taken place in the labor market during the past few decades, and agreed with other Progressive Era reformers and advocates of the Social Gospel that these economic changes had increased privation and public dependency. Such shifts not only hindered the temporarily unemployed and the unskilled, he argued, but also posed special challenges for the "incompetent persons who could not hold a job, and old and injured people who could not be placed."[22] At least early on, he insisted on paying "union prices" for labor despite long waiting lists of applicants; he also claimed to hire unemployed "union men" first.[23] Turn-of-the-century solicitations to other churches, in turn, highlighted the plight of printers replaced by typesetting machines, promising "strictly first-class work" and stressing, "We do NOT CUT PRICES but we will do it at living wages."[24] Reflecting back in the late 1920s, he observed, "Improved machinery, mass production, and competition are throwing into the industrial 'scrap heap' thousands of deserving men and women who now are in despair."[25]

Keenly aware of the popularity of scientific charity approaches—and a firm believer in many aspects—Helms stressed that Morgan Chapel's industrial programs helped to prevent the moral contagion that many believed came hand in hand with public dependency. "Because people are poor is no reason that we should treat them as beggars and paupers," he argued. Instead, as he explained, the chapel's Industries "combine[d] the virtues of scientific charity with the character stimulating quality of Christian sympathy for the unfortunate."[26] By offering work and helping them maintain their dignity, in part by providing them with access to secondhand but decent clothing, he sought to preserve the "character" and "independence" of the "self-respecting poor"—including disabled people.[27] While the chapel's staff followed scientific charity guidelines by carefully investigating any individuals who made outright requests for aid—monetary or in the form of garments, shoes, or fuel—early on Helms and his coworkers tended to allow anyone who was willing to labor in the Industries to do so provided there was space. Such practices echoed back to poorhouse work tests but would come under fire in 1910, when the Unitarian Benevolent Fraternity of Churches secretly hired an investigator to tarnish Morgan Chapel and thereby free themselves from their financial obligations to the organization.[28]

While Helms spoke to potential donors rather than the state legislators courted by idiot asylum superintendents such as Hervey Wilbur and Charles Bernstein, he also paid careful attention to the financial benefits to be accrued from marketing his programs as instilling the values of productive citizenship. Reflecting on his church's work some years later, for instance, Helms stated, "Hundreds have been helped in the time of their financial crisis, and have been delivered from becoming black-listed as paupers. They have asked for a chance to work, and it has been given them."[29] Reporting to the Methodist Bureau of Home Missions in the mid-1920s, in turn, he contended, "Those who appeal for work (not alms) come from the great army of the nation's producers" and, through Goodwill Industries' programs, would become "good citizens," restored to "independence," with "self-support . . . made possible and self-respect guaranteed."[30]

At Morgan Chapel, Helms sought to blend the sacred and the secular. After visiting Germany in 1899 and encountering Christian Socialism, he became ever more interested in how churches could drive social reform.[31] Upon his return, Helms assailed Methodist ministers for ignoring the poor, arguing in a 1901 lecture to the International Epworth League Convention—the Methodist organization for young people—that "the best examples of Christian brotherhood today are not found in the organized church, but in state institutions, and labor and philanthropic organizations, many of them independent of the church." He continued, "It costs more to be philanthropic than it does to be dogmatic. It is easier to propagate faith than to demonstrate love."[32]

While most institutional churches limited revivals in order to better attract the non-churchgoing, non-Protestant population, Helms maintained his evangelistic roots during his first two decades at Morgan Chapel. He organized multiple foreign-language services, prayer gatherings, and street-corner preaching, and even wrote a book of prayers for the chapel's nearly thirty departments, which employees used in morning devotions.[33] Handbills asked, "Are You Saved?" but at the same time, Helms modified the sanctuary's baptistry in order to provide the public with showers one story below.[34] Like other advocates of the Social Gospel, he believed that the best way to bring about the kingdom of heaven was to work toward "social salvation" and adopt "Christ's example of everyday religion."[35]

In succeeding years, Helms gradually reduced Morgan Memorial's evangelistic programs.[36] In part, he may have been responding to the community's decided lack of interest in church membership, which remained at the same level as before Helms took over—only ninety members and forty-five probationary members in 1910—as the Industries grew ever larger.[37] This shift toward secular programming also arose out of his growing conflict with the Unitarian Benevolent Fraternity of Churches, which temporarily suspended its funding of Morgan Memorial the same year.

Unbeknownst to Helms, the Unitarians had hired an investigator to evaluate his organization's practices. The investigator produced a scathing report that attacked everything from Morgan Memorial's bookkeeping system and Helms's mixing of religion and social service to the corporate structure and the organization's method of determining clients' worthiness for outright aid or work relief. Since 1904, perhaps earlier, the Unitarian Fraternity had been trying to find an excuse to stop funding Morgan Memorial because the institutional church "was draining the Fraternity's invested funds." Helms learned about the investigation only by accident and promptly "accused Fraternity delegates of committing an ethical malfeasance worthy of John D. Rockefeller in his early Standard Oil days."

Helms took particular exception to the investigator's claims that the Industries' work "relief" constituted a form of charitable aid and therefore required careful examination of clients beforehand; instead, he praised the moral benefits of work. The Unitarians' investigation would nevertheless have a lasting impact on disabled workers' prospects at Goodwill Industries. Once Helms calmed down, he agreed to all of the Benevolent Fraternity's modifications, including relinquishing his presidency and his shares in Morgan Memorial's cooperative and more thoroughly examining potential clients. The suspension of funding, however, led the church to miss its annual interest payment on the mortgage; the facilities were put up for auction that summer, but miraculously, the bank received no bids. In what Helms termed another miracle, he then raised $50,000 in one year to free Morgan Memorial from debt, at which time the Benevolent Fraternity of Churches ended its trusteeship with the approval of both Helms and the Methodists.[38] But in the aftermath of the turmoil, he hired efficiency expert Edward Buss to make Morgan Memorial's operations more professional and more efficient, reflecting the larger shift among charity workers toward scientific charity and professional social services. This move toward efficiency would have troubling consequences for the "disabled" people whom Helms increasingly sought to serve.[39]

In 1918 Helms formally separated the Industries from the church, ending Morgan Memorial's role as an institutional church. Nonetheless, he retained aspects of both his evangelistic roots and his commitment to "social theology," as did the Industries themselves.[40] A 1922 "Statement of Faith" suggested that "the Kingdom of God required an earthly salvation" and stressed the equal importance of "the Fatherhood of God" and "the Brotherhood of Man," demonstrating the lasting influence of the institutional church mind-set and the Social Gospel on Morgan Memorial.[41] Moreover, the 1922 *Prospectus and Manual of Morgan Memorial* stated, "Morgan Memorial in every department and fibre of its being is intended to be essentially missionary," and permanent employees were evaluated in part on their commitment to evangelism through at least the mid-1920s.[42]

As Helms moved away from evangelization, industrial programs became Morgan Memorial's raison d'être, bringing the organization considerable fame. At the 1904 world's fair in St. Louis, Morgan Memorial's industrial programs won a gold medal; at the 1905 Lewis and Clark Centennial Exposition in Portland, Oregon, the organization received the Grand Prix in Social Economy.[43] By 1910, the industrial programs extended from rug-weaving to rubber and paper salvage and employed 30 permanent workers and more than 500 temporary workers at a time; sales at the store reached $40,000, while wages amounted to nearly $30,000.[44] By the mid-1910s, Morgan Memorial's industrial programs occupied a six-story building in which a multiethnic workforce of men and women repaired a wide variety of items, from clothing and mirrors to dolls and furniture, as well as collecting paper and other materials that could be sold for salvage.[45] And in 1916, Morgan Memorial's industrial work (which Helms had named the National Cooperative Industrial Relief Association) acquired its eponymous name, Goodwill Industries, from a similar program in Brooklyn. That same year, Helms reported that the Industries had "repaired more than 100,000 garments, 50,000 pairs of shoes, and about 500,000 pieces of furniture." More than 3,000 workers had received $54,000 in wages.[46] By 1919, 75,000 homes in Boston contributed to Goodwill Industries, which did more than $200,000 in business each year.[47] Helms would maintain his broad focus on providing temporary employment and trade training to the "economically, physically, morally, and socially disabled" until the 1920s, after which he gradually began to focus primarily on aiding disabled people.[48]

The postwar years brought Helms and Morgan Memorial even more acclaim—and means for spreading the Goodwill Industries approach across the country. In 1918, the ringing endorsement of the Methodist Episcopal Centenary Survey garnered Helms the promise of $1 million from the Board of Home Missions to establish Goodwill Industries in urban "downtown" churches nationwide and to form a national Bureau of Goodwill Industries.[49] By 1925, there were Goodwill Industries in thirty-five major cities, and by 1930, the program had spread to fifty-eight cities.[50] By 1929, Helms claimed that Goodwill Industries was the "largest trade school in U. S. A." and that "these old and handicapped students could not get into a school but here they earn their way."[51]

Too Efficient Even for Disabled Workers

During Goodwill Industries' first major capital campaign in 1911 and following a sharp economic downturn, Edgar James Helms proclaimed, "Morgan Memorial has stood by the aged and handicapped and inefficient and has kept on operating at a loss for their sake until it has exhausted all its unrestricted funds." He explained, "It needs $25,000 now to recoup these losses and as much more to enable it to wisely minister to thousands of other handicapped folks like these who are coming." By no means would this be the only time that Helms would position elderly and disabled workers as the core population served by Goodwill Industries—at least in publicity materials. "From ... your aeroplane, you would witness a series of mostly motley processions," explained Helms in his 1926 annual report on Goodwill Industries. He continued, drawing a vivid picture of "the blind, the deaf, the crippled in wheelchairs and on crutches, those whose strength has been sapped by disease, the epileptic, the rheumatic; some come from jails and prisons to begin life anew; others mentally retarded, others environmentally handicapped, still others because of old age."[52] As these quotes indicate, elderly and "handicapped" workers often took center stage in Goodwill Industries' publicity. Reflecting the historical stigmatization of the "undeserving poor," Helms and his fellow superintendents assumed that donors preferred to support disabled and elderly workers over temporarily unemployed able-bodied workers. As it turned out, there was some truth to that assumption.

The Methodist Episcopal Board of Home Missions and Church Extension—the movement's most crucial funder—often cited the prospect of making disabled and elderly people self-supporting as its main reason for supporting the spread of Goodwill Industries.[53] But as aged and disabled workers who turned to Goodwill Industries discovered, Helms and other managers could not escape the same logic of efficiency that had led mainstream employers to screen out workers with a wide variety of disabilities. While Helms recognized the discrimination that disabled workers faced on the paid labor market, ironically, some found themselves labeled too slow even to labor at Goodwill—or at least to earn more than a pittance—let alone learn a profitable trade or skill. The complexity of disability posed additional hurdles—since clientele were rarely just "disabled"—as did the way in which Goodwill's origins in the scientific charity movement led managers to stress *temporary* work relief. That said, Goodwill Industries provided a limited number of individuals with disabilities with the means to continue working and at least stay on the fringes of the workforce.

Just as Henry Ford strove for efficiency, so too did the managers of Goodwill Industries. In fact, they adopted the piecework rates and time-motion studies customary in mainstream factories. During the 1910s, workers were paid for each piece they mended regardless of whether it required one or several repairs. In 1921, Helms succeeded in refining this "piecework" system, albeit against employees' wishes. Under the new "operations" system, Morgan Memorial paid employees for each individual operation done on a piece of clothing or furniture rather than for completing all of the repairs on a piece—a policy eventually adopted by other Goodwill Industries.[54] By 1922, Goodwill Industries, under the advice of efficiency expert Edward Buss, determined that sorters could sort seventy bags per day and expected sorters to meet that goal; within three years, managers expected the three sorters to handle 1,000 bags per week. And by the mid-1930s, Goodwill Industries nationwide used time-motion studies to determine the "actual earnings" of employees, reveal "a Goodwill worker's proportion of self-support," and thereby establish the necessary subsidies for workers who could not earn enough to cover their wages.[55]

Like his counterparts in the mainstream labor market, Helms found that a piecework system improved efficiency. But this scheme had other benefits as well. The operations system encouraged ambitious workers while also limiting tension between employees who worked at different rates—a not uncommon problem at Goodwill Industries and related workshops. At the Council of Goodwill Industries meeting in 1922, Helms explained: "As long as you allow this incompetent person who does poor and slow work to get a dollar a day, while here is one who can do twice as good and twice as much who is paid no more, you are pushing Mrs. Murphy down to the poor person's level and you are generating friction. But with the operation basis, Mrs. Maloney sees that she must spruce up to get as much as Mrs. Murphy."[56]

Helms's concern over the efficiency of Morgan Memorial's workforce reflected real fiscal challenges as well. Until at least the late 1920s, the Industries provided direct financial support to Morgan Memorial Chapel, supplying $1,200 during just 1922. Ironically, Helms had cautioned in 1918 that "it is both foolish and wicked to think of making this work a source of income for the church. That would be exploitation of the poor, not their evangelization." Revenue from Morgan Memorial's stores also supported much of its social services: the day nursery and kindergarten, the Children's Settlement, the Fresh Air camps, and the South Athol Farm for recovering alcoholic men. In addition, Helms had set lofty expectations when he first received funding from the Methodist Episcopal Bureau of Home Missions and Church Extension in the late 1910s, promising to make all of the Goodwill Industries self-supporting within a few years. By 1925, the Bureau of Home Missions and Church Extension supplied less than 1 percent of Goodwill Industries' funds nationwide, with 84 percent coming from the sale of goods salvaged by workers in the Industries and 12.7 percent supplied by local donors or Community Chests.[57]

Despite workers' hostility to the revised piecework system, Helms credited it with allowing the Industries to employ a more diverse workforce—including disabled and elderly workers. At the same Council of Goodwill Industries meeting, he explained that shifting entirely to paying by the operations performed on each piece reduced managers' concerns about efficiency: "In the old regime, when we were scarcely able to make ends meet Mr. Moore felt inclined to go up into the Industries and let a lot of those incompetent people go, for he knew we were losing 20 to 50 cents a day, and we ought to save it, and that was the first place that we could strike economy. They were the last people that ought to be discharged."[58] And in fact, Helms and his managers had altered the piecework system to protect the most vulnerable workers. Unlike mainstream employers, Goodwill Industries set the piecework rate at the speed of the average worker, not the fastest. Longer-term employees also earned part of their pay based on their personal interactions and involvement with other aspects of the institution, while managers subsidized workers who could not produce enough to earn the minimum wage via piecework.[59]

Even with the operations system, managers' concerns about efficiency led them to limit the hiring—and stays—of disabled and elderly workers. Indeed, Helms and his assistants sought to balance the ranks of "clumsy and inefficient" workers—that is, the disabled and elderly workers who tended to remain at the Industries—with workers who needed only temporary employment and who reportedly worked faster.[60] Helms cautioned, "It should be remembered that Morgan Memorial work is intended to provide as few permanent positions as possible."[61] Managers fretted, too, about the presence of slow workers who desperately needed help but stayed permanently at Goodwill Industries. A. G. Young complained in 1929, for instance: "The great danger faced by our workers is that the slowest person sets the pace. If there is anything that makes me sad as I go through our different Industries, it is the concrete evidence of this." Young added that he had designed the operation wage system "to overcome this crime."[62] Young, however, proved far more understanding than Morgan Memorial's treasurer, Fred C. Moore, who lamented the fact that Prohibition had virtually eliminated the recovering alcoholic tradesmen—able-bodied and skilled workers—who had previously served as inexpensive stalwarts for the Industries. He explained that, in the past, "good painters, printers, carpenters and others" would work for a "small wage" and "were able to produce more than they were being paid for." But with Prohibition, "only the inefficient and physically handicapped are coming to us." He complained that in "a great many cases they are unable to produce even what they are being paid."[63]

Although a visiting journalist from the *Christian Herald* characterized the entire workforce of Morgan Memorial as "handicapped poor" in 1933, temporary, able-bodied males comprised most of the workers at Morgan Memorial and often at other Goodwill Industries.[64] During 1917, for instance, 2,171 persons were given "opportunity labor" at Morgan Memorial, and in 1924 workers' stays at the Industries averaged 82.5 days; Buffalo Goodwill Industries, in turn, employed 364 workers between October 1920 and September 1921, with an average payroll of 50 people.[65] When Edgar M. Wahlberg, a radical Methodist minister and the superintendent of Grand Junction Goodwill Industries in Colorado, visited Morgan Memorial in 1927 for a month of training, he was astonished by how few "handicapped" he saw. He counted only eight workers with disabilities on the lower four stories of Morgan Memorial's six total floors.[66] Only in the fourth-floor sorting and repair departments did he see more disabled workers, reporting "a sprinkling of handicapped throughout these departments" and later recording "quite a number of handicapped" among the twenty-four employees in the clothing repair section.[67]

Most of the disabled employees seem to have fallen under the broad early twentieth-century category of "the crippled." In addition to three employees described as either "a hopeless cripple" or "badly crippled," Wahlberg reported seeing one man "slightly paralyzed to be somewhat childish," one slightly "lame" woman, a "one-armed man," a "hunch-backed" man, a deaf man, and one man with a glass eye. Other authors reported people who had lost limbs or digits to frostbite and a few men paroled from the Waverly School for the Feeble-Minded, along with the occasional blind person.[68]

Concerns about efficiency and profits led Helms and his managerial staff to restrict the best-paid and steadiest "regular" positions to temporarily unemployed, able-bodied workers.[69] Wahlberg suggested that Morgan Memorial kept speedy workers for the sake of efficiency and profits and called for them to transfer more employees on to industry.[70] Although other Goodwill Industries sites rarely provided full breakdowns of their workforce, the Brooklyn Industries reported in 1926 that they had served 150-some elderly and disabled workers since 1915, while employing 723 different people during 1925 alone. Brooklyn also refused all applicants who had lost both hands.[71] San Francisco's Goodwill Industries, however, seems to have broken the mold by employing mostly elderly workers in the early 1920s. At what local writers termed "The Old Curiosity Shop," the workforce averaged seventy years of age, with none of the women being under sixty.[72] Detroit, too, proved an exception, at least in its early years. During 1919, disabled people made up the entire workforce of nineteen workers, earning $1,193.22 during the year.[73]

Reflecting Goodwill Industries' roots in the scientific charity movement, its managers maintained low pay rates in order to encourage only temporary stays, a policy that posed a challenge for disabled workers who had nowhere else to go. E. C. E. Dorian explained in 1915, "But neither the rate of wages—about fifteen cents an hour—nor the work itself is designed to hold the men permanently."[74] Wahlberg, for instance, lambasted the Industries for failing to pay workers a living wage. He even suggested that the workers might consider unionizing. He recalled an "elevator helper" who earned only $1.50 per day and who was paying $2.00 for lodging per week. The worker complained, "I can't buy shaving cream and other things and I can't eat like I want. I feel hungry most of the time."[75] Wahlberg later added: "A $1.50 wage may be a very temporary opportunity wage, but is degrading over a long period. A man has a right to sour on Morgan under such circumstances."[76] In contrast, some of the furniture repair workers—whom operations manager A. G. Young characterized as "men and women of exceptional ability or those who have studied certain short cuts"—could earn up to $6 or $7 per day.[77]

The problem was, as Helms and his counterparts had feared, that most disabled workers employed at Goodwill Industries could not readily transition to the mainstream workforce—in part due to pervasive discrimination. As early as 1901, Morgan Chapel's Employment Bureau director, Mary E. French, observed that "many who are too poor to pay office fees and others, who, on account of age or disability of some kind, are pushed aside in the downtown Employment Bureaus come to free offices like ours." Despite her best efforts, that left the Industries with "a large number of persons whom it is hard to place."[78] As French suggested, returning dependent, unemployed people with disabilities to the mainstream wage labor market as self-supporting workers proved to be an increasingly impossible task. Although personnel records are limited, the stories recounted at annual meetings and periodically published in *Goodwill Tales* are suggestive. Of the fourteen disabled workers featured in the 1922 volume, only one found a job outside Goodwill Industries; another man who had lost half of his feet to frostbite remained at the Industries by choice after learning how to repair shoes. In *Goodwill Tales* stories from the mid- to late 1930s, eleven out of sixteen people with disabilities stayed permanently at Goodwill Industries.[79] Morgan Memorial's managers, in addition, often expressed frustration at the "number of handicapped people . . . [whom] we find very hard to place" and who "beg to remain with us" when encouraged to explore the wage labor market. As the economy worsened during the mid- to late 1920s, the treasurer, Fred C. Moore, regularly warned that such workers posed serious financial risks to the Industries; both he and operations director A. G. Young advised turning some handicapped laborers over to the Parish Welfare Bureau.[80]

In part, disabled workers tended to remain at Goodwill Industries because people with disabilities were seldom just disabled: many were the sole breadwinners for their families or had other characteristics that made them unattractive to employers. Indeed, most disabled workers were elderly or single women (and some fell into both categories).[81] In 1919 Denver Goodwill Industries employed, for instance, a sixty-five-year-old clothes presser who was deaf and "broken down in health," while the "cobbler was a man seventy-eight years old and a cripple."[82] The Brooklyn *Goodwill* journal reported, in turn: "A woman with a withered arm learned to run a sewing machine and was extremely grateful for the opportunity to earn a living, as her husband had deserted her."[83] The Buffalo Goodwill Industries, meanwhile, employed a "crippled widow" with four children, while a rheumatic Syrian man "earn[ed] two dollars a day [in Boston] by pulling the stuffing from shabby couches and arm-chairs."[84] Even younger disabled men tended to remain at the Industries—especially if they had a family to support. A veteran who had lost an arm and a leg in the Great War stayed permanently as a telephone operator, earning $2 a day, for instance, while a man with a wife and five children found stable work at Goodwill Industries after losing four fingers on his right hand and being refused employment everywhere he tried. Illustrating the pervasiveness of disability, some disabled individuals also sought work in order to support other family members with disabilities. Florence White Barbour reported in 1911, for instance, on "a cultured woman, wearing the carefully chosen clothes of five years ago, [who] asks for kitchen work or 'anything that anyone can do who has only one-tenth of vision left.' " As Barbour investigated further, she eventually learned that the "woman's husband ha[d] had influenza, an accident and a paralytic stroke and c[ould] no longer at seventy years give organ lessons."[85]

Disabled workers also stayed at Goodwill Industries because, as Wahlberg suggested, they rarely learned trades profitable on the mainstream labor market; in fact, the Industries divided its workforce partly on the basis of ability and disability. Able-bodied workers studied trades such as rug weaving, automobile driving, printing, and repairing shoes, clocks, and furniture. In contrast, workers with disabilities tended to work on unskilled tasks or semiskilled tasks such as sorting salvage or repairing clothing, presumably because of managerial concerns about efficiency. Wahlberg, for instance, found only a "sprinkling" of disabled workers in the printing and shoe, millinery, and furniture repair departments, along with several in the clothing repair department—many of these workers eventually moved along to positions outside Goodwill Industries. Six disabled people labored in the employment, industrial, and shipping departments combined, but clerical departments such as these employed only a small fraction of the overall workforce.[86] Foremen at Morgan Memorial also refused to hire the "deaf and dumb men who seem to be in desperate need" on account of it being "too difficult to tell them what they want done."[87]

Morgan Memorial also effectively barred most disabled workers from collections and driving work, the latter of which could be a profitable skill on the mainstream labor market. The 1922 manual noted that "the heavy articles to be lifted and other arduous duties makes physical weakness a handicap," while in 1924, operations manager A. G. Young commented, "The handicapped are unfit for our trucks and elevators. It would be impossible for them to lift the well filled bags, to say nothing of ice-chests . . . pianos, organs, etc." Young continued, warning, "To retain these stronger men we have to raise wages and thereby man our trucks and get sufficient help to make things 100% efficient if possible."[88]

Even when disabled people managed to learn trades at Goodwill Industries, their training did not always translate into marketable skills. In Brooklyn, for instance, "a man whose legs had been cut off was begging on the street. He heard of Goodwill Industries and was there taught to mend dolls. Instead of begging he earned enough to support himself and in time to buy artificial legs." The man, however, found that he could not support himself with his talents in doll repairing. Instead, he "later found employment running an elevator."[89]

Although managers of Goodwill Industries spoke about the potential for educating employers about disabled workers' capabilities, no evidence exists that they actually pressed local employers to hire workers with disabilities.[90] In 1927, Helms suggested that the superintendents of the various Goodwill Industries contact the "millions of Christian employers" through churches and publications. He cautioned employers, "There is no thought on the part of the Goodwill Industries that its sheltered employment or its teaching of trades should relieve commercial industry of its responsibility in employing handicapped people or providing employment training to eligible individuals."[91] Despite Helms's lofty rhetoric, Morgan Memorial's placement service seems to have exclusively served temporary, able-bodied workers.

Broader Struggles

Other sheltered workshops—notably, those targeted at blind adults—tried a slightly different approach to the question of how to return disabled workers to self-support.[92] In contrast to Goodwill Industries, the managers of workshops and industrial homes for blind adults provided their clients with training in skilled trades that could not easily be mechanized.[93] At workshops such as the Indiana Home for Blind Men and the Wisconsin Workshop for the Blind, blind men practiced (and in some cases learned) trades such as broom making, basketry, and chair caning. These trades built on the industrial training offered in state schools for the blind during the late nineteenth and early twentieth centuries.[94]

In the end, however, the workshops for blind people encountered just as much difficulty in addressing the separation of disabled people from the mainstream paid labor market as Goodwill Industries. Like Goodwill Industries, these workshops shared the concerns of mainstream employers about efficiency and barred male workers whom managers deemed inefficient—as well as nearly all blind women.[95] Moreover, even blind trades such as broom making and mattress making encountered competition from prison labor and mechanized factories.[96] As a result, workshops for blind people rarely returned their clients to the mainstream labor market and served only a small fraction of the adult blind population—by one estimate, just 700 of the 40,000 blind adults of working age in 1909.[97]

Pay at sheltered workshops, too, remained far below the standard of a living wage, as one hundred blind laborers argued when they engaged in a thirty-two-day sit-down strike in Manhattan in 1937. The Blind Workers Union's persistence paid off when the newly formed National Labor Relations Board intervened, recognizing their union, mandating the reinstatement of all striking workers, and helping to start negotiations on a $15 per week wage between the strikers and the Bourne Workshop and Community Craft Weavers Auxiliary. Reflecting sheltered workshops' roots in the scientific charity movement, the blind workshops' directors had contended that, "as charitable, non-profit-making groups they [we]re not subject to the provisions of the Wagner act."[98]

ULTIMATELY, GOODWILL INDUSTRIES AND other sheltered workshops did not—and in many ways could not—provide disabled workers with a viable alternative to the mainstream wage labor market. Disabled and elderly workers held a central place in the advertising campaigns of Goodwill Industries, but

Morgan Memorial and its counterparts proved unable to escape the imperatives of efficiency. Consequently, they managed to employ only a limited number of workers with disabilities, even fewer of whom managed to transition to the mainstream labor market as self-supporting workers. Instead, most disabled people stayed permanently at Goodwill Industries, doing unskilled or craft labor and earning low wages. Helms's passion for efficiency and his fears of encouraging pauperism and dependency fundamentally conflicted with the needs of disabled workers he sought to help. In effect, at both the various Goodwill Industries and other sheltered workshops, the simple act of laboring became more important than helping disabled people move to a living wage on the mainstream labor market.

Disability, too, proved a more complex problem than he and other workshop founders had expected. While Helms and his managers recognized the discrimination faced by disabled workers on the mainstream labor market, they could not single-handedly alter the dramatic economic changes and perverse public policies that drove disabled people out of the mainstream labor market during the late nineteenth and early twentieth centuries. At the same time, Goodwill Industries did provide some people with disabilities with very modest wages and the opportunity to continue to define themselves as workers.

The post–World War I program to rehabilitate disabled veterans would bear some striking similarities to sheltered workshops, especially the moralistic tone and fears about encouraging dependency. In different ways, the complexity and mutability of disabilities would pose serious challenges as rehabilitators sought to restore disabled veterans to the status of male breadwinners. Yet, unlike the civilian clientele served by Goodwill Industries and other workshops, many disabled veterans would ultimately return to the mainstream labor market. While their training—or at least the maintenance allowances that accompanied rehabilitation—helped to some degree, employers simply were far more willing to hire disabled veterans than disabled civilians.

CHAPTER SEVEN

The Duty to Make Himself a Useful, Self-Supporting Citizen
Disabled Veterans and the Limits of Vocational Rehabilitation, 1910s–1920s

The most precious gift to the war disabled is that of a useful employment to assure his complete independence and self-sufficiency of civil life. The new concept is of justice, and not alms, to the disabled. It is due of **right** to the disabled man, that his Government should restore, as nearly as possible, the *status quo ante*.[1]

John Aaron returned home from the Great War unable to continue farming in rural Alabama. While serving at Verdun, he had been wounded by shrapnel in the left thigh. The shrapnel left his left leg paralyzed below the knee, but after four surgeries and several years of hospitalization, he learned to walk again, albeit with a limp. Nevertheless, Aaron continued to suffer from a "drop foot," along with chronic pain and "atrophy of the muscles."[2] In 1921, he registered for vocational rehabilitation with the Veterans' Bureau, hoping to learn how to make pocketbooks in New York City. He made little progress in his training, however. While Aaron claimed that he "could not stand the work" physically, his supervisor contended that the veteran simply had a poor attitude. Shortly thereafter, Aaron left New York City for his parents' farm in Alabama.[3]

Unable to find work in his home state, Aaron contacted the Veterans' Bureau in 1923 to ask for further rehabilitation, this time as a tailor. He progressed well in his training for a few months, but then his wife left him. In the words of his supervisor, Aaron "began to get very 'wild,' running around with women of doubtful character or none at all, and gambling some."[4] Hoping that a change in environment would turn him around, the district supervisor transferred Aaron from Birmingham, Alabama, to the U.S. Vocational School nearly 300 miles away in Pascagoula, Mississippi. The veteran progressed well in his training for a year, then faltered once again; citing supposed mental limitations, bureau officials reduced his vocational objective to dry cleaner and presser. Soon afterward, Aaron requested that he be declared rehabilitated so that he could accept a position with the Hardwick Store Company at

$100 a month. But by the time of the 1930 census, he was no longer working as a dry cleaner and presser. Instead, he was once again living with his parents in Alabama and helping with his father's farm.[5]

The specific details of John Aaron's troubled encounter with the federal vocational rehabilitation program for disabled veterans are unique, but his experiences echoed those of many of his fellow veterans. More broadly, however, his tale highlights the difficulties faced by lawmakers in creating from scratch a rehabilitation program that could reintegrate disabled veterans into the mainstream workplace as breadwinners and "useful citizens."[6] Given how hostile employers had become toward workers with disabilities and how much workplaces had shifted during the late nineteenth and early twentieth centuries, this was no small ambition.

For many white veterans with disabilities, rehabilitation proved an economic boon. Some even regained their prewar earning power—in itself a major accomplishment, considering the fate of newly disabled civilians. Unlike managers at Goodwill Industries, rehabilitators insisted on training veterans in skilled jobs in growing sectors, a practice made possible in part due to the generous funding supplied by Congress. In fact, the Veterans' Bureau spent more per day during 1923 than any other federal agency: $1.25 million.[7] For some veterans, training provided an entrée to a long-desired career and a means of raising their class status, while for others, the maintenance payments served as a form of unemployment insurance during the postwar recession.

At the same time, many veterans left rehabilitation early or declined to enter entirely due to the challenges that administrators faced in creating a vast bureaucratic entity from scratch. Rehabilitation officials struggled to build enough capacity to handle nearly 180,000 trainees—more than ten times more than the 16,000 originally expected.[8] Administrative dysfunction and the inherently political nature of the rehabilitation program likewise discouraged veterans. Other disabled veterans, especially African American ones, found themselves largely barred or tracked into unskilled or semiskilled positions due to rehabilitators' racialized notions of fitness, class and racial prejudices, and pejorative assumptions about certain types of impairments.[9]

Veterans' rehabilitation also highlighted the challenges lawmakers faced in making disability policy. Not only was disability hard to quantify, as Isaac M. Rubinow had observed in regard to workmen's compensation, but impairments also evolved over time within individuals and reflected their particular economic contexts. Shifts in technology likewise produced unexpected new types of impairments, such as lung damage from gassing or chronic pain from shrapnel wounds, for which administrators had not accounted. Disability also proved far more complex and fluid in reality than rehabilitation officials had anticipated.

In the end, however, many veterans eventually found self-supporting work, but not necessarily because of their training. Instead, most employers turned out to be far more willing to hire disabled veterans than disabled civilians. Just like lawmakers, employers granted disabled veterans extra privileges for fulfilling the citizenship obligation of military service.[10]

At the same time, lawmakers' and rehabilitation officials' fears of encouraging public dependency—the same fears shared by labor law reformers, sheltered workshop managers, charity officials, and asylum superintendents—fundamentally shaped the program and blunted its impact. When faced with the fact that disabled veterans often could not locate a job that fit with their impairment and that paid a living wage, officials redefined what "rehabilitation" meant, declaring that simply completing the training process was enough. Undoing the broad exclusion of people with many different types of disabilities from the wage labor market would have required rehabilitators to focus on shifting the workplace rather than instilling the moral virtues of work in individual veterans. And while the framers of rehabilitation acts and the program's officials emphasized again and again that they aimed to turn disabled veterans into self-supporting breadwinners, their relentless rhetorical focus on preventing dependency helped to further inscribe the cultural link between disability and dependency.

The Goals of Vocational Rehabilitation

Unlike disabled civilians, who struggled to find employers willing to hire them, disabled veterans of the Great War came home to an enormous amount of public goodwill. Both the framers of the rehabilitation program and national-level administrators cast the project of returning disabled veterans to the status of breadwinners as a national obligation. Colonel Charles A. Forbes, director of the Veterans' Bureau, offered a typical perspective in 1921: "We must send these men back into society, mentally, physically, and morally fit to occupy their places as useful citizens."[11] But in some ways, disabled civilians and disabled veterans shared similar experiences. Just as with sheltered workshops, workmen's compensation, and idiot asylums, the specter of potential dependency loomed large in policy makers' minds.

Lawmakers and the public alike assumed that veterans would reenter the mainstream labor market, and employers actively sought to hire them. The National Association of Manufacturers (NAM), for instance, surveyed hundreds of employers in July 1917 and "managed to obtain promises of employment for over 5,000 disabled of all kinds and classes." The NAM reported, "Almost every manufacturer who replied stated that he would be perfectly willing to give employment to one or more war cripples, and many offered to make special openings for them." An electrical firm in New York not only promised to train and employ crippled veterans but also vowed to preferentially retain them if the postwar economy soured. A major manufacturer in Bridgeport, Connecticut, in turn, declared its willingness to take 200 to 300 war cripples with "good eyesight and at least one good arm," once fully trained.[12] Even more dramatically, when the state of Pennsylvania conducted an extensive survey of 30,000 industrial plants in 1917, investigators received several thousand replies that, in sum, promised to employ a total of 49,417 disabled workers with thirty-eight different types of disabilities.[13]

Disabled veterans, moreover, were an eclectic lot. Some had graduated from high school or college or worked in a trade. Most, however, had little education—in fact, many were illiterate. The majority of veterans had done only unskilled or semiskilled labor prior to the war. A significant minority had been too young when they enlisted (or were drafted) to have any record of employment at all.[14]

But in some ways, the experiences of disabled veterans echoed those of their civilian counterparts. As lawmakers debated how best to reintegrate disabled veterans into American society, the issue of public dependency once again rose to the fore. The specter of the Civil War pension system, in particular, worried framers of the rehabilitation acts. As had been the case during all prior wars, lawmakers had granted pensions to veterans who had suffered wounds or illnesses. But because Congress had repeatedly loosened the eligibility requirements for Civil War pensions, largely to curry favor with the public, costs ballooned massively over time. In fiscal year 1917, fifty-two years after the end of the war, the U.S. government disbursed nearly $160 million to Civil War veterans and their widows, orphans, or other dependents. All in all, the federal government paid $4.917 billion between 1866 and 1919—more than the actual cost of the war.[15] Rehabilitation promoters such as reformer Garrard Harris decried the waste and immorality produced by the pension system: "For a half century the lengthening chain of Civil War disability and service pensions, dragging on interminably, has fastened upon the country a burden of dependency merging more and more with each generation into pauperism and ever lending itself to widespread corruption and abuse of the Nation's gratitude towards its veteran warriors of the sixties."[16]

Just as policy makers had designed the workmen's compensation system partly to protect injured workers and the public from the civic and moral risks of public dependency, advocates of rehabilitation programs argued that disabled veterans needed to be protected from the moral corruption reportedly wrought by pensions. Leading rehabilitation promoter and sheltered workshop founder Douglas McMurtrie argued, for instance, that pensions were "always insufficient" and "socially demoralizing."[17] Worse yet, they encouraged veterans to leave the labor market. He noted, "Except in cases of men with unusual force of character and initiative, the crippled soldier almost starved in idleness on his pension, became partially dependent on kindly relatives, or obtained admission to a soldier home."[18]

Consequently, lawmakers designed the War Risk Insurance Act Amendments of 1917—which established the principle of rehabilitation, if not the actual program—specifically to discourage public dependency and encourage male breadwinning. Authored by Chicago-based Progressive reformers Julia Lathrop and Judge Julian W. Mack, the act did not follow the customary practice of granting disabled soldiers lifetime pensions based on military rank.[19] Instead, Mack proposed to defray the economic damage suffered by veterans by enacting a dual system of rehabilitation and compensation.[20] In contrast to the Civil War pension system or the schema used by Great Britain, he based compensation not on the percentage of physical damage or disfigurement but rather on how impairments reduced veterans' future capacity for wage labor, plus the number of dependents.[21]

Thereby, the act affirmed a traditional middle-class vision of family and gender relations: compensation would in effect allow disabled veterans to remain breadwinners for their families.[22] An American veteran with a total permanent disability such as complete blindness or loss of two limbs, for instance, would receive $100 every month, plus $20 if he was married and had two children; starting in 1923, any veterans who developed tuberculosis received an additional $50 a month. As a result, even severely disabled veterans could afford to marry and support children.[23] To discourage malingering, disabled veterans would be required to undergo periodic medical inspections. A veteran who did exceptionally well economically, however, would not lose his disability compensation unless his impairment improved markedly or vanished entirely. Unlike pensions, therefore, compensation would encourage veterans to return to work. Economist and future U.S. senator Paul Douglas explained, "The plain purpose ... is to give the injured man every inducement to rehabilitate himself."[24] But to qualify for compensation and apply for vocational rehabilitation, veterans first had to be rated for an occupational disability of at least 10 percent—a step that constituted a crucial stumbling block for African American veterans, since rehabilitation officials viewed them as inherently racially unfit.[25] Compensation could also be taken away entirely if veterans did not agree "to any reasonable medical or surgical treatment" aimed at lessening their disabilities.[26]

In rehabilitation, disabled veterans would learn skills ranging from automobile repair and electrical wiring to medicine and rubber salesmanship. Their training would, in theory, allow disabled veterans to eventually become self-supporting citizens.[27] The *Bulletin* of the Federal Board for Vocational Education (FBVE) argued, for instance, that vocational rehabilitation would "reestablish the disabled soldier or sailor as an independent, self-respecting economic unit. Any other policy will inevitably induce economic dependency with its inherent moral and social evils."[28] Rehabilitation also reflected the typical Progressive concern with efficiency, since it offered a means of salvaging "labor that would otherwise be unproductive" and prevent a permanent "economic loss to the community."[29]

The Misadministration of Vocational Rehabilitation

As American involvement in the war peaked in 1918, legislators and national-level administrators set about creating a workable vocational rehabilitation program. Reality would fall far short of their expectations, however. Indeed, chronic administrative dysfunction would ultimately prevent many veterans from accessing and fully benefiting from rehabilitation. Half of eligible veterans declined to enter training, and one-third of those who entered rehabilitation failed to complete their training.[30]

Congress placed a small, year-old agency—the FBVE—in charge of the vocational rehabilitation of disabled veterans. The result was a virtual catastrophe.[31] Previously, the FBVE had overseen vocational education programs for just a few thousand civilians. Experts on vocational rehabilitation, in turn, had predicted only 16,000 trainees, largely soldiers with amputations or those who had lost sight in one or both eyes.[32] Instead, 283,000 veterans registered for rehabilitation by November 1920—many with complex disabilities such as tuberculosis and other lung problems, multiple shrapnel wounds, and shell shock.[33] The agency lacked the capacity to suddenly manage the rehabilitation of hundreds of thousands of disabled veterans and had little choice but to use hundreds of local physicians to assess veterans' levels of disability, along with nearly 8,000 private schools and colleges to provide training.[34]

An unwieldy, split administrative system led to infighting among the four federal agencies responsible for caring for disabled veterans. Ex-soldiers had their disabilities medically certified by the army, received compensation from the Bureau of War Risk Insurance (BWRI) in the Treasury Department, and turned to the U.S. Public Health Service for medical care.[35] In addition, the central office of the FBVE in Washington, D.C., had to sign off on each case and refused nearly all offers of advice and volunteer work from organizations such as the NAM and the Red Cross Institute for Crippled and Disabled Men—and even from Ford Motor Company, whose successful employment of thousands of "cripples" was becoming widely known. McMurtrie, in turn, lambasted the FBVE for not accepting the offers of leading businessmen (and perhaps prominent rehabilitation experts such as himself) to serve on committees on a volunteer basis. He commented, "So instead of having the 'biggest' men in the communities throughout the country identified with its work the board was limited to men whom it could hire for salaries ranging from $2,000 to $4,000."[36] As a result of all of these problems, the FBVE enjoyed little success in rehabilitating trainees. By February 1920, the board had only 21,538 veterans in training; only 2,802 had completed their training. According to a 1920 investigation by the *New York Evening Post*, the FBVE placed just 217 rehabilitated veterans "in gainful employment."[37]

Congress responded to the FBVE's dysfunction—which one newspaper columnist termed "little short of criminal waste of the public's money"—by creating the Veterans' Bureau in August 1921.[38] The new agency centralized nearly all aspects of disabled veterans' compensation and rehabilitation. No longer did veterans need to negotiate the FBVE, the BWRI, and the army's medical department. At the same time, the Veterans' Bureau delegated some of its duties, employing private organizations such as the American Legion and the Red Cross, for instance, to help with the process of determining veterans' eligibility.[39] Congress also dramatically increased funding for rehabilitation, appropriating $447 million in 1923.[40]

The Veterans' Bureau's improved funding and coordination enabled the agency to speed the eligibility process. Between August and October 1921, for instance, the bureau interviewed 82,000 veterans, filed 35,000 claims for disability compensation and rehabilitation, and processed 30,000 claims with the help of local "clean-up squads" composed of national-level rehabilitation officials and volunteers from the American Legion and the Red Cross. This campaign presaged a large-scale decentralization of the eligibility process by the bureau's director, Colonel Charles R. Forbes (in 1923, General Frank T. Hines replaced Forbes). Veterans no longer had to send six copies of their files to Washington, D.C., and wait months for an answer; instead, local vocational officers ruled on veterans' eligibility for training. This simplified process, however, left African American veterans far more vulnerable to the prejudices of southern officials.[41]

Despite the Veterans' Bureau's efficiency in processing claims, the agency faced new pitfalls. By 1923, Forbes had fled to Europe, pending charges of defrauding the government. A Senate investigation in 1924 found that Forbes had embezzled or wasted nearly a quarter of the agency's funds ($223 million), primarily by diverting funds for hospital construction.[42] Among other schemes, Forbes arranged for the Veterans' Bureau to buy unbleached sheets at a price of $1.27, then "sold them to the Thompson-Kelly Company for 26 or 27 cents, and at the same time bought 25,000 new sheets for $1.02 apiece." In 1925, Forbes and John W. Thompson, a St. Louis building contractor, were sentenced to two years in Leavenworth and ordered to pay a $10,000 fine.[43]

Due to the fact that vocational rehabilitation was so new, the Veterans' Bureau struggled to find and retain qualified personnel, as had the FBVE. The men who oversaw the Rehabilitation Division included several public school superintendents, an insurance lawyer, a professor of vocational education at Columbia University, and a military officer who had coordinated technical training during the war.[44] Most officials, however, worked in one of the fourteen regional districts: the vocational advisers, registration officers, and district and subdistrict supervisors. Some of these local officials had earned degrees from normal schools, vocational high schools, or trade schools; others had served as foremen in a particular trade or as commissioned officers in the military; yet others had worked as agricultural extension agents or reporters for trade publications. Because civil service rules limited salaries to $2,000 to $4,000 apiece, neither the FBVE nor the Veterans' Bureau could retain rehabilitation officers. The manager of District 13 complained in 1922, for instance, that "42 percent of the rehabilitation assistants on our staff have been with us less than six months, and it is six months before a man is of very much value to you."[45]

Discouraging Public Dependency

Nearly every aspect of the vocational rehabilitation process reflected the intense interest of rehabilitation promoters, lawmakers, and D.C.-based rehabilitators in discouraging veterans from becoming dependent on public aid. Relatives—especially female ones—employers, and the public all had important roles to play. Edward T. Devine, the editor of the reform magazine *Survey* and the chairman of the Red Cross Institute for Crippled and Disabled Men, put it bluntly: "[The disabled veteran] is from start to finish to be looked upon as a producer."[46] Both rehabilitation experts and national-level rehabilitators intended to enable veterans to support their families. Consequently, disabled veterans—at least white ones—would undergo training not in the ill-paid crafts or menial labor offered to disabled civilians in sheltered workshops but rather in skilled trades that could pay a breadwinning wage.

Veterans' rehabilitation began as soon as injured soldiers emerged from surgery, since rehabilitation experts feared that even a few days would permanently suppress a soldier's "will to work." The *FBVE Bulletin* warned in 1918: "It has been said that the handicapped become employable in direct ratio to the promptness with which occupation is begun." The author noted, "Even a short period of idleness tends to hospitalize the patient, and seems to crush his ambition and kill his application. These can not be re-created by later systems of reeducation however elaborate."[47] Accordingly, bedridden veterans were taught to read and write (or to use Braille, if necessary), string beads, or make baskets, or on occasion skills like drafting. Those more mobile could study carpentry, jewelry making, or watch repair. Rehabilitation promoters viewed this "occupational therapy" as a means of addressing disabled soldiers' fears that their impairments meant a life of dependency. Devine explained: "The average man ... wakes up after the operation to black depression and dismay. He sees nothing before him but a life of idleness or a position as a watchman or doorkeeper."[48] In theory, however, learning even basic skills taught self-discipline, prevented self-pity, and persuaded disabled veterans that they could once again be productive.[49]

Yet rehabilitation experts noted the dual threats to soldiers' morals and morale posed by "useless busy work." The *FBVE Bulletin* recounted the tale of an "optimistic and cheerful" man who, upon hearing that he should learn raffia work, suddenly became aware of his disability and the fact that "others considered him worthless." The veteran saw raffia work as a "useless occupation" fit only for charity work. In this view, nonmarketable skills such as raffia work, drawing, or woodworking had their place in helping to retrain injured limbs or digits—but only briefly. The author cautioned: "If trivial and time-passing occupations are too long continued in the rehabilitation, disabled soldiers and sailors have been actually turned away from productive occupations and have taken up one of those 'semitrades' which are dependent upon charity or upon uncertain and fickle markets for support."[50]

The framers of the rehabilitation acts focused their attention on veterans with major vocational handicaps. Of the 670,000 veterans who requested rehabilitation, FBVE and Veterans' Bureau administrators deemed roughly half

(334,578) eligible for training.⁵¹ Any veteran whom administrators declared had a major "vocational handicap ... [that] prevent[ed] his return to his former occupation" received Section 2 training, which came with a monthly maintenance allowance of up to $145. Officials tracked veterans with "minor disabilities who [were] not prevented by their injuries from returning to gainful occupations" into Section 3 training. Trainees in both categories received free tuition for course work, supplies, training, and equipment, but Section 3 trainees received no maintenance allowances. As a result, veterans deemed eligible for Section 3 training made up only 11.4 percent of all trainees.⁵²

In contrast to the managers of sheltered workshops, the architects of the rehabilitation program rejected unskilled positions in heavy industry and manufacturing in favor of skilled, nonseasonal trades, at least for white veterans. National-level administrators argued that, even though the unskilled sectors of the economy were expanding rapidly, veterans would not be able to retain unskilled positions.⁵³ As McMurtrie explained, "The aim of re-education is to turn out the soldier as a skilled worker in a job *at which his disability is no handicap*."⁵⁴ Like Ford Motor Company, local rehabilitation officials sought to match disabled veterans to a job that fit their remaining capabilities and interests and which did not require veterans to rely on prosthetics.⁵⁵ *Carry On*, for instance, explained that a soldier who had lost an arm or a leg could be a telegrapher; in fact, so could a deafened man, since he could still hear the clicking of the telegraph.⁵⁶ Most white veterans entered training in skilled manufacturing or mechanical work (40 percent, combined, of all veterans), such as jewelry making, electrical work, or automobile repair. Thirteen percent each trained in agricultural, commercial work, and clerical work, with African American veterans being heavily concentrated in agriculture, while 16 percent of all veterans entered professional training programs such as medicine and law.⁵⁷ Almost exclusively, the FBVE and the Veterans' Bureau used existing educational institutions, as well as more than "8,000 shops, mills, factories, and business places of all sorts."⁵⁸ Vocational advisers placed veterans in both institutional (classroom) or placement (on-the-job) training; veterans entitled to Section 3 training often took correspondence courses. In theory, trainees were supposed to receive regular supervision from rehabilitation officials. More importantly, local rehabilitation officials were supposed to place veterans who had completed their training in a permanent job—a responsibility that federal officials soon tried to dismiss.

Rehabilitation promoters such as McMurtrie presented training as a crucial step for disabled veterans who sought to restore their status as "proper men." The veterans' advice magazine *Carry On* opened each issue with "The

Cartoon from "They Don't Want Your Charity—They Demand Their Chance," by H. T. Webster, *Carry On*, August 1918.

Creed of the Disabled Soldier": "Once more to be useful—to see pity in the eyes of my friends replaced with commendation—to work, produce, provide, and to feel that I have a place in the world—seeking no favors and given none—a *man* among *men* in spite of this physical handicap."[59] *Carry On* regularly carried features about how vocational rehabilitation had enabled a disabled veteran to keep his sweetheart, reflecting rehabilitators' intense interest in remasculinizing and normalizing disabled veterans.[60] For the first blind veteran of the war, Bill Zimmerman, finishing his rehabilitation program and finding a job was a precondition for returning to his prewar life. Zimmerman told his fellow veterans: "You see I have got to get a job now, because they sent for my girl to come down here to see me and she said, 'Bill, if you make good I am going to marry you.'"[61]

Advocates of rehabilitation argued that, like Zimmerman's girlfriend, family members and the general public had a crucial role to play in restoring disabled veterans to self-supporting citizenship. Commentators warned that veterans could easily slip into idleness and mendacity if allowed to do so by "hero-worship," excess sympathy, or the provision of charity.[62] Instead, relatives and friends needed to press disabled veterans to take advantage of vocational rehabilitation. James P. Munroe, the vice chairman of the FBVE, called upon veterans' families to help "re-establish initiative and a sense of individual responsibility in the soldier in order that through training the man may be returned to a self-respecting and independent status in the community."[63] Rehabilitators further fretted that the ease with which disabled workers could find employment during wartime labor shortages would discourage veterans with disabilities from entering rehabilitation. Here, too, rehabilitators called on relatives and employers to provide guidance. McMurtrie warned of the dire consequences of forgoing rehabilitation: "Even a disabled man may be able to go out and earn seven dollars a day in a munitions factory. This constitutes a very potent counter-attraction to representations of modest but permanent employment after a course of training. If he makes the opportunist choice he will, upon the return of employment conditions to normal, be reduced to the status of a casual laborer, perilously near the verge of mendicancy."[64] Rehabilitators further encouraged family, friends, and the public to monitor disabled veterans' progress, asking that they report any disabled veterans who tried to seek "charity under the guise of selling trinkets on the street corner" to the "proper authority."[65]

Rehabilitation promoters identified female relatives as having a particularly important role in encouraging veterans to pursue vocational rehabilitation. Writer and suffragist Alice Duer Miller drew on traditional ideas about women being the guardians of family morals. She argued: "The shock to the man who wakes up after the operation to find that he has lost an arm or a leg is not only the shock of his own handicap, but the horror of being a dependent—something useless and abnormal. The recovery of our disabled soldiers—their return to a useful life—is in the control of the women of this country. No war work that has ever been offered to us is as important—or perhaps as difficult." Rehabilitators' emphasis on the crucial role played by female relatives matched the prominent part taken by female physiotherapists in treating—and remasculinizing—wounded soldiers.[66]

In order to discourage veterans from public dependency, rehabilitation experts likewise urged employers to practice "tough love." McMurtrie, for instance, warned that misguided charity and prejudice on the part of employers would fatally doom rehabilitation programs. He pushed employers not to try to "'take care of,' from patriotic motives, a given number of disabled men, finding for them any odd jobs which are available, and putting ex-soldiers in them without much regard to whether they can earn the wages paid or not." Instead of helping disabled veterans, McMurtrie argued that these methods "pauperized" them and practically guaranteed that veterans would lose their job once the flush of wartime patriotism wore off.[67] Employers' prejudice against hiring disabled workers, he suggested, "helped make many cripples dependent." He criticized employers for preferring to give "the cripple alms" rather than "expend the thought necessary to place him in a suitable job."[68]

Finally, rehabilitation promoters urged employers and the public alike to be sensitive to disabled veterans with "invisible wounds." Like the framers of the rehabilitation acts, the general public initially assumed that disabled veterans would have visible disabilities such as amputations. As a result, veterans with invisible disabilities such as shell shock, lungs damaged by gassing, or chronic pain from shrapnel wounds encountered skepticism from the public and from employers. *Carry On* bemoaned "the present tendency [of the public] ... to spend most of its sympathy and encouragement on the man with visible wounds." Captain Arthur H. Samuels warned, "It is not the picturesque side of reconstruction that will afford the most troublesome problems of this country."[69]

Although rehabilitation promoters stressed the role of the public in remaking disabled veterans into self-supporting citizens, veterans also bore responsibilities. Rehabilitators argued that being disabled—and dependent—was a choice. *Carry On* argued, for instance: "The principle is that no one need be a cripple unless he himself wishes it.... *There is no such thing as being crippled, while there exists the iron will to overcome the handicap.*"[70] By returning to productive work, disabled veterans "chose" not to become crippled or disabled. *Carry On* commentator Herbert Kaufman argued, "The remarkable achievements of retinkered European soldiers indicate that the only hopeless cripple is a deliberate shirker."[71] The Red Cross Institute for Crippled and Disabled Men, in turn, advised veteran's families: "Demand of the cripple that he get back in the work of the world.... The cripple who is occupied is, in truth, no longer handicapped."[72] As institute director McMurtrie argued, the disabled veteran owed it to the nation not to "resign himself to dependence on his pension and to spending the rest of his life in demoralizing idleness." Instead, disabled veterans needed to fulfill their civic "duty" and become "worthy citizens."[73]

Who Could Access Rehabilitation?

Not all disabled veterans could even obtain approval to enter rehabilitation, however. Relying on a secret disability ratings schedule only belatedly released

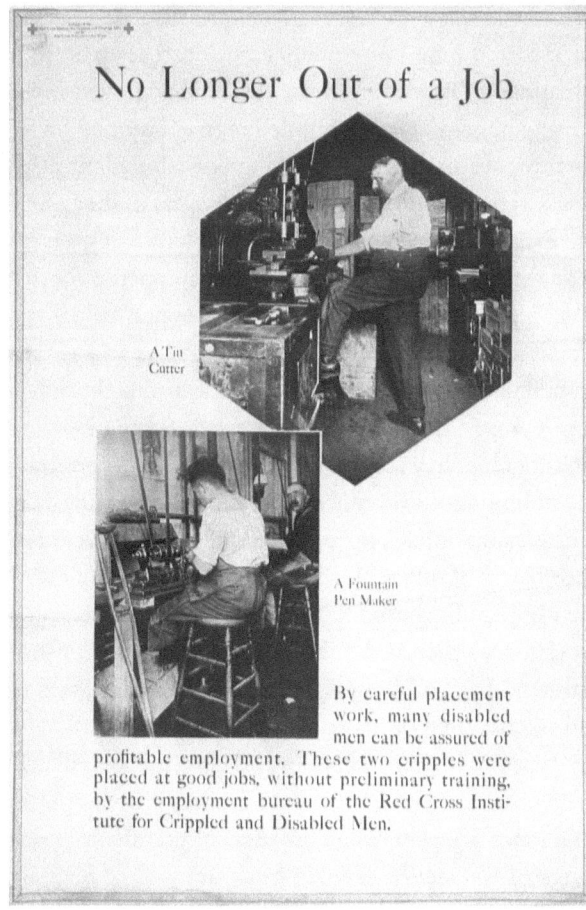

Poster from rehabilitation exhibit put together by the Red Cross Institute for Crippled and Disabled Men and the Red Cross Institute for the Blind, 1919. Courtesy of the Library of Congress, LC-USZC4-7377.

to Congress and the public, the FBVE and the Veterans' Bureau refused nearly half of compensation claims between 1917 and 1924.[74] And without a disability rating of at least 10 percent, veterans had no hope of entering training. Administrators' attempts to quantify disability in a ratings schedule reflected racialized notions of fitness and pejorative assumptions about certain types of impairments, as well as memories of the kinds of disabilities produced by past wars. As Rubinow had pointed out for workmen's compensation, lived experiences of disabilities rarely fit neatly into dismemberment schedules.[75]

Rehabilitation planners had expected soldiers to return with discrete and easily defined impairments such as amputations, blindness, and "crippling" injuries. But the new technologies and style of the war produced an unfamiliar, complex set of impairments that evolved and changed over time.[76] Nearly half of disabled veterans came home with "neuropsychiatric disorders" (shell shock), tuberculosis, or assorted lung impairments and heart lesions from gassing, often in combination.[77] Diagnosing these disabilities proved more complicated than the "dismembered men" or blinded men envisioned by rehabilitators. Lung and neuropsychiatric problems often developed months, if not years, after veterans returned home and, like physical and sensory disabilities, continued to evolve over time. Until 1923, disabled veterans were examined every ninety days for their disability rating and compensation, although they could still complete their training if they dropped below the 10 percent threshold. Veterans found the repeated examinations and adjustments in compensation taxing. Charles Grafe, for instance, had eight different disability ratings and compensation amounts between September 1921 and September 1923.[78] Although policy makers had initially been determined not to extend the statute of limitations on reporting a disability, fearing a repeat of the Civil War pension situation, Congress eventually allowed veterans up to three years to report cases of tuberculosis and neuropsychiatric disorders.[79] And whereas the minié bullets used in the Civil War produced such large wounds that many soldiers either died or had amputations, the gunshot and shrapnel wounds suffered by World War I soldiers caused high rates of chronic pain that limited veterans in training and employment.[80]

Veterans with certain types of impairments—especially neuropsychiatric disabilities—faced intense scrutiny from FBVE and Veterans' Bureau physicians that reflected the influence of eugenics and broader cultural assumptions about the "mad." Sufferers of war neuroses were often accused of feigning their impairments or acquiring them due to a syphilis infection (a noncompensable disability). The FBVE claimed in 1921: "The breakdown under the stress of military service of most neuropsychiatric cases was attributed to a defective nervous system."[81]

African American veterans had particular trouble gaining eligibility due to doctors' racialized concepts of "fitness." Physicians routinely denied compensation to African American veterans in the Carolinas, Georgia, Florida, and Tennessee, tracing their impairments to venereal diseases that purportedly existed before enlistment. Most doctors affiliated with the FBVE and the Veterans' Bureau viewed African Americans as inherently inferior and disease-ridden, and consequently ignored environmental conditions that led to higher rates of heart disease, tuberculosis, and physical disabilities.[82] Eligibility officers also feared that providing too many African American veterans with compensation benefits and vocational rehabilitation training would undermine southern labor markets and racial status hierarchies. Most African

American agricultural laborers earned just $30 a month, but disabled veterans received a maintenance allowance ranging between $80 and $145 per month, depending on the number of dependents and the cost of living.[83]

Returning to Wage Labor

Despite the slow and troubled start of the vocational rehabilitation program for veterans, national officials declared success in 1928, when the Veterans' Bureau terminated its rehabilitation program. General Hines, the director of the bureau, defined "success" in simple terms: as a majority of disabled veterans completing their training.[84] By 1928, 66 percent (or 118,355 veterans) of the 179,519 veterans who had entered training had finished their programs and, accordingly, been deemed "rehabilitated."[85] Hines did not attempt to draw larger conclusions about the impact of the rehabilitation program on the lives of disabled veterans, or even comment on whether veterans' training enabled them to regain the status of breadwinners.[86] On a more personal level, nevertheless, rehabilitation enabled many disabled veterans—at least white ones—to return to the wage labor market and maintain or even improve their economic standing.

This was, of course, a striking contrast with the fate of civilians with acquired physical or sensory impairments or chronic illnesses, who almost always suffered a dramatic drop in wages and who, by the 1920s, had increasing trouble retaining access to wage work. That said, some employers saw little difference between disabled veterans and other individuals with disabilities.

Even veterans with relatively serious impairments found that vocational rehabilitation allowed them to become self-supporting. John Heidecker, for example, received severe shrapnel wounds in his left arm at Soissons, France, that left his "elbow fixed at 130 degrees," his wrist capable of moving only thirty degrees, and his hand a "claw-hand."[87] The examiner declared his arm "very nearly useless in its present state" and granted him a 60 percent disability rating. Like most veterans with major impairments, Heidecker began rehabilitation immediately after being released from a stateside hospital. While in training to become a mechanical draftsman, he struggled with motivation and several illnesses unrelated to his wounds (pleurisy, stomach inflammation, and fainting, among others), ultimately missing over six months of his first eighteen months of training.[88] Several times in 1921 and 1922, Heidecker's supervisor threatened to discontinue his rehabilitation if his attitude did not improve. Once he entered placement training at Standard Oil in summer 1923, however, he proved to be such a strong employee that the company made plans to hire him as soon as he finished rehabilitation. After nearly three years of institutional and placement training, John Heidecker accepted a job as a mechanical draftsman, earning $145 a month, nearly on par with his prewar wages of $25 a week as a machinist apprentice, taking inflation into account.[89]

During economic downturns, veterans drew on the rehabilitation program as a form of unemployment insurance. During the postwar recession of 1920–1921, disabled veterans such as George Cathocalles flooded rehabilitation programs.[90] After being discharged in 1919, Cathocalles had returned to his home in Troy, New York, as well as to his prewar work as a collar turner. Initially, his wartime injury—a weak and arthritic right hand—caused no problems. But after a few months, Cathocalles could no longer find work. He tried running a pool room for a few months but could not support himself and his wife on his earnings in the midst of a recession. Only then did he request rehabilitation for his 10 percent disability. His approval for Section 2 training came, of course, with a maintenance allowance of at least $115 per month—which, in effect, served Cathocalles and many of his fellow veterans as unemployment compensation.[91] After two years of training as a shoe repairman, during which time he received glowing reports from supervisors, Cathocalles opened his own shoe repair shop in Troy. He received $9 per month in compensation until November 1928, when his disability was declared to be less than the 10 percent minimum.[92]

Heidecker's and Cathocalles's success in regaining their prewar incomes through rehabilitation was not a fluke. Studies done by national-level officials at both the FBVE and the Veterans' Bureau suggested that, even when allowing for inflation, many if not most rehabilitated veterans regained the same earning power as before the war. In fact, both agencies contended that rehabilitation dramatically increased veterans' incomes; such arguments, however, relied on fuzzy math. An FBVE study of 1,200 American men in 1921, for instance, indicated that those who had been through vocational rehabilitation earned dramatically more: $1,477 annually post-training versus $785 in prewar earnings.[93] In 1923, the Veterans' Bureau announced that a survey of one hundred rehabilitated veterans revealed that their average income had risen from $1,058 during the prewar years to $1,706. Some veterans had recorded far greater increases in income and even "jumped class." A former farm laborer now worked as an auto mechanic; his annual income had risen from $360 to $1,820.[94] On paper, these numbers seemed impressive, but inflation negated the value of veterans' increases in wages. In fact, rehabilitation had merely enabled disabled veterans to maintain their prewar wages.[95] This was nevertheless a significant accomplishment, particularly when contrasted with disabled civilians who typically had to cope with a considerable loss in income—if employers did not bar them entirely from the workplace.

Although the FBVE and the Veterans' Bureau focused on the financial rewards of rehabilitation, the program also provided veterans like George Adolfson with a means for personal fulfillment. Long passionate about art, Adolfson had not found a way to sustain himself as an artist before the war. Instead, he labored as a clerical worker and then as an electrician, earning $45 to $50 a month, working on his art in his free time. In summer 1918, Adolfson returned home from France with two relatively minor disabilities, rated collectively at 10 percent: chronic bronchitis, due to being gassed on the front, and a borderline case of tuberculosis. He received a minor amount of monthly compensation and soon began working as an electrical draftsman in the Brooklyn Navy Yard for $56 a month. In 1920, he petitioned the FBVE for rehabilitation, declaring that he wanted to work in commercial art, and the agency declared him eligible for Section 2 training. After three years of study, Adolfson fulfilled his heart's desire and became a commercial instructor of art at the Daily Vacation Bible School and increased his wages by $19 a month (to $75). As of the 1930 census, Adolfson was still teaching art.[96]

Clearly, disabled veterans also benefited from employers' and unions' goodwill. While by the 1920s nearly all firms saw disabled civilians as inefficient, liability-prone workers best screened out with preemployment physical examinations, companies actively sought out disabled veterans, even writing the bureau by the hundreds to offer positions. The American Guarantee Company of Columbus inquired whether the Veterans' Bureau had trained any men in operating multigraphs (early copying machines used for stamping addresses). Company president John L. Hamilton noted that such a position "could be easily handled by any ex-service man, with good intelligence, who has lost one or more of his feet or legs." He had previously tried and failed to hire a disabled veteran through the local American Legion post, but now requested one who was "ambitious, intelligent, and sober."[97] General Electric, in turn, commenced an extensive survey of its Schenectady plant in much the fashion that Ford Motor Company had. After analyzing fourteen potential categories of disability—arms, eyes, general debility, hernia, legs, lungs, and shell shock, among others—the Industrial Service Department determined that 24,538 "employment possibilities" existed in a plant that, at that time, employed only 14,000 workers.[98]

Likewise, unions sought to aid disabled veterans. Several major ones waived apprenticeship rules for disabled veterans, and one offered free membership to disabled veterans who had completed vocational rehabilitation.[99] Not only did Congress protect employers who hired disabled veterans from the disincentives of workmen's compensation laws, promising to cover any costs that arose from disabling second injuries, but insurance firms also promised that, unlike for disabled civilians, they would not raise rates for companies that hired veterans with disabilities. Given some employers' fears about the potential for second injuries, such promises were not without meaning. While corresponding with Veterans' Bureau officials about potential positions for disabled veterans, the American Ice Company of Jersey City, for instance, fretted that the "electrically driven machinery" involved with woodworking positions might be "too dangerous" for "a man of the type you represent."[100]

Not all employers, however, extended a welcome to disabled veterans; FBVE and Veterans' Bureau officials sometimes encountered the same sorts of dismissive attitudes and prejudices when trying to place their charges as did disabled civilians. As the personnel superintendent for Brooklyn's Sperry Gyroscope Company noted, many employers assumed that rehabilitated veterans were "all physically unfit" and that any type of "disability" made a man too weak to do physical labor. When the bureau queried whether the Abbott Ball Company in Hartford might be willing to hire disabled veterans, for instance, C. H. Abbott flatly stated, "We have no work in our factory which he could give to disabled men where they could learn a trade. Our work is all rather heavy and requires men capable of lifting and handling heavy parts." The General Phonograph Corporation in New York, in turn, contended that the labor in its plant was "extremely skilled" and required "peculiar training," following up with: "We hardly believe a disabled veteran could stand the arduous test of operating one of our record presses."[101]

The Political Gridlock of Rehabilitation

While Adolfson, Cathocalles, and Heidecker clearly benefited from vocational rehabilitation, other veterans found their encounter with the rehabilitation program so frustrating that they quit altogether. Veterans' tales of woe—which newspaper commentators and lawmakers viewed as the results of misadministration and unnecessary red tape—derived from the inherently political nature of designing and implementing the program. Furthermore, both the FBVE and the Veterans' Bureau struggled to build the administrative capacity necessary to supervise and place in employment the hundreds of thousands of veterans who demanded rehabilitation.[102] For veterans, the result was gridlock.

The way in which Congress initially structured the process of determining veterans' eligibility for rehabilitation meant that veterans waited for months to hear if they could enter rehabilitation.[103] In fact, the BWRI took so long to determine if disabled veterans were eligible for compensation—and therefore rehabilitation—that the FBVE decided in July 1919 to allow those still waiting on an eligibility ruling to begin training on a provisional basis. Veterans also had to undergo physical examinations by doctors from three different agencies: the military hospital from which they were discharged, the BWRI, and the FBVE itself.[104] As a result, most waited at least six months to learn if they were eligible for training; some waited nine.[105] Thirty percent of disabled veterans gave up before becoming eligible for training, and nearly half of those ruled eligible never entered training.[106] One convalescent veteran told a reporter for the *New York Times* that his buddy, who had a 23 percent disability and had been a salesman before the war, was promised training in rubber salesmanship. But "he got tired after waiting two months and went into another job."[107]

But the BWRI was not entirely to blame; the FBVE had its own brand of dysfunction, largely due to its lack of capacity. In fact, the board was so disorganized that it failed to properly publicize the rehabilitation program. When a reporter for the *New York Times* spoke with several disabled veterans at Baltimore's Fort McHenry Hospital in 1919, he discovered that none had heard of the program. The reporter recounted, "'That must be one of Uncle Sam's jokes,' said one of the crippled men. 'It sounds like War Risk,' and others nodded approval."[108] Even those veterans already engaged in occupational therapy—those training in the hospital's shoe repair, carpentry, jewelry-making, or watch repair shops—doubted that the rehabilitation program actually existed.

The board's centralized structure—with 1,000 of its 3,000 employees working in Washington, D.C.—meant that the Washington office approved all cases and disbursements, hired all of the agency's clerks, issued all of the regulations, and provided all supplies. According to a report in the *New York Evening Post*, the district vocational officer for the New York region, Arthur W. Griffin, became so frustrated with his status as a "figurehead" that he quit in July 1919. Griffin was only one of several district vocational officers to quit the New York district out of frustration with the FBVE.[109] Veterans, however, suffered the brunt of the FBVE's slowness and disorganization.

Some veterans waited so long to receive approval to begin training that their disabilities disappeared—along with their eligibility for rehabilitation. Edward M. Kalish, for instance, first requested rehabilitation from the FBVE's

New York district office in March 1919; he had been wounded on his left knee and right arm by a gas shell and had also developed rheumatism and breathing problems. In fact, Kalish had taken a leave of absence from the army for the specific purpose of signing up for rehabilitation, but officers told him that he first had to be discharged. He soon received his discharge, but the FBVE took four months to complete his paperwork—faster than the average of six months thanks to his regular visits to the office. In July 1919, the district vocational officer recommended the man for a course in commercial law but could not tell him when he would start his classes. Kalish went to the countryside to rest and returned to New York a month later to find that the FBVE still could not tell him when he would start training. In December, "he was informed that so much time had elapsed he would have to be examined again." At his medical examination in January 1920, the doctor "thumped him and finally pronounced him well," even though "the gas still bothered him and rheumatism gripped him at times. The board had delayed so long Kalish now had no disability." In frustration, he grabbed his papers off the doctor's desk and tore them into pieces; he did not respond to the FBVE's follow-up letters.[110]

Even after the Veterans' Bureau took over rehabilitation in 1921, proving eligibility remained a lengthy, complicated task. In 1928, veterans were still complaining that the eligibility procedure was "more involved than filing an accurate tax report." A veteran had to write "at least a dozen letters, must obtain from five to ten affidavits, [and] must see or communicate with every physician who treated him before or after his discharge from the service." According to one report, the vast majority of veterans filled out their applications incorrectly, while nearly two-thirds of physicians provided incomplete reports, which resulted in yet more correspondence and delays.[111]

The process of determining eligibility, moreover, proved susceptible to outside political influences. Veterans whose requests for rehabilitation were disapproved by local or national-level rehabilitation officials often turned to outside advocates such as congressmen, governors, the American Legion, or newspapers. When outside advocates contacted the Veterans' Bureau, D.C.-based rehabilitators invariably reopened the veteran's case, regardless of how many times it had already been considered.[112] Dissatisfied veterans could also appeal to the bureau's Central Office, which overturned 23 percent of regional office rulings, or to the director, who overruled 16 percent of Central Office decisions.[113] While such appeals were common in workmen's compensation programs as well, they nevertheless slowed the workings of the bureau.

Even when disabled veterans persisted through the tortuous process of becoming eligible for vocational rehabilitation, the FBVE's and the Veterans'

Bureau's lack of capacity meant that veterans' training and job placement often left much to be desired. The FBVE was particularly notorious for making laughable errors in training plans. A right-handed man who could not lift his right arm above his waist, for instance, was trained as a barber, and a man who fell when he bent over was tutored in automotive repair.[114] But the Veterans' Bureau, too, had a reputation for careless placement and supervision, likely due in part to the fact that nearly half of the bureau's ill-trained staff turned over each year. In 1924, the *New York Times* reported that 1,500 veterans in the city had not been supervised in at least five months.[115] And in an investigation the prior year, the New York City–based Merchants' Association found veterans with "poor eyes at watch-making," men with "withered feet at tailoring machines," and those with injured hands at jewelry making. The veterans "answered in most every case that they were there because their training officers ordered them there, sometimes under threat of having their compensation taken away if they disobeyed."[116] Veterans in placement training, in turn, found themselves running errands and cleaning up auto garages rather than learning how to repair cars. Many gave up on their training in disgust, which meant permanently losing their compensation.[117] The bureau's record of placing trained veterans in gainful employment was equally mixed, with more than a quarter unemployed or working in occupations outside their area of training in June 1924.[118]

The inherently political and bureaucratic nature of the rehabilitation program—and the lack of capacity on the part of the FBVE and the Veterans' Bureau—clearly prevented many veterans from pursuing rehabilitation. Veterans, however, bore some responsibility for the troubles of the program; some sometimes tried to "game" the rehabilitation system. With little supervision during placement training, some were tempted to extend their training as long as possible to continue receiving their maintenance allowance. At up to $145 per month, disabled veterans often earned more with maintenance pay than they could have earned in the open market, especially if they did not collect much compensation.[119]

Other veterans did not make good use of the training opportunities granted them. Donald Forbes, for instance, wrote to the FBVE himself to request rehabilitation (which was unusual), gained permission, and failed to complete several courses for which the Veterans' Bureau footed the bill. Forbes first contacted the FBVE in September 1920, asking to be evaluated for compensation and "vocational training." He had just been laid off from his position as a draftsman with New Departure Manufacturing in Connecticut. Reflecting an astute use of the bureau's own language, Forbes claimed, "I am not able to 'carry on' as mechanical draftsman, my pre-war occupation," due to a gas attack suffered in France.[120] He claimed that gassing had left him with a mild "bronchial condition."[121] By February 1921, Forbes had been approved for the correspondence course in mechanical engineering he had requested. He did not begin his course work for more than a year, during which time his lungs had healed enough that he became ineligible for compensation. Following standard procedure, rehabilitation officials still allowed him to continue (or in his case, enter) his training program, which he finally started in April 1922. By the end of 1922, however, Forbes had done so little of his course work that the Veterans' Bureau suspended him. He blamed his lack of progress during fall 1922 on two lung surgeries—of which the Veterans' Bureau had no record—and demanded to be transferred to a course in carpentry. A few weeks later, he asked for a correspondence course in architecture. The bureau denied both transfer requests, citing the fact that he was no longer receiving compensation, but offered to restart his course in mechanical engineering. By July 1923, he had again been suspended for failing to do any of his course work. This time, the bureau refused to budge, even when Forbes claimed that he had returned his books and equipment to the school out of a "misunderstanding."[122]

Debating "Disability"

Red tape was not the only factor that discouraged disabled veterans from entering rehabilitation. Equally critical was the fact that veterans and rehabilitation officials at both the local and the federal level did not agree on what constituted a disability or on who had the right to define that disability, especially those that produced chronic pain. Unlike rehabilitation officials, disabled veterans viewed their impairments in economic—rather than medical—terms: as the inability to find work or be self-supporting.[123] Likely reflecting most veterans' working-class backgrounds, an impairment, especially a minor one, became a disability only when they could not find employment (during an economic downturn, when employers raised their hiring standards, or because their impairment became worse). Rehabilitation officials, in contrast, required that veterans' disabilities be defined in medical terms: by doctors who, in effect, served as gatekeepers.[124] In the end, disability and its relation to the labor market proved far more complex and fluid than the architects of the rehabilitation program had expected.

To a limited degree, rehabilitation officials accommodated veterans' economic understanding of disability and strategic use of the rehabilitation program. Much as workers at Ford Motor Company chose not to report minor injuries in order to avoid the financial penalties of workmen's compensation, soldiers with minor disabilities often claimed full health in order to receive a quick discharge. Only later, once small injuries worsened into major disabilities—or when economic conditions made a minor impairment a larger liability—did veterans such as Harry Iverson contact the FBVE or the Veterans' Bureau, claiming that they could no longer "carry on." Iverson had developed two hernias during his time in the army, one while scaling a wall at Fort Leavenworth and another "while hiking on the Lorraine Front" as the company bugler; the latter had left him "unable to walk." When offered discharge in January 1919, he did not report his hernias. Iverson later explained that he "was anxious to be mustered out of service, and . . . was not having trouble at the time."[125] But once he returned home, he found himself unable to continue working as a butcher, since he could no longer lift carcasses or stand for long periods of time. In January 1920, Iverson requested rehabilitation with the hope of becoming a switchboard operator. The FBVE asked for an affidavit about the injuries he received while in the service and his current physical condition. District vocational officer William Clark noted, however, that disabilities often returned after discharge and acknowledged that "many of the men at the time of discharge were suffering from disabilities but because of general demobilization no record of the disability was made."[126] Despite the fact that the surgeon who examined Iverson at discharge proclaimed him "physically and mentally sound," officials deemed the veteran's surgery record enough evidence to grant him Section 2 rehabilitation.[127] Iverson's time in rehabilitation proved less than satisfactory due to the different ways in which he and Veterans' Bureau officials defined rehabilitation, but he had at least won the right to rehabilitation.

Most veterans who delayed reporting their injuries or disabilities—or whose injuries changed over time—did not fare as well as Iverson. Frank Roberts, for instance, claimed in 1920 that shelling on the French front had burst his eardrum, causing hearing loss, dizziness, and constant drainage from his ear. The Veterans' Bureau examiner concurred with most of Roberts's complaints, diagnosing him with a ruptured eardrum and chronic middle ear infections. The doctor thought that the man's complaints might have been the result of shelling, but could not say for sure. Nevertheless, the doctor reported that the infections had spread into the temporal bones of his skull and damaged the rest of Roberts's eardrum as well as some of the bones in his ear.[128] Remarkably, the veteran had only a mild hearing loss, which the doctor declared was "not a vocational or training handicap." He noted, however, that "the condition of the tympanic membrane is a menace to the Claimant's life."[129]

Roberts's delay in reporting his disability—as well as his inability to definitely connect his ear problems to his military service—was part of the reason why the FBVE denied him training. But his case also reflected the fact that impairments that veterans understood as economic disabilities often did not match up with the medical definitions used by local and national rehabilitation officials to determine eligibility for compensation and rehabilitation. The War Risk Insurance Act Amendments had defined disability in industrial terms, and veterans needed to have a vocational handicap to receive Section 2 training.[130] But veterans could become eligible for compensation and rehabilitation only if a doctor could put their disability in medical terms and use the Veterans' Bureau's secret disability rating schedule to confirm a vocational handicap of at least 10 percent. At least one of the bureau's assistant directors criticized the agency's focus on medical impairments over "industrial disability." He called for the bureau to rework its secret disability ratings with the aid of a committee composed not only of doctors but also of "at least one attorney, some laymen and if possible a practical business man."[131]

In fact, Roberts had found his ear problems to be an economic disability, but the FBVE determined his eligibility based solely on his medical diagnosis. Before the war, he had served as a detective for the Erie Railroad Company and had also worked as a tree trimmer for the Buffalo city parks department. Upon his return, he found himself unable to pass the railroad company's physical examination "on account of defective hearing and vision."[132] Nor could Roberts continue working for the parks department, because he could no longer safely climb trees. He could find work only as a laborer for Buffalo Structural Steel, and starting in 1923, he filled the proverbial disabled man's role as a watchman for the New York Central Railway.[133]

Despite the fact that Roberts's impairment constituted a clear *economic* disability, the FBVE denied his multiple petitions for training on medical grounds, arguing that his "mild hearing loss" constituted "no vocational handicap."[134] In fact, Board of Appeals member Benjamin Brod suggested in 1923 that the veteran could not find "a more suitable occupation than that of Park Attendant. He has no vocational handicap for this kind of work."[135] A local Veterans' Bureau official took Roberts's side against the board, noting that "the investigation plainly show[ed] that the man was employed as a watchman in a railroad shop. He could not get his job back with the Park Department. Man's extreme nervous condition, it would seem, precluded his ever being able to climb trees and do the work expected of park department employees."[136] Nevertheless, district vocational officer J. C. Wardlaw denied Roberts's petition, citing "lapsed eligibility."[137] In frustration, the veteran then refused to show up for his physical examinations; the bureau retaliated first by suspending his compensation, then by rating his disability as being less than 10 percent.[138] In 1924, Roberts finally contacted his congressman, Clarence McGregor, but to no avail. Buffalo subdistrict manager J. J. Kingsbury told Representative MacGregor that the man had no "vocational handicap for his pre-war occupation" and, in any case, he no longer met the 10 percent threshold to qualify for compensation or rehabilitation.[139]

Further reflecting veterans' economic understanding of disability and their strategic use of rehabilitation, some veterans found their training to be too costly financially. A first lieutenant who had developed tuberculosis in France, for instance, discovered that, in order to take the university courses for which he had been approved, he had to first undergo treatment in a tuberculosis sanatorium. During his treatment, he received only his compensation of $46 a month (based on his 23 percent disability) rather than the generous maintenance allowance offered to trainees. For two months he struggled to support his wife and child, but his family could not make ends meet. He left the sanatorium, got a job, and asked that his compensation be stopped. In a letter to the *New York Times*, he wrote, "When my lung doesn't ache I think it was a nightmare; when it does ache I know it all for grim reality."[140]

Veterans and rehabilitation officials on the local and national levels clashed not only over whether to define disability in medical or economic terms, but also over who had the right to determine how to evaluate the lived experience of a disability and even what constituted a disability. Such questions were particularly troublesome given the complicated nature of the injuries with which veterans returned home. Even veterans with seemingly simple injuries such as amputations struggled with chronic pain and ongoing medical problems; 9 percent of veterans "had to interrupt or abandon training for medical reasons alone."[141]

Local rehabilitation officials proved less than sympathetic to veterans who challenged the authority of rehabilitators and physicians by claiming the right to define their own experience of disability, especially when that experience involved chronic pain.[142] Sylvester Howland, for instance, battled with the Veterans' Bureau over the proper treatment for his impairment and what job he could reasonably be expected to accept. Due to a gunshot wound to his ankle, he had lost the bottom eight inches of his left leg. After spending nearly two years in a military hospital and undergoing a second amputation, Howland was released with a 50 percent disability rating and a stump that refused to heal. Like most veterans with major impairments, he immediately entered rehabilitation. After a brief trial in watchmaking and jewelry repair, Howland settled on auto repair. His stump continued to trouble him, however. In April 1923, two years into his training, he began complaining of pain in his stump; in part, he blamed the fact that his artificial leg was too loose. In December, Howland asked to be excused from training for a few days "to give my stump a chance to rest up a bit." The Veterans' Bureau declined his request, instead offering to send the man to New York to have his artificial leg altered. Ignoring the fact that the veteran's stump had never fully healed, Dr. C. F. Graham advised Howland that "the proper fitting of the socket . . . [would] undoubtedly allow your stump to heal up in a very short time."[143] It is unclear if Howland traveled to New York to visit the bureau's prosthetics workshop, but his previously sterling attendance and work record fell by the wayside in early 1924. He missed training, had his maintenance allowance suspended, and even asked to be transferred to another training site. But by May 1924, he and his instructor, a Mr. Lester, had made peace, but only temporarily. Lester promised Howland a place in his garage once he finished his training but reneged as soon as the Veterans' Bureau declared Howland rehabilitated in July 1924.[144]

As Howland reentered the labor market, he again found himself fighting rehabilitation officials who discounted his own knowledge of his disability and his capabilities. Following standard procedure, rehabilitation officials tried to locate a job for Howland. The only position that rehabilitators could find was in an auto repair shop in Albany, twelve miles from his home in Waterford. Howland said that he was willing to take the job if the Veterans' Bureau could find nothing else, but pleaded with them to find a closer position. He fretted about the cost of the streetcar fare, but mostly feared that "it will be hard on me to travel back and forth from Waterford, to Albany, each day . . . as I have only one leg."[145] Rehabilitators continued to offer jobs only in Albany. It is unclear if Howland accepted one of these positions; perhaps the fact that he and his wife had recently had their first child led him to do so. But by 1930, he had found a job as a mill foreman close by his home in Waterford, negating the value of his three years of training in auto repair. Curiously, his amputation does not seem to have prevented him from finding an industrial job; perhaps he had a personal connection with his employer or his boss was more willing to hire disabled veterans than disabled civilians.[146]

Rehabilitation: Training or a Real Job?

Veterans and rehabilitators battled not only over what constituted a disability and who had the right to define that condition, but also over the purpose and meaning of rehabilitation. Early promoters and, in particular, the advice magazine *Carry On*, promised that rehabilitation programs would enable veterans to improve their class status. The well-known poet, artist, and novelist Gelett Burgess wrote in 1918, for instance: "Many, even most disabled, men will have a chance to be better off... after the war than before. Not better off physically; that of course cannot be; but actually better off financially, socially and mentally.... Think what that means—a free technical education for your boy!"[147] Leading rehabilitation expert Douglas C. McMurtrie likewise argued that vocational rehabilitation would remedy the "former inequality of opportunity" that had limited most veterans to unskilled work before the war.[148] But in practice, rehabilitation officials' class and racial prejudices barred some veterans from even accessing training. Others discovered that their disabilities prevented them from actually securing employment in their chosen fields, only to find rehabilitators largely unsympathetic. As at Goodwill Industries, training and instilling the moral virtues of work had effectively replaced the more ambitious, yet complex, goal of integrating disabled veterans into the workplace.[149]

Carry On regularly featured success stories of veterans who had "jumped class." Burgess tantalized veterans' families, reporting: "Just look at these authentic cases and see: *A. Clay, of the Royal Engineers, was paralyzed in the right arm. Before the war he was a butcher. Now he is a telephone engineer.... C. E. James, of the British Royal Marines, lost his right leg. Before the war he was a gardener; now an electrician in C. A. V. Magneto Works.*"[150] Other writers described the grand ambitions of American veterans with disabilities. A Norwegian-born fisherman, for example, hoped to use his training in business and his knowledge of the fishing industry to become an executive. Another man had been guaranteed a job as a commercial chemist if he finished university, although he had finished only the first year of high school prior to entering the military and could receive only four years of vocational rehabilitation.[151] Burgess acknowledged, however, that not every disabled veteran could expect to "double his pay," but claimed that "almost every handicapped man can be educated to earn his own living."[152]

Local and national rehabilitation officials, however, were less interested than rehabilitation promoters in helping veterans raise their class status, perhaps reflecting a reluctance to challenge the dynamics of local economies.[153] National-level rehabilitators, for instance, discussed whether African Americans' maintenance allowances would upset the southern labor hierarchies. Local officials, in turn, denied all training to veterans who seemed unlikely to complete their course work. Veterans with tuberculosis and neuropsychiatric disorders were particularly likely to be judged "non-feasible."[154]

At the same time, rehabilitation officials at all levels sought to ensure that veterans' training would actually enable them to support themselves. Accordingly, vocational advisers sought to avoid placing disabled veterans in fields that officials viewed as overly popular among trainees, such as auto repair, chauffeuring, and motion picture operating; extremely competitive; or unlikely to pay well. Rehabilitators likewise tried to steer disabled veterans away from career objectives that veterans could not complete within the four-year time limit for training.[155] Yet, veterans struggled to obtain training in the fields in which they were interested, especially African American veterans, who often found themselves excluded from all but agricultural and semiskilled positions. In New York, conflicts between veterans and rehabilitators over training objectives and feasibility grew so heated that a rehabilitator at the Manhattan office advised his fellow officers to be hard-hearted when discussing training with veterans. In the infamous "Hard-Boiled Order," he recommended: "The organs used in approving cases are the eyes and the brain. The ears and the heart do not function. Be hard-boiled . . . . Put cotton in your ears and lock the door. If you are naturally sympathetic, work nights when nobody is there."[156]

Indeed, local and national rehabilitation officials were often contemptuous of veterans' desire to use their training as a means of improving their social standing. Most veterans came from working-class or rural communities, while rehabilitation officials readily revealed their middle-class backgrounds and prejudices. At the National Conference on Rehabilitation, Major Arthur Dean, for instance, attacked impoverished veterans who wanted to use their full four years of training. Dean grumbled: "This man here, an illiterate mountain white case, farmer, mechanic, a real illiterate, mental heavy weight; why, he thinks he ought to study four years because this man has four years. Perhaps he needs only four months."[157] Similarly, at the first national meeting of Veterans' Bureau district managers, Arthur W. Griffin, the head of the Rehabilitation Division, argued: "Rehabilitation is often pedagogically foolish: *Proof:* It tries to take a 6th grade graduate and make him into an accountant." Griffin asked, "Bluntly speaking, are we to put the man back into the economic and social status he had when he entered the service or are we to educate him as far as he wants to go?"[158] The district managers concurred with Griffin's bleak assessment of veterans' capabilities, citing veterans' poor educations and high rates of illiteracy.[159] Veterans' Bureau director Charles R. Forbes, for instance, suggested that the agency should consider stopping its efforts to teach illiterate veterans how to read and write.[160]

Rehabilitation officials' negative assessments of veterans' capabilities reflected racial prejudices as well. African American veterans who hoped to escape unskilled labor came in for particular criticism from national and local officials. Griffin complained, for instance, that when he entered the field of rehabilitation, "not one of us thought of negro illiterates who were day laborers in service in some camp where they caught a psycho something or other in camp and wanted to be accountants."[161] The FBVE and the Veterans' Bureau often advised African American veterans to enter low-skilled trades, agriculture, and the service industries and made more-limited efforts to contact them in the first place.[162] In part, rehabilitators feared, based on their labor market surveys, that African Americans trained in skilled labor or the professions would not be able to find work, or that vocational rehabilitation would further disrupt the southern labor market.[163] Major Arthur Dean, for instance, suggested that trying to turn an illiterate African American veteran into an "agricultural expert" raised questions about the meaning of rehabilitation itself.[164] Rehabilitation officials also discounted their disabilities.[165] Griffin, for instance, complained that the bureau was training "negro[es] who could not read before entering service and he received a mule kick in an army camp and [had] . . . flat feet which the service did or did not create."[166]

Officials and veterans fought not only over the purpose of rehabilitation but also over what "rehabilitation" itself meant. The architects of the rehabilitation acts did not make the terms of rehabilitation fully clear; the act stated that a veteran would be considered rehabilitated once he had a job and was earning a good wage. If a rehabilitated veteran lost his job for reasons related to his disability, furthermore, he could return to training or ask to be provided with another job.[167] But as soon as the Veterans' Bureau was established in 1921, officials at all levels proclaimed this definition of rehabilitation to be unworkable.[168] In part, bureau officials were responding to the fact that the FBVE had declared only 5,050 trainees rehabilitated by the time the bureau took over the rehabilitation program. What constituted "rehabilitation" was thus a far more pressing question for bureau officials than for their FBVE counterparts.

Bureau officials argued that Congress had set the agency an impossible task—the government simply could not intervene in the labor market to the degree originally promised. Major Arthur Dean declared, for instance, "No U.S. Veterans' Bureau or any other government bureau can control industry [without] . . . socialism and Russianism." Nor could the bureau "guarantee a man a job," since the bureau could not control factors such as "personality, physical condition, tact, and judgment. . . . These men fall down oftentimes, not because of their training, but because of themselves."[169] Rehabilitators further complained that veterans would not leave rehabilitation unless forced to do so—even when offered what rehabilitation officers considered to be good jobs. Dean grumbled that veterans seemed to "think that training should last until the law ends in 1926."[170] By late 1921, the Veterans' Bureau had settled on a new definition of rehabilitation: "To rehabilitate a disabled man who has a vocational handicap is to give him that vocational training which will equip him, as near as his disability will permit, for civil employment in an economic status approximating that which he would probably have occupied had he not seen war service." Unlike the FBVE, the bureau would not guarantee a veteran a job where he could earn a "good wage." The World War I Veterans' Act of 1924 incorporated this new definition for "rehabilitation": a Section 2 trainee became "rehabilitated and employable" as soon as he or she met one of the following conditions: "1. When the trainee has completed training as outlined in the individual training program, which meets the customary and essential requirements of employability in the occupation for which training is given. 2. When the trainee has graduated from, or completed a standardized course of instruction in college, university or higher technical institution having a definite occupational objective."[171] Although local rehabilitation officers continued to try to find each trainee a position, veterans had to retain those jobs. Even when veterans' impairments impinged on their ability to retain a job, placement officials would not locate multiple positions. Even when a veteran could not find a job, rehabilitators could declare that veteran thoroughly trained for his vocation and abruptly terminate his rehabilitation.[172]

Disabled veterans challenged rehabilitation officials' efforts to narrow the meaning of rehabilitation, demanding that the Veterans' Bureau retain the original, broader meaning of rehabilitation: permanent placement in a job with a living wage. Ernest Strickland, for instance, complained, "I understand that a person when rehabilitated is supposed to be able to earn a living wage ... [and] according to that [standard] I think that I am entitled to an extension in my training until I can earn a living wage." Working as an inside electrical wireman at a wage of $12 per week, he argued, "I can not live and keep my family."[173] Rehabilitation officials dismissed Strickland's petition, since his wages matched the prevailing wage for a wireman in the South; therefore, he met officials' criteria for a successful rehabilitation.

Veterans also protested bureau officials' attempts to redefine rehabilitation as simply completing training rather than actually being able to find a job. Harry Iverson had received eleven months of training in motion picture operating, passed the state written and practical examinations, and obtained a license. But due either to his disability—repeated double inguinal hernias—or the weeks that he had spent in the hospital, he was not yet fast enough to operate the projector by himself. As a result, the "theater for which he worked, discharged him saying that it was necessary to have him in the booth with another man"—which New York State law did not allow.[174] Iverson appealed for more training, even providing a notarized affidavit from his former employer that declared "Mr. Harry Iverson incapable of operating alone."[175] His petitions came to naught. District officials ruled, "Placement training cannot be given because the law allows only the operator in the booth, and no other person can enter the booth for instruction purposes; therefore according to Par. 32-B Miscl 150, Rev., Man is rehabilitated."[176] The Newark subdistrict manager even argued on Iverson's behalf with the head of the Rehabilitation Division, stating, "It is plainly shown that this man has spent more time in the hospital than in training."[177] The Board of Appeals was unmoved, declaring that Iverson "has had sufficient training to enter employment of the kind for which he was trained. The appeal is therefore denied."[178]

THE FEDERAL VOCATIONAL rehabilitation program for disabled veterans thus had decidedly mixed results. On the one hand, some veterans used their training to return to the workforce and self-support; in part, this success reflected the fact that, unlike Goodwill Industries, rehabilitation officials recognized the importance of training veterans for skilled jobs suitable for the economy of the 1920s. Trainees' maintenance allowances also proved invaluable during economic downturns. On the other hand, tens of thousands of veterans abandoned rehabilitation in disgust over the administrative dysfunction of the FBVE and the U.S. Veterans' Bureau, as well as the political nature of the program itself. Others could not even gain access to training due to racialized notions of fitness, officials' pejorative assumptions about individuals with certain types of disabilities, or the disjunction between the kinds of impairments expected and those produced by the new technologies of war. Yet others battled with rehabilitators over the meanings of disability—especially the experience of living with chronic pain—and rehabilitation. Eventually, many disabled veterans returned to the wage-based workforce, but not necessarily because of their training—a significant proportion of veterans did not continue in the field in which they had trained. Instead, most but not all employers generally accorded disabled veterans special status because of their wartime service.

Policy makers thus struggled to undo the ways in which people with a wide array of disabilities had become separated from the wage labor market—a separation created in part by public policies such as workmen's compensation. Disability and its relation to the labor market proved a far more fluid and complex concept than either the framers of rehabilitation programs or rehabilitation officials had expected. In many cases, impairments evolved over time, new technologies produced new types of disabilities, especially chronic pain, and the economic context played a crucial role in determining what veterans recognized as a disability. In the decades since World War I, the complexity and mutability of disability has continued to complicate policy makers' efforts to intervene in the labor market. Veterans' rehabilitation foreshadowed other key elements of twentieth-century disability policy as well. The rhetorical link that rehabilitators drew between disability and public dependency has remained a powerful influence on how both policy makers and the public understand disability. People with disabilities and policy makers continue to debate how best to define disability and what rehabilitation means. Finally, even as rehabilitators sought to decouple the rhetorical connections between public dependency and disability, they inadvertently reaffirmed disability as synonymous with the inability to work and be self-supporting.

Conclusion

By the 1920s, people with many different types and origins of disabilities—from tuberculosis and feeble-mindedness to amputations and blindness—had been pushed out of the paid labor market and, thereby, edged out from "good citizenship." Most people with disabilities kept on working, although their labors were rarely recognized or compensated as such. The "problem" of disability, however, lay not in the actual bodies of disabled people, but rather in the meanings assigned to those impairments by employers and policy makers, as well as how those meanings intersected with shifting family capacities, a rapidly changing workplace, public policies aimed at discouraging dependency, and the complexity and mutability of disability itself.

But as a concept, disability had become synonymous with dependency on public or charitable aid, poor citizenship, and the inability to care for oneself or do labor worthy of recompense—a status that threatened not only individuals' morals but also those of the nation. This situation had grave consequences for the social status of people with disabilities, as well as their families, excluding them from what Americans have long recognized as the very basis of social standing and economic citizenship. This definition of disability, moreover, would fundamentally shape policy making toward people with disabilities from the early twentieth century to the present.

Four interconnected factors served to largely exclude disabled people from paid work and "good citizenship" by the 1920s. The gradual mid-nineteenth-century shift away from farm and artisanal labor in rural and small communities to an urban wage economy left families smaller, more fragile, and less able to accommodate a partly productive relative. Households had long understood family members as falling on a spectrum of productivity that varied by gender, age, and ability. But the changing family context and the perennial contest for funding led proto-eugenicist superintendents and charity officials to characterize "idiots" as unproductive burdens in mainstream society and to create custodial asylums. Within these immense institutions for the "feeble-minded," inmates' labors—especially the vast amount of care work performed by women—no longer served as a pathway to release but rather as permanent "training" aimed at defraying asylums' costs.

Due to the rise of mechanized factory labor and the popularity of efficiency rhetoric, employers' visions of the ideal worker shifted dramatically in many economic sectors starting in the very late nineteenth century. "Disabilities" had long been just part of the job and an integral part of working-class life, costing status and skill but not producing stigma within the community. Employers had long accommodated their own newly disabled workers to some degree. But with the striking exception of Ford Motor Company, which actively hired workers with a wide array of disabilities, retaining them even during the Great Depression, companies soon began using the mechanisms of the modern corporation to identify "disabled" workers and screen them out in favor of those perceived as having intact, interchangeable bodies.

Well-intentioned public policies aimed at discouraging public dependency, moreover, had unexpectedly negative effects on disabled people's access to paid work and the mainstream labor market. Unaware that they were making disability policy, legislators and reformers struggled with the immense complexity of disability. Efforts to classify and segregate people from poorhouses into appropriate institutions, as well as attempts to aid disrupted families, inadvertently created a population in idiot asylums that could not be sent home, along with vast custodial asylums in which inmates labored without pay. And while workmen's compensation laws temporarily aided the families of industrial accident victims, the statutes unintentionally created powerful incentives for employers and insurers to exclude workers with even the most minor impairments.

Finally, the complexity and variability of disability itself posed great hurdles to both lawmakers and reformers. Not only does disability intersect with race, class, gender, and age, but it also evolves over time in individuals. New technologies, furthermore, further complicate an already vast range of impairments, while both economic and familial contexts help to define what actually constitutes a disability at any given time.

Reformers, lawmakers, and disabled people themselves all attempted to reintegrate people with disabilities into the mainstream labor market. Even as employers defined disabled people's bodies as unproductive, people with disabilities fought to maintain—or regain—access to paid work and the wage labor market. Among many other endeavors, they developed their own businesses and toiled in the hope of someday earning release from a custodial asylum for feeble-minded people.

Rehabilitators, in turn, had only mixed success, due in part to the fact that they understood disabled people's exclusion from the mainstream labor market through the lens of dependency and, especially in the case of Goodwill

Industries, the Protestant work ethic. Consequently, sheltered workshops focused more on instilling the moral virtues of work through craft labor than on preparing their disabled clientele for jobs that could pay a living wage. Although such organizations served people pushed to the fringes of the labor market, they, too, could not escape the economic imperatives of efficiency. Accordingly, sheltered workshops replicated some of the same exclusionary practices found on the mainstream labor market, although they did offer very modest incomes to some people with disabilities.

The rehabilitation of World War I veterans generally proceeded more smoothly, especially for white veterans, not because of the nature or administration of the rehabilitation program itself, but rather because employers were far more willing to hire disabled veterans than disabled civilians. Rehabilitators also offered veterans training in skilled positions. Nonetheless, as at sheltered workshops, the complexity and mutability of disability—the ways in which it was shaped by economic and family contexts, how it evolved over time in individuals, its sheer diversity, and its intersections with gender, race, and class—posed serious hurdles to disabled veterans who sought to reenter the labor market.

Paradoxically, a program to place "feeble-minded" people in domestic service and farm labor may have had the most success, at least until the Great Depression effectively ended it. At the Rome State Custodial Asylum, superintendent Charles Bernstein astutely analyzed the labor market, searching for niches that could accommodate and even benefit from a spectrum of ability. By creating labor colonies—even for feeble-minded women—he also developed a solution to the issues of family capacity that had so bedeviled Hervey Wilbur and led to the creation of immense custodial asylums such as Rome.

But in the end, most people with disabilities lost access to paid work, separating them and their families from the foundation of social standing and economic citizenship in the United States. Indeed, the economic, demographic, and policy shifts that took place between the 1840s and the 1930s left many disabled people and their relatives in poverty, not quite members of the deserving poor but not entirely undeserving either. Racialized and gendered notions about "fitness" and disability, along with the segmentation of the labor market, also meant that women and people of color had far less recourse either to gain compensation for their injuries or to access rehabilitation.

Since the 1920s, disabled people and policy makers have struggled to undo the shifts that took place in the late nineteenth and early twentieth centuries. One agency that could have helped unemployed workers with disabilities— the Works Progress Administration (WPA)—instead barred them. Like New

York City's Emergency Relief Bureau, WPA officials declared "crippled" people to be dependents suitable only for positions in sheltered workshops, not potential breadwinners worthy of relief work. After a lengthy sit-in in Manhattan and a protest trip to Washington, D.C., the League of the Physically Handicapped won access to WPA positions in New York City.[1] In the 1950s, Paul Strachan, the American Federation of the Physically Handicapped, and labor unions advocated for employment quotas for disabled people and building accessibility codes, as well as for National Employ the Handicapped Week.[2] And of course, a broad coalition fought for the enactment of the Rehabilitation Act of 1973 and the passage of the Americans with Disabilities Act of 1990—the two most important disability rights laws.

These laudable efforts, however, were hindered by the fact that for much of the twentieth century, lawmakers and reformers continued to view the problem of unemployed or underemployed disabled workers through the lens of dependency and often as a problem of individual immorality. This perspective made it hard to address the systemic discrimination against disabled people in workplaces. In the late 1930s, for instance, the federal Department of Labor exempted sheltered workshops from paying the national minimum wage required under the Fair Labor Standards Act of 1938. Workshop managers argued that their clientele were too inefficient for a minimum wage to be feasible. Being forced to offer the minimum wage would force them to close their doors, throwing clients out of work. Instead, workshops had to pay only a "fair wage," which, in the case of one workshop in the 1990s, turned out to be eleven cents an hour.[3] In effect, what mattered was that disabled clients worked, not whether they could earn a living wage that might lift them out of poverty.

Likewise, in the mid-twentieth century, vocational rehabilitators focused on adjusting the personalities of individuals with disabilities rather than making workplaces more accessible. Influenced by psychoanalysis, key rehabilitation figures such as Dr. Howard Rusk contended that disabled people saw themselves as exempt from normal social rules. In fact, protesting discriminatory treatment or demanding an accessible environment or workplace constituted evidence of psychological maladjustment that could undermine American society as a whole. Instead, disabled people needed to hide their disabilities and adjust to social norms.[4]

Harkening back to nineteenth-century debates over the deserving and undeserving poor, lawmakers also sought to discourage people with disabilities from relying on financial assistance except when absolutely necessary. Means-tested benefit programs such as Supplementary Security Income, which provides aid to disabled children as well as adults with minimal work histories and also qualifies recipients for Medicaid, require recipients to live below the poverty line. Consequently, people who need significant medical or attendant care have had to choose between living in poverty to ensure that they have health care and taking the risk of accepting a part-time job that might cost them their ventilators, attendant care, or life-preserving medications.[5]

The widespread assumption that disability is a problem of individual morality rather than of political economy has hindered efforts to address the larger reasons as to why disabled people lost access to the mainstream labor market, such as passage of the Americans with Disabilities Act of 1990 (ADA). Unlike in the case of other civil rights legislation, disabled people who wish to sue over employment discrimination must first prove that they are qualified to do the job and that their accommodation requests are reasonable; in other words, lawmakers presumed that people with disabilities were by and large unqualified. In addition, the judiciary has been almost unremittingly hostile to the anti–employment discrimination provisions of the ADA. The U.S. Supreme Court, for instance, created a catch-22 in which disabled workers could be fired for having a disability but were barred from suing. Nearly every case, moreover, has been decided in favor of employers.[6] Consequently, the ADA has had little impact on unemployment rates among people with disabilities, although it has made public spaces far more accessible. Almost thirty years after the passage of the ADA in 1990, nearly 30 percent of disabled people live in poverty and 70 percent of working-age adults with disabilities are unemployed.[7] In the 2008 ADA Amendments Act, Congress restored and even strengthened the employment protections, but the jury remains out as to whether the new Title I will truly expand opportunities for workers with disabilities. Disability-based employment discrimination remains pervasive and hard to battle. A 2015 study, for instance, demonstrated that accounting firms were 26 percent less likely to interview "well-qualified fictional applicants" who disclosed sensory processing or mobility disabilities.[8]

Although many employers remain skeptical of workers with disabilities today, Charles Bernstein and Henry Ford demonstrated long ago that people with disabilities could in fact fit quite well in mainstream workplaces, both traditional and modern. At the Rome State Custodial Asylum, Bernstein analyzed the labor market to locate economic sectors that could readily accommodate a range of ability, mainly in domestic service and nonmechanized farm labor. Bernstein focused not on what people labeled as "feeble-minded" could not do but rather where they might succeed, especially if provided with transition and placement services. Simultaneously, Ford Motor Company proved that the increasingly mechanized economy of the twentieth century did not actually require the interchangeable bodies so prized by most employers. Instead, by carefully analyzing the bodily requirements of each position, along with each worker's capabilities, Ford managers drew on a far broader workforce than their competitors, thereby reducing turnover. In sum, Bernstein and Ford demonstrated that disabled people's diverse capabilities did not necessarily constitute a disadvantage for employers and, in reality, could even provide an advantage. Furthermore, their approach—focusing not on what disabled people cannot do but rather on what they can do—foreshadowed the approach taken in the Americans with Disabilities Act of 1990.

At the same time, disability rights activists have also highlighted the fact that focusing on ensuring equal access to workplaces does not address the fact that not everyone *can* work. Some people cannot handle a part-time job, much less a forty-hour workweek. But by tying social standing and economic citizenship so closely to the ability to work, American social welfare policy leaves little space for those who are not able to labor.

Appendix

A Note on Sources

Rather than providing an all-inclusive discussion, I highlight here some of the most helpful sources and discuss both how I used them and their limitations.

Chapters 1 and 2: Records from the New York State Asylum for Idiots and Other State Custodial Asylums for "Feeble-Minded" People

These chapters draw primarily on pupil evaluations and admission, death, discharge, transfer, private pupil, and county admission registers from the New York State Asylum for Idiots, as well as on poorhouse census records and state and federal census records. Asylum records were intended for the private use of the superintendent and his staff and, later on, for research into pupils' heredity. As such, they are far more frank than the printed annual reports sent to legislators and the members of state charity boards, yet these records tend to offer only suggestive glimpses rather than detailed narratives of lives. Asylum administrators saved very little correspondence, unfortunately. Per agreement with the New York State Archives and the New York Office for People with Developmental Disabilities, all of the pupils' names, as well as occasionally other identifying details, were changed to preserve their and their families' privacy.

The descriptive and admissions registers for the New York State Asylum for Idiots overlap considerably and include multiple numbering systems; some individuals have four or five different numbers, making it a challenge to track them. The entries in these registers were based on information submitted by parents, sponsors, local poorhouse officials, or local doctors along with occasional notes from asylum staff on how a particular individual progressed skill-wise and, in many cases, whether and when an individual was discharged or transferred. The descriptive registers include categories such as head measurements; "peculiarities of face or form"; "cleanliness" and ability to walk, feed oneself, and dress oneself; habits; "idea of language" and "mental and moral condition"; commentary on the person's parents and suspected causes of idiocy; and finally, "improvement or results of education." When the second superintendent, James Carson, took over in 1884, he standardized the admissions registers, greatly expanded the list of questions, and reentered data for many of those admitted by the first superintendent, Hervey Wilbur. Carson's registers contained over eighty questions on topics ranging from parents' health and heredity to whether a child played and if he or she liked music.

Superintendents recorded "pupil evaluations" for about 15 percent of those in the asylum, but only very erratically. Some individuals have just a few lines for one year, while others' skills received extensive commentary; those included had a wide range of abilities.

Only a scattered few years of board of trustees' monthly minutes and reports exist for the New York State Asylum for Idiots, the New York Custodial Asylum for Feeble-Minded Women, and the Rome State Custodial Asylum for the period prior to 1920. The case files for the New York Custodial Asylum for Feeble-Minded Women appear to have been lost, along with any correspondence, although the records of a gubernatorial investigation into abuse have been preserved. At the time of this book's publication, inmates' case files for the Rome State Custodial Asylum had just recently been transferred to the New York State Archives from the Mohawk Correctional Facility, which now occupies the grounds of the former asylum.

CHARTS FOR CHAPTERS 1 AND 2

These charts are based primarily on data from the admissions and descriptive registers for people sent to and, in some cases, permanently incarcerated in the New York State Asylum for Idiots. Additional data came from the asylum's record of deaths, the pupil evaluations that exist for approximately 15 percent of admittees, and the register of private pay accounts, as well as from U.S. and New York State census records and the *New York Census of Inmates in Almshouses and Poorhouses, 1830–1921* searched via Ancestry.com. FileMaker was used to create a database, and the data were analyzed using SPSS and Excel. These charts include all individuals admitted from New York State (1,833 people between 1851 and 1893); they exclude the small number private pupils from out of state (68 in total) and those for whom there is no definite year of admission (20 individuals).

When possible, the terms used in the charts, such as "cleanly" and "filthy," reflect the language and categories of the time and those used in the asylum records. "Partly cleanly" indicates that individuals sometimes had trouble controlling their bladder or bowels, while "limited walking" includes those unstable on their feet for one reason or another. "Partial or no feeding" and "partial or no dressing" signifies that individuals required some or total assistance with feeding themselves and getting dressed or undressed.

The majority of people "transferred" out of the New York State Asylum for Idiots were sent to the New York State Custodial Asylum for Feeble-Minded Women at Newark (established in 1878) or the Rome State Custodial Asylum (opened in 1894); most of the remainder went to county poorhouses, as did some of those who spent time at the Rome or Newark asylums. Those "reinstitutionalized" generally either returned to the New York State Asylum for Idiots or went to one of the custodial asylums; many also wound up in county poorhouses.

A few categories used only in chapter 2 also bear further explanation. "Probably came from institution" includes people who arrived at the New York State Asylum for Idiots with the notation of "unknown family history" or only the barest hints at their family's history. Most such entries date from the late 1870s and early 1880s, when superintendent Hervey Wilbur was effectively running two asylums and, apparently, keeping less careful records. When cross-referenced with the asylum's county admission registers, it turned out that many of these inmates came from their county's poorhouse or an orphan asylum, or by application of the local superintendent of the poor. The label "separated from parents" indicates individuals who, for a variety of reasons, were no longer living with their parents but who did not come directly from an institution. Finally, "disabled parent" includes parents with a wide variety of impairments, from blindness, lameness, deafness, or consumption to amputations, epilepsy, general "feebleness" or debility, or the label "deficient" or "weak-minded." The point here is not whether parents actually had such disabilities, since that is impossible to determine in most cases, but rather that the family identified itself—or was perceived—as having a parent with some sort of disability and, therefore, often labeled as struggling.

Chapter 3: Rome Custodial Herald

Much of this chapter draws on the monthly paper "published . . . by and for the patients of the Rome Custodial Asylum," variously called the *Herald* or the *Custodial Herald*, which superintendent Charles Bernstein distributed all over the country in hopes of promoting his colony and parole programs. The newsletter contained brief historical or cultural pieces appropriate to the month, largely but not entirely uplifting accounts of inmates' labors and progress, reports from colonies, and letters from parolees and discharged inmates. The paper reinforced Bernstein's expectations that the potential candidates for parole, colony living, and discharge would be disciplined and self-sufficient. Obviously, the *Herald* was heavily edited and primarily reflects the experiences of a distinct subset of inmates. Nevertheless, the many dozens of letters from parolees and discharged inmates offer considerable detail about their lives after leaving the asylum as well as, at times, fond reminiscences of inmates, teachers, social events, and community at the asylum. Many of the individuals discussed in the *Herald* came from the New York State Asylum for Idiots; all names used in the chapter are pseudonyms.

Chapter 4: Consumers' League of Eastern Pennsylvania, "Commutations of Workmen's Compensation," circa 1928 (unpublished manuscript sent to John A. Fitch in March 1928)

This report, which was sent to social investigator John Fitch in draft form, traced the impact of lump-sum payments (or "commutations") of workmen's compensation on the lives of injured workers and their families in eastern Pennsylvania. In 1928, investigators successfully contacted 61 of the 112 people who had received lump-sum compensation payments in 1921 and 1922; the state had allowed commutations since at least 1915. The investigators provided only initials for each individual, as well as other demographic details.

Based on these interviews, the authors of the report argued in favor of allowing more commutations, especially for the discharge of small debts and purchases of homes or artificial limbs. They emphasized that most commutations for business ventures did not end successfully due to petitioners' lack of experience. Nevertheless, the report's authors noted that even failed endeavors seemed to have aided in the "readjustment of the injured person," since nearly all eventually returned to work afterward. Reflecting reformers' widely shared assumptions that even the deserving poor should undergo investigation before receiving aid, the report also stressed that, before granting commutations, administrators should thoroughly examine petitioners' plans. They also recommended conducting a follow-up interview in case applicants needed "a bit of timely advice [to] avert a disaster in home or business." Although the cover letter mentioned plans to publish the report, it appears to have been shared only with Fitch and the state compensation commissioner.

Chapter 6: Goodwill Industries Records

Because the Methodist Episcopal Bureau of Home Missions provided funding that enabled Edgar James Helms to expand the Goodwill Industries model across the nation and even abroad, the history of many locations of Goodwill Industries and, in particular, that of the flagship site in Boston is far better preserved than that of most other sheltered workshops. Historical records nevertheless remain scant due to the fact that many early workshops, including several Goodwill Industries locations, experienced devastating fires from the accumulation of salvage materials, especially rags. Few if any Goodwill Industries locations retained records of the early clientele; instead, records include correspondence, minutes of meetings, reports, newspaper clippings, and memorabilia.

Chapter 7: Regional Office Training Case Files, Rehabilitation, Veterans' Bureau, National Archives and Records Administration, Washington, D.C.

These case files were used to train rehabilitation officials—on both the local and national levels—and were specifically chosen to be representative of the 668,000 veterans who registered for vocational rehabilitation. Accordingly, the collection includes veterans with a wide range of outcomes, including being rejected for rehabilitation outright, fighting for several years to gain access to rehabilitation, dropping out of rehabilitation, completing rehabilitation but with many travails, and finishing rehabilitation smoothly. Every file includes the "Field Report of Physical Examination," the survey form on which Federal Board for Vocational Education (FBVE) officials recorded the veteran's biographical information, service history, employment before and after the war (including wages), and aspirations for rehabilitation. Most files also include one or more medical reports; rulings by FBVE and Veterans' Bureau officials on whether a veteran was eligible for rehabilitation; supervision reports by local rehabilitation officials; correspondence between veterans, physicians, educators, employers, and rehabilitation officials at all levels; reports from rehabilitation officers about their attempts to find employment for veterans; and the "Notice of Termination of Training" (which usually includes a few details about where veterans worked after completing rehabilitation). Many files include several years' worth of records and are at least a half-inch thick.

Notes

Abbreviations Used in Notes

AALL	American Association for Labor Legislation
BFRC	Benson Ford Research Center at the Henry Ford, Dearborn, Michigan
FBVE	Federal Board for Vocational Education
GII	Goodwill Industries International, Rockville, Maryland
MMGI	Morgan Memorial Goodwill Industries, Boston, Massachusetts
NARA	National Archives and Records Administration
NYSA	New York State Archives
RG15	Record Group 15
SAR	Syracuse Admission Registers
SBC	New York State Board of Charities
SDR	Syracuse Descriptive Registers
SPE	Syracuse Pupil Evaluation Reports
USVB	United States Veterans' Bureau

Introduction

1. The superintendent of the asylum identified Westbrooke's parents as "paupers" upon her admission. Syracuse Descriptive Registers, 1851–1945, vol. 2, entry 208, Syracuse State School, Admission, Discharge, Death, and Transfer Records, 1851–1945 (Acc. B1647, Subseries 1); Syracuse State Institution for Feeble-Minded Children, Pupil Evaluation Reports [ca. 1860–1909], vol. 1, p. 46 (Acc. B1666), Box 1; both held at New York State Archives (hereafter NYSA), Albany, NY. New York, Madison County, 1889, Record no. 591 in Ancestry.com, *Census of Inmates in Almshouses and Poorhouses, 1830–1920* (Provo, UT: Ancestry.com Operations), original data from New York State Board of Charities, Census of Inmates in Almshouses and Poorhouses, 1835–1921 (Acc. A1978), NYSA; U.S. Bureau of the Census, *Fourteenth Census of the United States, 1920*, New York, Madison County, Eaton, Enum. Dist. no. 106, sheet 8B.

2. Consumers' League of Eastern Pennsylvania, "Commutations of Workmen's Compensation" (unpublished manuscript sent to John A. Fitch in March 1928), pp. 32–33, John A. Fitch Papers (MS 937), Box 12, Folder 13, Wisconsin Historical Society, Madison, WI.

3. I am indebted to James W. Trent Jr. for introducing me to the idea of "unproductive citizens." James W. Trent Jr., *Inventing the Feeble Mind: A History of Mental Retardation in the United States* (Berkeley: University of California Press, 1994), 24.

4. George B. Mangold, untitled, in U.S. Federal Board for Vocational Education, *Proceedings of the First National Conference* (Washington, DC: Government Printing Office, 1922), 67.

5. T. H. Marshall, "Citizenship and Social Class," in *Class, Citizenship, and Social Development: Essays by T. H. Marshall* (New York: Doubleday, 1964), 65–122; Michael B. Katz, *The Price of Citizenship: Redefining the American Welfare State* (New York: Henry Holt, 2001); Alice Kessler-Harris, *In Pursuit of Equity: Women, Men and the Quest for Economic Citizenship in Twentieth-Century America* (Oxford: Oxford University Press, 2001); Linda K. Kerber, *No Constitutional Right to Be Ladies: Women and the Obligations of Citizenship* (New York: Hill and Wang, 1998); Judith N. Shklar, "Earning," in *American Citizenship: The Quest for Inclusion* (Cambridge, MA: Harvard University Press, 1991); Barbara Young Welke, *Law and the Borders of Belonging in the Long Nineteenth Century United States* (Cambridge: Cambridge University Press, 2010), 21–39.

6. At least 476 workers, if not as many 1,500, died as a result of their work on the dam. Union Carbide and Carbon Corporation had specifically recruited migrant black workers to drill the tunnel through rock filled with deadly silica because they were considered a cheap, pliable labor force. The disaster did, however, raise awareness about the dangers of silicosis. Martin Cherniack, *The Hawk's Nest Incident: America's Worst Industrial Disaster* (New Haven, CT: Yale University Press, 1986); Sarah F. Rose, " 'Crippled' Hands: Disability in Labor and Working-Class History," *Labor: Studies in Working-Class History of the Americas* 2, no. 1 (Spring 2005): 38–39.

7. Claudia Clark, *Radium Girls: Women and Industrial Health Reform, 1910–1935* (Chapel Hill: University of North Carolina Press, 1997), 23; Ruth Heifetz, "Women, Lead, and Reproductive Hazards: Defining a New Risk," in *Dying for Work: Workers' Safety and Health in Twentieth-Century America*, ed. David Rosner and Gerald Markowitz (Bloomington: Indiana University Press, 1987), 170.

8. Sarah F. Rose, "Gendering U.S. Disability Policy, 1895–1930" (paper presented at the Policy History Conference, Columbus, OH, June 2010). On the racialization and gendering of disability more generally, see, for instance, Douglas C. Baynton, "Disability and the Justification of Inequality in American History," in *The New Disability History: American Perspectives*, ed. Paul K. Longmore and Lauri Umansky (New York: New York University Press, 2001), 33–58; Douglas C. Baynton, *Defectives in the Land: Disability and Immigration in the Age of Eugenics*, (Chicago: University of Chicago Press, 2016); Douglas Baynton, "Defectives in the Land: Disability and American Immigration Policy, 1882–1924," *Journal of American Ethnic History* 24 (Spring 2005): 31–44; Douglas C. Baynton, " 'The Undesirability of Admitting Deaf Mutes': U.S. Immigration Policy and Deaf Immigrants, 1882–1924," *Sign Language Studies* 6, no. 4 (Summer 2006): 391–415; Natalia Molina, "Medicalizing the Mexican: Immigration, Race, and Disability in the Early-Twentieth-Century United States," *Radical History Review* 94 (Winter 2006): 22–37; Howard Markel, " 'The Eyes Have It': Trachoma, the Perception of Disease, the United States Public Health Service, and the American Jewish Immigration Experience, 1897–1924," *Bulletin of the History of Medicine* 74, no. 3 (Fall 2000): 525–60; Laura Briggs, "The Race of Hysteria: 'Overcivilization' and the 'Savage' Woman in Late Nineteenth-Century Obstetrics and Gynecology," *American Quarterly* 52, no. 2

(June 2000): 246–73; Susan M. Schweik, *Ugly Laws: Disability in Public* (New York: New York University Press, 2009), chaps. 6–8 passim; Michael A. Rembis, *Defining Deviance: Sex, Science, and Delinquent Girls, 1890–1960* (Urbana: University of Illinois Press, 2011).

9. W. Erickson, C. Lee, and S. von Schrader, "Disability Statistics from the 2012 American Community Survey (ACS)" (Ithaca, NY: Cornell University Employment and Disability Institute, 2014), www.disabilitystatistics.org (accessed 18 July 2014); U.S. Bureau of Labor Statistics, "Economics News Release: Persons with a Disability: Labor Force Characteristics Summary," http://www.bls.gov/news.release/disabl.nro.htm (accessed 16 June 2015).

10. "Disability" can be found in the Continental Congress's pension resolution of 1776, the succeeding Pension Acts of 1792 and 1793, and a variety of acts for the relief of "sick and disabled seamen." The 1793 act also introduced medical verification into the pension process. Worthington C. Ford et al., eds., *Journals of the Continental Congress, 1774–1789* (Washington, DC: Government Printing Office, 1904–1937), 5:702, quoted in Daniel Blackie, "Disabled Revolutionary War Veterans and the Construction of Disability in the Early United States, c1776–1840" (PhD diss., University of Helsinki, 2010), 81; see also ibid., 82–89; "Congress; House of Representatives, Tuesday, April 10," *Time Piece; and Literary Companion*, 13 April 1798, 2, 91.

11. Simon P. Newman, *Embodied History: The Lives of the Poor in Early Philadelphia* (Philadelphia: University of Pennsylvania Press, 2003), 78, 111; Dea H. Boster, *African American Slavery and Disability: Bodies, Property, and Power in the Antebellum South, 1800–1860* (New York: Routledge, 2013), 39.

12. Seth Delano (Dis) military pension file, US National Archives Microfilm Publication M804, *Revolutionary War Pension and Bounty-Land Warrant Application Files*, Records of the Department of Veterans Affairs, Record Group 15 (hereafter RG15), file number S15802, quoted in Blackie, "Disabled Revolutionary War Veterans," 166; Ava Baron and Eileen Boris, "'The Body' as a Useful Category for Working-Class History," *Labor: Studies in Working-Class History of the Americas* 4, no. 2 (Summer 2007): 28.

13. Coolidge held residency rights in Watertown; he arrived home in 1743 after Cambridge expelled him. He returned in 1749 after several years of wandering. Kim E. Nielsen, *A Disability History of the United States* (Boston: Beacon Press, 2012), 31–32, 36.

14. James Trowbridge (Dis), US National Archives Microfilm Publication M804, *Revolutionary War Pension and Bounty-Land Warrant Application Files*, Records of the Department of Veterans Affairs, RG15, file number S43205, quoted in Blackie, "Disabled Revolutionary War Veterans," 161.

15. Nielsen, *Disability History of the United States*, 33.

16. Parnel Wickham, "Idiocy in Virginia, 1616–1860," *Bulletin of the History of Medicine* 80, no. 4 (Winter 2006): 688, quoted in Nielsen, *Disability History of the United States*, 35.

17. Raymond A. Mohl, *Poverty in New York, 1783–1825* (Oxford: Oxford University Press, 1971), 95; John K. Alexander, *Render Them Submissive: Responses to Poverty in Philadelphia, 1760–1800* (Amherst: University of Massachusetts Press, 1980), 119–20; David M. Schneider, *The History of Public Welfare in New York State, 1609–1866* (Chicago: University of Chicago Press, 1938; reprint, Montclair, NJ: Patterson Smith, 1969), 152–55; Priscilla Ferguson Clement, *Welfare and the Poor in the Nineteenth-Century*

City: Philadelphia, 1800–1854 (Rutherford, NJ: Fairleigh Dickinson University Press, 1985), 74.

18. Timothy James Lockley, *Welfare and Charity in the Antebellum South* (Gainesville: University Press of Florida, 2007), 43; Mohl, *Poverty in New York*, 95; Alexander, *Render Them Submissive*, 119–20; Sonya Michel, "The Family, Civil Society, and Social Policy: A U.S. Perspective," in *The Golden Chain: Family, Civil Society and the State*, ed. Paul Ginsborg, Juergen Nautz, and Ton Nijhuis (Oxford: Berghahn Books, 2013), 1, 3; Newman, *Embodied History*, 28.

19. Under the 1601 Act for the Relief of the Poor and its 1607 amendment, each Anglican parish held responsibility for addressing its poor inhabitants. Funded by local taxes, the Poor Law Act mandated a joint system of outdoor and indoor relief: those unable to work received cash and food and lived in the community, while able-bodied "paupers" were forced to enter a "house of correction" and required to labor. Officials could also bind out poor children as apprentices. The law also required parents to care for their children and grandchildren, and vice versa. Walter I. Trattner, *From Poor Law to Welfare State: A History of Social Welfare in America*, 4th ed. (New York: Free Press, 1989), 8–11.

20. People obtained residency rights by being born in a town, living there for a particular period of time, or purchasing property. Ruth Wallis Herndon, *Unwelcome Americans: Living on the Margin in Early New England* (Philadelphia: University of Pennsylvania Press, 2001), 5, 110–11; Nielsen, *Disability History of the United States*, 75.

21. Baynton, "Disability and the Justification of Inequality," 38.

22. Dea H. Boster, "An 'Epeleptick' Bondswoman: Fits, Slavery, and Power in the Antebellum South," *Bulletin of the History of Medicine* 83, no. 2 (Summer 2009): 286.

23. See, for instance, Rosemarie Garland Thomson, *Extraordinary Bodies: Figuring Physical Disability in American Culture and Literature* (New York: Columbia University Press, 1997), 6; Simi Linton, *Claiming Disability: Knowledge and Identity* (New York: New York University Press, 1998); Catherine J. Kudlick, "Disability History: Why We Need Another 'Other,'" *American Historical Review* 108, no. 3 (2003): 763–64; Longmore and Umansky, *The New Disability History*; Nielsen, *Disability History of the United States*; Jeffrey A. Brune and Daniel J. Wilson, eds., *Disability and Passing: Blurring the Lines of Identity* (Philadelphia: Temple University Press, 2013); Beth Linker, "On the Borderland of Medical and Disability History: A Survey of the Fields," *Bulletin of the History of Medicine* 87, no. 4 (Winter 2013): 499–535. On disability and intersectionality, see Susan Burch and Hannah Joyner, *Unspeakable: The Story of Junius Wilson* (Chapel Hill: University of North Carolina Press, 2007); Rembis, *Defining Deviance*.

24. By and large, disability historians have focused on individuals with disabilities rather than on their family context. This trend likely reflects the political desire to foreground people with disabilities as well as the fact that families have at times been oppressive forces. On families as oppressive, see Linda V. Carlisle, *Elizabeth Packard: A Noble Fight* (Urbana: University of Illinois Press, 2010); Allison C. Carey, *On the Margins of Citizenship: Intellectual Disability and Civil Rights in Twentieth-Century America* (Philadelphia: Temple University Press, 2009), chap. 6 passim; Janice A. Brockley,

"Martyred Mothers and Merciful Fathers: Exploring Disability and Motherhood in the Lives of Jerome Greenfield and Raymond Repouille," in Longmore and Umansky, *The New Disability History*, 293–312. For work that engages directly with family context, see, for instance, the essays by Daniel Blackie, Penny L. Richards, Allison C. Carey, Pamela Block, and Fátima Gonçalves Cavalcante in "Part One: Family, Community, and Daily Life," in *Disability Histories*, ed. Susan Burch and Michael Rembis (Urbana: University of Illinois Press, 2014), 15–115; Kim E. Nielsen, "Property, Disability, and the Making of the Incompetent Citizen in the United States, 1860s–1940s," in Burch and Rembis, *Disability Histories*, 308–20; Burch and Joyner, *Unspeakable*; Robert Bogdan with Martin Elks and James A. Knoll, *Picturing Disability: Beggar, Freak, Citizen, and Other Photographic Rhetoric* (Syracuse, NY: Syracuse University Press, 2012), chaps. 3 and 10 passim; Marina Larsson, *Shattered Anzacs: Living with the Scars of War* (Sydney: University of New South Wales Press, 2009); David Wright, *Mental Disability in Victorian England: The Earlswood Asylum, 1847–1901* (Oxford: Oxford University Press, 2001).

25. Alexander, *Render Them Submissive*, 118–19; Clement, *Welfare and the Poor*, 69; Lockley, *Welfare and Charity in the Antebellum South*, 45; Mohl, *Poverty in New York*, 85; Trattner, *From Poor Law to Welfare State*, chap. 4 passim.

26. Deborah A. Stone, *The Disabled State* (Philadelphia: Temple University Press, 1984), 23. See also Schweik, *Ugly Laws*; John Williams-Searle, "Cold Charity: Manhood, Brotherhood, and the Transformation of Disability, 1870–1900," in Longmore and Umansky, *The New Disability History*, 163–65; K. Walter Hickel, "Medicine, Bureaucracy, and Social Welfare: The Politics of Disability Compensation for American Veterans of World War I," in Longmore and Umansky, *The New Disability History*, 245–48; Jeffrey A. Brune, "The Gilded Age State and America's Anti-malingering Backlash" (paper presented at the Society for Disability Studies Conference, Denver, CO, June 2012); Jeffrey A. Brune, "Fear of Malingering in the Era of Disability Rights" (paper presented at the Society for Disability Studies Conference, Atlanta, GA, June 2015).

27. Parnel Wickham, "Conceptions of Idiocy in Colonial Massachusetts," *Journal of Social History* 35, no. 4 (Summer 2002): 942–44, 949; Samuel Gridley Howe, *Report to the Legislature of Massachusetts upon Idiocy* (Boston: Coolidge and Wiley, 1848); John Fabian Witt, *The Accidental Republic: Crippled Workingmen, Destitute Widows, and the Remaking of American Law* (Cambridge, MA: Harvard University Press, 2004), 32–33, 118–20.

28. Peter B. Evans, Dietrich Rueschemeyer, and Theda Skocpol, eds., *Bringing the State Back In* (Cambridge: Cambridge University Press, 1985); Theda Skocpol, *Protecting Soldiers and Mothers: The Political Origins of Social Policy in the United States* (Cambridge, MA: Harvard University Press, 1992); Julian E. Zelizer, "Introduction: New Directions in Policy History," *Journal of Policy History* 17, no. 1 (2005): 1–11; Meg Jacobs, William J. Novak, and Julian E. Zelizer, eds., *The Democratic Experiment: New Directions in American Political History* (Princeton, NJ: Princeton University Press, 2003); Stephen Skowronek, *Building a New American State: The Expansion of National Administrative Capacities, 1877–1920* (Cambridge: Cambridge University Press, 1982).

238 Notes to Chapter One

29. James C. Scott, *Seeing Like a State: How Certain Schemes to Improve the Human Condition Have Failed* (New Haven, CT: Yale University Press, 1999).

30. Ava Baron, "Gender and Labor History: Learning from the Past, Looking to the Future," in *Work Engendered: Toward a New History of American Labor*, ed. Ava Baron (Ithaca, NY: Cornell University Press, 1991), 7–8; Jeanne Boydston, *Home and Work: Housework, Wages, and the Ideology of Labor in the Early Republic* (Oxford: Oxford University Press, 1990), 76; Baron and Boris, "'The Body' as a Useful Category," 23–43; Seth Rockman, *Scraping By: Wage Labor, Slavery, and Survival in Early Baltimore* (Baltimore: Johns Hopkins University Press, 2010), chap. 6 passim; Frank Tobias Higbie, *Indispensable Outcasts: Hobo Workers and Community in the American Midwest, 1880–1930* (Urbana: University of Illinois Press, 2003), chap. 3 passim.

Chapter One

1. Per agreement with the New York State Archives, all of the pupils' names, as well as occasionally other identifying details, have been changed to protect their privacy. In *Remembrance of Patients Past*, Geoffrey Reaume documents similar resistance by family members to inmate work programs at the Toronto Hospital for the Insane. Geoffrey Reaume, *Remembrance of Patients Past: Patient Life at the Toronto Hospital for the Insane, 1870–1940* (Toronto: University of Toronto Press, 2009; orig. publ. Oxford University Press, 2000), 175; Syracuse Descriptive Registers, vol. 2, entry 351, Syracuse State School, Admission, Discharge, Death, and Transfer Records, 1851–1945, Descriptive Registers, 1851–1913 (Acc. B1647, Subseries 1) (hereafter SDR), NYSA.

2. Although "idiot," "imbecile," and "feeble-minded" are problematic terms, there are no modern-day equivalents. Imbecile usually, but not always, referred to people who had more capability for self-care and useful labor than idiots. Charity officials often used the three terms interchangeably. Wickham, "Conceptions of Idiocy in Colonial Massachusetts," 940, 944, 947; Sharon L. Snyder and David T. Mitchell, "Out of the Ashes of Eugenics: Diagnostic Regimes in the United States and the Making of a Disability Minority," *Patterns of Prejudice* 36, no. 1 (2002): 88; Trent, *Inventing the Feeble Mind*, 5; Penny L. Richards, "Beside Her Sat Her Idiot Child: Families and Developmental Disability in Mid-Nineteenth-Century America," in *Mental Retardation in America: A Historical Reader*, ed. Steven Noll and James W. Trent Jr. (New York: New York University Press, 2004), 67–68; Walton O. Schalick, "Children, Disability, and Rehabilitation in History," *Pediatric Rehabilitation* 4, no. 2 (2001): 94.

3. Howe, *Report to the Legislature of Massachusetts upon Idiocy*.

4. As the founder of the first private asylum for idiots in the country and the superintendent of the first state asylum dedicated specifically to training idiots, Wilbur was the acknowledged expert on idiot education.

5. Even during the high period of eugenic institutionalization in the late nineteenth to mid-twentieth centuries, less than 10 percent of people with cognitive disabilities lived in asylums. During the 1850s and 1860s, furthermore, few of those who did enter idiot asylums remained for more than a couple of years. Penny L. Richards and

George H. S. Singer, "'To Draw Out of the Effort of His Mind': Educating a Child with Mental Retardation in Early-Nineteenth-Century America," *Journal of Special Education* 31, no. 4 (1998): 444; Philip M. Ferguson, *Abandoned to Their Fate: Social Policy and Practice toward Severely Retarded People in America, 1820–1920* (Philadelphia: Temple University Press, 1994); Gerald N. Grob, "Mental Retardation and Public Policy in America: A Research Agenda," *History of Education Quarterly* 26 (1986): 307–13; Carey, *On the Margins of Citizenship*; Noll and Trent, *Mental Retardation in America*.

6. Due to the nature of the sources available, this chapter does not entirely escape the bounds of institutions. Primarily, I focus on the lives of people who left idiot asylums through discharge home and, to a lesser extent, on their lives prior to entering the institution.

7. Such legal categories dated back to at least 1212 in English common law. Wickham, "Conceptions of Idiocy in Colonial Massachusetts," 939–40, 944, 947; Parnel Wickham, "Idiocy and the Law in Colonial New England," *Mental Retardation* 39, no. 2 (April 2001): 108, 110. See also Benjamin Joseph Klebaner, *Public Poor Relief in America, 1790–1860* (PhD diss., Columbia University, 1951; reprint, New York: Arno Press, 1976), 207–9; John V. N. Yates, *Report of the Secretary of State [of New York] on the Relief and Settlement of the Poor* (1824), reprinted in David Rothman, *The Almshouse Experience: Collected Reports* (New York: Arno Press and the New York Times, 1971), 952, 956–57; New York State Asylum for Idiots, *Fourth Annual Report of the Trustees of the New York State Asylum for Idiots, Transmitted to the Legislature, January 23, 1855* (Syracuse: Moser, Truax and DeGolia, 1891), 30, 37 (hereafter cited as NY Asylum, *Annual Report*).

8. Massachusetts Experimental School for Teaching and Training Idiotic Children, *Third and Final Report on the Experimental School for Teaching and Training Idiotic Children* (Cambridge, MA: Metcalf, 1852), 6 (hereafter cited as MA School, *Annual Report*).

9. Accordingly, even though idiots could generally not become church members, they were believed to be far more likely to receive salvation than those who actively rejected the Puritan faith. Wickham, "Conceptions of Idiocy in Colonial Massachusetts," 942–44, 949; Parnel Wickham, "Perspective: Images of Idiocy in Puritan New England," *Mental Retardation* 39, no. 2 (April 2001): 149.

10. Despite clear mathematical errors, the 1840 census was never corrected. At the turn of the twentieth century, eugenicists would attempt to similarly characterize southern and eastern European immigrants as feeble-minded. Baynton, "Defectives in the Land," 31–44; Samuel A. Cartwright, "Report on the Diseases and Physical Peculiarities of the Negro Race," *New Orleans Medical and Surgical Journal* 7 (May 1851): 693, quoted in Baynton, "Disability and the Justification of Inequality," 37.

11. Wickham, "Idiocy in Virginia, 1616–1860," 688, quoted in Nielsen, *Disability History of the United States*, 35.

12. Elizabethan poor laws served as the basis for the poor laws of all the New England and midwestern states as well as many in the South. Mohl, *Poverty in New York*, 22, 38, 55–65; Alan Bloom, "The Floating Population: Homelessness in Early Chicago, 1833–1871" (PhD diss., Duke University, 2001), 268–79; Michael Katz, *In the Shadow of the Poorhouse: A Social History of Welfare in America* (New York: Basic Books, 1986), 22;

David J. Rothman, *The Discovery of the Asylum: Social Order and Disorder in the New Republic* (Boston: Little, Brown, 1971), 190–91, 291–93; Stone, *The Disabled State*, 29–55; Newman, *Embodied History*, 17, 20–22, 32, 34, 67–68; Trattner, *From Poor Law to Welfare State*, 10, 17–25; Wickham, "Idiocy and the Law," 111.

13. Dorothea Lynde Dix, *Memorial: To the Legislature of Massachusetts* (Boston: Munroe and Francis, 1843), 5.

14. Dorothea L. Dix, *Memorial: To the Honorable the Legislature of the State of New-York* (1844), reprinted in Dorothea Lynde Dix, *On Behalf of the Insane Poor, Selected Reports* (New York: Arno / New York Times, 1979), 27, 54 (emphasis in original), quoted in Nicole Hahn Rafter, *Creating Born Criminals* (Urbana: University of Illinois Press, 1997), 25; Ferguson, *Abandoned to Their Fate*, chap. 2 passim.

15. Nielsen, *Disability History of the United States*, 36. On the role of familiarity in determining acceptance of people with disabilities, see Alice Wexler, "Chorea and Community in a Nineteenth-Century Town," *Bulletin of the History of Medicine* 76, no. 3 (Fall 2002): 495–527; Nora Ellen Groce, *Everyone Here Spoke Sign Language: Hereditary Deafness on Martha's Vineyard* (Cambridge, MA: Harvard University Press, 1985).

16. Cameron never managed his own money or the family plantation; rather, his younger brother Paul served as one of his trustees and ran the family's landholdings. Richards, "Beside Her Sat Her Idiot Child," 65–68; Richards and Singer, "'To Draw Out of the Effort of His Mind,'" 47, 451–56, 462–63.

17. Trent, *Inventing the Feeble Mind*, 10–12. The U.S. census did not tabulate idiots or the insane until 1840; Patricia Cline Cohen, *A Calculating People: The Spread of Numeracy in Early America*, 2nd ed. (Chicago: University of Chicago Press, 1982), 183.

18. Katz, *In the Shadow of the Poorhouse*, 11; D. Rothman, *Discovery of the Asylum*, 78–79; Richard Hofstadter, *The Age of Reform* (New York: Vintage Books, 1955), 135–73; David J. Rothman, "Perfecting the Prison: United States, 1789–1865," in *The Oxford History of the Prison*, ed. Norval Morris and David J. Rothman (Oxford: Oxford University Press, 1995), 120–28; Daniel T. Rodgers, *The Work Ethic in Industrial America, 1850–1920* (Chicago: University of Chicago Press, 1978), 16; Steven Mintz, *Huck's Raft: A History of American Childhood* (Cambridge, MA: Harvard University Press, 2004), 91; Reaume, *Remembrance of Patients Past*, 133.

19. Auburn was one of the most influential and widely copied penitentiaries in the antebellum United States. The equally influential "Pennsylvania Plan" likewise emphasized the importance of making inmates labor, but isolated the prisoners in their cells on a full-time basis. D. Rothman, *Discovery of the Asylum*, 103–4.

20. David Gollaher, *Voice for the Mad: The Life of Dorothea Dix* (New York: Free Press, 1995), 167–72; R. C. Scheerenberger, *A History of Mental Retardation* (Baltimore: P. H. Brookes, 1983), 105–7.

21. Moral treatment emerged nearly simultaneously in France, where Pinel famously broke the chains on inmates at Paris's Asylum de Bicêtre in 1793, and in England, where William Tuke, a Quaker, established the York Retreat in 1796. Tuke's fellow Quakers then helped spread moral treatment across the Atlantic. Roy Porter, *Madness: A Brief History* (Oxford: Oxford University Press, 2002), 103–7; Gerald Grob, *Mental Institutions in America, 1875–1940* (Princeton, NJ: Princeton University Press, 1983), 168–69;

Gerald Grob, *The Mad among Us: A History of the Care of America's Mentally Ill* (New York: Free Press, 2011), 27; Nathaniel Smith Kogan, "'Every Good Man Is a Quaker, and that None but Good Men Are Quakers': Transatlantic Quaker Humanitarianism, Disability, and Marketing Enlightened Reform, 1730–1834," (PhD diss., University of Texas at Arlington, 2015), chap. 4 passim; Bernard John Graney, "Hervey Backus Wilbur and the Evolution of Policies and Practices toward Mentally Retarded People" (PhD diss., Syracuse University, 1979), 32; Reaume, *Remembrance of Patients Past*, 11–14.

22. In 1842, Séguin published *Théorie et pratique de l'éducation des enfans arriérés et idiots: Leçons aux jeunes idiots de l'Hospice des incurables* (Paris: Germer Baillière, 1842) and, in 1846, his seminal work, *Traitement moral, hygiene, et education des idiots* (Paris: Germer Baillière, 1846). Common school advocate Horace Mann visited Séguin's school in Paris in 1843 and likely reported on his visit to his close friend Samuel Gridley Howe. In 1844, insane asylum superintendents in Ohio, Massachusetts, and New York began publicizing Séguin's work in their annual reports and via the founding conference of the Association of Medical Superintendents of American Institutions for the Insane. Séguin was not the only European to experiment with educating idiots in the late 1830s and early 1840s; in Switzerland, Johann Jakob Guggenbühl founded a small program for training cretins in 1839, and Carl Wilhelm Saegart had begun educating idiots in 1845. Peter L. Tyor and Leland V. Bell, *Caring for the Retarded in America: A History* (Westport, CT: Greenwood Press, 1984), 11; Harold Schwartz, *Samuel Gridley Howe: Social Reformer, 1801–1876* (Cambridge, MA: Harvard University Press, 1956), 138; Trent, *Inventing the Feeble Mind*, 284n1, 296n4; Graney, "Hervey Backus Wilbur," 34; Experimental School for Idiots and Feeble-Minded Children, *Second Annual Report of the Directors to the Governor and Legislature of Illinois, Together with the Report of the Superintendent, December 1866* (Springfield, IL: Baker, Bailhache, 1867), 15–16 (hereafter cited as IL School, *Annual Report*).

23. Ernest Freeberg, *The Education of Laura Bridgman: First Deaf and Blind Person to Learn Language* (Cambridge, MA: Harvard University Press, 2001), 83; R. A. R. Edwards, *Words Made Flesh: Nineteenth-Century Deaf Education and the Growth of Deaf Culture* (New York: New York University Press, 2012), 144–53; James W. Trent, Jr., *The Manliest Man: Samuel G. Howe and the Contours of Nineteenth-Century American Reform* (Amherst: University of Massachusetts Press, 2012), 7.

24. Howe first accepted an idiotic pupil in 1839; he took two more such students in the early 1840s. The American School for the Deaf, the Commercial Hospital and Lunatic Asylum, and the Ohio Deaf and Dumb Asylum all accepted a few idiots between the 1820s and the 1840s; the Hartford Retreat for the Insane also housed several adult idiots, who made up a significant proportion of long-staying incurable cases. Trent, *Manliest Man*, 5–7; Lawrence B. Goodheart, "Rethinking Mental Retardation: Education and Eugenics in Connecticut, 1818–1917," *Journal of the History of Medicine and Allied Sciences* 59, no. 1 (January 2004): 93–94; Tyor and Bell, *Caring for the Retarded*, 10–11.

25. Echoing Horace Mann, a close friend of both Howe and Sumner, Sumner's letter also suggested that each citizen had a "right" to the "full development of all his faculties." Tyor and Bell, *Caring for the Retarded*, 11–12.

26. Howe, *Report to the Legislature*, 5–6.

27. The *Oxford English Dictionary* defines a upas tree as "a fabulous tree alleged to have existed in Java, at some distance from Batavia, with properties so poisonous as to destroy all animal and vegetable life to a distance of fifteen or sixteen miles around it," and "a baleful, destructive, or deadly power or influence." The use of the word dates back to 1783. In the present day, upas tree refers to *Antiaris toxicaria* trees, which grow on the island of Java and which produce a poisonous sap. "Upas, n.," OED Online (Oxford University Press, June 2014), http://www.oed.com/view/Entry/219818?redirectedFrom=upas (accessed 8 July 2014). Howe, *Report to the Legislature*, 51–52; Trent, *Inventing the Feeble Mind*, 24–27.

28. Massachusetts Board of State Charities, *Fifth Annual Report* (1869), xvii, quoted in Amy Dru Stanley, *From Bondage to Contract: Wage Labor, Marriage, and the Market in the Age of Slave Emancipation* (Cambridge: Cambridge University Press, 1998), 130. Modeled on the infamous Black Codes of the South, Massachusetts's act enforced six months' labor in a workhouse or house of correction for convicted vagrants and vagabonds. This act, ironically, was enacted just a month after Congress passed the Civil Rights Act, "thereby voiding the southern Black Codes which, among other things, had punished free slaves for vagrancy and idleness. At the very moment when Republicans in Congress were enshrining the legal supremacy of free labor as a cornerstone of Reconstruction, their brethren in Massachusetts were engaged in constructing an apparatus of labor compulsions." Pennsylvania, Illinois, and New York, as well as the remaining New England states, followed Massachusetts's lead in the 1870s. Stanley, *From Bondage to Contract*, 108, and see also 99–100, 107–37; Freeberg, *Education of Laura Bridgman*, 97; Alexander Keyssar, *Out of Work: The First Century of Unemployment in Massachusetts* (Cambridge: Cambridge University Press, 1986), 135–39, 141, 253; Katz, *In the Shadow of the Poorhouse*, 92–93.

29. As early as 1854, Howe included proto-eugenic questions about parents' habits and abilities on the application form for the Perkins Institute for the Blind. Freeberg, *Education of Laura Bridgman*, 190–91, 198–202; MA School, *Seventh Annual Report, 1854*, 18.

30. Howe, *Report to the Legislature*, 40.

31. Tyor and Bell, *Caring for the Retarded*, 42; Freeberg, *Education of Laura Bridgman*, 21–22; Trent, *Manliest Man*, 187–88.

32. James B. Richards, not Howe, served as the first superintendent of the experimental idiot program. He departed Boston in 1852 to found a private school in Germantown, Pennsylvania, which became the Pennsylvania Training School for Idiotic and Feeble-Minded Children in 1854 (later renamed the Elwyn School). Richards remained a key figure among the small community of superintendents of idiot asylums until his death in 1886. Tyor and Bell, *Caring for the Retarded*, 15–16; Trent, *Manliest Man*, 188–91.

33. Graney, "Hervey Backus Wilbur," 12–13, 56–57; Trent, *Inventing the Feeble Mind*, 14.

34. Wilbur worked hard to build his clientele, advertising in newspapers, publishing several circulars, and cultivating a network of fellow physicians who could provide referrals. The *Boston Medical and Surgical Journal* also praised Wilbur's work in 1849.

Rafter, *Creating Born Criminals*, 18, 29–30; Catherine W. Brown, "Reminiscences," *Journal of Psycho-Asthenics* 1, no. 4 (June 1897): 134; Graney, "Hervey Backus Wilbur," 12–13, Trent, *Inventing the Feeble Mind*, 14; Tyor and Bell, *Caring for the Retarded*, 16; Hervey B. Wilbur, "Eulogy to Edouard Seguin: 'Remarks by Dr. H. B. Wilbur,'" in *The History of Mental Retardation, Collected Papers*, vol. 1, ed. Marvin Rosen, Gerald Robert Clark, and Marvin S. Kivitz (Baltimore: University Park Press, 1976), 183.

35. Backus was inspired by the 1845 census of New York State, which identified 1,610 idiots in New York, many of whom resided in poorhouses, as well as Utica State Lunatic Asylum superintendent's Amariah Brigham's 1844 call for an idiot asylum. Numerous reports on European experiments in idiot education, in particular John Conolly's accounts on the Bicêtre's program for idiots in the *British Foreign and Medical Review*, 1845 and 1847 respectively, provided practical evidence that idiots could indeed be educated. Backus also corresponded with a German educator, presumably Carl Wilhelm Saegert, who established a school affiliated with the Institute of Deaf-Mutes in Berlin in the mid-1840s. Despite New York legislators' skepticism and disinterest, Backus managed to interest two successive governors in his cause: Hamilton Fish (1849–1851) and Washington Hunt (1851–1853). Both pressed the legislature to establish an institution to train idiots. Trent, *Inventing the Feeble Mind*, 13–14; Graney, "Hervey Backus Wilbur," 49–50; Scheerenberger, *History of Mental Retardation*, 73; NY Asylum, *First Annual Report, 1851*, 11.

36. Starting in January 1850, Wilbur began pressing Howe for a recommendation for the potential position in New York. Wilbur confided to Howe, "Should a State Institution be founded in New York, I feel quite a disposition to secure the post of Supt. for myself. . . . Aside from yourself, I have devoted more time and attention to the subject, than anyone else in America." He bought one hundred copies of Howe's most recent annual report to distribute to New York legislators. Hervey B. Wilbur to Samuel Gridley Howe, 22 January 1850 and 26 February 1850, quoted in Graney, "Hervey Backus Wilbur," 45; see also 53, 170–71; Brown, "Reminiscences," 134. See also Freeberg, *Education of Laura Bridgman*, 14–19; Tyor and Bell, *Caring for the Retarded*, 15–16; Rafter, *Creating Born Criminals*, 19–20; NY Asylum, *First Annual Report, 1851*, 10–11; MA School, *First Annual Report, 1851*, 28.

37. Technically, the tavern was located in Watervliet on a road that connected Albany with the bridge to Troy. During the 1820s, the father of future railroad promoter Leland Stanford owned and operated the tavern. NY Asylum, *First Annual Report, 1851*, 9; *Third Annual Report, 1853*, 22; Graney, "Hervey Backus Wilbur," 54.

38. Trent, *Manliest Man*, chap. 6 passim, 223–29, 237–42; Edwards, *Words Made Flesh*, chap. 5 passim.

39. Graney, "Hervey Backus Wilbur," 169–72.

40. As Nathaniel Kogan has argued, such discussions simultaneously served to stigmatize people with disabilities as abnormal and less than human and laid the groundwork for efforts to educate children with disabilities. Freeberg, *Education of Laura Bridgman*, 30–35, 39–41; Lennard J. Davis, *Enforcing Normalcy: Disability, Deafness, and the Body* (New York: Verso, 1995), chap. 2 passim; Kogan, "'Every Good Man Is a

Quaker, and that None but Good Men Are Quakers,'" chap. 1 passim; Dwight Christopher Gabbard, "Disability Studies and the British Long Eighteenth Century," *Literature Compass* 8, no. 2 (2011): 85–86.

41. See, for instance, NY Asylum, *First Annual Report, 1851,* 16; *Second Annual Report, 1852,* 12; *Sixth Annual Report, 1856,* 12; *Seventh Annual Report, 1857,* 19–20; *Twenty-Seventh Annual Report, 1877,* 9.

42. IL School, *First Annual Report, 1865,* 12.

43. Ibid.; IL School, *Second Annual Report, 1866,* 6.

44. NY Asylum, *First Annual Report, 1851,* 16; IL School, *First Annual Report, 1865,* 12.

45. MA School, *Seventh Annual Report, 1854,* 8.

46. While Wilbur worked with Josephine Lowell Shaw to establish a eugenically oriented asylum in 1878 (the New York State Custodial Asylum for Feeble-Minded Women), he did so only reluctantly and for noneugenic reasons, as discussed in the next chapter.

47. NY Asylum, *First Annual Report, 1851,* 3; Schneider, *The History of Public Welfare in New York State,* 368; Trent, *Inventing the Feeble Mind,* 28–29; Ferguson, *Abandoned to Their Fate,* 54–60.

48. SDR, vol. 2, entry 10.

49. Nineteen received state funding because their families were too poor to pay even a small portion of their support; seven were pay pupils. The asylum's bylaws mandated that all students fall between the ages of seven and fourteen at the time of admission; accordingly, Wilbur admitted only pupils who were under twelve years of age. NY Asylum, *First Annual Report, 1851,* 9, 13.

50. Later on, however, Wilbur recorded that Mitchell's parents "regarded his [seven-year stay] in the asylum as a great benefit to him." SDR, vol. 2, entry 10.

51. Kathryn Irving, "To Be 'Useful and Happy': Paternalism, Politics, Experts, and the MA School for Idiotic Children, 1848–1883" (paper presented at the Society for Disability Studies Conference, Denver, CO, June 2012), copy in author's possession; MA School, *Third Annual Report, 1851,* 13.

52. IL School, *First Annual Report, 1865,* 15; *Second Annual Report, 1866,* 22, 25; *Fourth Annual Report, 1868,* 26–27.

53. NY Asylum, *Third Annual Report, 1853,* 18; *Twelfth Annual Report, 1862,* 28–29; *Twentieth Annual Report, 1871,* 7; IL School, *Fifth Annual Report, 1869,* 9.

54. In 1852, for instance, Wilbur rejected an applicant with hourly epileptic seizures and sent home two pupils: one whom he deemed to have consumption and hereditary insanity, and one with severe chorea. He excluded children with severe physical impairments or illness because such students required full-time personal attendants. He also tried to weed out pupils with moderate to severe epilepsy based on the rationale that their seizures frightened the other students, and he noted that one seizure could erase years of progress. NY Asylum, *Sixth Annual Report, 1856,* 11; *Twelfth Annual Report, 1862,* 21; *Sixteenth Annual Report, 1866,* 20; IL School, *First Annual Report, 1865,* 39; MA School, *First Annual Report, 1851,* 35.

55. NY Asylum, *Second Annual Report, 1852,* 33; *Forty-Eighth Annual Report, 1898,* 25. Natty: SDR, vol. 2, entry 19; SDR, vol. 5, entry 2. Willie: SDR, vol. 2, entry 20.

56. SDR, vol. 1.

57. Of the 309 pupils admitted in the 1850s, Wilbur deemed 38 "low-grade idiots" and described 27 as having one or more physical impairments. He accepted 26 "low-grade idiots" and 33 physically disabled children out of 249 admits in the 1860s; the numbers for the 1870s were 17 and 37, respectively. SDR, vol. 2; Syracuse Admission Registers, vols. 3–5, Syracuse State School, Admission, Discharge, Death, and Transfer Records, 1851–1945, Admission Registers, 1851–1920 (Acc. B1647, Subseries 2) (hereafter SAR), NYSA; NY Asylum, *First Annual Report, 1851,* 14. See also Trent, *Inventing the Feeble Mind,* 28–29; Edward Séguin, "Institutions for Idiots," *Appleton's Journal,* 12 February 1870, 182; NY Asylum, *Second Annual Report, 1852,* 33; *Fourth Annual Report, 1854,* 2; *Fifth Annual Report, 1855,* 11; *Sixth Annual Report, 1856,* 12; *Eighth Annual Report, 1858,* 9; *Twelfth Annual Report, 1862,* 8; *Fifteenth Annual Report, 1865,* 9; *Seventeenth Annual Report, 1867,* 11; *Twentieth Annual Report, 1871,* 16; *Twenty-Second Annual Report, 1872,* 12; *Twenty-Third Annual Report, 1873,* 9; *Twenty-Fourth Annual Report, 1874,* 11; *Twenty-Seventh Annual Report, 1877,* 9.

58. Superintendents of insane asylums likewise had trouble creating a "valid, reliable definition of mental health." NY Asylum, *Twenty-First Annual Report, 1871,* 10–11; IL School, *Eighth Biennial Report, 1880,* 23; MA School, *Third Annual Report, 1851,* 8–9; Tyor and Bell, *Caring for the Retarded,* 26–27; Ellen Dwyer, *Homes for the Mad: Life Inside Two Nineteenth-Century Asylums* (New Brunswick, NJ: Rutgers University Press, 1987), 149.

59. Admitted in 1872 at age fifteen, McDonogh never returned home. She "eloped" (departed without permission) in 1900 and then spent time in the Rome State Custodial Asylum and the Gowanda State Homeopathic Hospital. SDR, vol. 2, entry 574; Syracuse State Institution for Feeble-Minded Children, Pupil Evaluation Reports [ca. 1860–1909], vol. 1, p. 110 (Acc. B1666), Box 1(hereafter SPE), NYSA; U.S. Bureau of the Census, *Ninth Census of the United States, 1870,* New York, Cayuga County, Auburn, sheet 44; U.S. Bureau of the Census, *Thirteenth Census of the United States, 1910,* New York, Oneida County, Rome, Enum. Dist. no. 81, sheet 12; U.S. Bureau of the Census, *Fourteenth Census, 1920,* New York, Erie County, Collins, Enum. Dist. no. 280, sheet 14.

60. McNeil came from St. Mary's Institution for the Improved Instruction of Deaf-Mutes in Buffalo. After two years, Wilbur dismissed him as "unimprovable." SDR, vol. 3, p. 74; SPE, vol. 1, p. 101, Box 1; U.S. Bureau of the Census, *Tenth Census of the United States, 1880,* New York, Onondaga County, Geddes, Enum. Dist. no.173, sheet 82.

61. Roughly 8 percent of pupils had undergone "convulsions" or "fits" as infants, while nearly 12 percent had them as children prior to entering the asylum. Many, if not most, of these convulsions were likely not epileptic seizures. Parents attributed fits to teething as well as illnesses, among other reported causes. See, for instance, SDR, vol. 2, entry 453; SPE, vol. 1, p. 28; Syracuse State Institution for Feeble-Minded Children, Record of Deaths, 1851–1895, vol. 1, p. 61 (Acc. B1662) (hereafter Syracuse Death Records), NYSA; and SDR, vol. 3, p. 11; SAR, vol. 3, p. 118; SPE, vol. 1, p. 22; New York, Oneida County, 1881, Record no. 842 in Ancestry.com, *Census of Inmates in Almshouses*

and Poorhouses, 1830–1920 (Provo, UT: Ancestry.com Operations), original data from New York State Board of Charities, Census of Inmates in Almshouses and Poorhouses, 1835–1921 (Acc. A1978), NYSA (hereafter cited as *Almshouse Census*). Only a tiny fraction of students—less than 1 percent—appear to have had Down's syndrome, likely because of the high rate of untreatable congenital heart abnormalities associated with it. For examples of pupils whose impairment originated from thyroid disorders, see SDR, vol. 2, entry 154. Down's syndrome: SDR, vol. 2, entry 476. On abuse: SDR, vol. 2, entry 640; SAR, vol. 3, p. 49; U.S. Bureau of the Census, *Eighth Census of the United States, 1860*, New York, Fulton County, Ephratah, sheet 41; SDR, vol. 3, p. 77.

62. Chorea is a disorder that causes involuntary movements and is often associated with scarlet fever. See SDR, vol. 2, entries 297, 363, 450.

63. NY Asylum, *First Annual Report, 1851*, 20.

64. NY Asylum, *Second Annual Report, 1852*, 8, 23. Like Séguin, Wilbur defined idiocy fundamentally as a failure of the will. NY Asylum, *First Annual Report, 1851*, 15.

65. Paterson remained only a year at the asylum, departing when her family moved to rural Illinois. She continued to live with her parents for at least the next twenty years; her father farmed and served as a Presbyterian minister. SDR, vol. 2, entry 251. U.S. Bureau of the Census, *Seventh Census of the United States, 1850*, Illinois, Morgan County, sheet 89; *Eighth Census, 1860*, Illinois, Hancock County, La Harpe, sheet 737; *Ninth Census, 1870*, Illinois, Warren County, Ellison, sheet 10; *Tenth Census, 1880*, Illinois, Warren County, Ellison, Enum. Dist. no. 286, sheet 15.

66. NY Asylum, *Ninth Annual Report, 1860*, 17.

67. SDR, vol. 2, entry 141.

68. Wilbur dismissed Collins in 1867 after a four-year stay as "a bad epileptic." Heller remained at the asylum for ten years, departing in 1884; halfway through her stay, Wilbur noted that she was "still violent" and "cannot be trusted with beads, throws them away & puts them in her mouth." On "destructive habits," see SDR, vol. 3, p. 137; SAR, vol. 3, p. 260; SPE, vol. 1, p. 171. Frances Alden: SDR, vol. 2, entry 615; SAR, vol. 3, p. 23; SPE, vol. 1, p. 157. Diana Heller: SDR, vol. 2, entry 674; SAR, vol. 3, p. 83. Christopher Collins: Bureau of the Census, *Ninth Census, 1870*, New York, Hudson County, Hoboken, sheet 79; SDR, vol. 2, entry 340.

69. NY Asylum, *First Annual Report, 1851*, 20.

70. NY Asylum, *Fifth Annual Report, 1855*, 10. See also NY Asylum, *Second Annual Report, 1852*, 4. His younger brother, Charles Toppan Wilbur, meanwhile, contended that "hundreds of children of backward and imperfect mental development" who were "equally susceptible of improvement for usefulness and happiness" were being ignored. IL School, *First Annual Report, 1865*, 11.

71. Nelson never returned home; after he spent thirty-seven years in the asylum, Wilbur's successor, John Carson, transferred him at age forty-five to the Cayuga County Almshouse, whence he had come in 1867 and where he remained through at least 1910. SDR, vol. 2, entry 452; SDR, vol. 5, entry 14; SPE, vol. 1, p. 61; U.S. Bureau of the Census, *Twelfth Census of the United States, 1900*, New York, Onondaga County, Syracuse, 171, sheet 6; *Thirteenth Census, 1910*, New York, Cayuga County, Sennett, 59, sheet 3.

72. NY Asylum, *Annual Report, 1857*, 25; IL School, *Second Annual Report, 1866*, 6. NY Asylum, *Second Annual Report, 1852*, 15. See also NY Asylum, *Third Annual Report, 1853*, 20; *Twenty-First Annual Report, 1871*, 12.

73. SDR, vol. 2, entry 408. See also NY Asylum, *Eleventh Annual Report, 1861*, 12.

74. Wilbur noted that Buckner had "done a variety of farm-labor and made himself very useful at the Boys' Building" and was "always gentlemanly and well-behaved." Despite the fact that his father was a gardener, it is unclear whether he worked after leaving the asylum in 1878. According to the 1880 census, he had no occupation. By 1900, he was living in the Suffolk County Almshouse, presumably due to his elderly parents' deaths in the intervening years; poorhouse officials identified him as a laborer. SDR, vol. 2, entry 379; SPE, vol. 1, p. 6. Bureau of the Census, *Ninth Census, 1870*, New York, New York County, New York, sheet 33; *Tenth Census, 1880*, New York, Suffolk County, Orient, 329, sheet 8; *Twelfth Census, 1900*, New York, Suffolk County, Brookhaven, 817, sheet 2; *Thirteenth Census, 1910*, New York, Suffolk County, Brookhaven, 1349, sheet 9.

75. Gaffer became a "lifer" in asylums, remaining at Syracuse until 1902, when the superintendent, James Carson, transferred her to the Rome State Custodial Asylum. Her family may have lived too close to the margin to ever take her home; her father variously worked as a laborer and a market-man, while her sisters were employed as servants and, in one case, as a schoolteacher. Neither of her sisters married. SDR, vol. 2, entry 387; SDR, vol. 5, entry 11; SPE, vol. 1, p. 208. Bureau of the Census, *Seventh Census, 1850*, New York, Erie County, Buffalo, sheet 280; *Eighth Census, 1860*, New York, Erie County, Buffalo, sheet 16; *Ninth Census, 1870*, New York, Erie County, Buffalo, sheet 62; *Tenth Census, 1880*, New York, Erie County, Buffalo, Enum. Dist. no. 122, sheet 14; *Twelfth Census, 1900*, New York, Erie County, Buffalo, 30, sheet 5; *Thirteenth Census, 1910*, New York, Oneida County, Rome, Enum. Dist. no. 81, sheet 11.

76. NY Asylum, *Sixth Annual Report, 1856*, 14.

77. Ibid.; NY Asylum, *Seventh Annual Report, 1858*, 23.

78. Rodgers, *Work Ethic*, xi.

79. MA School, *Third Annual Report, 1851*, 16–18 (emphasis in original).

80. Pennsylvania Training School for Feeble-Minded Children, *Fifth Annual Report of the Board of Directors . . . with the Report of the Superintendent* (Philadelphia: Henry R. Ashmead, 1858), 36 (hereafter cited as PA School, *Annual Report*).

81. NY Asylum, *Sixth Annual Report, 1856*, 14; *Seventh Annual Report, 1857*, 23; IL School, *Second Annual Report, 1866*, 38.

82. Rather than reflecting middle-class status anxiety, a pervasive fear of social disorder, or superintendents' desires to justify and perpetuate their institution, idiot asylum training programs reflected the standard goals of public education in the nineteenth century: producing disciplined and productive, or at least not burdensome, inhabitants. By the late 1860s and early 1870s, most New York State insane asylums began to cancel inmate work programs; superintendents instead relied increasingly on mechanical and chemical restraints. Poor-law reformers, however, had less success enforcing work programs in almshouses, due to the ill health and disabilities common among permanent residents. D. Rothman, *Discovery of the Asylum*, 78–79; Hofstadter, *Age of*

Reform, 135–73; Mintz, *Huck's Raft*; Tyor and Bell, *Caring for the Retarded*, 24–39; Trent, *Inventing the Feeble Mind*, 24–39; Ferguson, *Abandoned to Their Fate*, 49–50; Dwyer, *Homes for the Mad*, 15–16; Thomas A. Krainz, *Delivering Aid: Implementing Progressive Era Welfare in the American West* (Albuquerque: University of New Mexico Press, 2005), 103–5, 112–19, 129–31; Bloom, "Floating Population," 268–79.

83. NY Asylum, *Tenth Annual Report, 1860*, 19. Personal communication from Rebecca McNulty Skrivin, 29 April 2007.

84. Idiot asylum superintendents occasionally experimented with menial tasks such as mat making, brush making, and shoe repairing, but such programs rarely lasted long or proved profitable. On provisions for deaf, blind, and "crippled" children, see John Vickrey Van Cleve and Barry A. Crouch, *A Place of Their Own: Creating the Deaf Community in America* (Washington, DC: Gallaudet University Press, 1989); Robert M. Buchanan, *Illusions of Equality: Deaf Americans in School and Factory, 1850–1950* (Washington, DC: Gallaudet University Press, 1999); Freeberg, *Education of Laura Bridgman*; Brad Byrom, "A Pupil and a Patient: Hospital-Schools in Progressive America," in *The New Disability History: American Perspectives*, ed. Paul K. Longmore and Lauri Umansky (New York: New York University Press, 2001), 133–56; NY Asylum, *Tenth Annual Report, 1861*, 20; Iowa State Asylum for Feeble Minded Children, *Second Biennial Report of the Trustees, Superintendent and Treasure of the Iowa State Asylum for Feeble Minded Children at Glenwood, November 1st, 1879* (Des Moines: F. M. Mills, 1880), 27 (hereafter cited as Iowa Asylum, *Biennial Report*); IL School, *Second Annual Report, 1866*, 9–10; PA School, *Thirteenth Annual Report, 1865*, 10; MA School, *Sixteenth Annual Report, 1863*, 10–11. For a detailed accounting of what Charles Toppan Wilbur called "instruction in trades" at various asylums, see IL School, *Seventh Biennial Report, 1878*, 14.

85. NY Asylum, *First Annual Report, 1852*, 23.

86. NY Asylum, *Ninth Annual Report, 1859*, 17; *Fifteenth Annual Report, 1865*, 32–33.

87. NY Asylum, *Fourth Annual Report, 1854*, 4; *Ninth Annual Report, 1859*, 18. See also NY Asylum, *Fifteenth Annual Report, 1866*, 32–33.

88. *Syracuse Daily Standard*, 5 June 1854, quoted in Graney, "Hervey Backus Wilbur," 56–57. On asylum tourism, see Freeberg, *Education of Laura Bridgman*, 14–16; Bogdan, *Picturing Disability*, 57–72.

89. Other prominent members of the first generation included James B. Richards, who taught at the experimental Massachusetts School and later founded the Pennsylvania School in 1854; Isaac N. Kerlin, who became superintendent of the Pennsylvania School in 1864; Henry M. Knight, who founded the Connecticut School for Imbeciles at Lakeville in 1858; and Gustavus A. Doren. In 1859, Doren took over the superintendency at the Ohio Institution for Feeble-Minded Youth at Columbus, founded in 1857. Tyor and Bell, *Caring for the Retarded*, 17–18.

90. Other than Kentucky, no southern states established idiot asylums or institutions for the feeble-minded until 1910, when economic, cultural, medical, and intellectual dynamics were substantially different; therefore, I have not included them. Wilbur to Howe, 21 December 1857, quoted in Graney, "Hervey Backus Wilbur," 67; see also 113,

115–16, 168. Steven Noll, *Feeble-Minded in Our Midst: Institutions for the Mentally Retarded in the South, 1900–1940* (Chapel Hill: University of North Carolina Press, 1995), 12.

91. NY Asylum, *First Annual Report, 1851*, 21; *Twentieth Annual Report, 1871*, 15–16; *Twenty-Fifth Annual Report, 1875*, 12; Graney, "Hervey Backus Wilbur," 169–72.

92. Séguin had earlier called for such an association. Wilbur and Kerlin cowrote the association's bylaws and constitution, and Wilbur nominated his friend Séguin as first president. At the association's annual meetings, superintendents shared not only their research on the causes of idiocy but also the details of their training programs, including industrial work.

93. Edouard Séguin, "Recent Progress in the Training of Idiots," *Proceedings of the Association of Medical Officers of American Institutions for the Idiotic and Feeble-Minded Persons* 3 (1879): 64.

94. IL School, *Second Annual Report, 1866*, 38.

95. MA School, *Tenth Annual Report, 1857*, 16.

96. IL School, *Fourth Annual Report, 1868*, 29.

97. Iowa Asylum, *Second Biennial Report, 1879*, 15, 27; IL School, *Second Annual Report, 1866*, 9.

98. By then, Howe was no longer serving as resident superintendent. He remained on as general superintendent, writing the annual reports and visiting regularly when in town, but he focused most of his attention on the Perkins Institution, abolitionism, and charity reform. MA School, *Twelfth Annual Report, 1859*, 10.

99. Ibid.; IL School, *Fourth Annual Report, 1868*, 30.

100. Howe did, however, question the standard practice of having boys learn farm work, declaring that farming "present[ed] the greatest variety of work, call[ed] into play the greatest number of mental faculties, and require[d] the most exercise of foresight, calculation, and discretion." Perhaps reflecting his state's pioneering textile mills, armories, and other industrial enterprises, as well as the Massachusetts School's location in urban Boston, he instead proposed placing idiots in "simple and monotonous" factory positions: in other words, doing piecework. Howe also suggested that an overseer could more easily manage a class of idiotic factory workers than could an individual farmer. In reality, male students at the Massachusetts asylum learned basic gardening as well as household skills such as digging, splitting wood, and sawing. Given how much trouble blind graduates of the Perkins Institution had finding work in an industrializing economy, Howe's suggestion was ironic. His counterparts in other states ignored this proposal, and he never followed through either; nevertheless, as we shall see in chapter 3, in the 1910s and 1920s Charles Bernstein used a similar strategy to successfully place thousands of "feeble-minded" inmates in the mainstream labor force. MA School, *Twelfth Annual Report, 1859*, 12; *Eleventh Annual Report, 1858*, 27; Freeberg, *Education of Laura Bridgman*, 194–196; Trent, *Manliest Man*, 64–66. On farm labor, see IL School, *Second Annual Report, 1866*, 9–10; PA School, *Thirteenth Annual Report, 1865*, 10.

101. Dwyer, *Homes for the Mad*, 24, 32, 41.

102. NY Asylum, *First Annual Report, 1851*, 18–19. See also NY Asylum, *Fourth Annual Report, 1854*, 30, 37; *Eighth Annual Report, 1858*, 10; *Eleventh Annual Report, 1861*, 15; *Seventeenth Annual Report, 1867*, 11, 13; *Twenty-Seventh Annual Report, 1877*, 9; Tyor and Bell, *Caring for the Retarded*, 31.

103. NY Asylum, *First Annual Report, 1851*, 4.

104. State legislators had originally budgeted $50,000 to build Utica State Lunatic Asylum; in the end, the asylum cost $435,100. NY Asylum, *First Annual Report, 1851*, 21; Dwyer, *Homes for the Mad*, 35–37; Graney, "Hervey Backus Wilbur," 98–99.

105. NY Asylum, *First Annual Report, 1851*, 3–4; Wilbur to Howe, 30 April 1850, cited in Graney, "Hervey Backus Wilbur," 41; see also 54.

106. Graney, "Hervey Backus Wilbur," 41. Much later, Wilbur's close friend Catherine Brown, who oversaw the Barre institution with her husband, George, described Wilbur as "scrupulously economical in the administration of finances of the State." Catherine Brown, "In Memoriam: Hervey Backus Wilbur, M.D.," *Archives of Medicine* 9 (1883): 277–79, quoted in Graney, "Hervey Backus Wilbur," 164. In 1853, the state legislature passed an act making the institution permanent. Rafter, *Creating Born Criminals*, 21.

107. It is not fully clear how Wilbur located these paying pupils; likely, they contacted him after reading newspaper or magazine coverage of the asylum or per recommendation from Samuel Gridley Howe. Income from paying pupils peaked in 1872 with thirty-two students paying a total of $5,710.20 and in 1874 with thirty-nine students paying a total of $5,904.89; fees for private pupils covered 16.77 percent and 17.88 percent of total regular expenditures in those years, respectively. Between 1866 and 1884, fees from paying pupils covered at least 9 percent of costs and likely a similar percentage before. Firm figures on total regular expenditures are missing for 1851–1856 and 1858–1865, but fees from paying pupils totaled between $2,000 and $3,000 during these years, enough to defray between one-third and one-half of the cost of all provisions. After Dr. James C. Carson took over as superintendent following Hervey B. Wilbur's death in 1883, however, the number of private pupils and the income from their fees plummeted to around 5 percent and, within a few years, to 2–3 percent of total regular expenditures. Carson also stopped reporting the numbers of paying pupils in residence. After O. H. Cobb's appointment as superintendent in 1908, paying pupils disappeared almost entirely. Data from NY Asylum, *Annual Reports*, 1851–1920. See also Trent, *Inventing the Feeble Mind*, 64–65.

108. For more on begging letters, see Scott A. Sandage, *Born Losers: A History of Failure in America* (Cambridge, MA: Harvard University Press, 2005), chap. 8 passim.

109. NY Asylum, *Annual Report, 1852*, 23.

110. NY Asylum, *Seventh Annual Report, 1857*, 24; *Ninth Annual Report, 1859*, 18. See also *Sixth Annual Report, 1856*, 14. The asylum used almost all of the farm produce itself, but occasionally sold a few hundred dollars' worth of produce between the 1850s and the mid-1870s. Starting in 1877, the asylum sold several hundred dollars' worth each year of farm products and shop products such as brushes.

111. NY Asylum, *Sixth Annual Report, 1856*, 14; *Tenth Annual Report, 1860*, 7–8.

112. The total cost of provisions and supplies was $10,892.66, while housing, clothing, and food totaled $20,773.80. NY Asylum, *Tenth Annual Report, 1860*, 7–8.

113. PA School, *Eighth Annual Report, 1860*, 25, 23.

114. NY Asylum, *Sixth Annual Report, 1856*, 14; *Tenth Annual Report, 1860*, 20; Iowa Asylum, *Second Biennial Report, 1879*, 11.

115. IL School, *Second Annual Report, 1866*, 7; *Fourth Annual Report, 1868*, 15; Iowa Asylum, *Fifth Biennial Report, 1887*, 11–12.

116. NY Asylum, *Twentieth Annual Report, 1871*, 20.

117. SDR, vol. 2, entry 80; Bureau of the Census, *Eighth Census, 1860*, New York, Onondaga County, Pompey, sheet 214; *Twelfth Census, 1900*, New York, Onondaga County, Pompey, Enum. Dist. no. 67, sheet 1; New York, *Almshouse Census*, Onondaga County, 1911, Record no. 6025.

118. Goode worked for the same family between 1880 and 1900. SDR, vol. 2, entry 105. Bureau of the Census, *Seventh Census, 1850*, New York, Saratoga County, Saratoga Springs, sheet 204/407; *Tenth Census, 1880*, New York, Oswego County, Pulaski, 262, sheet 18; *Twelfth Census, 1900*, New York, Oswego County, Pulaski, Enum. Dist. no. 142, sheet 8.

119. SDR, vol. 2, entry 351.

120. Chapter 2 focuses on those students who remained for decades—a fate that became increasingly common starting in the mid-1870s.

121. SDR, vols. 2–5; SAR, vols. 1–9.

122. MA School, *Third Annual Report, 1851*, 20; IL School, *Eighth Biennial Report, 1880*, 17.

123. Officially, the New York State Asylum for Idiots, as well as other asylums, had a trial period of one month, but in practice tended to keep pupils for considerably longer to see if they could be taught. SDR, vol. 2; NY Asylum, *Sixteenth Annual Report, 1866*, 20.

124. SDR, vol. 2, entry 2; SDR, vol. 5, entry 1.

125. In part, gendered discharge rates can be explained by the fact that New York opened a custodial institution for women in 1878 but did not open a comparable asylum for men until 1894. Nevertheless, female pupils were less likely to be discharged even during the asylum's first decade; 75.2 percent of male students admitted between 1851 and 1859 eventually returned home, while only 64.1 percent of female pupils did. Like its successors, the New York State Asylum for Idiots had more male applicants and male pupils than female; males comprised 66.6 percent of pupils admitted between 1851 and 1860. SDR, vol. 2; Syracuse Admission Registers, vols. 1–2, Syracuse State School, Admission, Discharge, Death, and Transfer Records, 1851–1945, Admission Registers, 1851–1920 (Acc. B1647, subseries 2) (hereafter SAR), NYSA; IL School, *Fourth Annual Report, 1868*, 22.

126. SDR, vol. 2, entry 184; SPE, vol. 1, p. 35; Syracuse Death Records, vol. 1, p. 54.

127. Between 1859 and 1862, Wilbur discharged twenty-two students whom he later described as working and supervised by either friends or relatives. These twenty-two students represented 36.7 percent of the sixty students discharged between 1859 and 1863. In 1864, Wilbur stopped regularly reporting discharges. Data from NY Asylum, *Annual Reports*, 1859–1864.

128. NY Asylum, *Fifteenth Annual Report, 1865*, 47–52. Joseph Calvert: SDR, vol. 2, entry 64. Nathaniel Bucher: SDR, vol. 3, p. 121; SAR, vol. 3, p. 245; SPE, vol. 1, p. 221.

Bureau of the Census, *Tenth Census, 1880*, New York, Onondaga County, Geddes, Enum. Dist. no. 173, sheet 79; *Twelfth Census, 1900*, New York, Onondaga County, Syracuse, Enum. Dist. no. 89, sheet 8; *Thirteenth Census, 1910*, New York, Onondaga County, Syracuse, Enum. Dist. no. 101, sheet 1.

129. NY Asylum, *Fifteenth Annual Report, 1865*, 55–58.

130. Tilton may have remained due to his family's marginal finances. Although his father farmed, which in many cases made it more likely that pupils would return home, he owned only $500 worth of land and $200 in personal property, while neighbors on average held $4,000 or $5,000 worth of land. SDR, vol. 2, entry 110. Bureau of the Census, *Seventh Census, 1850*, New York, Orleans County, Yates, sheet 607; *Eighth Census, 1860*, New York, Orleans County, Yates, sheet 26 and sheet 35; *Ninth Census, 1870*, New York, Orleans County, Yates, sheet 11; *Tenth Census, 1880*, New York, Onondaga County, Geddes, Enum. Dist. no. 173, sheet 79.

131. Carol Groneman, "'She Earns as a Child; She Pays as a Man': Women Workers in a Mid-Nineteenth Century New York City Community," in *Class, Sex, and the Woman Worker*, ed. Milton Cantor and Bruce Laurie (Westport, CT: Greenwood Press, 1977), 83–100; Alice Kessler-Harris, *Out to Work: A History of Wage-Earning Women in the United States*, 20th anniversary ed. (New York: Oxford University Press, 2003), 48, 51, 54–55, 58–59, 65–66, 68–69.

132. Melina's older sister Emily was admitted to the Syracuse asylum at the same time, but Wilbur soon arranged for her to be transferred to the New York Asylum for the Deaf and Dumb in Rochester. When the two girls were admitted to the New York State Asylum for Idiots, their father was already seventy-four years old. Melina's mother would have witnessed her domestic skills during the annual two-month vacations at home. SDR, vol. 2, entries 231 and 270; photograph of Melina and Emily Cogswell in SDR, vol. 2, on facing page from entries 693–95. Bureau of the Census, *Eighth Census, 1860*, New York, Jefferson County, Adams, sheet 32; *Ninth Census, 1870*, New York, Jefferson County, Adams, sheet 16; *Tenth Census, 1880*, New York, Jefferson County, Adams, Enum. Dist. no. 103, sheet 26; *Twelfth Census, 1900*, Michigan, Otsego County, Bagley, Enum. Dist. no. 140, sheet 4.

133. Sullivan continued to support himself as a laborer well after his mother's death. SDR, vol. 2, entry 223. Bureau of the Census, *Seventh Census, 1850*, New York, Washington County, Whitehall, sheet 38; *Tenth Census, 1880*, New York, Washington County, Whitehall, Enum. Dist. no. 158, sheet 28; *Twelfth Census, 1900*, New York, Washington County, Whitehall, Enum. Dist. no. 145, sheet 1.

134. Jane Carlisle: SDR, vol. 2, entry 15. Bureau of the Census, *Eighth Census, 1860*, New York, Otsego County, Otsego, sheet 27; *Ninth Census, 1870*, New York, Otsego County, Otsego, sheet 96; *Tenth Census, 1880*, New York, Otsego County, Otsego, Enum. Dist. no. 115, sheet 25; *Twelfth Census, 1900*, New York, Otsego County, Otsego, Enum. Dist. no. 132, sheet 7. PA School, *Fifth Annual Report, 1858*, 61–62.

135. SAR, vol. 7, p. 239. Bureau of the Census, *Tenth Census, 1880*, New York, Columbia County, Chatham, Enum. Dist. no. 4, sheet 30; *Twelfth Census, 1900*, New York, Columbia County, Hudson, Enum. Dist. no. 18, sheet 13; *Fourteenth Census, 1920*, New York,

Columbia County, Hudson, Enum. Dist. no. 25, sheet 7A; U.S. Bureau of the Census, *Fifteenth Census of the United States, 1930*, New York, Columbia County, Hudson, Enum. Dist. no. 11-22, sheet 3B; U.S. Bureau of the Census, *Sixteenth Census of the United States, 1940*, New York, Columbia County, Hudson, Enum. Dist. no. 11-37, sheet 11A.

136. Tyor and Bell, *Caring for the Retarded*, 49; George E. Shuttleworth, *Notes of a Visit to American Institutions for Idiots and Imbeciles* (Lancaster, Eng.: E. and J. L. Milner, 1877), 10.

137. Kentucky's Institute for the Feeble-Minded could enact such a policy in part because of the state's unusual policy of paying families an annual stipend to keep "pauper idiots" at home or, when necessary, board them out. Illinois reported similar numbers—52 out of 290 pupils discharged as able to perform "useful labor" by 1876, or just under 18 percent—but qualified this by noting "at home or elsewhere." Wolf Wolfensberger, *The Origin and Nature of Our Institutional Models* (Syracuse: Human Policy Press, 1975), 27; IL School, *Sixth Biennial Report, 1876*, 17.

138. MA School, *Eleventh Annual Report, 1858*, 31.

139. Blackie, "Disabled Revolutionary War Veterans," 134–38; Mintz, *Huck's Raft*, 135; Kessler-Harris, *Out to Work*, 121.

140. Eleanor Wills: SDR, vol. 2, entry 38. Bureau of the Census, *Seventh Census, 1850*, New York, Kings County, Williamsburg, sheet 392/666; *Eighth Census, 1860*, New York, Kings County, Brooklyn, sheet 138. Hannah Baxter: SDR, vol. 2, entry 480; Bureau of the Census, *Tenth Census, 1880*, New York, Wayne County, Arcadia, Enum. Dist. no. 171, sheet 30. William Gilbert: SDR, vol. 2, entry 436; Bureau of the Census, *Tenth Census, 1880*, Tennessee, Knox County, District 5, Enum. Dist. no. 152, sheet 13. James Barnes: SDR, vol. 2, entry 199; *Ninth Census, 1870*, New York, Oswego County, Oswego, sheet 59; *Tenth Census, 1880*, New York, Oswego County, Oswego, Enum. Dist. no. 224, sheet 25.

141. William Gilbert: "Cases of Paralysis" (undated sheet of notes included in volume), p. 1, SDR, vol. 2, near entries 567–74. James Barnes: SDR, vol. 2, entry 199.

142. SDR, vol. 2, entry 367.

143. Some parents, such as Simon Cowell's mother and father, simply desired to have their children at home. Wilbur noted about their son Simon, "Dismissed . . . or rather removed because his mother wanted him at home. He improved in the Asylum. Under a special teacher at home, he has since learned to some extent. Could be taught to work." The family employed a live-in teacher through at least 1870. IL School, *Fourth Annual Report, 1868*, 23; SDR, vol. 2, entry 329. Bureau of the Census, *Ninth Census, 1870*, New York, Cayuga County, Springport, sheet 55; *Tenth Census, 1880*, New York, Cayuga County, Springport, Enum. Dist. no. 37, sheet 24.

144. He later noted, "A large proportion of the new applications for admission each year come from localities or neighborhoods from which former pupils have been received." NY Asylum, *Fourth Annual Report, 1854*, 15–16; *Eighth Annual Report, 1858*, 10; *Seventeenth Annual Report, 1867*, 15; Tyor and Bell, *Caring for the Retarded*, 23; Graney, "Hervey Backus Wilbur," 75; NY Asylum, *Twenty-Third Annual Report, 1873*, 10.

145. IL School, *Fifth Annual Report, 1869*, 11, 18–21.

146. Ibid., 24–25. For a similar example from another state, see MA School, *Eleventh Annual Report, 1858*, 30–31.

147. Pensioners also had to document their wartime service and certify their injury's origin. The 1818 Pension Act eliminated the disability requirement, substituting poverty. Blackie, "Disabled Revolutionary War Veterans," 88, 104; John Phillips Resch, *Suffering Soldiers: Revolutionary War Veterans, Moral Sentiment, and Political Culture in the Early Republic* (Amherst: University of Massachusetts Press, 1999), 2, 10; Laura Jensen, *Patriots, Settlers, and the Origins of American Social Policy* (Cambridge: Cambridge University Press, 2003), 49.

148. See also Blackie, "Disabled Revolutionary War Veterans," 113–15, 124, 129, 165–66.

149. James E. Moran, "Asylum in the Community: Managing the Insane in Antebellum America," *History of Psychiatry* 9 (1998): 219, 223–26.

150. Boster, *African American Slavery and Disability*, 55–59, 65–72.

151. Rockman, *Scraping By*.

152. NY Asylum, *Fifteenth Annual Report, 1865*, 47–52; *Eleventh Annual Report, 1861*, 12; Albert Page: SDR, vol. 2, entry 141; NY Asylum, *Twelfth Annual Report, 1863*, 12.

153. Conrad Ulrich: SDR, vol. 3, p. 93; SAR, vol. 3, p. 201; Bureau of the Census, *Twelfth Census, 1900*, New York, Genesee County, Batavia, Enum. Dist. no. 5, sheet 33. Simon Thomas: SDR, vol. 2, entry 63; *Tenth Census, 1880*, New York, Tompkins County, Dryden, Enum. Dist. no. 226, sheet 46.

154. NY Asylum, *Twelfth Annual Report, 1863*, 12.

155. Eleanor Wills: SDR, vol. 2, entry 38. Bureau of the Census, *Eighth Census, 1860*, New York, Kings County, Brooklyn, sheet 138; *Twelfth Census, 1900*, West Virginia, Doddridge County, Cove, Enum. Dist. no. 19, sheet 1. Melissa Campbell: SDR, vol. 2, entry 461.

156. As Laurel Thatcher Ulrich, among others, has noted, families' need for care work has historically expanded and contracted over time. Laurel Thatcher Ulrich, *A Midwife's Tale: The Life of Martha Ballard, Based on Her Diary, 1785–1812* (New York: Vintage Books, 1990).

157. Geoffrey Reaume has likewise documented how challenges to family capacity led relatives to institutionalize people, often reluctantly. Reaume, *Remembrance of Patients Past*, 46–47; Simon Thomas: SDR, vol. 2, entry 63; New York, *State Census, 1892*, Tompkins County, Ulysses, Election District no. 4, sheet 2; Bureau of the Census, *Twelfth Census, 1900*, New York, Tompkins County, Ulysses, Enum. Dist. no. 163, sheet 3.

158. In fact, Barnes's father's business may have already been struggling when he was removed from the New York State Asylum for Idiots sometime in the 1860s. In 1860, the family had owned $30,000 in real estate and $5,000 in personal property, but by 1870, their circumstances had been reduced to $2,000 worth of land and $600 in personal property. By 1880, the family had collapsed; his father still worked as a baker but now lived as a boarder in another man's house. Barnes himself was employed elsewhere as a farm laborer. SDR, vol. 2, entry 199. Bureau of the Census, *Eighth Census, 1860*, New York, Onondaga County, Geddes, sheet 168; *Ninth Census, 1870*, New York, Oswego County, Oswego, sheet 59; *Tenth Census, 1880*, New York, Oswego County, Oswego,

Enum. Dist. no. 224, sheets 21 and 25; New York, *State Census, 1892,* Oswego County, Oswego, First Ward, sheet 13; New York, *Almshouse Census,* Oswego County, 1895, Record no. 757.

159. One brother was a cigar maker, another was a printer, and the third was a shoemaker turner. Other siblings, by contrast, such as Gordon Silverstein's brother, took in their "idiotic" relatives after parents died. Jason Cage: SDR, vol. 2, entry 638; SAR, vol. 3, p. 48; Bureau of the Census, *Tenth Census, 1880,* New York, Monroe County, Rochester, Enum. Dist. no. 10, sheet 31; New York, *Almshouse Census,* Monroe County, 1889, Record no. 4338; *Twelfth Census, 1900,* New York, Montgomery County, Amsterdam, Enum. Dist. no. 79, sheet 6; *Thirteenth Census, 1910,* New York, Monroe County, Rochester, Enum. Dist no 78, sheet 4B. Gordon Silverstein: SDR, vol. 2, entry 363. *Twelfth Census, 1900,* New York, Albany County, Albany, Enum. Dist. no. 48, sheet 1; *Thirteenth Census, 1910,* New York, Albany County, Albany, Enum. Dist. no. 65, sheet 18A.

160. SDR, vol. 2, entry 480; Bureau of the Census, *Tenth Census, 1880,* New York, Wayne County, Arcadia, Enum. Dist. no. 171, sheet 30.

161. Allison Carey has highlighted how the sentimental aspects of parent activism nearly a century later, in the 1950s and 1960s, constrained children's opportunities for self-advocacy. Carey, *On the Margins of Citizenship,* 112–13.

162. Grant's family had more resources than some; in 1860, his mother owned $800 worth of real estate and $500 in personal property. Nonetheless, their income had been modest enough that Grant qualified for full state funding at the asylum. His trail, as well as that of his family, goes cold after the 1880 census. SDR, vol. 2, entry 46. Bureau of the Census, *Eighth Census, 1860,* New York, Jefferson County, Watertown, sheet 128; *Ninth Census, 1870,* New York, Jefferson County, Watertown, sheet 19; *Tenth Census, 1880,* New York, Jefferson County, Watertown, Enum. Dist. no. 148, sheet 21.

163. According to census records, no one besides Robert lived with Helen James after her husband died. Paterson's parents also employed a farm laborer at times; only when her father reached the age of seventy-two and her mother (age sixty-two) developed diabetes did they finally recruit a housekeeper. Robert Jeffries: SDR, vol. 2, entry 80; Bureau of the Census, *Ninth Census, 1870,* New York, Onondaga County, Pompey, sheet 3; *Tenth Census, 1880,* New York, Onondaga County, Pompey, Enum. Dist. no. 192, sheet 16; *Twelfth Census, 1900,* New York, Onondaga County, Pompey, Enum. Dist. no. 67, sheet 1; New York, *Almshouse Census,* Onondaga County, 1911, Record no. 6025. Fanny Paterson: SDR, vol. 2, entry 251. *Seventh Census, 1850,* Illinois, Morgan County, sheet 89; *Eighth Census, 1860,* Illinois, Hancock County, La Harpe, sheet 737; *Ninth Census, 1870,* Illinois, Warren County, Ellison, sheet 10; *Tenth Census, 1880,* Illinois, Warren County, Ellison, Enum. Dist. no. 286, sheet 15.

164. SDR, vol. 2, entry 2; SDR, vol. 5, entry 1; SPE, vol. 1, p. 37. Bureau of the Census, *Eighth Census, 1860,* New York, Onondaga County, Geddes, sheet 167; *Ninth Census, 1870,* District of Columbia, Washington County, Washington City, sheet 45; *Tenth Census, 1880,* New York, Onondaga County, Geddes, Enum. Dist. no. 183, sheet 184; *Twelfth Census, 1900,* New York, Onondaga County, Syracuse, Enum. Dist. no. 171, sheet 6.

165. Orson Cobb: SDR, vol. 2, entry 314; Bureau of the Census, *Ninth Census, 1870*, New York, Wayne County, Galen, sheet 97; U.S. Bureau of the Census, *1880 Schedule of Defectives, Dependent, and Delinquent Classes*, New York, Cayuga County, Brutus, Enum. Dist. no. 114, sheet 561; *Tenth Census, 1880*, New York, Wayne County, Clyde, Enum. Dist. no. 145, sheet 50. See also SDR, vol. 2, entries 3, 32, 384; SDR, vol. 5, entry 3; *Tenth Census, 1880*, Pennsylvania, Philadelphia County, Philadelphia, Enum. Dist. no. 229, sheet 23. SDR, vol. 2, entry 352; SDR, vol. 5, entry 10; *Ninth Census, 1870*, New York, New York County, New York, sheet 1.

166. While such pupils often came from large families, as might be expected for farmers, few had siblings remain for long after discharge; instead, they generally lived with parents and, sometimes, farm laborers or servants as well. Farm families may also have chosen to retain more able, yet still idiotic, children rather than send them to the asylum. Blackie, "Disabled Revolutionary War Veterans," 128–29; David B. Danbom, *Born in the Country: A History of Rural America*, 2nd ed. (Baltimore: Johns Hopkins University Press, 2006), 87.

167. SDR, vol. 2, entry 280; Bureau of the Census, *Ninth Census, 1870*, New York, Broome County, Union, sheet 50; *Tenth Census, 1880*, New York, Broome County, Union, Enum. Dist. no. 58, sheet 4; New York, *Almshouse Census*, Chenango County, 1873, Record no. 34.

Chapter Two

1. New York State Custodial Asylum for Feeble-Minded Women, *Fourteenth Annual Report of the Managers of the State Custodial Asylum for Feeble-Minded Women at Newark, N.Y. for the Year Ending Sept. 30, 1898 to the Legislature of 1899* (Albany: Weed, Parsons, and Co., 1899), 4 (hereafter cited as Newark Asylum, *Annual Report*).

2. Syracuse Descriptive Register, vol. 4, p. 264, Syracuse State School, Admission, Discharge, Death, and Transfer Records, 1851–1945, Descriptive Registers, 1851–1913 (Acc. B1647, Subseries 1) (hereafter SDR); Syracuse Admission Registers, vol. 5, p. 69, Syracuse State School, Admission, Discharge, Death, and Transfer Records, 1851–1945, Admission Registers, 1851–1920 (Acc. B1647, Subseries 2) (hereafter SAR), both held at NYSA, Albany, NY.

3. Bureau of the Census, *Twelfth Census, 1900*, New York, Onondaga County, Syracuse, Enum. Dist. no. 171, sheet 1; *Thirteenth Census, 1910*, New York, Wayne County, Arcadia, Enum. Dist. no. 124, sheet 7.

4. In the late nineteenth century, charity officials and asylum superintendents began using "feeble-minded" as a catchall term for people previously referred to as idiots or imbeciles. Instead, "idiot," "imbecile," "moron," and, eventually, "borderline" came to represent a hierarchy within the larger category of people labeled "feeble-minded." For eugenicists, physical "stigmata of degeneracy" such as crossed eyes, cleft palate, irregular teeth, facial asymmetry, grimaces, or other physical impairments indicated mental weakness and aberrant morals, and vice versa. At the turn of the twentieth century, feeble-mindedness would also become associated with criminality. In 1963, Mark

Haller noted the central role that state idiot asylums and institutions for the feeble-minded played in laying the groundwork for the eugenics movement. Until recently, however, most scholars have started their accounts in 1883, when Francis Galton coined the term "eugenics." In recent years, scholars such as Sharon Snyder, David Mitchell, and Nicole Rafter have pushed back the origins of the eugenics movement to the Civil War years and even earlier. Snyder and Mitchell, "Out of the Ashes of Eugenics," 84–86; Trent, *Inventing the Feeble Mind*, 5, 80; Tyor and Bell, *Caring for the Retarded*, 26; Bogdan, *Picturing Disability*, 76–77, 83; Rafter, *Creating Born Criminals*, 36, 41, 49; Rembis, *Defining Deviance*, 1–8; Mark H. Haller, *Eugenics: Hereditarian Attitudes in American Thought* (1963; reprint, New Brunswick, NJ: Rutgers University Press, 1984), chaps. 3–4 passim; Daniel Kevles, *In the Name of Eugenics: Genetics and the Uses of Human Heredity* (Cambridge, MA: Harvard University Press, 1995), xiii; Stephen Jay Gould, *The Mismeasure of Man*, rev. and expanded ed. (New York: Norton, 1996); Sharon L. Snyder and David T. Mitchell, *Cultural Locations of Disability* (Chicago: University of Chicago Press, 2006), 5, 26–28.

5. Martin W. Barr, "The Imperative Call of Our Present to Our Future," *Journal of Psycho-Asthenics* 7 (1902): 5–8.

6. Although generation after generation of superintendents claimed that they were receiving more pupils with multiple and severe impairments, little evidence exists to support these complaints. New York State Asylum for Idiots, *First Annual Report of the Trustees of the New York State Asylum for Idiots for the Year 1851, Transmitted to the Legislature, January, 1852* (Albany: N.p., 1852), 3 (hereafter cited as NY Asylum, *Annual Report*); Schneider, *History of Public Welfare in New York State*, 368; Trent, *Inventing the Feeble Mind*, 28–29; Ferguson, *Abandoned to Their Fate*, 54–60; SDR, vol. 2; SAR, vols. 3–5.

7. SDR, vol. 2, entry 200.

8. *The Laws of the State of New-York, Passed at the Seventy-Fourth Session of the Legislature* (Albany: E. Croswell, 1851), chap. 502, p. 941; Massachusetts Experimental School for Teaching and Training Idiotic Children, *Third and Final Report on the Experimental School for Teaching and Training Idiotic Children; Also, the First Report of the Trustees of the Massachusetts School for Idiotic and Feeble-Minded Youth* (Cambridge, MA: Metcalf and Co., 1852), 9, 11, 36 (hereafter cited as MA School, *Annual Report*); MA School, *Seventh Annual Report, 1856*, 4–5, 11.

9. See, for instance, bakers: SDR, vol. 2, entry 199. Farmers: SDR, vol. 2, entry 323. Shoemakers: SDR, vol. 2, entry 44; Bureau of the Census, *Seventh Census, 1850*, New York, Chenango County, Greene, sheet 53. Unskilled laborers: SDR, vol. 2, entry 205; *Seventh Census, 1850*, New York, Onondaga County, Lafayette, sheet 30. Seamstresses: SDR, vol. 2, entry 63; *Eighth Census, 1860*, New York, Tompkins County, Dryden, sheet 108. Lawyers: SDR, vol. 2, entry 314; Bureau of the Census, *Eighth Census, 1860*, New York, Wayne County, Galen, sheet 117. Merchants: SDR, vol. 2, entry 1; *Seventh Census, 1850*, New York, Rensselaer County, Troy, sheet 139.

10. Directors of the Experimental School for Idiots and Feeble-Minded Children, *First Annual Report of the Directors to the Governor of Illinois, Together with the Report of*

the Superintendent, March 1866 (Springfield, IL: Illinois State Journal Steam Printing Co., 1866), 10 (hereafter cited as IL School, *Annual Report*).

11. The superintendents of the Massachusetts School for Idiotic and Feeble-Minded Youth did not always break down their pupils' origins, but in 1856, 23 percent of students' families paid at least part of their fees. In New York, approximately 30 percent of students were paying pupils during the asylum's first three years (1851–1854). With the exception of 1861–1866, when several wealthy southern families removed their children from New York's asylum, paying pupils comprised between 14 and 20 percent of students until 1875; at that point, the numbers of paying pupils dropped sharply. The families of others contributed toward their children's clothing when able. Following practices established by the American Asylum for the Deaf in Hartford, Connecticut, and the Perkins Institute for the Blind in Boston, Massachusetts, both Howe and Wilbur eagerly admitted paying pupils from states that had not yet established idiot asylums. New York State Asylum for Idiots, *Annual Reports*, 1851–1920; *Laws of the State of New-York*, chap. 502, p. 941; MA School, *First Report, 1851*, 36; *Third Report, 1851*, 9, 11; *Seventh Annual Report, 1856*, 4–5, 11.

12. Families of paying pupils paid a variety of rates, although it is not clear whether this differential reflected the varying levels of care required by their children or differences in relatives' ability or willingness to pay. Gannon's father contributed $112 annually in the 1850s, rising to $150 per year by the late 1870s; Stranger's parents paid $150 each year in the 1850s and $200 annually by the late 1870s. Gannon died in 1898 after a forty-six-year stay, and Stranger passed away in 1881 after twenty-four years. Rachel Gannon: SDR, vol. 2, entry 32; Syracuse State Institution for Feeble-Minded Children, Pupil Evaluation Reports [ca. 1860–1909], vol. 1, p. 48 (Acc. B1666), Box 1, NYSA (hereafter SPE); Bureau of the Census, *Seventh Census, 1850*, New York, New York County, New York, sheet 186; *Eighth Census, 1860*, New York, New York County, New York, sheet 154. James Stranger: SDR, vol. 2, entry 174; *Eighth Census, 1860*, New York, Ontario County, Seneca, sheet 177; *Ninth Census, 1870*, New York, Ontario County, Seneca, sheet 76. Private Pay Register (1853–1880), vol. 1, pp. 14–24, 128–40, Syracuse State Institution for Feeble-Minded Children Private Pay Accounts (Acc. B1684), Box 1, NYSA; New York State Asylum for Idiots, *Annual Reports*, 1851–1920.

13. On skilled trades, see SDR, vol. 2, entries 18 and 40; Bureau of the Census, *Seventh Census, 1850*, New York, New York County, New York, sheet 38, and Washington County, Jackson, sheet 6. On laborers, see SDR, vol. 2, entry 43; *Seventh Census, 1850*, New York, Monroe County, Rochester, sheet 346. For seamstresses, see SDR, vol. 2, entry 139; *Eighth Census, 1860*, New York, Delaware County, Franklin, sheet 76. On farmers, SDR, vol. 2, entries 66 and 175; *Seventh Census, 1850*, New York, Queens County, Jamaica, sheet 76; *Ninth Census, 1870*, New York, Westchester County, Eastchester, sheet 136. For small proprietors, see SDR, vol. 2, entry 46; *Seventh Census, 1850*, New York, Jefferson County, Watertown, sheet 110. Rockman, *Scraping By*.

14. In New York, parents of state-funded pupils at the schools for deaf, blind, and idiotic children had to provide enough clothing to outfit their child for their first six months; after that, the asylum charged maintenance to each child's county, although

some families occasionally contributed toward clothing. The first hints of change came with the Civil War, which temporarily reduced the ranks of paying pupils by a third, mostly southerners whose parents withdrew them from the asylum. Revenues from paying pupils remained constant, however; presumably, Wilbur began charging other families higher rates. Illinois Asylum for Feeble-Minded Children, *Sixth Biennial Report of the Trustees, Superintendent and Treasurer of the Illinois Asylum for Feeble-Minded Children at Lincoln, October 1st, 1876* (Springfield, IL: D. W. Lusk, 1877), 56–57. NY Asylum, *Seventh Annual Report, 1857,* 29. See, for instance, SDR, vol. 2, entries 8, 225, 235. Syracuse Private Pay Register, vol. 1, pp. 34, 40, 50.

15. Samuel Gridley Howe chaired Massachusetts's board. By 1886, a dozen states had established state charity boards. Thomas L. Haskell, *The Emergence of Professional Social Science: The American Social Science Association and the Nineteenth-Century Crisis of Authority* (Urbana: University of Illinois Press, 1977; revised, Baltimore: Johns Hopkins University Press, 2000), 93; Trattner, *From Poor Law to Welfare State,* 81–82; William R. Brock, *Investigation and Responsibility: Public Responsibility in the United States, 1865–1900* (Cambridge: Cambridge University Press, 1984), chap. 4 passim.

16. The New York State Board of Charities was established in 1867. Brock, *Investigation and Responsibility,* chap. 4 passim; Trattner, *From Poor Law to Welfare State,* 81–82, 88; Joan Waugh, *Unsentimental Reformer: The Life of Josephine Shaw Lowell* (Cambridge, MA: Harvard University Press, 1997), 127–29.

17. Louisa Lee Schuyler, *First Annual Report of the State Charities Aid Association* (New York: Slote and Janes, 1873), 16.

18. Brock, *Investigation and Responsibility,* 102–4; Trattner, *From Poor Law to Welfare State,* 114–15.

19. In 1875, the New York State legislature officially barred able-bodied children over one year old from poorhouses. Brock, *Investigation and Responsibility,* 102–4; Trattner, *From Poor Law to Welfare State,* 114–15.

20. All told, seven of the twelve were female. Brooklyn: SDR, vol. 2, entries 755–57; SDR, vol. 5, entries 53–55; SAR, vol. 3, pp. 163–65. New York City: SDR, vol. 5, pp. 52–55; Syracuse State Institution for Feeble-Minded Children, Record of Deaths, 1851–1895, vol. 1, p. 68 (Acc. B1662), NYSA (hereafter Syracuse Death Records). Erie County: SDR, vol. 5, p. 57; SDR, vol. 3, pp. 106–7; SAR, vol. 3, pp. 229–30.

21. Wilbur's successor, James Carson, noted of Butters two years before her discharge: "Uses judgment in planning, cutting, etc. As regards her intellectual capacity, I believe that with instruction she would have been equal in intelligence to the majority of girls of her age." John Weiman: SPE, vol. 1, p. 108. Mary Butters: SDR, vol. 3, p. 105; SAR, vol. 3, p. 228; SPE, vol. 1, p. 130.

22. Once at the asylum, Calhoun proved "willing to work at any kind of work that a boy of his age can do." But since he was a "foundling" with no known relatives, Wilbur's successor, James Carson, had few other options than eventually returning him to the Essex County poorhouse, which he reentered in 1895. NY Asylum, *Seventeenth Annual Report, 1867,* 12; SDR, vol. 4, p. 214; SAR, vol. 5, p. 19.

23. IL Institution, *Twelfth Biennial Report, 1888,* 8.

24. SDR, vol. 2, entry 200; Bureau of the Census, *Ninth Census 1870*, New York, Geneva County, Bethany, sheet 41; *Tenth Census, 1880*, New York, Geneva County, Bethany, Enum. Dist. no. 14, sheet 35. For Wilbur's view of poorhouses, see NY Asylum, *Fourth Annual Report, 1854*, 50; *Tenth Annual Report, 1860*, 18; *Twentieth Annual Report, 1871*, 22. See also Graney, "Hervey Backus Wilbur," 214. See also SDR, vol. 2, entry 539; *State Population Census Schedules, 1915* (NYSA, Albany, NY), Oneida, Rome Ward 2, Assembly District 3, Election District 1, p. 83, www.ancestry.com (accessed 12 June 2012).

25. Walter Goodrich: SDR, vol. 4, p. 89; SDR, vol. 5, entry 98; SAR, vol. 4, p. 196. Millie Landon: SDR, vol. 4, p. 294; SAR, vol. 5, p. 100. IL Institution, *Twelfth Annual Report, 1888*, 15.

26. Goodrich's story is discussed in the chapter. A poor woman had boarded Landon while she attended common school, but without relatives to advocate on her behalf, charity officials decided that "it would be to [Landon's] interest to be placed where she could have careful training and good moral surroundings." Landon remained at the Syracuse asylum for ten years. Like most homeless female pupils, she was transferred to the Custodial Asylum for Feeble-Minded Women in Newark by superintendent James Carson; five years later, officials there "charged [her] with insanity" and sent her to the Richmond County Almshouse, where she presumably died. The fate of the Kovacevich boys remains unclear. Millie Landon: *Almshouse Census*, New York, Richmond County, 1901, Record no. 1866.

27. Near-sighted and prone to "slight trouble with both ankles," Dassler was "never still, full of life & vigor." She never returned home; after she spent eleven years at the New York State Asylum for Idiots, superintendent James Carson transferred her to the Rome State Custodial Asylum. SDR, vol. 4, pp. 180; SAR, vol. 4, p. 284.

28. Straw remained only a brief time, relatively speaking, at the asylum, returning home after three years. By that time, his mother had presumably stabilized the household. Wiebe remained at the New York State Asylum for Idiots for close to two decades and was then transferred to the State Custodial Asylum for Feeble-Minded Women. Harvey Straw: SDR, vol. 4, p. 129; SAR, vol. 4, p. 233. Anna Wiebe: SDR, vol. 4, p. 166; SAR, vol. 4, p. 270.

29. Rudd died of diphtheria only a month after arriving at the asylum. Teesdale, in turn, was discharged after just three years' stay, despite the fact that his mother had died earlier on. He was relatively able upon arrival; he could read somewhat and do some work. Martha Rudd: SDR, vol. 3, p. 107; SAR, vol. 3, p. 230. Calvin Teesdale: SDR, vol. 4, p. 148; SAR, vol. 4, p. 252. Patrick J. Kelly, *Creating a National Home: Building the Veterans' Welfare State* (Cambridge, MA: Harvard University Press, 1997).

30. Despite the prevalence of tuberculosis at the time, few parents were actively identified as having "consumption," to use nineteenth-century parlance, but many had died of consumption. In fact, over 15 percent of pupils who had lost a parent could blame tuberculosis—a rate in line with the overall toll taken by consumption in the second half of the nineteenth century. O'Donnell and Rabinowitz never returned home; instead, they stayed at Syracuse for thirty-two and fourteen years, respectively,

and were then transferred to the Otsego County Poorhouse and the Rome State Custodial Asylum, respectively. Adaline O'Donnell: SDR, vol. 4, p. 249; SAR, vol. 5, p. 54. Bartholomew Rabinowitz: SAR, vol. 8, p. 99. Sheila M. Rothman, *Living in the Shadow of Death: Tuberculosis and the Social Experience of Illness in American History* (New York: BasicBooks, 1994), 131–32.

31. Matthew Frye Jacobson, *Barbarian Virtues: The United States Encounters Foreign Peoples at Home and Abroad, 1876–1917* (New York: Hill and Wang, 2000), chap. 4 passim; Daniel E. Bender, *Sweated Work, Weak Bodies: Anti-sweatshop Campaigns and Languages of Labor* (New Brunswick, NJ: Rutgers University Press, 2004), 5–6; Alan M. Kraut, *Silent Travelers: Germs, Genes, and the "Immigrant Menace"* (Baltimore: Johns Hopkins University Press, 1994), chap. 2 passim; Baynton, "Disability and the Justification of Inequality," 33–58; Baynton, "Defectives in the Land," 31–44; Howard Markel, "'The Eyes Have It,'" 525–60.

32. The original admission forms were generally completed by doctors, judges, superintendents of the poor, and, sometimes, the directors of other charitable institutions. SAR, vols. 1–7; Rafter, *Creating Born Criminals*, 36–41; Brent Ruswick, *Almost Worthy: The Poor, Paupers, and the Science of Charity in America, 1877–1917* (Bloomington: Indiana University Press, 2012), 72–73; Paul A. Lombardo, *Three Generations, No Imbeciles: Eugenics, the Supreme Court, and Buck v. Bell* (Baltimore: Johns Hopkins University Press, 2008), 7–20.

33. Margaret Lambeth: SDR, vol. 3, p. 104; SAR, vol. 3, p. 227; SPE, vol. 1, p. 124; Bureau of the Census, *Ninth Census, 1870*, New York, Monroe County, Rochester, sheet 23; New York, *Almshouse Census*, Monroe County, 1877, Record no. 975. On abuse, see SDR, vol. 2, entry 559; SAR, vol. 5, p. 180.

34. Trattner, *From Poor Law to Welfare State*, 82–83, 86; Stanley, *From Bondage to Contract*, 50–53, 105–6, 124–30; Philip Yale Nicholson, *Labor's Story in the United States* (Philadelphia: Temple University Press, 2004), 104–11.

35. During the 1850s, just 27 percent of pupils came from largely urban areas such as Brooklyn, Rochester, Troy, and Albany. But by the 1870s, roughly half of all new admits came from urban areas. Social Explorer Dataset, Census 1850 and 1890 (Oxford University Press), www.socialexplorer.com (accessed 13 June 2012); SDR, vols. 1–3; SAR, vols. 2–4.

36. New York was ahead of the country as a whole: in 1850, just 15.4 percent of Americans overall lived in urban areas, whereas in 1890, 35.1 percent did.

37. NY Asylum, *Thirty-Second Annual Report, 1882*, 4.

38. NY Asylum, *Tenth Annual Report, 1860*, 20; Dwyer, *Homes for the Mad*, 15–16; D. Rothman, "Perfecting the Prison," 120–28; D. Rothman, *Discovery of the Asylum*, 78–79.

39. SDR, vol. 2, entry 56; Bureau of the Census, *Ninth Census, 1870*, New York, New York County, New York, sheet 38; NY Asylum, *Sixth Annual Report, 1856*, 22.

40. Wetzel's father was a cooper. SDR, vol. 3, p. 52; SAR, vol. 3, p. 163; Bureau of the Census, *Ninth Census, 1870*, New York, Kings County, Brooklyn, sheet 243.

41. Johann and Wilfred Becker: SDR, vol. 2, entries 641, 644; SAR, vol. 3, pp. 51, 52; SPE, vol. 1, p. 78, 274. Bureau of the Census, *Ninth Census, 1870*, New York, Erie

County, Buffalo, sheet 233; *Tenth Census, 1880*, New York, Erie County, Buffalo, Enum. Dist. no. 136, sheet 14; SDR, vols. 2–5; SAR, vols. 1–7.

42. SDR, vols. 2–5; SAR, vols. 1–7; Nicholson, *Labor's Story in the United States*, 110.

43. IL Institution, *Twelfth Biennial Report, 1888*, 15.

44. In 1876, the Illinois legislature began allowing county officials to certify that families were too poor to cover traveling expenses, clothing, and incidentals. By 1890, nearly 60 percent of pupils at the Illinois asylum were county charges. NY Asylum, *Seventeenth Annual Report, 1867*, 12; IL Institution, *Sixth Biennial Report, 1876*, 56–57; *Thirteenth Biennial Report, 1890*, 10.

45. IL Institution, *Sixth Biennial Report, 1876*, 31; *Seventeenth Annual Report, 1867*, 9; *Twenty-Eighth Annual Report, 1878*, 11.

46. Trattner, *From Poor Law to Welfare State*, 88–89.

47. IL Institution, *Twelfth Annual Report, 1888*, 16; Trattner, *From Poor Law to Welfare State*, 115.

48. SDR, vol. 2; SAR, vols. 3–4.

49. Wheeler did not remain for long at the asylum, at least compared to his counterparts. After eight years, he "eloped" or, in other words, left of his own accord, returned for six months during the winter and early spring, and then promptly eloped again. SDR, vol. 3, p. 108; SAR, vol. 3, p. 231.

50. The 1892 New York State census listed both Straw and his mother as farmers and provided no occupation for the other six children, ages fourteen to twenty-eight; all but one was female. SDR, vol. 4, p. 129; SAR, vol. 4, p. 233; New York, *State Census, 1892*, Monroe County, Clarkson, First Ward, sheet 5; Find A Grave, "Robert Thomson Steele (1836–1883)," http://www.findagrave.com/cgi-bin/fg.cgi?page=gr&GSln=STEE&GSpartial=1&GSbyrel=all&GSst=36&GScntry=4&GSsr=1641&GRid=70402778& (accessed 11 July 2014).

51. Johann and Wilfred Becker: SDR, vol. 2, entries 641, 644; SAR, vol. 3, pp. 51, 52; *The Buffalo Directory* (Buffalo: Courier Co. of Buffalo, 1884), 273; *Buffalo City Directory* (Buffalo: Courier Co. of Buffalo, 1893), 292; New York, *State Census, 1892*, Erie County, Buffalo, Eleventh Ward, sheet 168; Bureau of the Census, *Twelfth Census, 1900*, New York, Erie County, Buffalo, Enum. Dist. no. 106, sheet 21; New York, *Almshouse Census*, Erie County, 1918, Record no. 8274.

52. Bagshaw died of epilepsy after ten years in the New York State Asylum for Idiots. Walter Goodrich: SDR, vol. 4, p. 89; SAR, vol. 4, p. 196; New York, *Almshouse Census*, Albany County, 1898, Record no. 3476; Bureau of the Census, *Thirteenth Census, 1910*, New York, Oneida County, Rome, Enum. Dist. no. 81, sheet 5B. Eileen Bagshaw: SDR, vol. 3, p. 86; SAR, vol. 3, p. 192.

53. SDR, vol. 3, p. 38; SAR, vol. 3, p. 148. Bureau of the Census, *Twelfth Census, 1900*, New York, Kings County, New York, Enum. Dist. no. 535, sheet 10; *Thirteenth Census, 1910*, New York, Kings County, New York, Enum. Dist. no. 920, sheet 8B; New York, *Almshouse Census*, Kings County, 1918, Record no. 9852; *Fifteenth Census, 1930*, New York, Richmond County, Farmer Colony, Enum. Dist. no. 43–87, sheet 3A.

54. NY Asylum, *Twenty-Fifth Annual Report, 1875*, 10.

55. Overall, only 29.8 percent of people admitted to the New York State Asylum for Idiots directly from institutions between 1871 and 1880 were eventually discharged, as opposed to 41.3 percent of others admitted during those decades. NY Asylum, *Thirty-First Annual Report, 1881*, 7.

56. IL Institution, *Eighth Biennial Report, 1880*, 11, 14; *Twelfth Biennial Report, 1888*, 15.

57. Isaac N. Kerlin, "Report of the Committee on the Care and Training of the Feeble-Minded," *Proceedings of the National Conference of Charities and Correction at the Fifteenth Annual Session Held in Buffalo, N.Y., July 5–11, 1888* (Boston: Geo. H. Ellis, 1888), 99–100 (hereafter cited as *NCCC Proceedings*).

58. NY Asylum, *Tenth Annual Report, 1860*, 18.

59. NY Asylum, *Twentieth Annual Report, 1870*, 22.

60. NY Asylum, *Eighteenth Annual Report, 1868*, 10; Graney, "Hervey Backus Wilbur," 214.

61. Graney, "Hervey Backus Wilbur," 214; Trent, *Inventing the Feeble Mind*, 80–82.

62. NY Asylum, *Twenty-First Annual Report, 1871*, 12–13.

63. Ibid., 12–13; NY Asylum, *Twenty-Second Annual Report, 1872*, 10–11.

64. Wilbur shared his concerns in correspondence with the Massachusetts-based charity reformer and statistician Edward Jarvis in 1860. Wilbur and the State Board of Charities made attempts between 1868 and 1870 and again in the mid-1870s. He also campaigned for an expansion of the Syracuse campus in 1871 with no luck. NY Asylum, *Eighteenth Annual Report, 1868*, 12; *Nineteenth Annual Report, 1869*, 7–8; *Twentieth Annual Report, 1871*, 7–9, 22; *Twenty-Second Annual Report, 1872*, 10–11; *Twenty-Fourth Annual Report, 1874*, 9; *Twenty-Fifth Annual Report, 1875*, 7; *Twenty-Eighth Annual Report, 1878*, 13; Graney, "Hervey Backus Wilbur," 139.

65. Keyssar, *Out of Work*, 252; Paul T. Ringenbach, *Tramps and Reformers, 1873–1916: The Discovery of Unemployment in New York* (Westport, CT: Greenwood Press, 1973), 114, 117.

66. Keyssar, *Out of Work*, 135–39, 141, 253; Katz, *In the Shadow of the Poorhouse*, 92–93; Stanley, *From Bondage to Contract*, 99–100, 107–37.

67. Trattner, *From Poor Law to Welfare State*, 88–89; Stanley, *From Bondage to Contract*, 135.

68. Although Dugdale's book was often used exclusively to support hereditarian, Social Darwinist, and eugenic arguments, Dugdale actually placed more weight on environmental factors. Rising charity reformer, scientific charity advocate, and newly appointed SBC member Josephine Shaw Lowell heard Dugdale's report at the 1877 meeting of the National Conference of Charities and Correction in Saratoga, New York. Rafter, *Creating Born Criminals*, 36, 38; Tyor and Bell, *Caring for the Retarded*, 56–59; Trent, *Inventing the Feeble Mind*, 71.

69. New York State Board of Charities, *Annual Report of the State Board of Charities* (Albany: Weed, Parsons, and Co., 1876), 288 (hereafter cited as SBC, *Annual Report*). Katz, *In the Shadow of the Poorhouse*, 87.

70. SBC, *Annual Report, 1874*, 100. Anderson was also the founding president of the University of Rochester.

71. Waugh, *Unsentimental Reformer*, 121. On the connections between social reformers and the development of modern social science, see Brock, *Investigation and Responsibility*; Haskell, *Emergence of Professional Social Science*, chap. 2 passim, 85–90, chap. 5 passim; P. Cohen, *A Calculating People*, chaps. 6–7 passim.

72. Waugh, *Unsentimental Reformer*, 85, 94, 111, 117, 138, 150; see also Brock, *Investigation and Responsibility*, 111; Katz, *In the Shadow of the Poorhouse*, 69–71.

73. Lowell, New York State Charities Aid Association, *Fourth Annual Report, 1876*, 27, quoted in Waugh, *Unsentimental Reformer*, 116.

74. S. J. Kleinberg, *Widows and Orphans First: The Family Economy and Social Welfare Policy, 1880–1939* (Urbana: University of Illinois Press, 2006).

75. NY Asylum, *Twenty-Seventh Annual Report, 1877*, 9.

76. NY Asylum, *Eleventh Annual Report, 1861*, 15; MA School, *Eleventh Annual Report, 1859*, 5; IL Institution, *Second Annual Report, 1866*, 19; *Twelfth Biennial Report, 1888*, 15; NY Asylum, *Thirtieth Annual Report, 1880*, 15.

77. Pennsylvania Training School superintendent Isaac N. Kerlin argued at the National Conference of Charities and Correction meeting in 1885 that "the wear and tear of an excitable idiot baby from two to ten years has wrecked many a family, and sent others down to pauperism." Iowa State Asylum for Feeble Minded Children, *Second Biennial Report of the Trustees, Superintendent and Treasurer of the Iowa State Asylum for Feeble Minded Children at Glenwood, November 1st, 1879* (Des Moines: F. M. Milles, 1880), 10; see also Isaac N. Kerlin, "Provision for Idiots: Report of Standing Committee," *Twelfth NCCC Proceedings, 1885*, 173.

78. IL Institution, *Twelfth Annual Report, 1888*, 15–16.

79. Such stories appeared far more frequently in the 1870s and 1880s. For earlier examples, see MA School, *Eleventh Annual Report, 1859*, 5; NY Asylum, *Eleventh Annual Report, 1862*, 15; IL Institution, *Second Annual Report, 1866*, 19; *Fourth Annual Report, 1868*, 15; Howe, *Report to the Legislature of Massachusetts*, 51–52.

80. Rafter, *Creating Born Criminals*, 41; William Rhinelander Stewart, *The Philanthropic Work of Josephine Shaw Lowell* (New York: Macmillan, 1911; reprint, Montclair, NJ: Patterson Smith, 1974), 116.

81. Lowell described her report as "extracts" from Hoyt's "Report on the Causes of Pauperism" with, of course, quite a bit of editorializing. She also employed this methodology in her 1878 and 1879 reports on the need for women's reformatories to the State Board of Charities and the National Conference of Charities. Stewart, *Philanthropic Work*, 87–117; Rafter, *Creating Born Criminals*, 41; Josephine Shaw Lowell, "One Means of Preventing Pauperism," *NCCC Proceedings* 6 (1879): 189–200.

82. New York Asylum for Idiots, *Twenty-Eighth Annual Report of the New York Asylum for Idiots for the Year 1878* (Syracuse, NY: Moser, Truax, and DeGolia, 1891), 13–14.

83. Rafter contends that Lowell defined feeble-minded women as "born criminals" who posed a "biological threat to society." But although hereditarianism clearly shaped Lowell's arguments in favor of custodial provisions for feeble-minded women, and although she emphasized the relationship among criminality, degeneracy, and dependency in her speeches on reformatories, she does not appear to have connected

criminality with feeble-mindedness. Rafter, *Creating Born Criminals*, 36, 41, 49; Tyor and Bell, *Caring for the Retarded*, 69.

84. Hervey B. Wilbur, "Status of the Work: New York," *Proceedings of the Association of Medical Officers of American Institutions for Idiotic and Feeble-Minded Persons* (1879), 100.

85. Graney, "Hervey Backus Wilbur," 100–102, 129–35, 140–49, 152–58.

86. SBC, *Annual Report, 1882*, 149–51.

87. Lillian Mallard: SDR, vol. 2, entry 528; SPE, vol. 1, p. 64. Lucy Halloran: SDR, vol. 2, entry 523.

88. NY Asylum, "Report of Special Committee," *Thirtieth Annual Report, 1880,* 11. See also NY Asylum, *Thirty-Second Annual Report, 1882,* 14–15, and *Thirty-Fourth Annual Report, 1884,* 20; Newark Asylum, *First Annual Report, 1885,* 10, 11.

89. Rafter, *Creating Born Criminals*, 46.

90. See, for instance, SDR, vol. 2, entry 425; SDR, vol. 2, entry 411; Newark Asylum, *Fourth Annual Report, 1888,* 5. On poorhouses sending women who were not feeble-minded, see NY Asylum, "Report of Special Committee," *Thirtieth Annual Report, 1880,* 9; *Thirty-Second Annual Report, 1882,* 14, 15. On inmates with epilepsy, see Newark Asylum, *Sixth Annual Report, 1890,* 10; *Seventh Annual Report, 1891,* 20; *Twelfth Annual Report, 1896,* 13; *Thirteenth Annual Report, 1897,* 8, 26–27; *Fourteenth Annual Report, 1898,* 5–6; *Thirty-First Annual Report, 1915,* 5, 7, 30.

91. Wages at the Newark asylum were significantly lower and hours were longer than at other nearby jobs. In 1906, for instance, the gardener received $50 per month but could earn $75 elsewhere. Ferguson, *Abandoned to Their Fate*, 72–75; NY Asylum, *Thirty-First Annual Report, 1881,* 4. See also Newark Asylum, *Seventh Annual Report, 1891,* 19–20; *Fifteenth Annual Report, 1899,* 20–21; *Twenty-Second Annual Report, 1906,* 11–12; *Twenty-Sixth Annual Report, 1910,* 12; *Thirtieth Annual Report, 1914,* 9–10. "Report of Board of Managers to the Governor," 9 April 1907 and 6 October 1909, and "Report of Visitation and Inspection," 8 March 1911, Monthly Reports and Minutes of Meetings of Boards of Managers of State Institutions (1902–1914) (Acc. A0283-78), Box 9, Newark Asylum Board Minutes, NYSA.

92. Trent, *Inventing the Feeble Mind*, 105.

93. On reformers' concerns about inmate care in poorhouses, see, for instance, SBC, *Annual Report, 1869*, lxx. On the growth of inmate care in asylums, see Trent, *Inventing the Feeble Mind*, 83–84, 104–5; Ferguson, *Abandoned to Their Fate*, 71–75.

94. SBC, *Annual Report, 1879*, 284.

95. Newark Asylum, *Third Annual Report, 1887,* 14–15; *Fifth Annual Report, 1889,* 6; *Fifteenth Annual Report, 1899,* 21; *Twenty-Third Annual Report, 1907,* 36.

96. Newark Asylum, *Second Annual Report, 1886,* 7; *Ninth Annual Report, 1893,* 12–13.

97. In 1907, the superintendent and the board began endorsing "outdoor work best suited to our inmates, the most pleasant and most healthful." This move was part of a campaign to gain more land, which they suggested would enable the asylum to produce its own supply of fruit and vegetables. Newark Asylum, *Twenty-Third Annual Report, 1907,* 9, 40; *Twenty-Fifth Annual Report, 1909,* 30–31. "Report of Visitation and Inspection," October 1907, Newark Asylum Board Minutes.

98. Although it is hard to compare the average weekly cost of care between institutions, Newark averaged $2.38 per person per week between 1880 and 1898 and $2.77 per week (excluding clothing) between 1895 and 1920. In contrast, the Syracuse asylum averaged $3.46 per person per week (excluding clothing) between 1878 and 1920 and $3.53 per week for board, instruction, and clothing between 1889 and 1911. Data from NY Asylum, *Annual Reports*, 1878–1920; Newark Asylum, *Annual Reports*, 1880–1920; Newark Asylum, *Twenty-Fifth Annual Report*, 1909, 30–31.

99. Newark Asylum, *First Annual Report*, 1885, 7.

100. In total, women discharged as not requiring custodial care, not imbecilic, much improved, and improved accounted for 61 of the 599 discharges (10.18 percent) between 1894 and 1920 (most women were classed as "improved"—39, or 6.51 percent). Newark Asylum, *Eighth Annual Report*, 1892, 24; *Tenth Annual Report*, 1894, 23–24; *Twenty-Eighth Annual Report*, 1912, 8. Data from Newark Asylum, *Annual Reports*, 1894–1920.

101. The next largest group of discharges from Newark between 1894 and 1920 comprised inmates deemed insane (18.70 percent), chronic invalids (2.17 percent), epileptics (0.83 percent), helpless cripples (0.67 percent), and those in need of a surgical operation (0.67 percent). Data from Newark Asylum, *Annual Reports*, 1894–1920; NY Asylum, *Annual Reports*, 1882–1920.

102. The Newark asylum did not have a commitment law until 1914. Consequently, parents or friends could remove inmates at will, but only after fulfilling the strict criteria established by the board and superintendent. In addition, many inmates had no relatives with whom they could live. In 1909, for instance, relatives gained the release of just 7 inmates out of a total population of 817; between 1894 and 1920, only 139 (23.20 percent of the 599 inmates discharged) returned to family or friends. In addition, one woman escaped from the institution in 1915 with help from her brother; the siblings then fled immediately to another state. Seven women in total absconded from the asylum between 1894 and 1920 (1.17 percent of discharges), while six were discharged after gaining writs of habeas corpus. NY Asylum, "Report of the Special Committee," *Twenty-Ninth Annual Report*, 1879, 13; Newark Asylum, *Twenty-Fifth Annual Report*, 1909, 29. (Names changed by Rafter), 19 June 1894, New York State Board of Charities Correspondence (Acc. 1977-1978), vol. 42, p. 199; quoted in Rafter, *Creating Born Criminals*, 45n56; see also 40–44; Newark Asylum, *Thirty-First Annual Report*, 1915, 29. Data on removals and elopements from Newark Asylum, *Annual Reports*, 1894–1920.

103. Tyor and Bell, *Caring for the Retarded*, 62; Trent, *Inventing the Feeble Mind*, 75–76, 81–82; Isaac N. Kerlin "Report of the Committee on Provision for Idiotic and Feeble-minded Persons," *Thirteenth NCCC Proceedings*, 1886, 291; Charles T. Wilbur, "Institutions for the Feeble-Minded: The Result of Forty Years' Effort in Establishing Them in the United States," *Fifteenth NCCC Proceedings*, 1888, 111.

104. Newark Asylum, *Sixth Annual Report*, 1890, 16.

105. Trent, *Inventing the Feeble Mind*, 81–84; Tyor and Bell, *Caring for the Retarded*, 62–65.

106. The Pennsylvania Training School served both paying and state-funded pupils. Kerlin, "Provision for Idiots, 162.

107. S. J. Barrows, "Discussion on Provision for the Feeble-Minded," *Fifteenth NCCC Proceedings, 1888*, 400. Barrows was the editor of the *Christian Register*. See also Kerlin, "Report of the Committee on Provision for Idiotic and Feebleminded Persons," 292.

108. Trent, *Inventing the Feeble Mind*, 64; Tyor and Bell, *Caring for the Retarded*, 76.

109. Kerlin, "Provision for Idiots, 162.

110. As with the Newark asylum, New York legislators intended for the Rome State Custodial Asylum to permanently contain "unteachable" adults at minimal cost and thereby protect society from the "burden" and "menace" of feeble-mindedness; initially, lawmakers and charity officials envisioned that Rome would serve a largely if not entirely male population. NY Asylum, *Thirtieth Annual Report, 1880*, 14; *Thirty-First Annual Report, 1881*, 8; *Thirty-Second Annual Report, 1882*, 5, 11.

111. Reformers working in Appalachia, with immigrants, and with Native Americans likewise sought to use handiwork as a form of rehabilitation. NY Asylum, *Forty-Ninth Annual Report, 1899*, 28–29; *Fiftieth Annual Report, 1900*, 35–36; Trent, *Inventing the Feeble Mind*, 109; Eileen Boris, *Art and Labor: Ruskin, Morris, and the Craftsman Ideal in America* (Philadelphia: Temple University Press, 1988); Jane E. Simonsen, *Making Home Work: Domesticity and Native American Assimilation in the American West, 1860–1919* (Chapel Hill: University of North Carolina Press, 2006).

112. NY Asylum, *Thirty-Eighth Annual Report, 1888*, 8; George G. Tarbell, "Status of the Work before the People and Legislatures: Massachusetts," *Proceedings of the Association of Medical Officers of American Institutions for Idiotic and Feeble-Minded Persons, Session: Barre, Mass., June 1880* (Philadelphia: J. B. Lippincott, 1880), 163 (hereafter cited as *AMO Proceedings*).

113. NY Asylum, *Annual Reports, 1884–1920*.

114. Yet Carson also routinely rejected many epileptic, low-grade, and multiply disabled inmates, and transferred "unteachable" inmates to the county poorhouses and the Rome asylum. NY Asylum, *Thirtieth Annual Report, 1880*, 14–15; *Thirty-Fifth Annual Report, 1885*, 20; *Thirty-Sixth Annual Report, 1886*, 19; *Thirty-Seventh Annual Report, 1887*, 20; *Thirty-Eighth Annual Report, 1888*, 21; *Thirty-Ninth Annual Report, 1889*, 22; *Forty-Fourth Annual Report, 1894*, 32–33; *Forty-Eighth Annual Report, 1898*, 23; *Fifty-Second Annual Report, 1902*, 12; *Fifty-Eighth Annual Report, 1908*, 36; *Sixty-Second Annual Report, 1912*, 11; *Sixty-Ninth Annual Report, 1918–1919*, 7; Trent, *Inventing the Feeble Mind*, 81.

115. NY Asylum, *Thirty-Second Annual Report, 1882*, 4; *Thirty-Fifth Annual Report, 1885*, 21.

116. NY Asylum, *Fiftieth Annual Report, 1900*, 35–36.

117. NY Asylum, *Thirty-Eighth Annual Report, 1888*, 27–28.

118. Based on his research, Carson acknowledged that "Mongolianism must be due, at least usually, to other than hereditary influences. So large a number as is shown by the statistics being last born, it would seem as if some inertia or lack of the essential vitality in the procreating powers of the mother during the last years of the child-bearing period might safely be considered a cause of imbecility of the Mongolian type." NY Asylum, *Thirty-Sixth Annual Report, 1886*, 21–22; *Forty-Sixth Annual*

Report, 1896, 36–39; *Forty-Eighth Annual Report*, 1898, 33–35; *Fifty-Sixth Annual Report*, 1905, 30, 36–37; *Sixty-First Annual Report*, 1911. See also Tyor and Bell, *Caring for the Retarded*, 60–61, 94–97.

119. NY Asylum, *Thirty-Sixth Annual Report*, 1886, 21; *Forty-Eighth Annual Report*, 1898, 39. See also *Thirty-Ninth Annual Report*, 1889, 21; *Fifty-Fourth Annual Report*, 1904, 29.

120. For Cobb's views, see NY Asylum, *Sixty-Second Annual Report*, 1912, 7–8; *Sixty-Fourth Annual Report*, 1914, 23–25; *Sixty-Sixth Annual Report*, 1915–1916, 4. Cobb did support discharging male pupils during World War I, but attributed their success in obtaining well-paid work to the "present unusual labor conditions." NY Asylum, *Sixty-Sixth Annual Report*, 1915–1916, 3; *Sixty-Seventh Annual Report*, 1916–1917, 12, 15; *Sixty-Ninth Annual Report*, 1918–1919, 13; *Seventieth Annual Report*, 1919–1920, 19.

121. These calculations are based on NY Asylum, *Annual Reports*, 1886–1920.

122. Neither Halford nor Ramsey came from institutions, nor did either seem to have come from a disrupted family. The New York State Asylum for Idiots was renamed the Syracuse State Institution for Feeble-Minded Children in 1891. Maud Halford: SDR, vol. 2, entry 499; SPE, vol. 1, p. 23; Bureau of the Census, *Twelfth Census, 1900*, New York, Erie County, Buffalo, Enum. Dist. no. 270, sheet 2. Irma Ramsey: SDR, vol. 3, p. 160; SDR, vol. 5, p. 76; SAR, vol. 3, p. 284; SPE, vol. 1, p. 135. On laundry work, see SDR, vol. 2, entry 528; SPE, vol. 1, p. 64.

123. Keene was an orphan whose wealthy uncle housed her prior to her arrival at the Syracuse asylum. Lancaster came from a seemingly intact farm family. Sybil Keene: SDR, vol. 1, entry 560, and vol. 5, p. 22; SPE, vol. 1, p. 115; New York, *Almshouse Census*, Orange County, 1925, Record no. 918. Lisa Lancaster: SDR, vol. 3, p. 16, and vol. 5, p. 40; SAR, vol. 3, p. 123; SPE, vol. 1, p. 235.

124. George G. Tarbell, "Status of the Work before the People and Legislatures: Massachusetts," *AMO Proceedings*, 1882, 271.

125. In 1895, Whitman turned up in a Brooklyn charities office trying to find his family and a new job. He had apparently lost touch with his sisters during his stay at the asylum, but retained his committal letter from 1879. The *Brooklyn Daily Eagle*'s coverage quickly reunited him with his relatives. NY Asylum, *Forty-Second Annual Report*, 1892, 25; *Forty-Fifth Annual Report*, 1895, 26; "Adolphus Whitman's Case: He Is a Credit to the Institution That Reared Him," *Brooklyn Daily Eagle*, 8 December 1895, 4, Syracuse Development Center Clipping Files (Acc. B1656), Box 1, NYSA; "His Family Found Again: Adolphus Whitman United with His Long Lost Relatives," *Brooklyn Daily Eagle*, 9 December 1895, 1; SDR, vol. 3, p. 205; SAR, vol. 4, p. 34.

126. "Very useful on the farm," see SDR, vol. 3, p. 69; SAR, vol. 3, p. 175; SPE, vol. 1, p. 103. On errands, see SDR, vol. 3, p. 39; SAR, vol. 3, p. 145; SPE, vol. 1, p. 179. On "do many useful things very nicely," see SDR, vol. 3, p. 5; SAR, vol. 3, p. 112; SPE, vol. 1, p. 213.

127. Carson described Willie as "sadly afflicted by a moderate degree of paralysis and physical infirmities, which gave him an awkward, unsteady gait and uncouth appearance." He noted that Willie had nonetheless "learned to talk so that he could be understood by those accustomed to his manner of speech and to read books and papers understandingly." NY Asylum, *Forty-Eighth Annual Report*, 1898, 25.

128. NY Asylum, *Sixtieth Annual Report, 1910*, 26–27. And in the late 1910s, superintendent Cobb introduced a merit system that allowed for trolley rides and trips to the movies. NY Asylum, *Sixty-Eighth Annual Report, 1917–1918*, 12.

129. Eileen Kavanaugh: SDR, vol. 3, p. 64; SAR, vol. 3, p. 170; SPE, vol. 1, p. 66. Clara Heinrich: SDR, vol. 3, p. 138; SAR, vol. 3, p. 262; SPE, vol. 1, p. 238. On pupils with palsy and chorea, see SDR, vol. 2, entry 622; SAR, vol. 3, p. 31; SPE, vol. 1, p. 91. On blind pupils, see SDR, vol. 2, entry 683; SAR, vol. 3, p. 91; SPE, vol. 1, p. 79.

130. Like virtually all asylum superintendents at this point, Bernstein held an MD and believed fervently in the moral benefits of work. Unlike most, he rejected most negative eugenics practices such as sterilization and expressed skepticism about eugenics in general.

131. Rome State Custodial Asylum, *Sixth Annual Report of the Board of Managers of the Rome State Custodial Asylum at Rome, N.Y., for the Year Ending September 30, 1900, Transmitted to the Legislature January 25, 1901* (Albany: James B. Lyon, 1901), 12, 16, 36; *Fifth Annual Report, 1901*, 38–39; *Ninth Annual Report, 1903*, 114 (hereafter cited as Rome Asylum, *Annual Report*).

132. Those inmates deemed "crippled" mostly seem to have done sewing. The Rome asylum still had the merit and demerit system in 1915; by this time, male inmates could also cash in their merits to acquire permits to go into the city of Rome. Rome Asylum, *Ninth Annual Report, 1903*, 50–51; *Tenth Annual Report, 1904*, 58, 64, 66; *Twelfth Annual Report, 1906*, 34; *Fourteenth Annual Report, 1908*, 21; *Twenty-First Annual Report, 1915*, 25–26; Trent, *Inventing the Feeble Mind*, 109.

133. SDR, vols. 2–5; SAR, vols. 1–6.

134. SDR, vol. 2, entry 604; SAR, vol. 3, p. 12; Syracuse Death Records, vol. 1. p. 47.

135. At 62.7 percent, the death rate for people with epilepsy nearly equaled that for "idiots." Ferguson argues that Bernstein did not care about the fate of "low-grade" inmates and saw the asylum's "custodial" designation as a threat to funding and his professional status. Ferguson, *Abandoned to Their Fate*, 102, 104, 113–14, 118–19, 123–27.

136. Rafter, *Creating Born Criminals*, 42; George W. Cowles, ed., *Landmarks of Wayne County, New York* (Syracuse, NY: D. Mason, 1895), 367; NY Asylum, "Report of the Special Committee," *Twenty-Ninth Annual Report, 1879*, 13. Newark Asylum, *Second Annual Report, 1886*, 9; *Fifth Annual Report, 1889*, 9; *Eighth Annual Report, 1892*, 14. "Report of Visitation and Inspection," 9 August 1911, Monthly Minutes and Reports (Acc. A0283-78), Box 9, Newark Asylum Board Minutes, NYSA.

137. "The State's Charities: Rome State Custodial Asylum," *New York Tribune*, 4 October 1897, Syracuse Development Center Clipping Files (Acc. B1656), Box 1, NYSA.

138. "The State's Charities"; Rome Asylum, *Fourth Annual Report, 1898*, 29, 32–33.

139. Ferguson, *Abandoned to Their Fate*, 91–93; Rome Asylum, *Fourth Annual Report, 1898*, 11.

140. Rome Asylum, *Twenty-First Annual Report, 1915*, 17.

141. Rome Asylum, *Ninth Annual Report, 1903*, 16; *Tenth Annual Report, 1904*, 64–65; *Eleventh Annual Report, 1905*, 43; *Twelfth Annual Report, 1906*, 34; *Thirteenth Annual Report, 1907*, 34; Trent, *Inventing the Feeble Mind*, 208.

142. Making matters worse, attendants faced excruciatingly long hours even when compared with their counterparts at other state asylums, working from 5:30 A.M. to 8:00 or 10:00 P.M. Turnover, consequently, was high. After years of advocacy, Bernstein managed to reduce their hours, while also giving them half of their evenings off plus sick time and two weeks of vacation; he also increased their salaries by 40 percent. In addition, he established dedicated recreation rooms and separate rooms for married couples, bus service between the asylum and the city of Rome, and, in 1920, an employee governance council to advise him on pension policies and social activities. "Meeting of the [Rome Asylum] Board of Managers," 1 February 1909, 3–4; [Report of the Board of Managers of Rome Asylum], 2 August 1909, p. 2, both from Rome Asylum Board Minutes; Rome Asylum, *Second Annual Report*, 1896, 39–40; *Herald*, 1 April 1914, 6; Charles Bernstein, "Training School for Attendants for the Feeble-Minded," *Journal of Psycho-Asthenics* 12 (1907): 31–43, 88–92; Rome Asylum, *Eighth Annual Report*, 1902, 11; *Ninth Annual Report*, 1903, 18; *Twenty-First Annual Report*, 1915, 22–24; Trent, *Inventing the Feeble Mind*, 128.

143. "Newark Women's Asylum: Report of the State Board of Charities Committee" [ca. spring 1893], Syracuse Development Center Clipping Files (Acc. B1656), Box 1, NYSA; SBC, *Annual Report*, 1894, xlii–xliv.

144. Rafter, *Creating Born Criminals*, 45–46; Newark Asylum, *Sixth Annual Report*, 1890, 16.

145. Newark Asylum, *Eighth Annual Report*, 1892, 26–27; *Ninth Annual Report*, 1893, 17; *Tenth Annual Report*, 1894, 18, 21, 23.

146. He deemed only 8–10 percent of inmates capable of benefiting from classes in 1907, which they attended in a hall with no desks. Seasonal activities included Halloween parties, Christmas cantatas performed by the inmates, musical programs for Easter, a Fourth of July picnic, and a September field day. Newark Asylum, *Twenty-Third Annual Report*, 1907, 36–37.

147. Newark Asylum, *Twenty-Seventh Annual Report*, 1911, 22; *Thirtieth Annual Report*, 1914, 6; "Report of Visitation and Inspection," 4 January 1911, 1 February 1911, 8 March 1911, 9 August 1911, and 1 August 1912, Newark Asylum Board Minutes.

148. Newark Asylum, *Twenty-Seventh Annual Report*, 1911, 42.

149. "Report of Visitation and Inspection," 6 June 1912, Newark Asylum Board Minutes. By 1916, Nevin had added classes in rug making, mattress making, chair caning, and cement work. *Twenty-Seventh Annual Report*, 1911, 22; *Twenty-Eighth Annual Report*, 1912, 6; *Twenty-Ninth Annual Report*, 1913, 26; *Thirtieth Annual Report*, 1914, 35; *Thirty-Second Annual Report*, 1916, 17.

150. "Report of Visitation and Inspection," 4 April 1912, Newark Asylum Board Minutes.

151. Newark Asylum, *Thirtieth Annual Report*, 1914, 7.

152. Henry M. Lechtrecker, [extract of February 1907 report to State Board of Charities on "Industrial Efforts"]; Henry M. Lechtrecker to Edwin Sanford, 4 June 1907; and Homer Folks to E. V. Stoddard, 11 February 1907; all from Newark Asylum Board Minutes.

153. Lechtrecker learned from Warnecke that "the matron is a chief offender and that much of the product is going to her immediate friends in the village of Newark, and at

Binghamton N.Y." Lechtrecker to Sanford, 4 June 1907, Newark Asylum Board Minutes; Cowles, *Landmarks of Wayne County*, 374.

154. Lechtrecker, "Industrial Efforts," Newark Asylum Board Minutes. Lechtrecker noted, "My personal observation in the premises is that they feel that they are acting entirely from commendable motives." He also suggested adding rug weaving and mat making since they could not be done in private and "could be better regulated." [Newark Asylum Board report], May 1907; [Newark Asylum Board report], 2 July 1907; Board of Managers to Charles E. Hughes, 19 June 1907, Newark Asylum Board Minutes; "Minutes of Adjourned Regular Meeting," 23 September 1909; all from Newark Asylum Board Minutes.

155. Lechtrecker, "Industrial Efforts," Newark Asylum Board Minutes; Henry M. Lechtrecker, [extract of February 1907 report to State Board of Charities on "Clothing" and "Observations and Defects"], Newark Asylum Board Minutes; "Report of Visitation and Inspection," 10 November 1909, 13 September 1911, and 10 October 1912; all from Newark Asylum Board Minutes.

156. Newark Asylum, *Eleventh Annual Report, 1895*, 21; "Report of Visitation and Inspection," 8 March 1911, Newark Asylum Board Minutes.

157. Flaherty and Hertzfeld never returned home. After eighteen years at the New York State Asylum for Idiots, superintendent Carson transferred Terrence Flaherty to the Rome State Custodial Asylum, where he remained for at least fourteen years. Hertzfeld, meanwhile, spent twenty-three years at the New York State Asylum for Idiots and was then transferred to the State Custodial Asylum for Women at Newark. Terrence Flaherty: SDR, vol. 3, p. 110; SAR, vol. 3, p. 233; Bureau of the Census, *Thirteenth Census, 1910*, New York, Oneida County, Rome, Enum. Dist. no. 81, sheet 5A. Frances Hertzfeld: SDR, vol. 4, p. 192; SAR, vol. 4, p. 296.

158. Despite Percy's inability to do productive work, Wilbur and his successor, Carson, retained Percy at the asylum, likely because her mother was a widow. In 1915, superintendent O. H. Cobb sent her to the Oneida County Poorhouse at age forty-nine. Painter had entered the same poorhouse twenty-two years earlier in 1893 after being discharged from the asylum as an "epileptic idiot." Myra Percy: SDR, vol. 3, p. 149, and vol. 5, p. 64; SAR, vol. 3, p. 273; *Tenth Census, 1880*, New York, Albany County, Albany, Enum. Dist. no. 32, sheet 55; New York, *Almshouse Census*, Oneida County, 1915, Record no. 6014. Arnold Painter: SDR, vol. 3, p. 151; SAR, vol. 3, p. 275; New York, *Almshouse Census*, Oneida County, 1893, Record no. 2333.

Chapter Three

1. "Letter Box: J.C. to Miss Sullivan," *Custodial Herald* 5, no. 4 (1 August 1917): 3. Pseudonyms have been used for inmates of the Rome State Custodial Asylum. The *Herald*, *Custodial Herald*, and *Rome Custodial Herald* are all the same publication.

2. "Colony News," *Herald* 9, no. 7 (1 July 1921): 5; "Letter Box: Mrs. W.F.P. (J. C. Cuyper) to Charles Bernstein," *Herald* 9, no. 11 (1 November 1921): 4.

3. Baynton, "Defectives in the Land," 31–44; Lombardo, *Three Generations, No Imbeciles*, chaps. 2 and 3 passim.

4. Bernstein's father, Abraham Bernstein, was presumably of Jewish descent, although his children were raised as Lutherans, possibly in deference to their mother, Eva Ann Young. The elder Bernstein ran a village store in the central New York town of Carlisle prior to his death. Both parents were "pioneer settlers" in the town. Maxwell C. Montgomery, "Memorial Tribute to Dr. Charles Bernstein," supplement, *Psychiatric Quarterly* 17, no. 1 (March 1943): 38.

5. J. G. Riggs, *Hello Doctor: A Brief Biography of Charles Bernstein, M.D.* (East Aurora, NY: Roycroft, 1936), 10.

6. Montgomery, "Memorial Tribute to Dr. Charles Bernstein," 38.

7. Rome Asylum, *Sixth Annual Report, 1900,* 12, 36. See also *Fifth Annual Report, 1899,* 12.

8. Rome Asylum, *Sixth Annual Report, 1900,* 16, 36. See also *Seventh Annual Report, 1901,* 38–39. On institutions in other states, see Tyor and Bell, *Caring for the Retarded,* 76; Wolf Wolfensberger, *Origin and Nature of Our Institutional Models,* 30, 44, 51; Rafter, *Creating Born Criminals,* 65; Trent, *Inventing the Feeble Mind,* 143–44. Bernstein built upon similar arguments made by his predecessors; in the 1880s, for instance, Ohio superintendent Gustavus Adolphus Doren told state legislators: "Give me the land [about 1,000 acres] and allow me to gather the idiotic and imbecile population now under public care together, and I agree that the institution shall be made self-sustaining, and I will pay back to the state the price of the land.'" A. Byers, "Discussion on Care of the Feeble-Minded," *Proceedings of the National Conference of Charities and Correction* 17 (1890): 441.

9. Inmates at the Rome State Custodial Asylum and the New York State Custodial Asylum for Feeble-Minded Women at Newark seem to have had significantly fewer new clothes than those at the Syracuse State Institution for Feeble-Minded Children. In 1902, for instance, inmates at Rome repaired 2,358 dresses but made only 227 new ones for a population of 142 women. In contrast, inmates in Newark's sewing workshops produced 784 new dresses for a population of 416 women. During the same year, pupils at Syracuse sewed 635 new dresses for the 253 female students. Rome Asylum, *Eighth Annual Report, 1902,* 23, 36–37; Newark Asylum, *Eighteenth Annual Report, 1902,* 6, 10; NY Asylum, *Fifty-Second Annual Report, 1902,* 18, 25–26.

10. Quote from Rome Asylum, *Thirteenth Annual Report, 1907,* 36. For details of inmates' work, see Rome Asylum, *Eleventh Annual Report, 1905,* 44–46; *Twelfth Annual Report, 1906,* 17, 20, 34; [Minutes of the Board of Managers of Rome Asylum], December 1909, pp. 2–3, Monthly Reports and Minutes of Meetings of Board of Managers of State Institutions (1902–1914) (Acc. A0283-78), Box 17, Rome Asylum Board Minutes, NYSA (hereafter Rome Asylum Board Minutes).

11. Rome Asylum, *Ninth Annual Report, 1903,* 50–51; *Tenth Annual Report, 1904,* 58, 64, 66; *Twelfth Annual Report, 1906,* 34; *Fourteenth Annual Report, 1908,* 21; and *Twenty-First Annual Report, 1915,* 25–26; Trent, *Inventing the Feeble Mind,* 109.

12. Ferguson, *Abandoned to Their Fate*; Rome Asylum, *Twelfth Annual Report, 1906,* 31–32. By 1909, inmate labor defrayed more than 25 percent of the cost of maintenance, and by 1914, Bernstein and the board of managers suggested that inmate labor saved the state 25–40 percent of costs. Rome Asylum, *Fifteenth Annual Report, 1909,* 21, 28–40;

[Rome Asylum Board of Managers Report], 5 January 1914, pp. 3–4; Rome Asylum, *Twenty-First Annual Report, 1915,* 33.

13. Philip Ferguson wryly describes the history of Rome as "a tale of 40 colonies and a warehouse." Ferguson, *Abandoned to Their Fate,* 153; Rome Asylum, *Ninth Annual Report, 1903,* 23–25.

14. Charles Bernstein, "Discussion of [Mason paper]," *Proceedings of the New York State Conference of Charities and Correction* 4 (1903): 201, quoted in Ferguson, *Abandoned to Their Fate,* 106.

15. Discussion of A. Gertrude Jacob, "Systematic Physical Training for the Mentally Deficient," *Journal of Psycho-Asthenics* 9, no. 4 (June 1905): 110.

16. Discussion of H. G. Hardt, "Accidents in Institutions for Feeble-Minded and Epileptics," *Journal of Psycho-Asthenics* 13, nos. 1–4 (September 1908–June 1909): 102–3.

17. Rome Asylum, *Thirteenth Annual Report, 1907,* 31. On similar views held by other superintendents, see Henry H. Goddard, "Impressions of European Institutions and Special Classes," *Journal of Psycho-Asthenics* 13, no. 1–4 (September 1908–June 1909): 21; Trent, *Inventing the Feeble Mind,* chap. 5 passim. When Bernstein discharged women past the age of menopause, he tried to discharge only those who could aid their family with their labors. See *Ninth Annual Report, 1903,* 52.

18. Rome Asylum, *Seventeenth Annual Report, 1911,* 40; *Nineteenth Annual Report, 1913,* 16; and *Twentieth Annual Report, 1914,* 13.

19. Rome Asylum, *Sixteenth Annual Report, 1910,* 11, 12; *Seventeenth Annual Report, 1911,* 11, 23; *Documents of the Assembly of the State of New York* (Albany: J. B. Lyon, 1917), 155–58; Rome Asylum, *Eighteenth Annual Report, 1912,* 15; "The Regular Monthly Meeting of the Board of Managers," 3 February 1913, p. 1, Rome Asylum Board Minutes; Trent, *Inventing the Feeble Mind,* 106, 208, 213–14; Ferguson, *Abandoned to Their Fate,* 109–10.

20. Rome Asylum, *Nineteenth Annual Report,* 21. Afterward, he was asked to lecture on mental degeneracy and eugenics at Syracuse University.

21. On familiarity and disability, see Wexler, "Chorea and Community," 495–527; Groce, *Everyone Here Spoke Sign Language;* see also Rome Asylum, *Nineteenth Annual Report,* 22; Trent, *Inventing the Feeble Mind,* 213–14.

22. Trent, *Inventing the Feeble Mind,* 184–92.

23. "Minutes: Address of Welcome, W. W. Swan," *Journal of Psycho-Asthenics* 12, nos. 1–4 (September 1907–June 1908): 68; Discussion of W. E. Fernald, "Farm Colony in Massachusetts," *Journal of Psycho-Asthenics* 7, no. 4 (June 1903): 77; Trent, *Inventing the Feeble Mind,* 105–7.

24. Trent, *Inventing the Feeble Mind,* 296n11.

25. Quote from Rome Asylum, *Tenth Annual Report, 1904,* 23; see also 61–64.

26. Rome Asylum, *Eleventh Annual Report, 1905,* 14–15.

27. Rome Asylum, *Twelfth Annual Report, 1906,* 17.

28. Ferguson, *Abandoned to Their Fate,* 119; Trent, *Inventing the Feeble Mind,* 200.

29. On eugenicists, the phenomenon of "feeble-minded women," and how such fears affected the lives of many girls and women with and without disabilities, see, for

instance, Rembis, *Defining Deviance*; Rafter, *Creating Born Criminals*; Snyder and Mitchell, *Cultural Locations of Disability*; Baynton, *Defectives in the Land*.

30. Orphanages, half-orphan asylums, and prisons for women also employed "cottage" systems. Isaac N. Kerlin, "President's Annual Address," *Proceedings of the Association of Medical Officers of American Institutions for Idiotic and Feeble-Minded Persons* (Philadelphia: J. B. Lippincott, 1892): 275–76; William L. Parry-Jones, "The Model of the Geel Lunatic Colony and Its Influence on the Nineteenth-Century Asylum System in Britain," in *Madhouses, Mad-Doctors, and Madmen: The Social History of Psychiatry in the Victorian Era*, ed. Andrew Scull (Philadelphia: University of Pennsylvania Press, 2015), 201–17.

31. Ada Fitts, "How to Fill the Gap between the Special Classes and Institutions," *Journal of Psycho-Asthenics* 20, nos. 3–4 (March and June 1916): 82–83; "Minutes of the Association [Discussion of Elizabeth E. Farrell, "Results of After-Care Work with Special Class Children"]," *Journal of Psycho-Asthenics* 22, no. 1 (September 1917): 33.

32. "News and Notes," *Journal of Psycho-Asthenics* 20, nos. 1–2 (September and December 1915): 49.

33. In March 1919, the editors outlined the "Colony System" for the benefit of the inmates and other interested parties, explaining that the "privilege of life in the colonies is given only to self respecting girls and boys of reasonable intelligence who wish to make an effort to be self sustaining, law-abiding citizens." "Colony System," *Custodial Herald* 7, no. 3 (1 March 1919): 1; "The Girls' Colony," *Rome Custodial Herald* 2, no. 7 (1 November 1914): 3; Rome Asylum, *Twenty-First Annual Report, 1915*, 19–20, and *Twenty-Third Annual Report, 1917*, 26.

34. In 1919, 19.4 percent of inmates in the asylum were either paroled or in a colony; Bernstein discharged 0.4 percent. Rome Asylum, *Twenty-Fifth Annual Report, 1919*, 14–16.

35. Bernstein established the Adirondack reforestation colonies in conjunction with the State Conservation Commission. These colonies provided savings to both entities, serving as sources of outings for asylum inmates and cheap labor. Rome Asylum, *Nineteenth Annual Report, 1913*, 24; *Twenty-First Annual Report, 1915*, 21–22; *Twenty-Second Annual Report, 1916*, 25.

36. Rome Asylum, *Twenty-Third Annual Report, 1917*, 28.

37. Charles Bernstein, "Self-Sustaining Feeble-Minded," *Journal of Psycho-Asthenics* 22, nos. 3–4 (March and June 1918): 157.

38. McMann was listed in the 1910 census as "Mex" or, more likely, "Mulatto." "School Items," *Rome Custodial Herald* 2, no. 10 (1 February 1915): 6; Bureau of the Census, *Thirteenth Census, 1910*, New York, Oneida County, Rome, 2nd Ward, sheet 12B.

39. "School Items," *Rome Custodial Herald* 2, no. 10 (1 February 1915): 5; "School Items," *Rome Custodial Herald* 4, no. 6 (1 October 1916): 6; "Our Discharges, 'Our Inspiration,'" *Herald* 14, no. 9 (1 September 1916): 5.

40. By the end of the year, residents had earned a grand total of $1,800 in wages. "News and Notes," 50–52; Bernstein, "Self-Sustaining Feeble-Minded," 158.

41. Rome Asylum, *Nineteenth Annual Report, 1913*, 16; *Twenty-Second Annual Report, 1916*, 34.

42. Charles Bernstein, "Colony Care for Isolation and Dependent Cases," *Social Hygiene* 7, no. 1 (January 1921): 52–53.

43. Rome Asylum, *Twenty-First Annual Report, 1915*, 17.

44. "Our Discharges: Our Inspiration," *Herald* 14, no. 9 (1 September 1926): 5.

45. Families were so desperate for servants in 1910 that the Maine Bureau of Industrial and Labor Statistics placed an advertisement in 500 newspapers: "WANTED—10,000 girls to help around the house. Must be honest and willing to work. Good homes for those who suit." David A. Katzmann, *Seven Days a Week: Women and Domestic Service in Industrializing America* (New York: Oxford University Press, 1978), 38; Rome Asylum, *Twenty-First Annual Report, 1915*, 17; *Twenty-Second Annual Report, 1916*, 21–22; and *Twenty-Third Annual Report, 1917*, 25; Charles Bernstein, "A State's Policy towards the Care of the Feeble-Minded," *Journal of Psycho-Asthenics* 16, no. 2 (December 1914): 51–53.

46. After Bernstein opened the working girls' colony in 1914, a "series of anonymous post cards [were] sent to the women who were employing the girls stating that they should be ashamed to employ scab labor, etc., all apparently from one source, a discharged and disgruntled former employee." Rome Asylum, *Twenty-Third Annual Report, 1917*, 28.

47. Bernstein, "Self-Sustaining Feeble-Minded," 160.

48. "Favor Colony Here for Feebleminded," *New York Times*, 27 January 1918, 10.

49. Ward Millias, "Charles Bernstein, 1872–1942: Bernstein as a Humanist," *American Journal of Mental Deficiency* 47 no. 1 (1942–1943): 17–19, quoted in Ferguson, *Abandoned to Their Fate*, 110.

50. Carey, *On the Margins of Citizenship*, 165–69.

51. Rome Asylum, *Twenty-Second Annual Report, 1916*, 28.

52. Ibid., 34; Bernstein, "Self-Sustaining Feeble-Minded," 159.

53. "What Our Boys and Girls Are Doing," *Rome Custodial Herald* 1, no. 2 (1 June 1913): 4; "Puzzledom," *Rome Custodial Herald* 1, no. 3 (1 July 1913): 2; "Our Willing Workers," *Rome Custodial Herald* 1, no. 5 (1 September 1913): 3; "School Items," *Rome Custodial Herald* 1, no. 4 (1 February 1914): 4; "School Items," *Rome Custodial Herald* 2, no. 6 (1 October 1914): 6; "School Items," *Rome Custodial Herald* 2, no. 9 (Holiday Number 1914): 5. In October 1913, Matilda Connor escorted another parolee to the Douglasses' home so that the latter could work there. "Building News," *Rome Custodial Herald* 1, no. 5 (1 September 1913): 6. In 1915, Bernstein suggested that some parolees and colony residents returned because "they preferred to work at the Asylum." Rome Asylum, *Twenty-First Annual Report, 1915*, 19–20.

54. See, for instance, "Letterbox, A.C. to Miss Samson," 7 March 1917, *Rome Custodial Herald* 4, no. 12 (1 April 1917): 4. Most letters were addressed to the matron, Miss Bayne, or the head teacher and editor of the *Herald*, Mary Douglass (no apparent relation to board member James Douglass).

55. Discussion of A. W. Wilmarth, "To Whom May the Term, Feeble-Minded, Be Applied?," *Journal of Psycho-Asthenics* 10, no. 4 (June 1906): 217–18. See also Trent, chap. 5 passim.

56. George H. Knight, "The Feeble-Minded," *Proceedings of the Association of Medical Officers of American Institutions for Idiotic and Feeble-Minded Persons* (Philadelphia: J. B. Lippincott, 1895): 561.

57. Fitts, "How to Fill the Gap," 83.

58. Bernstein, "A State's Policy," 51–53.

59. Anne Moore, *The Feeble-Minded in New York: A Report Prepared for the Public Education Association of New York* (New York: State Charities Aid Association and Special Committee on Provision for the Feeble-Minded, 1911); State of New York, State Board of Charities, Bureau of Analysis and Investigation, *Report on Fifty-Two Border-Line Cases in the Rome State Custodial Asylum* (Albany, 1914) (published in *Eugenics and Social Welfare Bulletin* no. 4); State of New York, State Board of Charities, Bureau of Analysis and Investigation, *Second Report on Fifty-Two Border-Line Cases in the Rome State Custodial Asylum* (Albany, 1915) (published in *Eugenics and Social Welfare Bulletin* no. 4); *Report of the State Commission to Investigate Provision for the Mentally Deficient, Pursuant to the Provisions of Chapter 2727 of the Laws of 1914* (Albany: J. B. Lyon, 1915); Clara Harrison Town and Grace E. Hill, *How the Feeble-Minded Live in the Community: A Report of a Social Investigation of the Erie County Feeble-Minded Discharged from the Rome State School, 1905–1924* (Buffalo: Children's Aid Society, 1930).

60. Trent, *Inventing the Feeble Mind*, 296n11; Kevles, *In the Name of Eugenics*, 82, 129–30 [Report of the Rome Asylum Board of Managers], October 1914, pp. 2–3, Rome Asylum Board Minutes.

61. Joseph P. Byers, "A State Plan for the Care of the Feeble-Minded," *Journal of Psycho-Asthenics* 21, no. 1–2 (September and December 1916): 38.

62. "Minutes of the Association [Discussion of Charles Bernstein, "Self-Sustaining Feeble-Minded," and of Walter Fernald's paper on twenty-five years of discharges]," *Journal of Psycho-Asthenics* 22, no. 1 (September 1917): 41.

63. "Minutes of the Association [Discussion of Charles Bernstein, "Self-Sustaining Feeble-Minded]," *Journal of Psycho-Asthenics* 22, no. 1 (September 1917): 39.

64. E. J. Emerick, "Progress in the Care of the Feeble-Minded in Ohio," *Journal of Psycho-Asthenics* 22, no. 2 (December 1917): 78–79 [President's Address from June 1917 meeting of American Association of Institutions for Feeble Minded].

65. As other superintendents began to imitate Bernstein's programs, he continued to stir up hornets' nests with his decidedly noneugenic views. In 1921, he argued that "in many instances we have seen such matings [between borderline cases] bring forth children the equal of so-called non-tainted stock." Bernstein, "Colony Care, quoted in Trent, *Inventing the Feeble Mind*, 213. W. E. Fernald, "The Burden of Feeble-Mindedness," *Journal of Psycho-Asthenics* 17 (1912): 91, quoted in Graney, "Hervey Backus Wilbur," 191; Tyor and Bell, *Caring for the Retarded*, 124, 127; Trent, *Inventing the Feeble Mind*, 180, 204, 215; Graney, "Hervey Backus Wilbur," 196; Discussion of A. W. Wilmarth, "To Whom May the Term, Feeble-Minded, Be Applied?," 207–8.

66. Trent, *Inventing the Feeble Mind*, 214; "Report to the Directors of the Morgan Memorial Cooperative Industries and Stores," Morgan Memorial (1920–1921) Folder, Box 2, Morgan Memorial—Goodwill Industries Records, Boston University School of Theology Archives, Boston, MA.

67. For the most complete account of the lives of those Rome inmates deemed less able, see Ferguson, *Abandoned to Their Fate*. Bernstein usually refused to release low-grade inmates to their families (even one who worked as a teamster in a local railroad yard before being killed by a train) and punished higher-grade inmates by making them eat with the low-grade inmates and wear the same outfits. Ibid., 114–17, 146–48.

68. "Tied to Tree, Lost Legs," *Washington Post*, 7 December 1906, 11.

69. "What Our Boys and Girls Are Doing," *Rome Custodial Herald* 1, no. 2 (1 June 1913): 4; "School Items," *Rome Custodial Herald* 1, no. 12 (1 April 1914): 2; "School Items," *Rome Custodial Herald* 2, no. 6 (1 October 1914): 6; "Letter Box," L.T. to Mary Douglass, 29 January 1915, *Rome Custodial Herald* 2, no. 11 (1 March 1915): 4; Bureau of the Census, *Thirteenth Census, 1910*, New York, Oswego County, Enum. Dist. no. 104, sheet 5B; *Fourteenth Census, 1920*, New York, Cortland County, New York, Enum. Dist. 12–17, sheet 14B; *Fifteenth Census, 1930*, New York, Cortland County, Enum. Dist. no. 14, sheet 2A; U.S. Selective Service System, in *World War I Selective Service System Draft Registration Cards, 1917–1918* (Washington, DC: NARA, 1917–1918), Entry for L.J.T., Marathon, Cortland County, New York.

70. "Letter Box: M.S. to All at Home," *Custodial Herald* 7, no. 4 (March 1919): 7; "Nurse's Training Class," *Herald* 10, no. 12 (1 December 1922): 6; "Nurses' Training Class," *Herald* 13, no. 3 (1 March 1925): 4; "Girls' Letter Box: T.H. to Miss Stebbins," *Herald* 13, no. 7 (1 July 1925): 7; "Nurses' Training Class: M.H. to Mrs. Chamberlain," *Herald* 15, no. 7 (1 July 1927): 8.

71. L.E.W. to Dr. and Mrs. Montgomery, *Herald* 9, no. 7 (1 July 1921): 4.

72. "Letter Box," L.W. to Dr. and Mrs. Montgomery, 6 June 1921, *Custodial Herald* 9, no. 7 (July 1921): 4; "Our Discharges, 'Our Inspiration,'" *Herald* 14, no. 9 (1 September 1921): 5.

73. Barny and Herschel Obermeyer were two out of the approximately two dozen Rome inmates whom Bernstein sent to Institution for Male Defective Delinquents at Napanoch just after it opened. All of the "boys"—really men—stood accused of sexual activity such as fellatio, pederasty, or public masturbation. In every case, the Napanoch superintendent declared them to not qualify as "defective delinquents" and sent them back to Rome. Both Obermeyers also attended the Western Institution for the Instruction of Deaf-Mutes (now the Rochester School for the Deaf) and the Institution for Improved Instruction of Deaf Mutes in New York City (now the Lexington School for the Deaf). Syracuse Admissions Register, vol. 9, entries 2197 and 2302, Syracuse State School, Admission, Discharge, Death, and Transfer Records, 1851–1945, Admissions Registers, 1851–1920 (Acc. B1647, Subseries 2), NYSA; New York State Institution for Male Defective Delinquents inmate case files, 1920–1956 (Acc. 14610-88B), House Numbers 185 and 186, Box 5, NYSA.

74. Trent, *Inventing the Feeble Mind*, 219–20.

Chapter Four

1. Chapter title from "Cripples in the Ford Plant," *Elevator Constructor* 20, no. 8 (August 1923): 16.

2. "Rehabilitation: Training and Employment of Disabled Workmen in the Ford Plant," *Monthly Labor Review* 17, no. 5 (November 1923): 174. This article reprinted a speech given by Dr. James E. Mead, the head of the Medical Department, at the International Conference on Rehabilitation of the Disabled in March 1919.

3. "More Help Urged for the Disabled," *New York Times*, 28 March 1927, 11; Victoria Saker Woeste, *Henry Ford's War on Jews and the Legal Battle against Hate Speech* (Stanford, CA: Stanford University Press, 2012).

4. John Edward P. Williams-Searle, "Broken Brothers and Soldiers of Capital: Disability, Manliness, and Safety on the Rails, 1863–1908" (PhD diss., University of Iowa, 2004), 46. See also Edward Slavishak, *Bodies of Work: Civic Display and Labor in Industrial Pittsburgh* (Durham: Duke University Press, 2008), 159–60; Richard White, *Railroaded: The Transcontinentals and the Making of Modern America* (New York: Norton, 2011), 282; Christopher Sellers, *Hazards on the Job: From Industrial Disease to Environmental Health Science* (Chapel Hill: University of North Carolina Press, 1997), 35–36; Arwen Mohun, "Mitigating the Violence of the Machine: Accidents, Bodies, and the Creation of a Risk Society" (paper presented at the Annual Meeting of the Organization of American Historians, Memphis, TN, April 2003), 2, 15; Bender, *Sweated Work*, 7.

5. "The Reminiscences of Mr. John Wagner," 22, Oral History Collection (Acc. 65), Benson Ford Research Center, Dearborn, MI (hereafter BFRC).

6. There is considerable debate among historians about whether and how accident rates increased during the late nineteenth century and the twentieth century. In certain industries, such as railroads, accident rates rose significantly, but rates did not rise across the overall economy. Mark Aldrich, perhaps the foremost historian of the American safety movement, suggests that "risk perception, not risk itself, [was] the issue" that motivated labor reformers such as Carroll Wright. Mark Aldrich, review of *The Accidental Republic: Crippled Workingmen, Destitute Widows, and the Remaking of American Law*, by John Fabian Witt, EH.Net, June 2004, http://eh.net/bookreviews/library/0794 (accessed 22 June 2008); Witt, *Accidental Republic*, 2–3, 24–27, 187–89; Mark Aldrich, *Safety First: Technology, Labor, and Business in the Building of American Work Safety, 1870–1939* (Baltimore: Johns Hopkins University Press, 1997), 10–11, 15–16, 23, 41, 47, 56–58.

7. Crystal Eastman, *Work-Accidents and the Law* (Philadelphia: Russell Sage Foundation, 1910; reprint, New York: Arno Press, 1969), 227; Mohun, "Mitigating the Violence of the Machine," 8–9. Funded by the Russell Sage Foundation, the Pittsburgh Survey was a massive investigation of Pittsburgh undertaken by some seventy investigators in 1907 and 1908. The most prominent of the many Progressive Era social surveys, the Pittsburgh Survey aimed to expose the social problems of industrial cities with the hope of inspiring lawmakers to improve the urban environment, defined broadly. The survey spanned topics ranging from women workers and working-class households to immigrants' assimilation and the lives of steelworkers; investigators released their conclusions in social reform magazines, especially *Charities and the Commons* (the forerunner of *Survey*), then published six volumes of results between 1909 and 1914.

8. Fitch used his interviews to highlight the individual physical and larger social costs of how working conditions had worsened since unions had been driven out of the Pittsburgh steel industry: speedups, intense mechanization, an increase in the length of shifts from eight to twelve hours, and the emergence of the "long turn," in which workers labored for twenty-four hours straight. He hoped that *The Steel Workers* would aid calls for industrial democracy and efforts to rejig the balance of power away from employers—goals that may well have shaped his depictions of injured workers and led him to stress their stoic approach to workplace dangers. John A. Fitch, Cd-5-6 (Cards 7-8), John A. Fitch Papers (MS 937), Box 4, Folder 1, Wisconsin Historical Society; John A. Fitch, *The Steel Workers* (New York: Russell Sage Foundation, 1910; reprint, Pittsburgh: University of Pittsburgh Press, 1989), 4-6.

9. Fitch, Nubia-4 (Cards 5-6), Box 4, Folder 3; see also Fitch, Ch-1 (Card 2) and Ch-3 (Cards 3-4), Box 4, Folder 1, both from Fitch Papers.

10. Alan Derickson, *Black Lung: Anatomy of a Public Health Disaster* (Ithaca, NY: Cornell University Press, 1998), 30-33. See also Arwen Mohun, *Steam Laundries: Gender, Technology, and Work in the United States and Great Britain, 1880–1940* (Baltimore: Johns Hopkins University Press, 1990), 138; and James Ducker, *Men of the Steel Rails: Workers on the Atchison, Topeka & Santa Fe Railroad, 1869–1900* (Lincoln: University of Nebraska Press, 1983), 43-46.

11. Baron, "Gender and Labor History," 7, 18-29; Dorothy Sue Cobble, "'Drawing the Line': The Construction of a Gendered Work Force in the Food Service Industry," in *Work Engendered: Toward a New History of American Labor*, ed. Ava Baron (Ithaca, NY: Cornell University Press, 1991), 216-18, 221, 226; Nancy Gabin, "Time Out of Mind: The UAW's Response to Female Labor Laws and Mandatory Overtime in the 1960s," in *Work Engendered*, 355-57, 362, 366; Kessler-Harris, *In Pursuit of Equity*, 21-58; Kessler-Harris, *Out to Work*, 68-69, 139-42, 157-58, 185-86, 203-4, 230-34.

12. See, for instance, Aldrich, *Safety First*, chaps. 1-2 passim; Mark Aldrich, *Death Rode the Rails: American Railroad Accidents and Safety, 1828–1965* (Baltimore: Johns Hopkins University Press, 2006); Witt, *Accidental Republic*.

13. Barbara Young Welke, *Recasting American Liberty: Gender, Race, Law, and the Railroad Revolution* (Cambridge: University of Cambridge Press, 2001), 18.

14. Judith Rollins, *Between Women: Domestics and Their Employers* (Philadelphia: Temple University Press, 1985), 63; Mohun, *Steam Laundries*, 84; Alison Hepler, *Women in Labor: Mothers, Medicine, and Occupational Health in the United States, 1890–1980* (Columbus: Ohio State University Press, 2000), 38.

15. Clark, *Radium Girls*, 23-25.

16. Oscar Handlin, *The Uprooted: The Epic Story of the Great Migration That Made the American People* (Philadelphia: University of Pennsylvania Press, 2002), 63.

17. Kevin Kenny, *Making Sense of the Molly Maguires* (Oxford: Oxford University Press, 1998), 11, 26-28, 60, 128; Gary R. Mormino and George E. Pozzetta, *The Immigrant World of Ybor City: Italians and Their Latin Neighbors in Tampa, 1885–1985* (Gainesville: University Press of Florida, 1998), 177. On injuries and workers' activism, see Rose, "'Crippled' Hands,'" 36-45; Bender, *Sweated Work*, 52-60, chaps. 4 and 6 passim.

18. Farmers hired whites for cotton and the fruit crops that required working from a ladder. James Gregory, *American Exodus: The Dust Bowl Migration and Okie Culture in California* (Oxford: Oxford University Press, 1989), 58.

19. Ford also viewed African American workers as more efficient than whites; consequently, he went against white employees' wishes and allowed African Americans to take supervisory positions in the River Rouge blast furnace. Robert Lacey, *Ford: The Men and the Machine* (Boston: Little, Brown, 1986), 222–23.

20. Jesse Pope, *The Clothing Industry in New York* (Columbia, MO: E. W. Stephens Publishing, 1905), quoted in Bender, *Sweated Work*, 48.

21. Amy M. Hamburger, "The Cripple and His Place in the Community," *Annals of the American Academy of Political and Social Science* 77 (May 1918): 44, quoted in Halle Gayle Lewis, "'Cripples Are Not the Dependents One Is Led to Think': Work and Disability in Industrializing Cleveland, 1861–1916" (PhD diss., Binghamton University, 2004), 14.

22. Williams-Searle suggests that this lack of "hiring discrimination" stemmed in part from "the empty sleeves of Civil War veterans" being "a common sight." Williams-Searle, "Broken Brothers," 47.

23. This report traced the impact of lump-sum payments (or "commutations") of workmen's compensation on the lives of sixty-one injured workers and their families in eastern Pennsylvania. Investigators provided a wealth of demographic information about individuals but only gave the initials of their names; I created pseudonyms, paying particular attention to individuals' ethnicities. Consumers' League of Eastern Pennsylvania, "Commutations of Workmen's Compensation" (unpublished manuscript sent to John A. Fitch in March 1928), 1–8, quotes from 7–8, 10, Fitch Papers, Box 12, Folder 13.

24. Winthrop's artificial leg was "so heavy that it worrie[d] him and cause[d] pain through congestion of blood vessels in the groin." Consequently, he discarded it and used crutches instead. Winthrop lived with his supportive brother while he adjusted to his injury and the artificial leg. The Consumers' League also reported on the case of a man who had lost his leg below the knee and could not work for three years. The man eventually used his commuted workmen's compensation to purchase an artificial limb and "returned to his old job as a foreman out at the quarry," where he "evidently makes good money again." Consumers' League, "Commutations of Workmen's Compensation," 19, 57.

25. Welfare Federation of Cleveland, Committee on Cripples, "Education and Occupations of Cripples: Juvenile and Adult," *Publications of the Red Cross Institute for Crippled and Disabled Men* 2, no. 3 (1918): 50 (hereafter cited as "Survey of Cleveland Cripples." The survey did not assess the prospects of deaf or blind people, but suggested that the latter faced extremely high rates of unemployment.

26. Consumers' League, "Commutations of Workmen's Compensation," 20.

27. With both of their sons away from home, in the navy and a seminary, Sampson and his wife struggled at first. Eventually, both sons came home and worked for the telephone company. Ibid., 22–23.

28. H. Lewis, "'Cripples Are Not the Dependents,'" 116–25.

29. Eastman, *Work-Accidents*, 223.
30. Welke, *Recasting American Liberty*, 65.
31. "Survey of Cleveland Cripples," 57.
32. Occupational illnesses such as black lung often had the same effect. "Survey of Cleveland Cripples," 58; Derickson, *Black Lung*, 30–33.
33. "Sawyer" referred to men who cut lumber using pit saws as well as those who cut lumber to the lengths desired by builders. Welke, *Recasting American Liberty*, 67–68; Consumers' League, "Commutations of Workmen's Compensation," 36; Randolph E. Bergstrom, *Courting Danger: Injury and Law in New York City, 1870–1910* (Ithaca, NY: Cornell University Press, 1992), 147.
34. *John Schappner v. The Second Avenue Railroad Company*, 1870 Number S392, N.Y.C. Supreme Court; quoted in Bergstrom, *Courting Danger*, 110.
35. Consumers' League, "Commutations of Workmen's Compensation," 36.
36. Slavishak, *Bodies of Work*, 159–60, 174.
37. Fitch, "Andrew Gallagher," Fitch Papers, Box 4, Folder 2. For a similar tale by a Pittsburgh glassblower, see also Tibbey Glass Works (Cards 1–2), Fitch Papers, Box 4, Folder 2.
38. "Wages Represent Gross Receipts," *Official Journal [of the Amalgamated Meat Cutters and Butcher Workmen of America]* 6, no. 4 (January 1905): 1–2.
39. "Survey of Cleveland Cripples," 225.
40. Of course, such practices reduced lawsuits and mitigated the need for companies to pay gratuities to injured workers. Williams-Searle, "Broken Brothers," 265–66.
41. *Peters v. Standard Oil*, Cuyahoga County Court of Common Pleas case no. 48501, 1894, plaintiff's petition, March 8, 1894; amendment to plaintiff's petition, n.d.; quoted in H. Lewis, "'Cripples Are Not the Dependents,'" 1. Peters was discharged after he filed his lawsuit.
42. Bergstrom, *Courting Danger*, 51.
43. Finnie later sued the streetcar line. The Crown Suspender Company likewise allowed Dora Reynolds to work a light schedule, often alternating days, after she had an injury outside work. Ibid., 150–51.
44. Charles W. Holmes, "Some Recent Experiments in the Employment of the Blind, I. By the Massachusetts Commission for the Blind," in American Association of Workers for the Blind (hereafter AAWB), *Eleventh Convention, 1911*, 18. See also H. E. Parrott, "Ohio's Work for the Blind: The Dayton Association for the Blind," *Outlook for the Blind* 3 (April 1909): 97.
45. In the case of a middle-aged bookbinder who had voluntarily left his position after gradually losing his eyesight, the agent had to demonstrate how easy the man's longtime task was (hammering the edges of books after stitching to prepare them for binding) in order to persuade the factory owners to take the man back. The agent later reported, "Then I had my chance, and I said, 'If I, who was never in a bindery in my life, can in five minutes learn to do this thing, being myself blind, can you question for a moment that your old employee, who for twenty-three years has stood at this bench and done this work, can still do it?'" The bookbinder returned to work the very next

week. Edward G. Pease, "Some Recent Experiments in the Employment of the Blind: II. By the Dayton Association for the Blind," in AAWB, *Eleventh Convention, 1911*, 22; Charles W. Holmes, "Employment Bureau," AAWB, *Ninth AAWB Convention, 1907*, 107; Holmes, "Some Recent Experiments in the Employment of the Blind," 18.

46. Liberio Delfino, "Some Recent Experiments in the Employment of the Blind: III. By the Pennsylvania Institution for the Instruction of the Blind," AAWB, *Eleventh Convention, 1911*, 25

47. "Survey of Cleveland Cripples," 225.

48. *Railroad Trainmen's Journal* 17 (January 1900): 89, quoted in Williams-Searle, "Broken Brothers," 372. See also Consumers' League, "Commutations of Workmen's Compensation," 16–18. Elderly workers also became watchmen. See International Association of Machinists, *Proceedings of the Conference of Officers, General Organizers, and Business Agents* (St. Louis: International Association of Machinists, 1920): 491; Eastman, *Work-Accidents*, 148–49; Mrs. W. Phillips to Mrs. Henry Ford, 2 August 1914, Fair Lane Papers (Acc. 1), Box 139, Folder 139–2, BFRC; and W. E. Powers to F. W. Andrews, "Re: Hugh McDonald, X-9535," 28 March 1923, Charles E. Sorenson Papers (Acc. 38), Box 50, Safety Reports—1924, BFRC; Fitch, Smith Johnson (Cards 1–2), Fitch Papers, Box 4, Folder 2.

49. During the same years, the Dayton Association also placed two blind people in a paper box factory and nine broom makers in the Plating Department of the Davis Sewing Company. The Dayton Association's efforts were modeled on the pioneering work of the Massachusetts Association for the Blind, which began placing small numbers of blind workers in factories in 1904. These and other such associations arose in response to the 1890 and 1900 censuses, which provided detailed new data about blind people's lives, especially the disproportionately large numbers of people who lost their sight as adults and who received no assistance from state governments. Unlike earlier advocacy efforts by wealthy graduates of state schools for the blind, these associations were led primarily by sighted reformers. "New Factory Employment for the Blind," *Outlook for the Blind* (Autumn 1917): 52; Catherine J. Kudlick, "The Outlook of *The Problem* and the Problem with the *Outlook*: Two Advocacy Journals Reinvent Blind People in Turn-of-the-Century America," in *The New Disability History: American Perspectives*, ed. Paul K. Longmore and Lauri Umansky (New York: New York University Press, 2001), 193; E. J. Nolan, "A Sketch of the History of Organization among the Blind People of Chicago," *The Problem* 1, no. 2 (April 1900): 50–52; *The Michigan Employment Institution for the Blind: Its Recognized Necessity and Proper Policy; Erroneous Current Impressions Seem to Require Correction; A Remonstrance from Those Who Should Know* (Lansing, MI: Board of the Directors for the Michigan Association of Workers for the Blind, 1928); Belle Hymen, "Journal of Proceedings of Sixth General Convention of the American B. P. H. E. and G. I. Association, Held at Kansas City, Kansas, August 27–29th Inclusive, 1901," *The Problem* 2, no. 4 (October 1901): 87.

50. *Des Moines Capital*, quoted in "Jobs for Cripples Only," *American Journal of Care for Cripples* 3, no. 4 (December 1916): 270; "Employment Results in Philadelphia," *American Journal of Care for Cripples* 3, no. 1 (May 1916): 42–43.

51. Pease, "Some Recent Experiments in the Employment of the Blind: II," 22.

52. Robert Buchanan notes, "There is no available evidence that other employers followed Automatic Electric's lead." Deaf workers did, however, find an occupational niche in the printing industry, since state schools for the deaf often trained male students in typography. Buchanan, *Illusions of Equality*, 73–74.

53. "Survey of Cleveland Cripples," 56. Others, such as those targeted by the "unsightly beggar" ordinances or ugly laws that spread across the United States and beyond in the postbellum decades, peddled trinkets or begged. As Susan Schweik and Robert Bogdan, among others, have argued, begging is itself a form of work. Susan M. Schweik, *The Ugly Laws: Disability in Public* (New York: New York University Press, 2009), 230–54; Robert Bogdan with Martin Elks and James A. Knoll, *Picturing Disability: Beggar, Freak, Citizen, and Other Photographic Rhetoric* (Syracuse, NY: Syracuse University Press, 2012), 22–41.

54. The interviewer noted that the Italian immigrant seemed to still be adjusting to his disability; while he had been a reliable worker before his injury, afterward he spent most of his time carousing with friends. Consumers' League, "Commutations of Workmen's Compensation," 4–5, 11–12. See also Massachusetts Association for Promoting the Interests of the Blind, *Report, 1912–1913* (Boston: Association for Promoting the Interests of the Blind, 1913), 11.

55. Consumers' League, "Commutations of Workmen's Compensation," 14–16.

56. Suggestively, a number of working-class memoirists, among them Jack Metzgar, connect their parents' experiences of seeing their "own family and many others decimated by industrial accidents" with "fanatical commitment[s] . . . to 'saving for an education'" that would put their children safely into the middle class. Jack Metzgar, *Striking Steel: Solidarity Remembered* (Philadelphia: Temple University Press, 2000), 6, 41; Elaine Scarry, *The Body in Pain: The Making and Unmaking of the World* (Oxford: Oxford University Press, 1987), 262. See also Richard Sennett and Jonathan Cobb, *The Hidden Injuries of Class* (New York: Knopf, 1972), 32–33; and Cheri Register, *Packinghouse Daughter: A Memoir* (New York: Perennial, 2001), 12–13.

57. Consumers' League, "Commutations of Workmen's Compensation," 36.

58. *Lacy at Ninety: A Tribute*, comp. and ed. David H. Townsend (Alamogordo, NM: Human Science Associates, 1976), 24, 34–35, 38–39.

59. E. G. Liebold to C. E. Mitchell, 14 October 1912; M. J. Shear to E. G. Liebold, 8 January 1913; Lacy Simms to E. G. Liebold, 11 April 1915; Lacy Simms to Carnes Artificial Limb Company, 26 March 1913; Henry Ford Office Papers (Acc. 62), Box 31, Lacy Simms, BFRC.

60. Simms's rejection of the arms caused him some difficulty with Ford's longtime secretary E. G. Liebold, who requested regular updates on Simms's progress with his artificial arms and his plans for paying back the loan. Liebold and Simms maintained an extensive and often acrimonious correspondence for a period of three years, during which Simms concealed that he had already disposed of the artificial arms. Several times, Liebold complained to Charles W. Williams of the Cleveland Chamber of Commerce about not receiving updates or payments on the loan from Simms. In addition,

Liebold wrote to Carnes Artificial Limb Company to complain that the limbs "furnished to Mr. Simms are still useless and from his letters it would appear that it takes more time and practice than the ordinary person has at his command"; Liebold asked that a representative call on Simms in person. Simms, however, seemingly convinced Liebold that he could not adapt to the arms while attending school and working. Liebold to Carnes Artificial Limb Company, 21 June 1915, Henry Ford Office Papers (Acc. 62), Box 31, Lacy Simms, BFRC.

61. "Survey of Cleveland Cripples," 215–18.

62. Anne Finger, *Elegy for a Disease: A Personal and Cultural History of Polio* (New York: St. Martin's Press, 2006), 258.

63. Harry Crews, *A Childhood: A Biography of a Place* (New York: Harper and Row, 1978), 54, quoted in Mohun, "Mitigating the Violence of the Machine," 2.

64. On the safety first movement, see Aldrich, *Safety First*, chaps. 3–4 passim.

65. Mohun, "Mitigating the Violence of the Machine," 6; Peter Linebaugh and Marcus Rediker, *The Many-Headed Hydra: Sailors, Slaves, Commoners, and the Hidden History of the Revolutionary Atlantic* (Boston: Beacon Press, 2000), 160–61, 164; H. Lewis, "'Cripples Are Not the Dependents,'" 63.

66. Walter Licht, *Working for the Railroad: The Organization of Work in the Nineteenth Century* (Princeton, NJ: Princeton University Press, 1983), 184.

67. The public was notoriously skeptical of railroad safety or the lack thereof. Newspapers regularly printed stories with titles such as "Another Railway Horror." States began regulating railroad safety in the 1840s, aiming to inspire greater awareness of safety by tracking and reporting on accidents and by mandating safety devices that would protect passengers and workers. Federal lawmakers began trying to address railroad safety in the 1870s. Williams-Searle, "Cold Charity," 157–86; Williams-Searle, "Broken Brothers," 50; Ducker, *Men of the Steel Rails*, 121–22; Aldrich, *Safety First*, 25–26, 33–34.

68. Trainmen who remained in the industry for thirty years had a 24 percent chance of dying in a work accident, for instance. Such programs offered benefits for permanent disability and death; locals decided whether to also provide temporary disability insurance. The Brotherhood of Locomotive Engineers pioneered a mutual insurance program in 1867. Aldrich, *Death Rode the Rails*, 161; Aldrich, *Safety First*, 15; Witt, *Accidental Republic*, 113–14.

69. Williams-Searle, "Broken Brothers," 390.

70. These early exams focused on testing trainmen for color-blindness and poor hearing. Brotherhood leaders shared railroad managers' fears that recently disabled workers would make fraudulent insurance claims. Aldrich, *Death Rode the Rails*, 91, 172–73; Williams-Searle, "Cold Charity," 163.

71. The Burlington Railroad established a surgical program in 1870; most carriers had full-scale medical bureaucracies by the 1890s. The Baltimore & Ohio Railroad checked applicants for kidney disease, venereal disease, tuberculosis, and cancer as well. Aldrich, *Death Rode the Rails*, 91, 156–59, 163, 172; Witt, *Accidental Republic*, 113–14.

72. Williams-Searle, "Broken Brothers," 390.

73. Ibid., 392, 517. See also William John Pinkerton, *His Personal Record: Stories of Railroad Life* (Kansas City, MO: Pinkerton Publishing, 1904), 9, quoted in Williams-Searle, "Broken Brothers," 50.

74. Williams-Searle, "Cold Charity," 161, 164, 168; Williams-Searle, "Broken Brothers," 71, chap. 3 passim, 394; Aldrich, *Death Rode the Rails*, 4–6. See also Rose, "'Crippled Hands,'" 41–45, 48–49.

75. "Survey of Cleveland Cripples," 214–15. Douglas Baynton contends that efficiency rhetoric was so pervasive by the early twentieth century that people with a wide array of disabilities were often seen not as "afflicted" but rather as "handicapped in the race for life." Baynton, *Defectives in the Land*, 48–58.

76. Consumers' League, "Commutations of Workmen's Compensation," 36.

77. Ibid., 16–18. Apparently, his new employer had "given [the motor company] a rather plain piece of his mind, saying that he thought a firm of the standing of [the motor company] . . . could look after its own industrial disabled, but if they couldn't, the shop would do what they could as a matter of charity."

78. Leading rehabilitator Douglas C. McMurtrie published *American Journal of Care for Cripples* between 1914 and 1919. He is discussed in chapter 7. The *Journal* offered advice to employers in a wide variety of industries on how to make use of "cripples," as well as profiles of institutions that sought to provide medical and vocational rehabilitation to those deemed cripples, as well as reports on the Red Cross Institute for the Crippled and Disabled, which opened in 1917 in New York City. "A Crippled Farm Worker," *American Journal of Care for Cripples* 3, no. 3 (September 1916): 128; Selene Armstrong Harmon, "The Government an Employment Agency," *World's Work* 23, no. 5 (September 1916): 578; John M. Kinder, *Paying with Their Bodies: American War and the Problem of the Disabled Veteran* (Chicago: University of Chicago Press, 2015), 144.

79. The Civil Service added total deafness and loss of speech to the list of exclusionary conditions in 1906; the Deaf community mobilized and won the reversal of the rule in 1908. Buchanan, *Illusions of Equality*, 37, 147n6.

80. Fitch, Woods Mill (Larkin) (Cards 2–3), Fitch Papers, Box 4, Folder 3. See also "Old Men Not Wanted," *Official Journal [of the Amalgamated Meat Cutters and Butcher Workmen of America]* 2, no. 35 (August 1902): 81; United Mine Workers of America, *Proceedings of the Twenty-Seventh Consecutive and Fourth Biennial Convention* (Indianapolis, IN: Bookwalter-Ball Printing, 1919), 834; Gregory Wood, *Retiring Men: Manhood, Labor, and Growing Old in America, 1900–1960* (Lanham, MD: University Press of America, 2012), chap. 1 passim.

81. Fitch, *Steel Workers*, 183–84; Slavishak, *Bodies of Work*, 174.

82. Frank Barkley Copley, "A Great Corporation Investigates Itself," *American Magazine* 74, no. 6 (October 1912): 652, in Fitch Papers, Box 4, Folder 7.

83. Rachel Bryant Marks, "The Problem of Second Injuries: History and Analysis of Second-Injury Provisions of Workmen's Compensation Laws in the United States" (PhD diss., University of Chicago, 1950), 45; "Physical Examination of Workmen," *Square Deal* 15, no. 63 (December 1914): 444, reprinted from *Knights of Labor Journal*.

84. Safety posters at Ford Motor Company featured gory images of workers' injured eyes accompanied by headlines that blared claims such as "He Removed the Guard and Lost an Eye!" Aldrich, *Safety First*, 114–21.

85. Buchanan, *Illusions of Equality*, 79–81.

86. Mohun, "Mitigating the Violence of the Machine," 11. For more on the survey, see Emil Frankel, "The Vocational Adjustment of Physically and Mentally Handicapped Children," in Section IV B of the *Special Report of the White House Conference on Child Health and Protection* (Washington, DC: Government Printing Office, 1928), 10–12; Henry Kessler, *The Crippled and the Disabled: Rehabilitation of the Physically Handicapped* (New York: Columbia University Press, 1935), 22–24. The spread of "unsightly beggar" ordinances or "ugly laws" across the United States during the postbellum decades posed additional challenges for the most desperate workers with physical disabilities. These codes outlawed the display of "unsightly" or "mutilated" bodies for peddling and begging and, at times, the presence of such bodies on public streets. Although it is challenging to trace how extensively these codes were enforced, their rapid spread—from San Francisco in 1867 and Chicago in 1881 to Pennsylvania in 1891 and Manila in 1902, to give just a few examples—testifies to disabled people's increasingly tenuous place in the public sphere. Schweik, *Ugly Laws*, 291–96.

87. John R. Commons, "Henry Ford, Miracle Maker," *The Independent*, 1 May 1920, 160–61; "Reminiscences of William P. Baxter," pp. 14–15, Oral History Collection (Acc. 65), BFRC (hereafter cited as Baxter reminiscences); Edsel Ford, "Why We Employ Aged and Handicapped Workers," *Saturday Evening Post*, 6 February 1943, 16–17.

88. While the tale might seem apocryphal, Medical Transfer Department head Norman McLeod detailed the man's age (twenty-eight) and explained that he had been placed in the Stock Department due to the limited work available in the two other departments that employed blind workers. Totally blind men continued to do such work through at least the 1930s. Norman McLeod, "What Sick and Crippled Men Are Doing for the Ford Motor Company," *Modern Hospital* 12, no. 1 (January 1919): 3; Henry Ford, *My Life and Work* (Garden City, NJ: Doubleday, Page, 1922; reprint, North Stratford, NH: Ayer, 2000), 108–9. P. L. Atkinson, "Smooth-Running Henry Ford," *Physical Culture Magazine* (June 1923): 126, in Vertical File—Ford, Henry—Philosophy of Life, BFRC.

89. Until 1918, Ford Motor Company tried to suppress any news about its hiring of disabled workers, reportedly "because they cannot employ all the cripples in the United States, and the number of applications which follow each burst of publicity is very pathetic." Ford managers also feared that disabled workers would travel en masse to Dearborn to seek employment, much like the near-riots that happened at the Highland Park plant after the company announced the five-dollar-day policy. "Rehabilitation: Training and Employment of Disabled Workmen," 174; Atkinson, "Smooth-Running Henry Ford," 126; James E. Mead, "Salvage of Men," *American Medicine* 14, no. 6 (June 1919): 372–78; Elliot, "Henry Ford and What He Stands For in America," 268; all from BFRC. See also R. D. Meyer, "An Experiment in Rehabilitation," *Forbes* 54, no. 6 (15 September 1944): 20.

90. When Marquis arrived at Ford, he changed the name of the Sociological Department to the Educational Department, but the old name stuck in newspaper articles and internal company reports. The Sociological, Medical, and Employment Departments were those most involved in hiring and dealing with disabled and injured workers. Allan Nevins, *Ford: Expansion and Challenge, 1915–1931* (New York: Scribner and Sons, 1957), 345; Steve Meyer, *The Five-Dollar Day: Labor Management and Social Control in the Ford Motor Company, 1908–1921* (Albany: State University of New York Press, 1981), 129–30. Baxter reminiscences, pp. 14–15.

91. This practice may have arisen after the company hired a few deaf workers in its earliest years. Robert Buchanan reports that "according to lore within the deaf [sic] community, [Art] Tremaine and his peers demonstrated such extraordinary diligence and efficiency that they soon won over skeptical supervisors, who later informed Henry Ford." Buchanan, *Illusions of Equality*, 74.

92. S. Meyer, *The Five-Dollar Day*, 72; H. Ford, *My Life and Work*, 106–7; Allan Nevins, *Ford: The Times, the Man, the Company* (New York: Arno Press, 1976), 561. *Factory Facts from Ford* (Dearborn, MI: Ford Motor Co., 1915), p. 14, Ford Non-Serial Imprints Collection (Acc. 951), Box 11; E. G. Liebold to C. L. Gould, 26 January 1914, Five Dollar Day Papers (Acc. 683), Box 1; both from BFRC. Of course, if applicants proved inefficient or unfaithful, they would be discharged. Press release about profit-sharing plan (untitled), 2, Fair Lane Papers (Acc. 1), Box 178 (Personnel), Folder 178-16, BFRC. Allan Nevins reports that in 1919, the head of the Medical Department claimed that not one worker had ever been discharged because of a physical disability. He adds, "Anyone incapacitated by illness or accident was granted leave of absence and told his job would be waiting for him." Nevins, *Ford: The Times, the Man, the Company*, 562.

93. *Factory Facts from Ford*, 14. The company introduced minimal physical exams along with the five-dollar day; potential hires were checked for hernias, heart and chest problems, and contagious diseases. Baxter reminiscences, pp. 2–3; Cyrus W. Phillips to Ford Motor Company, 2 September 1914, and L. B. Robertson to Cyrus W. Phillips, 9 September 1914, Legal Department (Ford Motor Company) Records (Acc. 75), Box 27, New York Workmen's Complaints—1917—Personnel; J. E. Mead to Executive Committee on Hospitals, 22 March 1916, Ford Motor Company Incorporation Records (Acc. 85), Box 4, Operating Committee Minutes; all from BFRC.

94. Medical transfer director Norman McLeod noted that "the percentage of crippled men on the labor market at this time is exceptionally high on account of the fact that so many of our young and physically perfect men are at war," but also predicted that disabled veterans would comprise a large proportion of the postwar workforce. McLeod, "What Sick and Crippled Men Are Doing," 1.

95. The head of the Employment Department, John R. Lee, argued that transferring workers was far cheaper than replacing them. S. Meyer, *The Five-Dollar Day*, 37, 54–55, 80, 105–6. "Henry Ford Gives $10,000,000.00 in 1914 Profits to His Employees," *Detroit Journal*, 5 January 1914, typescript, Fair Lane Papers (Acc. 1), Box 178, Folder 178-18; press release, 1914, Fair Lane Papers (Acc. 1), Box 178, Folder 178-16; Samuel Marquis, "Testimony in Arbitration before Hon. Judge Samuel Alschuler, Arbitrator, between

the Packers and Their Employees regarding a General Increase in Wage Rates," 23 November 1920, pp. 59–60, Samuel Simpson Marquis Papers (Acc. 293), Box 1, Marquis Testimony at Packers v. Employees Arbitration—1920 (hereafter cited as "Testimony at Packers v. Employees Arbitration"), BFRC. The Employment Department also kept applications of disabled people on file until appropriate positions in the Ammeter, Coil, and Commutator Departments opened up during the 1910s. Baxter reminiscences, p. 15. See also U.S. Commission on Industrial Relations, *Final Report and Testimony Submitted to Congress*, 64th Cong., 1st sess., 1916, S. Doc. 415, 7628, 7631.

96. J. E. Mead, "Rehabilitating Cripples at Ford Plant," *Iron Age* 102, no. 13 (26 September 1918): 740; Mead, "Salvage of Men," 374.

97. Meyer notes that "the entire system rested on the productivity of the individual worker.... The inefficient workman always faced the threat, and sometimes the fact, of discharge." S. Meyer, *The Five-Dollar Day*, 106. See also, H. Ford, *My Life and Work*, 107; "The Reminiscences of Harold M. Cordell," p. 106, Oral History Collection (Acc. 65), BFRC; Mead, "Rehabilitating Cripples at Ford Plant," 741.

98. Each department had a specific quota of "crippled" men. [Minutes of the second meeting of the Operating Committee of the Ford Motor Company], 23 March 1916, pp. 9–10, Ford Motor Company Incorporation Records (Acc. 85), Box 40, Operating Committee Minutes, BFRC; Baxter reminiscences, p. 15; McLeod, "What Sick and Crippled Men Are Doing," 2. For more on the Magneto Department, see Douglas Brinkley, *Wheels for the World: Henry Ford, His Company, and a Century of Progress, 1903–2003* (New York: Penguin, 2003), 103, 153; S. Meyer, *The Five-Dollar Day*, 32–33.

99. C. A. Zahnow, [Re: Edward J. Jeffries], 21 November 1918, Henry Ford Office Papers (Acc. 62), Box 28, Reports (Safety Standings, Attendance, Socio., Housing); Baxter reminiscences, p. 15; C. E. Sorenson to Raymond E. Kennedy, 20 August 1937, Nevins and Hill Research—Original Documents and Notes Series (hereafter Nevins and Hill Research) (Acc. 572), Box 28, Folder 12.7.3; all from BFRC.

100. C. E. Sorenson to Raymond E. Kennedy, 20 August 1937, Nevins and Hill Research (Acc. 572), Box 28, Folder 12.7.3, BFRC.

101. J. H. McFarland to Mr. Andrews, 17 March 1923, Nevins and Hill Research (Acc. 572), Box 28, Folder 12.7.3, BFRC. The small number of totally blind men seems to have been the one group allowed to work at significantly less than 100 percent efficiency. In 1929, Howard M. Cordell explained to a Dutch rehabilitator, G. H. Aldus, that three blind men in the Body Assembly Department worked at "not more than 20%" efficiency placing ignition switch plates in the switch mounting collar for the instrument panel. Two men placed washers on bolts for the transmission in the Motor Assembly Department at 80 percent efficiency, and several others labored in the Valve Bushing Department placing bushings in a block at approximately "75% efficiency." According to Cordell, only the "three men [who worked] in the Gasket Department placing brass and asbestos rings on an arbor" reached 100 percent efficiency. H. M. Cordell to G. H. Aldus, 28 February 1929, Vertical File—Ford Motor Company—History of—Personnel, 1917–1929, BFRC.

102. "The Reminiscences of Mr. W. Griffith," p. 30, Oral History Collection (Acc. 65); C. E. Sorenson to Raymond E. Kennedy, 20 August 1937, Nevins and Hill Research (Acc. 572), Box 28, Folder 12.7.3; both from BFRC.

103. C. E. Sorenson to Raymond E. Kennedy, 20 August 1937, Nevins and Hill Research (Acc. 572), Box 28, Folder 12.7.3, BFRC.

104. "Ford Motor Company Medical Organization: Medical Sub-departments," p. 7, Woodry Papers (Acc. 611), Industrial Relations Medical–Highland Park, BFRC; *The Ford Industries: Facts about the Ford Motor Company and Its Subsidiaries* (Detroit, MI: Ford Motor Co., 1924), p. 113, pamphlet available at BFRC library.

105. The program for tubercular employees arose in 1916 when four men declined to be sent to a nearby sanatorium, citing the fact that they would not be able to support their large families. The men had a dedicated physician. "Ford Motor Company Medical Organization: Medical Sub-departments," p. 2, Woodry Papers (Acc. 611), Industrial Relations Medical–Highland Park, BFRC. At times, the company shifted particularly ill workers to branches with better climates "in the hopes that they would recover." [Minutes of the second meeting of the Operating Committee of the Ford Motor Company], 23 March 1916, p. 9, Ford Motor Company Incorporation Records (Acc. 85), Box 40, Operating Committee Minutes, BFRC; Marquis, "Testimony at Packers v. Employees Arbitration," 23 November 1920, p. 45. See also H. Ford, *My Life and Work*, 110; McLeod, "What Sick and Crippled Men Are Doing," 2; Mead, "Salvage of Men," 377.

106. Henry Ford eventually hired his first cousin, Arthur Litogot, to do home work. Given that they never met, it is unlikely that he served as the source of Ford's interest in hiring workers with disabilities or even the use of home work. Originally a collar maker, Litogot became totally blind sometime in the late 1910s or early 1920s; his World War I draft registration showed no such disability. After his wife wrote to say that he would love to meet his first cousin, Ford's longtime personal secretary, E. G. Liebold, visited and left quite impressed. After telling Ford that Litogot could not work, the industrialist suggested that his secretary give Litogot $100 to $150 on every visit—money that he accepted only reluctantly. Ford eventually hit upon the idea of having him do home work, with which his cousin was "very highly elated." To Liebold's knowledge, however, Ford never visited Litogot. "The Reminiscences of Mr. E. G. Liebold," pp. 233–34, Oral History Collection (Acc. 65), BFRC; Mead, "Salvage of Men," 178–79; "Proceedings of National and Local Societies: International Conference on the Rehabilitation of the Disabled (1919): American Employers and Rehabilitation," *International Record of Medicine and General Practice Clinics* 109 (1919): 659.

107. H. Ford, *My Life and Work*, 105–9. On flexible specialization, see David Hounshell, *From the American System to Mass Production, 1800–1932* (Baltimore: Johns Hopkins University Press, 1985).

108. S. J. Woolf, "What of the Next 25 Years?," *Rotarian* 48, no. 6 (June 1936): 7, Henry and Edsel Ford Quotations Collection (Acc. 511), Box 1, BFRC. Labor historians have a mixed perspective on the physical impact of mechanization on workers. As Mohun explains, "Technological innovations could either ease the strain of a

particularly dreaded job, or they could worsen it by facilitating expectations of speed or by straining one particular part of the body." Mechanization initially made many types of work—especially mining and other jobs involving dust—far more dangerous, although technological innovations such as ventilation systems and wet-drilling eventually lowered the incidence of dust diseases such as black lung, white lung, and brown lung. Mohun, *Steam Laundries*, 74; Barbara Ellen Smith, *Digging Our Own Graves: Coal Miners and the Struggle over Black Lung Disease* (Philadelphia: Temple University Press, 1987), 50–51; Alan Derickson, "Industrial Refugees: The Migration of Silicotics from the Mines of North America and South Africa in the Early Twentieth Century," *Labor History* 29, no. 1 (1988): 68; Alan Derickson, *Workers' Health, Workers' Democracy: The Western Miners' Struggle, 1891–1925* (Ithaca, NY: Cornell University Press, 1988), 40, 54–56; David Rosner and Gerald Markowitz, *Deadly Dust: Silicosis and the Politics of Occupational Disease in Twentieth-Century America* (Princeton, NJ: Princeton University Press, 1991), 9, 38–41, 51–62.

109. Henry Ford, *Quotations from the Unusual Henry Ford* (Redondo Beach, CA: Quotamus Press, 1978), 115. See also H. Ford, *My Life and Work*, 209.

110. Unlike Taylor, Gilbreth focused more on simplifying the number of motions required for a particular job than on timing motions with a stopwatch; he hoped thereby to improve workers' welfare. See, for instance, Katherine M. H. Blackford, "Rating Men," *Efficiency Society Journal* 3, no. 6 (March 1914): 4–6; Frank B. Gilbreth and Lillian Moller Gilbreth, *Motion Study for the Handicapped* (London: George Routledge and Sons, 1920).

111. "Rehabilitation: Training and Employment of Disabled Workmen," 174.

112. Mead, "Salvage of Men," 375.

113. "Reminiscences of Robert A. Shaw," p. 66, Oral History Collection (Acc. 65), BFRC; U.S. Commission on Industrial Relations, *Final Report and Testimony*, 7631. Marquis claimed in 1923, "I do not recall that a cripple ever received an additional injury while in the employ of the company, and the only instance on record of injury to an old man was the case of one who went to sleep and fell off his chair." Marquis, *Henry Ford*, 111. See also "Elevators," 9 December 1924, Nevins and Hill Research (Acc. 572), Box 27, Folder 12.1, BFRC.

114. "The Reminiscences of Mr. William C. Klann," pp. 89–91, Oral History Collection (Acc. 65), BFRC.

115. Ibid., 90.

116. Ibid., 91.

117. On Ford's interest in hiring felons and African Americans, see U.S. Commission on Industrial Relations, *Final Report and Testimony*, 7630; Clarence Hooker, *Life in the Shadows of the Crystal Palace, 1910–1927: Ford Workers in the Model T Era* (Bowling Green, OH: Bowling Green State University Popular Press, 1997), 141–43; Olivier Zunz, *The Changing Face of Inequality: Urbanization, Industrial Development, and Immigration in Detroit, 1880–1920* (Chicago: University of Chicago Press, 1982), 396–97.

118. Ford viewed charity as a waste because it did not remove the cause of the problem. H. Ford, *My Life and Work*, 107; *Facts from Ford* (Detroit: Ford Motor Co., 1920),

Vertical File—Ford Motor Company—Sociological Department; George Edward Lyndon Jr., "Ford and Labor," *Pipp's Weekly* 4, no. 18 (25 August 1923): 1, Vertical File—Ford Motor Company—Sociological Department; Interview with Henry Ford by George Sylvester Viereck, *N.Y. American*, 5 August 1928, and Interview with Henry Ford by Meigs Frost, *New Orleans Times-Picayune*, 22 July 1934, Henry and Edsel Ford Quotations Collection (Acc. 511), Box 1; Henry Ford, "Looking under the Human Hood: As Told to William L. Stidger," *Rotarian*, January 1947, 10; Samuel Marquis, [speech to meeting of Indianapolis Branch Efficiency Club], 17 May 1916, p. 59, S. S. Marquis Correspondence (Acc. 63), Box 1, Speeches–1916; "The Reminiscences of Mr. George Brown," p. 98, and "The Reminiscences of Harold M. Cordell," p. 106, Oral History Collection (Acc. 65); all from BFRC. See also U.S. Commission on Industrial Relations, *Final Report and Testimony*, 7630.

119. Marquis reports that there were over 1,700 "cripples" working at Ford at "the outbreak of the war," and "in addition to these, some four or five thousand more men, disabled more or less by disease, and who for that reason would be rejected by industry, were on its payroll." Marquis also claims that after the war, Ford "agreed to take a thousand handicapped men as fast as they came out of the hospital." Samuel S. Marquis, *Henry Ford: An Interpretation* (Boston: Little, Brown, 1923), 111. In the mid-1920s, Henry Ford began discussing his hiring of disabled workers in interviews. C. Esco Obermann, *A History of Vocational Rehabilitation in America* (Minneapolis: T. S. Denison, 1965), 154–155; Mead, "Rehabilitating Cripples at Ford Plant," 739–42. See also "Rehabilitation: Training and Employment of Disabled Workmen," 174; Atkinson, "Smooth-Running Henry Ford," 126; Mead, "Salvage of Men"; Elliot, "Henry Ford and What He Stands for in America," 268; all from BFRC. See also R. Meyer, "An Experiment in Rehabilitation," 20.

120. "Cases of Total Disability Resulting from the War," *Economic World*, n.s., 26, no. 17 (26 October 1918): 601–2; "Employment of Cripples in a Large Industrial Plant," *Monthly Labor Review* 7, no. 6 (December 1918): 85–86; "A Problem in Efficiency," *Modern Hospital* 12, no. 2 (January 1919): 45–46. See also "9,500 Partially Disabled Employees Working in Ford Motor Plant," *National Safety News* 3, no. 3 (17 January 1921): 4; reprinted in *Labour Gazette* (March 1919): 320 and *Journal of Industrial Hygiene and Toxicology* 3, no. 4 (August 1921): 89.

121. In fact, Mead challenged the government's entire approach to rehabilitation, arguing that "if every large industrial concern would adopt a similar plan, showing no discrimination towards the disabled in the hiring of men and using discretion in their assignment to work, it would hardly be necessary for the Government to institute such an elaborate and comprehensive plan of rehabilitation as is now under way." "A Problem in Efficiency," 45; Mead, "Salvage of Men," 378.

122. H. Ford, *My Life and Work*, 108–9. See also H. Ford, "Looking under the Human Hood," 10. In 1944, Ford declared that "laziness and idleness are the cause of all the world's trouble." *Detroit Times*, 20 March 1944 (see also *Detroit Times*, 5 November 1944), in Henry and Edsel Ford Quotations Collection (Acc. 511), Box 1, BFRC. On sheltered workshops, see Byrom, "A Pupil and a Patient," 133–56; Obermann, *History of*

Vocational Rehabilitation, 147–59; Edward D. Berkowitz, *Disabled Policy: America's Programs for the Handicapped* (Cambridge: Cambridge University Press, 1987); Richard K. Scotch, "American Disability Policy in the Twentieth Century," in *The New Disability History: American Perspectives*, ed. Paul K. Longmore and Lauri Umansky (New York: New York University Press, 2001), 375–92.

123. H. Ford, "Looking under the Human Hood," 10. For more on Henry Ford's hatred of charity, see "The Reminiscences of Harold M. Cordell," p. 106, Oral Histories (Acc. 65), and "The Reminiscences of George Brown," p. 98, Oral Histories (Acc. 65), both from BFRC; "Cripples in the Ford Plant," 16.

124. "Editorial: The Paradox of Henry Ford," *Boston Herald*, 7 May 1923, and "Inspire Men to Keep Job, Marquis' Aim," [undated newspaper article], in S. S. Marquis Correspondence (Acc. 63), Box 1, Newspaper Clippings 1915–1925, BFRC.

125. Samuel Marquis, "Address Delivered by Dean Marquis, May 17, 1916, before the Convention of the National Conference of Charities on Corrections, Y.M.C.A.," p. 5, S. S. Marquis Correspondence (Acc. 63), Box 1, Speeches—1916, BFRC (hereafter cited as "Address before NCCC").

126. On the company's rehiring of injured workers, see R. D. McClure to Sorenson, 20 September 1923, Charles E. Sorenson Papers (Acc. 38), Box 48, Henry Ford Hospital; W. E. Powers to F. W. Andrews, "Re: Hugh McDonald, X-9535," 28 March 1923; Marquis, "Testimony at Packers v. Employees Arbitration," 23 November 1920, pp. 88–89; both from BFRC. On fitting employees to jobs, see Baxter reminiscences, pp. 14–15; Marquis, "Address before NCCC," p. 5; both from BFRC. During the 1910s, the Legal Department also sometimes hired the widows of workers killed in industrial accidents and, occasionally, the widows of men who died in noncompensable ways while at work. See, for instance, the file on Millie Dunbar: Legal Department (Ford Motor Company) Records (Acc. 75), Box 50, Millie Dunbar—1917, BFRC.

127. J. E. Mead, "Assistance to Sick or Injured Employees," 8 May 1923, Nevins and Hill Research (Acc. 572), Box 31, Folder 12.20, BFRC. At times, Ford Motor Company could be extraordinarily generous toward ill or disabled employees. In the case of H.G., an employee who developed tuberculosis while working for Ford, B. J. Craig, the secretary to Edsel B. Ford (president in 1919), claimed in 1919 that the company had spent $3,825.33 attempting to cure H.G.'s tuberculosis. Apparently, either H.G. or the asylum in which he was living (in Rochester, NY) had contacted Ernest Liebold in hopes of receiving additional aid. Craig stated to Liebold, "When it was found that he probably never would be in a position to return to his work we decided that he was a proper case for the authorities in the community from which he came." B. J. Craig to E. G. Liebold, 2 May 1919, and E. G. Liebold to B. F. Craig, 29 April 1919, Henry Ford Office Papers (Acc. 62), Box 89, "Ford Motor Company Sociological Department and Service Department," BFRC.

128. The company also hired back 383 draftees rejected by the U.S. Armed Forces and committed itself to rehiring disabled veterans of World War I who had previously worked at Ford. Mead, "Rehabilitating Cripples at Ford Plant," 742.

129. Peter Banionis, Frank W. McCracken, Compensation Department (Ford Motor Company) records (Acc. 789), Box 1, BFRC.

130. Baxter reminiscences, p. 15. The Bay Cliff health homes were supported by the Couzens Fund; Walter Beesley also noted Henry Ford's interest in them. "The Reminiscences of Mr. Wallace G. Beesley," p. 24, Oral History Collection (Acc. 65), BFRC.

131. L. B. Robertson to P. E. Martin, 1 April 1913, and note by Martin, 2 April 1913, Legal Cases Numerical Records (Acc. 297), Box 1, Folder L-2—Unreported Accidents—1913–1915 (personnel), BFRC.

132. Charles F. F. Campbell to Mrs. Henry Ford, Fair Lane Papers (Acc. 1), Box 144, Folder 144-11; Charles F. F. Campbell to Mrs. Henry Ford, 22 May 1930, Fair Lane Papers (Acc. 1), Box 178, Folder 178-9; both from BFRC.

133. For correspondence between Clara Ford and Helen Keller, see Fair Lane Papers (Acc. 1), Box 144, Folders 144-11 and 144-12, BFRC. On Henry Ford's and Samuel Marquis's efforts to aid crippled children, see Dr. Peabody to Henry Ford, [ca. mid-1920s], Henry Ford Office Papers (Acc. 23), Box 15, Health and Medicine; Marquis, "Address before NCCC," p. 15; both from BFRC. In 1924, Ford Motor Company paid $4,232.30 for aid to "handicapped children." F. W. Andrews, "Sociological Department: Summary of Outside Investigations for the Year 1924," Nevins and Hill Research (Acc. 572), Box 31, Folder 12.20, BFRC.

134. "The Reminiscences of Miss Elba Morse," pp. 1–8, Oral History Collection (Acc. 65), BFRC.

135. General Photographs Series (Acc. 833), Box 31, Folder 57A, BFRC.

136. H. Ford, "Looking under the Human Hood," 10; E. Ford, "Why We Employ Aged and Handicapped Workers"; "How Can Industry Find Jobs for Disabled Veterans?," *Machinery* 50, no. 8 (April 1944): 132–38. Between March 1941 and 1943, the ranks of employees with permanent physical handicaps grew by more than 450 percent, from 2,563 to 11,652. "The Following Report Shows the Number of Men at the Rouge Plant Who Have Permanent Physical Handicaps and the Number on Each Rate," C. L. Martindale / Otto H. Husen Files (Acc. 157), Box 196, Handicapped Employees (Statistics) 1941–, BFRC. Publicity Release #21, "Ford Employs Many Handicapped Persons," 18 February 1943, C. L. Martindale / Otto H. Husen Files (Acc. 157), Box 196, Handicapped Employees (Statistics) 1941–, BFRC. David L. Lewis, *The Public Image of Henry Ford: An American Folk Hero and His Company* (Detroit: Wayne State University Press, 1976), 387.

137. O'Brien, *Crippled Justice*, 34, 42–45; Sarah F. Rose, "Teaching Blind People to Walk by Taking Away Their Canes: The Influence of World War II on Conceptions of Disability in the United States" (MA thesis, University of Chicago, 2001), 27–46.

Chapter Five

1. Harry E. Mock, *Industrial Medicine and Surgery* (Philadelphia: W. B. Saunders, 1919), 372.

2. I am grateful to Trevor Engel for locating and suggesting the quotation in the chapter title. U.S. Bureau of Labor Statistics, "Proceedings of the Sixth Annual Meeting of the International Association of Industrial Accident Boards and Commissions,"

Bulletin of the United States Bureau of Labor Statistics 273 (Washington, DC: Government Printing Office, 1920), 353.

3. Twenty-two states passed laws between 1910 and 1914; another twenty-one states enacted programs between 1915 and 1920.

4. For more on this 1928 survey of 600 major employers, see Frankel, "Vocational Adjustment of Physically and Mentally Handicapped Children," 10–12; Kessler, *The Crippled and the Disabled*, 22–24.

5. Robert Asher, "The Limits of Big Business Paternalism: Relief for Injured Workers in the Years before Workmen's Compensation," in *Dying for Work: Workers' Safety and Health in Twentieth-Century America*, ed. David Rosner and Gerald Markowitz (Bloomington: Indiana University Press, 1987), 19–33; Anthony Bale, "America's First Compensation Crisis: Conflict over the Value and Meaning of Workplace Injuries under the Employers' Liability System," in Rosner and Markowitz, *Dying for Work*, 34–52; Robert Asher, "Failure and Fulfillment: Agitation for Employers' Liability Legislation and the Origins of Workmen's Compensation in New York State, 1876–1910," *Labor History* 24, no. 2 (1983): 221–22; Skocpol, *Protecting Soldiers and Mothers*, 293–98; Eliza K. Pavalko, "State Timing of Policy Adoption: Workmen's Compensation in the United States, 1909–1929," *American Journal of Sociology* 95, no. 3 (1989): 592–94; Edward Berkowitz, "How to Think about the Welfare State," *Labor History* 32, no. 4 (1991): 493–95; Price V. Fishback and Shawn Everett Kantor, "The Durable Experiment: State Insurance of Workers' Compensation Risk in the Early Twentieth Century," *Journal of Economic History* 56, no. 4 (1996): 809–11.

6. Eastman, *Work-Accidents*, 165.

7. Of course, Eastman's assumption that working-class women in Pittsburgh were not already working outside the home reflected her own middle-class background. Eastman omitted women's experiences with industrial accidents from her book, reflecting her presumption that working-class families relied on a single male breadwinner. S. J. Kleinberg, "Seeking the Meaning of Life: The Pittsburgh Survey and the Family," in *Pittsburgh Surveyed: Social Science and Social Reform in the Early Twentieth Century*, ed. Maurine W. Greenwald and Margo Anderson (Pittsburgh: University of Pittsburgh Press, 1996), 98. Eastman, *Work-Accidents*, 119, 123, 125–26, 135–52; Witt, *Accidental Republic*, 131.

8. Crystal Eastman, *"Employers' Liability": A Criticism Based on Facts* (New York: New York Branch of the American Association for Labor Legislation, 1909), 13.

9. Eastman died in 1928 of kidney disease at age forty-five, leaving behind two orphaned children. Crystal Eastman to Annie Eastman, 21 September 1907, Crystal Eastman Papers (Acc. 82-M4), Box 6, Folder 169, Schlesinger Library, Harvard University, Cambridge, MA.

10. Eastman, *Work-Accidents*, appendix 1, quoted in Aldrich, *Safety First*, 91.

11. Eastman, *Work-Accidents*, 127–28.

12. Lattimore participated in the Pittsburgh Survey, investigating issues surrounding child care; her contribution was entitled "Pittsburgh as Foster Mother." Graham Taylor, "The National Conference at St. Louis: Occupational Standards," *Survey* 24 (11 June 1910): 453.

13. Graham Taylor, "The Industrial Viewpoint: Investigation of Industrial Accidents," *Charities and the Commons* 19 (4 January 1908): 1374; see also Henry R. Seager, "Outline of a Program of Social Legislation with Special Reference to Wage-Earners," in American Association for Labor Legislation, *Proceedings of the First Annual Meeting* (Madison, WI: American Association for Labor Legislation, 1907), 86, 95, 100.

14. Edward T. Devine, "Social Forces: Personal Depravity or Social Mal-adjustment," *Charities and the Commons* 21 (31 October 1908): 142. See also Robert Emmet Chaddock, "Needed Legislative Changes Requiring the Notification of Accidents and Diseases," *American Labor Legislation Review* 3, no. 1 (March 1913): 67–68 (hereafter *ALLR*).

15. Belle Lindner Israels, "Poverty and Insurance for the Unemployed," *Charities and the Commons* 20 (6 June 1908): 344. Israels later became Franklin Delano Roosevelt's publicist. See also William H. Matthews, "Widows' Families: Pensioned and Otherwise," *Survey* 32 (6 June 1914): 270.

16. Strikingly, the labor reformers who studied work accidents and advocated for workmen's compensation programs did not highlight Civil War pensions as a cautionary example. Nevertheless, Theda Skocpol claims that Congress's many expansions and extensions of Civil War pensions influenced the development of workmen's compensation. The Civil War pension system also served northerners as an early form of Social Security. Daniel T. Rodgers, *Atlantic Crossings: Social Politics in a Progressive Age* (Cambridge, MA: Harvard University Press, 1998), 213. Also see Skocpol, *Protecting Soldiers and Mothers*, 3, 59, 267–70.

17. Katherine Coman, "General Discussion [on comprehensive plans of social insurance]," *ALLR* 3, no. 2 (June 1913): 237, 239. See also William Hard, "General Discussion [on comprehensive plans of social insurance]," *ALLR* 3, no. 2 (June 1913): 233–34.

18. Witt, *Accidental Republic*, 130; Gwendolyn Mink, "The Lady and the Tramp: Gender, Race, and the Origins of the American Welfare State," in *Women, the State, and Welfare*, ed. Linda Gordon (Madison: University of Wisconsin Press, 1990), 100, 105–6.

19. Advances in medical care during the second half of the nineteenth century—including amputation, asepsis, anesthesia, and follow-up surgeries—meant that more workers survived their injuries to live with disabilities. Eastman, *Work-Accidents*, 144; James D. Schmidt, *Industrial Violence and the Legal Origins of Child Labor* (Cambridge: Cambridge University Press, 2010), 93–97.

20. William Hard, "The Legal Doctrine of Assumed Risk," *Machinists Monthly Journal* 23, no.2 (February 1911): 122 (hereafter *MMJ*); "Miners' Tribute to Moloch," *MMJ* 23, no. 3 (March 1911): 221.

21. Henry R. Seager, "Work Accidents and the Law," *Survey* 24 (6 August 1910): 664; Aldrich, *Safety First*, 114–21.

22. "The Trend of Things," *Charities and the Commons* 19 (18 January 1908): 1439.

23. William Hard, "The Ideal for Compensation," *MMJ* 21, no. 7 (July 1909): 610; Hard, "The Legal Doctrine of Assumed Risk," 122; "Miners' Tribute to Moloch," 221.

24. See also Elizabeth Beardsley Butler, "Pittsburgh's Steam Laundry Workers," *Charities and the Commons* 20 (1 August 1908): 554.

25. Miners also resisted the Bureau of Mines' efforts to popularize safer "permissible explosives," largely because such shifts eroded miners' ability to control blasting. Aldrich, *Safety First*, 219, 223; Thomas G. Andrews, *Killing for Coal: America's Deadliest Labor War* (Cambridge, MA: Harvard University Press, 2008), 140–41, 145–46.

26. Graham Taylor, "The Month's Industrial Survey: Preventing Mine Disasters," *Survey* 22 (3 April 1909): 79; Paul U. Kellogg, "Cannon: Test-Tubes: Swords: Plow-Shares," *Survey* 27 (2 December 1911): 1299–1302.

27. Witt, *Accidental Republic*, 119.

28. Crystal Eastman, "Employers' Liability," in *Thirty-Third Annual Report of the Proceedings of the New York Bar* [ca. 1910], p. 14, American Association for Labor Legislation Pamphlet Collection (hereafter AALL Pamphlet Collection) (Acc. 5001pam), Box 11, Folder 17 (B-3) (emphasis in original), Kheel Center for Labor-Management Documentation and Archives, M. P. Catherwood Library, Cornell University, Ithaca, NY (hereafter Kheel Center).

29. Alice Hamilton, "Lead Poisoning in Illinois," *ALLR* 1, no. 1 (January 1911): 20–23. See also Edward E. Platt, "Lead Poisoning in New York City," *ALLR* 2, no. 2 (June 1912): 278; Eastman, *Work-Accidents*, 87, 89, 95, 101.

30. Isaac M. Rubinow, *Social Insurance, with Special Reference to American Conditions* (New York: H. Holt, 1913; reprint, New York: Arno Press, 1969), 49. See also Emile E. Watson, *Report to the Legislature of the State of Ohio of the Investigation Made for the Ohio Employers Liability Commission into Industrial Accidents Occurring in Cuyahoga County, Ohio, for the Period of November, 1905, to January 1, 1911* (Columbus, OH: F. J. Heer Printing, 1910), 33; David A. Moss, *Socializing Security: Progressive-Era Economists and the Origins of American Social Policy* (Cambridge, MA: Harvard University Press, 1996), 121–22; Robert Asher, "Workmen's Compensation in the United States, 1880–1935" (PhD diss., University of Minnesota, 1971), 67–68; Eastman, *Work-Accidents*, 151–52.

31. *Survey* was the AALL's main means of reaching other Progressive reformers. From 1911 on, the AALL published the quarterly *American Labor Legislation Review*, which summarized developments in labor legislation around the country and featured the organization's policy proposals. Moss, *Socializing Security*, 1–3, 5, 11–12, 21–22; Asher, "Workmen's Compensation in the United States," 704; Skocpol, *Protecting Soldiers and Mothers*, 178–79.

32. Witt, *Accidental Republic*, 130.

33. These rules, usually referred to as the common-law doctrines or common-law defenses, had been developed by judges in the 1830s and 1840s as a means of ensuring that tort lawsuits would not damage economic growth and industrialization. Skocpol, *Protecting Soldiers and Mothers*, 258–59, 287; Bale, "America's First Compensation Crisis," 36–37.

34. Carl Gersuny, *Work Hazards and Industrial Conflict* (Hanover, NH: University Press of New England, 1981), 25.

35. Asher, "Workmen's Compensation in the United States," 33, 37–38.

36. Eastman, "Employers' Liability," 5; Eastman, *Work-Accidents*, 124. See also Bale, "America's First Compensation Crisis," 36; Skocpol, *Protecting Soldiers and Mothers*, 288–90.

37. Industrial accident victims in a few states, most notably Minnesota, had exceptionally high rates of success with liability lawsuits, with 73 percent winning awards in 1908 and 1909. During the same years, 43 percent of plaintiffs won in Pennsylvania, 46 percent in Michigan, 53 percent in Wisconsin, and 63 percent in Iowa. In New York, however, only 52,427 of the 414,681 workers who filed injury claims between 1906 and 1908 received any compensation. Asher, "Workmen's Compensation in the United States," 422–23; Berkowitz, *Disabled Policy*, 17, quoted in Willis J. Nordlund, *A History of the Federal Employees' Compensation Act* (Washington, DC: U.S. Department of Labor, Employee Standards Administration, Office of Workers' Compensation Programs, 1992), 19–20; George M. Gillette, "Competition or Co-operation in Workmen's Compensation," *Survey* 22 (13 September 1909): 820; "The Common Welfare: Little Variation in Work-Accident Rates," *Survey* 25 (8 October 1910): 85; Nate Holdren, "Disability, Passion, and Commodification in Early Twentieth Century American Workplace Injury Lawsuits" (paper presented at the Conference of the American Society for Legal History, Philadelphia, PA, November 2010).

38. Asher, "Workmen's Compensation in the United States," 36; Henry Rogers Seager, *Social Insurance: A Program of Social Reform* (New York: Macmillan, 1910), 62; Watson, *Report to the Legislature*, 44, 46–47; Eastman, "Employers' Liability," 17; Edward Berkowitz and Monroe Berkowitz, "The Survival of Workers' Compensation," *Social Service Review* 58, no. 2 (June 1984): 262–63.

39. Eastman, "Employers' Liability," 9.

40. "The Common Welfare: Liability vs. Compensation as Applied to Actual Cases," *Survey* 24 (14 May 1910): 277.

41. Hard, "The Ideal for Compensation," 610.

42. State of Wisconsin, *Report of the Special Committee on Industrial Insurance [to the] Wisconsin Legislature, 1909–1910* (Madison, WI: Committee on Industrial Insurance, 1911), 5–6; Asher, "Workmen's Compensation in the United States," 286; Seager, *Social Insurance*, 62; Bale, "America's First Compensation Crisis," 39–40.

43. Asher, "Workmen's Compensation in the United States," 138–56, 423–24; "Social Forces: Compensation for Industrial Accidents," *Survey* 22 (29 May 1909): 298; Gillette, "Competition or Co-operation in Workmen's Compensation," 821.

44. Paul U. Kellogg, "Monongah," *Charities and the Commons* 19 (4 January 1908): 1328; "Social Forces: Compensation for Industrial Accidents," 298.

45. The AALL did not invent the idea of internalization but did popularize it via both its workmen's compensation advocacy and its sickness insurance campaigns later on in the 1910s. Moss, *Socializing Security*, 65, 70.

46. William F. Willoughby, "The Problem of Social Insurance: An Analysis," *ALLR* 3, no. 2 (June 1913): 160–61.

47. Eastman, *"Employers' Liability,"* 21.

48. "Social Forces: Compensation for Industrial Accidents," 298.

49. "The Common Welfare: United Effort for Labor Legislation," *Survey* 22 (24 April 1909): 143; "Social Forces: The Conservation of Labor," *Survey* 24 (2 April 1910): 1–2; Taylor, "The Industrial Viewpoint," 1374–75.

50. John R. Commons, "Labor Legislation," *Survey* 22 (17 April 1909): 133. See also Asher, "Workmen's Compensation in the United States," 279–283; State of Wisconsin, *Report of the Special Committee on Industrial Insurance*, 6.

51. "Casualties on the Railroads," *MMJ* 21, no. 4 (April 1909): 294.

52. These figures were based on 1910 estimates. James T. Patterson, *America's Struggle against Poverty in the Twentieth Century* (Cambridge, MA: Harvard University Press, 2000), 25. As Skocpol notes, Commons and the Wisconsin school had a "distinctive mode of social reform.... Its essential premise was the notion that employment could be stabilized, industrial accidents reduced, and the general welfare of workers enhanced through the crafting of labor regulations that offered financial rewards to employers who behaved in efficient and humane ways." Theda Skocpol, *Social Policy in the United States: Future Possibilities in Historical Perspective* (Princeton, NJ: Princeton University Press, 1995), 149.

53. John B. Andrews, "A Clinic for Industrial Diseases," *Survey* 25 (12 November 1910): 269; "Social Forces: The Conservation of Labor," 1; Eastman, *Work-Accidents*, 165–66; "Quotations from First Report of New York State Employers' Liability Commission," appendix 4 in Eastman, *Work-Accidents*, 285.

54. "Sanctum Notes," *MMJ* 21, no. 1 (January 1909): 68.

55. Rodgers, *Atlantic Crossings*, 246; State of Washington, *Report of Commission Appointed by Governor M. E. Hay to Investigate the Problems of Industrial Accidents and to Draft a Bill on the Subject of Employes' Compensation to Be Submitted to the 1911 Session of the Washington Legislature* (Olympia, WA: E. L. Boardman, 1910), 6; Kansas City Board of Public Welfare, "Industrial Accidents in Missouri," [ca. 1914 or 1915], p. 13, AALL Pamphlet Collection, Box 12, Folder 2 (B-9).

56. American Association for Labor Legislation, *Proceedings of the Annual Meeting* (1907), quoted in Asher, "Workmen's Compensation in the United States," 195.

57. Asher, "Workmen's Compensation in the United States," 197–201, 205–12, 218–20, 275. See also State of Wisconsin, *Report of the Special Committee on Industrial Insurance*, 38; Eastman, "Employers' Liability," 18.

58. By the early 1910s, most medium to large employers supported an automatic industrial accident compensation system that included contributions from both employers and workers; most small companies, however, did not. Nevertheless, employers utterly failed to convince legislators to include employee contributions, except for two years in Ohio. Asher, "Workmen's Compensation in the United States," 129–56, 164–66, 174–80, 294–304, 672–73.

59. Skocpol, *Protecting Soldiers and Mothers*, 293.

60. "Administration of Labor Laws," *ALLR* 1, no. 2 (June 1911): 59; John Andrews and Irene Andrews, "Scientific Standards in Labor Legislation," *ALLR* 1, no. 2 (June 1911): 123; Abram I. Elkus, "General Discussion [on factory inspection]," *ALLR* 3, no. 1 (March 1913): 35; Skocpol, *Protecting Soldiers and Mothers*, 188–89.

61. Skocpol, *Protecting Soldiers and Mothers*, 295.

62. Moss, *Socializing Security*, 129–30; Witt, *Accidental Republic*, 128–29, 146–48; Berkowitz, *Disabled Policy*, 19. Theodore Roosevelt advocated for workmen's

compensation in his annual speeches to Congress between 1904 and 1908—the "only major labor reform Roosevelt endorsed while he was President." Asher, "Workmen's Compensation in the United States," 194.

63. The *Ives* decision pushed lawmakers toward elective compensation programs, although within a few years states such as Illinois and California required all employers to participate. Moss, *Socializing Security*, 125–26.

64. On the rise of the administrative state, see, for instance, Skowronek, *Building a New American State*; Skocpol, *Protecting Soldiers and Mothers*, 44–46; Witt, *Accidental Republic*, 190; William J. Novak, "The Legal Origins of the Modern American State," in *Looking Back at Law's Century*, ed. Austin Sarat, Bryant Garth, and Robert A. Kagan (Ithaca, NY: Cornell University Press, 2002), 249–50.

65. Roosevelt and other American labor law reformers feared creating what is now termed a "moral hazard": a situation in which beneficiaries received the same amount or more than they had earned via work and therefore had no incentive to return to work. *Message of the President of the United States Transmitting the Report of the Employer's Liability and Workingmen's Compensation Commission*, 62nd Cong., 2nd Sess., Senate Doc. No. 338, vol. 1: 68–70, quoted in I. M. Rubinow, "American Compensation Acts" [undated manuscript, ca. 1924], pp. 38–39, Isaac Max Rubinow Papers (Acc. 5616), Box 12, Permanent Partial (2/3), Kheel Center; personal communication from Edward Berkowitz, 1 July 2008.

66. By 1921, eleven of the forty-seven states with compensation acts provided retroactive compensation if the disability lasted from four to eight weeks. "Compensation of Federal Employees for Accidents and Diseases [part of immediate legislative program]," *ALLR* 2, no. 4 (December 1912): 560–61, 563. Rodgers, *Atlantic Crossings*, 221–41.

67. The federal act did, however, provide full wages for the year of compensation, a provision that was roundly critiqued by *Survey* for encouraging malingering. The federal law was revised in 1916 to cover over 90 percent of workers and provide several years of coverage at 66 ⅔ percent of wages. It covered both occupational diseases and industrial accidents. "Social Legislation: Compensation Laws Upheld by Supreme Court," *Survey* 37 (17 March 1917): 698; John B. Andrews, "New Federal Workmen's Compensation Law," *Survey* 36 (23 September 1916): 617–18; "The Common Welfare: Federal Employer's Liability Law," *Survey* 20 (25 April 1908): 127–28; "Compensation of Federal Employees for Accidents and Diseases," 560–61; Charles Earl, "The Need of a New Federal Employees' Accident Compensation Law," *ALLR* 3, no. 1 (March 1913): 43–52; "Workmen's Compensation for the Employees of the United States," *ALLR* 4, no. 2 (May 1914): 518–83; Nordlund, *A History of the Federal Employees' Compensation Act*, 5–8.

68. Eventually, most states added "loss of use" clauses that provided similar compensation for disabilities that were not dismemberments, such as frozen joints or a shortened leg. By 1918, thirty-three out of forty-one state acts incorporated dismemberment schedules and, by 1924, forty out of the forty-six states with workmen's compensation used them. New York State, Department of Labor, *The Workmen's Compensation Law, with Amendments, Additions, and Annotations to July 1, 1915* (Albany:

J. B. Lyon, 1915), 8; I. M. Rubinow, "Dismemberment Schedule under American Compensation Acts" (undated manuscript, ca. 1917–1918, revised 1924), pp. 1, 7, Rubinow Papers, Box 12, Permanent Partial (2/3).

69. Legislators were attracted by the simplicity of dismemberment schedules and the idea that all permanent injuries required compensation, regardless of whether there was a loss of earning capacity. Rubinow also traced their origin to the "voluntary contracts for accident insurance written by casualty companies for many years in which the amount of insurance in dollars is specified for every possible loss of members or loss of a combination of members." I. M. Rubinow, "Memorandum for the International Labor Office; Subject: Measurement of Permanent Incapacity under Social Insurance Schemes" [undated, ca. 1929–1935], p. 5, Rubinow Papers, Box 8, Folder 42; A. W. Whitney, "Schedules in Workmen's Compensation," *Transactions of the Actuarial Society of America* 14 (1913): 308–21; G. P. Michelbacher, "Schedule Rating of Permanent Injuries," *Proceedings of the Casualty Actuarial and Statistical Society of America* 1 (1914): 257–74; Rubinow, "Dismemberment Schedule under American Compensation Acts," 46; I. M. Rubinow to Royal Meeker, 28 January 1914, Rubinow Papers, Box 1, Folder 16; Berkowitz, *Disabled Policy*, 29.

70. "Workmen's Compensation: Period of Waiting Time Required under Workmen's Compensation Laws," *Monthly Labor Review* 36 (January 1933): 122–23.

71. The New Jersey act—one of the first workmen's compensation programs passed—provided an important precedent for the 50 percent rate and for the dismemberment schedules that would become popular nationwide. France offered a 65 percent lifetime pension for permanent total disability and a 50 percent lifetime pension for permanent partial disability, while Germany provided 65 percent of wages for lifetime disabilities. National Metal Trades Association, *Report of Committee on Employers' Liability Insurance to the Thirteenth Annual Convention* (New York: National Metal Trades Association, 1911), 73–74; Asher, "Workmen's Compensation in the United States," 482; P. Tecumseh Sherman, "The Compensation Commissions: A Review of Legislation Proposed in Seven States with Respect to Work Accidents," *Survey* 22 (4 March 1911): 949–62; John B. Andrews, "Workmen's Compensation in New Jersey—The Wrong Way," *Survey* 33 (27 March 1915): 696–97.

72. In 1910, steelworkers averaged $697 per year, or $13.40 per week. Semiskilled workers averaged from $15.12 to $18.00 per week; skilled workers averaged $21.60 to $36.00 per week. David Brody, *Steelworkers in America: The Nonunion Era* (Cambridge, MA: Harvard University Press, 1960; reprint, New York: Harper and Row, 1969), 46–48; P. Tecumseh Sherman, *Memorandum Relative to the Respective Advantages and Disadvantages of Various Forms of Compensation Law before the Congressional Employers' Liability and Workmen's Compensation Commission* (New York: National Civic Federation, 1911), 46–47.

73. I. M. Rubinow, "The Rate of Weekly Benefits" [undated manuscript, ca. 1917, revised 1924], p. 1, Rubinow Papers, Box 12, The Rate of Weekly Benefits.

74. The ruling was a heavy blow to AALL leaders; Eastman left the field of workmen's compensation afterward. Employers in nonhazardous industries ignored the

elective program. Moss, *Socializing Security*, 125–26; Witt, *Accidental Republic*, 183. See also Edward T. Devine, "Editorial Grist: Compensation Bills at Albany," *Survey* 29 (22 February 1913): 722–24; Henry R. Seager, "Introductory Address," *ALLR* 1, no. 4 (December 1911): 11.

75. Watson, *Report to the Legislature*, 56; Asher, "Workmen's Compensation in the United States," 668.

76. Some compensation statutes, such as Washington State's and the much-criticized 1908 federal employees' compensation act, covered only workers in specified hazardous injuries. Interstate commerce workers, along with sailors and any harbor workers injured on a vessel, were ineligible for compensation, while children could receive compensation, but generally received less money.

77. I. M. Rubinow to Hazel Kyrk, 11 December 1931, Rubinow Papers, Box 5, Folder 23; Edson S. Lott, *Workmen's Compensation Laws as Distinguished from Employers' Liability Laws: An Address . . . before the Insurance Society of New York* ([New York?], 1912), 8s. Legislators in states such as Michigan acknowledged the dangers of mechanized farm labor but rejected defining such work as "industrial." In California, farmers could elect to come under the compensation act and, by 1917, 12,000 farmers had done so. *Report of the Employers' Liability and Workmen's Compensation Committee of the State of Michigan* (Lansing, MI: Wynkoop Hallenbeck Crawford, 1917), 12. A. J. Pillsbury, *Changes in the [California] Compensation Law: What They Are and Why They Were Made* (San Francisco: Rincon Publishing, [ca. 1917]), 8.

78. Lott, *Workmen's Compensation Laws*, 8s.

79. Yet the AALL's compensation campaign, by its very existence, implicitly acknowledged new environmentalist views of poverty as caused not by "individual failings" by but "systemic risks." Moss, *Socializing Security*, 8.

80. Witt, *Accidental Republic*, 127, 132.

81. Wet-drilling, masks, and good ventilation could have reduced workers' exposure; the company instituted none of these practices. A radical magazine exposed the disaster and its cover-up in 1935; Congress soon held hearings on the disaster, and Secretary of Labor Frances Perkins organized a national conference on silicosis. By the late 1930s, states began compensating workers for silicosis, making it the first occupational illness routinely covered under compensation statutes. Rosner and Markowitz, *Deadly Dust*, 10, 97, 105.

82. Union Carbide and Carbon collected the 99 percent pure silica and transferred it to another division of the company for use. Cherniack, *The Hawk's Nest Incident*, quote from 3; see also 17–20, 24–34, 41, 53, 66–67; Rosner and Markowitz, *Deadly Dust*, 98.

83. "The Common Welfare: The New York Liability Bills," *Survey* 24 (21 May 1910): 303; "Social Forces," *Survey* 26 (2 September 1911): 768. *Survey* did criticize U.S. Steel's workmen's compensation program for its low rates. "The Common Welfare: Accident Relief of the U.S. Steel Corporation," *Survey* 24 (23 April 1910): 137; "To Stop Wasting Human Life," *MMJ* 21 (June 1909): 487–88; Hard, "The Ideal for Compensation," 610.

84. Jane Addams, "Human Conservation in Industry: A National Responsibility," *Survey* 24 (3 September 1910): cover page.

85. Testimony by Arthur Holder, "Employers' Liability Commission Hearings," *MMJ* 24 (February 1912): 62. Holder was a member of the IAM and part of the Legislative Committee of the AFL. Despite Samuel Gompers's long-held doubts about workmen's compensation, the AFL endorsed the principle of compensation in 1909. Asher, "Workmen's Compensation in the United States," 249.

86. M. J. McMahon, "Letter to the Editor: In Advocacy of Insurance," *MMJ* 21 (July 1909): 648–49; Hard, "The Legal Doctrine of Assumed Risk," 122; A. A. Graham, "Desired Legislation," *MMJ* 23 (April 1911): 327; William Forbath, *Law and the Shaping of the American Labor Movement* (Cambridge, MA: Harvard University Press, 1991), 29–124.

87. "Sanctum Notes," *MMJ* 21 (November 1909): 1107.

88. "The Common Welfare: Liability vs. Compensation," 277; Hard, "The Ideal for Compensation," 610. See Bale, "America's First Compensation Crisis," 48; Skocpol, *Protecting Soldiers and Mothers*, 288–91.

89. J. Andrews, "Workmen's Compensation in New Jersey—The Wrong Way," 696–97; Skocpol, *Protecting Soldiers and Mothers*, 193.

90. "Social Forces," *Survey* 26 (2 September 1911): 768; "Industry: 22 Years as a Mill Surgeon," *Survey* 28 (21 September 1912): 778–79.

91. Rodgers, *Atlantic Crossings*, 225.

92. Bismarck began to support sickness and disability insurance in 1878 precisely for this purpose. Ibid., 223.

93. "Petition to the President for a Federal Commission on Industrial Relations," *Survey* 27 (30 December 1911): 1430. See also "Industry: 22 Years as a Mill Surgeon," 778–79.

94. Willoughby, "The Problem of Social Insurance," 158.

95. J. Lee Kreader, "America's Prophet for Social Security: A Biography of Isaac Max Rubinow," (PhD diss., University of Chicago, 1988), 36.

96. He later reflected, "In Professor Seligman's [1903] seminar . . . I was first bitten by the social insurance bug." I. M. Rubinow to E. E. Agger, 21 February 1935, Rubinow Papers, Box 9, Folder 10, quoted in Kreader, "America's Prophet for Social Security," 48.

97. Kreader, "America's Prophet for Social Security," 75–77, 78–86, 98–99; U.S. Commissioner of Labor, *Twenty-Fourth Annual Report: Workmen's Insurance and Compensation Systems in Europe* (Washington, DC: Government Printing Office, 1911).

98. Rubinow was attracted in part to the AALL by its professed nonpartisanship and his growing realization that, unlike in Europe, where beneficiaries or government pushed for legislation, in the United States "legislation usually starts as a 'reform movement' initiated by private individuals and groups." His first encounter with the organization was at the 1911 annual meeting, where he presented a paper listing all of the faults of the 1908 federal employees' compensation act. I. M. Rubinow, *The Quest for Security* (New York: H. Holt, 1934), 604; Kreader, "America's Prophet for Social Security," 152–53, 156.

99. Laura Rubinow Lebow, Interview by J. Lee Kreader, 6 April 1978, Rubinow Papers, quoted in Kreader, "America's Prophet for Social Security," 203.

100. Kreader, "America's Prophet for Social Security," 209. In addition, Rubinow spent part of 1914 calculating real trends in wages, a project that the Bureau of Labor Statistics had abandoned in 1890. He "not only documented swift and dramatic declines in both the hourly and weekly real wages since 1907, but also found real wages to have peaked in 1896." Ibid., 206–7.

101. Roy Lubove, "Economic Security and Social Conflict in America: The Early Twentieth Century, Part II," *Journal of Social History* 1, no. 4 (Summer 1968): 337–38. The standard accident table involved three different projects: estimating the frequency of accidents in the United States, deriving the spread of the comparative seriousness of accidents from European statistics (i.e., the proportions of fatalities and different types of permanent disabilities), and applying the results to American compensation scales.

102. The pure premium was "the actual cost of the insurance after subtracting agents' commissions and an insurance company's administrative expenses ... based on accident rates, the relative degrees of seriousness among accidents, and the compensation scale prescribed by any given state." Kreader, "America's Prophet for Social Security," 210.

103. Not only did Rubinow routinely dress down authors of journal articles and book reviews for failing to recognize his expertise and contributions, but he was also wont to criticize current and potential employers. While negotiating with the California Industrial Accident Board about a position as chief actuary, for instance, he wrote, "I could have easily pointed out to the Board that there is not a single man in the country (and that is no exaggeration) who has had the experience such as I have had to prepare me for taking charge of a State insurance fund." Ibid., 589; Barbara [Nachtrieb] Armstrong, Interview by J. Lee Kreader, Oral History Collection of Columbia University, Butler Library, p. 7, quoted in Kreader, "America's Prophet for Social Security," 634; Henriette C. Epstein, Interview by Lee Kreader, 16 and 22 March 1979, New York, Rubinow Papers; quoted in Kreader, "America's Prophet for Social Security," 675; I. M. Rubinow to Robert F. Foester, 6 June 1914, Box 3, Folder 45; I. M. Rubinow to His Excellency, Governor of the State of New York, 23 April 1918, Box 6, Folder 25; I. M. Rubinow to Clarence W. Hobbs, 21 October 1935, Box 2, Folder 36, Box 2; Ira B. Cross to I. M. Rubinow, 25 September 1913, Rubinow Papers, Box 7, Folder 2; all from Rubinow Papers.

104. Rubinow followed compensation statutes in distinguishing between total and partial permanent disability. In the 1920s and 1930s, he expanded on his articles for the *ALLR* and *Survey* in several unpublished manuscripts on disability. Intriguingly, in the 1930s Rubinow developed a definition of disability remarkably similar to that of the American with Disabilities Act: "Physical disability [he prefers that term or "physical incapacity" over "physical invalidity"] is a condition limiting the individual in normal exercises of life's functions and the concept need not be limited to economically productive work. Loss, total or partial, of ability to move around, to see, to exercise any of the senses or functions or even impairment of general health constitutes physical invalidity or disability, for at least that principle must be recognized that full exercises in economic functions must presuppose at least an average level of health and well being." I. M. Rubinow, "Memorandum for the International Labor Office," 9.

105. I. M. Rubinow, "Social Insurance: The New York Compensation Act; An Appreciation and a Criticism," *Survey* 31 (21 February 1914): 643; see also I. M. Rubinow, "First American Conference on Social Insurance," *Survey* 30 (5 July 1913): 478–80; I. M. Rubinow, "The Pension Plan for the Brewing Industry," *Survey* 29 (21 December 1912): 360–63; I. M. Rubinow, "Industry: Accident Compensation for Federal Employees," *Survey* 30 (16 August 1913): 624–28; I. M. Rubinow, "Editorials: The Specter of Malingering," *Survey* 31 (25 October 1913): 97–98; I. M. Rubinow, "Social Insurance: What the New Phrase Means and Why," *Survey* 31 (6 December 1913): 268–69, 278–83; I. M. Rubinow, "General Discussion [on insurance aspects of workmen's compensation]," *ALLR* 3, no. 2 (June 1913): 280–81; I. M. Rubinow, "Accident Compensation for Federal Employees," *ALLR* 2, no. 1 (February 1912): 29.

106. Rubinow, "Memorandum for the International Labor Office," 1. See also I. M. Rubinow, "The Theory and Practice of Law Differentials," *Proceedings, Casualty Actuarial and Statistical Society of America* 4, no. 9 (1917): 23.

107. Rubinow, "Dismemberment Schedule under American Compensation Acts," 2.

108. Rubinow, "Memorandum for the International Labor Office," 6. See also Rubinow, "Dismemberment Schedule under American Compensation Acts," 3.

109. Rubinow, "Memorandum for the International Labor Office," 9. Rubinow observed that "cases of total permanent disability are very rare," resulting from less than one-eighth of 1 percent of all industrial accidents. Most states required loss of both arms, hands, legs, feet, or eyes; the sight in both eyes; or loss of any two parts. Despite the tiny numbers of permanent total disability cases, Rubinow argued that the fear of such cases had exerted undue influence on compensation statutes. Rubinow, "Dismemberment Schedule under American Compensation Acts," 2; Rubinow, "Total Permanent Disabilities" [undated manuscript, ca. 1917–1918, revised 1924], p. 19, Rubinow Papers, Box 12, Permanent Partial (3/3). On the stringent criteria for proving total permanent disability, see Royal Meeker to I. M. Rubinow, 6 February 1915, Rubinow Papers, Box 10, Folder 33; E. H. Downey to I. M. Rubinow, 5 April 1915, Rubinow Papers, Box 3, Folder 10, Box 3.

110. *Iowa Law in Regard to Employer's Liability or Workmen's Compensation Enacted by the Thirty-Fifth General Assembly*, comp. W. S. Allen, Senate File no. 3, pp. 13–14, AALL Pamphlet Collection, Box 12, Folder 3 (B-3).

111. Rubinow, "Memorandum for the International Labor Office," 8–9.

112. Dismemberment schedules provided a specified period of compensation (usually measured in weeks) for various injuries. Rubinow's suggestion foreshadowed the so-called occupational grid in the Social Security Disability Insurance program by several decades. Rubinow, "Social Insurance: The New York Compensation Act," 643. See also Rubinow, "Editorials: The Specter of Malingering," 97; personal communication from Edward Berkowitz, 1 July 2008.

113. West Virginia also provided a dismemberment schedule that took into account both age and occupation. Both California and West Virginia provided lifetime pensions for disabilities above 70 percent, at 10 percent and 40 percent of wages, respectively. I. M. Rubinow, "Partial Permanent Disability" (undated manuscript, ca. 1917–1918, revised

1924), p. 50, Rubinow Papers, Box 12, Partial Permanent Disability (1/3); Whitney, "Schedules in Workmen's Compensation," 308–21; Michelbacher, "Schedule Rating of Permanent Injuries," 257–74; Albert W. Whitney, "General Discussion [on insurance aspects of workmen's compensation]," *ALLR* 3, no 2 (June 1913): 273.

114. Rubinow, "Memorandum for the International Labor Office," 7.

115. I. M. Rubinow to E. H. Downey, 25 March 1915, Rubinow Papers, Box 3, Folder 10. See also I. M. Rubinow to Royal Meeker, 28 January 1914, Box 1, Folder 16; and I. M. Rubinow to A. J. Pillsbury, 25 October 1911, Box 2, Folder 31, both from Rubinow Papers.

116. Rubinow, "Dismemberment Schedule under American Compensation Acts," 13; Berkowitz, *Disabled Policy*, 29.

117. Some states covered medical costs for injured workers. Rubinow, "General Discussion [on insurance aspects of workmen's compensation]," 280–81.

118. Rubinow, "Social Insurance: The New York Compensation Act," 643.

119. "The Common Welfare: Compensation Bills Proposed by Pennsylvania Commission," *Survey* 29 (15 March 1913): 828; Florence L. Sanville, "Social Legislation in the Keystone State: Seven Years of Suffering since the Tale of Industrial Accidents was First Tallied in a Great Industrial District; The Administration's Compensation Bills in 1915," *Survey* 34 (10 April 1915): 45; Rubinow, "The Pension Plan for the Brewing Industry," 361.

120. Rubinow, "Dismemberment Schedule under American Compensation Acts," 5–7; Rubinow, "Memorandum for the International Labor Office," 7. See also Stephen Mihm, "'A Limb Which Shall Be Presentable in Polite Society": Prosthetic Technologies in the Nineteenth Century," in *Artificial Parts, Practical Lives: Modern Histories of Prosthetics*, edited by Katherine Ott, David Serlin, and Stephen Mihm (New York: New York University Press, 2002): 282–99; Schweik, *Ugly Laws*, 52–62; Baynton, *Defectives in the Land*, 106–32.

121. Rubinow, "Dismemberment Schedule under American Compensation Acts," 41–42; I. M. Rubinow to Crystal Eastman, 17 February 1927, Rubinow Papers, Box 3, Folder 12. In September 1918, Rubinow actually applied for the position of superintendent of case work at the Federal Board of Vocational Education. I. M. Rubinow to C. A. Prosser, 28 September 1918, Rubinow Papers, Box 3, Folder 36, Box 3.

122. Rubinow, "Editorials: The Specter of Malingering," 97–98. Fears of malingering extended to war veterans as well, as discussed in chapter 7.

123. I. M. Rubinow to Royal Meeker, 28 January 1914, Rubinow Papers, Box 1, Folder 16; Bruno Lasker, "Rebuilt Men: New Trades and Fresh Courage for French War Cripples," *Survey* 37 (7 April 1917): 11.

124. Rubinow to Meeker, 28 January 1914, Rubinow Papers, Box 1, Folder 16.

125. See, for instance, "The Common Welfare: The New York Liability Bills," 303; "Social Forces," *Survey* 26 (2 September 1911): 768; "The Common Welfare: Liability vs. Compensation," 277; "Industry: 22 Years as a Mill Surgeon," 778–79; William M. Leiserson, "The Wisconsin Legislation of 1911," *Survey* 27 (14 October 1911): 1001.

126. Prior to 1912, the AALL focused on policy research rather than on promoting specific legislation. It had officially expanded its mission to include the writing and

publicizing of model bills in 1910, but little action took place on this front until 1912, when the Committee on Social Insurance was founded. Skocpol, *Protecting Soldiers and Mothers*, 198–99. See, for instance, "The Common Welfare: Paragraphs in Philanthropy and Social Advance: Liability Law Void," *Charities and the Commons* 19 (18 January 1908): 1402–3; "Plan Uniform Law on Accident Compensation," *Survey* 25 (10 December 1910): 423.

127. "A Platform of Industrial Minimums," *Survey* 28 (6 July 1912): 518; "The Common Welfare: Recent Developments in Accident Compensation," *Survey* 28 (3 August 1912): 596–97; "The Common Welfare: New Committee on Social Insurance," *Survey* 29 (15 March 1913): 827; Rubinow, "First American Conference on Social Insurance," 479; McSweeney, "Industry: Medical Men and Workmen's Compensation in Massachusetts," *Survey* 31 (8 November 1913): 31.

128. "Standards for Workmen's Compensation Laws Recommended by the American Association for Labor Legislation," *ALLR* 4, no. 4 (December 1914): 585 (scale endorsed by the AFL in November 1914). Throughout the 1910s, the Social Insurance Committee served as the AALL's focal point for social insurance research and legislative proposals. Skocpol, *Protecting Soldiers and Mothers*, 199.

129. John B. Andrews, "Outline of Work: 1913," *ALLR* 4, no. 1 (March 1914): 150; "Standards for Workmen's Compensation Laws Recommended by the American Association for Labor Legislation," 587–88. This scale was endorsed by the AFL in November 1914. Prompted by Andrews, the AALL had decided to start proposing model legislation in 1910, but did not actually do so until early 1913, after the formation of the Committee on Social Insurance. In its proposed standards for workmen's compensation statutes, the AALL did not address the problems created by dismemberment schedules, perhaps because the schedules were so widespread as to be unchangeable.

130. "Immediate Legislative Program," *ALLR* 2, no. 4 (December 1912): 516; J. Andrews, "Outline of Work: 1913," 150; John B. Andrews, "Report of Work: 1916," *ALLR* 7, no. 1 (March 1917): 188. Some AALL members demurred, notably Ernst Freund of the University of Chicago. Freund fretted in *Survey* about whether providing even a small amount of compensation would make workers greedy for more. He stated, "Experience demonstrates that a scale of compensation once adopted is not likely to be reduced. On the other hand, there will be constant clamor and pressure for increase of rates." Ernst Freund, "Editorial Grist: The Federal Workmen's Compensation Act," *Survey* 27 (3 February 1912): 1671. See also Gertrude Vaile, "Some Social Problems of Public Outdoor Relief," *Survey* 34 (3 April 1915): 15.

131. J. Andrews, "Report of Work: 1916," 188.

132. I. M. Rubinow to C. A. Prosser, 28 September 1918, Rubinow Papers, Box 3, Folder 36.

133. Berkowitz, *Disabled Policy*, 15.

134. Only thirteen states raised compensation scales between 1915 and 1925. Insurance Department of the Chamber of Commerce of the United States, "Tendencies in Workmen's Compensation," *Insurance Bulletin*, no. 18: 971–75; Asher, "Workmen's Compensation in the United States," 659.

135. Asher, "Workmen's Compensation in the United States," 661.

136. John B. Andrews to I. M. Rubinow, 29 May 1924, and 13 June 1924, Box 1, Folder 17; and John B. Andrews to I. M. Rubinow, 30 July 1913, Box 1, Folder 18, all in Rubinow Papers; Witt, *Accidental Republic*, 197.

137. Rubinow left Ocean Accident & Insurance Guarantee in 1916 over a spat about his advocacy on behalf of the health insurance movement. He struggled to find a permanent position for several years and finally moved to Palestine to run the American Zionist Medical Unit. When he returned to the United States in 1923, he could not find a place in the weakened social insurance movement and became further isolated after he began fighting with AALL leaders such as Andrews and Commons over whether to prioritize preventing social problems or eradicating poverty. As a result, Rubinow spent the rest of his life working for B'nai Brith and was almost totally excluded from the process of developing and administering Social Security in the early 1930s, despite being the foremost visionary of the Social Security system: a devastating disappointment. E. H. Downey to Walter S. Bucklin (recommendation to president of Liberty Mutual Insurance Company for Rubinow), 16 September 1920, Box 3, Folder 10; I. M. Rubinow to William J. Gardner, 8 March 1916, Box 7, Folder 2; I. M. Rubinow to J. J. Smick, 4 November 1935, Box 2, Folder 36; I. M. Rubinow to Edwin R. A. Seligman, 13 May 1917, Box 9, Folder 14; all from Rubinow Papers. Raymond Rubinow to Paul U. Kellogg [ca. 1936], Survey Associates Papers, Box 106, Folder 800, Social Welfare History Archives, University of Minnesota, Minneapolis, MN; Rubinow, *Social Insurance*, 170–71, 480–81; Moss, *Socializing Security*, 160–61; Lubove, "Economic Security and Social Conflict," 344, 346, 348–49.

138. When Franklin Roosevelt learned in 1936 that Rubinow was dying from lung cancer, he sent him a copy of *The Quest for Security*, inscribed, "For the Author—Dr. I. M. Rubinow. This reversal of the usual process is because of the interest I have had in reading your book." Inscribed copy of *The Quest for Security* in the possession of Raymond S. Rubinow; Kreader, "America's Prophet for Social Security," 694. According to former senator Paul Douglas, Roosevelt considered Rubinow to be the "greatest single authority upon social security in the United States." Paul H. Douglas, "Dr. I. M. Rubinow's Contribution to Social Security," *Forum Report* 1, no. 1 (Fall 1970): 14.

139. The commission did not seem particularly concerned about the unexpected outcome of the compensation statute, devoting only a paragraph to discrimination against disabled workers. The report's authors instead spent several pages discussing the possibility that compensation statutes might encourage malingering among workers. Chicago-based industrial surgeon Harry E. Mock dated the popularization of physical examinations to 1912, explicitly linking them to compensation statutes. He commented, "The enactment of these laws gave a marked stimulus to the method because many concerns felt that it was necessary to rule out the defectives in order to protect themselves from liabilities." Mock served as a medical examiner or surgeon for Sears, Roebuck & Company; Chicago, Milwaukee & St. Paul Railroad Company; Lincoln Motor Car Works; and Mutual Insurance Company of New York. Commonwealth of Massachusetts Industrial Accident Board, *First Annual Report of the Industrial*

Accident Board (Boston: Wright and Potter Printing, 1914), 44; Mock, *Industrial Medicine and Surgery*, 371.

140. G. L. Avery, "Avery Company's Plan under the Illinois Workmen's Compensation and Employers' Liability Act," *Proceedings of the First Cooperative Safety Congress* (Milwaukee, 1912), 266, quoted in Marks, "The Problem of Second Injuries," 38–39 (emphasis in original).

141. Ralph J. Brodsky, *The Workmen's Compensation Act of the State of Pennsylvania Explained for Employers and Employees* (Philadelphia: Ralph J. Brodsky, 1915), 17, Box 12, Folder 8 (B-15). See also State of Michigan, Industrial Accident Board, "Workmen's Compensation Law (Act No. 10 of Public Acts Extra Session, 1912): Provisions and Operation," *Bulletin* (1912): 12, Box 12, Folder 2 (B-9); and W. S. Allen, "Iowa Law in Relation to Employer's Liability or Workmen's Compensation, Enacted by Thirty-Fifth General Assembly, Senate File No. 3" (State of Iowa, 1913), pp. 12–14, Box 12, Folder 3 (B-10); all from AALL Pamphlet Collection (Acc. 5001pam), Kheel Center.

142. "General Discussion of Conference: Loss of Remaining Eye," *National Compensation Journal* 1, no. 4 (May 1914): 44 (reprint of "Proceedings of the First National Conference of Industrial Accident Boards and Commissions Held at Lansing, Mich., April 14 and 15, 1914").

143. The chairman of Pennsylvania's Workmen's Compensation Board downplayed these developments, arguing that the board had not found any real instances of discrimination even after investigation. Taking a view reminiscent of Ford Motor Company's approach to placing disabled workers, he commented: "Of course, it is the employer's right, as well as his duty, to cause physical examinations of his employee. Their mutual interests are thus served. Many employers, by this examination, discover that the employee is in the wrong place, in view of his physical infirmities, and then a transfer takes place to the advantage of the employee himself as well as for the better safety of his fellows." He grudgingly noted, however, "There are always individual cases, undoubtedly, but they do not establish the rule." The New York State Compensation Commission made a similar argument to the *Jewish Deaf*. Denying seeing any cases of discrimination, the deputy commissioner contended that "the employer has not discharged his old help, even if they are afflicted, but rather has given more attention to their abilities and transferred them to other departments where they are safer.... The employer takes more care of them and puts them at work where they can be more useful." National Association of the Deaf, "Proceedings of the Twelfth Convention of the National Association of the Deaf," *The Nad* 3, no. 1 (February 1918): 80–81; Nate Holdren, "Incentivizing Safety and Discrimination: Employment Risks under Workmen's Compensation in the Early Twentieth Century United States," *Enterprise and Society* 15, no. 1 (March 2014): 36–39.

144. Employers may have feared that workers with hernias and other preexisting injuries that were difficult to diagnose would use compensation acts to malinger. Industrial physicians, in turn, promoted physical examinations as a means of improving public health. "Physical Examination of Workmen," *Square Deal* 15, no. 63 (December

1914): 443–44, article reprinted from Knights of Labor *Journal*; Commonwealth of Massachusetts Industrial Accident Board, *First Annual Report*, 44; "Does the Workmen's Compensation Law Change the Old Time Relations between the Physician and His Patient?," *National Compensation Journal* 1, no. 1 (January 1914): 28–29; Marks, "The Problem of Second Injuries," 10; L. L. Gilbert, "Physical Examination of Railway Employees from a Medico-Legal Standpoint," *Medico-Legal Journal* 17, no. 3 (1899): 337–39; Edwin W. De Leon, *The Relation of the Medical Examination of Employes to Insurance under Workmen's Compensation Laws* (White Sulphur Springs, WV: Annual Convention of International Association of Casualty and Surety Underwriters, 1914), 6; "Medical Examination of Employes: Experience of Seven Chicago Firms," special number, *Bulletin of the Chicago Tuberculosis Institute* 1, no. 3 (June 1913): 4–14; Angela Nugent, "Fit for Work: The Introduction of Physical Examinations in Industry," *Bulletin of the History of Medicine* 57, no. 4 (Winter 1983): 578–583, 585.

145. Marks, "The Problem of Second Injuries," 10.

146. Ibid.; "Physical Exams for Republic I. & S. Employes," *Steel and Iron* 48 (20 April 1914): v.

147. Mock, *Industrial Medicine and Surgery*, 371; Holdren, "Incentivizing Safety," 41; see also Slavishak, *Bodies of Work*, 351–52.

148. *Weaver v. Maxwell Motor Co.*, 186 Mich. 588 (1915); *National Compensation Journal* 1, no. 11 (November 1914): 6, quoted in Marks, "The Problem of Second Injuries," 50. See also *Schwab v. Emporium Forestry Co.*, 167 A.D. 614 (1915); *In re Madden, Appeal of American Mut. Liability Ins. Co.*, 222 Mass. 487 (1916).

149. *Nease v. Hughes Stone Co., et al.*, 114 Okla. 170 (1925); Marks, "The Problem of Second Injuries," 55.

150. Wallace D. Yaple, "State Insurance Experience in Ohio," *National Compensation Journal* 1, no. 4 (May 1914): 37 (reprint of "Proceedings of the First National Conference of Industrial Accident Boards and Commissions Held at Lansing, Mich., April 14 and 15, 1914"); Marks, "The Problem of Second Injuries," 5.

151. "Physical Examination of Workmen prior to Employment Becoming Necessary," *Problem* 1, no. 3 (May 1915): 9, quoted in Marks, "The Problem of Second Injuries," 48. According to Marks, the Colorado Industrial Commission found in 1931 and 1932 that insurance companies refused to sell insurance to mining firms that retained "men who had suffered major loses." As a result, the coal operators were forced to discharge lifelong employees. Marks, "The Problem of Second Injuries," 94. Insurance firms tended to deny using rates to encourage discrimination against disabled and elderly workers, citing the fact that insurance companies aggregated risks over many firms. Holdren, "Incentivizing Safety," 45.

152. The chairman of Pennsylvania's Workmen's Compensation Board argued that for "the man who insures his own risk, the physical condition of his employees is of no consequence so far as that insurance proposition is concerned." Marks, "The Problem of Second Injuries," 5; National Association of the Deaf, "Proceedings of the Twelfth Convention," *The Nad*, 80–81, "Special Convention Issue," 80; Holdren, "Incentivizing Safety," 46–52; John Andrews's opening comments on "rehabilitating men" in New

York State, Industrial Commission, *Proceedings of the First Industrial Safety Conference of New York State* (Albany: J. B. Lyon, 1917), 162.

153. Witt reports that "work-fatality rates per manhour ... dropped by two-thirds" between 1907 and 1920 and notes that nonfatal work accidents "appear to have declined by half." Witt, *Accidental Republic*, 187; Lescohier, "The Lumberman's Hazard," *Survey* 26 (5 August 1911): 640; "The Common Welfare: Accident Prevention in Minnesota," *Survey* 32 (23 May 1914): 210; "The Common Welfare: Safety First and Sickness Last," *Survey* 33 (7 November 1914): 121; John Calder, "Industry: Some Methods in Safety Engineering, II: Guarding Wood-Working Saws and Cutters," *Survey* 27 (18 November 1911): 1215.

154. Don D. Lescohier, "Some Work-Hazards Which Go into a Loaf of Bread," *Survey* 26 (2 September 1911): 805; John A. Fitch, "Industry: A Safety Movement That Is Becoming Nation Wide," *Survey* 31 (11 October 1913): 49.

155. Fitch, "Industry: A Safety Movement," 49.

156. "Social Forces: Pittsburgh in Perspective," *Survey* 27 (7 October 1911): 917–18.

157. Eastman, *Work-Accidents*, 84–87; *Report of the Proceedings of the First National Conference on Vocational Rehabilitation of Persons Disabled in Industry or Otherwise* (Washington, DC: Government Printing Office, 1922), 59–61.

158. Industrial physicians echoed this distrustful attitude, generally favoring their diagnostic exams over workers' own medical histories and prioritizing diagnosis over treatment or prevention. John H. Weller, "General Discussion of Conference: Physical Examinations," *National Compensation Journal* 1, no. 4 (May 1914): 43 (reprint of "Proceedings of the First National Conference of Industrial Accident Boards and Commissions Held at Lansing, Mich., April 14 and 15, 1914"); Nugent, "Fit for Work," 588–91.

159. Hookstadt's views evolved with time. After researching the frequency of second injuries that led to "major disabilities," he declared the "increased costs of second injuries" to be "negligible," at less than .3 percent of all compensation costs. Carl Hookstadt, "Problem of the Handicapped in Industry," *Monthly Labor Review* 4 (March 1918): 579; Carl Hookstadt, "Comparison of Compensation Laws of the United States and Canada up to January 1, 1920," *Bulletin of the United States Bureau of Labor Statistics* 275 (Washington, DC: Government Printing Office, 1920): 74–75.

160. Peter J. Brady, "General Discussion on Workmen's Compensation," *ALLR* 5, no. 1 (March 1915): 25.

161. "Strike Threat over Compensation Law," *New York Times*, 12 August 1914, 13; Marks, "The Problem of Second Injuries," 45; "Physical Examination of Workmen," *Square Deal* 15, no. 63 (December 1914): 444. On statements against medical examinations by the AFL, the United Garment Workers of America, and Samuel Gompers, see Marks, "The Problem of Second Injuries," 45–47.

162. American Federation of Labor, *Report of the Proceedings of the Thirty Fourth Convention*, 67, quoted in Holdren, "Incentivizing Safety," 35; see also Nugent, "Fit for Work," 591–592.

163. Edwin W. De Leon, "General Discussion on Workmen's Compensation," *ALLR* 5, no. 1 (March 1915): 20.

164. Marks, "The Problem of Second Injuries," 17–23.

165. Great Britain, Home Office, Departmental Committee on Workmen's Compensation, *Report of Departmental Committee Appointed to Enquire into the Law Relating to Compensation for Injured Workmen*, vol. 2, *Minutes of Evidence*, Cmd. 2334, Parliamentary Papers, vol. 75 (1905): 487, sec. 4442, quoted in Marks, "The Problem of Second Injuries," 19. Ironically, the opponents of the 1897 British compensation act had predicted that employers would require physical examinations of job applicants and bar some men from employment entirely. Marks, "The Problem of Second Injuries," 17–18.

166. Rodgers, *Atlantic Crossings*, chap. 6 passim. The U.S. Department of State asked consuls in European cities to report on the functioning of compensation statutes, including the impact of the laws on disabled workers. Marks suggests that American policy makers ignored the issue based on the testimony of labor leaders, who swore that compensation statutes would not cause discrimination against disabled or elderly workers. Marks, "The Problem of Second Injuries," 24–33.

167. Williams-Searle, "Broken Brothers," 390, 392, 517. See also William John Pinkerton, *His Personal Record: Stories of Railroad Life* (Kansas City, MO: Pinkerton Publishing, 1904), 9, quoted in Williams-Searle, "Broken Brothers," 50.

168. The study was coordinated by the State City Free Labor Exchange. Marks, "The Problem of Second Injuries," 88.

169. Consumers' League of Eastern Pennsylvania, "Commutations of Workmen's Compensation," [unpublished manuscript sent to John A. Fitch in March 1928], pp. 33–34, John A. Fitch Papers (MS 937), Box 12, Folder 13, Wisconsin Historical Society.

170. In 1925, Pullman had eighty-eight one-eyed employees; only eight remained by 1931. Nate Holdren, "Screening for 'Impaired Risks': Risk, Medical Examinations, and Hiring at the Pullman Company in the Early Twentieth-Century United States" (paper presented at the Annual Meeting of the Business History Conference, St. Louis, MO, April 2011), 14; Holdren, "Incentivizing Safety," 54.

171. Montgomery Ward's policy stemmed from the company's adoption of a self-insurance plan in 1912. Workers were screened after one year and, if deemed unfit, were fired. De Leon, *Relation of the Medical Examination of Employes to Insurance*, 6.

172. With some success, France sought to limit discrimination against disabled workers, requiring all companies with a "concession, monopoly, or subvention from the state" to reserve a certain proportion of positions for disabled soldiers. Brodsky, *The Workmen's Compensation Act*, 5; "Compensation's Effect on Employees," *Weekly Underwriter* 91, no. 6 (8 August 1914): 155; "Legal Advances in 1919," *Modern Hospital* 14, no. 3 (March 1919): 195; "Vocational Rehabilitation: Interrelation of the Programs of Vocational Rehabilitation and Workmen's Compensation," *Bulletin of the Federal Board for Vocational Education* 76 (June 1922): 14–15; "Laws concerning the Employment of Disabled Men," *American Journal of Care for Cripples* 7, no. 1 (March 1918): 67; Marks, "The Problem of Second Injuries," 34–36, 56, 76–77, 89, 114–15.

173. Many states maintained second-injury funds until quite recently; some disappeared only after the passage of the Americans with Disabilities Act of 1990.

Howard A. Rusk, "Rehabilitation: Handicapped Veterans Complain That Compensation Laws Are Quoted by Some Employers in Turning Them Down for Jobs," *New York Times*, 1 September 1946, 30. See also "Early Change in Compensation Law Urged for Employment of Handicapped Workers," *New York Times*, 18 June 1944, S5; Charles Hurd, "The Veteran: Uniform State Insurance Laws Held Need for Handicapped Men," *New York Times*, 27 May 1945, 24; "War Casualty Hiring Urged on Employers," *New York Times*, 23 October 1945, 8; David Tobenkin, "Don't Overlook Second-Injury Funds: Special State Funds for Workers with Pre-existing Conditions Can Help Defray Long-Term Costs for Workers' Compensation," *HR Magazine* 57, no. 7 (July 2009): 51.

174. S. Meyer, *The Five-Dollar Day*, 197–98. Nevins reports that Sorenson "despised the Sociological Department and tried to thwart it." Nevins, *Ford: Expansion and Challenge*, 349. See also Steven Watts, *The People's Tycoon: Henry Ford and the American Century* (New York: Knopf, 2005), 285–95.

175. Marquis, *Henry Ford: An Interpretation*, 155, quoted in S. Meyer, *The Five-Dollar Day*, 198–99. Nevins suggests that during this time, Ford's interests were shifting from social reform to politics and journalism. Nevins, *Ford: Expansion and Challenge*, 350.

176. "Reminiscences of Robert A. Shaw," p. 66, Oral History Collection (Acc. 65), BFRC.

177. In 1913, for instance, Robertson had tried to fire a worker with epilepsy because of the "danger of serious injury from such cause with resulting compensation to be paid." Ford personally overruled the recommendation for discharge. L. B. Robertson to P. E. Martin, 1 April 1913, and note by Martin, 2 April 1913, Legal Cases Numerical Records (Acc. 297), Box 1, Folder L-2—Unreported Accidents—1913–1915 (personnel), BFRC.

178. B. C. Forbes, "Slave Driving in Ford Factories: Pictured by Ford's Own Workers," *Forbes*, 1 May 1927, 20, Vertical File—Ford Motor Company—Labor, BFRC; "Reminiscences of William P. Baxter," pp. 14–15, Oral History Collection (Acc. 65), BFRC.

179. The Ford Motor Company had opposed Michigan's workmen's compensation law before its passage in 1912, arguing that a voluntary system would better compensate workers. Nevins, *Ford: Expansion and Challenge*, 345–46. Legal Department to Mr. Shaw, 28 December 1916, and L. B. Robertson to James Couzens, 29 September 1915, Legal Cases Numerical Records (Acc. 297), Box 2, Folder L-10 (Lichtenberg, John, 1915 [personal]), BFRC.

180. Robertson to Couzens, 29 September 1915, BFRC.

181. Nevins, *Ford: Expansion and Challenge*, 345. These pro-business exemptions may derive from the fact that Michigan's original workmen's compensation law was written largely in an open-shop state by major employers, unlike the workmen's compensation laws passed in Wisconsin, New York, Washington, and Illinois.

182. McKenzie nevertheless remained at Ford Motor Company; he served as a general foreman by 1940. David McKenzie, Compensation Department (Ford Motor Company) records (hereafter Compensation Department records) (Acc. 789), Box 1. See also Alphonso M. Boyer, Jake Cohen, Box 2, all BFRC; Bureau of the Census, *Sixteenth Census, 1940*, Michigan, Highland Park City, Enum. Dist. 82–125, Sheet 6B.

183. Francesco Aiello, Compensation Department records (Acc. 789), Box 2.

184. "More Help Urged for the Disabled," *New York Times*, 28 March 1927, 11.

185. In fact, many if not most of the workers who filed delayed compensation claims and who can be located in census records seem to have remained at Ford Motor Company. Frank Alampi, Fred Albers; see also George Benko, Norman Davis, and John Heckleman, who lost his "first right finger" due to "misconduct" but who retained his position at Ford; Compensation Department records (Acc. 789), Box 2; Bureau of the Census, *Sixteenth Census, 1940*, Michigan, Detroit, Ward 21, Enum. Dist. 84-1466, Sheet 12A, and Enum. Dist. 84-1458, Sheet 13A; Michigan, Detroit, Ward 3, Enum. Dist. 84-137, Sheet 10B; and Michigan, Highland Park City, Enum. Dist. 82-148, Sheet 2A. See also *Fifteenth Census, 1930*, Michigan, Detroit, Enum. Dist. 82-195, Sheet 6B.

186. Nationwide, most workers were accorded temporary total disability while they recovered from accidents; once healed, they were reclassified as having a temporary partial, permanent partial, or permanent total disability. Like most states, Michigan relied on a dismemberment schedule, and limited compensation for total disabilities to 300 weeks until 1919, when legislators raised the time limit to 500 weeks. Until 1919, injured or disabled workers also received only 50 percent of their wages, with a minimum of $4 per week and a maximum of $10. If workers were injured for more than eight weeks, they received compensation for the two-week waiting period. Industrial Accident Board [of Michigan], *Workmen's Compensation Law: Provisions and Operation*, p. 9; Industrial Accident Board [of Michigan], *Workmen's Compensation Law of the State of Michigan, as Amended and in Force on and after August 10, 1917*, p. 5, AALL Pamphlet Collection, Box 12, Folder 13; *Rules of the Michigan Industrial Accident Board, Effective August 14, 1919* (Lansing, MI: Department of Labor, 1917), 10, 13, 28.

187. Nevins, *Ford: Expansion and Challenge*, 345–46.

188. See chap. 4.

189. Vahan Harootian, Compensation Department records (Acc. 789), Box 2, as well as Jacob Patrick, Herman Warmack, Ardro Hardymek, and James Hastings, also in Box 2; Bureau of the Census, *Sixteenth Census, 1940*, Michigan, Detroit, Ward 21, Enum. Dist. 84-1430, Sheet 61B. By 1940, Hastings worked as a machine operator at Ford. For an example of an unsuccessful delayed compensation case, see Lawrence Hansen, in Box 2; Hansen, too, remained at Ford through at least 1930, at which time he labored as a ball pinion machine operator. *Fifteenth Census, 1930*, Michigan, Detroit, Enum. Dist. 82-83, Sheet 17B. See also Schmidt, *Industrial Violence*, 187–90.

190. The author claimed, "The output of condemnatory letters from Ford plants, it has been the experience of this publication, exceeds that from any other plant or plants in America." Forbes, "Slave Driving," 19–20. See also Peter Skatus, Sam Trojanek, Paul Vokes, and John Zahaski, Compensation Department records (Acc. 789), Box 2.

191. S. Alex Marshall, Compensation Department records (Acc. 789), Box 2. See also Joseph Omasta and Peter Banionis for cases where disabilities worsened, workers were laid off, and then could not find other jobs. Compensation Department records (Acc. 789), Box 1.

192. For hernia claims, see Peter Skatus, Sam Trojanek, Paul Vokes, and John Zahaski, Compensation Department records (Acc. 789), Box 2. A few workers did receive delayed compensation for hernias during this period. See Henry Zygaj, Compensation Department records (Acc. 789), Box 2, and Joseph Midalla (Box 1). Some workers made more colorful claims. Stanley Stempnik alleged in 1933 that he "lost his mind from [the] heat of [the] blast furnace" in 1923. Don Mettetal "claim[ed in 1931] that lifting rubber was such heavy work, it caused detachment of [the] retina" in 1915. Compensation Department records (Acc. 789), Box 1 (Don Mettetal) and 2 (Stanley Stempnik).

193. Flori Popovich, Compensation Department records (Acc. 789), Box 2.

Chapter Six

1. "Human wreckage" and the "industrial scrap heap" were two of several such terms commonly used by rehabilitators. "Scrap heap" referred to both disabled and elderly workers who had been thrown out of the mainstream labor market due to concerns about efficiency; "human wreckage" appeared most often in discussions of war injuries. See, for instance, J. J. Kennedy, "Safety and Efficiency," *Safety Engineering* 40 (December 1920): 216; W. F. Bradley, "French War Repair Shops Models of Systematism," *Motor Age* 29 (29 June 1916): 20; "No Trouble," *Christian Advocate* 81 (9 August 1906): 81; Edgar J. Helms, "Eighth Annual Report of the Bureau of Goodwill Industries of the Department of City Work of the Board of Home Missions and Church Extension of the Methodist-Episcopal Church," 1926, p. 5, Chronological File, Goodwill Industries International Archives, Bethesda, MD (hereafter GII).

2. E. J. Helms, "Religious and Welfare Work of Morgan Memorial," in [Morgan Memorial Co-operative Industries and Stores, Inc., Report for 1910], p. 12, Chronological File, GII.

3. Edgar J. Helms, "Ninth Annual Report of the Bureau of Goodwill Industries," 1927, p. 1, Chronological File, GII.

4. By the 1920s, hundreds of sheltered workshops and industrial homes served blind people, those labeled as "cripples," people with epilepsy, individuals with cognitive disabilities, and disabled people in general. See, for instance, Bradley Byrom, "A Vision of Self Support: Disability and the Rehabilitation Movement in Progressive America" (PhD diss., University of Iowa, 2004); Frances A. Koestler, *The Unseen Minority: A Social History of Blindness in the United States* (New York: David McKay, 1976); Williams-Searle, "Broken Brothers," chap. 6 passim.

5. Frederick C. Moore, *The Golden Threads of Destiny* (Boston: Morgan Memorial Goodwill Press, 1952; reprint, Bethesda, MD: Goodwill Industries International, 2001), 69. E. J. Helms to Bishop Fred Leete, 8 January 1919, Chronological File, GII. E. C. E. Dorion's 1915 treatise on Morgan Memorial includes no mention of disabled workers. Dorion, *The Redemption of the South End: A Study in City Evangelization* (New York: Abingdon Press, 1915; reprint, Bethesda, MD: Goodwill Industries International, 2001), chap. 5 passim and chap. 12 passim.

6. Herbert Kliebard notes that, as a whole, the vocational education movement had little positive impact on graduates' wages and selection of jobs. Herbert Kliebard, *Schooled to Work: Vocationalism and the American Curriculum, 1876–1946* (New York: Teachers College Press, 1999), 212–15.

7. The "Not Charity but a Chance" slogan came from a 1918 article in a veterans' rehabilitation magazine, *Carry On*, by way of a circular from Cleveland Goodwill Industries, but Helms had deployed similar phrases in fund-raising pamphlets for years. Frank M. Baker to Oliver Friedman, 18 March 1925, City File, Cleveland, GII; Florence White Barbour, *"Just Folks: They Are Like You and You Are Like Them ("Only More So") Because Conditions Are Different—That's All,"* Folder 1911, Box 1, Morgan Memorial—Goodwill Industries Records, Boston University School of Theology Archives, Boston, MA (hereafter MMGI). The origins of the slogan "Saving the Waste in Men and Things" remain obscure.

8. Reformers of all stripes created rehabilitative work programs in the late nineteenth century, from vocational education for immigrant children and reformatories to manual labor boarding schools for Native American and African American children. On vocational education, see Arthur F. McClure, James Riley Chrisman, and Perry Mock, *Education for Work: The Historical Evolution of Vocational and Distributive Education in America* (Rutherford, NJ: Fairleigh Dickinson University Press, 1985); Harvey Kantor, *Learning to Earn: School, Work, and Vocational Reform in California, 1880–1930* (Madison: University of Wisconsin Press, 1988); Kliebard, *Schooled to Work*. On reformatories, see Barbara M. Brenzel, *Daughters of the State: A Social Portrait of the First Reform School for Girls in North America, 1856–1905* (Cambridge, MA: Massachusetts Institute of Technology Press, 1983); Mary E. Odem, *Delinquent Daughters: Protecting and Policing Adolescent Female Sexuality in the United States, 1885–1920* (Chapel Hill: University of North Carolina Press, 1995).

9. The chapel was founded in 1859 by Methodist Episcopal preacher Henry Morgan. In 1903, the *Boston Sunday Journal* described Morgan Memorial as the "oddest church in the whole country," in part because "Unitarians paid the bills for a Methodist preacher." "Boston Has the Oddest Church in the Whole Country," *Boston Sunday Journal*, 19 April 1903, 11, quoted in Jonathan Andrew Dorn, "'Our Best Gospel Appliances': Institutional Churches and the Emergence of Social Christianity in the South End of Boston" (PhD diss., Harvard University, 1994), 286.

10. Dorion, *The Redemption of the South End*, 116, quoted in Dorn, "'Our Best Gospel Appliances,'" 14; see also 147, 149.

11. Institutional churches such as Boston's Congregationalist Berkeley Temple emerged out of the doctrines of the Social Gospel and Thomas Beecher's "practical Christianity," which defined social services as a key form of evangelism. Such churches also aimed to prevent the decline of mainline Protestantism in urban areas by discarding pew fees and keeping their doors open all week long. Berkeley Temple provided a reading room, evangelical services, and young people's choirs. Helms's predecessor at Morgan Chapel in the 1860s and 1870s, Henry Morgan, had experimented with providing some services later instituted by Helms: a night school, employment office, and

"benevolent sewing school," among others. Dorn, "'Our Best Gospel Appliances,'" 1–4, 45–57, 137, 165–67; Benjamin L. Hartley, "Holiness Evangelical Urban Mission and Identity in Boston, 1860–1910" (ThD diss., Boston University School of Theology, 2005), 132, 134, 136, 317–18.

12. Sydney E. Ahlstrom, *A Religious History of the American People* (New Haven, CT: Yale University Press, 1972), chap. 47 passim; Martin E. Marty, *Modern American Religion*, vol. 1, *The Irony of It All, 1893–1919* (Chicago: University of Chicago Press, 1986), chap. 14 passim; Henry F. May, *Protestant Churches and Industrial America* (New York: Octagon Books, 1963), 170–203.

13. Helms seemed unaware that Yiddish, not Hebrew, served as the neighborhood's lingua franca. In contrast to most Methodists at that time, Helms still believed in the evangelistic doctrines of "instantaneous sanctification" and "entire sanctification." Quote from Hartley, "Holiness Evangelical Urban Mission," 299; see also 259–60, 288, 290–93, 296, 306.

14. Helms also studied at Harvard University with Francis Greenwood Peabody, a professor of social ethics and a leading advocate of the Social Gospel. Although Peabody was Unitarian, he was not hostile toward the Methodist Helms. Hartley, "Holiness Evangelical Urban Mission," 260–61.

15. Dorn, "'Our Best Gospel Appliances,'" 138–41; Hartley, "Holiness Evangelical Urban Mission," 256, 319, 329, 331, 340, 345.

16. Dorn, "'Our Best Gospel Appliances,'" 136, 154.

17. The Unitarian Benevolent Fraternity of Churches had already helped to develop another institutional church in the South End: Unitarian Parker Memorial Church. Ibid., 136–37.

18. Bill Stidger, "Shirt Sleeve Christianity," *Christian Herald*, July 1933, 8; Edgar James Helms, *Pioneering in Modern City Missions* (Boston: Morgan Memorial Printing Department, 1927; reprint, Bethesda, MD: Goodwill Industries International, 2001), 25; John Fulton Lewis, *Goodwill: For the Love of People* (Bethesda, MD: Goodwill Industries of America, 1977), 57, 60; H. May, *Protestant Churches and Industrial America*, 189; Beatrice Plumb, *The Goodwill Man: Edgar James Helms* (Minneapolis: T. S. Denison, 1965), 122–23; E. J. Helms, "Spiritual Values of Social, Institutional, and Industrial Efforts," *First Annual Meeting of the Council of Cities* (Philadelphia: Department of City Work of the Board of Home Missions and Church Extension of the Methodist Episcopal Church, 1917), 16. Helms was also inspired by the founder of the Methodist Church, John Wesley, who established a workshop in 1740 in which twelve impoverished people repaired donated items and then sold them to other poor people. Like Helms, Wesley aimed to simultaneously prevent both idleness and want. "Excerpts from John Wesley's Journal, Tuesday, November 25, 1740: Passage from a Speech by E. J. Helms, Founder of Goodwill Industries," Chronological File, GII.

19. E. J. Helms, "Annual Report of the Boston Missionary and Church Extension Society, 1897–98," *Our City* 3, no. 1 (October–December 1898): 13, in Morgan Chapel (1898), Box 1, MMGI.

20. Dorn, "'Our Best Gospel Appliances,'" 306–7.

21. Morgan Chapel was staffed largely by Iowans in the early years. [Morgan Memorial Co-operative Industries and Stores, Inc., Report for 1910], Chronological File, GII.

22. Helms, *Pioneering in Modern City Missions*, 59, 96, 130.

23. Scrapbook for 1895–1900, p. 305, Morgan Chapel 1895–1900, Box 1, MMGI; Dorn, "'Our Best Gospel Appliances,'" 156, 157n82.

24. E. J. Helms to My Dear Friend, 1896, unnamed folder, Box 1, MMGI; *Arts and Industries* (April 1906): 10, 1906 Folder, Box 1, MMGI.

25. Edgar J. Helms, "Radio Talk over WHAS," 5 May 1929, Chronological File, GII; Dorn, "'Our Best Gospel Appliances,'" 157.

26. Helms, "Religious and Welfare Work of Morgan Memorial"; "The Morgan Memorial Situation," p. 2, Morgan Chapel scrapbook for 1900, Box 1, MMGI.

27. E. J. Helms, "The Relation of the Church to Industrial Relief," *Second Annual Meeting of the Council of Cities of the Methodist Episcopal Church* (Philadelphia: Board of Home Missions and Church Extension of the Methodist Episcopal Church, 1918), 39–40, MMGI.

28. Morgan Memorial Co-operative Industries and Stores, Inc., *Report of 1909*, pp. 2–3, Chronological File, GII; *Atlanta Goodwill Industries Incorporated* (Atlanta: Atlanta Goodwill Industries, ca. 1931), 4; E. J. Helms, "Morgan Chapel, Boston," *Christian City: Devoted to City Evangelization* 40, nos. 3–4 (March–April 1899), 62–64; E. J. Helms, "To the Member of the Joint Committee, and Delegates of the Women's Auxiliary, the Co-operative Industries, and Local Church" [1910], "Joint Committee: Sub-committees, Morgan Memorial" journal, pp. 110–11, Box 1, MMGI.

29. Helms, "Religious and Welfare Work of Morgan Memorial"; "Darkness Dispelled, for the Light Came," *Goodwill* (Brooklyn), n.s., 5, no. 2 (December 1926–February 1927): 1, City File, Brooklyn—Newsletters/Brochures, GII. See also *Arts and Industries*, April 1906, p. 5, Chronological File, GII.

30. E. J. Helms, "Report of the Bureau of Goodwill Industries to the Annual Meeting of the Board of Home Missions and Church Extension of the Methodist Episcopal Church (1924)," Methodist Church records, Bureau—1924, GII.

31. Helms was particularly inspired by Johann Wichern's Inner Mission movement, which had established orphanages, asylums, and workhouses to aid the poor in the mid-nineteenth century. Once back in Boston, he joined the Boston chapter of Walter Rauschenbusch's Brotherhood of the Kingdom—one of the key Social Gospel organizations in the early twentieth century—and developed a friendship with Harry Ward, the pro-labor secretary of the Methodist Federation for Social Service. Dorn, "'Our Best Gospel Appliances,'" 305.

32. Edgar J. Helms, "Church and Workingman," *Zion's Herald* 79 (17 July 1901): 919, quoted in Hartley, "Holiness Evangelical Urban Mission," 264. In the same lecture, Helms criticized premillennialist evangelicals such as Dwight Moody for doing damage to evangelicalism with their theories of a second coming. Helms's growing interest in Social Gospel and liberal theology also reflected the ways in which Methodists

were "'mainstreaming' and increasingly resembling their upper-class Protestant neighbors in their social gospel emphases." Hartley, "Holiness Evangelical Urban Mission," 331.

33. Helms changed the church's name from Morgan Chapel to Morgan Memorial in 1902, after building a new facility. Dorn, "'Our Best Gospel Appliances,'" 303–4.

34. Ibid., 161; Hartley, "Holiness Evangelical Urban Mission," 319–20. Helms also held temperance and evangelism meetings in conjunction with concerts on Saturday night. Dorn, "'Our Best Gospel Appliances,'" 147.

35. Dorn, "'Our Best Gospel Appliances,'" 158, 378.

36. Hartley defines the turning point as 1902, when Morgan Memorial constructed a new church building that "critics chastised as looking more like a warehouse than a church." In response to the criticism, Helms erected "what would have been seen as a very modern electric cross on the top of the building that announced the priorities of his church: 'Life, Love, Hope, Faith, and Brotherhood.'" Quote from Hartley, "Holiness Evangelical Urban Mission," 322; Dorn, "'Our Best Gospel Appliances,'" 292–93.

37. Hartley, "Holiness Evangelical Urban Mission," 322–23; Dorn, "'Our Best Gospel Appliances,'" 295–96, 367.

38. Dorn, "'Our Best Gospel Appliances,'" 362–64 (quote from 362).

39. Trattner, *From Poor Law to Welfare State*, 211–27; Regina Kunzel, *Fallen Women, Problem Girls: Unmarried Mothers and the Professionalization of Social Work, 1890–1945* (New Haven, CT: Yale University Press, 1995), chap. 5 passim; Alice O'Connor, *Poverty Knowledge: Social Science, Social Policy, and the Poor in Twentieth-Century U.S. History* (Princeton, NJ: Princeton University Press, 2001), chap. 1 passim; Katz, *In the Shadow of the Poorhouse*, 163–71.

40. The institutional church movement came to an end in the late 1910s amid the rise of professional charity and social work and continued turnover in downtown neighborhoods, which made it difficult to develop a committed membership. Dorn, "'Our Best Gospel Appliances,'" 364–66, 378, 381–82.

41. Ibid., 378.

42. *Prospectus and Manual of Morgan Memorial* (Boston: Goodwill Press of Morgan Memorial, 1922), 189; *Annual Report of the Board of Home Missions and Church Extension of the Methodist Episcopal Church, 1925*, 105 (hereafter cited as *Board of Home Missions Annual Report*).

43. Dorn, "'Our Best Gospel Appliances,'" 299. Josiah Strong, head of the American Institute for Social Service, praised Morgan Memorial, along with many ministers from all different Protestant denominations. Helms had a reputation as a talented publicist.

44. Ibid., 297–98.

45. Goodwill Industries tended to employ significant numbers of elderly women in clothing repair. *Goodwill* (Milwaukee) 1, no. 1 (1921): 3, City File, Milwaukee, GII; "The Old Ladies' Corner," *Goodwill* (Brooklyn), o.s., 9, no. 40 [n.s., 1, no. 2] (December 1922–February 1923): 4, City File, Brooklyn—Newsletters/Brochures, GII. See also Earl Christmas, *The House of Goodwill: A Story of Morgan Memorial* (Boston:

Morgan Memorial Press, 1924), 62; *Atlanta Goodwill Industries Incorporated*, 6–7. The six-story workshop was a gift of George and John Henry, New Hampshire paper mill magnates; after the workshop opened, Helms had one hundred applicants each day. Dorn, "'Our Best Gospel Appliances,'" 371.

46. Helms, "Spiritual Values of Social, Institutional, and Industrial Efforts," 16.

47. *Board of Home Missions Annual Report, 1919*, 58.

48. F. Moore, *The Golden Threads of Destiny*, 69. Helms's motivations for shifting the focus of Goodwill Industries toward disabled people remain unclear. Nonetheless, Goodwill Industries worked with the Federal Vocational Bureau and the Reconstruction Committee to rehabilitate disabled veterans at the Industries themselves or through home work. E. J. Helms to Bishop Fred Leete, 8 January 1919, Chronological File, GII. Dorion, *The Redemption of the South End*, chap. 5 passim and chap. 12 passim.

49. The Centenary, as originally planned, was a five-year-long program aimed at expanding Methodist Episcopal missions both abroad and domestically; the program commemorated the hundredth anniversary of Methodist Episcopal mission work. The Centenary grant to Goodwill Industries reflected the deep concern of the Board of Home Missions about reconnecting the church to "polyglot" urban communities, generally through large downtown institutional churches, and preventing the spread of industrial unrest and radicalism. See, for instance, Melvin P. Burns, "The New City Program and the Centenary Campaign," *Second Annual Meeting of the Council of Cities of the Methodist Episcopal Church* (Philadelphia: Board of Home Missions and Church Extension of the Methodist Episcopal Church, 1918), 11; George B. Dean, "Report of the Superintendent of the Department of City Work," *Board of Home Missions Annual Report, 1917*, 51–88; Ralph Welles Keeler, "Report of the Superintendent of the Department of City Work," *Board of Home Missions Annual Report, 1918*, 53; J. Lewis, *Goodwill*, 87. The Board of Home Missions provided less support than promised (in part because the Centenary did not meet its donation goals), one of several factors that helped lead to an uneasy partnership between Helms and the board and, in the 1930s, the entire separation of Goodwill Industries from Methodist control. *The Centenary Survey of the Board of Home Missions and Church Extension of the Methodist Episcopal Church* (New York: Joint Centenary Committee, 1918), 49–51; *Board of Home Missions Annual Report, 1920*, 58; *Board of Home Missions Annual Report, 1928*, 28; J. Lewis, *Goodwill*, 108, 119, 137–45, 151–56.

50. The schism between the Methodist Episcopal Church North and the Methodist Church South delayed the establishment of Goodwill Industries in the South, since white ministers there would not work with Helms or offer any support, probably due to the integrated services offered at Morgan Memorial and other northern Goodwill Industries. An Atlanta minister contended that the postwar labor shortage meant that, in the South, only African Americans would use Goodwill Industries. F. D. Leete to E. J. Helms, 13 January 1919, Chronological File, GII.

51. Helms, "Radio Talk over WHAS."

52. Barbour, "*Just Folks*," 3; Edgar J. Helms, "Eighth Annual Report of the Bureau of Goodwill Industries," 1926, pp. 1–2, Chronological File, GII; Russell S. James, "Report

of Training at Morgan Memorial," 1920, pp. 7–8 (quote from 7), Chronological File, GII; Helms, "Radio Talk over WHAS."

53. See, for instance, *Annual Report of the Board of Home Missions, 1919*, 58; *Annual Report of the Board of Home Missions, 1920*, 59; E. J. Helms, "Report on the Goodwill Industries for Dr. Burns," 1920, People File, Edgar J. Helms—Correspondence, 1920–1929, GII.

54. Helms battled employees for a year before replacing the piecework system with the operations system. Growing competition from church rummage sales helped in part to drive the concern with improving efficiency; in 1930, Helms termed such activities un-Christian. A. G. Young, "Exhibit No. 16: Standards in Manufacture," in "Minutes and Proceedings of the Second Annual Council of the Goodwill Industries of America, Buffalo, New York, February 22–27, 1921," p. 92, Methodist Church records, Bureau—1921, GII (hereafter cited as "Minutes and Proceedings of the Second Annual Council of the Goodwill Industries of America, 1921"); "A Goodwill Sale versus a Rummage Sale," *The Goodwill: Morgan Memorial Edition*, o.s., 9, no. 40, n.s., 1, no. 2 (December 1922, January and February 1923: 2 (5521), Folder for 1923, Box 2, MMGI; E. J. Helms, "Superintendent's Report," 21 May 1930, p. 1, Morgan Memorial, 1930–1931 Folder, Box 4, MMGI.

55. *Prospectus and Manual of Morgan Memorial*, 130; "A Trip through Morgan Memorial and a Biographical Sketch of Rev. Henry Morgan," n.d., Folder for 1925, Box 3, MMGI; Oliver A. Friedman, "Accounting and Cooperation with Other Agencies," in *The Goodwill Industries: A Manual* (Boston: Morgan Memorial Goodwill Press, 1935), 133–34.

56. "Minutes and Proceedings of the Second Annual Council of the Goodwill Industries of America, 1921," pp. 23–24, Methodist Church records, Bureau—1921, GII.

57. Helms, "The Relation of the Church to Industrial Relief," 41. *Prospectus and Manual of Morgan Memorial*, 59. *Annual Report of the Board of Home Missions, 1925*, 105.

58. "Minutes and Proceedings of the Second Annual Council of the Goodwill Industries of America, 1921," pp. 23–24, Methodist Church records, Bureau—1921, GII.

59. "Memorandum concerning Minimum Wage in the Morgan Memorial Goodwill Industries" [ca. 1927–1930], City File, Boston—Reports, GII; *Prospectus and Manual of Morgan Memorial*, 91.

60. Helms, *Pioneering in Modern City Missions*, 94; "Do You Know That?," *Goodwill* (Milwaukee) 4, no. 3 (1926): 6, City File, Milwaukee, GII; Bureau of Goodwill Industries and the National Association of Goodwill Industries, *Purposes and Policies of Goodwill Industries* (Boston: Morgan Memorial Goodwill Industries Press, 1936), 26–27; Edgar M. Wahlberg, "Daily Record of Work at Morgan Memorial, 21 November 21, 1927–December 1927," p. 16, City File, Boston—History (2), GII.

61. "Memorandum concerning Minimum Wage in the Morgan Memorial Goodwill Industries"; Dorion, *The Redemption of the South End*, 49–50.

62. A. G. Young, "The Piecework System in Goodwill Industries," *Goodwill Glimpses*, July 1929, p. 2, Goodwill Scribbler, GII; Young, "Exhibit No. 16: Standards in Manufacture," p. 92, Methodist Church records, Bureau—1921, GII. See also H. A. R.

Carleton, "Steps Necessary to Put the Goodwill Industries on a Trade School Basis," *Papers Presented at the First Annual Meeting of the Goodwill Industries at Pittsburgh, Pennsylvania, February 10–12, 1920*, p. 18, Delegate Assemblies (1920), GII.

63. F. C. Moore, "Report of the Assistant Superintendent and Treasurer to the Board of Directors of the Morgan Memorial Cooperative Industries and Stores, Inc. for the Meeting September 20, 1920," Morgan Memorial (1920–1921), Box 2, MMGI.

64. "Our First Woman Cabinet Officer," *Christian Herald* (July 1933): 6–7, 1929 Folder, Box 4, MMGI.

65. By 1922, Morgan Memorial employed about 5,000 workers per year. J. S. Nicholson, "Safest and Shortest Methods to Self-Support," *Papers Presented at the First Annual Meeting of the Goodwill Industries at Pittsburgh, Pennsylvania, February 10–12, 1920*, Delegate Assemblies (1920), GII; *Prospectus and Manual of Morgan Memorial*, 57, 59; *Annual Report of the Board of Home Missions*, 1924, 82; "Financial Statements," *Goodwill* (Buffalo) 1, no. 3 (1922): 2, City File, Buffalo—Newsletters and Memos, GII.

66. These eight disabled workers were employed in the employment, industrial, storage, receiving, collecting, and shipping departments. During the first nine months of 1928, Morgan Memorial employed 1,342 people, roughly 150–200 of whom were likely regular employees.

67. A Methodist minister like Helms, Wahlberg supported miners' efforts to unionize in Utah in the mid-1920s; established consumers' cooperatives, unemployed cooperatives, and a credit union, among many other initiatives, in Denver in the 1930s and 1940s; directed the first Denver chapter of the American Civil Liberties Union; and fought for civil rights for migrant workers and nonwhites in Colorado. Wahlberg, "Daily Record of Work at Morgan Memorial," pp. 3–7, 15, 39, 41. Auraria Library, "Inventory of the Edgar M. Wahlberg Papers, 1920–1990," Auraria Library, Denver, CO, http://carbon.cudenver.edu/public/library/archives/wahlberg/wahlberg.html (accessed 30 June 2008).

68. James, "Report of Training at Morgan Memorial," 1920, pp. 7–8 (quote from 7); "Meet Charles Please!," *Goodwill News* (Baltimore), September 1921, p. 2, Chronological File, GII. See also Lauretta Joy, "Cleveland *Plain Dealer* Visits Us and Reports," *Good Samaritan* (Cleveland) 1, no. 1 (1920): 2, City File, Cleveland—Newsletters, GII; Barbour, "Just Folks," 9–10; "Report to the Directors of the Morgan Memorial Cooperative Industries and Stores," Morgan Memorial (1920–1921) Folder, Box 2, MMGI.

69. Wahlberg, "Daily Record of Work at Morgan Memorial," p. 17; "Just Folks," *Goodwill News* (Buffalo) 1, no. 2 (1920): 3, City File, GII.

70. Wahlberg, "Daily Record of Work at Morgan Memorial," p. 16.

71. "Work of Goodwill Industries Shows," *Brooklyn Daily Times*, 12 November 1922, City File, Brooklyn—Clippings, GII.

72. Ralph Welles Keeler, *The Goodwill Industries* (Philadelphia: Department of City Work, 1923), 10. Women made up one-third of the sixty-member workforce.

73. "Background Material on [Detroit] Goodwill Industries" [ca. 1966], City File, Detroit—History, GII.

74. Dorion, *The Redemption of the South End*, 49–50.

75. Wahlberg, "Daily Record of Work at Morgan Memorial," p. 21. Wahlberg supported the labor movement throughout his life.

76. Ibid., 27. At the same time, workers had a voice in the management of the Industries and served on the board of each Goodwill Industries. *Annual Report of the Board of Home Missions, 1920*, 59.

77. Young briefly recalled a strike that took place among the shoe repairmen when he first arrived in the 1910s, which led him to raise their wages from $1.20–$1.60 per day to $4–$6 each day. A. G. Young, "Goodwill Industries and the Human Element," 17 September 1929, Folder for 1929–1930, Box 4, MMGI.

78. Mary E. French, "Employment Bureau Report," *Morgan Chapel Mirror* (n.d. but after March 1901): 11–12 (4962–4963), Morgan Chapel (1898) Folder, Box 1, MMGI.

79. Lowell Brestel Hazzard, *Goodwill Tales* (Boston: Morgan Memorial Goodwill Press, 1922); *Goodwill Tales* (Boston: Morgan Memorial Goodwill Press, ca. 1938), Subject Files (E–G), GII.

80. The Associated Charities and other charitable agencies apparently sent many clients to Morgan Memorial. In 1920, Helms reported, "Industrial conditions are so good on the outside that we are having very few able-bodied persons looking for employment, [illegible] handicapped people are sent to us from all over Boston." F. C. Moore to the Members of the Board of Directors of the Morgan Memorial Cooperative Industries and Stores, Inc., 18 May 1927, Morgan Memorial (1927–1928) Folder, Box 3; A. G. Young to the President and Members of the Board of Directors of the Morgan Memorial Co-operative Industries and Stories, Inc., Morgan Memorial (1927–1928) Folder, Box 3; "Report to the Directors of the Morgan Memorial Cooperative Industries and Stores," presumably June 1920, Morgan Memorial (1920–1921), Box 2, MMGI; F. C. Moore, "Treasurer's Report to the Directors of the Morgan Memorial Cooperative Industries & Stores, Inc.," 24 September 1930, p. 3, Morgan Memorial (1930–1931) Folder, Box 4, all MMGI.

81. As the historian Gregory Wood has shown, in the early twentieth century employers barred not only disabled workers but also elderly workers. Gregory Wood, *Retiring Men: Manhood, Labor, and Growing Old in America, 1900–1960* (Lanham MD: University Press of America, 2012), chap. 1 passim. Single women, in turn, could rarely find work that paid a living wage, which led them to stay permanently at Goodwill Industries. "Back on the Pay Roll—Help Keep Him There!," *Goodwill News* (Springfield, MA) 2, no. 4 (1935): 1, City File, Springfield, MA, GII; Dorion, *The Redemption of the South End*, 51.

82. Keeler, *The Goodwill Industries*, 15.

83. Ethel M. Sandry, "It's Love's Way," *Goodwill* (Brooklyn), n.s., 5, no. 2 (December 1926–February 1927): 1, City File, Brooklyn—Newsletters/Brochures, GII; Keeler, *The Goodwill Industries*, 15.

84. "Just Folks," 3. Able-bodied women with a disabled or ill spouse also made up some of the ranks of long-term employees. "Service, Not Profit, Our Slogan," *Goodwill* (Brooklyn), n.s., 6, no. 1 (September–November 1927): 1, City File, Brooklyn—Newsletters/Brochures, GII; Barbour, "Just Folks," 9.

85. Keeler, *The Goodwill Industries*, 15, 24; Barbour, "Just Folks," 7.

86. Wahlberg, "Daily Record of Work at Morgan Memorial," pp. 3–7; "A Trip through Morgan Memorial and a Biographical Sketch of Rev. Henry Morgan," n.d., Folder for 1925, Box 3, MMGI. At least two other Goodwill Industries employed disabled men primarily in their furniture repair department. Jennie Cole Gilbert, "Not Charity, but a Chance," *Western Christian Advocate*, 6 July 1921, 682; *Prospectus and Manual of Morgan Memorial*, 139; Ethel M. Sandry, "Glimpses of Goodwill," *Goodwill* (Brooklyn), n.s., 5, no. 1 (September–November 1926): 1, City File, GII. It is unclear why Helms and other Goodwill managers did not train more disabled people in trades. Perhaps the complexity of disabled workers' situations led Helms to invest fewer resources in them.

87. Rose H. Greenleaf, "Report of the Employment Office of Morgan Memorial for the Year Ending September 1, 1928," Morgan Memorial (1928) Folder, Box 3, MMGI.

88. *Prospectus and Manual of Morgan Memorial*, 115; A. G. Young, "To the Members of the Board of the Directors of the Morgan Memorial Co-Operative Industries & Stores, Inc.," 19 May 1924, Morgan Memorial (1924, #3) Folder, Box 3, MMGI. The Denver Goodwill Industries, however, allowed a tubercular man to drive a truck. Keeler, *The Goodwill Industries*, 12.

89. Sandry, "It's Love's Way," 1.

90. Helms, "Ninth Annual Report of the Bureau of Goodwill Industries," p. 5.

91. Ibid.

92. Notably, blind people themselves helped to establish sheltered workshops for blind adults. See, for instance, E. J. Nolan, "A Sketch of the History of Organization among the Blind People of Chicago," *The Problem* 1, no. 2 (April 1900): 50–52; "Journal of Proceedings of Sixth General Convention of the American B. P. H. E. and G. I. Association, Held at Kansas City, Kansas, August 27–29th Inclusive, 1901," *The Problem* 2, no. 4 (October 1901): 87; *The Michigan Employment Institution for the Blind*, 2; "A Paper on the Industrial Education of the Blind," *The Problem* 2, no. 3 (July 1901): 54, 57–60; Edward J. Nolan, "Historical Sketch of the Association," in *Origin, Constitution, Proceedings, Papers, and Compiled Discussions of the American Association of Workers for the Blind, Formerly the American Blind People's High Education and General Improvement Association, at the Eighth General Convention, Held at the Michigan Employment Institution for the Blind, Saginaw, W. S., Mich., August 22–25, 1905* (Hartford, CT: Connecticut Institute for the Blind, 1905), 50 (hereafter cited as *Eighth AAWB Convention, 1905*).

93. Joseph Sanders, "Boarding in an Institution vs. Boarding Outside," *Proceedings and Addresses, Ninth General Convention, American Association of Workers for the Blind* (Cambridge, MA: Outlook for the Blind, 1907); also reprinted in *Outlook for the Blind* 2, no. 1 ([April 1908]), 89 (hereafter cited as *Ninth AAWB Convention, 1907*); J. Perrine Hamilton, "The Necessity of Public Provision for the Employment of the Blind," in *Ninth AAWB Convention, 1907*, 118.

94. Freeberg, *The Education of Laura Bridgman*, 11–13, 71–72; Koestler, *The Unseen Minority*, 209.

95. J. Perrine Hamilton, *The Chief Needs of Adult Blind Persons and the Chief Aims of the Michigan Employment Institution for the Blind: A Circular of Information and Inquiry*

(Saginaw, MI: Michigan Employment Institution for the Blind, 1904), 4; Lucy Wright, "Field Work of the Massachusetts Commission for the Blind," *Outlook for the Blind* 2, no. 3 (October 1908): 123; Oscar Kustermann, "Inventory of Work for the Blind in America: Wisconsin: Workshop for the Blind, Milwaukee," in American Association of Workers for the Blind, *Tenth Convention* (reprinted in *Outlook for the Blind* 3, nos. 2–4, and 4, nos. 1–2 [Summer 1909–Summer 1910]: 55) (hereafter cited as *Tenth AAWB Convention, 1909*).

96. E. J. Nolan, "Hat-Frame Making," in *Ninth AAWB Convention, 1907*, 98; R. E. Colby, "Broom Making," in *Ninth AAWB Convention, 1907*, 92–93; Charles F. F. Campbell, "Hand Weaving," in *Ninth AAWB Convention, 1907*, 95–97; Mrs. C. E. Main, "Inventory of Work for the Blind in America: District of Columbia: The Aid Association for the Blind," in *Tenth AAWB Convention, 1909*, 21; Edward M. Van Cleve, "Ohio Commission for the Blind: Its New Work and New Workers," *Outlook for the Blind* 5, no. 3 (Autumn 1911): 68; E. Stagg Whiting, "The Competition between Prison Labor and the Labor of the Blind," in *American Association of Workers for the Blind, Eleventh Convention, 1911* (reprinted in *Outlook for the Blind* 5, no. 2 [Summer 1911]: 35–36). See also Charles H. Van Etten, "Remonstrance against Prison Broom Making," *Outlook for the Blind* 4, no. 4 (Winter 1911): 172, reprinted from the *Saginaw Courier-Herald*, 4 December 1910.

97. Kustermann, "Inventory of Work for the Blind in America: Wisconsin: Workshop for the Blind, Milwaukee," 54; C. S. McGriffin, "Indiana Industrial Home for Blind Men," in *Eighth AAWB Convention, 1905*, 34–35; H. E. Parrott, "Ohio's Work for the Blind: The Dayton Association for the Blind," in *Tenth AAWB Convention, 1909*, 97. For a discussion of piecework rates, see B. S. Riedle, "Inventory of Work for the Blind in America: Illinois: Industrial Home for the Blind, Chicago," in *Tenth AAWB Convention, 1909*, 23–24; Nolan, "Hat-Frame Making," 99; R. E. Colby, "Inventory of Work for the Blind in America: Connecticut: Department of Trades," in *Tenth AAWB Convention, 1909*, 19.

98. I am grateful to Trevor Engel for locating this intriguing story. "17 Blind Strikers Joined by 83 More," *New York Times*, 9 April 1937, 2; "40 Blind Strikers March on City Hall," *New York Times*, 14 April 1937, 18; "30 Blind Sit-Downers to End Strike Today," *New York Times*, 1 May 1937, 4.

Chapter Seven

1. Charles Prosser served as the first director of the Federal Board for Vocational Education, which oversaw veterans' rehabilitation between 1918 and 1921. Charles A. Prosser, "Two Hundred Ways to Salvage Wounded Men," *New York Times*, 28 July 1918, 54 (emphasis in original). See also John Cummings, "Vocational Rehabilitation of Disabled Soldiers and Sailors: A Preliminary Study," *Federal Board for Vocational Education Bulletin*, no. 5 (1918): 15 (hereafter cited as *FBVE Bulletin*). Chapter title from Garrard Harris, *The Redemption of the Disabled: A Study of Programmes of Rehabilitation for the Disabled of War and of Industry* (New York: D. Appleton, 1919), 214.

2. "Report of Neuro-Psychiatric Examination," 6 February 1922, Records of the Veterans Administration (RG15), Regional Office Training Case Files 1918–1928 (Entry 15A), Box 11, John Aaron case file, NARA, Washington, DC (hereafter Training Case Files).

3. John Aaron to T. J. Calvert, 12 January 1923; "Supervision Report," 9 October 1923, both in Training Case Files, Box 11, John Aaron case file.

4. "Supervision Report," 9 October 1923, Training Case Files, Box 11, John Aaron case file.

5. Training Case Files, Box 11, John Aaron case file.

6. Colonel Forbes, [opening speech to the National Conference on Rehabilitation and Its Problems], 29 and 30 December 1921, p. 3, Records of the Veterans Administration (RG15), Rehabilitation Division Records (PC-15), Minutes of Conferences (Entry 10), Box 2, NARA (hereafter NCRIP).

7. Karl Walter Hickel, "Entitling Citizens: World War I, Progressivism, and the Origins of the American Welfare State, 1917–1928" (PhD diss., Columbia University, 1999), 132.

8. On the rise of the administrative state and challenges of capacity, see, for instance, Skowronek, *Building a New American State*; Skocpol, *Protecting Soldiers and Mothers*, 44–46; Witt, *Accidental Republic*, 190; Novak, "Legal Origins of the Modern American State," 249–50.

9. Paul R. D. Lawrie, "'Salvaging the Negro': Race, Rehabilitation, and the Body Politic in World War I America, 1917–1924," in *Disability Histories*, ed. Susan Burch and Michael Rembis (Urbana: University of Illinois Press, 2014), 321–44.

10. Kerber, *No Constitutional Right to Be Ladies*, 225–28, 251–52; David A. Gerber, "Introduction: Finding Disabled Veterans in History," in *Disabled Veterans in History*, ed. David A. Gerber (Ann Arbor: University of Michigan Press, 2001), 11–24; Scotch, "American Disability Policy in the Twentieth Century," 375–79.

11. Colonel Forbes, [opening speech], NCRIP, 29 and 30 December 1921, p. 3.

12. Edan Dane, "Agencies Which Aided War-Crippled," *New York Times*, 24 August 1919, 49.

13. Lew R. Palmer, "Employment Opportunities for Pennsylvanians Disabled in War Service," *Annals of the American Academy of Political and Social Science* 80 (November 1918): 70–75.

14. Hickel, "Entitling Citizens," 188.

15. Skocpol, *Protecting Soldiers and Mothers*, 110; Obermann, *A History of Vocational Rehabilitation in America*, 149; Harris, *Redemption of the Disabled*, 32; Beth Linker, *War's Waste: Rehabilitation in World War I America* (Chicago: University of Chicago Press, 2011), 12; Blackie, "Disabled Revolutionary War Veterans."

16. Harris, *Redemption of the Disabled*, 178. See also Paul H. Douglas, "The War Risk Insurance Act," *Journal of Political Economy* 26, no. 5 (May 1918): 461; Hickel, "Entitling Citizens," 110; Linker, *War's Waste*, chap. 1 passim.

17. By trade, Douglas McMurtrie was a bibliographer, typographer, and printer. He became involved with the movement to aid crippled children by chance in 1910. For ten years, McMurtrie devoted vast amounts of time to that movement as well to as the larger vocational rehabilitation movement. The historian Bradley Byrom describes him as the "mouthpiece" of the movement. By 1917, McMurtrie had amassed the largest library on "cripples" and rehabilitation in the country, while in 1918 he began directing the new Red Cross Institute for Crippled and Disabled Men (which was endowed

by Jeremiah Milbank) and began advising the federal government on how best to rehabilitate disabled veterans. In 1920, however, McMurtrie abruptly left the rehabilitation movement, never to return. Byrom, "A Vision of Self Support," 73–76; Kinder, *Paying with Their Bodies*, 121.

18. Douglas C. McMurtrie, *Care of Crippled Soldiers and Sailors: A Letter Published in the New York Evening Post of August 31, 1917* (New York: N.p., 1917), 3.

19. Mack was a well-known child welfare reformer, a former judge on the Cook County juvenile court, and a current judge on the federal circuit court in Chicago as well a prominent American Zionist. Gerber, "Introduction: Finding Disabled Veterans," 11–18; Hickel, "Entitling Citizens," 3.

20. The original War Risk Insurance Act was passed in 1914. The amendments also added voluntary life insurance (since lawmakers feared that commercial insurance companies would refuse to insure disabled veterans after the war) and disability compensation. Judge Mack modeled the program in part on workmen's compensation. The rehabilitation program thus represented a continuation of the "veterans' welfare state" that had developed after the Civil War. Obermann, *History of Vocational Rehabilitation*, 147–51; Hickel, "Entitling Citizens," 111–12, 117–30; Hickel, "Medicine, Bureaucracy, and Social Welfare, 239; Kelly, *Creating a National Home*, 4.

21. In Great Britain, in contrast, the devastation of the war limited veterans' pensions and prevented the enactment of marriage allowances. British rates for pensions were low; a private with a total permanent disability and no children born before the war received 27 shillings, 6 pence a week. Allowances for children were also minimal: 6 shillings, 8 pence for the first child, 5 shillings for the second, and 4 shillings, 2 pence for any others. These rates were simply not adequate to support a family. The average working-class family spent 39 shillings a week on food alone in late 1917, and about 37 shillings in 1918. During the war, the cost of living for an average working-class family rose by over 100 percent, but pensions did not rise. Harris, *Redemption of the Disabled*, 189; Hickel, "Entitling Citizens," 118, 239, 246; Deborah Cohen, *The War Come Home: Disabled Veterans in Britain and Germany, 1914–1939* (Berkeley: University of California Press, 2001), 16, 21, 26, 44, 107; "The New Royal Warrant," *Reveille* 1, no. 1 (August 1918): 150–53; J. M. Winter, *The Great War and the British People* (Cambridge, MA: Harvard University Press, 1986), 215–45.

22. Like other Progressive reformers, Mack believed that families should follow the male breadwinner model. In 1909, he identified female wage work outside the home as a cause of juvenile delinquency. Hickel, "Entitling Citizens," 118.

23. Julian W. Mack, "A Chance—with a Running Start: Government Compensation Provides Means for the Handicapped Fighter," *Carry On* 1, no. 2 (August 1918), 12; Hickel, "Medicine, Bureaucracy, and Social Welfare," 240, 256; Obermann, *History of Vocational Rehabilitation*, 158, 168.

24. Douglas, "The War Risk Insurance Act," 473–74. Unlike in Great Britain, veterans' disability compensation did not disqualify them from other social benefits such as unemployment. Jeffrey Reznick, "Work-Therapy and the Disabled British Soldier in Great Britain in the First World War: The Case of Shepherd's Bush Military Hospital,

London," in *Disabled Veterans in History*, ed. David Gerber (Ann Arbor: University of Michigan Press, 2001), 197; D. Cohen, *The War Come Home*, 112.

25. War Risk Insurance Act of October 6, 1917, H.R. 5723, 65th Cong., 1st sess., 28, reprinted in "To the Disabled Soldier and Sailor in the Hospital," *FBVE Bulletin*, no. 1 (1918): 13; Lawrie, "'Salvaging the Negro,'" 325, 336–37.

26. War Risk Insurance Act of October 6, 1917, reprinted in "To the Disabled Soldier and Sailor in the Hospital," 15.

27. American policy makers were inspired by European, Canadian, and American precedents. See Edward T. Devine, *Disabled Soldiers and Sailors Pensions and Training* (Oxford: Oxford University Press, 1919), chaps. 4–8 passim; Douglas C. McMurtrie, *The Disabled Soldier* (New York: Macmillan, 1919); Harris, *Redemption of the Disabled*, chaps. 4–12 passim.

28. Cummings, "Vocational Rehabilitation of Disabled Soldiers and Sailors," 12.

29. Douglas C. McMurtrie, "The Duty of the Employer in the Reconstruction of the Crippled Soldier," *Journal of the American Society of Heating and Ventilating Engineers*, July 1918, 678; Cummings, "Vocational Rehabilitation of Disabled Soldiers and Sailors," 14. See also John Turner Wakeman, "A Tuberculosis Background for Advisors and Teachers," *FBVE Bulletin*, no. 59 (1920): 25; Hickel, "Entitling Citizens," 174–75; Harris, *Redemption of the Disabled*, 48–49.

30. Harold A. Littledale, "Disabled Soldiers Untrained after 19 Months of Red Tape," *New York Evening Post*, 16 February 1920, 1, 4. Of veterans eligible for vocational rehabilitation, 53.6 percent entered training, and 46.4 percent (155,059 out of 334,578 veterans) did not. Federal Board for Vocational Education, *Annual Report to Congress of the Federal Board for Vocational Education* (Washington, DC: Government Printing Office, 1920), 330 (hereafter cited as FBVE, *Annual Report*); U.S. Veterans' Bureau, *Annual Report of the Director* (Washington, DC: Government Printing Office, 1927), 101 (hereafter cited as USVB, *Annual Report*); USVB, *Annual Report of the Director, 1928*, p. 33; Colonel Forbes, [opening speech], NCRIP, 29 and 30 December 1921, p. 3.

31. The Soldier Rehabilitation Act of 1918 (Pub. L. 178, 65th Congress) made the FBVE responsible for coordinating the rehabilitation of disabled veterans. Obermann, *History of Vocational Rehabilitation*, 149–51; David R. B. Ross, *Preparing for Ulysses: Politics and Veterans during World War II* (New York: Columbia University Press, 1969), 29.

32. NCRIP, 29 and 30 December 1921, pp. 6–7.

33. Ibid.; USVB, *Annual Report, 1922*, 336.

34. Obermann, *History of Vocational Rehabilitation*, 156–64.

35. Roughly 930,000 veterans applied for disability under the War Risk Insurance Act. Ross, *Preparing for Ulysses*, 26; "Legion Attacks Vocation Board," *New York Times*, 19 September 1919, 24; Lawrie, "'Salvaging the Negro,'" 328.

36. Douglas C. McMurtrie, *The Essentials of a National System for Rehabilitation of Disabled Service Men of the American Forces: A Statement Presented to the Committee on Education of the House of Representatives* (Greenwich, CT: Arbor Press, 1920), 11–12. In 1919, the FBVE reluctantly accepted the offer of the Elks Club and the American Red Cross to provide loans to soldiers who had waited for months to learn if they were

eligible for disability compensation and rehabilitation. Dane, "Agencies Which Aided War-Crippled," 49.

37. Littledale, "Disabled Soldiers Untrained after 19 Months of Red Tape," 1; USVB, *Annual Report, 1922,* 336.

38. Public Law 47 (67th Congress) established the Veterans' Bureau; Obermann, *History of Vocational Rehabilitation,* 164–66; Dane, "Agencies Which Aided War-Crippled," 49.

39. Obermann, *History of Vocational Rehabilitation,* 158, 164–69.

40. Hickel, "Entitling Citizens," 132.

41. "Details New Plan for Veteran Relief," *New York Times,* 24 October 1921, 27. The first report of the Veterans' Bureau proclaimed that the bureau had contacted 227,302 prospective trainees in just ten and a half months, while the FBVE had taken thirty-seven and a half months to contact 404,396 prospective trainees. USVB, *Annual Report, 1922,* 284; Lawrie, "'Salvaging the Negro,'" 331–32.

42. Ross, *Preparing for Ulysses,* 31. Forbes was a friend of President Harding and had a checkered history. As a young man, he had deserted the army and served his first prison term at Leavenworth. He later earned the Distinguished Service Medal and Croix de Guerre in France. "A Pretty Mess," *Time,* 5 November 1923, http://www.time .com/time/magazine/article/0,9171,716844-1,00.html (accessed 6 July 2008).

43. "Veterans' Scandal Approaching Climax," *New York Times,* 9 March 1924, XX4; Kinder, *Paying with Their Bodies,* 99.

44. Hickel, "Entitling Citizens," 189–90.

45. "District Managers' Conference," 20 September 1922, 10:00–10:45 A.M., p. 9, RG15, Rehabilitation Division Records (PC-15), Minutes of Conferences (Entry 10), Box 2, NARA (hereafter "District Managers' Conference," 20 September 1922). District 13 included Washington State, Oregon, and Idaho.

46. Devine, *Disabled Soldiers,* 259.

47. "Ward Occupations in Hospitals," *FBVE Bulletin,* no. 25 (December 1918): 6. See also "Putting Our War Cripples Back on the Payroll," *New York Times,* 12 May 1918, 80.

48. Devine, *Disabled Soldiers,* 436.

49. Many policy makers and commentators worried that veterans would falter once released from military discipline. Elizabeth Green Upham, "Training of Teachers for Occupational Therapy for the Rehabilitation of Disabled Soldiers and Sailors," *FBVE Bulletin,* no. 6 (February 1918): 12–13, 18; L. G. Brock, "The Re-Education of the Disabled," *American Journal of Care for Cripples* 4, no. 1 (March 1917): 24; Cummings, "Vocational Rehabilitation of Disabled Soldiers and Sailors," 25.

50. Upham, "Training of Teachers for Occupational Therapy," 37, 52–53.

51. USVB, *Annual Report, 1927,* 101. At least initially, compensation was suspended if a man refused to enter training. Douglas, "The War Risk Insurance Act," 475.

52. FBVE, *Third Annual Report, 1919,* 7–8, 17; Hickel, "Entitling Citizens," 182–83; USVB, *Annual Report, 1928,* 33; FBVE, "Manual of Procedure (Misc. 150 Rev., Art II-F)," pp. 3–5, RG15, Rehabilitation Division Records (PC-15), Minutes of Conferences (Entry 10), Box 1.

53. Charles A. Prosser, "A Federal Program for the Vocational Rehabilitation of Disabled Soldiers and Sailors," *Annals of the American Academy of Political and Social Science* 80 (November 1918): 118; Elizabeth Green Upham, "The Absorption of Handicapped Labor into Industry," *Vocational Summary* 2, no. 3 (July 1919): 44, quoted in Hickel, "Entitling Citizens," 199. Rehabilitators relied on detailed industrial surveys similar to those pioneered by the Red Cross Institute for Crippled and Disabled Men and other organizations aimed at helping cripples. See, for instance, Helen E. Redding, "Opportunities for the Employment of Disabled Men: Preliminary Survey of the Piano, Leather, Rubber, Paper Goods, Shoe, Sheet Metal Goods, Candy, Drug and Chemical, Cigar, Silk, Celluloid, Optical Goods, and Motion Picture Industries," *Publications of the Red Cross Institute for Crippled and Disabled Men* 1, no. 16 (24 July 1918): 1–33. Hickel argues, "Rehabilitation . . . required a case-by-case mode of application unprecedented in federal welfare policy." Hickel, "Entitling Citizens," 234.

54. McMurtrie, *The Disabled Soldier*, 95 (emphasis in original).

55. FBVE, *Annual Report, 1919*, 17.

56. "Reconstruction—Before and After," *Carry On* 1, no. 2 (August 1918): 20–21.

57. USVB, *Annual Report* (1928), 33; Lawrie, "'Salvaging the Negro,'" 323.

58. FBVE, *Fourth Annual Report, 1920*, 282. The Veterans' Bureau also established four government-funded training centers.

59. "The Creed of the Disabled Soldier," *Carry On* 1, no. 6 (March 1919): i. *Carry On* was published jointly by the U.S. Public Health Service, the army, and McMurtrie's Red Cross Institute for Crippled and Disabled Men.

60. David Gerber has argued that disabled veterans fill an uncomfortable position in national mythology. On the one hand, they are celebrated as veterans who gave their health for the nation. On the other hand, disabled veterans' status as *disabled* people has often placed them in a vulnerable position. Because rehabilitators have often been particularly disturbed by disabled veterans' apparent dependency (and supposed lack of masculinity), disabled veterans have faced far more pressure than disabled civilians to undergo "aggressive socioeconomic normalization" so that they can pass in society at large. Gerber, "Introduction: Finding Disabled Veterans," 19. Sarah F. Rose, "Normalizing the Disabled: Rehabilitation in Blind Veterans," in Rose, "Teaching Blind People to Walk by Taking Away Their Canes: The Influence of World War II on Conceptions of Disability in the United States" (MA thesis, University of Chicago, 2001), 65–81.

61. "Our First Blinded Soldier," *Carry On* 1, no. 1 (June 1918): 14; Alice Duer Miller, "How Can a Woman Best Help?," *Carry On* 1, no. 1 (June 1918): 18; W. H. Zimmerman; "A Message," *Carry On* 1, no. 10 (July 1919): 26; Joanna Bourke, *Dismembering the Male: Men's Bodies, Britain, and the Great War* (Chicago: University of Chicago Press, 1996), 74. Bourke states that single men were discouraged from thinking about marriage, partly because of the lack of marriage allowances in Britain.

62. Major General Merritte W. Ireland, "Carry On," *Carry On* 1, no. 6 (March 1919): 4.

63. "Rehabilitation Begins," *New York Times*, 30 June 1918, 23. See also Red Cross Institute for Crippled and Disabled Men, "A Square Deal for the Crippled Soldier" [advertisement], *New York Times*, 23 March 1918, 8; Colonel Frank Billings, M.C., U.S.A.,

"A Message: To the Fathers, Mothers, Wives, Sisters, and Brothers of Disabled Soldiers," *Carry On* 1, no. 8 (May 1919): 4; "Editorials: A Carry On Association," *Carry On* 1, no. 9 (June 1919): 16; McMurtrie, *The Disabled Soldier*, 96; Kinder, *Paying with Their Bodies*, 143.

64. Douglas C. McMurtrie, "The High Road to Self-Support," *Carry On* 1, no. 1 (June 1918): 6. See also Harris, *Redemption of the Disabled*, 16; Lucy Wright, "Offsetting the Handicap of Blindness," *Annals of the American Academy of Political and Social Science* 77 (May 1918): 28; John Galsworthy, "The Need for Reality: Consider What Will Happen Five or Ten Years from Now," *Carry On* 1, no. 2 (August 1918): 29–30 (reprint from *British War Pensions Gazette*); "Vocation Offices Opened," *New York Times*, 11 November 1918, 4.

65. "Employment of Disabled Soldiers," *Carry On* 1, no. 6 (March 1919): 17; Kinder, *Paying with Their Bodies*, 100.

66. Miller, "How Can a Woman Best Help?," 17–18; Hickel, "Entitling Citizens," 219; see also Linker, *War's Waste*, chap. 3 passim.

67. McMurtrie, *The Disabled Soldier*, 101–2.

68. Ibid., 4.

69. Captain Arthur H. Samuels, S.C., U.S.A., "Invisible Wounds," *Carry On* 1, no. 3 (September 1918): 13–15; see also Gertrude Atherton, "Beggars No More," *Carry On* 1, no. 4 (October–November 1918): 18; "What About the Tuberculous?," *Carry On* 1, no. 8 (April 1919): 22; FBVE, *Fourth Annual Report, 1920*, 285; Kinder, *Paying with Their Bodies*, 71.

70. "The Enemy Was Ready: How Germany Made Preparation for Her Wounded," *Carry On* 1, no. 1 (June 1918): 24, 26; Devine, *Disabled Soldiers*, 51.

71. Herbert Kaufman, "The Only Hopeless Cripple," *Carry On* 1, no. 4 (October–November 1918): 22.

72. Red Cross Institute for Crippled and Disabled Men, *Your Duty to the War Cripple*; quoted in McMurtrie, *The Disabled Soldier*, 110–11. Rehabilitators' arguments were bolstered by disabled civilians. Michael Dowling, one of the most famous disabled men in the early twentieth century, was a banker and former Speaker of the Minnesota House of Representatives who lost his left arm, both legs, and the fingers of his right hand to frostbite. Nonetheless, Dowling insisted on attending public school and eventually became a teacher. Dowling rejected the term "cripple" and argued that his impairments did not matter; instead, he contended that even the most physically impaired man could be "worth $100,000 from the neck up." "From His Neck Up: A Man May Be Worth $100,000 a Year," *Carry On* 1, no. 1 (June 1918): 23.

73. McMurtrie, *The Disabled Soldier*, 34. See also Harris, *Redemption of the Disabled*, 214.

74. Hickel suggests that the Veterans' Bureau kept the schedule secret so that veterans could not "tailor their claims or rehearse for their medical examination" and prevent interference by the American Legion or congressmen. Even congressmen could not obtain copies of the schedule. Veterans could declare new disabilities only through the end of 1924. The bureau released the rating schedule in 1933. Other veterans lacked sufficient evidence to prove that their disabilities arose during their military service. Hickel, "Entitling Citizens," 139–40; Hickel, "Medicine, Bureaucracy, and Social Welfare," 247.

75. Deborah Stone and Edward Berkowitz have discussed the challenges of quantifying disability in administrative programs. See Stone, *The Disabled State*, chap. 3 passim; Berkowitz, *Disabled Policy*, 23 and chap. 3 passim.

76. Hickel, "Entitling Citizens," 133. Only 5,000 American soldiers had amputations, and less than 200 became totally blind during the war. Just 2,300 disabled veterans were female (35,000 women served in the Army and Navy Nurse Corps). Half of female disabled veterans gained compensation benefits. Hickel, "Medicine, Bureaucracy, and Welfare," 244, 260n6.

77. Harris, *Redemption of the Disabled*, 127; I. M. Rubinow, "A Statistical Consideration of the Number of Men Crippled in War, and Disabled in Industry," *Publications of the Red Cross Institute for Crippled and Disabled Men* 1, no. 4 (February 1918), 3; FBVE, *Annual Report, 1920*, 285; "What About the Tuberculous?," 22; "First National Meeting of the District Managers of the U.S. Veterans' Bureau," 18 October 1918, 3:00 P.M., pp. 1, 3–4, RG15, Rehabilitation Division Records (PC-15), Minutes of Conferences (Entry 10), Box 1, NARA (hereafter "First National District Managers Meeting"); Kinder, *Paying with Their Bodies*, 119.

78. The number of veterans claiming disability compensation for neuropsychiatric disorders and tuberculosis continued to rise during the 1920s. Between June 1924 and June 1928, the number of veterans receiving compensation for neuropsychiatric disabilities increased from 32,103 to 54,958, and the ranks of veterans claiming compensation for tuberculosis grew from 39,099 to 60,690. In 1923, General Hines, the director of the Veterans' Bureau, advised that temporary disability ratings should be made permanent if at all possible. USVB, *Annual Report, 1928*, 20; W. J. Blake to Charles W. Grafe, 29 April 1924; Board of Appeals to W. J. Blake, "Appeal for Increased Compensation," 23 April 1924; D. T. Powell to Charles W. Grafe, 3 July 1924; W. F. Lent to John J. McGovern, 23 October 1923, RG15, Training Case Files (Entry 15A), Box 11, Charles Grafe case file, NARA.

79. "House Passes Veteran Bill," *New York Times*, 3 March 1923, 2.

80. Initially, Congress required that veterans be rated for disability within one year of their discharge and file for compensation within five years. Lawmakers eventually extended the date for getting a certificate of disability to 1922. "Moves to Expedite Relief of Soldiers," *New York Times*, 3 June 1921, 14; Jennifer Davis McDaid, "How a One-Legged Rebel Lives: Confederate Veterans and Artificial Limbs in Virginia," in *Artificial Parts, Practical Lives: Modern Histories of Prosthetics*, ed. Katherine Ott, David Serlin, and Stephen Mihm (New York: New York University Press, 2002), 119–43; Shauna Devine, *Learning from the Wounded: The Civil War and the Rise of American Medical Science* (Chapel Hill: University of North Carolina Press, 2014), 202–3.

81. FBVE, *Annual Report, 1921*, 407; Hickel, "Medicine, Bureaucracy, and Social Welfare," 250; Lawrie, "'Salvaging the Negro,'" 325.

82. Hickel suggests that FBVE and Veterans' Bureau administrators feared that compensation and trainees' maintenance allowances "had the potential to undermine racial inequality rooted in labor markets, income distribution, and the relationship between the state and racially defined groups of citizens." Lawrie notes that the nearly

wholesale exclusion of African American veterans from combat meant that, unlike many white veterans, they did not receive disability ratings in military hospitals but rather had to claim disability under the War Risk Insurance Act. Hickel, "Medicine, Bureaucracy, and Social Welfare," 240, 255–58; Hickel, "Entitling Citizens," 155, 157; Lawrie, "'Salvaging the Negro,'" 328–30, 336–37.

83. Hickel, "Medicine, Bureaucracy, and Social Welfare," 256.

84. USVB, *Annual Report, 1928*, 30–34.

85. Bureau officials had classified another 10,392 veterans (5.8 percent of trainees) as having "completed" their training. Ibid., 33.

86. Indeed, Hines's final report on the activities of the Rehabilitation Division was only five pages long.

87. "Report of Physical Examination," 13 August 1923, RG15, Training Case Files (Entry 15A), Box 10, John Heidecker case file, NARA.

88. Heidecker suffered from medical complaints other than his war injuries, and his motivation clearly flagged during training. In March 1922, the Veterans' Bureau doctor "stated that he d[id] not consider [Heidecker] very ill, and that he has positively not been coming for treatments." E. B. Klauder to Mr. Snyder, 24 March 1922, Training Case Files, Box 10, John Heidecker case file.

89. Training Case Files, Box 10, John Heidecker case file.

90. Half of all of the veterans who registered for vocational rehabilitation did so during the eighteen months of the recession. As of June 30, 1920, 207,724 disabled veterans had been contacted about vocational rehabilitation by the FBVE or inquired themselves. The recession ran from roughly June 1920 to December 1921. Although monthly registration data is not available for June 1920, 301,002 disabled veterans registered for rehabilitation between July 1920 and December 1921; 137,237 of these veterans were "dropped after investigation." FBVE, *Annual Report, 1920*, 449; USVB, *Annual Report, 1922*, 336–37.

91. Hickel, "Entitling Citizens," 237n17.

92. RG15, Training Case Files (Entry 15A), Box 10, George Cathocalles case file, NARA.

93. FBVE, *Annual Report, 1921*, 376, 387.

94. "How Training Aids Disabled Veterans," *New York Times*, 29 January 1923, 18.

95. Taking inflation into account, $744 in 1916 was the equivalent of $1,320.63 (using the Consumer Price Index) or $1,359.73 (using the unskilled wage) in 1921; while $1,058 in 1916 equaled $1,697.37 and $1,856.22 in 1923 (using the Consumer Price Index and the unskilled wage, respectively). Figures from "Six Ways to Compute the Relative Value of a U.S. Dollar Amount, 1790–2006," www.MeasuringWorth.com/uscompare/ (accessed 16 February 2008).

96. RG15, Training Case Files (Entry 15A), Box 10, George S. Adolfson case file, NARA; Bureau of the Census, *Fifteenth Census, 1930*, New York, Kings County, Enum. District no. 24-51, sheet 2A, George Adolfson household.

97. John L. Hamilton to Bureau of Vocational Training, 19 May 1921, Records of the Veterans Administration (RG15), Veterans' Bureau Rehabilitation Division (PC-15), General Correspondence File (Entry 2), Box 6, NARA.

98. Industrial Service Department, "Rehabilitation: General Electric Company, Schenectady Works, New York," November 1918, RG15, PC-15, General Correspondence File (Entry 2), Box 93A, NARA.

99. The NAM, moreover, led a drive in 1925 to find jobs for 25,000 disabled veterans. FBVE, *Fourth Annual Report, 1920*, 425; "Drive on for Jobs for Rehabilitated," *New York Times*, 4 July 1925, 3.

100. Douglas McMurtrie argued that such a provision would prevent employers who hired disabled veterans from incurring higher insurance premiums. McMurtrie, *The Disabled Soldier*, 174; "Considering Status of Disabled Men," *Eastern Underwriter* 19, no. 32 (9 August 1918): 17–18; Wesley M. Oler to C. R. Forbes, 14 April 1922, RG15, PC-15, General Correspondence File (Entry 2), Box 6, NARA.

101. Merrill R. Lott to U.S. Veterans' Bureau, 13 June 1925, Box 6; C. H. Abbott to United States Veterans' Bureau, 24 February 1922, Box 4; and President of General Phonograph Corporation to C. R. Forbes, 24 January 1922, Box 93A, all from RG15, PC-15, General Correspondence File (Entry 2), NARA.

102. On issues of capacity, see Skowronek, *Building a New American State*; Kinder, *Paying with Their Bodies*, 99.

103. Lawmakers may have feared that individual agencies did not possess the capacity to handle the entire eligibility process or may have intended to prevent a repeat of the pension scandals by making the process of gaining eligibility difficult.

104. "Crippled Soldiers Disheartened by Delays," *New York Times*, 24 August 1919, 43.

105. Harold A. Littledale, "Thousands of Disabled Men Untrained in This District," *New York Evening Post*, 18 February 1920, 1, 7.

106. Littledale, "Disabled Soldiers Untrained after 19 Months of Red Tape," 1, 4. For statistics on the veterans eligible for rehabilitation, as well as how many chose to enter training, see chap. 7, note 30. FBVE, *Fourth Annual Report, 1920*, 330; USVB, *Annual Report of the Director, 1927*, 101; USVB, *Annual Report of the Director, 1928*, 33.

107. "Crippled Soldiers Disheartened by Delays," 43. The much smaller federal-state vocational rehabilitation program for civilians suffered from some of the same problems. In particular, disabled industrial workers were not very interested in entering rehabilitation. "Activities of Bureau of Rehabilitation, Pennsylvania Department of Labor and Industry, up to Aug. 1, 1920: Address of Commissioner Clifford B. Connelley of the Pennsylvania Department of Labor and Industry," *Seventh Annual Meeting of the International Association of Industrial Accident Boards and Commissions* (1920): 2, pamphlet available at M. P. Catherwood Library, Cornell University, Ithaca, NY.

108. "Crippled Soldiers Disheartened by Delays," 43.

109. Littledale, "Thousands of Disabled Men Untrained in This District," 7. District 2, which encompassed New York State, Connecticut, and New Jersey, was noted for its dysfunction, although the district's bad reputation may have been more a function of the activity of New York City media (and the ease with which historians can access the New York newspapers). Scott Gelber, "A 'Hard-Boiled Order': The Reeducation of Disabled WWI Veterans in New York City," *Journal of Social History* 39, no. 1 (Fall 2005): 161–80.

110. Littledale, "Thousands of Disabled Men Untrained in This District," 1, 7; Kinder, *Paying with Their Bodies*, 103–4.

111. "Disabled Men Seek to Untie Red Tape," *New York Times*, 15 June 1928, 1.

112. "Veterans' Bureau Called Wasteful," *New York Times*, 29 March 1923, 6; Clarence MacGregor to J. J. Kingsbury, 24 June 1924, RG15, Training Case Files (Entry 15A), Box 11, Frank Roberts case file, NARA; Obermann, *History of Vocational Rehabilitation*, 162–63.

113. "Disabled Men Seek to Untie Red Tape," 1, 6.

114. Ross, *Preparing for Ulysses*, 26; "Legion Attacks Vocation Board," 24.

115. "Klan's Hand Seen in Veterans' Bureau," *New York Times*, 10 October 1924, 1.

116. "Veterans' Bureau Called Wasteful," 6.

117. Rose C. Feld, "The New War Cripples' School," *New York Times*, 19 March 1922, 107.

118. Hickel, "Entitling Citizens," 281.

119. Some veterans—especially those placed in auto garages for training—colluded with their employers to extend their training indefinitely. See, for instance, "$2,000,000,000 Spent for Aid, but War Veterans Suffer," *New York Times*, 25 February 1923, XX3.

120. Donald L. Forbes to R. T. Fisher, 8 September 1920, RG15, Training Case Files (Entry 15A), Box 10, Donald L. Forbes case file, NARA.

121. Forbes blamed his disability on the "narrowness of the trenches," which left him "handicapped in adjusting [his] mask." He said that he was "burnt on right cheek and inhaled quite a bit of several different gasses." "Federal Board for Vocational Education: Survey," 11 February 1921, Training Case Files, Box 10, Donald L. Forbes case file.

122. Joseph C. O'Rane to J. C. Wardlaw, 28 June 1923, and J. C. Wardlaw to Hartford Sub-District Manager, 12 July 1923; "Notice of Termination of Training," 21 July 1923, Training Case Files, Box 10, Donald L. Forbes case file.

123. Hickel argues that veterans and their families had a "social and cultural" understanding of disability that was "influenced by notions about an individual's prerogatives and obligations toward his dependents, his local community, and the state." Veterans expected that their military service would be rewarded with compensation, medical treatment, and vocational rehabilitation. Hickel draws on the "social model of disability," but seems to be imposing a present-day theoretical model on the past. It seems more accurate to say that disabled veterans had an "economic" understanding of disability. Veterans defined their impairments as disabilities once they could no longer earn a living or support their families, no doubt spurred by federal vocational rehabilitation policy. See Hickel, "Medicine, Bureaucracy, and Social Welfare," 252–53.

124. Deborah Stone and Edward Berkowitz have explored the challenges of defining disability for administrative programs.

125. Harry Iverson, "Affidavit concerning Disability with Service," 26 February 1920, RG15, Training Case Files (Entry 15A), Box 11, Harry Iverson case file, NARA.

126. William A. Clark to Harry H. Iverson, 20 February 1920, Training Case Files, Box 11, Harry Iverson case file.

127. "Federal Board for Vocational Education," 18 January 1919, Training Case Files, Box 11, Harry Iverson case file.

128. The official diagnosis was "purulent discharge from the ear with destruction of the tympanic membrane and necrosis of the bone" and "chronic purulent otitis media with chronic mastoiditis of the left ear." Until the invention of antibiotics, mastoiditis was a leading cause of death among children. W. Scott Renner to U. B. Stein, 2 November 1921 and 14 November 1921, Training Case Files, Box 11, Frank Roberts case file.

129. Ibid.

130. Hickel, "Entitling Citizens," 140.

131. Hickel also notes that the 1933 disability schedule was filled with nonmedical criteria. Fraser, "Memorandum for the Director," p. 2, quoted in Hickel, "Entitling Citizens," 140; see also 139, 141; Lawrie, " 'Salvaging the Negro,' " 327.

132. "Federal Board for Vocational Education: Survey," 16 October 1920, Training Case Files, Box 11, Frank Roberts case file.

133. Training Case Files, Box 11, Frank Roberts case file. "Entitling Citizens," 107.

134. J. C. Wardlaw to Chairman, District Board of Appeals [ca. May–July 1923], Training Case Files, Box 11, Frank Roberts case file.

135. Ibid.

136. Joseph Bell to J. C. Wardlaw, 7 July 1923, Training Case Files, Box 11, Frank Roberts case file.

137. J. C. Wardlaw to Sub-District Manager, 11 July 1923, Training Case Files, Box 11, Frank Roberts case file.

138. W. J. Blake to Frank J. Roberts, 15 February 1924, and W. J. Blake to Frank Roberts, 4 April 1924, Training Case Files, Box 11, Frank Roberts case file.

139. In 1922, the Veterans' Bureau offered Roberts a temporary partial rating of 30–35 percent, which gave him compensation and treatment but no access to rehabilitation. Roberts's compensation was contingent on his willingness to undergo surgery on his ear and temporal bones, which he declined to do. As a result, Roberts was declared "non-feasible" in December 1922, and his compensation was taken away. Clarence MacGregor to J. J. Kingsbury, 24 June 1924, and J. J. Kingsbury to Clarence MacGregor, 27 June 1924; J. C. Wardlaw to Frank J. Roberts, 9 November 1922; W. F. Lent to Buffalo Sub-District Manager, U. S. Veterans' Bureau, 26 March 1923; J. C. Wardlaw to Chairman, District Board of Appeals [ca. May–July 1923]; William W. Verner to Claims Division, 9 June 1922; "Report of Physical Examination," 17 December 1922, all from Training Case Files, Box 11, Frank Roberts case file.

140. A Disabled Soldier, "Letter to the Editor: Failures in Rehabilitation," *New York Times*, 27 August 1919, 10. The soldier was from Meriden, Connecticut.

141. Hickel, "Entitling Citizens," 239; Kinder, *Paying with Their Bodies*, 99.

142. For more on the importance of experience, see Alexa Schriempf, "(Re)fusing the Amputated Body: An Interactionist Bridge for Feminism and Disability," *Hypatia* 16, no. 4 (Fall 2001): 53–79.

143. Bessie C. Garrah to Dr. Graham, 3 April 1923; Sylvester J. Howland to Dr. C. F. Graham, 20 December 1923; C. F. Graham to Sylvester J. Howland, 22 December 1923, RG15, Training Case Files (Entry 15A), Box 10, Sylvester Howland case file, NARA.

336 Notes to Chapter Seven

144. Lester suddenly decided to go out of business. "Albany, New York," 7 March 1924; Sylvester Howland to Mr. Arends, 2 April 1924; "Sylvester Howland, C-482913"; "Notice of Change of Status During Training," 1 April 1924 and 10 April 1924; "Supervision Report," 16 May 1924; "Notice of Termination of Training," 7 July 1924; Sylvester Howland to Edwin C. Carry, 8 July 1924; E. C. Carry to J. W. Jones, 11 July 1924; Training Case Files, Box 10, Sylvester Howland case file.

145. Sylvester Howland to Albany branch of U. S. Veterans' Bureau, 25 July 1924; Training Case Files, Box 10, Sylvester Howland case file.

146. E. C. Cary, "Employment Placement and Follow-Up Report," 7 August 1924; E. C. Cary to E. K. Foley, 13 August 1924, Training Case Files, Box 10, Sylvester Howland case file; Bureau of the Census, *Fifteenth Census, 1930*, New York, Saratoga County, Enum. District no. 46-52, sheet 27A, Sylvester Howland household.

147. Gelett Burgess, "Victim *versus* Victor," *Carry On* 1, no. 1 (June 1918): 20. Burgess was a poet, artist, art critic, novelist, and humorist. He coined the term "blurb." See also "Getting Down to Cases," *Carry On* 1, no. 7 (April 1919): 26–28.

148. McMurtrie, "Vocational Re-education," 58–59, quoted in "A 'Hard-Boiled Order,'" 165; Linker, *War's Waste*, 157.

149. Lawrie, "'Salvaging the Negro,'" 327.

150. Burgess, "Victim *versus* Victor," 20 (emphasis in original).

151. "Getting Down to Cases," 26–28.

152. Burgess, "Victim *versus* Victor," 22.

153. Hickel, "Entitling Citizens," 173–74.

154. Hickel, "Medicine, Bureaucracy, and Social Welfare," 250, 255–58; Lawrie, "'Salvaging the Negro,'" 332.

155. Gelber, "A 'Hard-Boiled Order,'" 165–70.

156. The rehabilitation officer was fired, but not before the memorandum had spurred investigations by both the American Legion and the U.S. House Committee on Education. U.S. House Committee on Education, *Charges against the Federal Board for Vocational Education*, 4, 7, quoted in Gelber, "A 'Hard-Boiled Order,'" 162.

157. NCRIP, 29 December 1921, p. 9; Kinder, *Paying with Their Bodies*, 123.

158. "First National District Managers Meeting," 18 October 1918, 3:00 P.M., pp. 1, 3–4.

159. Depending on the region, between 25 and 62 percent of veterans had only a primary school education. NCRIP, 29 December 1921, p. 31; Hickel, "Entitling Citizens," 35, 246; FBVE, *Annual Report, 1920*, 316, 349, 383, 405. To some degree, the Veterans' Bureau used IQ tests to place veterans, but the practice was not widespread. The bureau also labeled some veterans morons. Hickel, "Entitling Citizens," 243–46; USVB, *Annual Report, 1922*, 332–35.

160. "First National District Managers Meeting," 19 October 1921, 9:30 A.M., p. 3; Kinder, *Paying with Their Bodies*, 136–37.

161. "First National District Managers Meeting," 18 October 1918, 3:00 P.M., pp. 1, 3–4.

162. Hickel, "Entitling Citizens," 255–56, 262–65, 268; Lawrie, "'Salvaging the Negro,'" 331–32.

163. In the *Vocational Summary*, rehabilitators argued that vocational rehabilitation would make African American veterans "content to remain in the region of their birth and fulfilling '[t]he hope of the South for an improved labor supply.'" "War-Disabled Negroes in Training," *The Vocational Summary* 4, no. 2 (June 1921): 33; quoted in Hickel, "Entitling Citizens," 255. Rehabilitators' fears were not groundless. During the war, the dependent allowances of War Risk Insurance had helped discourage African American women from working in the mainstream labor market. After the war, trainees' monthly maintenance allowance of $115 granted relative freedom to the few African American veterans who gained compensation, as well as their families. Hickel, "Entitling Citizens," chap. 2 passim, 270; Lawrie, "'Salvaging the Negro,'" 332; Kinder, *Paying with Their Bodies*, 134–35.

164. Major Arthur Dean, NCRIP, 29 December 1921, p. 8; FBVE, *Annual Report, 1920*, 316, 349.

165. Hickel, "Medicine, Bureaucracy, and Social Welfare," 257.

166. "First National District Managers Meeting," 18 October 1918, 3:00 P.M., pp. 1, 3–4.

167. NCRIP, 29 December 1921, p. 8; Hickel, "Entitling Citizens," 184–85.

168. "First National District Managers Meeting," 18 October 1921, 4:15 P.M., pp. 2–3.

169. Ibid.

170. NCRIP, 29 December 1921, pp. 12, 16, 28. In part, rehabilitators blamed veterans' maintenance allowances, which many officers thought were set too high, especially for veterans in placement training. Like Rubinow, rehabilitators worried that the veterans would be accustomed to a "false standard of living" by receiving both a maintenance allowance and partial or full wages from their placement training. NCRIP, 29 December 1921, p. 56; "District Managers' Conference," 20 September 1922, p. 12.

171. U.S. Veterans' Bureau Rehabilitation Division, "Manual of Procedure," November 1921, p. 1, RG15, Rehabilitation Division Records (PC-15), Minutes of Conferences (Entry 10), Box 2, NARA; USVB, *Annual Report, 1925*, 197.

172. "District Managers' Conference," 20 September 1922, p. 43; NCRIP, 30 December 1921, pp. 16, 19; Kinder, *Paying with Their Bodies*, 99.

173. Ernest Strickland to Board of Appeals, USVB, Knoxville, Tennessee, 29 April 1925, and H. B. Garland to Strickland, 23 April 1925, file "Strickland, Ernest M.," Box 23, Regional Office Training Case Files, 1918–1928, Records of the Veterans Administration, RG15, NARA; quoted in Hickel, "Entitling Citizens," 224–25.

174. "Appeal for Further Training," 14 August 1922, Training Case Files, Box 11, Harry Iverson case file.

175. William Steininger to "To Whom It May Concern," 8 August 1922 [original date 14 March 1922], Training Case Files, Box 11, Harry Iverson case file.

176. "Statistical Information," 16 March 1922, Training Case Files, Box 11, Harry Iverson case file.

177. William H. Myers to Harry H. Iverson, 16 February 1922; "Appeal—Further Training," 17 March 1922; William H. Meyers to Chief of Rehabilitation Division, 17 March 1922, Training Case Files, Box 11, Harry Iverson case file.

178. J. C. Wardlaw, the Manager of District no. 2, recommended that the Board of Appeals deny Iverson's petition for additional training. J. C. Wardlaw to Chief of

Administrative Division and Chairman of Board of Appeals, 8 August 1922; "Appeal for Further Training," 14 August 1922; George E. Ijems to Newark Sub-District Manager, 17 August 1922, Training Case Files, Box 11, Harry Iverson case file; Kinder, *Paying with Their Bodies*, 133.

Conclusion

1. Paul K. Longmore and David Goldberger, "The League of the Physically Handicapped and the Great Depression: A Case Study in the New Disability History," *Journal of American History* 87, no. 3 (December 2000): 888–922.

2. Nielsen, *Disability History of the United States*, 150–51.

3. Starting in 1966, the Fair Labor Standards Act amendments required workshops to pay most employees "at least 50 percent of the current minimum wage." Only in 1973 were sheltered workshops required to pay a "fair wage." In 2014, President Barack Obama signed an executive order extending minimum wage rules to all workers employed as federal contractors, including many sheltered workshops. The same year, Congress sought to limit placements of young adults with disabilities in sheltered workshops via the Workforce Innovation and Opportunity Act. Yet, as of 2016, 3,400 workshops still hold certificates giving them right to pay subminimum wages—sometimes less than a dollar per hour. Marta Russell, *Beyond Ramps: Disability at the End of the Social Contract* (Monroe, ME: Common Courage Press, 1998), 136; Michelle Diament, "Obama Signs Law Limiting Sheltered Workshop Eligibility," disabilityscoop, 22 July 2014, https://www.disabilityscoop.com/2014/07/22/obama-law-limiting-sheltered/19538/ (accessed 28 August 2016); Lydia DePillas, "Disabled People Are Allowed to Work for Pennies Per Hour—But Maybe Not for Much Longer," *Washington Post*, 12 February 2016, https://www.washingtonpost.com/news/wonk/wp/2016/02/12/disabled-people-are-allowed-to-work-for-pennies-per-hour-but-maybe-not-for-much-longer/ (accessed 28 August 2016).

4. Ruth O'Brien, *Crippled Justice: The History of Modern Disability Policy in the Workplace* (Chicago: University of Chicago Press, 2001), 6–8.

5. Paul K. Longmore, "Why I Burned My Book," in *Why I Burned My Book and Other Essays on Disability* (Philadelphia: Temple University Press, 2003), 248–51.

6. In 1999 the Supreme Court ruled that if disabled persons could mitigate their disability with equipment or medication—insulin, a wheelchair, glasses, crutches—then they no longer qualified for protection under the Americans with Disabilities Act. Yet they could still be fired by their employer for being disabled. The Americans with Disabilities Amendments Act of 2008 removed this loophole and broadened the definition of disability. O'Brien, *Why I Burned My Book*, chap. 6 passim.

7. Erickson, Lee, and von Schrader, "Disability Statistics from the 2012 American Community Survey (ACS)"; U.S. Bureau of Labor Statistics, "Economics News Release."

8. Mason Ameri, Lisa Schur, Meera Adya, Scott Bentley, Patrick McKay, and Douglas Kruse, "The Disability Employment Puzzle: A Field Experiment on Employer Hiring Behavior," NBER Working Paper no. 21560 (September 2015).

Bibliography

Primary Sources

MANUSCRIPT COLLECTIONS

Ancestry.com
    United States Censuses, 1850–1940
Benson Ford Research Center, Dearborn, Michigan
    Charles E. Sorenson Papers (Acc. 38)
    C. L. Martindale / Otto H. Husen Files (Acc. 157)
    Compensation Department Records (Acc. 789)
    Fair Lane Papers (Acc. 1)
    Five Dollar Day Papers (Acc. 683)
    Ford Motor Company Incorporation Records (Acc. 85)
    Ford Motor Company Non-Serial Publications Collection (Acc. 951)
    Henry and Edsel Ford Quotations Collection (Acc. 511)
    Henry Ford Office Papers (Acc. 23 and 62)
    General Photographs Series (Acc. 833)
    Legal Cases Numerical Records (Acc. 297)
    Legal Department (Ford Motor Company) Records (Acc. 75)
    Norman L. Woodry Papers (Acc. 611)
    Samuel Simpson Marquis Papers (Acc. 293)
    S. S. Marquis Correspondence (Acc. 63)
    Nevins and Hill Research, Original Documents and Notes (Acc. 572)
    Oral History Collection (Acc. 65)
    Vertical File
Boston University School of Theology Archives, Boston, Massachusetts
    Morgan Memorial—Goodwill Industries Records
Goodwill Industries International, Rockville, Maryland
    Chronological File
    City File
    Delegate Assemblies
    Edgar J. Helms Correspondence
    Methodist Church records
    Morgan Memorial Goodwill Industries Records
    Training Lectures
Kheel Center for Labor-Management Documentation and Archives, M. P.
Catherwood Library, Cornell University, Ithaca, New York
    American Association for Labor Legislation Pamphlet Collection (Acc. 5001pam)

Isaac Max Rubinow Papers (Acc. 5616)

National Archives, Washington, DC
  Records of the Veterans Administration, Record Group 15, Regional Office Training Case Files, 1918–1928 (Entry 15A)
  Records of the Veterans Administration, Record Group 15, Rehabilitation Division Records (PC-15)

New York State Archives, Albany, New York
  Governor. Investigation case files of charges and complaints against public officials and agencies, 1857–1919 (Acc. A0531)
  Monthly Reports and Minutes of Meetings of Boards of Managers of State Institutions, 1902–1914 (Acc. A0283-78)
    Newark Custodial Asylum
    Rome Custodial Asylum
    Syracuse State Institution
  New York Census of Inmates in Almshouses and Poorhouses, 1830–1921 (Acc. A1978), accessed through Ancestry.com. Provo, UT: Ancestry.com Operations
  New York State Censuses, 1855, 1875, 1892, 1905, 1915, 1925, accessed through Ancestry.com
  New York State Institution for Male Defective Delinquents inmate case files, 1920–1956 (Acc. 14610-88B)
  State Board of Charities. Census of non-institutionalized insane and idiots, 1871 (Acc. A1979)
  State Board of Charities. Correspondence (Acc. 1977-1978)
  Syracuse Developmental Center. Clipping Files (Acc. B1656)
  Syracuse Developmental Center. County Admission Registers, 1866–1974 (Acc. B1665)
  Syracuse State Institution for Feeble-Minded Children. Private Pay Accounts, 1835–1903 (Acc. B1684)
  Syracuse State Institution for Feeble-Minded Children. Pupil Evaluation Reports [ca. 1860–1909] (Acc. B1666)
  Syracuse State Institution for Feeble-Minded Children. Record of Deaths, 1851–1895 (Acc. B1662)
  Syracuse State School, Admission, Discharge, Death, and Transfer Records, 1851–1945 (Acc. B1647)
    Admission/Discharge Registers, 1884–1924 (Subseries 5)
    Admissions Registers, 1851–1920 (Subseries 2)
    Descriptive Registers, 1851–1913 (Subseries 1)

Schlesinger Library, Harvard University, Cambridge, Massachusetts
  Crystal Eastman Papers (Acc. 82-M4)

Social Welfare History Archives, University of Minnesota, Minneapolis, Minnesota
  Survey Associates records (Acc. SWA1)

Wisconsin Historical Society, Madison, Wisconsin
  John A. Fitch Papers (MS 937)

PERIODICALS

Amalgamated Meat Cutters and Butcher Workmen of North America. *Official Journal.* 1899–1908.

———. *Report of the Proceedings of the General Convention.* 1899–1906, 1914–1926.

American Association for Labor Legislation. *American Labor Legislation Review.* 1911–1919.

———. *Legislative Review.* 1909–1910.

———. *Proceedings of the Annual Meeting.* 1907–1909.

American Association of Workers for the Blind. *Outlook for the Blind.* 1908–1913.

———. *Proceedings of the Convention.* 1905, 1907, 1909, 1911.

American Blind People's Higher Education and General Improvement Association. *The Problem.* 1900–1903.

Association of Medical Officers of American Institutions for Idiotic and Feeble-Minded Persons. *Proceedings* (became *Journal of Psycho-Asthenics* in 1896). 1876–1902.

Charity Organization Society of New York. *Charities and the Commons.* 1908.

———. *Survey.* 1909–1918.

Efficiency Society. *Journal.* 1912–1914.

Federation of Associations for Cripples and Welfare Commission for Cripples. *American Journal of Care for Cripples.* 1914–1916.

International Association of Industrial Accident Boards and Commissions. *Proceedings.* 1919–1922.

International Association of Machinists. *Machinists Monthly Journal.* 1909–1918.

———. Grand Lodge Convention. *Proceedings, . . . Convention / Grand Lodge, International Association of Machinists.* 1889–1924.

Methodist Episcopal Church. Board of Home Missions and Church Extension. *Annual Report.* 1916–1929.

———. Board of Home Missions and Church Extension. *Council of Cities.* 1918–1919.

———. Board of Home Missions and Church Extension. Department of City Work. *Annual Meeting of the Council of Cities.* 1917–?

National Conference of Charities and Corrections. *Proceedings of the National Conference of Charities and Corrections.* 1874–1920.

Office of the Surgeon General, U.S. Army, and the Red Cross Institute for Crippled and Disabled Men. *Carry On: A Magazine for the Reconstruction of Disabled Soldiers and Sailors.* 1918–1919.

Red Cross Institute for Crippled and Disabled Men. *Publications of the Red Cross Institute for Crippled and Disabled Men.* 1918–1919.

State Charities Aid Association. *Annual Report of the State Charities Aid Association to the State Commissioners of Public Charities of the State of New York.* 1873–1890.

United Mine Workers of America. *Proceedings.* 1898–1924.

GOVERNMENT PUBLICATIONS

Commonwealth of Massachusetts Industrial Accident Board. *First Annual Report of the Industrial Accident Board.* Boston: Wright and Potter Printing, 1914.

Documents of the Assembly of the State of New York. Albany: J. B. Lyon, 1917.

Federal Board for Vocational Education. *See* U.S. Federal Board for Vocational Education

Illinois, State of. Illinois Institution for the Education of Feeble-Minded Children. *Annual Report of the Directors and Superintendent.* 1866–1890.

Iowa, State of. *Biennial Report of the Board of Trustees of the Asylum for Feeble Minded Children of the State of Iowa at Glenwood.* 1877–1891.

Laws of the State of New-York, Passed at the Seventy-Fourth Session of the Legislature. Chapter 502. Albany: E. Croswell, 1851.

Massachusetts, State of. Experimental School for Teaching and Training Idiotic Children. *Third and Final Report on the Experimental School for Teaching and Training Idiotic Children; Also, the First Report of the Trustees of the Massachusetts School for Idiotic and Feeble-Minded Youth.* Cambridge, MA: Metcalf, 1852.

———. *Report of the Trustees of the Massachusetts School for Idiotic and Feeble-Minded Youth.* 1852, 1854, 1856–1860.

Michigan, State of. *Report of the Employers' Liability and Workmen's Compensation Committee of the State of Michigan.* Lansing, MI: Wynkoop Hallenbeck Crawford, 1911.

New York State. Board of State Commissioners of Public Charities. *Annual Report of the Board of State Commissioners of Public Charities of the State of New York.* Albany. 1867–1872.

———. Department of Labor. *The Workmen's Compensation Law, with Amendments, Additions, and Annotations to July 1, 1915.* Albany: J. B. Lyon, 1915.

———. Industrial Commission. *Proceedings of the First Industrial Safety Conference of New York State.* Albany: J. B. Lyon, 1917.

———. *Proceedings of the State Convention of the County Superintendents of the Poor.* 1872–1881.

———. State Board of Charities. *Annual Report of the State Board of Charities of the State of New York.* Albany. 1873–1903.

———. State Board of Charities. Bureau of Analysis and Investigation. *Report on Fifty-Two Border-Line Cases in the Rome State Custodial Asylum.* Albany, 1914.

———. State Board of Charities. Bureau of Analysis and Investigation. *Second Report on Fifty-Two Border-Line Cases in the Rome State Custodial Asylum.* Albany, 1915.

———. State Commission to Investigate Provision for the Mentally Deficient. *Report of the State Commission to Investigate Provision for the Mentally Deficient, Pursuant to the Provisions of Chapter 2727 of the Laws of 1914.* Albany: J. B. Lyon, 1915.

———. State Custodial Asylum for Feeble Minded Women. *Annual Report of the Board of Managers.* 1878–1920.

———. State Custodial Asylum, Rome. Board of Managers. *Annual Report of the Board of Managers of the Rome State Custodial Asylum at Rome, N.Y.* 1896–1930.

———. State Custodial Asylum, Rome. *Custodial Herald* (name varies among *Rome Custodial Herald*, *Custodial Herald*, and *Herald*). Rome, NY: Rome State Custodial Asylum. 1913–1919.

———. State School, Syracuse. *Annual Report.* Albany. 1851–1920.

Ohio, State of. *Report to the Legislature of the State of Ohio of the Investigation Made for the Ohio Employers Liability Commission into Industrial Accidents Occurring in*

Cuyahoga County, Ohio, for the Period of November, 1905, to January 1, 1911. Columbus, OH: F. J. Heer, 1910.

Pennsylvania. Training School for Feeble-Minded Children, *Annual Report of the Board of Directors of the Pennsylvania Training School for Feeble-Minded Children with the Report of the Superintendent.* 1857–1906.

U.S. Bureau of Labor Statistics. *Bulletin.* Washington, D.C.: Government Printing Office. 1912–1920.

U.S. Bureau of the Census. *Census of the United States.* 1840–1940.

U.S. Commissioner of Labor. *Twenty-Fourth Annual Report: Workmen's Insurance and Compensation Systems in Europe.* Washington, DC: Government Printing Office, 1911.

U.S. Commission on Industrial Relations. *Final Report and Testimony Submitted to Congress.* 64th Cong., 1st sess., 1916, S. Doc. 415.

U.S. Federal Board for Vocational Education. *Annual Reports.* Washington, DC: Government Printing Office. 1917–1922.

———. *Bulletin.* Washington, D.C.: Government Printing Office. 1917–1922.

———. *Proceedings of the First National Conference on Vocational Rehabilitation of Persons Disabled in Industry or Otherwise.* Washington, DC: Government Printing Office, 1922.

U.S. Selective Service System. *World War I Selective Service System Draft Registration Cards, 1917–1918.* Washington, DC: National Archives and Records Administration, 1917–1918, accessed through Ancestry.com.

U.S. Veterans' Bureau. *Annual Report of the Director.* Washington, D.C.: Government Printing Office. 1922–1928.

Washington, State of. *Report of Commission Appointed by Governor M. E. Hay to Investigate the Problems of Industrial Accidents and to Draft a Bill on the Subject of Employes' Compensation to Be Submitted to the 1911 Session of the Washington Legislature.* Olympia, WA: E. L. Boardman, 1910.

Wisconsin, State of. *Report of the Special Committee on Industrial Insurance [to the] Wisconsin Legislature, 1909–1910.* Madison, WI: Committee on Industrial Insurance, 1911.

Yates, John V. N. *Report of the Secretary of State [of New York] on the Relief and Settlement of the Poor.* 1824. Reprinted in David Rothman, *The Almshouse Experience: Collected Reports.* New York: Arno Press and the New York Times, 1971.

LEGAL CASES

In re Madden, Appeal of American Mut. Liability Ins. Co., 222 Mass. 487 (1916).
Nease v. Hughes Stone Co., et al., 114 Okla. 170 (1925).
Schwab v. Emporium Forestry Co., 167 A.D. 614 (1915).
Weaver v. Maxwell Motor Co., 186 Mich. 588 (1915).

BOOKS AND PAMPHLETS

Atlanta Goodwill Industries Incorporated. Atlanta: Atlanta Goodwill Industries, ca. 1931.
Buffalo City Directory. Buffalo: Courier Co. of Buffalo, 1893.

The Buffalo Directory. Buffalo: Courier Co. of Buffalo, 1884.
Bureau of Goodwill Industries and the National Association of Goodwill Industries. *Purposes and Policies of Goodwill Industries*. Boston: Morgan Memorial Goodwill Industries Press, 1936.
The Centenary Survey of the Board of Home Missions and Church Extension of the Methodist Episcopal Church. New York: Joint Centenary Committee, 1918.
Christmas, Earl. *The House of Goodwill: A Story of Morgan Memorial*. Boston: Morgan Memorial Press, 1924.
Cowles, George W. *Landmarks of Wayne County, New York*. Syracuse, NY: D. Mason, 1895.
De Leon, Edwin W. *The Relation of the Medical Examination of Employes to Insurance under Workmen's Compensation Laws*. White Sulphur Springs, WV: Annual Convention of International Association of Casualty and Surety Underwriters, 1914.
Devine, Edward T., with Lilian Brandt. *Disabled Soldiers and Sailors Pensions and Training*. Preliminary Economic Studies of the War No. 12. Oxford: Oxford University Press, 1919.
Dix, Dorothea Lynde. *Memorial: To the Legislature of Massachusetts*. Boston: Munroe and Francis, 1843.
Dorion, E. C. E. *The Redemption of the South End: A Study in City Evangelization*. New York: Abingdon Press, 1915. Reprint, Bethesda, MD: Goodwill Industries International, 2001.
Eastman, Crystal. *"Employers' Liability": A Criticism Based on Facts*. New York: New York Branch of the American Association for Labor Legislation, 1909.
———. *Work-Accidents and the Law*. New York: Russell Sage Foundation, 1910. Reprint, New York: Arno Press, 1969.
Fitch, John A. *The Steel Workers*. New York: Russell Sage Foundation, 1910. Reprint, Pittsburgh: University of Pittsburgh Press, 1989.
Ford, Henry. *My Life and Work*. Garden City, NJ: Doubleday, Page, 1922. Reprint, North Stratford, NH: Ayer, 2000.
———. *Quotations from the Unusual Henry Ford*. Redondo Beach, CA: Quotamus Press, 1978.
Gilbreth, Frank B., and Lillian Moller Gilbreth. *Motion Study for the Handicapped*. London: George Routledge and Sons, 1920.
The Goodwill Industries: A Manual. Boston: Morgan Memorial Goodwill Press, 1935.
Goodwill Tales. Boston: Morgan Memorial Goodwill Press, ca. 1938.
Hamilton, J. Perrine. *The Chief Needs of Adult Blind Persons and the Chief Aims of the Michigan Employment Institution for the Blind: A Circular of Information and Inquiry*. Saginaw, MI: Michigan Employment Institution for the Blind, 1904.
Harris, Garrard. *The Redemption of the Disabled: A Study of Programmes of Rehabilitation for the Disabled of War and of Industry*. New York: D. Appleton, 1919.
Hazzard, Lowell Brestel. *Goodwill Tales*. Boston: Morgan Memorial Goodwill Press, 1922.
Helms, Edgar James. *Pioneering in Modern City Missions*. Boston: Morgan Memorial Printing Department, 1927. Reprint, Bethesda, MD: Goodwill Industries International, 2001.

Howe, Samuel Gridley. *Report to the Legislature of Massachusetts upon Idiocy*. Boston: Coolidge and Wiley, 1848.
International Association of Machinists. *Proceedings of the Conference of Officers, General Organizers, and Business Agents*. St. Louis: International Association of Machinists, 1920.
Keeler, Ralph Welles. *The Goodwill Industries*. Philadelphia: Department of City Work, 1923.
Kessler, Henry. *The Crippled and the Disabled: Rehabilitation of the Physically Handicapped*. New York: Columbia University Press, 1935.
Lacy at Ninety: A Tribute. Compiled and edited by David H. Townsend. Alamogordo, NM: Human Science Associates, 1976.
Lott, Edson S. *Workmen's Compensation Laws as Distinguished from Employers' Liability Laws: An Address... before the Insurance Society of New York*. [New York?], 1912.
Marquis, Samuel S. *Henry Ford: An Interpretation*. Boston: Little, Brown, 1923.
Massachusetts Association for Promoting the Interests of the Blind. *Report, 1912–1913*. Boston: Association for Promoting the Interests of the Blind, 1913.
McMurtrie, Douglas C. *Care of Crippled Soldiers and Sailors: A Letter Published in the New York "Evening Post" of August 31, 1917*. New York: n.p., 1917.
———. *The Disabled Soldier*. New York: Macmillan, 1919. Reprint, New York: Arno Press.
———. *The Essentials of a National System for Rehabilitation of Disabled Service Men of the American Forces: A Statement Presented to the Committee on Education of the House of Representatives*. Greenwich, CT: Arbor Press, 1920.
The Michigan Employment Institution for the Blind: Its Recognized Necessity and Proper Policy; Erroneous Current Impressions Seem to Require Correction; A Remonstrance from Those Who Should Know. Lansing, MI: Board of the Directors of the Michigan Association of Workers for the Blind, 1928.
Mock, Harry E. *Industrial Medicine and Surgery*. Philadelphia: W. B. Saunders, 1919.
Moore, Anne. *The Feeble-Minded in New York: A Report Prepared for the Public Education Association of New York*. New York: State Charities Aid Association and Special Committee on Provision for the Feeble-Minded, 1911.
Moore, Frederick C. *The Golden Threads of Destiny*. Boston: Morgan Memorial Goodwill Press, 1952. Reprint, Bethesda, MD: Goodwill Industries International, 2001.
National Metal Trades Association. *Report of Committee on Employers' Liability Insurance to the Thirteenth Annual Convention*. New York: National Metal Trades Association, 1911.
Pillsbury, A. J. *Changes in the [California] Compensation Law: What They Are and Why They Were Made*. San Francisco: Rincon Publishing [ca. 1917].
Prospectus and Manual of Morgan Memorial. Boston: Goodwill Press of Morgan Memorial, 1922.
Rosen, Marvin, Gerald Robert Clark, and Marvin S. Kivitz, eds. *The History of Mental Retardation, Collected Papers*. Vol. 1. Baltimore: University Park Press, 1976.

Rubinow, I. M. *The Quest for Security.* New York: H. Holt, 1934.

———. *Social Insurance, with Special Reference to American Conditions.* New York: H. Holt, 1913. Reprint, New York: Arno Press, 1969.

Seager, Henry Rogers. *Social Insurance: A Program of Social Reform.* New York: Macmillan, 1910.

Séguin, Edouard. *Théorie et pratique de l'éducation des enfans arriérés et idiots: Leçons aux jeunes idiots de l'Hospice des incurables.* Paris: Germer Baillière, 1842.

———. *Traitement moral, hygiene, et education des idiots.* Paris: Germer Baillière, 1846.

Sherman, P. Tecumseh. *Memorandum Relative to the Respective Advantages and Disadvantages of Various Forms of Compensation Law before the Congressional Employers' Liability and Workmen's Compensation Commission.* New York: National Civic Federation, 1911.

Shuttleworth, George E. *Notes of a Visit to American Institutions for Idiots and Imbeciles.* Lancaster, Eng.: E. and J. L. Milner, 1877.

Town, Clara Harrison, and Grace E. Hill. *How the Feeble-Minded Live in the Community: A Report of a Social Investigation of the Erie County Feeble-Minded Discharged from the Rome State School, 1905–1924.* Buffalo, NY: Children's Aid Society, 1930.

Watson, Emile E. *Report to the Legislature of the State of Ohio of the Investigation Made for the Ohio Employers Liability Commission into Industrial Accidents Occurring in Cuyahoga County, Ohio, for the Period of November, 1905, to January 1, 1911.* Columbus, OH: F. J. Heer Printing, 1910.

Welfare Federation of Cleveland. *Education and Occupations of Cripples, Juvenile and Adult: A Survey of All the Cripples of Cleveland, Ohio, in 1916.* New York: Red Cross Institute for Crippled and Disabled Men, 1918.

ARTICLES

"Adolphus Whitman's Case: He Is a Credit to the Institution That Reared Him." *Brooklyn Daily Eagle,* 8 December 1895, 4.

Barr, Martin W. "The Imperative Call of Our Present to Our Future." *Journal of Psycho-Asthenics* 7 (1902): 5–8.

Bernstein, Charles. "Colony Care for Isolation and Dependent Cases." *Social Hygiene* 7, no. 1 (January 1921): 52–53.

———. "Self-Sustaining Feeble-Minded." *Journal of Psycho-Asthenics* 22, nos. 3–4 (March and June 1918): 150–61.

———. "A State's Policy towards the Care of the Feeble-Minded." *Journal of Psycho-Asthenics* 16, no. 2 (December 1914): 51–54.

———. "Training School for Attendants for the Feeble-Minded." *Journal of Psycho-Asthenics* 12 (1907): 31–43, 88–92.

Bradley, W. F. "French War Repair Shops Models of Systematism." *Motor Age* 29 (29 June 1916): 20–21, 36

"Cases of Total Disability Resulting from the War." *Economic World,* n.s., 26, no. 17 (26 October 1918): 601–2.

Commons, John R. "Henry Ford, Miracle Maker." *The Independent*, 1 May 1920, 160–61.
"Compensation's Effect on Employees." *Weekly Underwriter* 91, no. 6 (8 August 1914): 155.
"Congress; House of Representatives, Tuesday, April 10." *Time Piece; and Literary Companion*, 13 April 1798, 2, 91.
"Considering Status of Disabled Men." *Eastern Underwriter* 19, no. 32 (9 August 1918): 17–18.
Crary, David. "Employer Bias Locks Blind Out: Despite Leaps in Technology and the Law, the Visually Impaired Still Have Trouble Getting Hired." *Chicago Tribune*, 17 March 2008, 3.
"Crippled Soldiers Disheartened by Delays." *New York Times*, 24 August 1919, 43.
"Cripples in the Ford Plant." *Elevator Constructor* 20, no. 8 (August 1923): 16.
Dane, Edan. "Agencies Which Aided War-Crippled." *New York Times*, 24 August 1919, 49.
"Details New Plan for Veteran Relief." *New York Times*, 24 October 1921, 27.
"Disabled Men Seek to Untie Red Tape." *New York Times*, 15 June 1928: 1, 6.
A Disabled Soldier. "Letter to the Editor: Failures in Rehabilitation." *New York Times*, 27 August 1919, 10.
"Does the Workmen's Compensation Law Change the Old Time Relations between the Physician and His Patient?" *National Compensation Journal* 1, no. 1 (January 1914): 28–30.
Douglas, Paul H. "The War Risk Insurance Act." *Journal of Political Economy* 26, no. 5 (May 1918): 461–83.
"Drive on for Jobs for Rehabilitated." *New York Times*, 4 July 1925, 3.
"Early Change in Compensation Law Urged for Employment of Handicapped Workers." *New York Times*, 18 June 1944, S5.
"Employment of Cripples in a Large Industrial Plant." *Monthly Labor Review* 7, no. 6 (December 1918): 85–86.
"Favor Colony Here for Feebleminded," *New York Times*, 27 January 1918, 10.
Feld, Rose C. "The New War Cripples' School." *New York Times*, 19 March 1922, 107.
Ford, Edsel. "Why We Employ Aged and Handicapped Workers." *Saturday Evening Post*, 6 February 1943, 16–17.
"40 Blind Strikers March on City Hall." *New York Times*, 14 April 1937, 18.
Frankel, Emil. "The Vocational Adjustment of Physically and Mentally Handicapped Children." In Section IV B of the *Special Report of the White House Conference on Child Health and Protection*, 10–12. Washington, DC: Government Printing Office, 1928.
Gilbert, Jennie Cole. "Not Charity, but a Chance." *Western Christian Advocate*, 6 July 1921, 682.
Gilbert, L. L. "Physical Examination of Railway Employees from a Medico-Legal Standpoint." *Medico-Legal Journal* 17, no. 3 (1899): 333–39.
Harmon, Selene Armstrong. "The Government an Employment Agency." *World's Work* 23, no. 5 (September 1916): 575–79.
Helms, E. J. "Morgan Chapel, Boston." *Christian City: Devoted to City Evangelization* 40, nos. 3–4 (March–April 1899), 62–64.

"His Family Found Again: Adolphus Whitman United with His Long Lost Relatives." *Brooklyn Daily Eagle*, 9 December 1895, 1.

Hookstadt, Carl. "Problem of the Handicapped in Industry." *Monthly Labor Review* 4 (March 1918): 579–92.

"House Passes Veteran Bill." *New York Times*, 3 March 1923, 2.

"How Can Industry Find Jobs for Disabled Veterans?" *Machinery* 50, no. 8 (April 1944): 132–38.

"How Training Aids Disabled Veterans." *New York Times*, 29 January 1923, 18.

Hurd, Charles. "The Veteran: Uniform State Insurance Laws Held Need for Handicapped Men." *New York Times*, 27 May 1945, 24.

Kennedy, J. J. "Safety and Efficiency." *Safety Engineering* 40 (December 1920): 216.

"Klan's Hand Seen in Veterans' Bureau." *New York Times*, 10 October 1924, 1.

"Legal Advances in 1919." *Modern Hospital* 14, no. 3 (March 1919): 195.

"Legion Attacks Vocation Board." *New York Times*, 19 September 1919, 24.

Littledale, Harold A. "Disabled Soldiers Untrained after 19 Months of Red Tape." *New York Evening Post*, 16 February 1920, 1, 4.

———. "Thousands of Disabled Men Untrained in This District." *New York Evening Post*, 18 February 1920, 1, 7.

Lowell, Josephine Shaw. "One Means of Preventing Pauperism." *Proceedings of the National Conference of Charities and Correction* 6 (1879): 189–200.

McLeod, Norman. "What Sick and Crippled Men Are Doing for the Ford Motor Company." *Modern Hospital* 12, no. 1 (January 1919): 1–3.

McMurtrie, Douglas C. "The Duty of the Employer in the Reconstruction of the Crippled Soldier." *Journal of the American Society of Heating and Ventilating Engineers*, July 1918, 675–78.

Mead, J. E. "Rehabilitating Cripples at Ford Plant." *Iron Age* 102, no. 13 (26 September 1918): 739–42.

———. "Salvage of Men." *American Medicine* 14, no. 6 (June 1919): 372–78.

"Medical Examination of Employes: Experience of Seven Chicago Firms." Special number, *Bulletin of the Chicago Tuberculosis Institute* 1, no. 3 (June 1913): 4–14.

Meyer, R. D. "An Experiment in Rehabilitation." *Forbes* 54, no. 6 (15 September 1944): 20.

Michelbacher, G. P. "Schedule Rating of Permanent Injuries." *Proceedings of the Casualty Actuarial and Statistical Society of America* 1 (1914): 257–74.

Montgomery, Maxwell C. "Memorial Tribute to Dr. Charles Bernstein." Supplement, *Psychiatric Quarterly* 17, no. 1 (March 1943): 38–39.

"More Help Urged for the Disabled." *New York Times*, 28 March 1927, 11.

"Moves to Expedite Relief of Soldiers." *New York Times*, 3 June 1921, 14.

National Association of the Deaf. "Proceedings of the Twelfth Convention of the National Association of the Deaf." *The Nad* 3, no. 1 (February 1918): 1–183.

"The New Royal Warrant." *Reveille* 1, no. 1 (August 1918): 150–53.

"9,500 Partially Disabled Employees Working in Ford Motor Plant." *National Safety News* 3, no. 3 (17 January 1921): 4.

"No Trouble." *Christian Advocate* 81 (9 August 1906): 81.

Palmer, Lew R. "Employment Opportunities for Pennsylvanians Disabled in War Service." *Annals of the American Academy of Political and Social Science* 80 (November 1918): 70–78.
"Physical Exams for Republic I. & S. Employes." *Steel and Iron* 48 (20 April 1914): v.
"A Pretty Mess." *Time*, 5 November 1923. http://www.time.com/time/magazine/article/0,9171,716844-1,00.html (accessed 6 July 2008).
"Physical Examination of Workmen." *Square Deal* 15, no. 63 (December 1914): 444, reprinted from *Knights of Labor Journal*.
"A Problem in Efficiency." *Modern Hospital* 12, no. 2 (January 1919): 45–46.
"Proceedings of National and Local Societies: International Conference on the Rehabilitation of the Disabled (1919): American Employers and Rehabilitation." *International Record of Medicine and General Practice Clinics* 109 (1919): 659.
Prosser, Charles A. "A Federal Program for the Vocational Rehabilitation of Disabled Soldiers and Sailors." *Annals of the American Academy of Political and Social Science* 80 (November 1918): 117–22.
———. "Two Hundred Ways to Salvage Wounded Men." *New York Times*, 28 July 1918, 54.
"Putting Our War Cripples back on the Payroll." *New York Times*, 12 May 1918, 80.
"Rehabilitation Begins." *New York Times*, 30 June 1918, 23.
"Rehabilitation: Training and Employment of Disabled Workmen in the Ford Plant." *Monthly Labor Review* 17, no. 5 (November 1923): 173–74.
Rubinow, I. M. "The Theory and Practice of Law Differentials." *Proceedings, Casualty Actuarial and Statistical Society of America* 4, no. 9 (1917): 8–44.
Rusk, Howard A. "Rehabilitation: Handicapped Veterans Complain That Compensation Laws Are Quoted by Some Employers in Turning Them Down for Jobs." *New York Times*, 1 September 1946, 30.
Séguin, Edward. "Institutions for Idiots." *Appleton's Journal*, 12 February 1870, 182.
"17 Blind Strikers Joined by 83 More." *New York Times*, 9 April 1937, 2.
"A Square Deal for the Crippled Soldier" [advertisement]. *New York Times*, 23 March 1918, 8.
Stidger, Bill. "Shirt Sleeve Christianity." *Christian Herald*, July 1933, 8.
"Strike Threat over Compensation Law." *New York Times*, 12 August 1914, 13.
"30 Blind Sit-Downers to End Strike Today." *New York Times*, 1 May 1937, 4.
"Tied to Tree, Lost Legs." *Washington Post*, 7 December 1906, 11.
Tobenkin, David "Don't Overlook Second-Injury Funds: Special State Funds for Workers with Pre-existing Conditions Can Help Defray Long-Term Costs for Workers' Compensation," *HR Magazine* 57, no. 7 (July 2009): 51.
"$2,000,000,000 Spent for Aid, but War Veterans Suffer." *New York Times*, 25 February 1923, XX3.
"Veterans' Bureau Called Wasteful." *New York Times*, 29 March 1923, 6.
"Veterans' Scandal Approaching Climax." *New York Times*, 9 March 1924, XX4.
"Vocation Offices Opened." *New York Times*, 11 November 1918, 4.
"War Casualty Hiring Urged on Employers." *New York Times*, 23 October 1945, 8.

Whitney, A. W. "Schedules in Workmen's Compensation." *Transactions of the Actuarial Society of America* 14 (1913): 308–21.

Wilbur, Charles T. "Institutions for the Feeble-Minded: The Result of Forty Years' Effort in Establishing Them in the United States." *Proceedings of the National Conference of Charities and Correction* 15 (1888): 106–13.

Wilbur, Hervey B. "Status of the Work: New York." *Proceedings of the Association of Medical Officers of American Institutions for Idiotic and Feeble-Minded Persons* (1879): 96–101.

"Workmen's Compensation: Period of Waiting Time Required under Workmen's Compensation Laws." *Monthly Labor Review* 36 (January 1933): 122–23.

Wright, Lucy. "Offsetting the Handicap of Blindness." *Annals of the American Academy of Political and Social Science* 77 (May 1918): 28–35.

Secondary Sources

BOOKS

Ahlstrom, Sydney E. *A Religious History of the American People*. New Haven, CT: Yale University Press, 1972.

Aldrich, Mark. *Death Rode the Rails: American Railroad Accidents and Safety, 1828–1965*. Baltimore: Johns Hopkins University Press, 2006.

———. *Safety First: Technology, Labor, and Business in the Building of American Work Safety, 1870–1939*. Baltimore: Johns Hopkins University Press, 1997.

Alexander, John K. *Render Them Submissive: Responses to Poverty in Philadelphia, 1760–1800*. Amherst: University of Massachusetts Press, 1980.

Andrews, Thomas G. *Killing for Coal: America's Deadliest Labor War*. Cambridge, MA: Harvard University Press, 2008.

Baynton, Douglas C. *Defectives in the Land: Disability and Immigration in the Age of Eugenics*. Chicago: University of Chicago Press, 2016.

Bender, Daniel E. *Sweated Work, Weak Bodies: Anti-sweatshop Campaigns and Languages of Labor*. New Brunswick, NJ: Rutgers University Press, 2004.

Bergstrom, Randolph E. *Courting Danger: Injury and Law in New York City, 1870–1910*. Ithaca, NY: Cornell University Press, 1992.

Berkowitz, Edward D., ed. *Disability Policies and Government Programs*. New York: Praeger and the Bureau of Economic Research, 1979.

———. *Disabled Policy: America's Programs for the Handicapped*. Cambridge: Cambridge University Press, 1987.

Bogdan, Robert, with Martin Elks and James A. Knoll. *Picturing Disability: Beggar, Freak, Citizen, and Other Photographic Rhetoric*. Syracuse, NY: Syracuse University Press, 2012.

Boris, Eileen. *Art and Labor: Ruskin, Morris, and the Craftsman Ideal in America*. Philadelphia: Temple University Press, 1988.

Boster, Dea H. *African American Slavery and Disability: Bodies, Property, and Power in the Antebellum South, 1800–1860*. New York: Routledge, 2013.

Brinkley, Douglas. *Wheels for the World: Henry Ford, His Company, and a Century of Progress, 1903–2003*. New York: Penguin, 2003.
Bourke, Joanna. *Dismembering the Male: Men's Bodies, Britain, and the Great War*. Chicago: University of Chicago Press, 1996.
Boydston, Jeanne. *Home and Work: Housework, Wages, and the Ideology of Labor in the Early Republic*. Oxford: Oxford University Press, 1990.
Brock, William R. *Investigation and Responsibility: Public Responsibility in the United States, 1865–1900*. Cambridge: Cambridge University Press, 1984.
Brody, David. *Steelworkers in America: The Nonunion Era*. Cambridge, MA: Harvard University Press, 1960. Reprint, New York: Harper and Row, 1969.
Brune, Jeffrey A., and Daniel J. Wilson, eds. *Disability and Passing: Blurring the Lines of Identity*. Philadelphia: Temple University Press, 2013.
Buchanan, Robert M. *Illusions of Equality: Deaf Americans in School and Factory, 1850–1950*. Washington, DC: Gallaudet University Press, 1999.
Burch, Susan. *Signs of Resistance: American Deaf Cultural History, 1900 to World War II*. New York: New York University Press, 2002.
Burch, Susan, and Hannah Joyner. *Unspeakable: The Story of Junius Wilson*. Chapel Hill: University of North Carolina Press, 2007.
Burch, Susan, and Michael Rembis, eds. *Disability Histories*. Urbana: University of Illinois Press, 2014.
Carey, Allison C. *On the Margins of Citizenship: Intellectual Disability and Civil Rights in Twentieth-Century America*. Philadelphia: Temple University Press, 2009.
Carlisle, Linda V. *Elizabeth Packard: A Noble Fight*. Urbana: University of Illinois Press, 2010.
Cherniack, Martin. *The Hawk's Nest Incident: America's Worst Industrial Disaster*. New Haven, CT: Yale University Press, 1986.
Clark, Claudia. *Radium Girls: Women and Industrial Health Reform, 1910–1935*. Chapel Hill: University of North Carolina Press, 1997.
Clement, Priscilla Ferguson. *Welfare and the Poor in the Nineteenth-Century City: Philadelphia, 1800–1854*. Rutherford, NJ: Fairleigh Dickinson University Press, 1985.
Cohen, Deborah. *The War Come Home: Disabled Veterans in Britain and Germany, 1914–1939*. Berkeley: University of California Press, 2001.
Cohen, Patricia Cline. *A Calculating People: The Spread of Numeracy in Early America*. 2nd ed. Chicago: University of Chicago Press, 1982.
Crews, Harry. *A Childhood: A Biography of a Place*. New York: Harper and Row, 1978.
Danbom, David B. *Born in the Country: A History of Rural America*. 2nd ed. Baltimore: Johns Hopkins University Press, 2006.
Davis, Lennard J. *Enforcing Normalcy: Disability, Deafness, and the Body*. New York: Verso, 1995.
Derickson, Alan. *Black Lung: Anatomy of a Public Health Disaster*. Ithaca, NY: Cornell University Press, 1998.
———. *Workers' Health, Workers' Democracy: The Western Miners' Struggle, 1891–1925*. Ithaca, NY: Cornell University Press, 1988.

Deutsch, Albert. *The Mentally Ill in America: A History of Their Care and Treatment from Colonial Times.* New York: Columbia University Press, 1949.

Devine, Shauna. *Learning from the Wounded: The Civil War and the Rise of American Medical Science.* Chapel Hill: University of North Carolina Press, 2014.

Donohue, Kathleen G. *Freedom from Want: American Liberalism and the Idea of the Consumer.* Baltimore: Johns Hopkins University Press, 2003.

Ducker, James. *Men of the Steel Rails: Workers on the Atchison, Topeka & Santa Fe Railroad, 1869–1900.* Lincoln: University of Nebraska Press, 1983.

Dwyer, Ellen. *Homes for the Mad: Life inside Two Nineteenth-Century Asylums.* New Brunswick, NJ: Rutgers University Press, 1987.

Edwards, R. A. R. *Words Made Flesh: Nineteenth-Century Deaf Education and the Growth of Deaf Culture.* New York: New York University Press, 2012.

Evans, Peter B., Dietrich Rueschemeyer, and Theda Skocpol, eds. *Bringing the State Back In.* Cambridge: Cambridge University Press, 1985.

Ferguson, Philip M. *Abandoned to Their Fate: Social Policy and Practice toward Severely Retarded People in America, 1820–1920.* Philadelphia: Temple University Press, 1994.

Finger, Anne. *Elegy for a Disease: A Personal and Cultural History of Polio.* New York: St. Martin's Press, 2006.

Forbath, William. *Law and the Shaping of the American Labor Movement.* Cambridge, MA: Harvard University Press, 1991.

Freeberg, Ernest. *The Education of Laura Bridgman: First Deaf and Blind Person to Learn Language.* Cambridge, MA: Harvard University Press, 2001.

Gersuny, Carl. *Work Hazards and Industrial Conflict.* Hanover, NH: University Press of New England, 1981.

Gollaher, David. *Voice for the Mad: The Life of Dorothea Dix.* New York: Free Press, 1995.

Goodwin, Joanne L. *Gender and the Politics of Welfare Reform: Mothers' Pensions in Chicago, 1911–1929.* Chicago: University of Chicago Press, 1977.

Gould, Stephen Jay. *The Mismeasure of Man.* Rev. and expanded ed. New York: Norton, 1996.

Gregory, James. *American Exodus: The Dust Bowl Migration and Okie Culture in California.* Oxford: Oxford University Press, 1989.

Grob, Gerald. *The Mad among Us: A History of the Care of America's Mentally Ill.* New York: Free Press, 2011.

———. *Mental Institutions in America, 1875–1940.* Princeton, NJ: Princeton University Press, 1983.

Groce, Nora Ellen. *Everyone Here Spoke Sign Language: Hereditary Deafness on Martha's Vineyard.* Cambridge, MA: Harvard University Press, 1985

Haller, Mark H. *Eugenics: Hereditarian Attitudes in American Thought.* 1963. Reprint, New Brunswick, NJ: Rutgers University Press, 1984.

Handlin, Oscar. *The Uprooted: The Epic Story of the Great Migration That Made the American People.* Philadelphia: University of Pennsylvania Press, 2002.

Haskell, Thomas L. *The Emergence of Professional Social Science: The American Social Science Association and the Nineteenth-Century Crisis of Authority.* Rev. ed. Baltimore: Johns Hopkins University Press, 2000.

Hepler, Alison. *Women in Labor: Mothers, Medicine, and Occupational Health in the United States, 1890–1980.* Columbus: Ohio State University Press, 2000.

Herndon, Ruth Wallis. *Unwelcome Americans: Living on the Margin in Early New England.* Philadelphia: University of Pennsylvania Press, 2001.

Higbie, Frank Tobias. *Indispensable Outcasts: Hobo Workers and Community in the American Midwest, 1880–1930.* Urbana: University of Illinois Press, 2003.

Hofstadter, Richard. *The Age of Reform.* New York: Vintage Books, 1955.

Hooker, Clarence. *Life in the Shadows of the Crystal Palace, 1910–1927: Ford Workers in the Model T Era.* Bowling Green, OH: Bowling Green State University Popular Press, 1997.

Hounshell, David. *From the American System to Mass Production, 1800–1932.* Baltimore: Johns Hopkins University Press, 1985.

Jacobs, Meg, William J. Novak, and Julian E. Zelizer, eds. *The Democratic Experiment: New Directions in American Political History.* Princeton, NJ: Princeton University Press, 2003.

Jacobson, Matthew Frye, *Barbarian Virtues: The United States Encounters Foreign Peoples at Home and Abroad, 1876–1917.* New York: Hill and Wang, 2000.

Jensen, Laura. *Patriots, Settlers, and the Origins of American Social Policy.* Cambridge: Cambridge University Press, 2003.

Kanner, Leo. *A History of the Care and Study of the Mentally Retarded.* Springfield, IL: Charles C. Thomas, 1964.

Kantor, Harvey. *Learning to Earn: School, Work, and Vocational Reform in California, 1880–1930.* Madison: University of Wisconsin Press, 1988.

Katz, Michael B. *In the Shadow of the Poorhouse: A Social History of Welfare in America.* New York: Basic Books, 1986.

———. *The Price of Citizenship: Redefining the American Welfare State.* New York: H. Holt, 2001.

Katzmann, David A. *Seven Days a Week: Women and Domestic Service in Industrializing America.* New York: Oxford University Press, 1978.

Kelly, Patrick J. *Creating a National Home: Building the Veterans' Welfare State.* Cambridge, MA: Harvard University Press, 1997.

Kendrick, Asahel C. *Martin B. Anderson, LL.D.: A Biography.* Philadelphia: American Baptist Publication Society, 1895.

Kenny, Kevin. *Making Sense of the Molly Maguires.* Oxford: Oxford University Press, 1998.

Kerber, Linda K. *No Constitutional Right to Be Ladies: Women and the Obligations of Citizenship.* New York: Hill and Wang, 1998.

Kessler-Harris, Alice. *In Pursuit of Equity: Women, Men and the Quest for Economic Citizenship in Twentieth-Century America.* Oxford: Oxford University Press, 2001.

———. *Out to Work: A History of Wage-Earning Women in the United States.* 20th anniversary ed. New York: Oxford University Press, 2003.

Kevles, Daniel. *In the Name of Eugenics: Genetics and the Uses of Human Heredity.* Cambridge, MA: Harvard University Press, 1995.

Keyssar, Alexander. *Out of Work: The First Century of Unemployment in Massachusetts.* Cambridge: Cambridge University Press, 1986.

———. *The Right to Vote: The Contested History of Democracy in the United States.* New York: Basic Books, 2000.

Kinder, John M. *Paying with Their Bodies: American War and the Problem of the Disabled Veteran.* Chicago: University of Chicago Press, 2015.

Klebaner, Benjamin Joseph. *Public Poor Relief in America, 1790–1860.* PhD diss., Columbia University, 1951. Reprint, New York: Arno Press, 1976.

Kleinberg, S. J. *Widows and Orphans First: The Family Economy and Social Welfare Policy, 1880–1939.* Urbana: University of Illinois Press, 2006.

Kliebard, Herbert. *Schooled to Work: Vocationalism and the American Curriculum, 1876–1946.* New York: Teachers College Press, 1999.

Koestler, Frances A. *The Unseen Minority: A Social History of Blindness in the United States.* New York: David McKay, 1976.

Krainz, Thomas A. *Delivering Aid: Implementing Progressive Era Welfare in the American West.* Albuquerque: University of New Mexico Press, 2005.

Kraut, Alan M. *Silent Travelers: Germs, Genes, and the "Immigrant Menace."* Baltimore: Johns Hopkins University Press, 1994.

Kunzel, Regina. *Fallen Women, Problem Girls: Unmarried Mothers and the Professionalization of Social Work, 1890–1945.* New Haven, CT: Yale University Press, 1995.

Lacey, Robert. *Ford: The Men and the Machine.* Boston: Little, Brown, 1986.

Larsson, Marina. *Shattered Anzacs: Living with the Scars of War.* Sydney: University of New South Wales Press, 2009.

Lewis, David L. *The Public Image of Henry Ford: An American Folk Hero and His Company.* Detroit: Wayne State University Press, 1976.

Lewis, John Fulton. *Goodwill: For the Love of People.* Bethesda, MD: Goodwill Industries of America, 1977.

Licht, Walter. *Getting Work: Philadelphia, 1840–1950.* Cambridge, MA: Harvard University Press, 1992.

———. *Working for the Railroad: The Organization of Work in the Nineteenth Century.* Princeton, NJ: Princeton University Press, 1983.

Linebaugh, Peter, and Marcus Rediker. *The Many-Headed Hydra: Sailors, Slaves, Commoners, and the Hidden History of the Revolutionary Atlantic.* Boston: Beacon Press, 2000.

Linker, Beth. *War's Waste: Rehabilitation in World War I America.* Chicago: University of Chicago Press, 2011.

Linton, Simi. *Claiming Disability: Knowledge and Identity.* New York: New York University Press, 1998.

Lockley, Timothy James. *Welfare and Charity in the Antebellum South.* Gainesville: University Press of Florida, 2007.

Lombardo, Paul A. *Three Generations, No Imbeciles: Eugenics, the Supreme Court, and Buck v. Bell.* Baltimore: Johns Hopkins University Press, 2008.

Longmore, Paul K., and Lauri Umansky, eds. *The New Disability History: American Perspectives.* New York: New York University Press, 2001.
Marty, Martin E. *Modern American Religion.* Vol. 1, *The Irony of It All, 1893–1919.* Chicago: University of Chicago Press, 1986.
May, Arthur J. *A History of the University of Rochester, 1850–1962.* Edited and abridged by Lawrence Eliot Klein. Rochester, NY: University of Rochester Press, 1977.
May, Henry F. *Protestant Churches and Industrial America.* New York: Octagon Books, 1963.
McClure, Arthur F., James Riley Chrisman, and Perry Mock. *Education for Work: The Historical Evolution of Vocational and Distributive Education in America.* Rutherford, NJ: Fairleigh Dickinson University Press, 1985.
Metzgar, Jack. *Striking Steel: Solidarity Remembered.* Philadelphia: Temple University Press, 2000.
Meyer, Steve. *The Five-Dollar Day: Labor Management and Social Control in the Ford Motor Company, 1908–1921.* Albany: State University of New York Press, 1981.
Mintz, Steven. *Huck's Raft: A History of American Childhood.* Cambridge, MA: Harvard University Press, 2004.
Mitchell, David T., and Sharon L. Snyder. *Narrative Prosthesis: Disability and the Dependencies of Discourse.* Ann Arbor: University of Michigan Press, 2000.
Mohl, Raymond A. *Poverty in New York, 1783–1825.* Oxford: Oxford University Press, 1971.
Mohun, Arwen. *Steam Laundries: Gender, Technology, and Work in the United States and Great Britain, 1880–1940.* Baltimore: Johns Hopkins University Press, 1990.
Mormino, Gary R. and George E. Pozzetta, *The Immigrant World of Ybor City: Italians and Their Latin Neighbors in Tampa, 1885–1985.* Gainesville: University Press of Florida, 1998.
Moss, David A. *Socializing Security: Progressive-Era Economists and the Origins of American Social Policy.* Cambridge, MA: Harvard University Press, 1996.
Nevins, Allan. *Ford: Expansion and Challenge, 1915–1931.* New York: Scribner and Sons, 1957.
———. *Ford: The Times, the Man, the Company.* New York: Arno Press, 1976.
Newman, Simon P. *Embodied History: The Lives of the Poor in Early Philadelphia.* Philadelphia: University of Pennsylvania Press, 2003.
Nicholson, Philip Yale. *Labor's Story in the United States.* Philadelphia: Temple University Press, 2004.
Nielsen, Kim E. *Beyond the Miracle Worker: The Remarkable Life of Anne Sullivan Macy and Her Extraordinary Friendship with Helen Keller.* Boston: Beacon Press, 2009.
———. *A Disability History of the United States.* Boston: Beacon Press, 2012.
———. *The Radical Lives of Helen Keller.* New York: New York University Press, 2004.
Noll, Steven. *Feeble-Minded in Our Midst: Institutions for the Mentally Retarded in the South, 1900–1940.* Chapel Hill: University of North Carolina Press, 1995.
Nordlund, Willis J. *A History of the Federal Employees' Compensation Act.* Washington, DC: U.S. Department of Labor, Employee Standards Administration, Office of Workers' Compensation Programs, 1992.

Obermann, C. Esco. *A History of Vocational Rehabilitation in America*. Minneapolis: T. S. Denison, 1965.
O'Brien, Ruth. *Crippled Justice: The History of Modern Disability Policy in the Workplace*. Chicago: University of Chicago Press, 2001.
O'Connor, Alice. *Poverty Knowledge: Social Science, Social Policy, and the Poor in Twentieth-Century U.S. History*. Princeton, NJ: Princeton University Press, 2001.
Patterson, James T. *America's Struggle against Poverty in the Twentieth Century*. Cambridge, MA: Harvard University Press, 2000.
Perman, Michael. *Struggle for Mastery: Disfranchisement in the South, 1888–1908*. Chapel Hill: University of North Carolina Press, 2001.
Pernick, Martin S. *The Black Stork: Eugenics and the Death of "Defective" Babies in American Medicine and Motion Pictures since 1915*. Oxford: Oxford University Press, 1996.
Plumb, Beatrice. *The Goodwill Man: Edgar James Helms*. Minneapolis: T. S. Denison, 1965.
Porter, Roy. *Madness: A Brief History*. Oxford: Oxford University Press, 2002.
Rafter, Nicole Hahn. *Creating Born Criminals*. Urbana: University of Illinois Press, 1997.
Reaume, Geoffrey. *Remembrance of Patients Past: Patient Life at the Toronto Hospital for the Insane, 1870–1940*. Toronto: University of Toronto Press, 2009; orig. publ. Oxford University Press, 2000.
Register, Cheri. *Packinghouse Daughter: A Memoir*. New York: Perennial, 2001.
Reiss, Benjamin. *Theaters of Madness: Insane Asylums and Nineteenth-Century American Culture*. Chicago: University of Chicago Press, 2008.
Rembis, Michael A. *Defining Deviance: Sex, Science, and Delinquent Girls, 1890–1960*. Urbana: University of Illinois Press, 2011.
Resch, John Phillips. *Suffering Soldiers: Revolutionary War Veterans, Moral Sentiment, and Political Culture in the Early Republic*. Amherst: University of Massachusetts Press, 1999.
Richards, Laura E. *Samuel Gridley Howe*. New York: D. Appleton-Century, 1935.
Riggs, J. G. *Hello Doctor: A Brief Biography of Charles Bernstein, M.D.* East Aurora, NY: Roycroft, 1936.
Ringenbach, Paul T. *Tramps and Reformers, 1873–1916: The Discovery of Unemployment in New York*. Westport, CT: Greenwood Press, 1973.
Rockman, Seth. *Scraping By: Wage Labor, Slavery, and Survival in Early Baltimore*. Baltimore: Johns Hopkins University Press, 2010.
Rodgers, Daniel T. *Atlantic Crossings: Social Politics in a Progressive Age*. Cambridge, MA: Harvard University Press, 1998.
———. *The Work Ethic in Industrial America, 1850–1920*. Chicago: University of Chicago Press, 1978.
Rollins, Judith. *Between Women: Domestics and Their Employers*. Philadelphia: Temple University Press, 1985.
Rosner, David, and Gerald Markowitz. *Deadly Dust: Silicosis and the Politics of Occupational Disease in Twentieth-Century America*. Princeton, NJ: Princeton University Press, 1991.

Ross, David R. B. *Preparing for Ulysses: Politics and Veterans during World War II*. New York: Columbia University Press, 1969.
Rothman, David J. *The Discovery of the Asylum: Social Order and Disorder in the New Republic*. Boston: Little, Brown, 1971.
Rothman, Sheila M. *Living in the Shadow of Death: Tuberculosis and the Social Experience of Illness in American History*. New York: BasicBooks, 1994.
Russell, Marta. *Beyond Ramps: Disability at the End of the Social Contract*. Monroe, ME: Common Courage Press, 1998.
Ruswick, Brent. *Almost Worthy: The Poor, Paupers, and the Science of Charity in America, 1877–1917*. Bloomington: Indiana University Press, 2012.
Sandage, Scott A. *Born Losers: A History of Failure in America*. Cambridge, MA: Harvard University Press, 2005.
Scarry, Elaine. *The Body in Pain: The Making and Unmaking of the World*. Oxford: Oxford University Press, 1987.
Scheerenberger, R. C. *A History of Mental Retardation*. Baltimore: Paul H. Brookes, 1983.
Schmidt, James D. *Industrial Violence and the Legal Origins of Child Labor*. Cambridge: Cambridge University Press, 2010.
Schneider, David M. *The History of Public Welfare in New York State, 1609–1866*. Chicago: University of Chicago Press, 1938. Reprint, Montclair, NJ: Patterson Smith, 1969.
Schudson, Michael. *The Good Citizen: A History of American Civic Life*. New York: Free Press, 1998.
Schwartz, Harold. *Samuel Gridley Howe: Social Reformer, 1801–1876*. Cambridge, MA: Harvard University Press, 1956.
Schweik, Susan M. *Ugly Laws: Disability in Public*. New York: New York University Press, 2009.
Scott, James C. *Seeing Like a State: How Certain Schemes to Improve the Human Condition Have Failed*. New Haven, CT: Yale University Press, 1999.
Sellers, Christopher. *Hazards on the Job: From Industrial Disease to Environmental Health Science*. Chapel Hill: University of North Carolina Press, 1997.
Sennett, Richard, and Jonathan Cobb. *The Hidden Injuries of Class*. New York: Knopf, 1972.
Simonsen, Jane E. *Making Home Work: Domesticity and Native American Assimilation in the American West, 1860–1919*. Chapel Hill: University of North Carolina Press, 2006.
Skocpol, Theda. *Protecting Soldiers and Mothers: The Political Origins of Social Policy in the United States*. Cambridge, MA: Harvard University Press, 1992.
———. *Social Policy in the United States: Future Possibilities in Historical Perspective*. Princeton, NJ: Princeton University Press, 1995.
Skowronek, Stephen. *Building a New American State: The Expansion of National Administrative Capacities, 1877–1920*. Cambridge: Cambridge University Press, 1982.
Slavishak, Edward. *Bodies of Work: Civic Display and Labor in Industrial Pittsburgh*. Durham: Duke University Press, 2008.

Smith, Barbara Ellen. *Digging Our Own Graves: Coal Miners and the Struggle over Black Lung Disease*. Philadelphia: Temple University Press, 1987.
Smith, Rogers. *Civic Ideals: Conflicting Visions of Citizenship in U.S. History*. New Haven, CT: Yale University Press, 1997.
Snyder, Sharon L., and David T. Mitchell. *Cultural Locations of Disability*. Chicago: University of Chicago Press, 2006.
Stanley, Amy Dru. *From Bondage to Contract: Wage Labor, Marriage, and the Market in the Age of Slave Emancipation*. Cambridge: Cambridge University Press, 1998.
Stern, Alexandra Minna. *Eugenic Nation: Faults and Frontiers of Better Breeding in Modern America*. Berkeley: University of California Press, 2005.
Stewart, William Rhinelander. *The Philanthropic Work of Josephine Shaw Lowell*. New York: Macmillan, 1911. Reprint, Montclair, NJ: Patterson Smith, 1974.
Stone, Deborah A. *The Disabled State*. Philadelphia: Temple University Press, 1984.
Stromquist, Shelton. *Solidarity and Survival: An Oral History of Iowa Labor in the Twentieth Century*. Iowa City: University of Iowa Press, 1993.
Stuckey, Zosha. *A Rhetoric of Remnants: Idiots, Half-Wits, and Other State-Sponsored Inventions*. Albany: State University of New York Press, 2014.
Thomson, Rosemarie Garland. *Extraordinary Bodies: Figuring Physical Disability in American Culture and Literature*. New York: Columbia University Press, 1997.
Trattner, Walter I. *From Poor Law to Welfare State: A History of Social Welfare in America*. 4th ed. New York: Free Press, 1989.
Trent, James W., Jr. *Inventing the Feeble Mind: A History of Mental Retardation in the United States*. Berkeley: University of California Press, 1994.
———. *The Manliest Man: Samuel G. Howe and the Contours of Nineteenth-Century American Reform*. Amherst: University of Massachusetts Press, 2012.
Tyor, Peter L., and Leland V. Bell. *Caring for the Retarded in America: A History*. Westport, CT: Greenwood Press, 1984.
Ulrich, Laurel Thatcher. *A Midwife's Tale: The Life of Martha Ballard, Based on Her Diary, 1785–1812*. New York: Vintage Books, 1990.
Van Cleve, John Vickrey, and Barry A. Crouch. *A Place of Their Own: Creating the Deaf Community in America*. Washington, DC: Gallaudet University Press, 1989.
Watts, Steven. *The People's Tycoon: Henry Ford and the American Century*. New York: Knopf, 2005.
Waugh, Joan. *Unsentimental Reformer: The Life of Josephine Shaw Lowell*. Cambridge, MA: Harvard University Press, 1997.
Welke, Barbara Young. *Law and the Borders of Belonging in the Long Nineteenth Century United States*. Cambridge: Cambridge University Press, 2010.
———. *Recasting American Liberty: Gender, Race, Law, and the Railroad Revolution*. Cambridge: University of Cambridge Press, 2001.
White, Richard. *Railroaded: The Transcontinentals and the Making of Modern America*. New York: Norton, 2011.
Wilson, Daniel J. *Living with Polio: The Epidemic and Its Survivors*. Chicago: University of Chicago Press, 2005.

Winter, J. M. *The Great War and the British People.* Cambridge, MA: Harvard University Press, 1986.
Witt, John Fabian. *The Accidental Republic: Crippled Workingmen, Destitute Widows, and the Remaking of American Law.* Cambridge, MA: Harvard University Press, 2004.
Woeste, Victoria Saker. *Henry Ford's War on Jews and the Legal Battle against Hate Speech.* Stanford, CA: Stanford University Press, 2012.
Wolfensberger, Wolf. *The Origin and Nature of Our Institutional Models.* Syracuse, NY: Human Policy Press, 1975.
Wood, Gregory. *Retiring Men: Manhood, Labor, and Growing Old in America, 1900–1960.* Lanham, MD: University Press of America, 2012.
Wright, David. *Mental Disability in Victorian England: The Earlswood Asylum, 1847–1901.* Oxford: Oxford University Press, 2001.
Zunz, Olivier. *The Changing Face of Inequality: Urbanization, Industrial Development, and Immigration in Detroit, 1880–1920.* Chicago: University of Chicago Press, 1982.

ARTICLES AND BOOK CHAPTERS

Ameri, Mason, Lisa Schur, Meera Adya, Scott Bentley, Patrick McKay, and Douglas Kruse. "The Disability Employment Puzzle: A Field Experiment on Employer Hiring Behavior." NBER Working Paper no. 21560 (September 2015).
Asch, Adrienne, and Michelle Fine. "Introduction: Beyond Pedestals." In *Women with Disabilities: Essays in Psychology, Culture, and Politics*, edited by Michelle Fine and Adrienne Asch, 12–26. Philadelphia: Temple University Press, 1988.
Asher, Robert. "Failure and Fulfillment: Agitation for Employers' Liability Legislation and the Origins of Workmen's Compensation in New York State, 1876–1910." *Labor History* 24, no. 2 (1983): 198–222.
———. "The Limits of Big Business Paternalism: Relief for Injured Workers in the Years before Workmen's Compensation." In *Dying for Work: Workers' Safety and Health in Twentieth-Century America*, edited by David Rosner and Gerald Markowitz, 19–33. Bloomington: Indiana University Press, 1987.
Bale, Anthony. "America's First Compensation Crisis: Conflict over the Value and Meaning of Workplace Injuries under the Employers' Liability System." In *Dying for Work: Workers' Safety and Health in Twentieth-Century America*, edited by David Rosner and Gerald Markowitz, 34–52. Bloomington: Indiana University Press, 1987.
Baron, Ava. "Gender and Labor History: Learning from the Past, Looking to the Future." In *Work Engendered: Toward a New History of American Labor*, edited by Ava Baron. Ithaca, NY: Cornell University Press, 1991.
Baron, Ava and Eileen Boris. "The Body as a Category for Working-Class History." *Labor: Studies in Working-Class History of the Americas* 4, no. 2 (Summer 2007): 23–43.
Baynton, Douglas C. "Defectives in the Land: Disability and American Immigration Policy, 1882–1924." *Journal of American Ethnic History* 24 (Spring 2005): 31–44.

———. "Disability and the Justification of Inequality in American History." In *The New Disability History: American Perspectives*, edited by Paul K. Longmore and Lauri Umansky, 33–58. New York: New York University Press, 2001.

———. "'The Undesirability of Admitting Deaf Mutes': U.S. Immigration Policy and Deaf Immigrants, 1882–1924." *Sign Language Studies* 6, no. 4 (Summer 2006): 391–415.

Berkowitz, Edward. "How to Think about the Welfare State." *Labor History* 32, no. 4 (1991): 489–502.

Berkowitz, Edward and Monroe Berkowitz. "The Survival of Workers' Compensation." *Social Service Review* 58, no. 2 (June 1984): 259–80.

Boster, Dea H. "An 'Epeleptick' Bondswoman: Fits, Slavery, and Power in the Antebellum South." *Bulletin of the History of Medicine* 83, no. 2 (Summer 2009): 271–301.

Briggs, Laura. "The Race of Hysteria: 'Overcivilization' and the 'Savage' Woman in Late Nineteenth-Century Obstetrics and Gynecology." *American Quarterly* 52, no. 2 (June 2000): 246–73.

Brockley, Janice A. "Martyred Mothers and Merciful Fathers: Exploring Disability and Motherhood in the Lives of Jerome Greenfield and Raymond Repouille." In *The New Disability History: American Perspectives*, edited by Paul K. Longmore and Lauri Umansky, 293–312. New York: New York University Press, 2001.

Byrom, Brad. "A Pupil and a Patient: Hospital-Schools in Progressive America." In *The New Disability History: American Perspectives*, edited by Paul K. Longmore and Lauri Umansky, 133–56. New York: New York University Press, 2001.

Davis, Lennard. Introduction to *The Disability Studies Reader*, edited by Lennard Davis, 1–8. New York: Routledge, 1997.

Davis, Michael. "Forced to Tramp: The Perspective of the Labor Press, 1870–1900." In *Walking to Work: Tramps in America, 1790–1935*, edited by Eric H. Monkkonen, 141–70. Lincoln: University of Nebraska Press, 1984.

Derickson, Alan. "Industrial Refugees: The Migration of Silicotics from the Mines of North America and South Africa in the Early Twentieth Century." *Labor History* 29, no. 1 (1988): 66–89.

Douglas, Paul H. "Dr. I. M. Rubinow's Contribution to Social Security." *Forum Report* 1, no. 1 (Fall 1970): 8–16.

Fishback, Price V., and Shawn Everett Kantor. "The Durable Experiment: State Insurance of Workers' Compensation Risk in the Early Twentieth Century." *Journal of Economic History* 56, no. 4 (1996): 809–36.

Forestell, Nancy M. "'And I Feel Like I'm Dying from Mining for Gold': Disability, Gender, and the Mining Community, 1920–1950." *Labor: Studies in Working-Class History of the Americas* 3, no. 3 (Fall 2006): 77–93.

Gabbard, Dwight Christopher. "Disability Studies and the British Long Eighteenth Century." *Literature Compass* 8, no. 2 (2011): 85–86.

Gabin, Nancy. "Time Out of Mind: The UAW's Response to Female Labor Laws and Mandatory Overtime in the 1960s." In *Work Engendered: Toward a New History of American Labor*, edited by Ava Baron. Ithaca, NY: Cornell University Press, 1991.

Gelber, Scott. "A 'Hard-Boiled Order': The Reeducation of Disabled WWI Veterans in New York City." *Journal of Social History* 39, no. 1 (Fall 2005): 161–80.

Gerber, David A. "Introduction: Finding Disabled Veterans in History." In *Disabled Veterans in History*, edited by David A. Gerber, 1–54. Ann Arbor: University of Michigan Press, 2001.

Gill, Michael. "The Myth of Transition: Contractualizing Disability in the Sheltered Workshop." *Disability and Society* 20, no. 2 (2005): 613–23.

Goodheart, Lawrence B. "Rethinking Mental Retardation: Education and Eugenics in Connecticut, 1818–1917." *Journal of the History of Medicine and Allied Sciences* 59, no. 1 (January 2004): 90–111.

Grob, Gerald N. "Mental Retardation and Public Policy in America: A Research Agenda." *History of Education Quarterly* 26 (1986): 307–13.

Groneman, Carol. " 'She Earns as a Child; She Pays as a Man': Women Workers in a Mid-Nineteenth Century New York City Community." In *Class, Sex, and the Woman Worker*, edited by Milton Cantor and Bruce Laurie, 83–100. Westport, CT: Greenwood Press, 1977.

Hacker, Jacob S. "Bringing the Welfare State Back In: The Promise (and Perils) of the New Social Welfare History." *Journal of Policy History* 17, no. 1 (2005): 125–54.

Heifetz, Ruth. "Women, Lead, and Reproductive Hazards: Defining a New Risk." In *Dying for Work: Workers' Safety and Health in Twentieth-Century America*, edited by David Rosner and Gerald Markowitz, 160–74. Bloomington: Indiana University Press, 1987.

Hickel, K. Walter. "Medicine, Bureaucracy, and Social Welfare: The Politics of Disability Compensation for American Veterans of World War I." In *The New Disability History: American Perspectives*, edited by Paul K. Longmore and Lauri Umansky, 237–67. New York: New York University Press, 2001.

Holdren, Nate. "Incentivizing Safety and Discrimination: Employment Risks under Workmen's Compensation in the Early Twentieth Century United States." *Enterprise and Society* 15, no. 1 (March 2014): 31–67.

Jennings, Audra. " 'The Greatest Numbers . . . Will Be Wage Earners': Organized Labor and Disability Activism, 1945–1953." *Labor: Studies in Working-Class History of the Americas* 4, no. 4 (Winter 2007): 55–82.

Kleinberg, S. J. "Seeking the Meaning of Life: The Pittsburgh Survey and the Family." In *Pittsburgh Surveyed: Social Science and Social Reform in the Early Twentieth Century*, edited by Maurine W. Greenwald and Margo Anderson, 88–105. Pittsburgh: University of Pittsburgh Press, 1996.

Kudlick, Catherine J. "Disability History: Why We Need Another 'Other.' " *American Historical Review* 108, no. 3 (2003): 763–93.

———. "The Outlook of *The Problem* and the Problem with the *Outlook*: Two Advocacy Journals Reinvent Blind People in Turn-of-the-Century America." In *The New Disability History: American Perspectives*, edited by Paul K. Longmore and Lauri Umansky, 187–213. New York: New York University Press, 2001.

Lawrie, Paul R. D. " 'Salvaging the Negro': Race, Rehabilitation, and the Body Politic in World War I America, 1917–1924." In *Disability Histories*, edited by Susan Burch and Michael Rembis, 321–44. Urbana: University of Illinois Press, 2014.

Linker, Beth. "On the Borderland of Medical and Disability History: A Survey of the Fields." *Bulletin of the History of Medicine* 87, no. 4 (Winter 2013): 499–535.

Longmore, Paul K. "Why I Burned My Book." In *Why I Burned My Book and Other Essays on Disability*, 230–259. Philadelphia: Temple University Press, 2003.

Longmore, Paul K., and David Goldberger. "The League of the Physically Handicapped and the Great Depression: A Case Study in the New Disability History." *Journal of American History* 87, no. 3 (December 2000): 888–922.

Longmore, Paul K., and Lauri Umansky. "Introduction: Disability History; From the Margins to the Mainstream." In *The New Disability History: American Perspectives*, edited by Paul K. Longmore and Lauri Umansky, 1–32. New York: New York University Press, 2001.

Lubove, Roy. "Economic Security and Social Conflict in America: The Early Twentieth Century, Part II." *Journal of Social History* 1, no. 4 (Summer 1968): 325–50.

Markel, Howard. " 'The Eyes Have It': Trachoma, the Perception of Disease, the United States Public Health Service, and the American Jewish Immigration Experience, 1897–1924." *Bulletin of the History of Medicine* 74, no. 3 (Fall 2000): 525–60.

Markowitz, Gerald, and David Rosner. "Death and Disease in the Fall of the House of Labor." *Labor History* 30, no. 1 (1989): 113–17.

Marshall, T. H. "Citizenship and Social Class." In *Class, Citizenship, and Social Development: Essays by T. H. Marshall*, 65–122. New York: Doubleday, 1964.

McDaid, Jennifer Davis. "How a One-Legged Rebel Lives: Confederate Veterans and Artificial Limbs in Virginia." In *Artificial Parts, Practical Lives: Modern Histories of Prosthetics*, edited by Katherine Ott, David Serlin, and Stephen Mihm, 119–43. New York: New York University Press, 2002.

McGovern, Charles. "Consumption and Citizenship in the United States, 1900–1940." In *Getting and Spending: European and American Consumer Societies in the Twentieth Century*, edited by Susan Strasser, Charles McGovern, and Matthias Judt, 37–58. Cambridge: Cambridge University Press, 1998.

Michel, Sonya. "The Family, Civil Society, and Social Policy: A U.S. Perspective." In *The Golden Chain: Family, Civil Society and the State*, edited by Paul Ginsborg, Juergen Nautz, and Ton Nijhuis. Oxford: Berghahn Books, 2013.

Mihm, Stephen. " 'A Limb Which Shall Be Presentable in Polite Society": Prosthetic Technologies in the Nineteenth Century." In *Artificial Parts, Practical Lives: Modern Histories of Prosthetics*, edited by Katherine Ott, David Serlin, and Stephen Mihm, 282–99. New York: New York University Press, 2002.

Mink, Gwendolyn. "The Lady and the Tramp: Gender, Race, and the Origins of the American Welfare State." In *Women, the State, and Welfare*, edited by Linda Gordon, 92–122. Madison: University of Wisconsin Press, 1990.

Molina, Natalia. "Medicalizing the Mexican: Immigration, Race, and Disability in the Early-Twentieth-Century United States." *Radical History Review* 94 (Winter 2006): 22–37.

Moran, James E. "Asylum in the Community: Managing the Insane in Antebellum America." *History of Psychiatry* 9 (1998): 217–240.

Nielsen, Kim E. "Property, Disability, and the Making of the Incompetent Citizen in the United States, 1860s–1940s." In *Disability Histories*, edited by Susan Burch and Michael Rembis, 308–20. Urbana: University of Illinois Press, 2014.

Noll, Steven, and James W. Trent Jr., eds. *Mental Retardation in America: A Historical Reader* (New York: New York University Press, 2004).

Nordlund, Willie J. "The Federal Employees' Compensation Act." *Monthly Labor Review* 114, no. 9 (1991): 3–14.

Novak, William J. "The Legal Origins of the Modern American State." In *Looking Back at Law's Century*, edited by Austin Sarat, Bryant Garth, and Robert A. Kagan, 249–86. Ithaca, NY: Cornell University Press, 2002.

———. "The Legal Transformation of Citizenship in Nineteenth-Century America." In *The Democratic Experiment: New Directions in American Political History*, edited by Meg Jacobs, William J. Novak, and Julian E. Zelizer, 85–119. Princeton, NJ: Princeton University Press, 2003.

Nugent, Angela. "Fit for Work: The Introduction of Physical Examinations in Industry." *Bulletin of the History of Medicine* 57, no. 4 (Winter 1983): 578–95.

Parry-Jones, William L. "The Model of the Geel Lunatic Colony and Its Influence on the Nineteenth-Century Asylum System in Britain." In *Madhouses, Mad-Doctors, and Madmen: The Social History of Psychiatry in the Victorian Era*, edited by Andrew Scull, 201–17. Philadelphia: University of Pennsylvania Press, 2015.

Pavalko, Eliza K. "State Timing of Policy Adoption: Workmen's Compensation in the United States, 1909–1929." *American Journal of Sociology* 95, no. 3 (1989): 592–615.

Pierson, Paul. "The Study of Policy Development." *Journal of Policy History* 17, no. 1 (2005): 34–51.

Reznick, Jeffrey. "Work-Therapy and the Disabled British Soldier in Great Britain in the First World War: The Case of Shepherd's Bush Military Hospital, London." In *Disabled Veterans in History*, edited by David Gerber, 185–203. Ann Arbor: University of Michigan Press, 2001.

Richards, Penny L. "Beside Her Sat Her Idiot Child: Families and Developmental Disability in Mid-Nineteenth-Century America." In *Mental Retardation in America: A Historical Reader*, edited by Steven Noll and James W. Trent Jr., 130–64. New York: New York University Press, 2004.

Richards, Penny L., and George H. S. Singer. "'To Draw Out of the Effort of His Mind': Educating a Child with Mental Retardation in Early-Nineteenth-Century America." *Journal of Special Education* 31, no. 4 (1998): 443–66.

Rose, Sarah F. "'Crippled' Hands: Disability in Labor and Working-Class History." *Labor: Studies in Working-Class History of the Americas* 2, no. 1 (Spring 2005): 27–54.

Rosner, David, and Gerald Markowitz. "Safety and Health as a Class Issue: The Workers' Health Bureau of America during the 1920s." In *Dying for Work: Workers' Safety and Health in Twentieth-Century America*, edited by David Rosner and Gerald Markowitz, 53–64. Bloomington: Indiana University Press, 1987.

Rothman, David J. "Perfecting the Prison: United States, 1789–1865." In *The Oxford History of the Prison*, edited by Norval Morris and David J. Rothman, 111–29. Oxford: Oxford University Press, 1995.

Russell, Marta. "Backlash, Political Economy, and Structural Exclusion." In *Backlash against the ADA: Reinterpreting Disability*, edited by Linda Hamilton Krieger, 254–96. Ann Arbor: University of Michigan Press, 2003.

Schalick, Walton O. "Children, Disability, and Rehabilitation in History." *Pediatric Rehabilitation* 4, no. 2 (2001): 91–95.

Schriempf, Alexa. "(Re)fusing the Amputated Body: An Interactionist Bridge for Feminism and Disability." *Hypatia* 16, no. 4 (Fall 2001): 53–79.

Scotch, Richard K. "American Disability Policy in the Twentieth Century." In *The New Disability History: American Perspectives*, edited by Paul K. Longmore and Lauri Umansky, 375–92. New York: New York University Press, 2001.

Shklar, Judith N. "Earning." In *American Citizenship: The Quest for Inclusion*, 63–104. Cambridge, MA: Harvard University Press, 1991.

Snyder, Sharon L., and David T. Mitchell. "Out of the Ashes of Eugenics: Diagnostic Regimes in the United States and the Making of a Disability Minority." *Patterns of Prejudice* 36, no. 1 (2002): 79–103.

Wexler, Alice. "Chorea and Community in a Nineteenth-Century Town." *Bulletin of the History of Medicine* 76, no. 3 (Fall 2002): 495–527.

Wickham, Parnel. "Conceptions of Idiocy in Colonial Massachusetts." *Journal of Social History* 35, no. 4 (Summer 2002): 935–54.

———. "Idiocy and the Law in Colonial New England." *Mental Retardation* 39, no. 2 (April 2001): 104–13.

———. "Idiocy in Virginia, 1616–1860." *Bulletin of the History of Medicine* 80, no. 4 (Winter 2006): 677–701.

———. "Perspective: Images of Idiocy in Puritan New England." *Mental Retardation* 39, no. 2 (April 2001): 147–51.

Williams-Searle, John. "Cold Charity: Manhood, Brotherhood, and the Transformation of Disability, 1870–1900." In *The New Disability History: American Perspectives*, edited by Paul K. Longmore and Lauri Umansky, 157–86. New York: New York University Press, 2001.

Zelizer, Julian E. "Introduction: New Directions in Policy History." *Journal of Policy History* 17, no. 1 (2005): 1–11.

UNPUBLISHED THESES, DISSERTATIONS, AND CONFERENCE PAPERS

Asher, Robert. "Workmen's Compensation in the United States, 1880–1935." PhD diss., University of Minnesota, 1971.

Blackie, Daniel. "Disabled Revolutionary War Veterans and the Construction of Disability in the Early United States, c1776–1840." PhD diss., University of Helsinki, 2010.
Bloom, Alan. "The Floating Population: Homelessness in Early Chicago, 1833–1871." PhD diss., Duke University, 2001.
Brune, Jeffrey A. "Fear of Malingering in the Era of Disability Rights." Paper presented at the Society for Disability Studies Conference, Atlanta, GA, June 2015.
———. "The Gilded Age State and America's Anti-malingering Backlash." Paper presented at the Society for Disability Studies Conference, Denver, CO, June 2012.
Byrom, Bradley. "A Vision of Self Support: Disability and the Rehabilitation Movement in Progressive America." PhD diss., University of Iowa, 2004.
Dorn, Jonathan Andrew. "'Our Best Gospel Appliances': Institutional Churches and the Emergence of Social Christianity in the South End of Boston, 1880–1920." PhD diss., Harvard University, 1994.
Graney, Bernard John. "Hervey Backus Wilbur and the Evolution of Policies and Practices toward Mentally Retarded People." PhD diss., Syracuse University, 1979.
Gutman, Herbert George. "Social and Economic Structure and Depression: American Labor in 1873 and 1874." PhD diss., University of Wisconsin, 1959.
Hartley, Benjamin L. "Holiness Evangelical Urban Mission and Identity in Boston, 1860–1910." ThD diss., Boston University School of Theology, 2005.
Hickel, Karl Walter. "Entitling Citizens: World War I, Progressivism, and the Origins of the American Welfare State, 1917–1928." PhD diss., Columbia University, 1999.
Holdren, Nate. "Disability, Passion, and Commodification in Early Twentieth Century American Workplace Injury Lawsuits." Paper presented at the Conference of the American Society for Legal History, Philadelphia, PA, November 2010.
———. "Screening for 'Impaired Risks': Risk, Medical Examinations, and Hiring at the Pullman Company in the Early Twentieth-Century United States.'" Paper presented at the Annual Meeting of the Business History Conference, St. Louis, MO, April 2011.
Irving, Kathryn. "To Be 'Useful and Happy': Paternalism, Politics, Experts, and the MA School for Idiotic Children, 1848–1883." Paper presented at the Society for Disability Studies Conference, Denver, CO, June 2012.
Kogan, Nathaniel Smith. "'Every Good Man Is a Quaker, and that None but Good Men Are Quakers': Transatlantic Quaker Humanitarianism, Disability, and Marketing Enlightened Reform, 1730–1834." PhD diss. University of Texas at Arlington, 2015.
Kreader, J. Lee. "America's Prophet for Social Security: A Biography of Isaac Max Rubinow." 3 vols. PhD diss., University of Chicago, 1988.
Lewis, Halle Gayle. "'Cripples Are Not the Dependents One Is Led to Think': Work and Disability in Industrializing Cleveland, 1861–1916." PhD diss., Binghamton University, 2004.
Marks, Rachel Bryant. "The Problem of Second Injuries: History and Analysis of Second-Injury Provisions of Workmen's Compensation Laws in the United States." PhD diss., University of Chicago, 1950.

Mohun, Arwen. "Mitigating the Violence of the Machine: Accidents, Bodies, and the Creation of a Risk Society." Paper presented at the Annual Meeting of the Organization of American Historians, Memphis, TN, April 2003.

Rose, Sarah F. "Gendering U.S. Disability Policy, 1895–1930." Paper presented at the Policy History Conference, Columbus, OH, June 2010.

———. "Teaching Blind People to Walk by Taking Away Their Canes: The Influence of World War II on Conceptions of Disability in the United States." MA thesis, University of Chicago, 2001.

Williams-Searle, John Edward P. "Broken Brothers and Soldiers of Capital: Disability, Manliness, and Safety on the Rails, 1863–1908." PhD diss., University of Iowa, 2004.

INTERNET SOURCES

Aldrich, Mark. Review of *The Accidental Republic: Crippled Workingmen, Destitute Widows, and the Remaking of American Law*, by John Fabian Witt. EH.Net, June 2004. http://eh.net/bookreviews/library/0794 (accessed 22 June 2008).

Auraria Library. "Inventory of the Edgar M. Wahlberg Papers, 1920–1990." Auraria Library, Denver, CO. http://carbon.cudenver.edu/public/library/archives/wahlberg/wahlberg.html (accessed 30 June 2008).

DePillas, Lydia. "Disabled People Are Allowed to Work for Pennies Per Hour—But Maybe Not for Much Longer." *Washington Post*, 12 February 2016, https://www.washingtonpost.com/news/wonk/wp/2016/02/12/disabled-people-are-allowed-to-work-for-pennies-per-hour-but-maybe-not-for-much-longer/ (accessed 28 August 2016).

Diament, Michelle. "Obama Signs Law Limiting Sheltered Workshop Eligibility." disabilityscoop, 22 July 2014, https://www.disabilityscoop.com/2014/07/22/obama-law-limiting-sheltered/19538/ (accessed 28 August 2016).

Erickson, W., C. Lee, and S. von Schrader. "Disability Statistics from the 2012 American Community Survey (ACS)." Ithaca, NY: Cornell University Employment and Disability Institute, 2014. www.disabilitystatistics.org (accessed 18 July 2014).

Find A Grave. "Robert Thomson Steele (1836–1883)." http://www.findagrave.com/cgi-bin/fg.cgi?page=gr&GSln=STEE&GSpartial=1&GSbyrel=all&GSst=36&GScntry=4&GSsr=1641&GRid=70402778& (accessed 11 July 2014).

Jernigan, Kenneth. "Lighthouse for the Blind Closes Sheltered Shop and Feels That It Got a Bum Rap." National Federation of the Blind. http://www.nfb.org/Images/nfb/Publications/bm/bm97/bm970301.htm (accessed 19 March 2007).

McNeil, John M. "Employment, Earnings, and Disability (1991/92, 1993/94, 1994/95, and 1997 data from the Survey of Income and Program Participation)." Prepared for the 75th Annual Conference of the Western Economic Association International, June 29–July 3, 2000. U.S. Census Bureau. http://www.census.gov/hhes/www/disability/emperndis.pdf (accessed 6 July 2008).

"Six Ways to Compute the Relative Value of a U.S. Dollar Amount, 1790–2006." http://www.MeasuringWorth.com/uscompare/ (accessed 16 February 2008).

Taylor, Steven J. "Disabled Workers Deserve Real Choices, Real Jobs." Center for an Accessible Society, 2002. http://www.accessiblesociety.org/topics/economics-employment/shelteredwksps.html (accessed 19 March 2007).

"Upas, n." OED Online. June 2014. Oxford University Press. http://www.oed.com/view/Entry/219818?redirectedFrom=upas (accessed 8 July 2014).

U.S. Bureau of Labor Statistics. "Economics News Release: Persons with a Disability: Labor Force Characteristics Summary." http://www.bls.gov/news.release/disabl.nro.htm (accessed 16 June 2015).

Index

Aaron, John, 190–91
Able-bodied: in asylums, 77, 93; definition of, 2, 40, 48; Goodwill Industries' preference for, 172–73, 176, 181, 183–84, 186–87, 322n80, 322n84; injuries to, 143; in poorhouses, 6, 53–54, 69–70, 236n19, 259n19; versus disabled workers on labor market, 111, 124, 127, 129, 131, 136, 138, 163. *See also* Disability; Discrimination against disabled workers
Abrams, Moishe, 61
ADA. *See* Americans with Disabilities Act of 1990
ADA Amendments Act of 2008, 227
Addams, Jane, 152
Administrative state, 144, 148–49, 158
Adolfson, George, 207–8
African Americans: at asylums, 103, 274n38, 315n8; disability and proslavery rhetoric, 7, 16; disabled slaves, 5, 42; disabled veterans and rehabilitation, 191, 194, 197, 199, 204, 217–19, 332n82, 337n163; disabled workers, 120; at Ford Motor Company, 131, 280n19; at Goodwill Industries, 319n50. *See also* Race: racism and occupational safety
Aged. *See* Elderly workers
Agricultural labor. *See* Farm labor
Alden, Frances, 28
Almshouse. *See* Poorhouse
American Association for Labor Legislation, 142–43, 305n126, 306n128, 307n137; work accidents and employers' liability, 139, 144, 146–48, 151, 297n45; workmen's compensation, 152, 156, 158, 160–61, 166, 171, 300n74, 301n79, 302n98, 306nn129–30. *See also* *American Labor Legislation Review*; John Andrews
American Association for the Study of the Feeble-Minded. *See* Association of Medical Officers of American Institutions for Idiotic and Feeble-Minded Persons
American Guarantee Company, 207
American Labor Legislation Review, 148, 156, 160, 296n31. *See also* American Association for Labor Legislation; John Andrews
American Legion, 196, 207, 210, 330n74, 336n156
Americans with Disabilities Act of 1990 (ADA), 5, 226–28, 338n6
Amputees: employers' discrimination against, 7, 111, 123–24, 159, 166; at Ford Motor Company, 128–29; historical "normality" of, 11, 112–13, 115, 122, 295n19; as workers, 3, 116, 118, 120–21, 124–25, 130, 184, 186, 207, 215–17; workmen's compensation, 9, 145, 149, 157, 163; World War I veterans, 195, 199, 201–4, 215–16, 331n76. *See also* Chronic pain; One-eyed workers; Lacy Simms
Andrews, John, 143, 147, 161
Artisanal labor, 48, 57, 60, 172–73, 189, 198, 223, 225
Association of Medical Officers of American Institutions for Idiotic and Feeble-Minded Persons, 32, 50, 95, 104–5, 241n22, 249n92
Asylums: academic training, 1, 10, 14–15, 28–29, 77, 88–90, 95–96; admission

Asylums: academic training (cont.)
  policies, 24–27, 52–57, 63, 74, 266n101;
  asylum-building movement, 14, 18–19;
  community within, 86, 103; custodial
  care, shift to, 51–53, 65–90; discharge
  practices, 36–48, 63–69, 75–86, 91,
  96–110; families, interactions with, 15,
  36, 40–48, 50, 57–66; funding schemes,
  31, 34–36, 73–78, 94–95, 97–98, 105–107;
  labor programs, 1, 10–11, 27–34, 61,
  73–76, 77–80, 82, 84–86, 92–94; living
  conditions, 49, 74, 82–87, 97; moral
  treatment, 18–20, 53, 240n21; rural
  focus, 15, 23, 33, 36, 42, 51, 57, 60–61, 65.
  See also Charles Bernstein; Care work;
  Eugenics; Samuel Gridley Howe; Idiot
  asylums; Illinois Institution for the
  Education of Feeble-Minded Children;
  Institute for Idiots (Barre, Massachusetts); George Knight; Massachusetts
  School for Idiotic and Feeble-Minded
  Youth; New York State Custodial
  Asylum for Feeble-Minded Women;
  New York State Asylum for Idiots;
  James B. Richards; Rome State
  Custodial Asylum; Edouard Séguin;
  Unpaid labor at asylums; Charles
  Toppan Wilbur; Hervey Backus
  Wilbur
Automatic Electric, and hiring of deaf
  workers, 120, 283n52. *See also* Deaf

Backus, Frederick F., 22. *See also* New
  York State Asylum for Idiots:
  founding
Bagshaw, Ellen, 64, 262n52
Barnes, James, 40, 43, 254n153
Barr, Martin W., 50, 243n35
Barre, Massachusetts. *See* Institute for
  Idiots (Barre, Massachusetts)
Baxter, Hannah, 40, 44
Becker, Johann, 61, 64
Becker, Wilfred, 61, 64

Bernstein, Charles: as asylum superintendent, 78, 82, 84–85, 88, 93–98, 269n130, 270n142; childhood, 93, 272n4; colony and parole program, 11, 91–92, 99–110, 274nn34–35, 275n46; disability experience and, 93; eugenics and, 97–98, 103, 105, 109, 249n100, 269n130, 273n20; feeble-minded, evolving views of, 92–93, 95–96, 276n67; influence, national, 11, 90, 103–7; labor market analysis, 106, 109–11, 225, 227–28, 275n45; political skills, 94–95, 97–98, 101, 105, 111, 231. *See also* Eugenics; Parole program; Rome State Custodial Asylum
Blind: Blind Workers Union, 188;
  deserving poor, as part of, 5–6, 8, 140;
  disabled veterans, 194, 200, 203–4,
  331n76; employment discrimination,
  118–21, 137, 181, 249n100, 280n25,
  284n70; Enlightenment and, 23;
  family care and, 5, 40, 44; idiocy and,
  27, 74, 88, 231; placement on job
  market, 118–20, 249n29, 281n45,
  282n49; in poorhouses, 54, 63;
  rehabilitative and educational
  campaigns, 18–22, 28, 30, 32, 34, 62,
  118–20, 188, 242n29, 258n11; as workers
  at Ford Motor Company, 127–28,
  130–31, 135, 286n88, 288n101, 289n106;
  as workers generally, 3, 11, 42, 78, 111,
  122, 127, 184, 223, 249n100, 281n45;
  workshops for, 188, 314n4, 323n92. *See
  also* African Americans: disabled
  slaves; One-eyed workers; Perkins
  Institution for the Blind
Brain injuries. *See* Head injuries
Bridgman, Laura, 20
Bucher, Nathaniel, 38
Buckner, Charles, 29, 247n74
Bureau of War Risk Insurance (BWRI).
  See War Risk Insurance
Butters, Mary, 54, 259n21

Cage, Jason, 43
Cahn, Amanda, 103
Calhoun, Fred, 55, 259n22
California Home for the Care and Training of the Feeble-Minded, 23, 32
Calvert, Joseph, 38
Cameron, Thomas, 17, 240n16
Campbell, Melissa, 43
Care work, 1–2, 10–11, 42–44, 48, 51, 74–75, 78, 80–82, 89. *See also* Gender: discharge from asylums; Gender: feeble-minded women; Rehabilitation; Unpaid labor at asylums
Carlisle, Jane, 39
Carry On, 199–200, 202, 217
Carson, James C., approach to inmate labor, 77–78; discharge practices as superintendent, 1, 64, 81–82, 246n71, 247n75, 259n212, 260nn26–27, 267n114, 268n127, 271nn157–58; hereditarian views, 80, 229; paying pupils and, 250n107
Cathocalles, George, 206, 208
Charities and the Commons. See *Survey*
Charity organization societies, 63, 141, 143. *See also* Charles S. Hoyt; Josephine Shaw Lowell; Poorhouse: reform campaigns; Scientific charity movement
Chronic pain: workers, 3, 181, 186, 280n24; World War I veterans, 13, 190–91, 202, 204, 206, 212, 215–16, 221–22
Citizenship: disabled veterans and, 190–92, 195, 201–2; idiots and, 23, 241n25; poverty and, 154; work and, 2–4, 9–10, 12–13, 23, 134, 141, 173, 223, 225, 228; "unproductive citizens," 13, 112, 122, 233n3
Civil War. *See* Pensions
Cleveland Cripples Survey. *See* Survey of Cleveland Cripples
Cobb, O. H., 60, 80, 250n107, 268n120, 269n128, 271n158

Cobb, Orson, 46
Cogswell, Emily, 39
Cogswell, Melina, 39, 40
Collins, Christopher, 28, 246n68
Colony and parole program. *See* Charles Bernstein; Parole program; Rome State Custodial Asylum
Commons, John R., 143, 307n137
Company physicians. *See* Industrial surgeons
Connor, Matilda, 103, 275n53
Consumers' League of Eastern Pennsylvania, 1–2, 115–16, 120, 167, 231–32, 280nn23–24
Coolidge, Samuel, 5–6, 235n13
Cowell, Simon, 253n143
Cripple: concept, 3, 5, 8; disabled veterans as, 193–94, 196–97, 202–3, 209; employment discrimination, 123–26, 137, 226; at Ford Motor Company, 128, 132, 134, 168; at Goodwill Industries, 172, 186; industrial accidents and, 146, 156, 159–60; as workers, 1, 94, 111, 115, 118–19, 121, 125, 269n132. *See also* Asylums, admission policies; Physical examinations; Second-injury problem
Custodial Herald. See *Rome Custodial Herald*
Cuyper, Julia, 91–92

Dassler, Irma, 58, 260n27
Deaf: deserving poor, as part of, 5, 8; disabled veterans, 199; employment discrimination, 126–27, 187, 285n79, 308n143; Enlightenment and, 23; idiocy and, 14, 25, 27, 29, 231, 245n60, 252n132, 277n73; in poorhouses, 54; rehabilitative and educational campaigns, 18–20, 23, 28, 30, 34, 53, 62, 243n35, 252n132, 258n11; as workers at Ford Motor Company, 128, 130, 134, 287n91; as workers generally, 38–39,

Deaf: deserving poor, as part of (cont.) 86, 108, 120, 127, 184, 186, 283n52; workshops for, 181. *See also* Hard-of-hearing

Defective: disabled veterans, in reference to, 204; disabled workers, in reference to, 129, 156, 163–64, 214, 307n139; feeble-minded, as part of, 74, 102, 106, 108, 277n73. *See also* African Americans: disability and proslavery rhetoric; Physical examinations; Second-injury problem

Delano, Seth, 5

Dependency, 2–4, 9, 11–13, 20, 222–26; charity reformers' fears about, 50–57, 67–73, 88–90; disabled veterans and, 192–94, 197–98, 201; Goodwill Industries, 172, 177, 189; industrial accidents and, 136–41, 146–51, 153; workmen's compensation and, 160, 162–63, 171. *See also* Josephine Shaw Lowell; Scientific charity movement

Devine, Edward T., 141, 143, 145–47, 197–98

Disability, 3, 8, 13, 156, 161, 222–24; antebellum notions of, 5–7; Enlightenment and, 23

Disabled slaves, 5, 7, 16, 42

Disabled veterans: dependency and, 192–94, 197–98, 201; gender and, 191–92, 194, 205, 326n22, 329n60, 331n76; Revolutionary War, 5–6, 42; workmen's compensation and, 167; World War I, 12–13, 131–32, 186, 189–222, 225. *See also* Federal Board for Vocational Education; Charles T. Forbes; Douglas C. McMurtrie; Pensions: Civil War; Rehabilitation; Veterans' Bureau

Discrimination against disabled workers: amputees, 7, 111, 123–24, 159, 166; blind, 118–21, 137, 181, 249n100, 280n25, 284n70; competition with able-bodied workers, 111, 124, 127, 129, 131, 136, 138, 163; cripples, 123–26, 137, 226; deaf, 126–27, 187, 285n79, 308n143; elderly workers, 159, 162–63, 166, 309n151, 311n166, 314n1, 322n81; at Goodwill Industries, 183–84, 186–87, 322n80; insurance companies and, 123, 161–62, 164, 166–67, 208, 309nn151–52, 311n171; one-eyed workers, 2, 137, 164, 166, 311n170; unions and, 112, 122–24, 126; worn-out workers, 1, 5, 113, 117, 126, 132, 137, 146. *See also* Gender: employers' concepts of workers' fitness; Physical examinations; Second-injury problem

Dismemberment schedules and workmen's compensation, 149, 157–59, 163, 167, 170, 203, 299n68, 300n69, 306n129, 313n186

Dix, Dorothea, 17–19, 68. *See also* Poorhouse, Psychosocial impairments

Domestic labor, 3, 11, 114; at asylums, 27, 30, 33, 39, 74, 252n132; in Bernstein's colony and parole program, 15, 90–92, 99–102, 109, 111, 225, 228; workmen's compensation and, 151. *See also* Asylums: labor programs; Care work; Gender: feeble-minded women; Unpaid labor at asylums

Downs, Jack, 17

Down's Syndrome, 16, 27, 267n118. *See also* Idiocy: causes; Idiocy: definitions

Eastman, Crystal, 139, 153; poverty and disability, views of, 116, 139–42, 145, 159, 171; research on industrial accidents and the employers' liability system, 113, 116, 119, 139–46; workmen's compensation, 146, 148, 151

Efficiency movement and disabled workers, 102, 119, 122–26. *See also* Henry Ford: understanding of mechanization; Physical examinations

Elderly workers: employment discrimination, 159, 162–63, 166, 309n151, 311n166, 314n1, 322n81; at Goodwill Industries, 173, 181, 183–86, 188, 318n45; parents and institutionalization, 43, 57; in poorhouses and asylums, 53–54, 74, 84; as workers, 40, 57, 120, 129, 282n48. *See also* Goodwill Industries; Physical examinations

Elizabethan poor law. *See* Poor law: English roots

Employers' liability: critiques of, 139, 144–49, 151, 152; legal doctrines, 144–45, 297n37. *See also* Crystal Eastman

Enlightenment and disability, 23

Epilepsy: admissions to idiot asylums and, 25, 71, 74, 78, 88, 231, 234n54, 262n52, 265n90, 269n135; definition of idiocy and, 14; disabled slaves with, 7, 42; employers and, 126, 314n4; Ford Motor Company and, 111, 128, 130, 134, 312n177

Eugenics: disabled veterans and, 204; hereditarianism and proto-eugenics, 20, 50, 59, 69–75, 80, 105, 242n29, 257n4, 263n68, 264n83; sterilization, 109, 269n130. *See also* Charles Bernstein; Samuel Gridley Howe; Charles Toppan Wilbur; Hervey Backus Wilbur

Fahey, Alice, 39

Fair Labor Standards Act of 1938, 226, 338n3. *See also* Sheltered workshops

Family capacity: Bernstein's colony program and, 91, 99, 108, 110, 225; industrial accidents, adjustment to, 121; institutionalization and, 9, 13–15, 35–39, 41, 43–44, 48–50, 57–65, 67, 80, 89–91, 254n157. *See also* Charles Bernstein: colony and parole program; Parole program

Family economies. *See* Family capacity; Household economies; Spectrum of productivity

Farm labor: disabled veterans, 199, 205, 219; discharged inmates and, 35, 40, 42, 46–47, 81; economy and, 10, 15, 223, 225, 227; families and, 28, 47–48; idiot asylums and, 11, 15, 33, 52–53, 57, 60–61, 64–65, 78. *See also* Asylums: labor programs; Charles Bernstein: colony and parole program; Family capacity; Household economies; Spectrum of productivity; Wage labor economy

Farmer, Janette, 82

FBVE Bulletin, 195, 198

Federal Board for Vocational Education (FBVE), 232; administrative dysfunction, 195–97, 203, 209–11, 221; approach to rehabilitation, 198–99, 201, 213–14, 220; attitude towards veterans, 204, 219; impact on veterans, 206–8. *See also* African Americans; disabled veterans; rehabilitation; Veterans' Bureau

Feeble-minded. *See* Charles Bernstein; James C. Carson; O. H. Cobb; Eugenics; Gender: Feeble-minded women; Idiocy; Josephine Shaw Lowell; New York State Asylum for Idiots; New York State Custodial Asylum for Feeble-Minded Women; Parole program; Rome State Custodial Asylum; Charles Toppan Wilbur; Hervey Backus Wilbur

Fernald, Walter E., 98, 106. *See also* Eugenics

Fitch, John A., 113, 117, 126, 231–32. *See also* Pittsburgh Survey

Fitzgerald, John, 84, 93, 95

Five Dollar Day, 128, 132, 169, 286n89, 287n92

Flaherty, Terrence, 88, 271n157

Forbes, Charles T., 192, 196–97, 218, 328n42

374 Index

Forbes, Donald, 211–12
Ford, Henry: charity and, 131–33; people with disabilities and, 121, 127, 130, 132–34, 134–35; sheltered workshops and, 132, 134; understanding of mechanization, 11–12, 42, 111, 127, 130, 135
Ford Motor Company: disabled workers, placement of, 12, 118–19, 127–33, 134–35, 288n98, 308n143; Employment Department, 131, 133, 287n90, 287n95; Legal Department, 134, 168–69, 292n126, 312n179; Medical Department, 128–29, 131–34; physical examinations, use of, 128; publicity about hiring disabled workers, 135, 286n89; Sociological Department, 127–28, 131, 133–34, 167, 287n90, 312n174; workmen's compensation and, 133, 167–71. *See also* Henry Ford; Samuel Marquis; Charles Sorenson
Foster, John, 27

Gaffer, Lillian, 29
Gannon, Rachel, 52, 258n12
Gender: asylum labor programs and, 33–36, 43, 73–85, 98–102; dependency and male breadwinner ideology, 3–4, 12, 72, 112, 119, 137, 139, 142, 151, 159; disability and, 7, 9–10, 12, 223–25; disabled veterans and, 191–92, 194, 205, 326n22, 329n60, 331n76; discharge from asylums, 9, 37–39, 42–44, 50–51, 67, 80–82, 251n125, 260n26, 273n17; employers' concepts of workers' fitness and, 4, 138, 148; feeble-minded women, 71–76, 89, 92, 98–102, 104–5, 225, 230, 244n46, 264n83, 266n100, 266n102; industrial accidents and, 12, 111–12, 114, 137, 139, 141, 151, 159, 294n7; poorhouses and, 6, 59; rehabilitation and, 14, 30, 37, 40, 175–77, 180, 185, 186, 188, 226, 322n81; workmen's compensation and, 12, 150–51, 194. *See also* Care work; Josephine Shaw Lowell; New York State Custodial Asylum for Feeble-Minded Women at Newark; Unpaid labor at asylums
General Electric and disabled workers, 126, 166, 207
Gilbert, William, 40, 43
Gilbreth, Frank, 131, 290n110. *See also* Efficiency movement and disabled workers
Goode, Sally, 36, 251n118
Goodnow, Henry, 24, 241n48
Goodrich, Walter, 57, 64, 65, 262n52
Goodwill Industries, 4, 12, 172–73, 189, 191, 221; advertising of aged and disabled workers, 181; disabled workers and efficiency movement at, 179, 181–87, 320n54, 323n86; evangelical roots, 174–80, 182; founding and development, 173–80; preference for able-bodied workers, 183–84, 186–87, 322n80; Prohibition and, 183–84; secularization and, 178–80, 182; sources on, 232; spread of, 180, 182–83, 319n49; John Wesley, influence of, 316n18. *See also* Edgar James Helms
Goodwill Tales, 185
Grant, Winston, 44–45, 255n162
Griffin, Arthur W., 209, 218–19
Group homes, 11, 92, 99, 102. *See also* Charles Bernstein: colony and parole program; Parole program

Halford, Maud, 80, 268n122
Halloran, Lucy, 74
Hamilton, Alice, 143
Hard-of-hearing, workers: idiocy and, 16, 25, 27, 74; physical examinations for, 124, 128, 137, 163, 214, 284n70; World War I veterans' rehabilitation, 213–14. *See also* Deaf
Harlow, Amelia, 49–50, 89

Hawk's Nest Tunnel disaster, 4, 151–52, 234n6, 301n81
Head injuries: idiocy and, 5, 14, 16, 27; industrial accidents and, 169
Heidecker, John, 205, 206, 208
Heinrich, Clara, 81–82
Helms, Edgar James: early career, 173–76; efficiency movement and, 179, 181–87; evangelism, 174–76, 178–80; influence of John Wesley, 316n18; labor market, understanding of, 177; scientific charity and, 177, 189, 315n7; settlement houses and, 174–75. *See also* Goodwill Industries; Morgan Chapel
Henry, Patrick, 6, 17
Henry, Sarah Shelton, 6, 17
Herald. See *Rome Custodial Herald*
Hereditarianism. *See* Eugenics
Hertzfeld, Frances, 88, 271n157
Hines, Frank T., 196, 205, 331n78
Household economies, 2, 10, 15, 40, 42–43, 48, 72, 75, 110, 121. *See also* Family capacity; Spectrum of productivity
Howe, Samuel Gridley: early career, 15, 19, 23; hereditarian and proto-eugenic beliefs, 20–21, 35, 40; idiot asylums, advocacy for, 14–15, 19–22, 25, 30, 32–34, 40, 48. *See also* Asylums; Eugenics; Massachusetts School for Idiotic and Feeble-Minded Youth; Perkins Institution for the Blind
Howland, Sylvester, 215–16
Hoyt, Charles S., 55, 70, 72, 264n81. *See also* Charity organization societies; Josephine Shaw Lowell; Poorhouse: reform campaigns; Scientific charity movement
Human resources departments, 128
Hutmacher, Tina, 108

Idiocy: arguments for humanity, 20–21; causes (perceived), 27, 60; definitions, 15–19; family views of, 14, 36–48; language about, 14; surveys of, 19–20, 22. *See also* Frederick Backus; Charles Bernstein; Eugenics; Samuel Gridley Howe; Idiot asylums; George Knight; James B. Richards; Edouard Séguin; Charles Toppan Wilbur; Hervey Backus Wilbur
Idiot asylums: admission policies, 24–27, 54–55, 63, 266n101; charity reform, effect of, 51–57; colony and parole programs, 91–110; custodial care, shift to, 51–53, 65–90; discharge practices, 36–48, 75–86; founding, 17–18, 21–22; funding schemes, 31, 34–36; living conditions, 49, 74, 83–84, 87, 97; rural focus, 15, 23, 33, 36, 42, 51, 57, 60–61, 65; spread, 31–33; training programs, 27–31, 33 wage labor economy, effect of, 57–65. *See also* Charles Bernstein; Care work; Eugenics; Samuel Gridley Howe; Illinois Institution for the Education of Feeble-Minded Children; Institute for Idiots (Barre, Massachusetts); George Knight; Massachusetts School for Idiotic and Feeble-Minded Youth; New York State Custodial Asylum for Feeble-Minded Women; New York State Asylum for Idiots; James B. Richards; Rome State Custodial Asylum; Edouard Séguin; Unpaid labor at asylums; Charles Toppan Wilbur; Hervey Backus Wilbur
Illinois Institution for the Education of Feeble-Minded Children, 23, 25, 32–33, 36–37, 41, 52–53, 57, 62–63, 67, 72, 76–77, 97
Imbecility. *See* Idiocy
Industrial accidents, 2, 4, 9; debates over, 137–48, 156–61; employers' views of, 162–71; prevention efforts, 148–53; workers' experiences of, 112–22. *See also* American Association for Labor

376 Index

Industrial accidents (cont.)
  Legislation; Crystal Eastman;
  Employers' liability; Gender:
  industrial accidents and; Occupa-
  tional diseases and illnesses; Physical
  examinations; Isaac Max Rubinow;
  Second-injury problem; *Survey*;
  Workmen's compensation
Industrial surgeons, 128, 137, 163, 168,
  307n139, 310n158. *See also* Harry E.
  Mock
Insane. *See* Psychosocial impairments
Institute for Idiots (Barre, Massachu-
  setts), 22, 27, 250n106
Insurance companies discriminating
  against disabled workers, 123, 161–62,
  164, 166–67, 208, 309nn151–52, 311n171.
  See also Medical departments;
  Physical examinations
International Association of Machinists
  (IAM) and industrial accidents, 142,
  144, 147, 152
Iowa Asylum for Feeble-Minded
  Children at Glenwood, 33, 35, 72, 76
Itard, Jean-Marc, 18
Iverson, Harry, 213, 220–21

Kalish, Edward M., 209–10
Kansas State Asylum for Idiotic and
  Imbecile Youth, 32, 76
Kavanaugh, Eileen, 82
Keene, Sybil, 81
Kellogg, Paul U., 143, 146
Knight, George, 248n89, 276n56

Labor. *See* Artisanal labor; Asylums:
  labor programs; Care work; Discrim-
  ination against disabled workers;
  Domestic labor; Farm labor;
  Gender; Household economies; Life
  jobs; Mechanization; Self-employ-
  ment; Sheltered workshops;
  Spectrum of productivity; Unpaid
  labor at asylums; Wage labor
  economy
Labor market, informal, 10–11, 136. *See
  also* Care work; Household econo-
  mies; Wage labor economy
Labor unions. *See* Unions
Lambeth, Mary, 59–60
Lancaster, Lisa, 81
Landon, Millie, 57, 260n26
League of the Physically Handicapped, 226
Life jobs, 116, 118, 129
Little, Irene, 41
Lowell, Josephine Shaw, 11, 69–74, 89,
  172, 244n46. *See also* Eugenics; New
  York State Custodial Asylum for
  Feeble-Minded Women; Scientific
  charity movement; State Board of
  Charities
Lunatic. *See* Psychosocial impairments;
  Shell shock

Mack, Julian W., 194, 326n19
Mad. *See* Psychosocial impairments;
  Shell shock
Malingering, 150, 158, 194, 299n67,
  307n139, 308n144
Mallard, Lillian, 74
Marquis, Samuel, 128, 133–34, 167–68,
  287n90, 290n113, 291n119
Massachusetts School for Idiotic and
  Feeble-Minded Youth, 21, 24, 32–34,
  36–37, 48, 52–54, 72, 76, 78, 97–99
Mather, Cotton, 16
McDonagh, Mary, 27, 245n59
McMann, Bettina, 100, 274n38
McMurtrie, Douglas C., 194, 196, 199,
  201–2, 217, 285n78, 325n17
McNeil, Walter, 27, 245n60
Mead, James E., 128–29, 132, 278n2
Mechanization: Henry Ford and, 11–12,
  42, 111, 127, 130, 135; industrial acci-
  dents and, 279n8, 289n108; sheltered
  workshops and, 172–73

Medicaid, 227
Medical departments, 123, 126, 163, 166, 196. *See also* Ford Motor Company: Medical Department; Physical examinations
Medical examinations. *See* Physical examinations
Methodist Episcopal Church: Goodwill Industries and, 180–82, 232, 319nn49–50; Morgan Chapel and, 173–74, 315n9. *See also* Social Gospel movement
Mexican Americans, 114–15, 274n38
Minimum-wage, sheltered workshops and, 183, 226, 338n3
Mitchell, Alexander, 24
Mock, Harry E., 164, 307n139
Moore, Fred C., 183, 186
Moral treatment. *See* Asylums
Morgan, Henry, 315n9, 315n11
Morgan Chapel, 174–78, 185, 315n9, 318n33
Morgan Memorial Goodwill Industries. *See* Edgar James Helms; Goodwill Industries; Morgan Chapel
Munson, Carrie, 29

National Association of Manufacturers (NAM), 148, 192–93
National Cash Register Company, 119
National Employ the Handicapped Week, 5
Nelson, Floyd, 29, 246n71
Neuropsychiatric disabilities. *See* Shell shock
Neuropsychiatric disorders. *See* Psychosocial impairments; Shell shock
New York State Asylum for Idiots, 1, 10, 14–15, 88–90; academic training at, 28–29, 77; admission policies, 24–27, 52–57; approach to training, 27–29; custodial care, shift to, 65–68, 77–80; discharge practices, 36–48, 63–69, 78, 80–83; founding, 22; funding schemes, 34–35, 77–78; labor programs and occupational training, 29–31, 61, 77–80; move to Syracuse, 31; shifting population, 51–65; sources for, 229–31. *See also* Asylums; Frederick Backus; James C. Carson; O. H. Cobb; Eugenics; Family capacity; Samuel Gridley Howe; Idiocy; Idiot asylums; Josephine Shaw Lowell; Spectrum of productivity; Hervey Backus Wilbur
New York State Board of Charities. *See* State Board of Charities
New York State Custodial Asylum for Feeble-Minded Women: 49, 51; admission policies, 74; discharge practices, 75–76, 80; founding, 67, 73; funding schemes, 73–77; influence, 73; inmate labor, 73–76, 84–86; living conditions, 83–86. *See also* Asylums; Eugenics; Family capacity; Idiocy; Idiot asylums; Josephine Shaw Lowell; Hervey Backus Wilbur
New York State Institution for Male Defective Delinquents (at Napanoch), 108, 277n73
Newark State Custodial Asylum. *See* New York State Custodial Asylum for Feeble-Minded Women

Obermeyer, Barny, 108, 277n73
Obermeyer, Herschel, 108, 277n73
Occupational diseases and illnesses, 4, 112, 114, 143, 151–152, 234n6; workmen's compensation and, 148, 153, 160–61, 299n67, 301n81. *See also* Gender: industrial accidents and; Race: racism and occupational safety
O'Donnell, Adaline, 59
One-eyed workers, 2, 137, 164, 166, 311n170. *See also* Amputees; Blind; Physical examinations

Oneida State Custodial Asylum for Unteachable Idiots. *See* Rome State Custodial Asylum
Otis, James, Jr., 6

Page, Albert, 28
Parkes, Henry, 48
Parole program: at Rome State Custodial Asylum, 3, 91–92, 96, 98–101, 103–9, 231, 274n34, 275n53; opposition to Rome plan, 96, 103–5; spread of Rome plan, 105–7, 184. *See also* Charles Bernstein; Eugenics; Rome State Custodial Asylum
Paterson, Fanny, 28, 45, 246n65, 255n163
Pennsylvania Training School for Idiotic and Feeble-minded Children, 30, 32–33, 35, 67, 76–77, 107
Pensions: Civil War, 141, 193–94, 204, 295n16; Revolutionary War, 5, 42, 235n10, 254n147; for work accidents, 118, 149, 300n71; World War I-era commentary, 193–94, 204
Percy, Myra, 88, 271n158
Perkins Institution for the Blind, 19, 21, 32, 242n29, 249n98, 258n11
Phossy-jaw, 114
Physical examinations: compensation and, 160, 307n139; disabled veterans and, 204, 207, 209–10, 214–15, 220, 232, 330n74; discrimination and, 1–2, 12, 111, 126, 138, 162–67, 308n144, 311nn170–71; at Ford Motor Company, 127–28, 287n93, 308n143; origins, 123–24, 284n70; protests against, 167–68, 311n165. *See also* Discrimination against disabled workers; Medical departments
Pinel, Philippe, 18, 240n21
Pittsburgh Survey, 113, 117, 138–40, 143, 146, 278n7, 294n7. *See also* Crystal Eastman; John A. Fitch
Poor law: boarding out, 46; charity organization societies; deserving versus undeserving poor, 6, 8–9, 17, 51, 67, 69–71, 133, 137, 177, 181, 225–26, 232; English roots, 8, 17, 236n19; residency requirements, 6–7. *See also* Poorhouse
Poorhouse: disabled people in, 5, 9, 17–19, 25, 259n19; families and, 44–45; finances of, 34; idiot asylum inmates from, 51–52, 54–56, 59, 63, 74, 92, 243n35; living conditions, 6, 17–19, 68, 75; reform campaigns, 11, 17–19, 30, 36, 44, 47, 53–54, 70–72, 140, 224; as sources, 229–30; transfer and reinstitutionalization of inmates, 1–2, 48–49, 56, 60, 63–65, 68, 76, 80–81, 247n74, 259n22, 260n26, 260n30, 267n114, 271n158; work requirements, 69, 75, 98, 177. *See also* Charity organization societies; Dorothea Dix; Charles S. Hoyt; Josephine Shaw Lowell; Malingering; Poor law; Scientific charity movement; State Board of Charities
Pratt, Walter, 1–3, 7–8, 13
Prosthetic limbs, 107, 121, 199, 216. *See also* Amputees; Chronic pain
Protestant work ethic, 4, 12, 23, 29, 172, 174, 225, 316n18
Psychosocial impairments, 5, 7, 16, 22, 42, 47, 57, 59, 99, 159, 219, 245n58, 266n101; conditions for asylum and poorhouse inmates labeled as insane, 17–18, 45, 75, 84–85; state insane asylums, 17–19, 30, 34, 53–54, 68–69, 73–75, 97, 247n82. *See also* Dorothea Dix; Shell shock; Utica State Lunatic Asylum; Willard Asylum for the Chronic Insane; Worcester State Lunatic Hospital

Rabinowitz, Bartholomew, 59, 260n30
Race, 4, 7, 9, 16, 224; racism and occupational safety, 4, 12, 112, 114–15, 151, 155. *See also* African Americans; Mexican Americans

Radium poisoning, 114
Ramsey, Irma, 80–81, 268n122
Red Cross Institute for Crippled and Disabled Men, 196–98, 202–3
Rehabilitation: access for disabled veterans, 202–5; of civilians, 132, 193; disabled veterans' views of, 212–22; ideology regarding disabled veterans, 192–95, 197–202; misadministration of veteran' rehabilitation, 195–97, 208–12; Section 2 training, 199, 206–7, 214, 220; Section 3 training, 199; World War I veterans, 190–92, 205–8. *See also* Disabled veterans; Federal Board for Vocational Education; Pensions: Civil War; Veterans' Bureau
Richards, James B., 24, 242n32, 248n89
Roberts, Frank, 213–15
Robertson, L. B., 134, 168, 312n177
Rome Custodial Herald, 100, 103, 109, 231
Rome State Custodial Asylum, 10–11, 16, 54, 61, 64, 77, 91–92; academic training at, 95–96; colony and parole program, 96–110; discharge practices, 83, 91, 96–110; founding, 77; funding schemes, 94–95, 97–98, 105–107; inmate labor, 78, 82, 92–94; living conditions, 82, 84–85. *See also* Asylums; Charles Bernstein; Eugenics; Family capacity; Group homes Idiocy; Idiot asylums; Parole program
Rubinow, Isaac Max (I. M.): biography, 154–55, 161, 302n96, 302n98, 303n100, 303n103; disability, understanding of, 156–60, 167, 169–70, 191, 203, 303n104; industrial accidents, understanding of, 143, 151, 156; workmen's compensation, critique of, 150–51, 153–62, 167, 169, 191, 203, 304n109. *See also* American Association for Labor Legislation; *American Labor Legislation Review*; Discrimination against disabled workers; Dismemberment schedules and workmen's compensation; Physical examinations; Workmen's compensation
Rudd, Mary, 59, 260n29

Safety First movement: disabled workers and, 122–23, 126, 286n84; at Ford Motor Company, 113, 130, 168; race and, 4, 114–15, 151; on railroads, 123, 284n67; safety devices, 147, 153; workers' attitudes towards, 7, 142, 165
Scientific charity movement: blind workshops, influence on, 188; Goodwill Industries, influence on, 172, 174, 177, 179, 181, 185; idiot asylums and, 11, 69–71, 81, 263n68
Scientific management, 128
Second-injury problem, 163–64, 166–68, 311n173
Séguin, Edouard, 15, 18–19, 21, 27, 32
Self-employment, 120
Settlement house movement, 140, 174, 176
Shell shock, 131, 195, 202, 204, 207, 217, 331n78
Sheltered workshops: for blind adults, 188, 323n92; development, 172–73, 188, 314n4; exemption from minimum-wage laws, 226, 338n3; Henry Ford and, 132, 134; ideology, 4, 10, 188–89, 192, 194, 198–99, 225; John Wesley; as sources, 232; strikes against, 188, 226. *See also* Goodwill Industries; Rehabilitation
Sherbourne, Robert, 45
Silicosis, 4, 151–52, 234n6, 301n81
Silverstein, Gordon, 255n159
Simms, Lacy, 121, 283n60
Slavery. *See* African Americans: disability and proslavery rhetoric; Disabled slaves
Social Gospel movement, 148, 174, 176–79, 315n11, 316n14, 317nn31–32

Social insurance, 143, 153–56, 158, 160–61, 306nn128–29, 307n137
Social Security Disability Insurance (SSDI), 161, 304n112
Sociological Department. *See* Ford Motor Company: Sociological Department
Sorenson, Charles, 168–69, 312n174
Spectrum of productivity, 10–11, 14–15, 36–48, 90, 92, 101, 106, 112, 136, 223, 225. *See also* Family capacity; Household economies
Stahl, Rebecca, 37
State Board of Charities: asylums and poorhouses, inspections of, 53, 63, 69, 87–88, 260n26; development of, 20, 30, 53, 55, 63, 69, 259nn15–16; hereditarian views, 69–72, 97, 263n54; industrial accidents and, 105; as sources, 229
State Charities Aid Association, 53, 105
Stebbins, Inez F., 99–100, 103
Stranger, James, 52, 258n12
Straw, Harvey, 58, 63, 260n28, 262n50
Sullivan, Paddy, 39–40, 252n133
Supplementary Security Income (SSI), 226
Survey, 139, 141–43, 145–47, 152–53, 155–56, 160–61
Survey of Cleveland Cripples, 115, 120–21
Sutton, Randolph, 65
Syracuse State Institution for Feeble-Minded Children. *See* James C. Carson; New York State Asylum for Idiots; Hervey Backus Wilbur

Tangemann, Luke, 107
Tedesco, Prudence, 101
Teesdale, Calvin, 59, 260n29
Thomas, Simon, 43
Tilton, Alexander, 39, 252n130
Treby, John, 6–8
Trowbridge, James, 6

Tuberculosis: in asylums, 83–84; compensation and; disabled veterans and, 194–95, 204, 207, 215, 217, 331n78; Ford Motor Company and, 111, 128, 130–31, 292n127; hereditarianism and, 37, 59, 260n30; medical examinations and, 126, 163, 284n71; workers with, 3, 114, 126, 223
Tucker, Emily, 14–15, 36

Ulrich, Conrad, 43
Union Carbide and Carbon, 4, 151–52, 234n6, 301n81
Unions: advocacy on behalf of disabled workers, 166, 226; Blind Workers Union, 188; disabled veterans and, 207; discrimination against disabled workers, 112, 122–24, 126; Goodwill Industries and, 177, 185; industrial accidents, views of, 138, 142, 146–47, 279n8; Rome State Custodial Asylum's colony and parole program, 102; workmen's compensation and, 152, 161. *See also* Physical examinations: protests against
United States Veterans' Bureau (USVB). *See* Veterans' Bureau
Unpaid labor at asylums, 1, 10–11, 49, 51, 73, 75–76, 80, 85, 89–90. *See also* Asylums: labor programs; Care work; Gender: asylum labor programs; Gender: feeble-minded women; Sheltered workshops: exemption from minimum-wage laws
Utica State Lunatic Asylum, 22, 30, 34, 243n35, 250n104. *See also* Psychosocial impairments

Veterans. *See* Disabled veterans
Veterans' Bureau, 4, 190–92; administration, 191–92, 196, 199, 218–20; corruption and dysfunction, 196–98; disability, views of, 204, 214–15; mixed

success of, 203–8, 210–16, 221; sources on, 232
Vocational rehabilitation. *See* Douglas C. McMurtrie; Rehabilitation

Wage labor economy: disabled veterans and, 194, 198, 205–7, 219, 221, 223; exclusion of disabled workers, 2–3, 112, 136–38, 162, 171–73, 192, 223–26; Goodwill Industries and, 177, 182, 184–89; industrial accidents and, 141–42, 156; institutionalization and, 48–49, 51, 57–65, 67, 88; integration into, 90–92, 99, 109, 111; rehabilitators and, 12; workmen's compensation and, 146–47, 149, 158–59. *See also* Asylums: labor programs; Care work; Family capacity; Household economies; Parole program; Physical examinations; Rehabilitation; Sheltered workshops: exemption from minimum-wage laws; Spectrum of productivity; Unpaid labor at asylums
Wahlberg, Edgar M., 184–87, 321n67, 322n75
Wainwright Commission, 146, 148, 151
War Risk Insurance, 194, 196, 209, 214
Waverly School for the Feeble-Minded, and Goodwill Industries, 107, 184
Wearing out, 1, 5, 113, 117, 126, 132, 137, 146. *See also* Elderly workers
Wegener, Lucy, 108
Weiman, John, 54
Welfare capitalism, and disabled workers, 111, 122, 126
Westbrooke, Lily, 1–3, 7–8, 13, 233n1
Wetzel, Beatrix, 61, 261n40
Wheeler, Wallace, 63, 262n49
Whitman, Adolphus, 81, 268n125
Wiebe, Anna, 58, 260n28
Wilbur, Charles Toppan, 23–25, 33, 41, 52, 62, 76, 246n70

Wilbur, Hervey Backus: discharge practices, 36–48; early career, 21–23; founding of New York State Asylum for Idiots; idiot asylums, vision for, 27–31; idiots, views of, 24; influence on other asylum superintendents, 23–24, 31–35; shift to custodial care, 60, 65–74. *See also* Association of Medical Officers of American Institutions for Idiotic and Feeble-Minded Persons; Asylums; Idiocy; Idiot asylums; Institute for Idiots (Barre, Massachusetts)
Willard Asylum for the Chronic Insane, 47, 59, 69. *See also* Psychosocial impairments
Wills, Eleanor, 40, 41, 43, 253n140, 254n155
Women. *See* Gender
Worcester State Lunatic Hospital, 17–19. *See also* Dorothea Dix; Psychosocial impairments
Work. *See* Artisanal labor; Asylums: labor programs; Care work; Domestic labor; Family capacity; Farm labor; Gender: asylum labor programs; Gender: feeble-minded women; Household economies; Labor market, informal; Mechanization; Self-employment; Sheltered workshops; Spectrum of productivity; Unpaid labor at asylums; Wage labor economy
Work accidents. *See* Industrial accidents
Workers' compensation. *See* Workmen's compensation
Workmen's compensation, 135–36; American versus European systems, 149–50; critiques of, 153–61, 170; design of, 148–53; disabled veterans, 167; disabled workers' experiences with, 161–71; *Ives v. South Buffalo Railway*; medical expenses and; motivation behind, 136–48. *See also* American Association for Labor

Workmen's compensation (cont.) Legislation; Amputees: workmen's compensation; Discrimination against disabled workers; Dismemberment schedules and workmen's compensation; Crystal Eastman; Employers' liability; Ford Motor Company: workmen's compensation and; Gender: workmen's compensation and; Occupational diseases and illnesses; Physical examinations; Isaac Max Rubinow: disability, understanding of; Second-injury problem; Unions: workmen's compensation and; Wage labor economy: workmen's compensation and; Wainwright Commission

Worn-out workers. *See* Wearing out

Young, A. G., 183, 185–87

www.ingramcontent.com/pod-product-compliance
Lightning Source LLC
Chambersburg PA
CBHW020637300426
44112CB00007B/142